Table of Contents

Books 1 and 2

by
Osamu Tezuka

translation and introduction
Frederik L. Schodt

lettering and retouch
Digital Chameleon

Dark Horse Manga™

INTRODUCTION

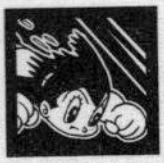

Astro Boy first blasted into American consciousness in 1963, when he starred in a popular black-and-white animated television series of the same name. In an age when most American superheroes fought for a patriotic form of justice and had special powers derived from mysterious, almost cosmic sources, Astro Boy was utterly original. He was an autonomous robot boy – an advanced android – with a computer brain and rockets in his feet. Whether flying through the air or outwitting enemies, his powers were based on semi-scientific or mechanical principles, and instead of fighting for justice, he fought for peace. To most young American viewers, the *Astro Boy* TV series was so cleverly dubbed they had no idea it was originally from Japan or based on a Japanese manga titled *Tetsuwan Atom*, or "Mighty Atom," created in 1951 by Osamu Tezuka.

From childhood Osamu Tezuka had been a huge fan of comics and animation, especially U.S. animation, but he began drawing *Mighty Atom* while still a medical student at Osaka University. Atom's huge success encouraged him to abandon his career as a doctor and pursue his true love, of becoming an artist. Ironically, he first drew Atom not as the star, but as a side character in a story titled *"Atom Taishi,"* ("Ambassador Atom," occasionally rendered as "Captain Atom"), in the monthly boys' magazine *Shonen* in April 1951. When Tezuka made Atom the hero and changed the series name to *Mighty Atom* it proved sensationally popular, and he continued drawing it for the next eighteen years.

A physician who never practiced medicine, Tezuka brought an extraordinary creativity into a then-underdeveloped medium of entertainment for children. By experimenting in *Mighty Atom* and other works, he helped create a Japanese-led revolution in comics and animation that reverberates around the world to this day. In Japan, where he is known as the "God of Manga," Tezuka is regarded as one of the more important people of the 20th century. Readers will notice, however, that his stories have many references to science and to medicine.

In 1963, Tezuka turned his *Mighty Atom* manga into Japan's first animated black-and-white television series, making Atom a true national phenomenon. In the United States, NBC took notice and had veteran producer Fred Ladd localize 104 episodes of the series for the U.S. market, rewriting many of the scripts, dubbing the dialogue with American voice talent, and changing the name of the hero and series title from *Mighty Atom* to *Astro Boy*. An American-style *Astro Boy* comic book was produced under the Gold Key imprint in 1965, but it was not drawn by Tezuka, and it was based on the animated TV show. In the 1980s, another unlicensed English-language *Astro Boy* comic book was created, but it too was not drawn by Tezuka. As a result, until the publication of this series by Dark Horse Comics in 2002, English-speaking fans of Astro Boy have had no way of knowing what the original manga story – the original *Mighty Atom* – was like.

Before reading this English version of the *Mighty Atom* manga collection – herein titled *Astro Boy* – a few comments are in order.

First, Japanese manga are usually black-and-white line drawings, but when initially published in magazines the first few pages of the episodes are often in color. When compiled into inexpensive paperback books all the pages, including the color ones, are reproduced in monochrome. As a result, some of the pages in this edition, while all monochrome, have a different tone to them, with more shading.

The *Astro Boy* series is made up of many individual stories, which in paperback editions are self-contained and concluding. Since Tezuka drew the series over an extremely long period of time, careful readers can see how he developed many of his storytelling skills and refined his art style. Astro became more modern and "cute," to satisfy the core audience of elementary school children. Page layouts became more creative, and in the design of supporting characters Tezuka sometimes included homages to American animators such as Walt Disney and Max Fleischer, whom he admired greatly.

Over the years, different publishers have reissued the *Astro Boy* stories in different paperback and hardback editions. As was Tezuka's tendency, he sometimes went back and redrew parts of stories if he felt they did not live up to his standards or if he felt that discontinuities had crept into the story line. For this reason, of two episodes drawn at nearly the same time, the artwork in one may sometimes look more modern than in the other.

Publishers issuing the entire collection of *Astro Boy* stories have always faced the dilemma of what order to introduce them. This collection was originally issued by Akita Shoten under its Sunday Comics imprint, as a series of twenty-three paperbacks. Rather than begin with the very first story created in April 1951, it begins with "The Birth of Astro Boy," which Tezuka specially authored in 1975 to make the entire collection easier to understand; the 1951 episode is contained in volume fifteen. Similarly, other stories also appear in the order that Tezuka or the collection editors felt most appropriate, regardless of when they were created. Tezuka also drew introductions to many of the older stories, using himself as an interlocutor. It is this charming technique that tells us, in the first volume of this collection, of his frustration over the restrictions placed on him by American television in the 1960s.

In Japan, *Mighty Atom/Astro Boy* is so famous that most people know the basic construct behind the story. For new readers, however, some elements may need reinforcing. Briefly, Astro was created on April 7, 2003 by Dr. Tenma, of the Ministry of Science, as a robot replacement for his beloved son, Tobio, who was killed in an accident. When Tenma realizes Astro will never grow like a real boy he is crushed, and he sells Astro to a robot vendor. Tenma becomes unbalanced and leaves the Ministry of Science, thereafter to become a somewhat shadowy figure. His successor, Professor Ochanomizu, finds Astro at a robot circus and thereafter becomes his guardian. Ochanomizu creates a normal-looking robot family for Astro, who thereafter lives with his robot mother, father, sister (Uran), and brother (Cobalt). Despite his amazing powers, Astro attends regular third-grade class with other human children at Ochanomizu Elementary School, where his teacher is the eccentric Higeoyaji, or "Mr. Mustachio." Mustachio is a surrogate father-friend to Astro and an amateur sleuth who is always getting involved in all sorts of adventures with him. In his early manga

Tezuka made many innovations, and one of the more unique ones was to create what he called a "star system," a stable of "actors" who appear in different roles in different stories much like a theater repertory company. Thus fans of *Astro Boy* will note that many of the same cast of supporting characters also appear in other famous Tezuka stories.

New readers may at first also find Tezuka's visual gags confusing. He created so many stories in his lifetime that he developed a type of dialog with his readers, and he loved to insert nonsensical characters at random into scenes that seemed to be getting too serious. Thus a gourd-like character would sometimes come sailing out of the air and bounce off the floor, or an odd, cartoony little creature would come out and say *"omukae de gonsu"* (roughly, "Here ta meet ya").

Translating Tezuka's work always presents challenges, but in rendering the names of the characters I have tried to be as faithful to the originals as possible. This may disappoint some fans of the TV animation shown in North America in the sixties. In that series, names were cleverly adjusted to American tastes, Professor Ochanomizu, for example, becoming Dr. Packadermus J. Elephun. Nonetheless, this collection presents the original unedited manga story, which is firmly set in Japan, with Japanese characters, so I felt it more appropriate to retain Japanese names where-ever possible. One exception is Astro's teacher, who is always called by his nick-name of Higeoyaji ("Mr. Mustache") instead of his real name of Shunsaku Ban; because it is a nickname, I have rendered him as "Mr. Mustachio." Occasionally the original Japanese names of characters also have double meanings that cannot be conveyed in translation. For example, *tawashi* means "scrub brush," and *shibugaki* means "bitter perimmon." Nonetheless, I felt it more important to retain the original sound of the character names, especially if they are famous, and to intimate the double meaning elsewhere in the translation. For minor characters with humorous names, I have tried to find equivalent English puns whenever possible. The one central character whose American name I have chosen to retain is that of Astro Boy himself. *Astro* is quite close to *atom*, which is an English word anyway, and at this point in history I felt that using *atom* in an American edition of the story would be going against too much history

As Tezuka himself laments in this volume, the many stories in the collection are sometimes of uneven quality. Whether in manga or animation, *Astro Boy* became by far his most famous work, and he sometimes felt trapped by the need to satisfy young male fans' desires for scenes of battling robots. Still, *Astro Boy* developed extraordinary longevity and appeal across cultures. Tezuka created Astro in the ashes of Japan's defeat in World War II, when Japan did not have the reputation for science and technology that it has today. He used Astro to imagine – from the perspective of the very analog 1950s – a world of advanced technology where man and machine coexist, and the problems that might emerge. Tezuka once wrote that he had created Astro to be a 21st-century reverse-Pinocchio, a nearly perfect robot who strove to become more human and emotive and to serve as an interface between man and machine. The closer we get to a true age of robots, the more meaning *Astro Boy* therefore assumes.

– Frederik L. Schodt

A NOTE TO READERS

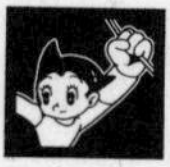

Many non-Japanese, including people from Africa and Southeast Asia, appear in Osamu Tezuka's works. Sometimes these people are depicted very differently from the way they actually are today, in a manner that exaggerates a time long past, or shows them to be from extremely undeveloped lands. Some feel that such images contribute to racial discrimination, especially against people of African descent. This was never Osamu Tezuka's intent, but we believe that as long as there are people who feel insulted or demeaned by these depictions, we must not ignore their feelings.

We are against all forms of discrimination and intend to continue to work for its elimination. Nonetheless, we do not believe it would be proper to revise these works. Tezuka is no longer with us, and we cannot erase what he has done, and to alter his work would only violate his rights as a creator. More importantly, stopping publication or changing the content of his work would do little to solve the problems of discrimination that exist in the world.

We are presenting Osamu Tezuka's work as it was originally created, without changes. We do this because we believe it is also important to promote the underlying themes in his work, such as love for mankind and the sanctity of life. We hope that when you, the reader, encounter this work, you will keep in mind the differences in attitudes, then and now, toward discrimination, and that this will contribute to an even greater awareness of such problems.

– Tezuka Productions and Dark Horse Comics

publisher
MIKE RICHARDSON

editor
CHRIS WARNER

consulting editor
TOREN SMITH for STUDIO PROTEUS

collection designer
DAVID NESTELLE

English-language version produced by **DARK HORSE COMICS** and **STUDIO PROTEUS**

ASTRO BOY® BOOKS 1&2

This volume collects material previously published as the Dark Horse graphic novels *Astro Boy Book 1* and *Astro Boy Book 2*.

Dark Horse Manga
A division of Dark Horse Comics, Inc.
10956 SE Main Street
Milwaukie, OR 97222

DARKHORSE.COM

To find a comics shop in your area, call the Comic Shop Locator Service toll-free at 1-888-266-4226

First edition: September 2008
ISBN 978-1-59582-153-9

10 9 8 7 6 5 4 3 2
Printed in the United States of America

THE BIRTH OF
ASTRO BOY

First published June 20, 1975, as part of an
original story for Volume 1 of Asahi
Sonorama's edition of the *Tetsuwan Atomu*
("Mighty Atom") series.

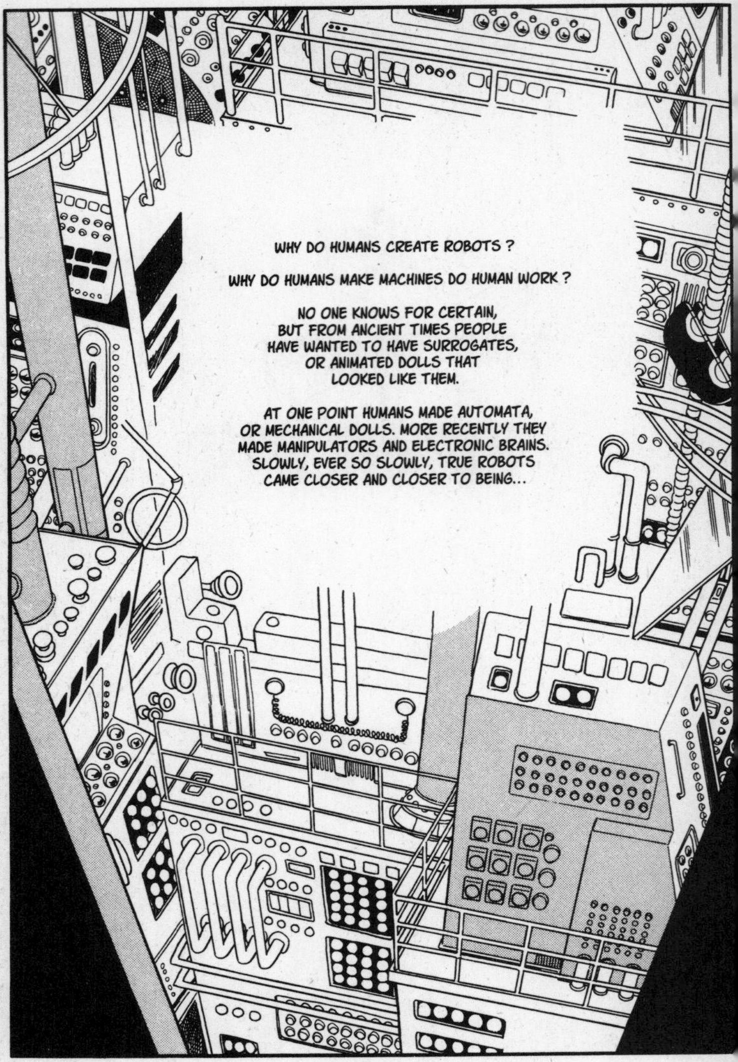
WHY DO HUMANS CREATE ROBOTS ?
WHY DO HUMANS MAKE MACHINES DO HUMAN WORK ?
NO ONE KNOWS FOR CERTAIN, BUT FROM ANCIENT TIMES PEOPLE HAVE WANTED TO HAVE SURROGATES, OR ANIMATED DOLLS THAT LOOKED LIKE THEM.
AT ONE POINT HUMANS MADE AUTOMATA, OR MECHANICAL DOLLS. MORE RECENTLY THEY MADE MANIPULATORS AND ELECTRONIC BRAINS. SLOWLY, EVER SO SLOWLY, TRUE ROBOTS CAME CLOSER AND CLOSER TO BEING...

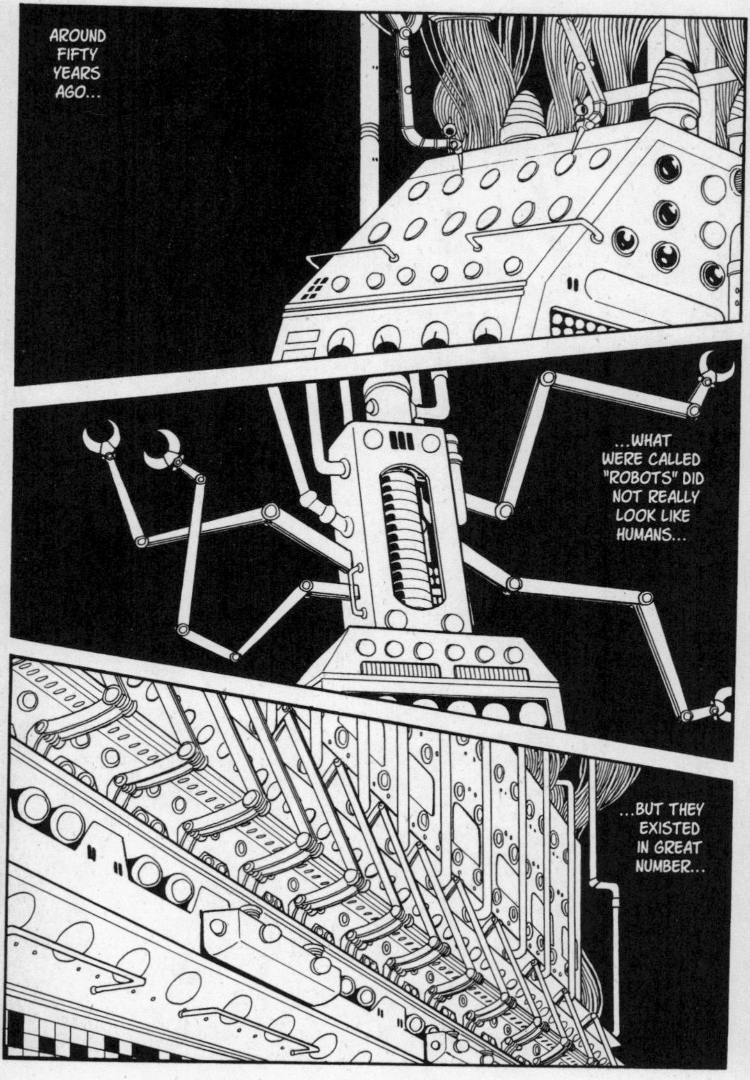
AROUND FIFTY YEARS AGO...
...WHAT WERE CALLED "ROBOTS" DID NOT REALLY LOOK LIKE HUMANS...
...BUT THEY EXISTED IN GREAT NUMBER...

IT TOOK TOO MANY MACHINES TO PERFORM THE SAME WORK AS A HUMAN...

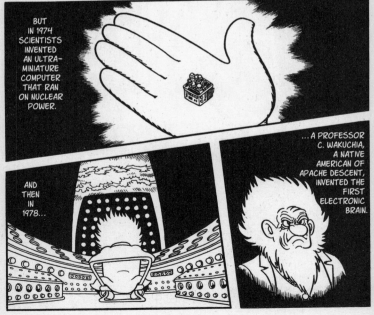

BUT IN 1974 SCIENTISTS INVENTED AN ULTRA-MINIATURE COMPUTER THAT RAN ON NUCLEAR POWER.

AND THEN IN 1978...

...A PROFESSOR C. WAKUCHIA, A NATIVE AMERICAN OF APACHE DESCENT, INVENTED THE FIRST ELECTRONIC BRAIN.

12

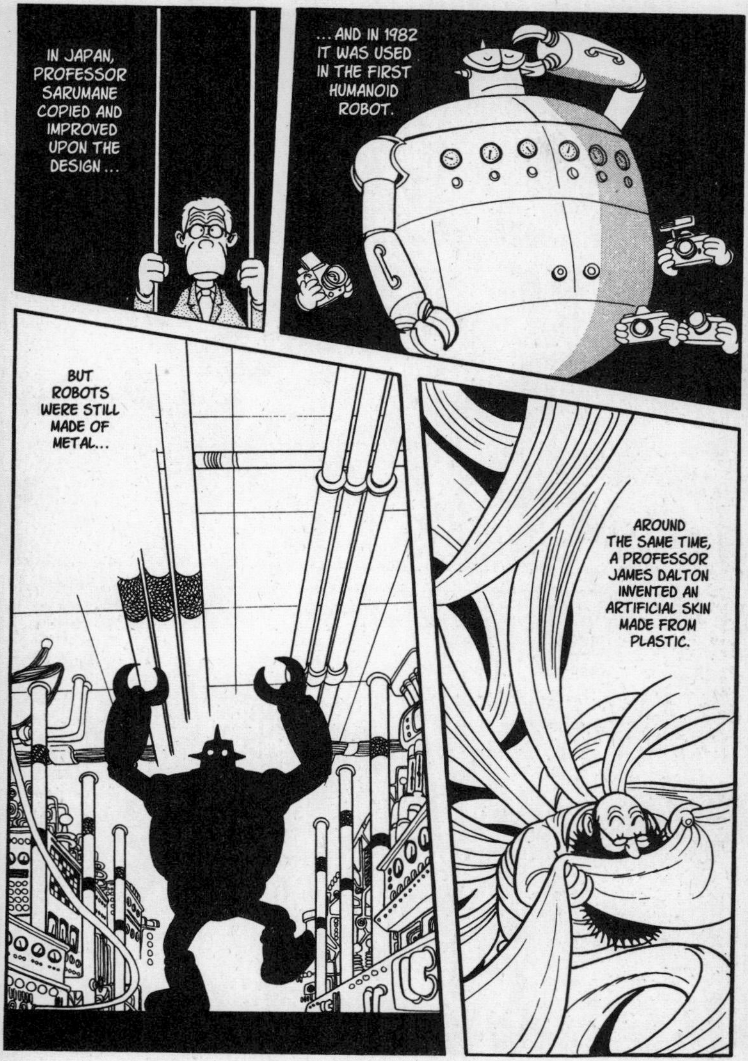
IN JAPAN, PROFESSOR SARUMANE COPIED AND IMPROVED UPON THE DESIGN...
...AND IN 1982 IT WAS USED IN THE FIRST HUMANOID ROBOT.
BUT ROBOTS WERE STILL MADE OF METAL...
AROUND THE SAME TIME, A PROFESSOR JAMES DALTON INVENTED AN ARTIFICIAL SKIN MADE FROM PLASTIC.

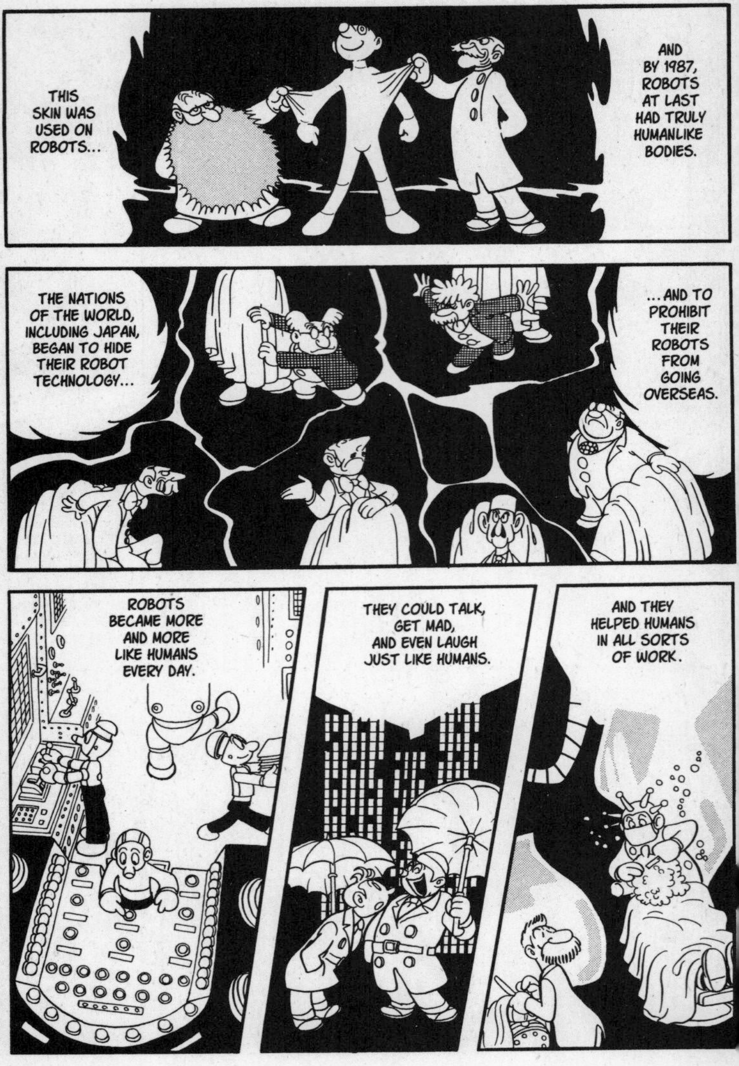
THIS SKIN WAS USED ON ROBOTS...
AND BY 1987, ROBOTS AT LAST HAD TRULY HUMANLIKE BODIES.
THE NATIONS OF THE WORLD, INCLUDING JAPAN, BEGAN TO HIDE THEIR ROBOT TECHNOLOGY...
...AND TO PROHIBIT THEIR ROBOTS FROM GOING OVERSEAS.
ROBOTS BECAME MORE AND MORE LIKE HUMANS EVERY DAY.
THEY COULD TALK, GET MAD, AND EVEN LAUGH JUST LIKE HUMANS.
AND THEY HELPED HUMANS IN ALL SORTS OF WORK.

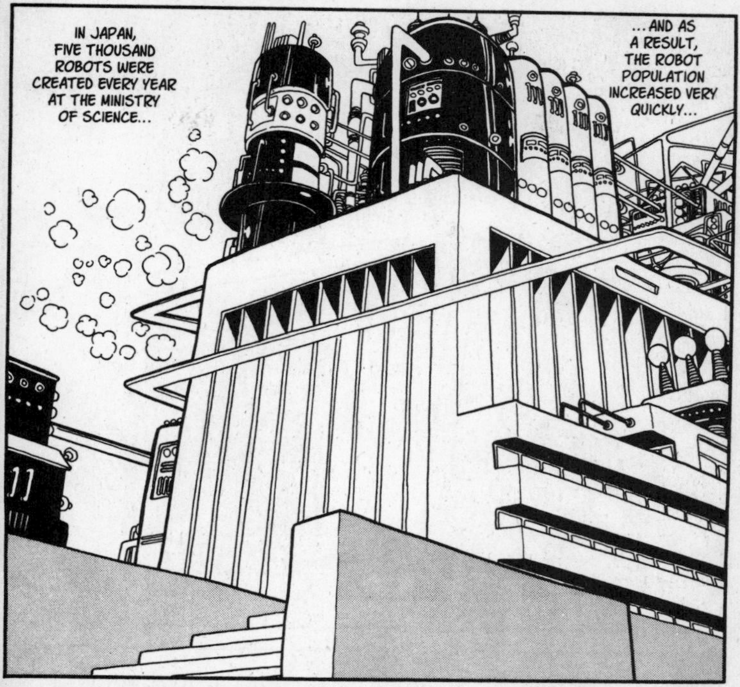
IN JAPAN, FIVE THOUSAND ROBOTS WERE CREATED EVERY YEAR AT THE MINISTRY OF SCIENCE...
...AND AS A RESULT, THE ROBOT POPULATION INCREASED VERY QUICKLY...
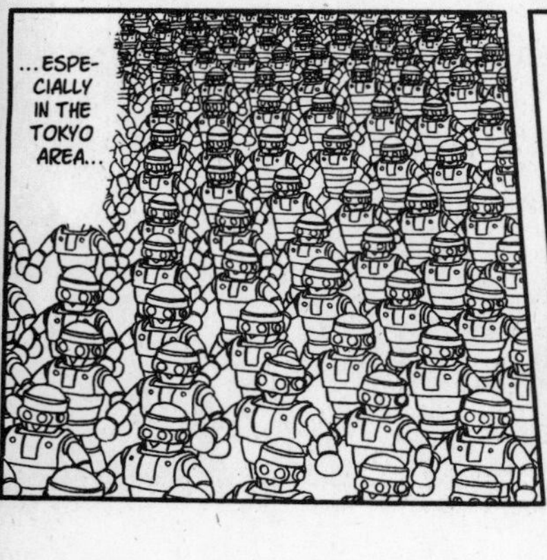
...ESPE- CIALLY IN THE TOKYO AREA...
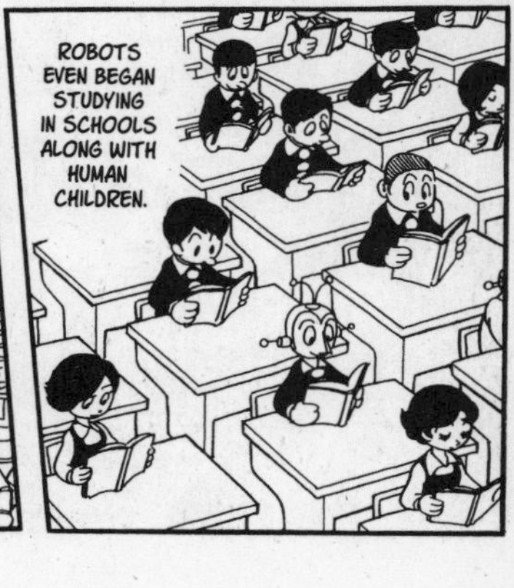
ROBOTS EVEN BEGAN STUDYING IN SCHOOLS ALONG WITH HUMAN CHILDREN.

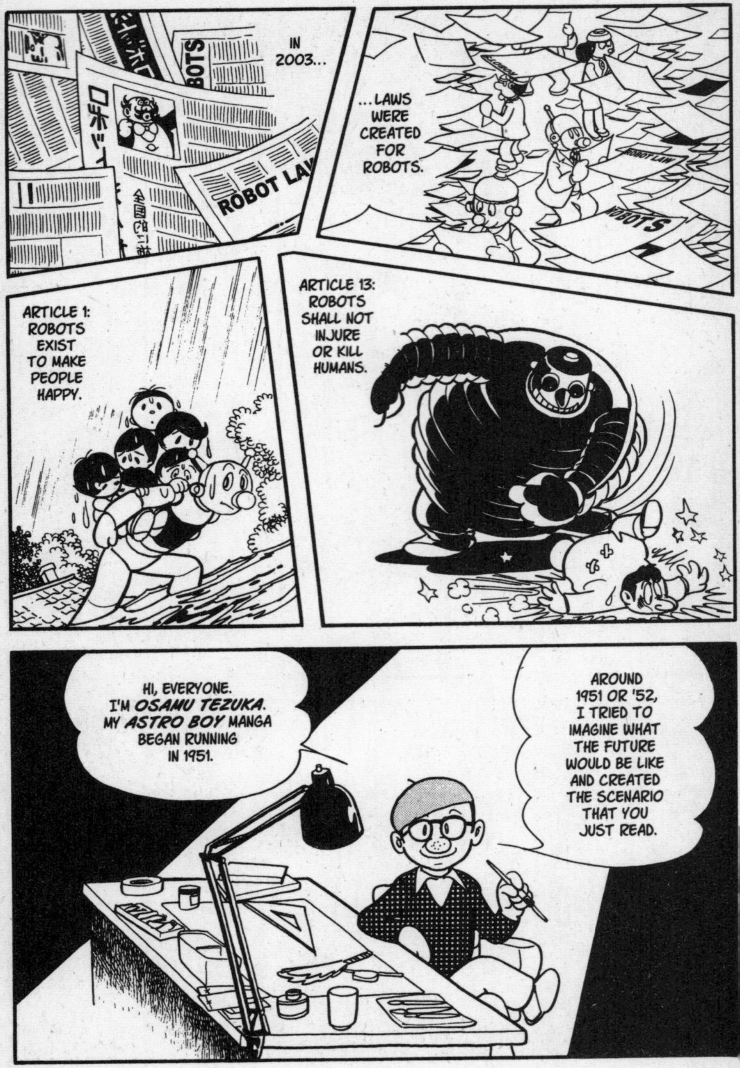
IN 2003...
...LAWS WERE CREATED FOR ROBOTS.
ROBOT LAW
ARTICLE 1: ROBOTS EXIST TO MAKE PEOPLE HAPPY.
ARTICLE 13: ROBOTS SHALL NOT INJURE OR KILL HUMANS.
HI, EVERYONE. I'M *OSAMU TEZUKA*. MY *ASTRO BOY* MANGA BEGAN RUNNING IN 1951.
AROUND 1951 OR '52, I TRIED TO IMAGINE WHAT THE FUTURE WOULD BE LIKE AND CREATED THE SCENARIO THAT YOU JUST READ.

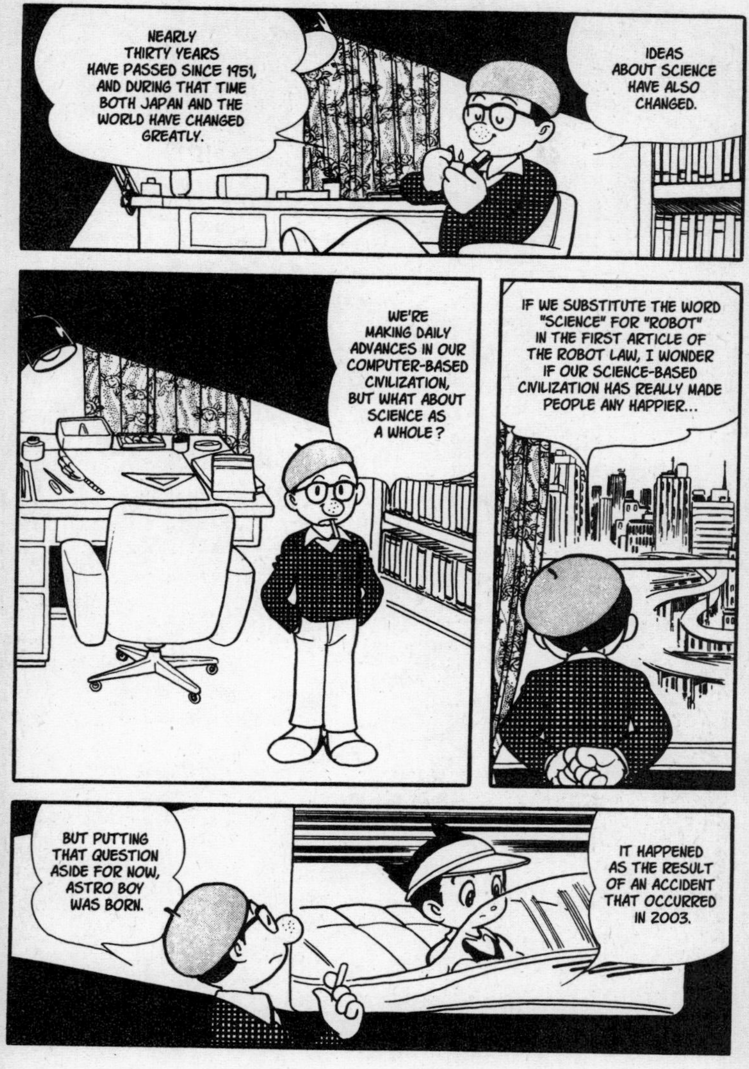
NEARLY THIRTY YEARS HAVE PASSED SINCE 1951, AND DURING THAT TIME BOTH JAPAN AND THE WORLD HAVE CHANGED GREATLY.
IDEAS ABOUT SCIENCE HAVE ALSO CHANGED.
WE'RE MAKING DAILY ADVANCES IN OUR COMPUTER-BASED CIVILIZATION, BUT WHAT ABOUT SCIENCE AS A WHOLE?
IF WE SUBSTITUTE THE WORD "SCIENCE" FOR "ROBOT" IN THE FIRST ARTICLE OF THE ROBOT LAW, I WONDER IF OUR SCIENCE-BASED CIVILIZATION HAS REALLY MADE PEOPLE ANY HAPPIER...
BUT PUTTING THAT QUESTION ASIDE FOR NOW, ASTRO BOY WAS BORN.
IT HAPPENED AS THE RESULT OF AN ACCIDENT THAT OCCURRED IN 2003.

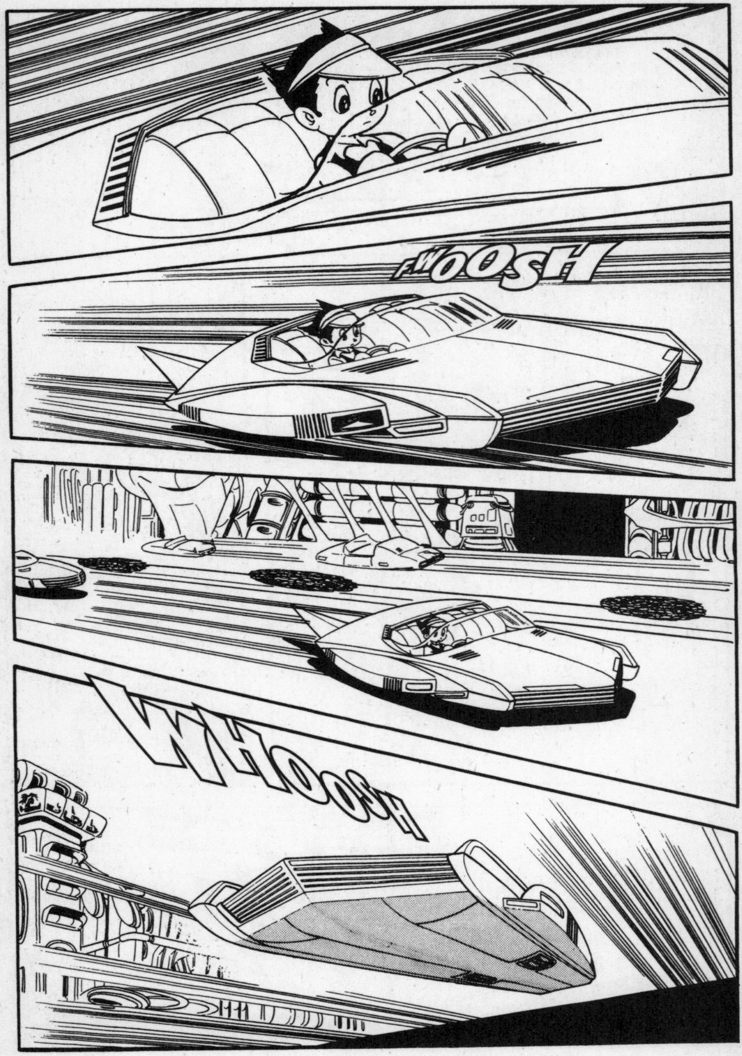
FWOOSH
WHOOSH

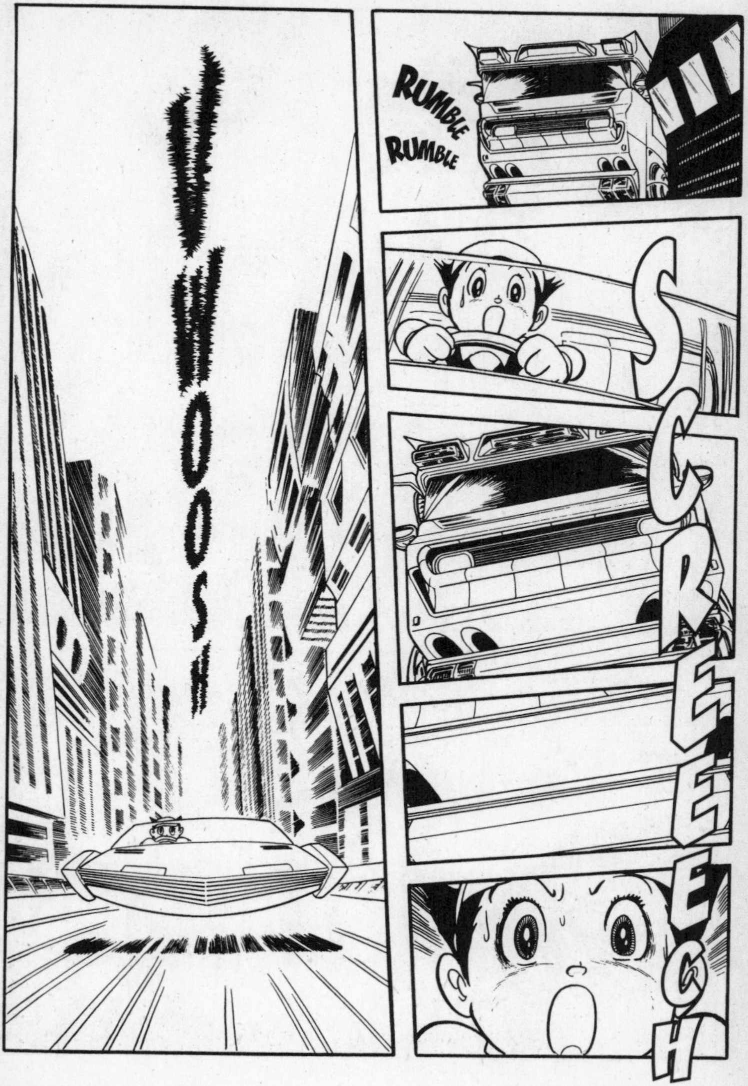
WHOOOSH
RUMBLE
RUMBLE
SCREEECH

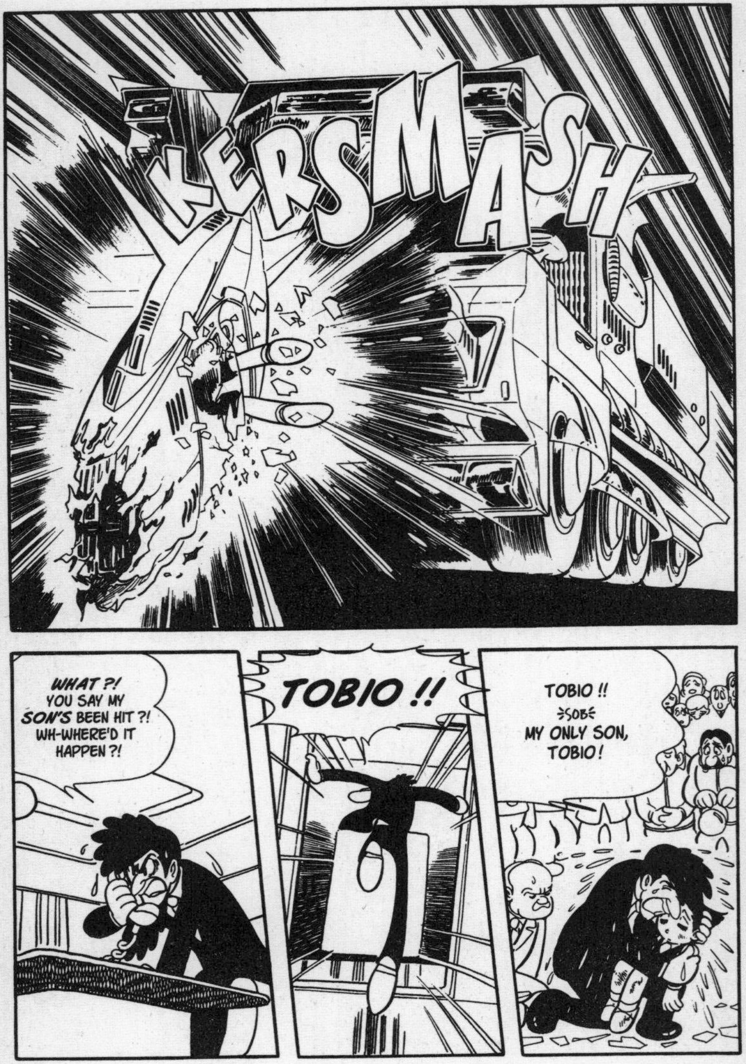
KERSMASH
WHAT ?! YOU SAY MY SON'S BEEN HIT ?! WH-WHERE'D IT HAPPEN ?!
TOBIO !!
TOBIO !! SOB MY ONLY SON, TOBIO !

⇒SOB SOB⇐

TOBIO... TOBIO...

I KNOW! TOBIO, I'LL RE-CREATE YOU, WITH AN IMMORTAL BODY!

THAT'S IT! I'LL CREATE A ROBOT IDENTICAL TO YOU... *HEH HEH HEH HAH HAH HA HAH!*

ALL RIGHT, MEN... WE'RE GOING TO USE THE CREAM OF TECHNOLOGY AT THE MINISTRY OF SCIENCE AND CREATE THIS ROBOT.

...IT'LL BE A ROBOT UNLIKE ANY OTHER IN THE WORLD. IT'LL BE MODERN SCIENCE'S SUPREME WORK OF ART!

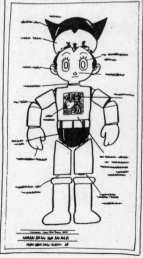

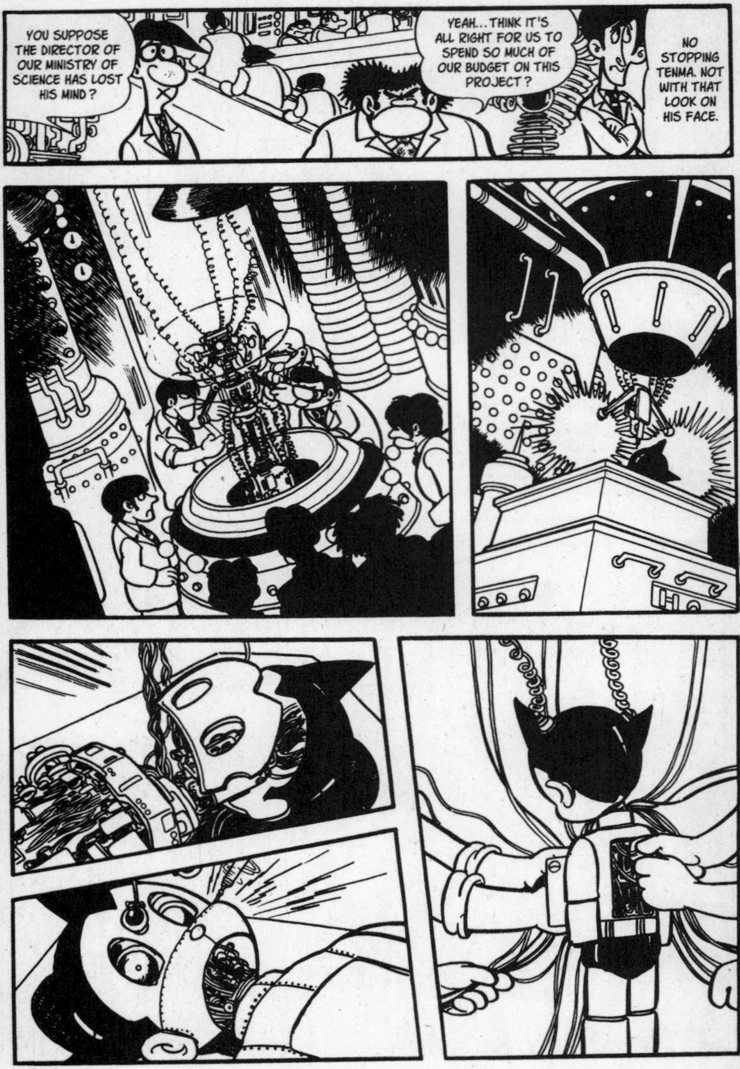
YOU SUPPOSE THE DIRECTOR OF OUR MINISTRY OF SCIENCE HAS LOST HIS MIND ?
YEAH... THINK IT'S ALL RIGHT FOR US TO SPEND SO MUCH OF OUR BUDGET ON THIS PROJECT ?
NO STOPPING TENMA. NOT WITH THAT LOOK ON HIS FACE.

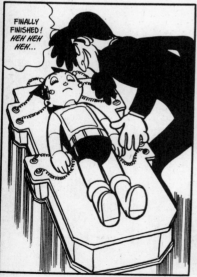

FINALLY FINISHED! HEH HEH HEH...

JUST WAIT, TOBIO...

I'M GOING TO BRING YOU BACK TO LIFE...

23

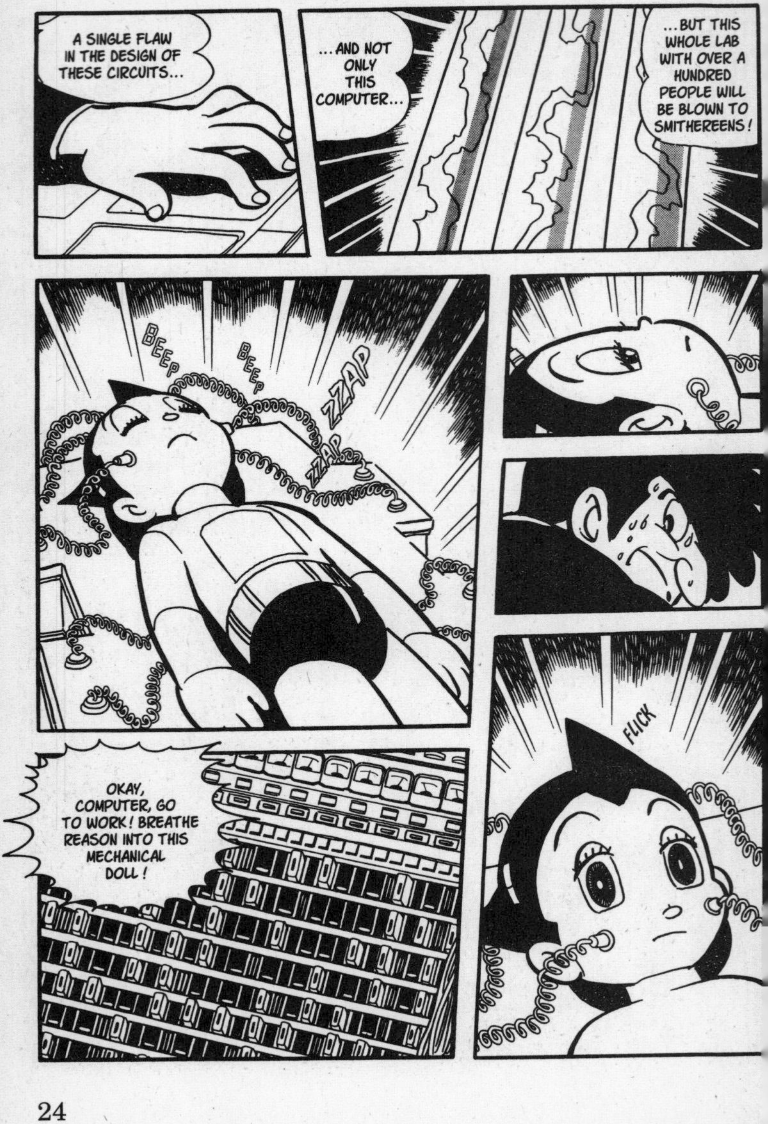

A SINGLE FLAW IN THE DESIGN OF THESE CIRCUITS...
...AND NOT ONLY THIS COMPUTER...
...BUT THIS WHOLE LAB WITH OVER A HUNDRED PEOPLE WILL BE BLOWN TO SMITHEREENS!
BEEP
BEEP
ZZAP
ZZAP
OKAY, COMPUTER, GO TO WORK! BREATHE REASON INTO THIS MECHANICAL DOLL!
FLICK

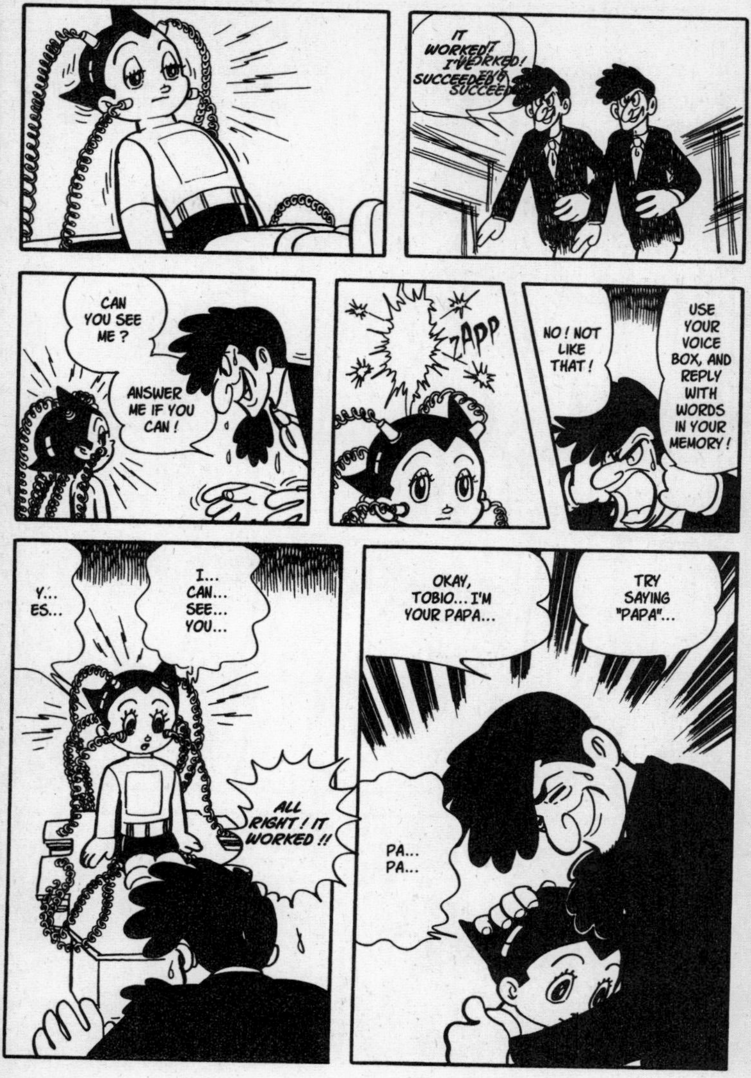
IT WORKED! I'VE SUCCEEDED!
CAN YOU SEE ME?
ANSWER ME IF YOU CAN!
ZAPP
NO! NOT LIKE THAT!
USE YOUR VOICE BOX, AND REPLY WITH WORDS IN YOUR MEMORY!
Y... ES...
I... CAN... SEE... YOU...
ALL RIGHT! IT WORKED!!
OKAY, TOBIO... I'M YOUR PAPA...
TRY SAYING "PAPA"...
PA... PA...

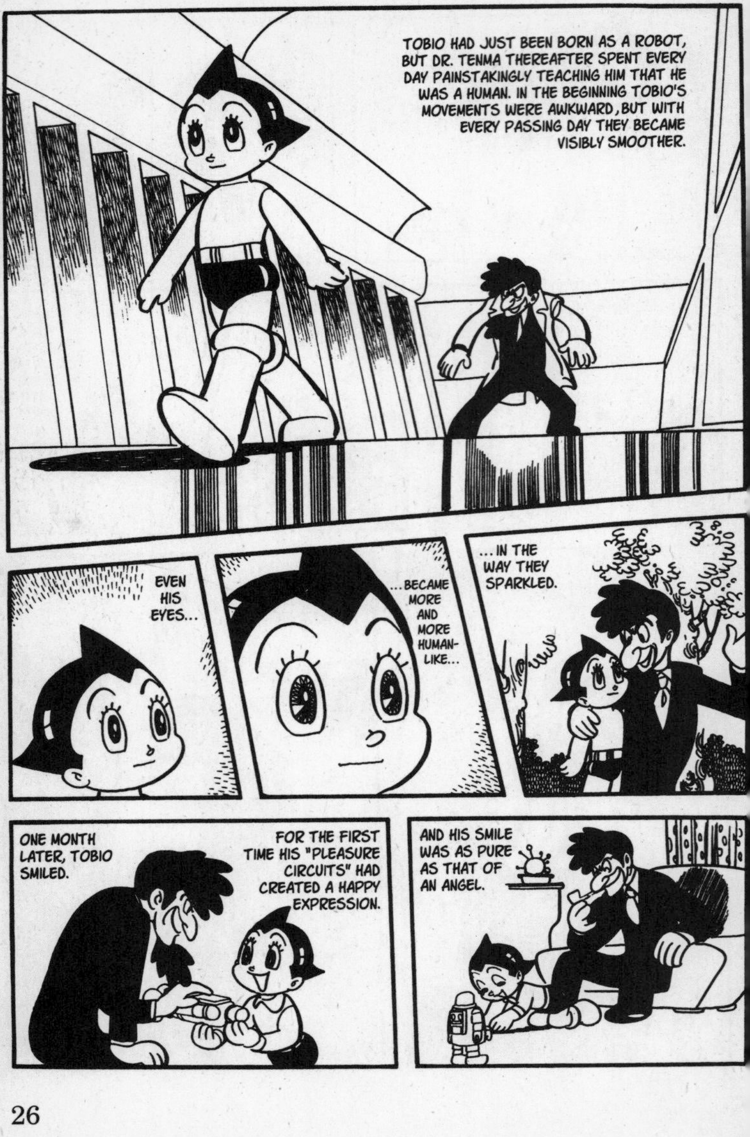
TOBIO HAD JUST BEEN BORN AS A ROBOT, BUT DR. TENMA THEREAFTER SPENT EVERY DAY PAINSTAKINGLY TEACHING HIM THAT HE WAS A HUMAN. IN THE BEGINNING TOBIO'S MOVEMENTS WERE AWKWARD, BUT WITH EVERY PASSING DAY THEY BECAME VISIBLY SMOOTHER.
EVEN HIS EYES...
...BECAME MORE AND MORE HUMAN-LIKE...
...IN THE WAY THEY SPARKLED.
ONE MONTH LATER, TOBIO SMILED.
FOR THE FIRST TIME HIS "PLEASURE CIRCUITS" HAD CREATED A HAPPY EXPRESSION.
AND HIS SMILE WAS AS PURE AS THAT OF AN ANGEL.

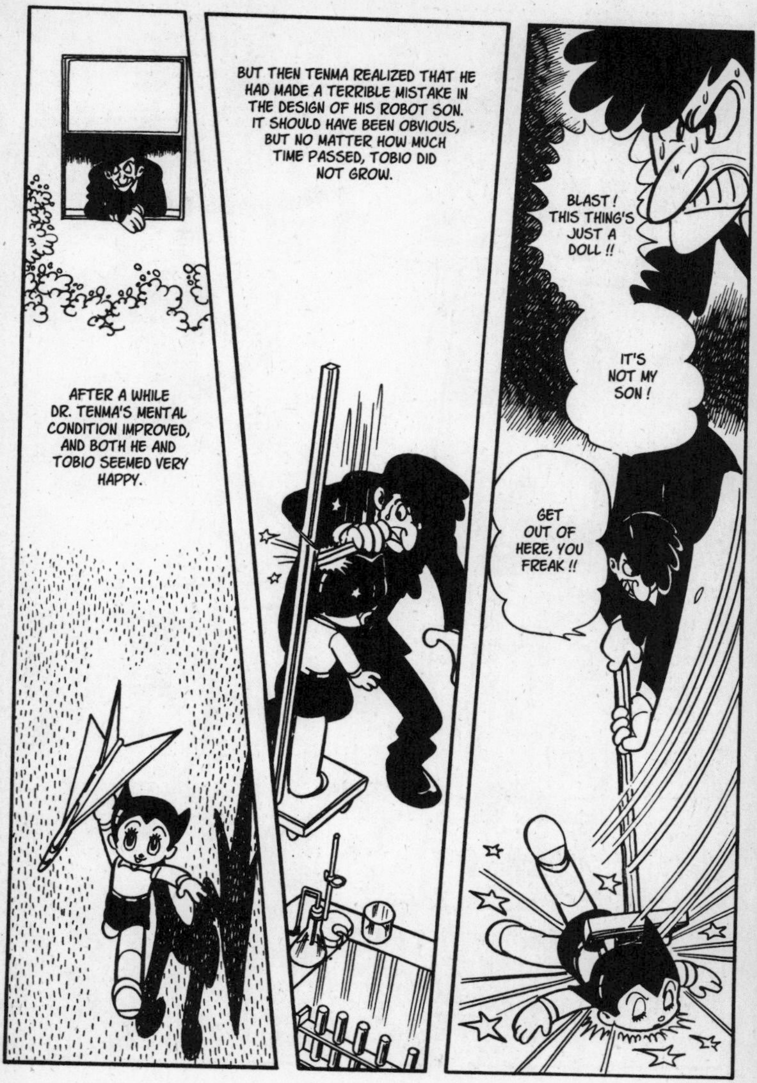
AFTER A WHILE DR. TENMA'S MENTAL CONDITION IMPROVED, AND BOTH HE AND TOBIO SEEMED VERY HAPPY.
BUT THEN TENMA REALIZED THAT HE HAD MADE A TERRIBLE MISTAKE IN THE DESIGN OF HIS ROBOT SON. IT SHOULD HAVE BEEN OBVIOUS, BUT NO MATTER HOW MUCH TIME PASSED, TOBIO DID NOT GROW.
BLAST! THIS THING'S JUST A DOLL!!
IT'S NOT MY SON!
GET OUT OF HERE, YOU FREAK!!

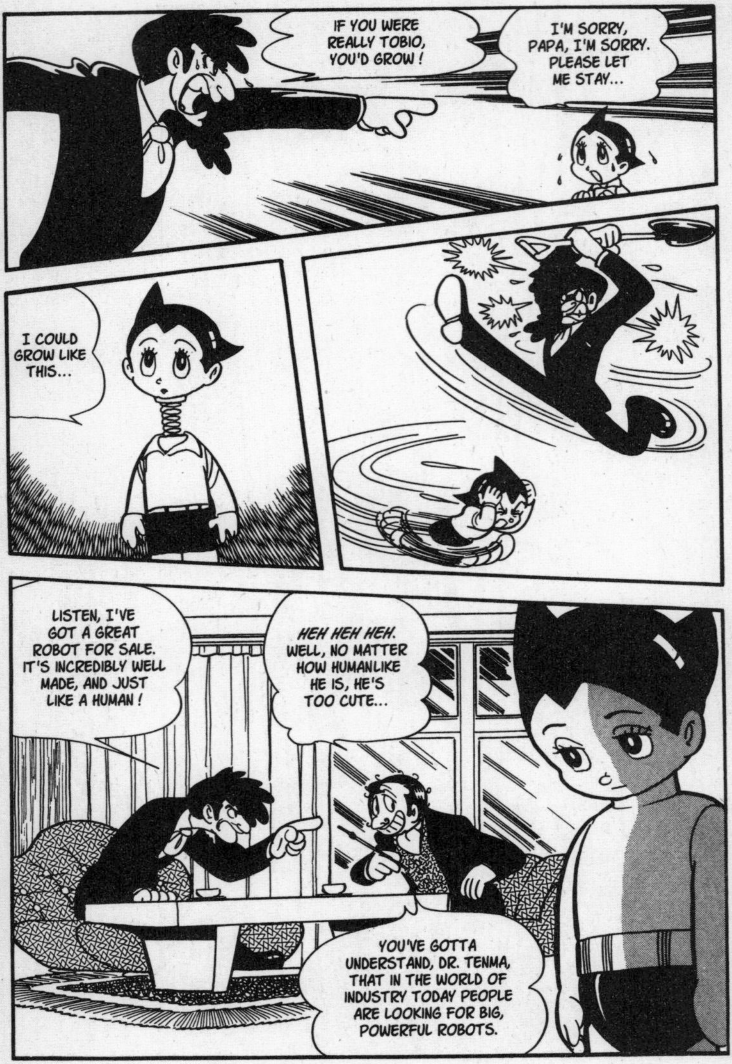
IF YOU WERE REALLY TOBIO, YOU'D GROW !
I'M SORRY, PAPA, I'M SORRY. PLEASE LET ME STAY...
I COULD GROW LIKE THIS...
LISTEN, I'VE GOT A GREAT ROBOT FOR SALE. IT'S INCREDIBLY WELL MADE, AND JUST LIKE A HUMAN !
HEH HEH HEH. WELL, NO MATTER HOW HUMANLIKE HE IS, HE'S TOO CUTE...
YOU'VE GOTTA UNDERSTAND, DR. TENMA, THAT IN THE WORLD OF INDUSTRY TODAY PEOPLE ARE LOOKING FOR BIG, POWERFUL ROBOTS.

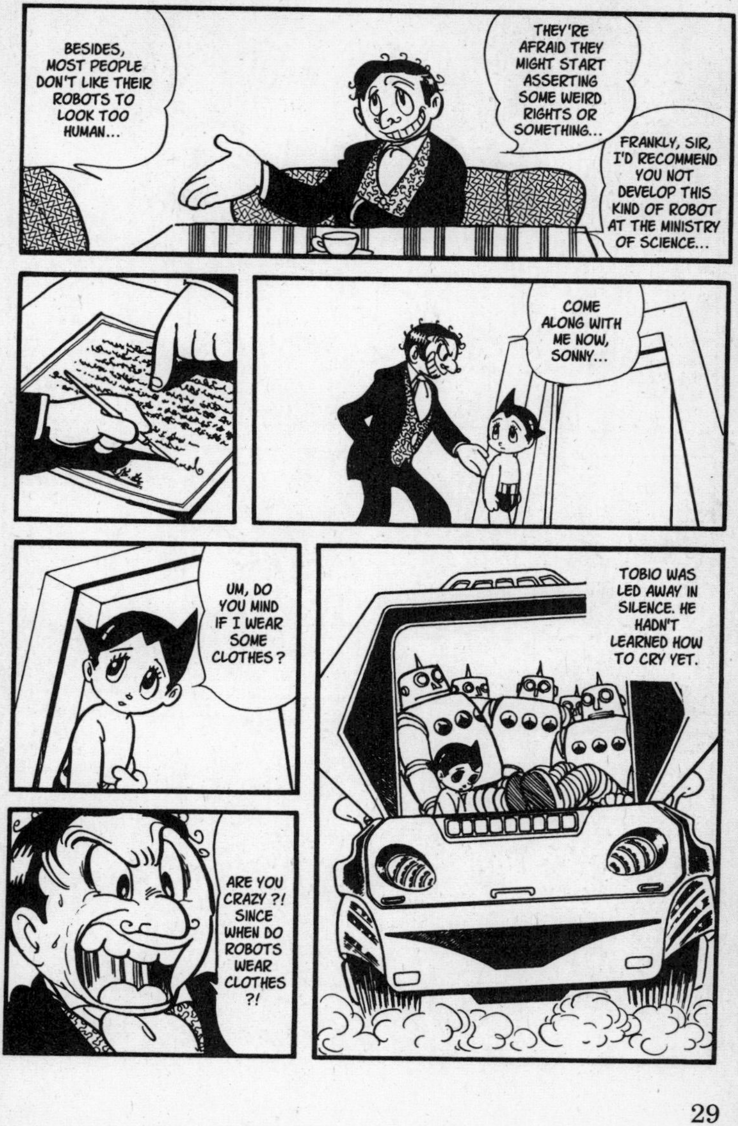
BESIDES, MOST PEOPLE DON'T LIKE THEIR ROBOTS TO LOOK TOO HUMAN...
THEY'RE AFRAID THEY MIGHT START ASSERTING SOME WEIRD RIGHTS OR SOMETHING...
FRANKLY, SIR, I'D RECOMMEND YOU NOT DEVELOP THIS KIND OF ROBOT AT THE MINISTRY OF SCIENCE...
COME ALONG WITH ME NOW, SONNY...
UM, DO YOU MIND IF I WEAR SOME CLOTHES?
ARE YOU CRAZY?! SINCE WHEN DO ROBOTS WEAR CLOTHES?!
TOBIO WAS LED AWAY IN SILENCE. HE HADN'T LEARNED HOW TO CRY YET.

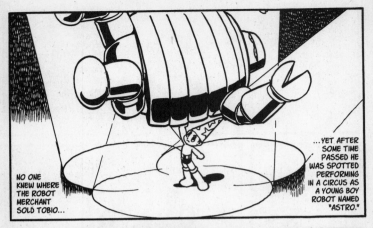

NO ONE KNEW WHERE THE ROBOT MERCHANT SOLD TOBIO...
...YET AFTER SOME TIME PASSED HE WAS SPOTTED PERFORMING IN A CIRCUS AS A YOUNG BOY ROBOT NAMED "ASTRO."
AS IT HAPPENED, A PROFESSOR OCHANOMIZU, THE HEAD OF THE OCHANOMIZU RESEARCH LAB, CAME TO SEE THE CIRCUS.
HE REALIZED RIGHT AWAY THAT "ASTRO" WAS NO ORDINARY ROBOT.
I HAD THEM GIVE YOU TO ME, SO YOU CAN COME WITH ME.
FROM NOW ON, YOU'RE NO LONGER A SLAVE TO BE BOUGHT AND SOLD !
I'LL BE LIKE A FATHER TO YOU, SO YOU DON'T NEED TO WORRY. IF YOU STUDY HARD YOU'LL TURN INTO A WONDERFUL BOY.
REALLY ?

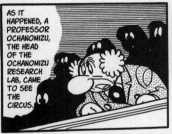

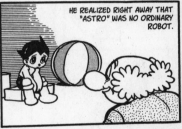

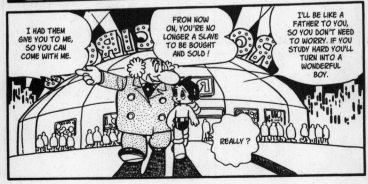

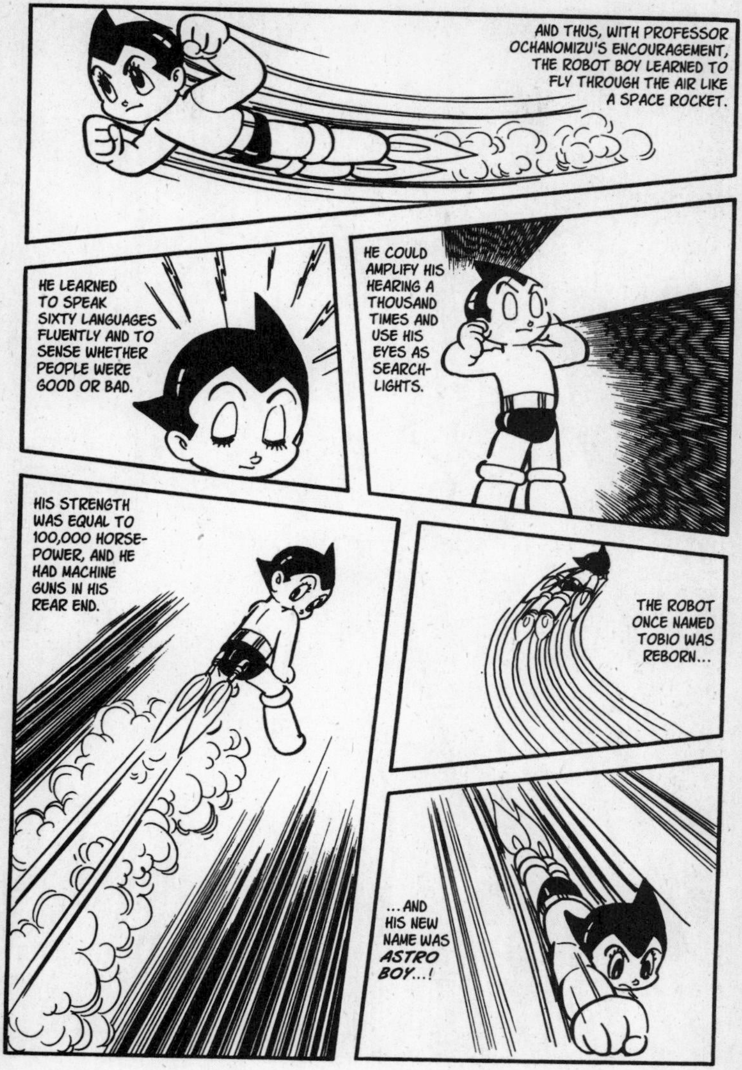
AND THUS, WITH PROFESSOR OCHANOMIZU'S ENCOURAGEMENT, THE ROBOT BOY LEARNED TO FLY THROUGH THE AIR LIKE A SPACE ROCKET.
HE LEARNED TO SPEAK SIXTY LANGUAGES FLUENTLY AND TO SENSE WHETHER PEOPLE WERE GOOD OR BAD.
HE COULD AMPLIFY HIS HEARING A THOUSAND TIMES AND USE HIS EYES AS SEARCH-LIGHTS.
HIS STRENGTH WAS EQUAL TO 100,000 HORSE-POWER, AND HE HAD MACHINE GUNS IN HIS REAR END.
THE ROBOT ONCE NAMED TOBIO WAS REBORN...
...AND HIS NEW NAME WAS *ASTRO BOY*...!

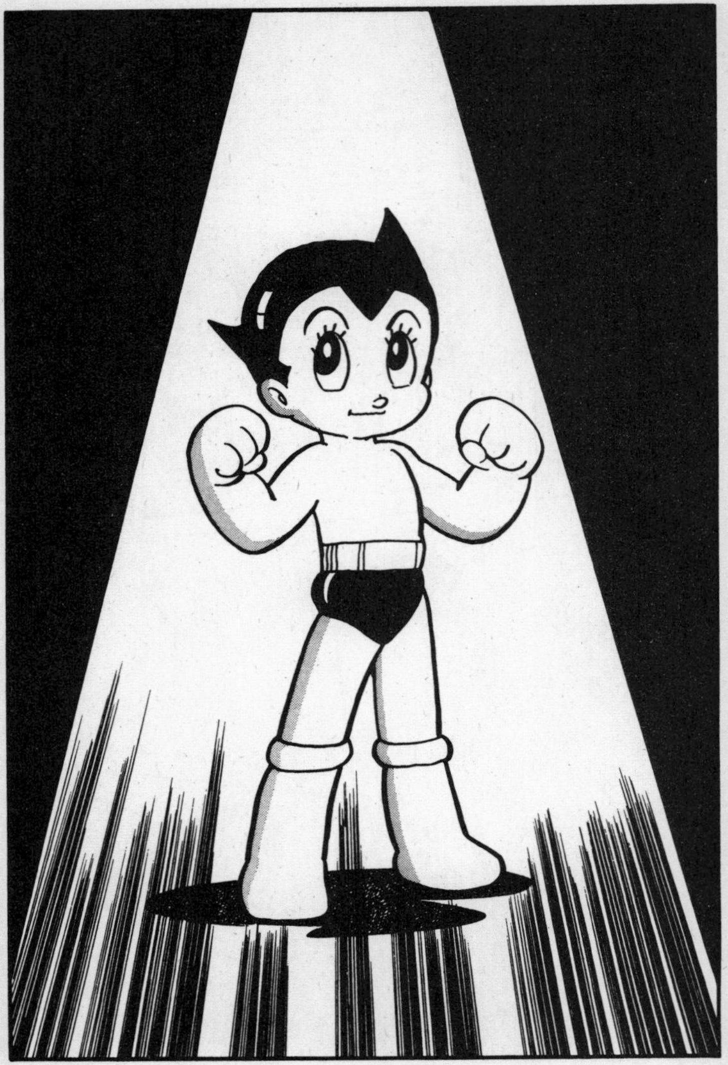

THE HOT
DOG CORPS

Originally serialized between March and
October 1961 in *Shonen* magazine.

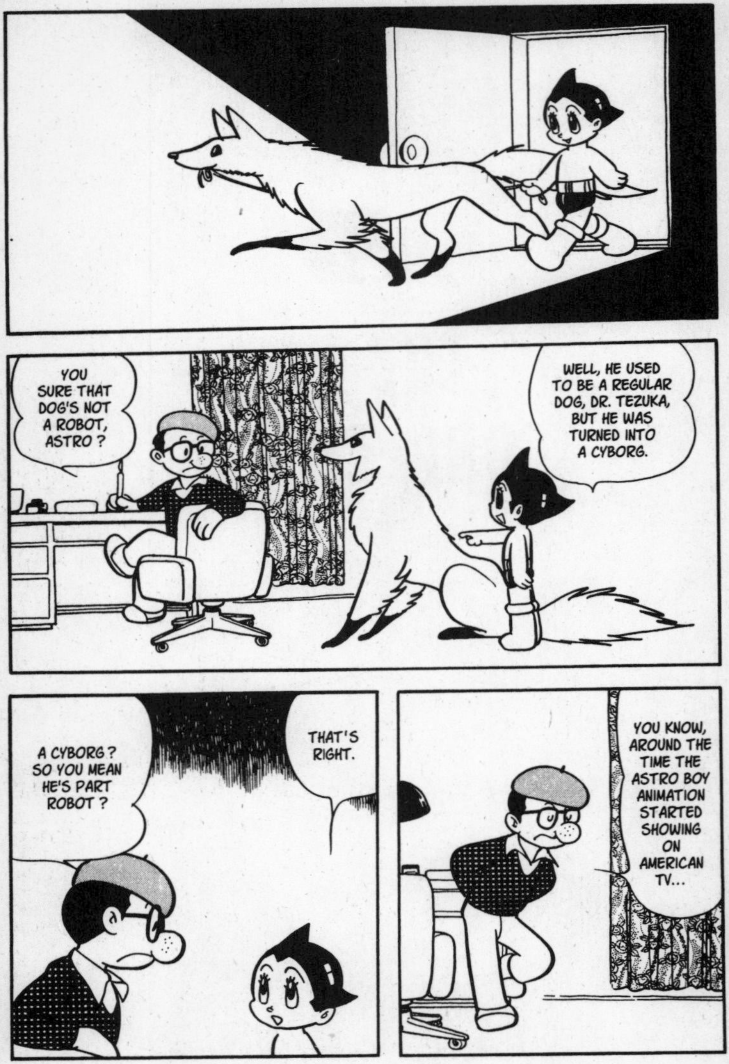
YOU SURE THAT DOG'S NOT A ROBOT, ASTRO ?
WELL, HE USED TO BE A REGULAR DOG, DR. TEZUKA, BUT HE WAS TURNED INTO A CYBORG.
A CYBORG ? SO YOU MEAN HE'S PART ROBOT ?
THAT'S RIGHT.
YOU KNOW, AROUND THE TIME THE ASTRO BOY ANIMATION STARTED SHOWING ON AMERICAN TV...

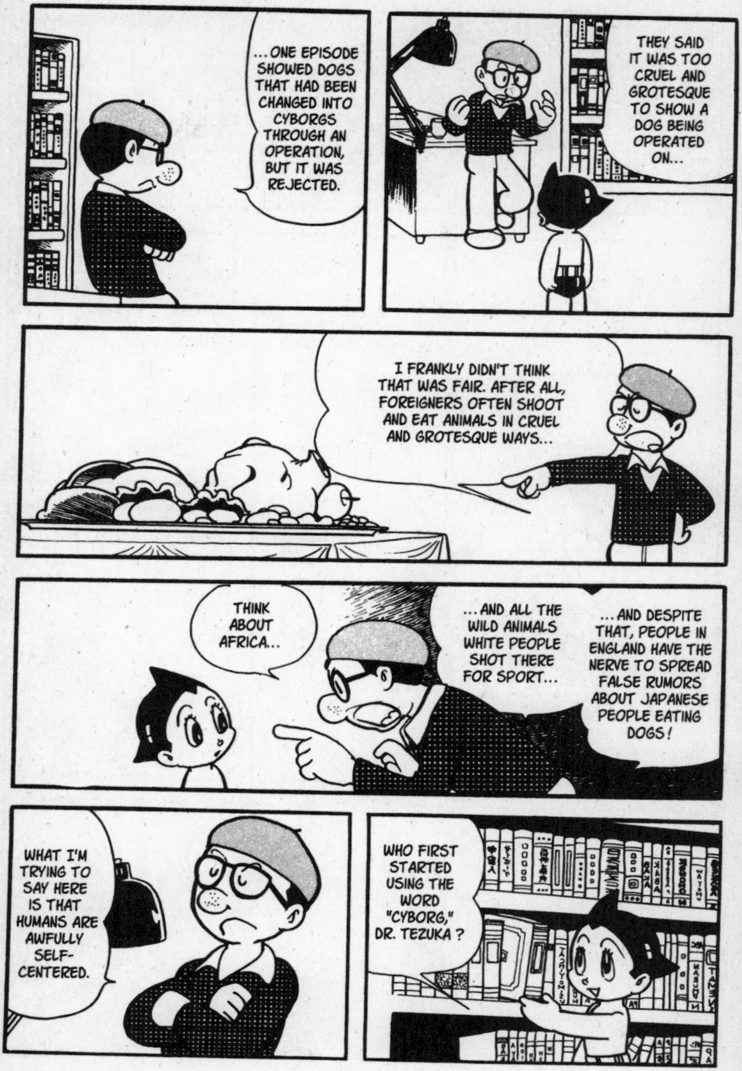
...ONE EPISODE SHOWED DOGS THAT HAD BEEN CHANGED INTO CYBORGS THROUGH AN OPERATION, BUT IT WAS REJECTED.
THEY SAID IT WAS TOO CRUEL AND GROTESQUE TO SHOW A DOG BEING OPERATED ON...
I FRANKLY DIDN'T THINK THAT WAS FAIR. AFTER ALL, FOREIGNERS OFTEN SHOOT AND EAT ANIMALS IN CRUEL AND GROTESQUE WAYS...
THINK ABOUT AFRICA...
...AND ALL THE WILD ANIMALS WHITE PEOPLE SHOT THERE FOR SPORT...
...AND DESPITE THAT, PEOPLE IN ENGLAND HAVE THE NERVE TO SPREAD FALSE RUMORS ABOUT JAPANESE PEOPLE EATING DOGS!
WHAT I'M TRYING TO SAY HERE IS THAT HUMANS ARE AWFULLY SELF-CENTERED.
WHO FIRST STARTED USING THE WORD "CYBORG," DR. TEZUKA?

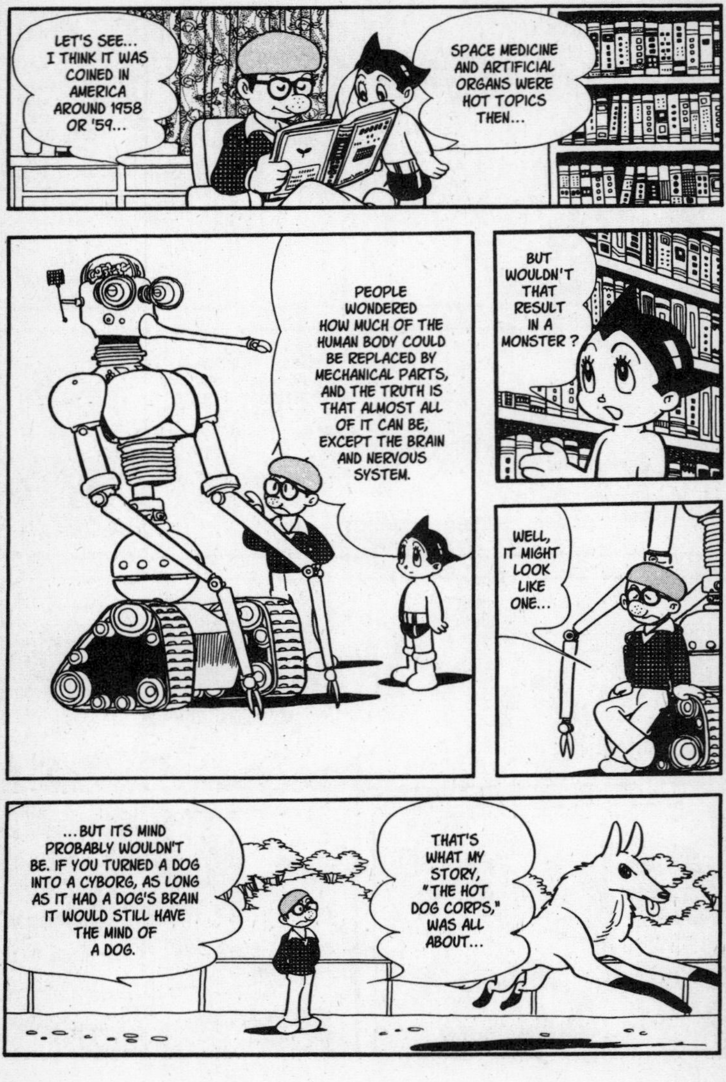
LET'S SEE... I THINK IT WAS COINED IN AMERICA AROUND 1958 OR '59...
SPACE MEDICINE AND ARTIFICIAL ORGANS WERE HOT TOPICS THEN...
PEOPLE WONDERED HOW MUCH OF THE HUMAN BODY COULD BE REPLACED BY MECHANICAL PARTS, AND THE TRUTH IS THAT ALMOST ALL OF IT CAN BE, EXCEPT THE BRAIN AND NERVOUS SYSTEM.
BUT WOULDN'T THAT RESULT IN A MONSTER?
WELL, IT MIGHT LOOK LIKE ONE...
...BUT ITS MIND PROBABLY WOULDN'T BE. IF YOU TURNED A DOG INTO A CYBORG, AS LONG AS IT HAD A DOG'S BRAIN IT WOULD STILL HAVE THE MIND OF A DOG.
THAT'S WHAT MY STORY, "THE HOT DOG CORPS," WAS ALL ABOUT...

DEAR OLD PERO

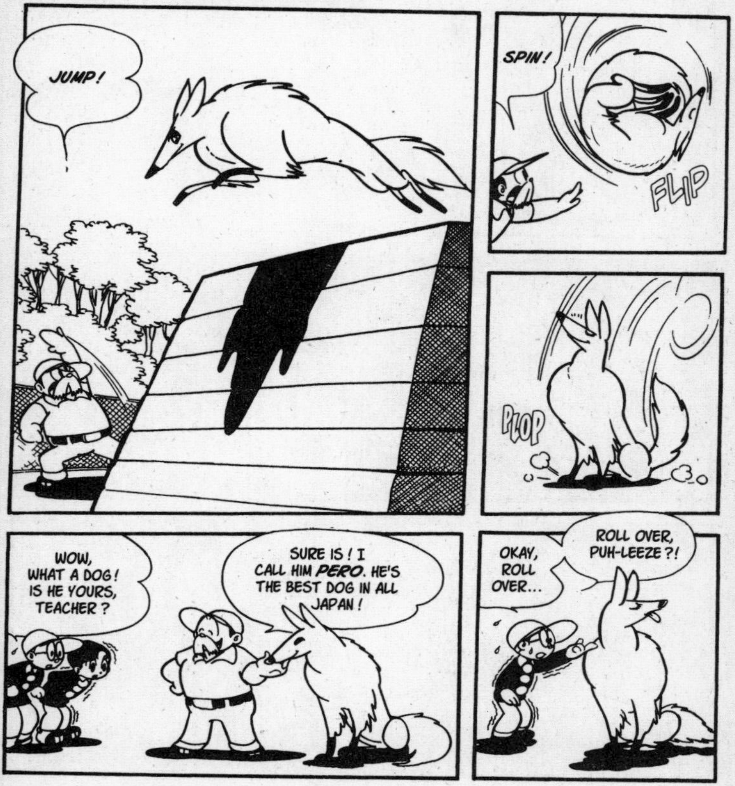
JUMP!
SPIN!
FLIP
PLOP
WOW, WHAT A DOG! IS HE YOURS, TEACHER?
SURE IS! I CALL HIM *PERO*. HE'S THE BEST DOG IN ALL JAPAN!
OKAY, ROLL OVER...
ROLL OVER, PUH-LEEZE?!

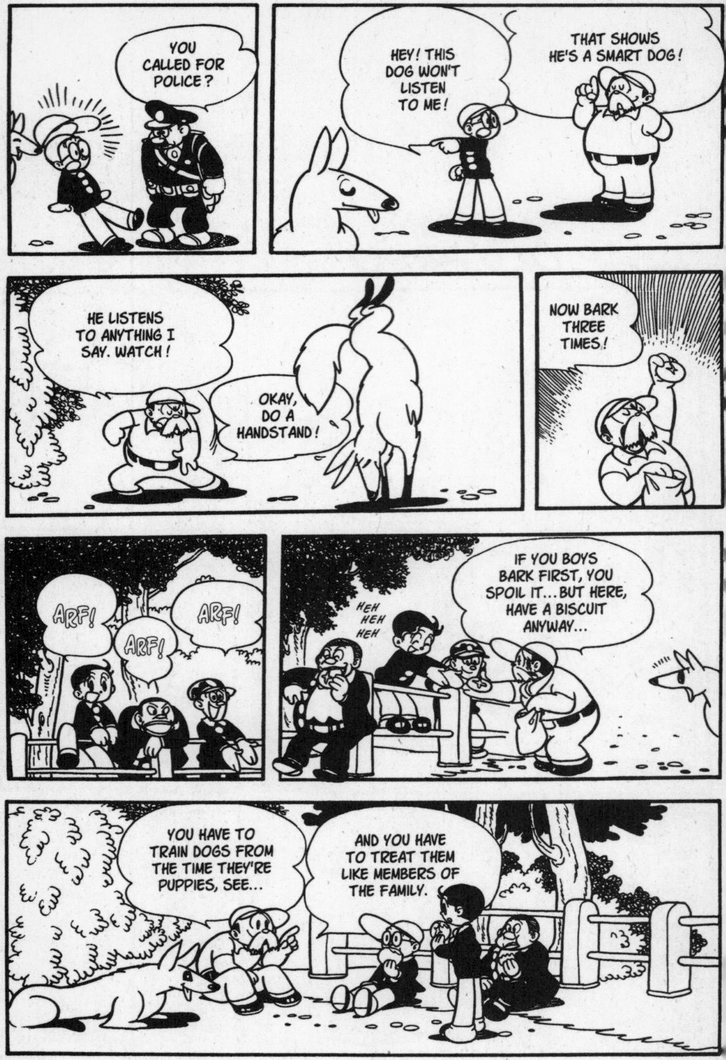
YOU CALLED FOR POLICE?
HEY! THIS DOG WON'T LISTEN TO ME!
THAT SHOWS HE'S A SMART DOG!
HE LISTENS TO ANYTHING I SAY. WATCH!
OKAY, DO A HANDSTAND!
NOW BARK THREE TIMES!
ARF!
ARF!
ARF!
HEH HEH HEH
IF YOU BOYS BARK FIRST, YOU SPOIL IT... BUT HERE, HAVE A BISCUIT ANYWAY...
YOU HAVE TO TRAIN DOGS FROM THE TIME THEY'RE PUPPIES, SEE...
AND YOU HAVE TO TREAT THEM LIKE MEMBERS OF THE FAMILY.

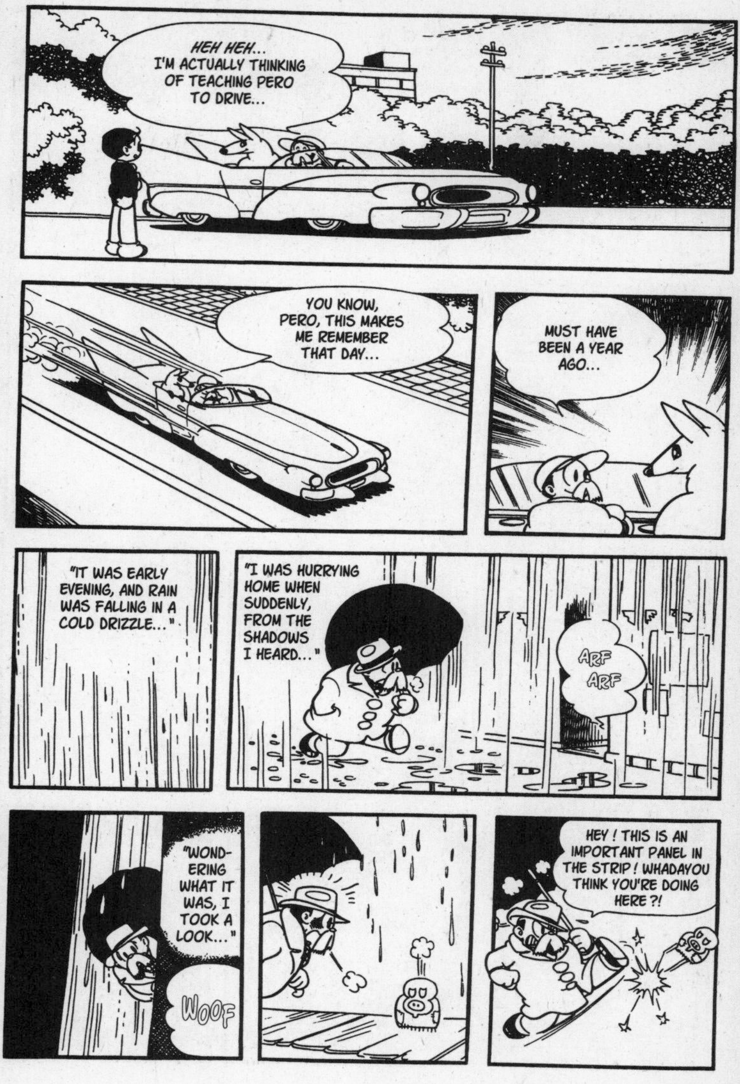
HEH HEH... I'M ACTUALLY THINKING OF TEACHING PERO TO DRIVE...
YOU KNOW, PERO, THIS MAKES ME REMEMBER THAT DAY...
MUST HAVE BEEN A YEAR AGO...
"IT WAS EARLY EVENING, AND RAIN WAS FALLING IN A COLD DRIZZLE..."
"I WAS HURRYING HOME WHEN SUDDENLY, FROM THE SHADOWS I HEARD..."
ARF ARF
"WONDERING WHAT IT WAS, I TOOK A LOOK..."
WOOF
HEY ! THIS IS AN IMPORTANT PANEL IN THE STRIP ! WHADAYOU THINK YOU'RE DOING HERE ?!

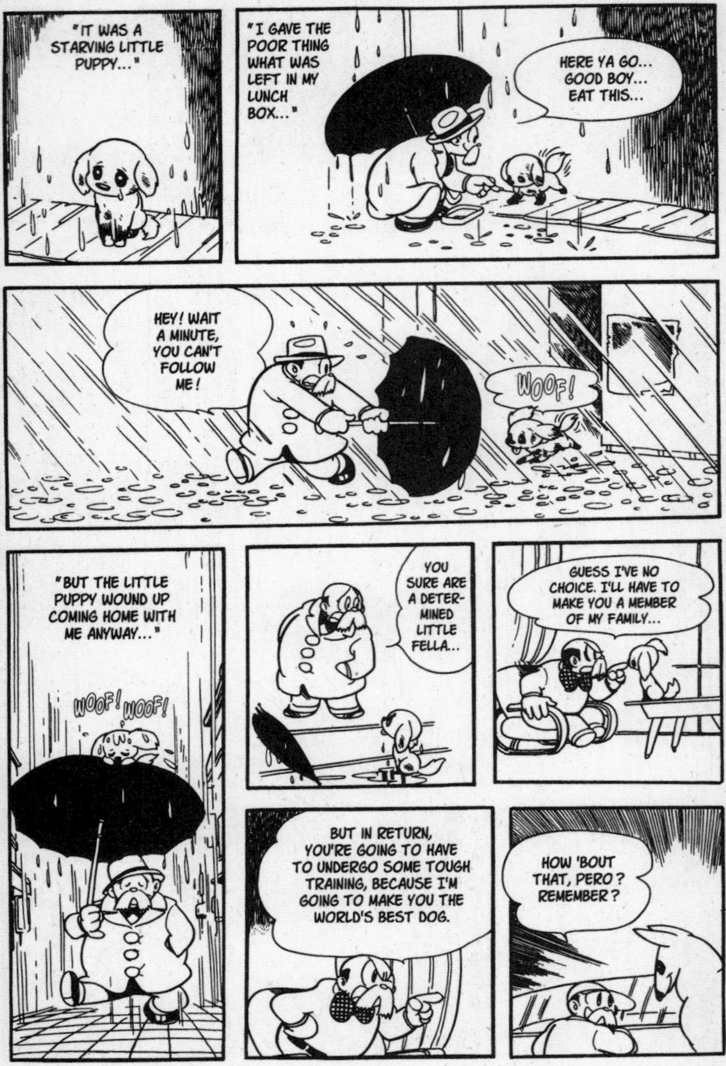
"IT WAS A STARVING LITTLE PUPPY..."
"I GAVE THE POOR THING WHAT WAS LEFT IN MY LUNCH BOX..."
HERE YA GO... GOOD BOY... EAT THIS...
HEY! WAIT A MINUTE, YOU CAN'T FOLLOW ME!
WOOF!
"BUT THE LITTLE PUPPY WOUND UP COMING HOME WITH ME ANYWAY..."
WOOF! WOOF!
YOU SURE ARE A DETERMINED LITTLE FELLA...
GUESS I'VE NO CHOICE. I'LL HAVE TO MAKE YOU A MEMBER OF MY FAMILY...
BUT IN RETURN, YOU'RE GOING TO HAVE TO UNDERGO SOME TOUGH TRAINING, BECAUSE I'M GOING TO MAKE YOU THE WORLD'S BEST DOG.
HOW 'BOUT THAT, PERO? REMEMBER?

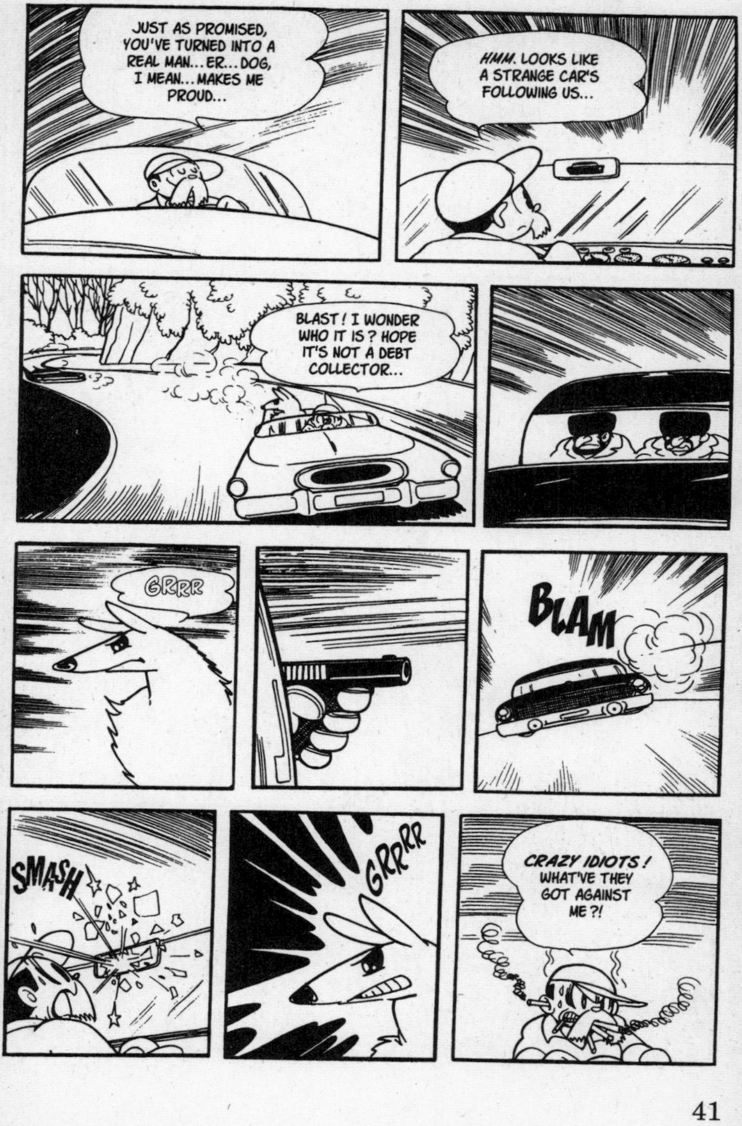
JUST AS PROMISED, YOU'VE TURNED INTO A REAL MAN... ER... DOG, I MEAN... MAKES ME PROUD...
HMM. LOOKS LIKE A STRANGE CAR'S FOLLOWING US...
BLAST! I WONDER WHO IT IS? HOPE IT'S NOT A DEBT COLLECTOR...
GRRR
BLAM
SMASH
GRRRR
CRAZY IDIOTS! WHAT'VE THEY GOT AGAINST ME?!

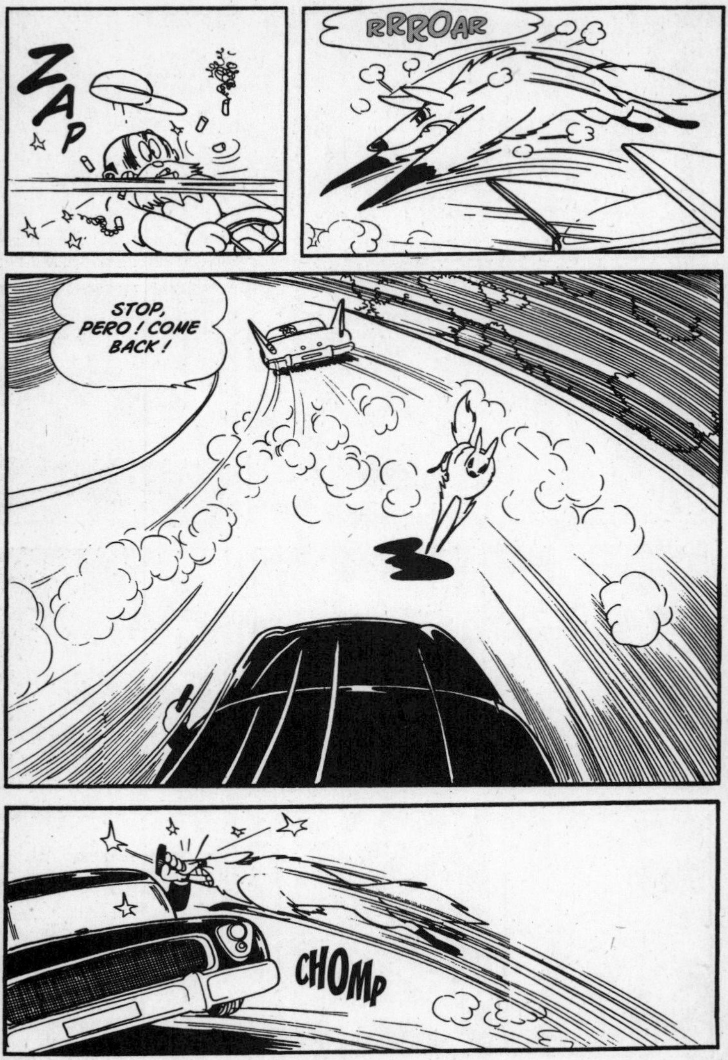

ZAP
RRROAR
STOP, PERO! COME BACK!
CHOMP

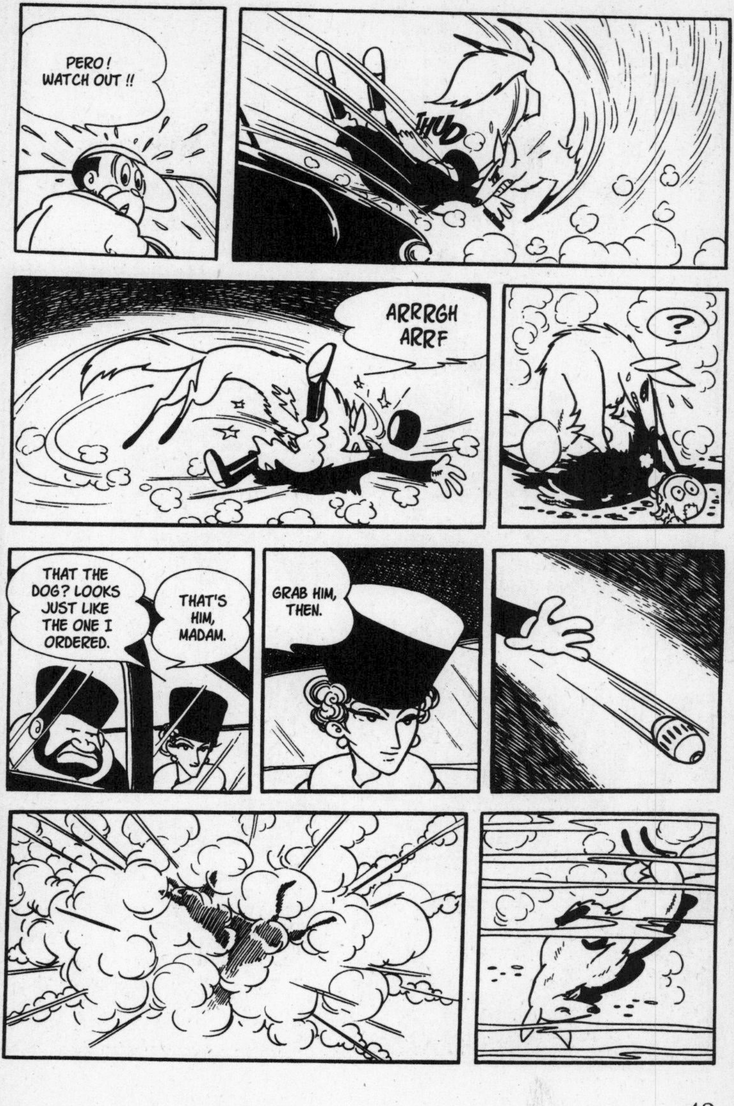
PERO! WATCH OUT!!
THUD
ARRRGH ARRF
?
THAT THE DOG? LOOKS JUST LIKE THE ONE I ORDERED.
THAT'S HIM, MADAM.
GRAB HIM, THEN.

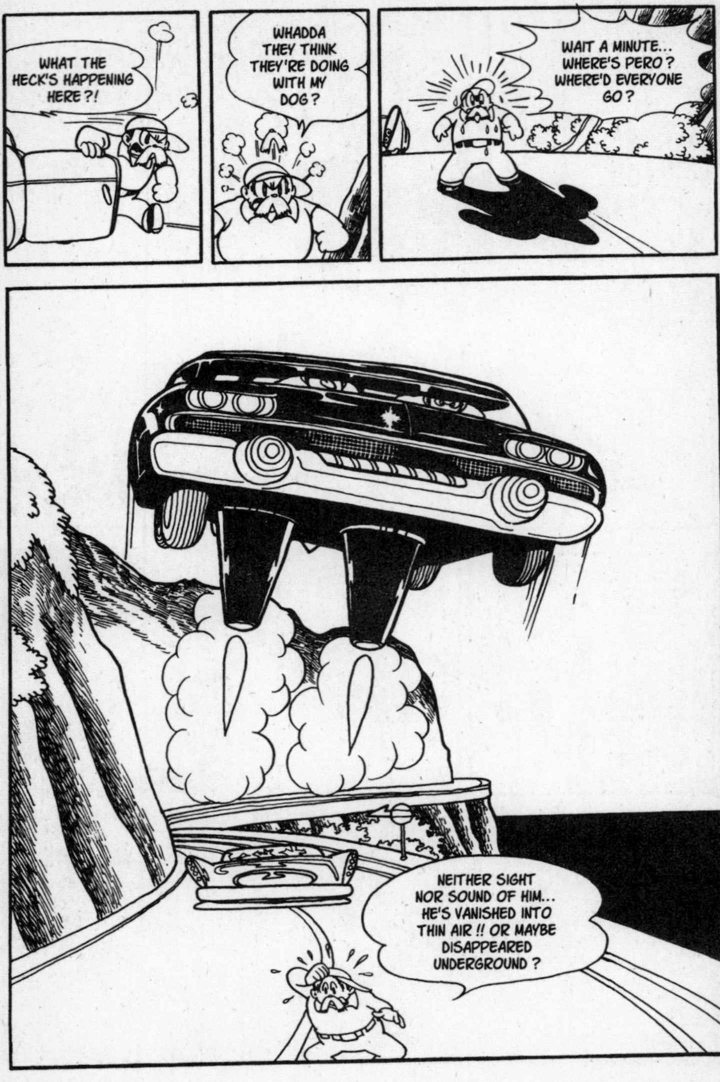
WHAT THE HECK'S HAPPENING HERE?!
WHADDA THEY THINK THEY'RE DOING WITH MY DOG?
WAIT A MINUTE... WHERE'S PERO? WHERE'D EVERYONE GO?
NEITHER SIGHT NOR SOUND OF HIM... HE'S VANISHED INTO THIN AIR !! OR MAYBE DISAPPEARED UNDERGROUND?

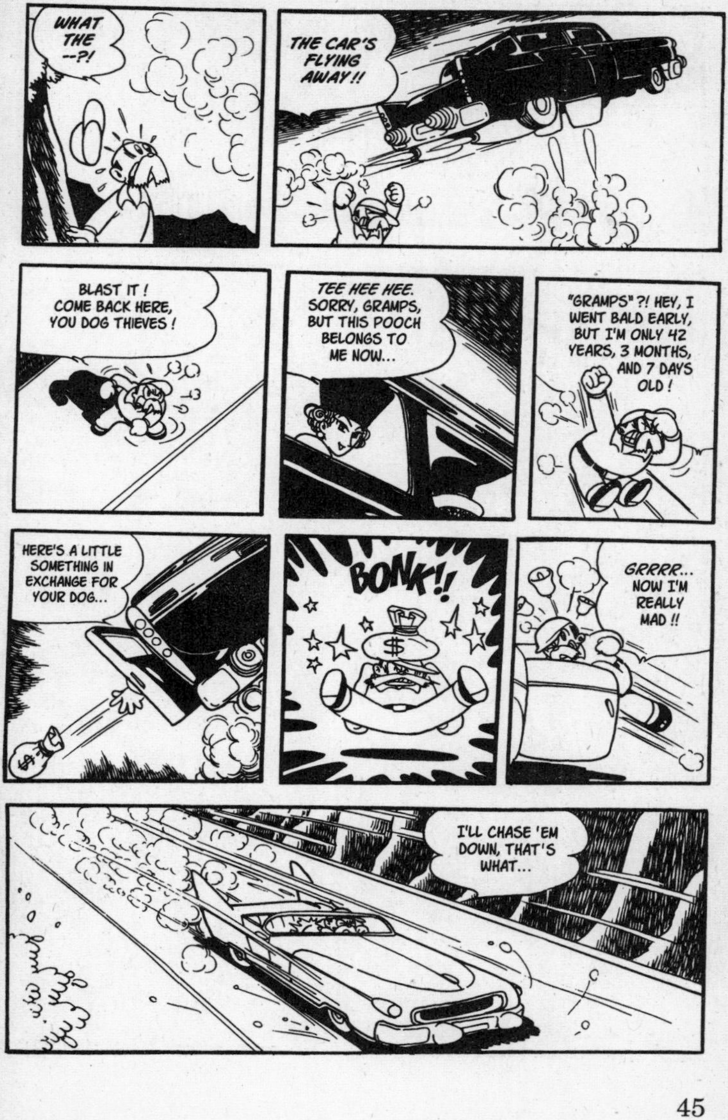
WHAT THE --?!
THE CAR'S FLYING AWAY!!
BLAST IT! COME BACK HERE, YOU DOG THIEVES!
TEE HEE HEE. SORRY, GRAMPS, BUT THIS POOCH BELONGS TO ME NOW...
"GRAMPS"?! HEY, I WENT BALD EARLY, BUT I'M ONLY 42 YEARS, 3 MONTHS, AND 7 DAYS OLD!
HERE'S A LITTLE SOMETHING IN EXCHANGE FOR YOUR DOG...
BONK!!
GRRRR... NOW I'M REALLY MAD!!
I'LL CHASE 'EM DOWN, THAT'S WHAT...

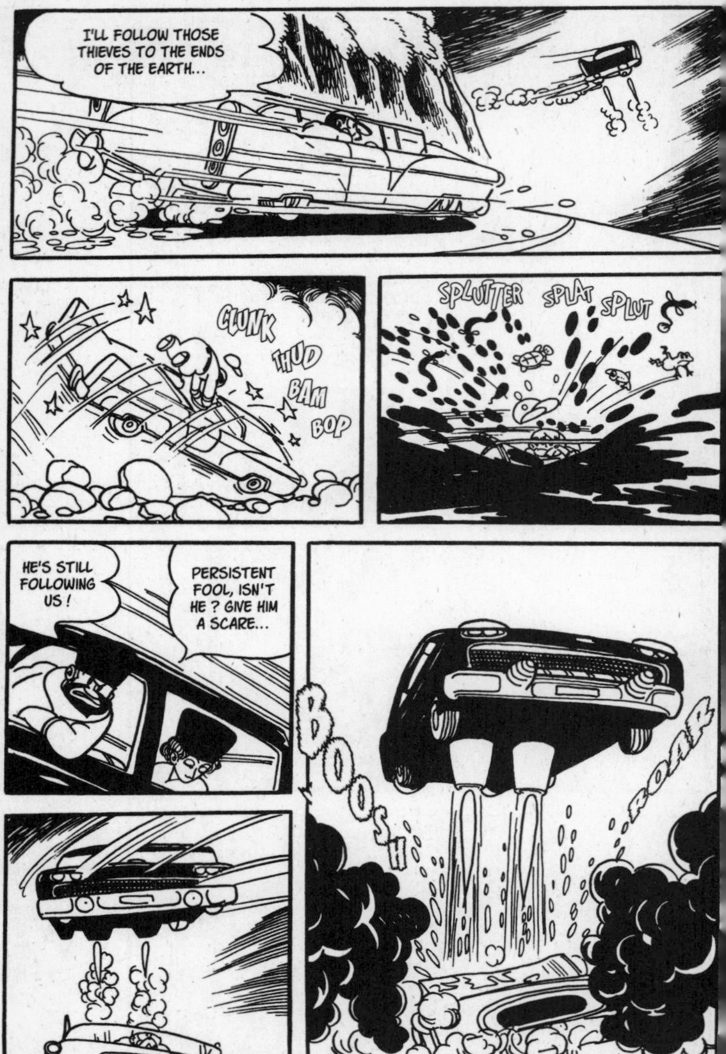
I'LL FOLLOW THOSE THIEVES TO THE ENDS OF THE EARTH...
CLUNK
THUD
BAM
BOP
SPLUTTER
SPLAT
SPLUT
HE'S STILL FOLLOWING US !
PERSISTENT FOOL, ISN'T HE ? GIVE HIM A SCARE...
BOOSH
ROAR

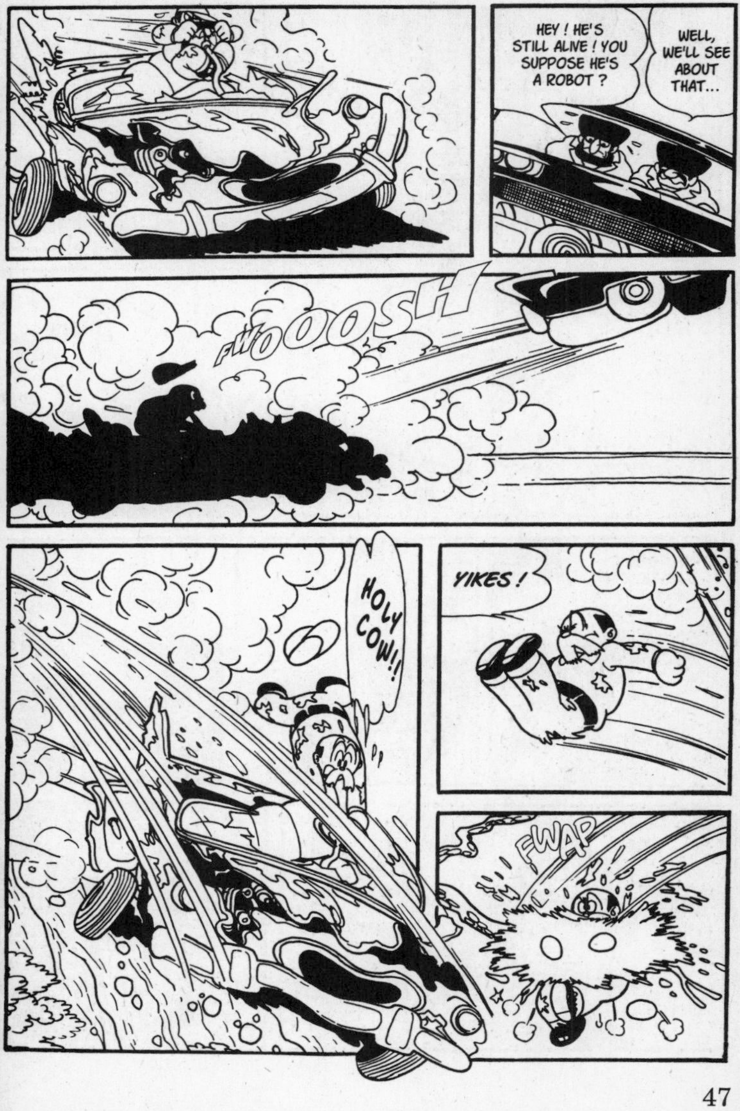
HEY ! HE'S STILL ALIVE ! YOU SUPPOSE HE'S A ROBOT ?
WELL, WE'LL SEE ABOUT THAT...
FWOOOSH
HOLY COW!!
YIKES !
FWAP

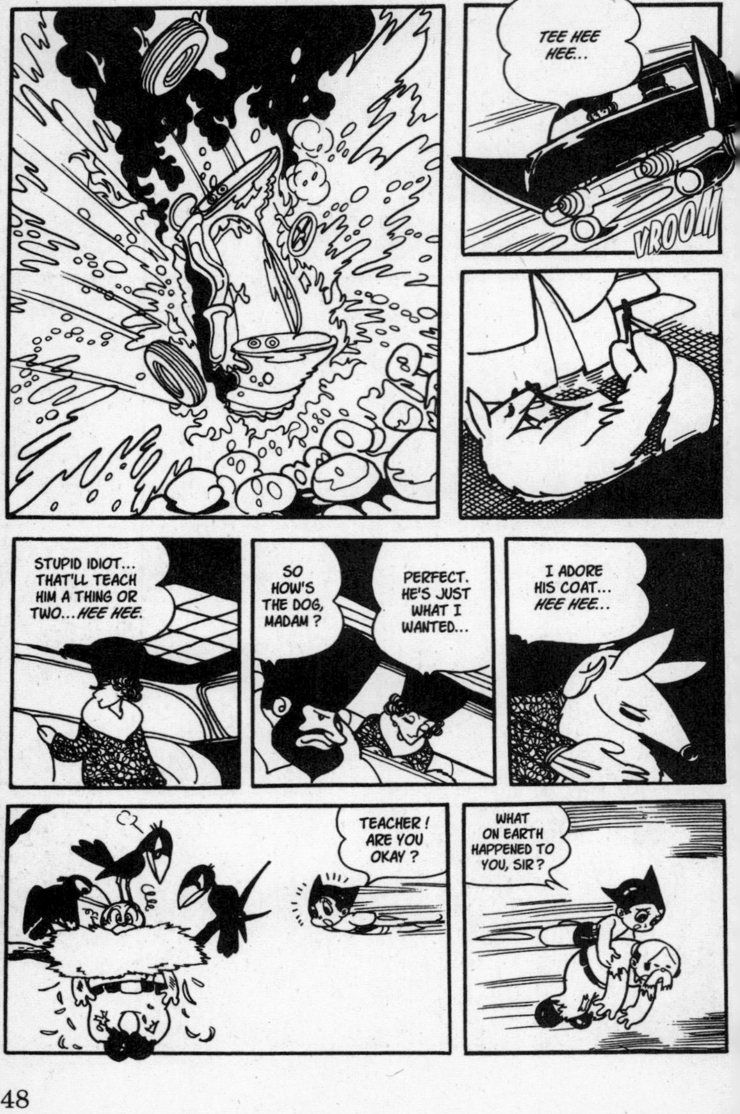
TEE HEE HEE...
VROOM
STUPID IDIOT... THAT'LL TEACH HIM A THING OR TWO... *HEE HEE.*
SO HOW'S THE DOG, MADAM?
PERFECT. HE'S JUST WHAT I WANTED...
I ADORE HIS COAT... *HEE HEE...*
TEACHER! ARE YOU OKAY?
WHAT ON EARTH HAPPENED TO YOU, SIR?

A STRANGE PILOT ARRIVES

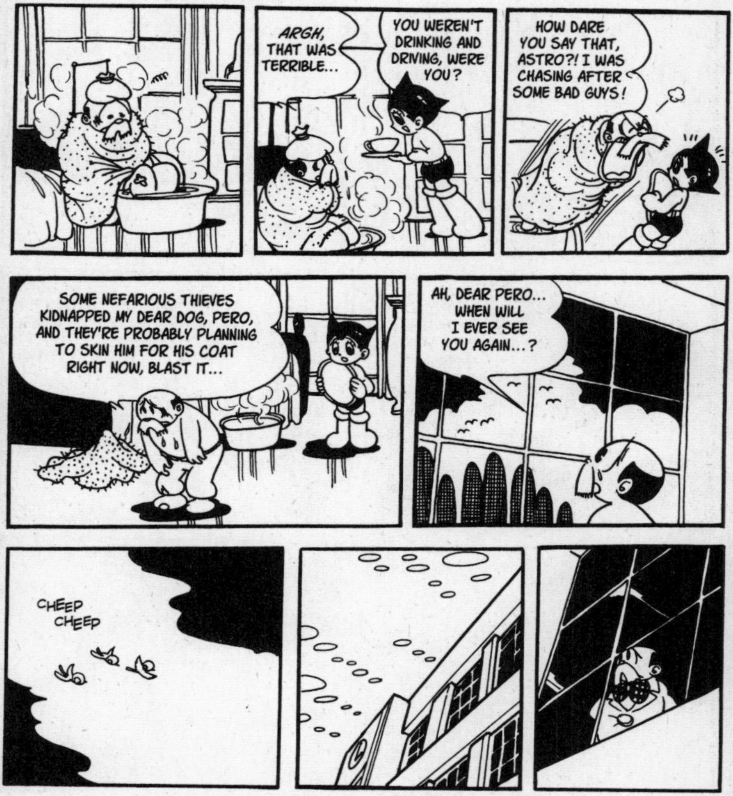

ARGH, THAT WAS TERRIBLE...
YOU WEREN'T DRINKING AND DRIVING, WERE YOU?
HOW DARE YOU SAY THAT, ASTRO?! I WAS CHASING AFTER SOME BAD GUYS!
SOME NEFARIOUS THIEVES KIDNAPPED MY DEAR DOG, PERO, AND THEY'RE PROBABLY PLANNING TO SKIN HIM FOR HIS COAT RIGHT NOW, BLAST IT...
AH, DEAR PERO... WHEN WILL I EVER SEE YOU AGAIN...?
CHEEP CHEEP

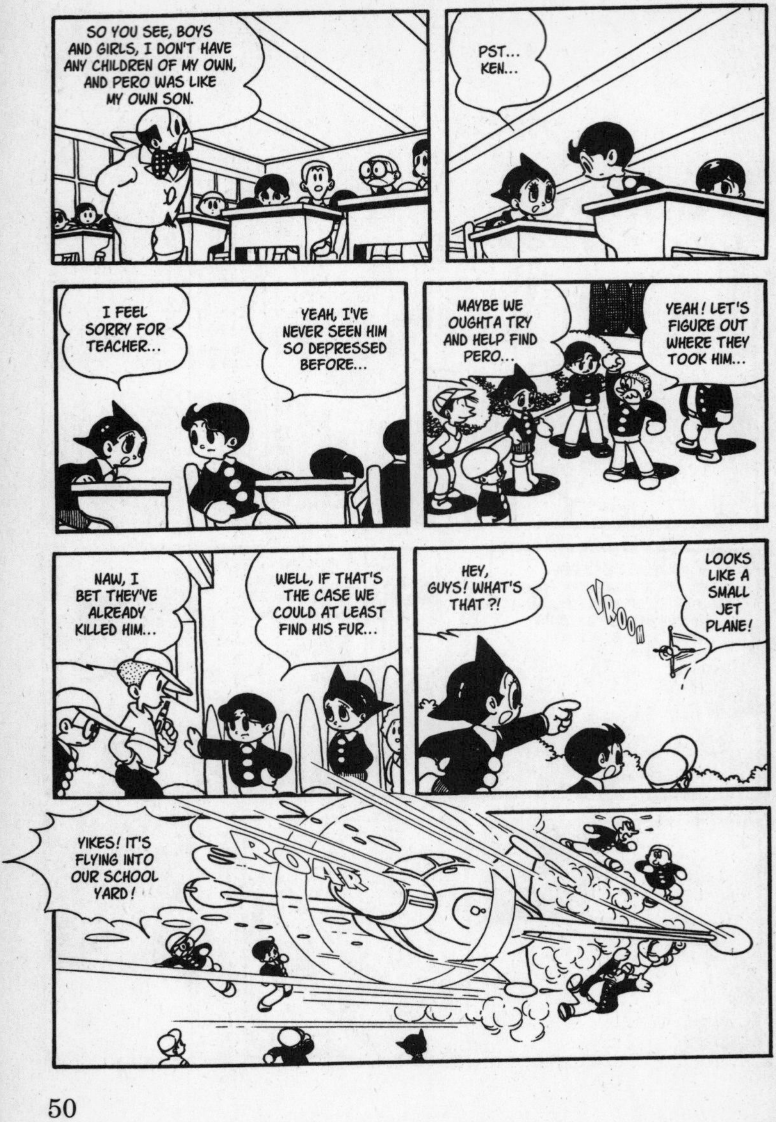
SO YOU SEE, BOYS AND GIRLS, I DON'T HAVE ANY CHILDREN OF MY OWN, AND PERO WAS LIKE MY OWN SON.
PST... KEN...
I FEEL SORRY FOR TEACHER...
YEAH, I'VE NEVER SEEN HIM SO DEPRESSED BEFORE...
MAYBE WE OUGHTA TRY AND HELP FIND PERO...
YEAH! LET'S FIGURE OUT WHERE THEY TOOK HIM...
NAW, I BET THEY'VE ALREADY KILLED HIM...
WELL, IF THAT'S THE CASE WE COULD AT LEAST FIND HIS FUR...
HEY, GUYS! WHAT'S THAT?!
VROOM
LOOKS LIKE A SMALL JET PLANE!
YIKES! IT'S FLYING INTO OUR SCHOOL YARD!
ROAR

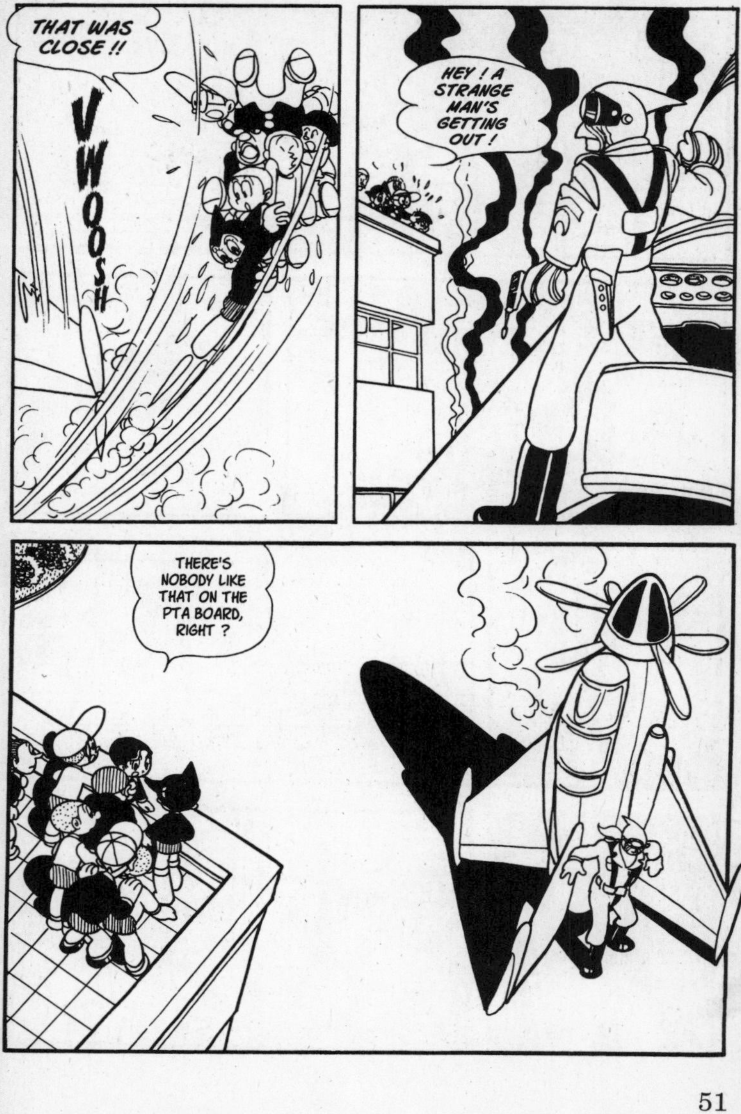
THAT WAS CLOSE !!
VWOOSH
HEY ! A STRANGE MAN'S GETTING OUT !
THERE'S NOBODY LIKE THAT ON THE PTA BOARD, RIGHT ?

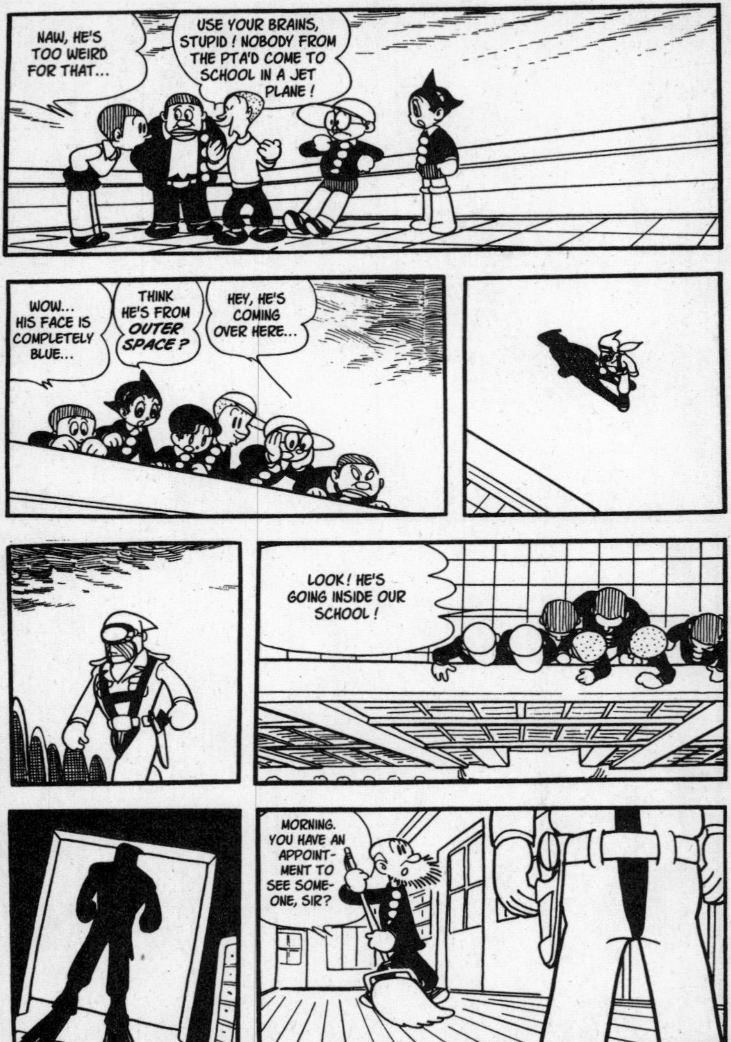
NAW, HE'S TOO WEIRD FOR THAT...
USE YOUR BRAINS, STUPID! NOBODY FROM THE PTA'D COME TO SCHOOL IN A JET PLANE!
WOW... HIS FACE IS COMPLETELY BLUE...
THINK HE'S FROM OUTER SPACE?
HEY, HE'S COMING OVER HERE...
LOOK! HE'S GOING INSIDE OUR SCHOOL!
MORNING. YOU HAVE AN APPOINT-MENT TO SEE SOME-ONE, SIR?

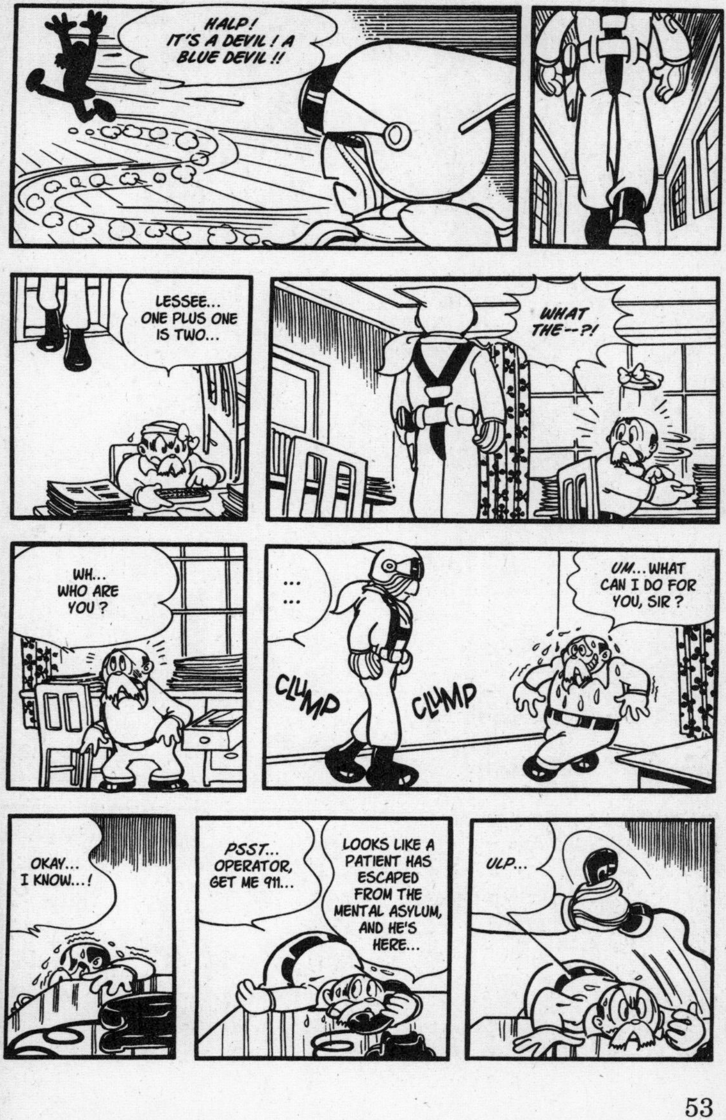
HALP! IT'S A DEVIL! A BLUE DEVIL!!
LESSEE... ONE PLUS ONE IS TWO...
WHAT THE--?!
WH... WHO ARE YOU?
...
...
CLUMP
CLUMP
UM... WHAT CAN I DO FOR YOU, SIR?
OKAY... I KNOW...!
PSST... OPERATOR, GET ME 911...
LOOKS LIKE A PATIENT HAS ESCAPED FROM THE MENTAL ASYLUM, AND HE'S HERE...
ULP...

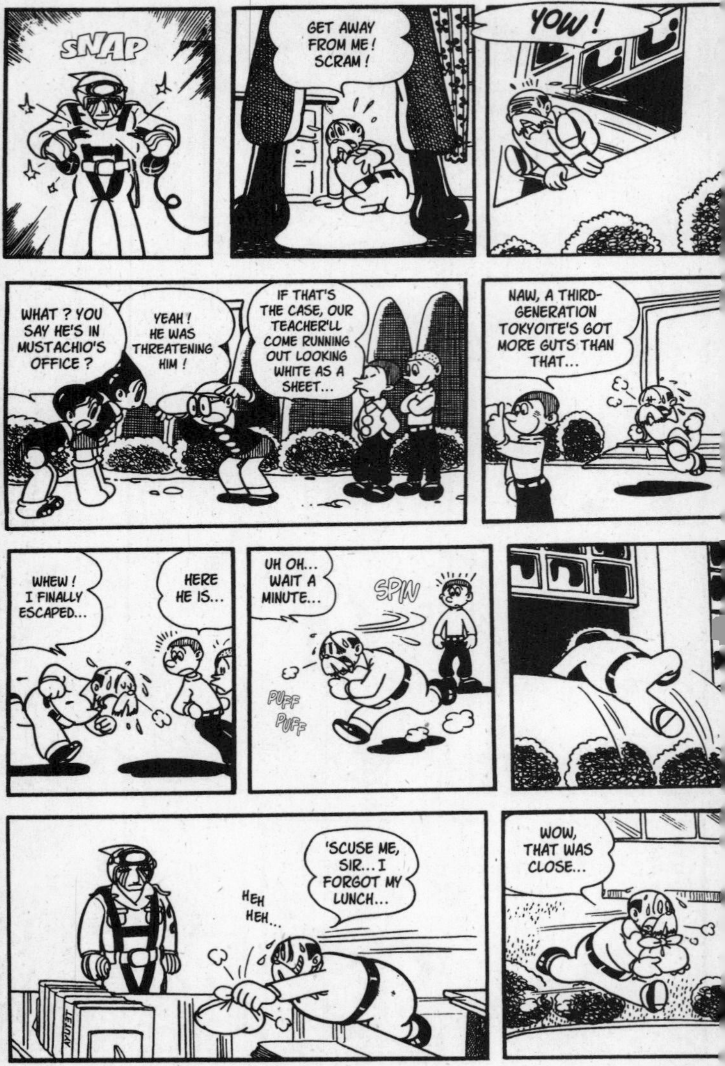
SNAP
GET AWAY FROM ME! SCRAM!
YOW!
WHAT? YOU SAY HE'S IN MUSTACHIO'S OFFICE?
YEAH! HE WAS THREATENING HIM!
IF THAT'S THE CASE, OUR TEACHER'LL COME RUNNING OUT LOOKING WHITE AS A SHEET...
NAW, A THIRD-GENERATION TOKYOITE'S GOT MORE GUTS THAN THAT...
WHEW! I FINALLY ESCAPED...
HERE HE IS...
UH OH... WAIT A MINUTE...
SPIN
PUFF PUFF
HEH HEH...
'SCUSE ME, SIR... I FORGOT MY LUNCH...
WOW, THAT WAS CLOSE...

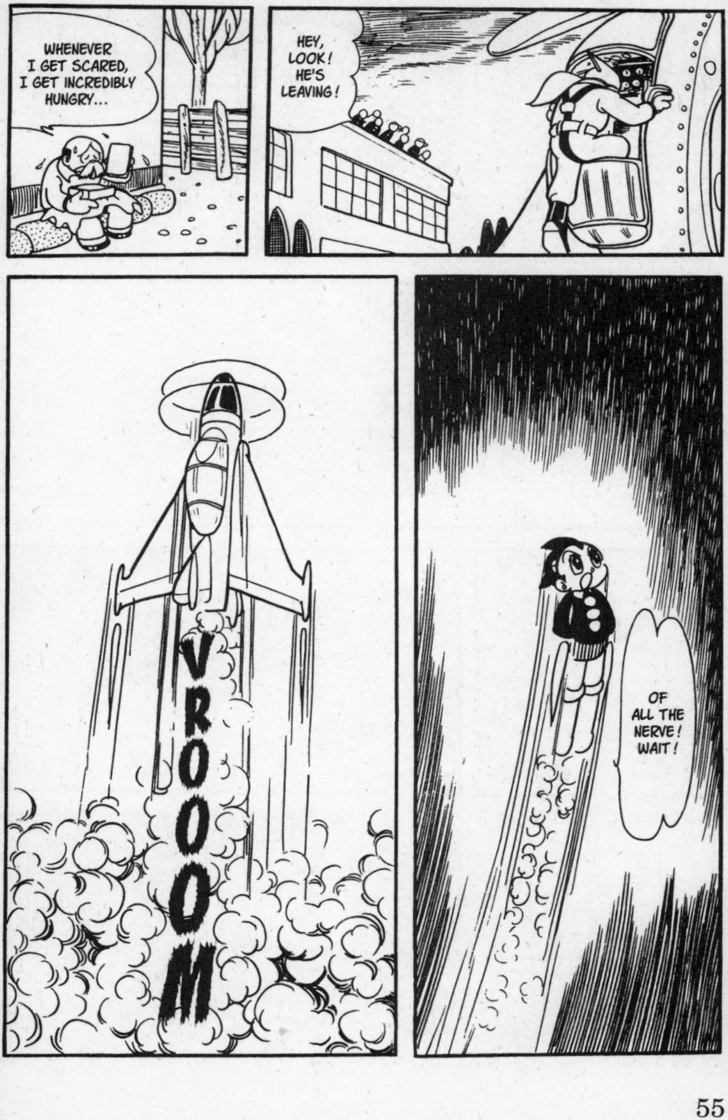
WHENEVER I GET SCARED, I GET INCREDIBLY HUNGRY...
HEY, LOOK! HE'S LEAVING!
VROOOM
OF ALL THE NERVE! WAIT!

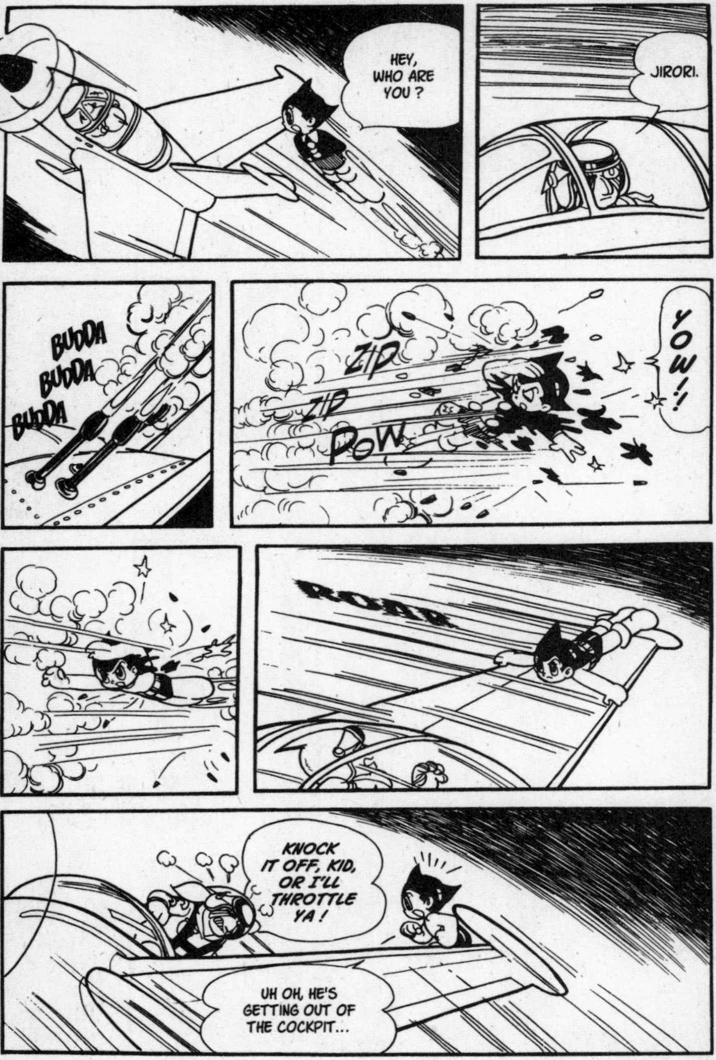
HEY, WHO ARE YOU ?
JIRORI.
BUDDA BUDDA BUDDA
ZIP
ZIP
POW
YOW!!
ROAR
KNOCK IT OFF, KID, OR I'LL THROTTLE YA !
UH OH, HE'S GETTING OUT OF THE COCKPIT...

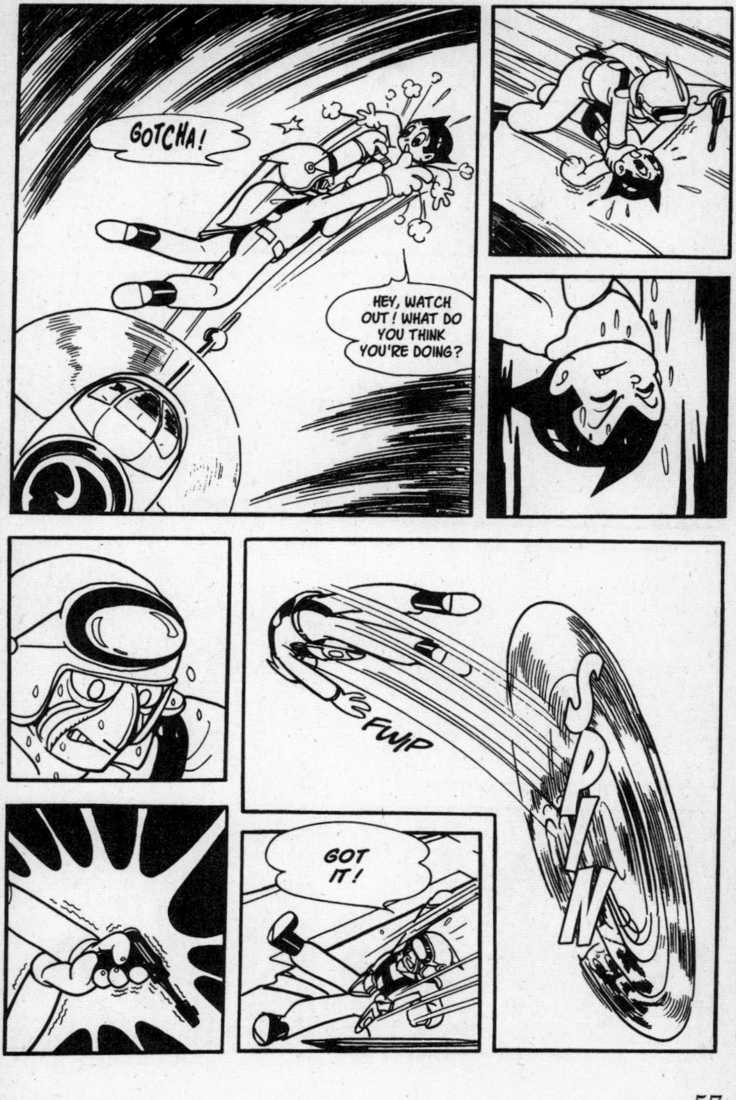
GOTCHA!
HEY, WATCH OUT! WHAT DO YOU THINK YOU'RE DOING?
FWIP
SPIN
GOT IT!

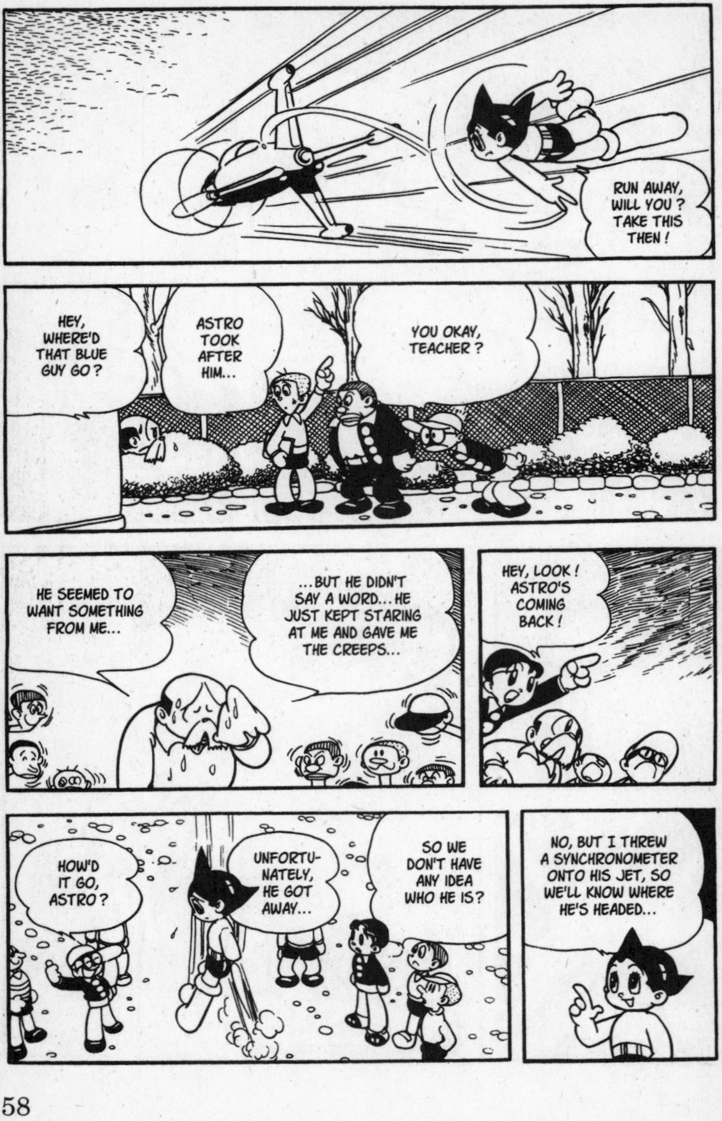
RUN AWAY, WILL YOU? TAKE THIS THEN!
HEY, WHERE'D THAT BLUE GUY GO?
ASTRO TOOK AFTER HIM...
YOU OKAY, TEACHER?
HE SEEMED TO WANT SOMETHING FROM ME...
...BUT HE DIDN'T SAY A WORD... HE JUST KEPT STARING AT ME AND GAVE ME THE CREEPS...
HEY, LOOK! ASTRO'S COMING BACK!
HOW'D IT GO, ASTRO?
UNFORTUNATELY, HE GOT AWAY...
SO WE DON'T HAVE ANY IDEA WHO HE IS?
NO, BUT I THREW A SYNCHRONOMETER ONTO HIS JET, SO WE'LL KNOW WHERE HE'S HEADED...

THE FAR REACHES OF THE ARCTIC OCEAN

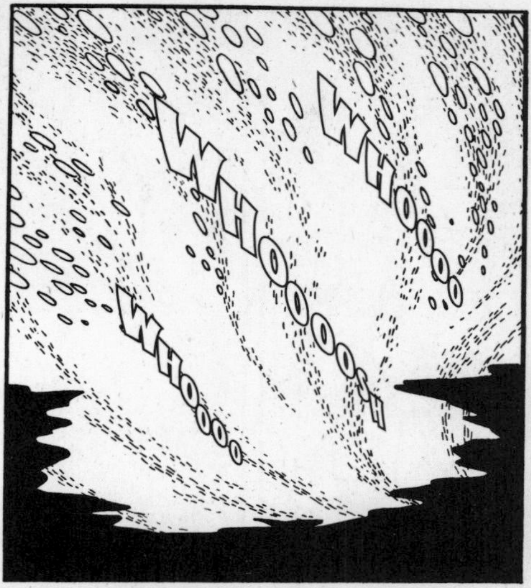
WHOOOO
WHOOOOOSH
WHOOOO

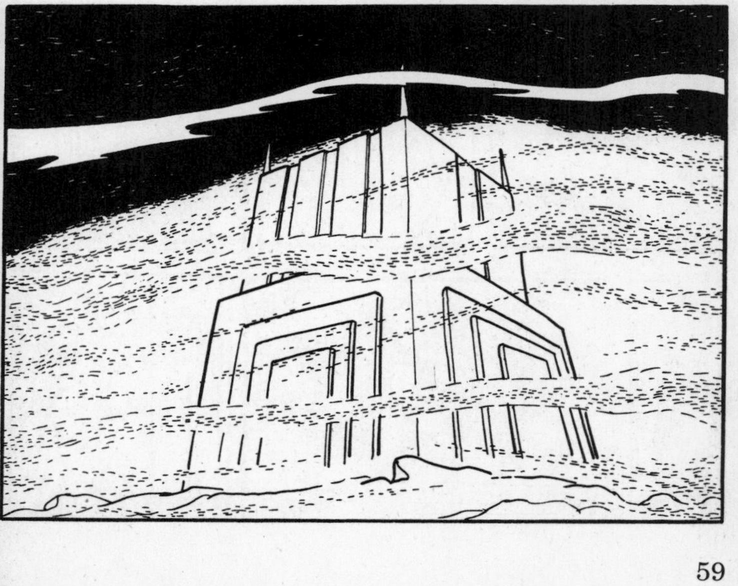

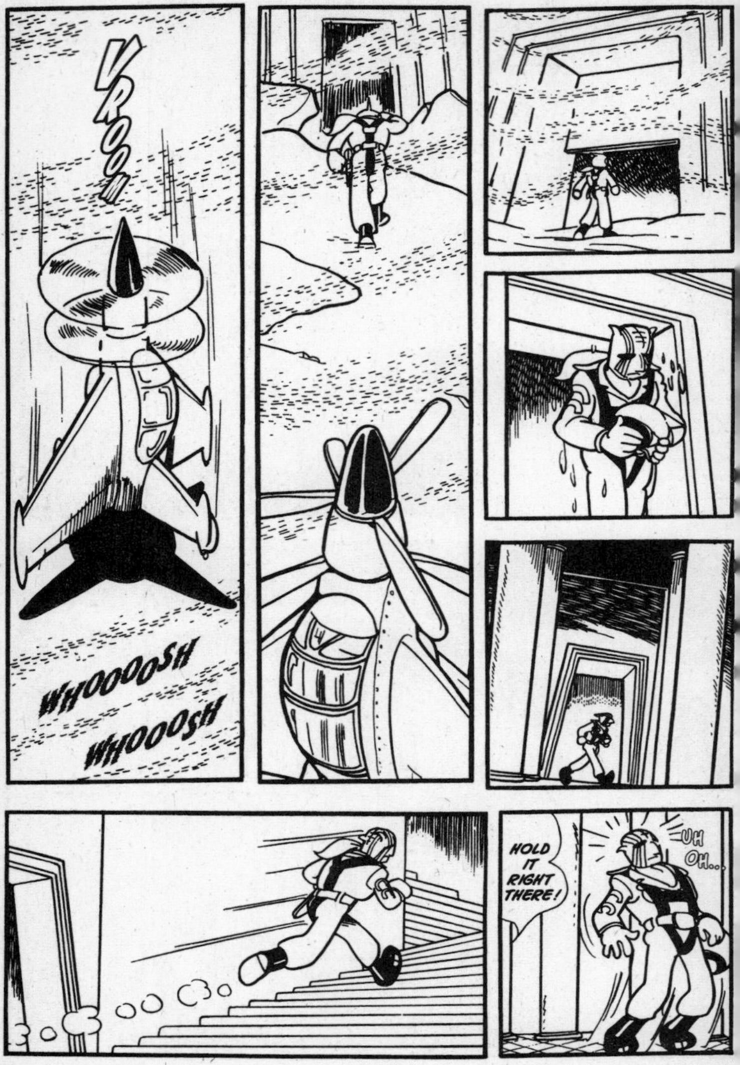
VROOM
WHOOOOSH
WHOOOSH
HOLD IT RIGHT THERE!
UH OH...

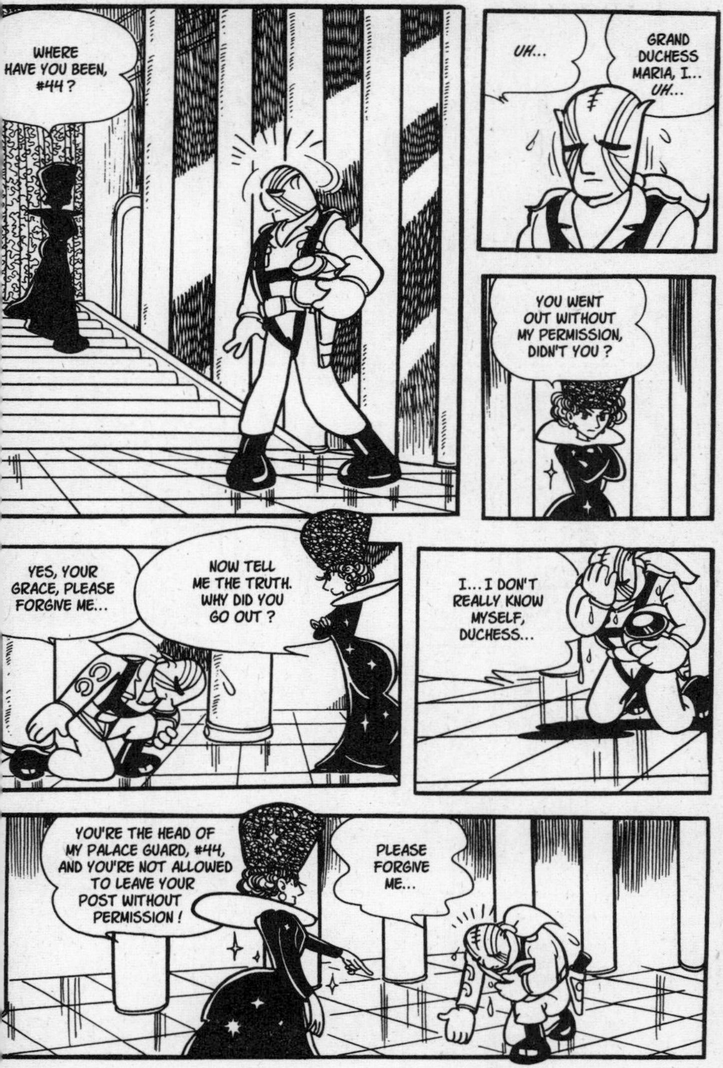
WHERE HAVE YOU BEEN, #44?
UH...
GRAND DUCHESS MARIA, I... UH...
YOU WENT OUT WITHOUT MY PERMISSION, DIDN'T YOU?
YES, YOUR GRACE, PLEASE FORGIVE ME...
NOW TELL ME THE TRUTH. WHY DID YOU GO OUT?
I... I DON'T REALLY KNOW MYSELF, DUCHESS...
YOU'RE THE HEAD OF MY PALACE GUARD, #44, AND YOU'RE NOT ALLOWED TO LEAVE YOUR POST WITHOUT PERMISSION!
PLEASE FORGIVE ME...

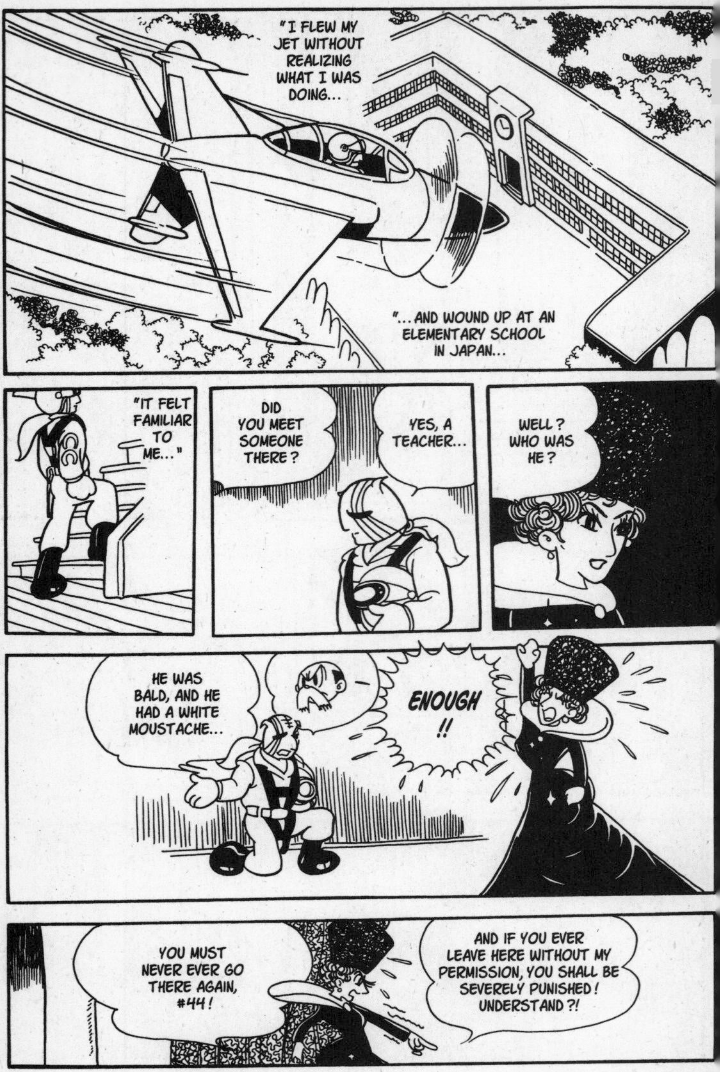
"I FLEW MY JET WITHOUT REALIZING WHAT I WAS DOING...
"...AND WOUND UP AT AN ELEMENTARY SCHOOL IN JAPAN...
"IT FELT FAMILIAR TO ME..."
DID YOU MEET SOMEONE THERE?
YES, A TEACHER...
WELL? WHO WAS HE?
HE WAS BALD, AND HE HAD A WHITE MOUSTACHE...
ENOUGH !!
YOU MUST NEVER EVER GO THERE AGAIN, #44!
AND IF YOU EVER LEAVE HERE WITHOUT MY PERMISSION, YOU SHALL BE SEVERELY PUNISHED! UNDERSTAND?!

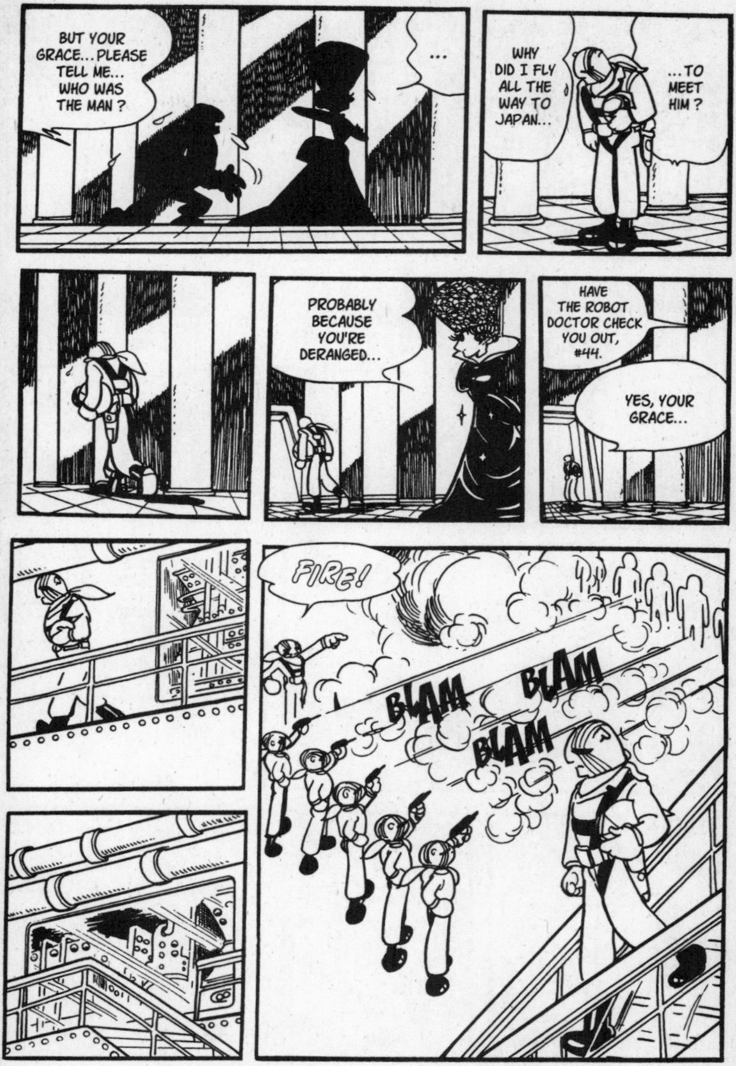

BUT YOUR GRACE... PLEASE TELL ME... WHO WAS THE MAN ?
...
WHY DID I FLY ALL THE WAY TO JAPAN...
...TO MEET HIM ?
PROBABLY BECAUSE YOU'RE DERANGED...
HAVE THE ROBOT DOCTOR CHECK YOU OUT, #44.
YES, YOUR GRACE...
FIRE!
BLAM
BLAM
BLAM

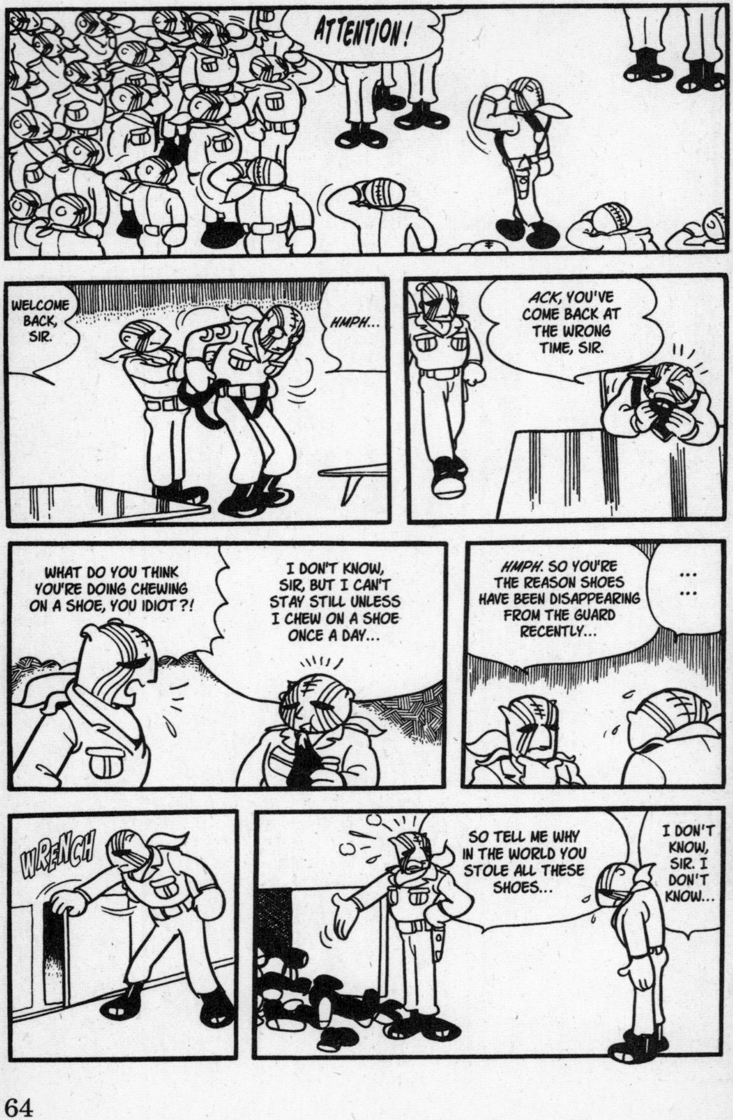
ATTENTION!
WELCOME BACK, SIR.
HMPH...
ACK, YOU'VE COME BACK AT THE WRONG TIME, SIR.
WHAT DO YOU THINK YOU'RE DOING CHEWING ON A SHOE, YOU IDIOT?!
I DON'T KNOW, SIR, BUT I CAN'T STAY STILL UNLESS I CHEW ON A SHOE ONCE A DAY...
HMPH. SO YOU'RE THE REASON SHOES HAVE BEEN DISAPPEARING FROM THE GUARD RECENTLY...
...
...
WRENCH
SO TELL ME WHY IN THE WORLD YOU STOLE ALL THESE SHOES...
I DON'T KNOW, SIR. I DON'T KNOW...

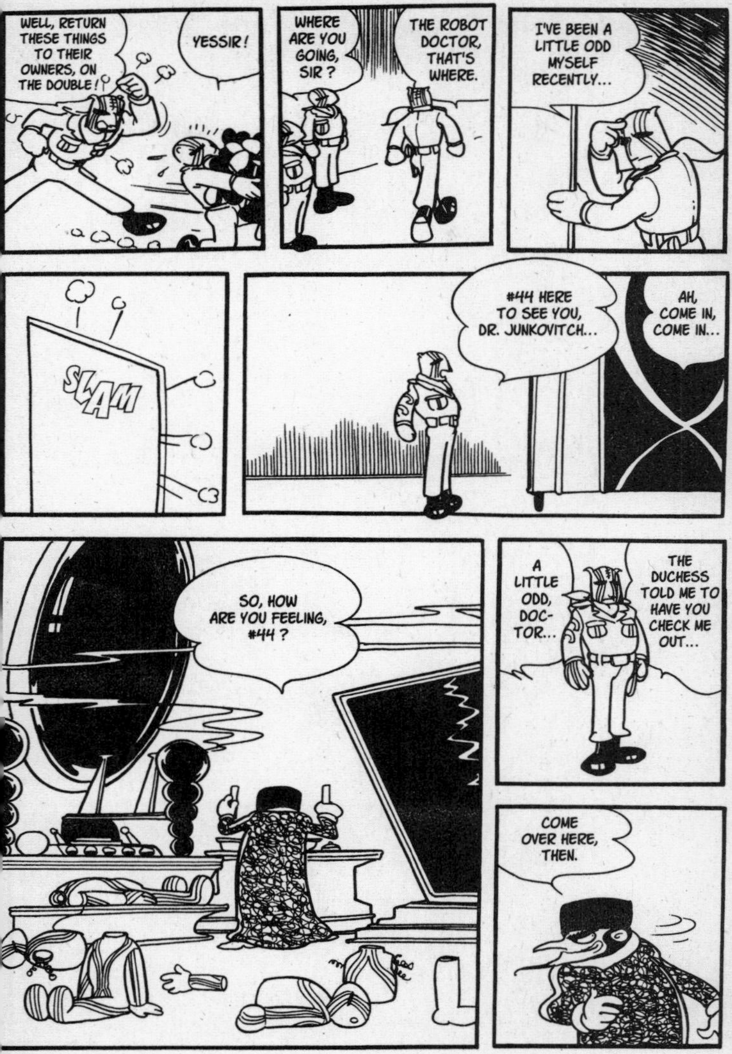
WELL, RETURN THESE THINGS TO THEIR OWNERS, ON THE DOUBLE!
YESSIR!
WHERE ARE YOU GOING, SIR?
THE ROBOT DOCTOR, THAT'S WHERE.
I'VE BEEN A LITTLE ODD MYSELF RECENTLY...
SLAM
#44 HERE TO SEE YOU, DR. JUNKOVITCH...
AH, COME IN, COME IN...
SO, HOW ARE YOU FEELING, #44?
A LITTLE ODD, DOC-TOR...
THE DUCHESS TOLD ME TO HAVE YOU CHECK ME OUT...
COME OVER HERE, THEN.

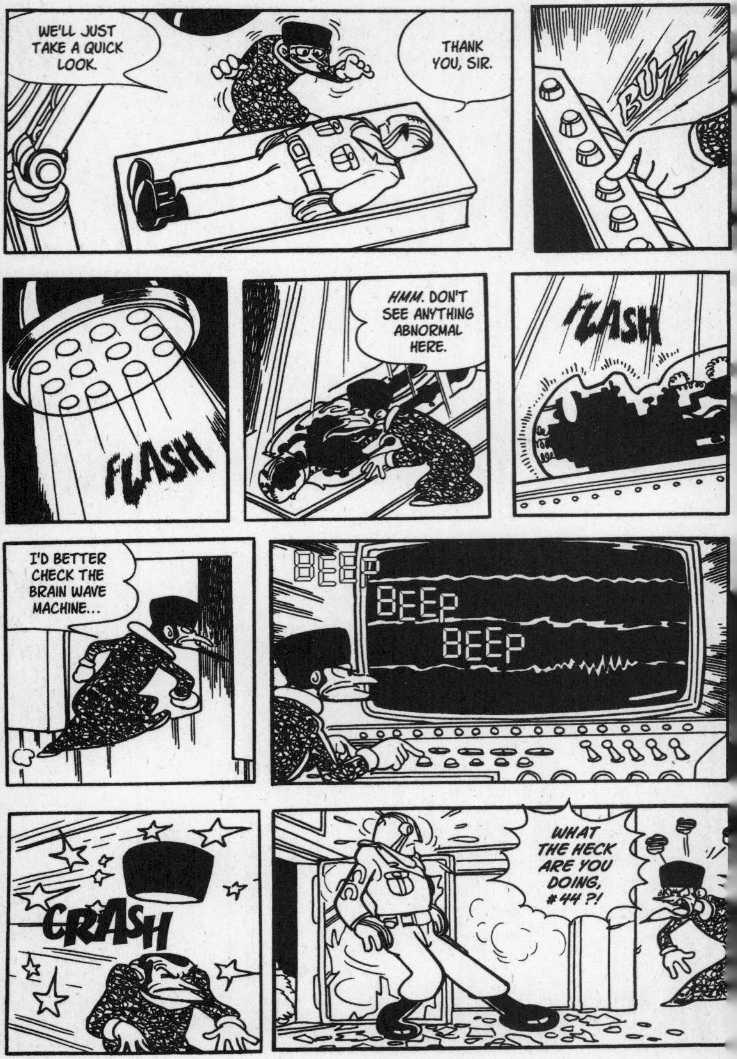
WE'LL JUST TAKE A QUICK LOOK.
THANK YOU, SIR.
BUZZ
FLASH
HMM. DON'T SEE ANYTHING ABNORMAL HERE.
FLASH
I'D BETTER CHECK THE BRAIN WAVE MACHINE...
BEEP
BEEP
BEEP
CRASH
WHAT THE HECK ARE YOU DOING, #44 ?!

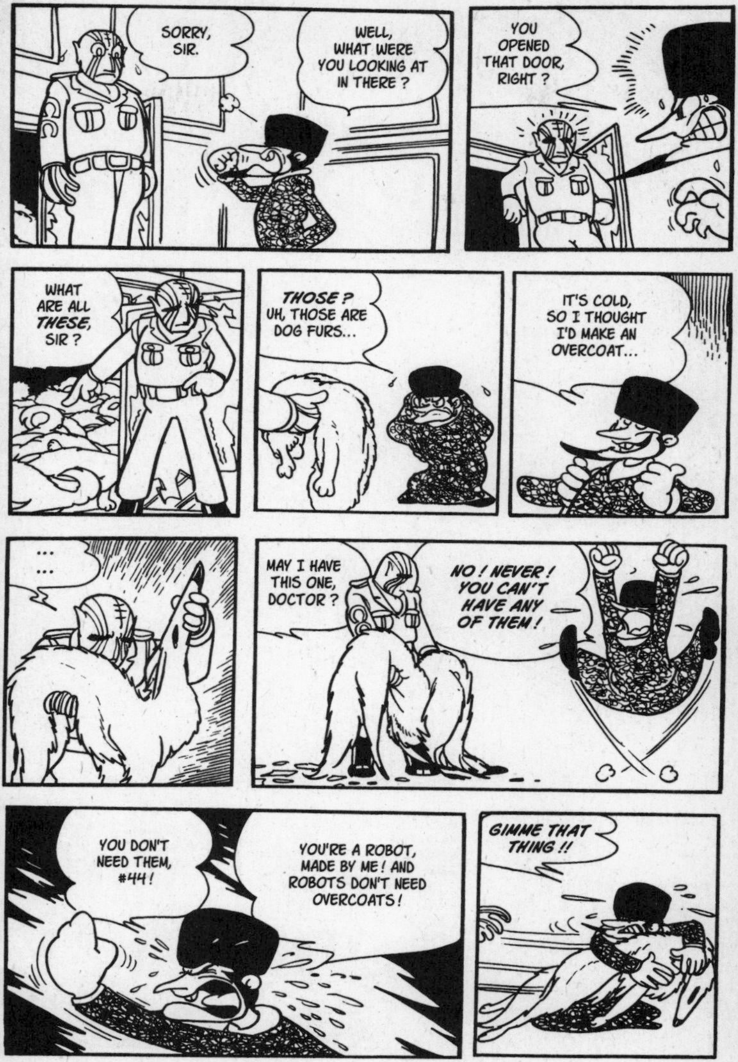
SORRY, SIR.
WELL, WHAT WERE YOU LOOKING AT IN THERE ?
YOU OPENED THAT DOOR, RIGHT ?
WHAT ARE ALL *THESE,* SIR ?
THOSE ? UH, THOSE ARE DOG FURS...
IT'S COLD, SO I THOUGHT I'D MAKE AN OVERCOAT...
...
...
MAY I HAVE THIS ONE, DOCTOR ?
NO ! NEVER ! YOU CAN'T HAVE ANY OF THEM !
YOU DON'T NEED THEM, #44 !
YOU'RE A ROBOT, MADE BY ME ! AND ROBOTS DON'T NEED OVERCOATS !
GIMME THAT THING !!

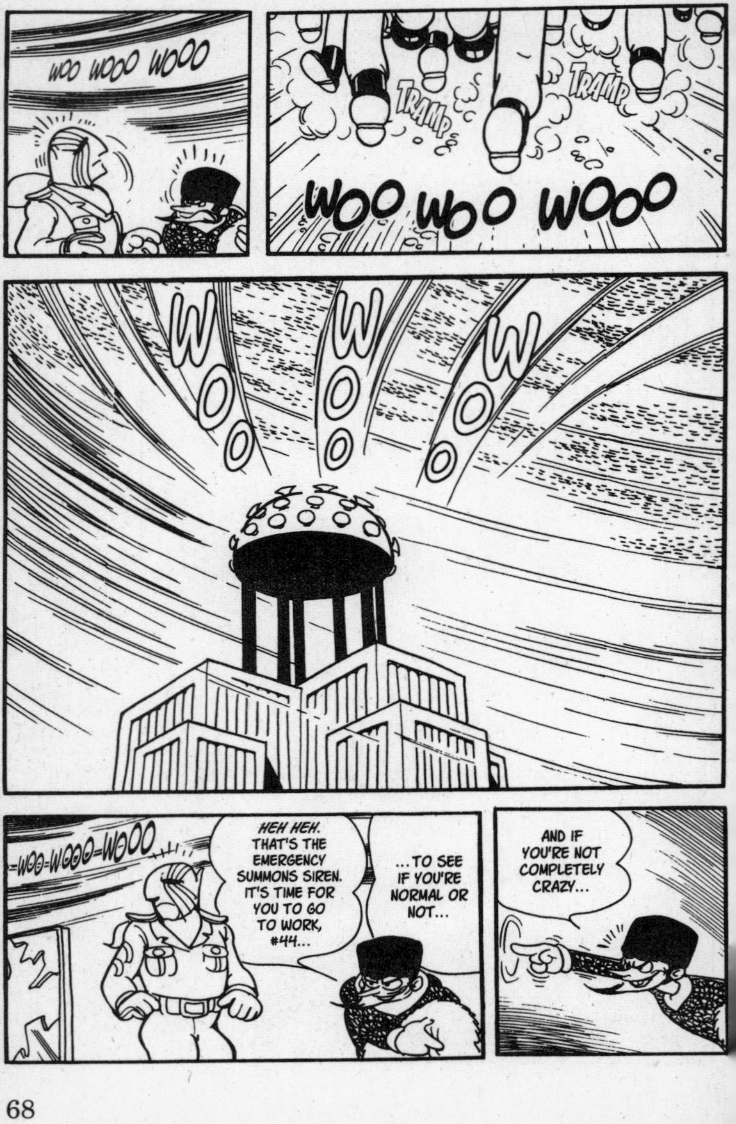
WOO WOOO WOOO
TRAMP
TRAMP
WOO WOO WOOO
WOO
WOO
WOO
=WOO=WOOO=WOOO
HEH HEH. THAT'S THE EMERGENCY SUMMONS SIREN. IT'S TIME FOR YOU TO GO TO WORK, #44...
...TO SEE IF YOU'RE NORMAL OR NOT...
AND IF YOU'RE NOT COMPLETELY CRAZY...

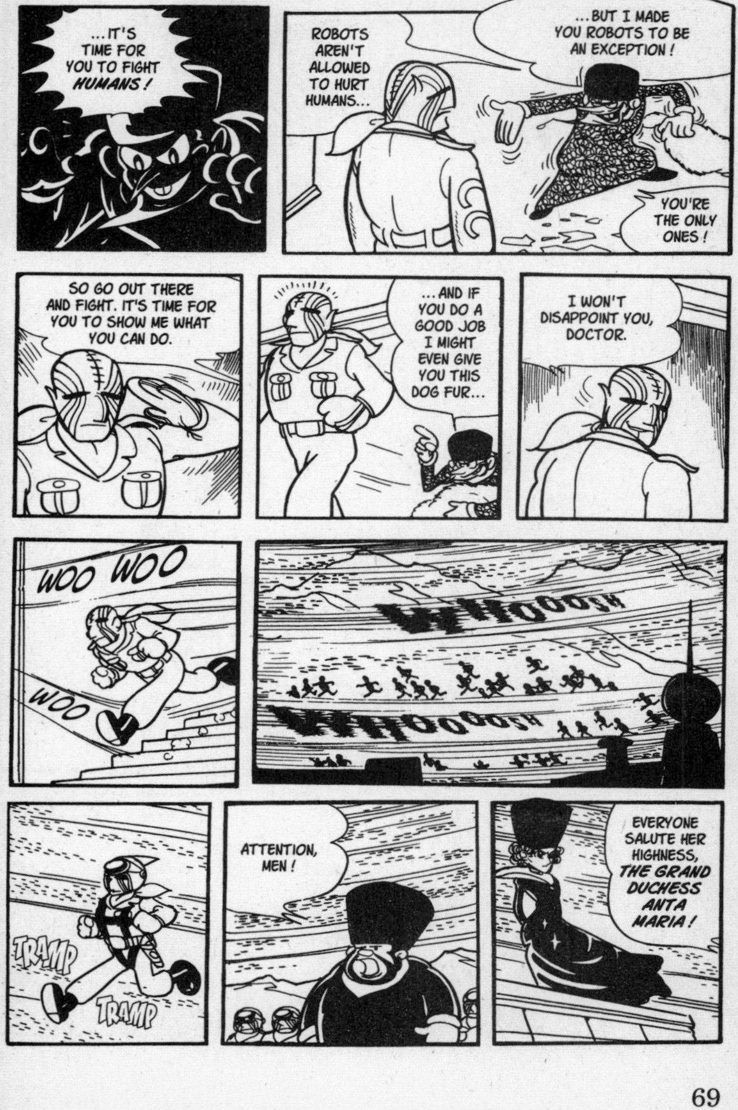

...IT'S TIME FOR YOU TO FIGHT HUMANS!
ROBOTS AREN'T ALLOWED TO HURT HUMANS...
...BUT I MADE YOU ROBOTS TO BE AN EXCEPTION!
YOU'RE THE ONLY ONES!
SO GO OUT THERE AND FIGHT. IT'S TIME FOR YOU TO SHOW ME WHAT YOU CAN DO.
...AND IF YOU DO A GOOD JOB I MIGHT EVEN GIVE YOU THIS DOG FUR...
I WON'T DISAPPOINT YOU, DOCTOR.
WOO WOO
WOO
WHOOOSH
WHOOOOSH
TRAMP
TRAMP
ATTENTION, MEN!
EVERYONE SALUTE HER HIGHNESS, THE GRAND DUCHESS ANTA MARIA!

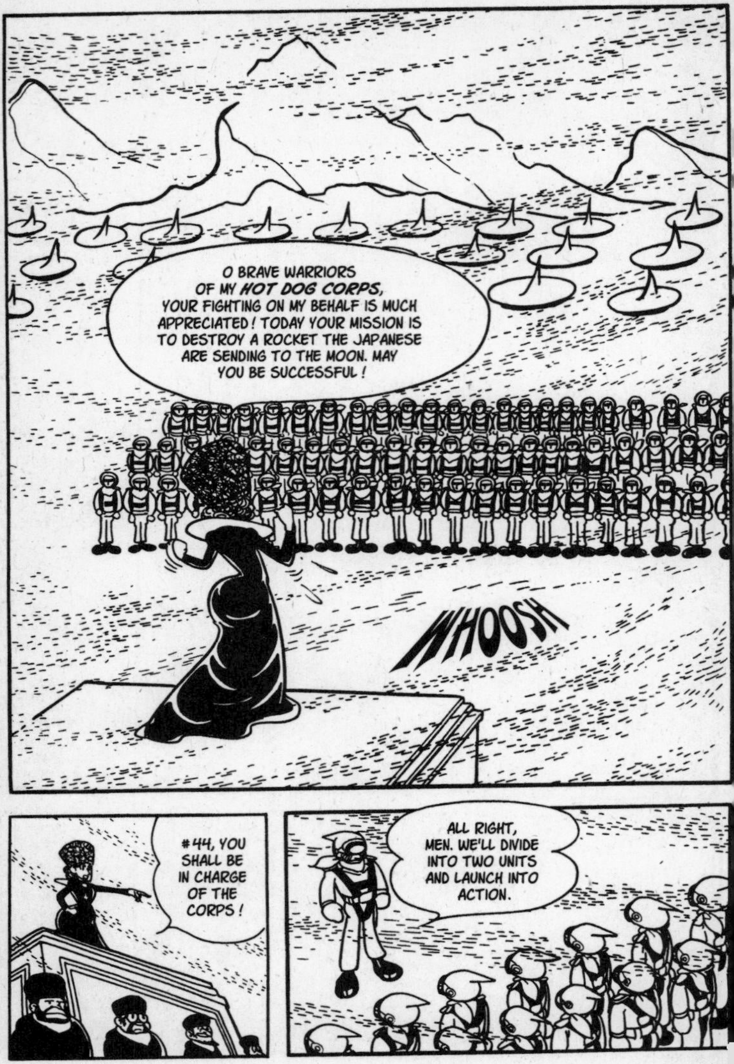
O BRAVE WARRIORS OF MY HOT DOG CORPS, YOUR FIGHTING ON MY BEHALF IS MUCH APPRECIATED! TODAY YOUR MISSION IS TO DESTROY A ROCKET THE JAPANESE ARE SENDING TO THE MOON. MAY YOU BE SUCCESSFUL!
WHOOSH
#44, YOU SHALL BE IN CHARGE OF THE CORPS!
ALL RIGHT, MEN. WE'LL DIVIDE INTO TWO UNITS AND LAUNCH INTO ACTION.

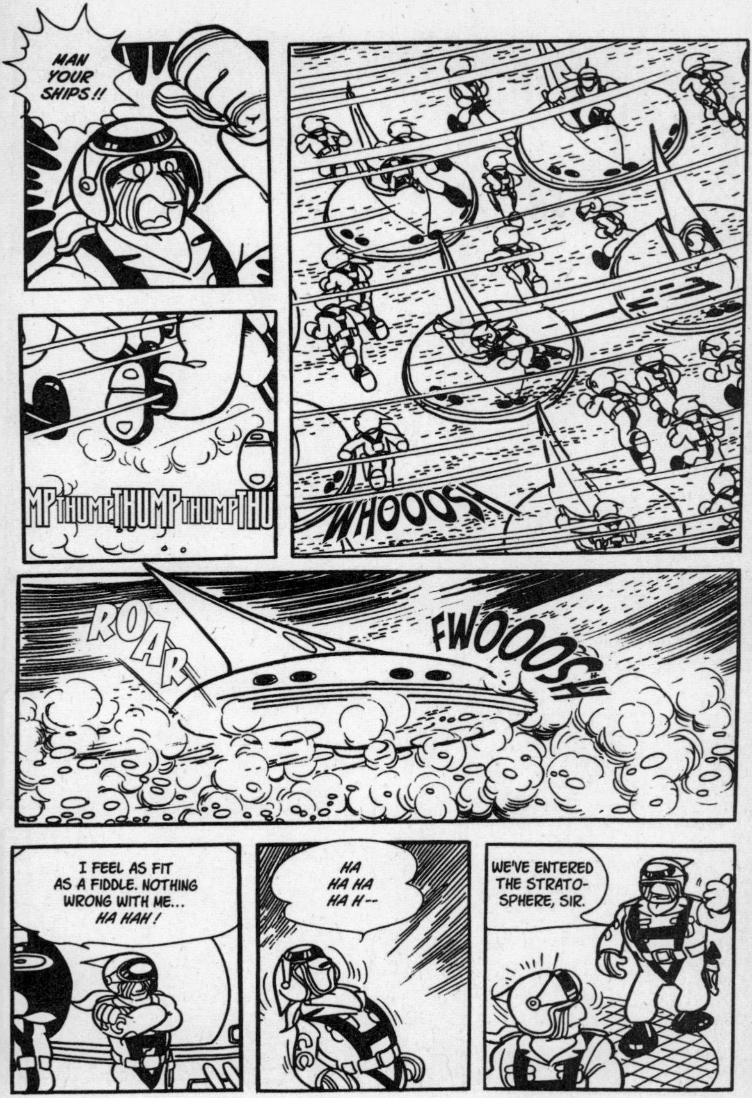
MAN YOUR SHIPS!!
WHOOOSH
MPTHUMPTHUMPTHUMPTHU
ROAR
FWOOOSH
I FEEL AS FIT AS A FIDDLE. NOTHING WRONG WITH ME... HA HAH!
HA HA HA HA H--
WE'VE ENTERED THE STRATO-SPHERE, SIR.

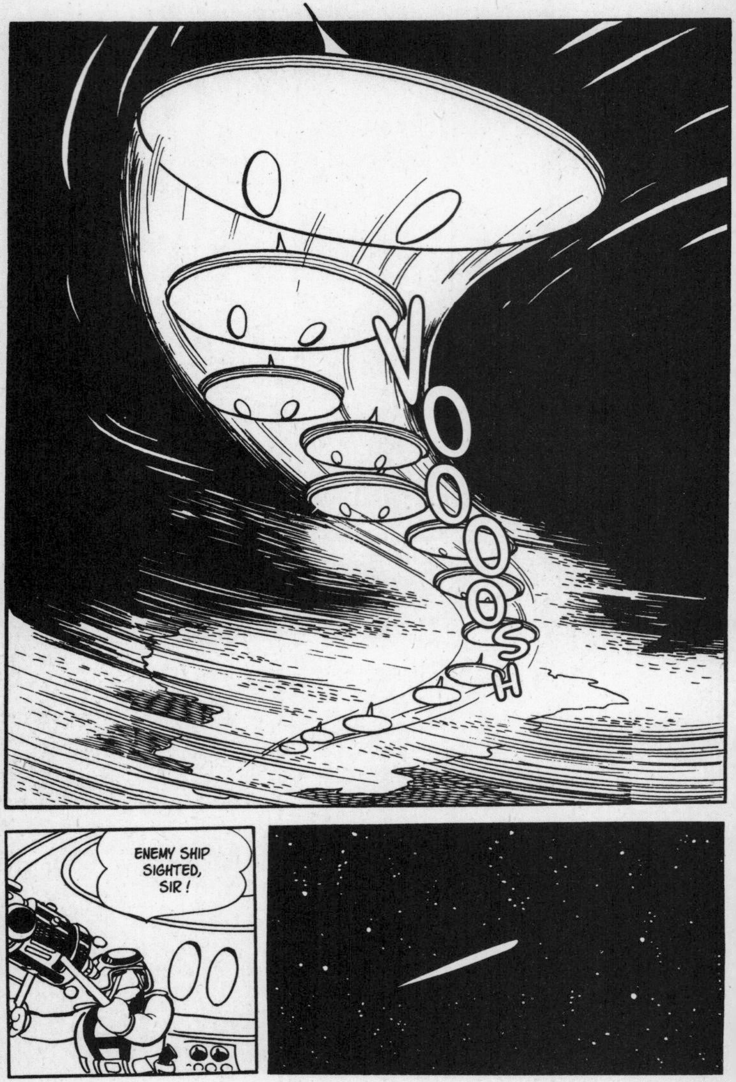
VOOOOSH
ENEMY SHIP SIGHTED, SIR!

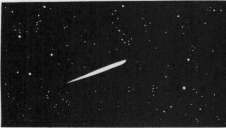

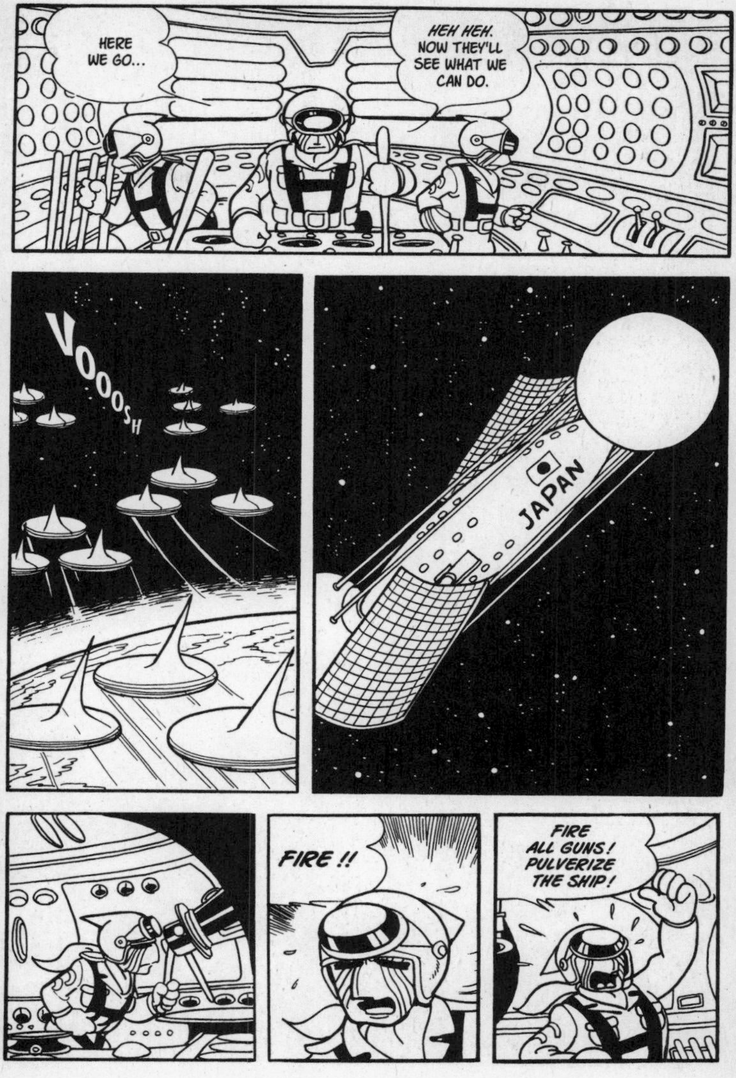
HERE WE GO...
HEH HEH. NOW THEY'LL SEE WHAT WE CAN DO.
VOOOOSH
JAPAN
FIRE !!
FIRE ALL GUNS! PULVERIZE THE SHIP!

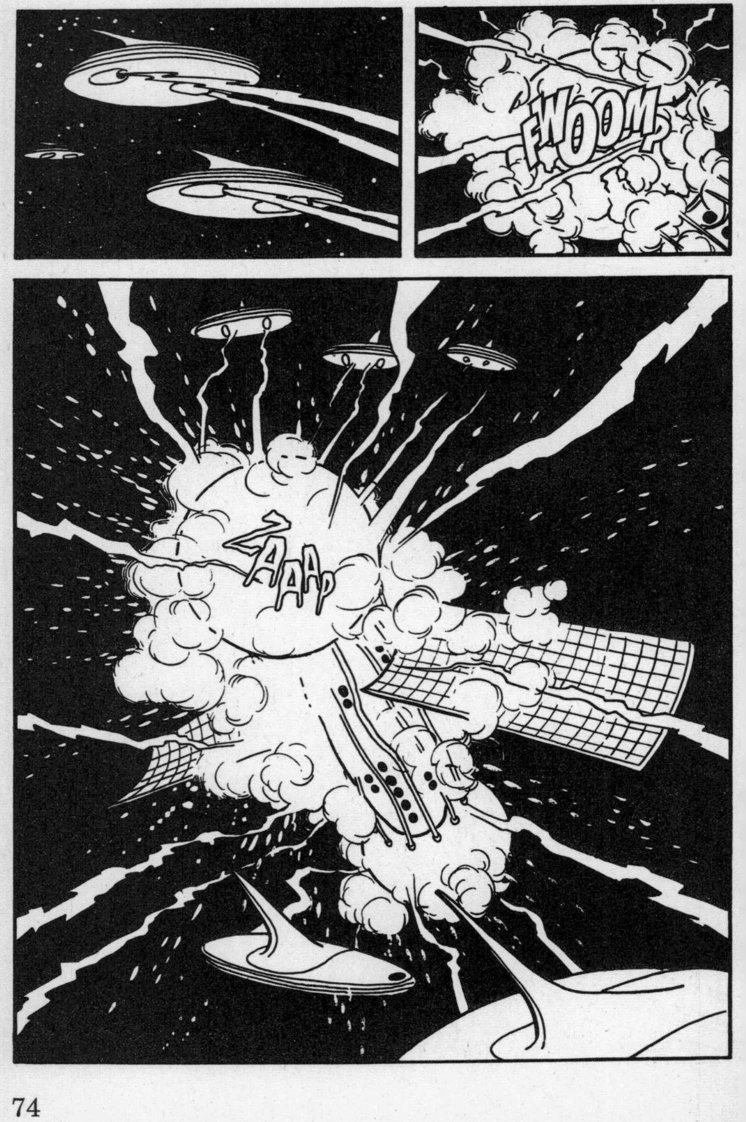
FWOOM
ZAAAP

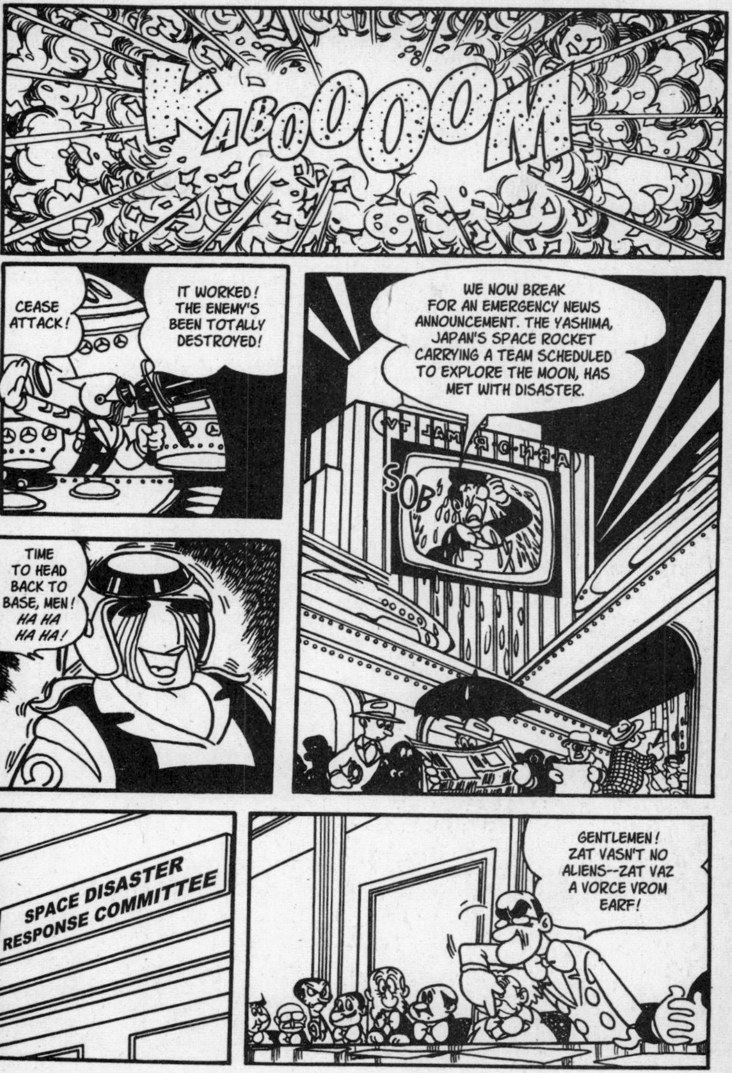
KABOOOOM
CEASE ATTACK!
IT WORKED! THE ENEMY'S BEEN TOTALLY DESTROYED!
TIME TO HEAD BACK TO BASE, MEN! *HA HA HA HA!*
WE NOW BREAK FOR AN EMERGENCY NEWS ANNOUNCEMENT. THE YASHIMA, JAPAN'S SPACE ROCKET CARRYING A TEAM SCHEDULED TO EXPLORE THE MOON, HAS MET WITH DISASTER.
SOB
SPACE DISASTER RESPONSE COMMITTEE
GENTLEMEN! ZAT VASN'T NO ALIENS--ZAT VAZ A VORCE VROM EARF!

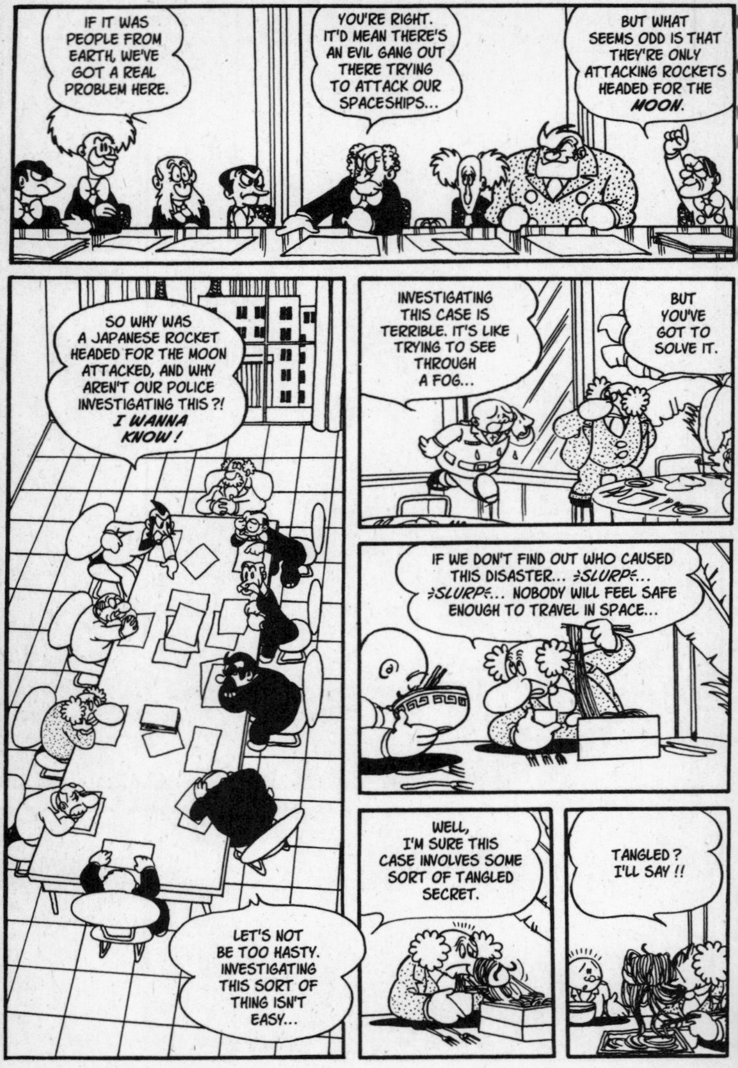
IF IT WAS PEOPLE FROM EARTH, WE'VE GOT A REAL PROBLEM HERE.
YOU'RE RIGHT. IT'D MEAN THERE'S AN EVIL GANG OUT THERE TRYING TO ATTACK OUR SPACESHIPS...
BUT WHAT SEEMS ODD IS THAT THEY'RE ONLY ATTACKING ROCKETS HEADED FOR THE *MOON*.
SO WHY WAS A JAPANESE ROCKET HEADED FOR THE MOON ATTACKED, AND WHY AREN'T OUR POLICE INVESTIGATING THIS ?! *I WANNA KNOW !*
LET'S NOT BE TOO HASTY. INVESTIGATING THIS SORT OF THING ISN'T EASY...
INVESTIGATING THIS CASE IS TERRIBLE. IT'S LIKE TRYING TO SEE THROUGH A FOG...
BUT YOU'VE GOT TO SOLVE IT.
IF WE DON'T FIND OUT WHO CAUSED THIS DISASTER... *SLURP*... *SLURP*... NOBODY WILL FEEL SAFE ENOUGH TO TRAVEL IN SPACE...
WELL, I'M SURE THIS CASE INVOLVES SOME SORT OF TANGLED SECRET.
TANGLED? I'LL SAY !!

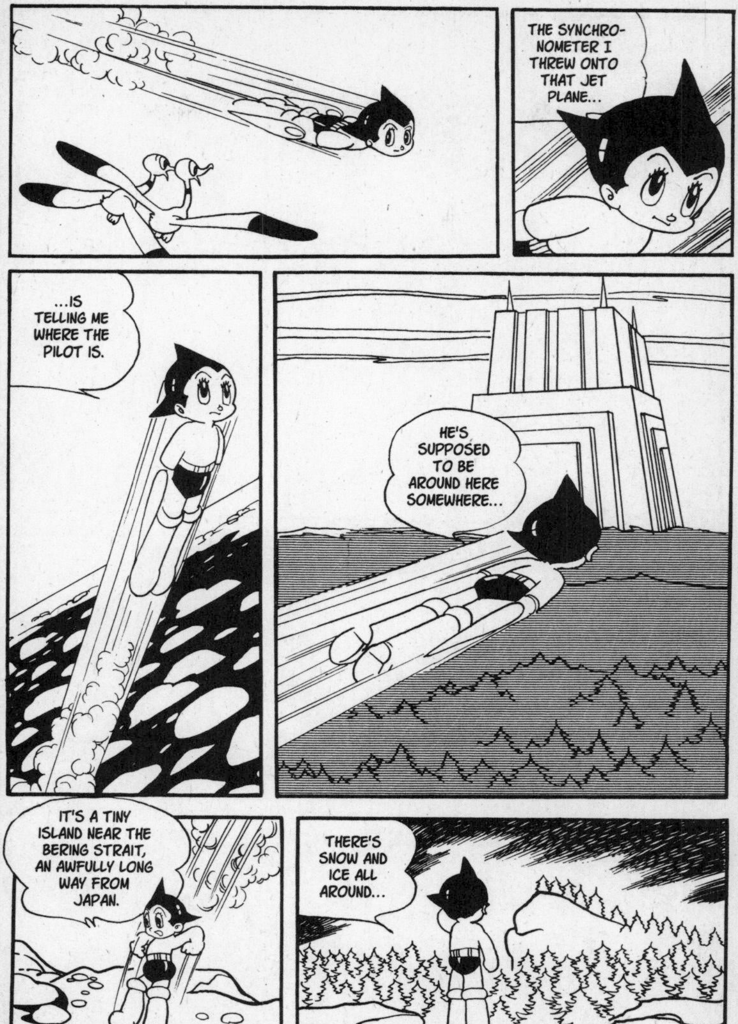
THE SYNCHRO-NOMETER I THREW ONTO THAT JET PLANE...
...IS TELLING ME WHERE THE PILOT IS.
HE'S SUPPOSED TO BE AROUND HERE SOMEWHERE...
IT'S A TINY ISLAND NEAR THE BERING STRAIT, AN AWFULLY LONG WAY FROM JAPAN.
THERE'S SNOW AND ICE ALL AROUND...

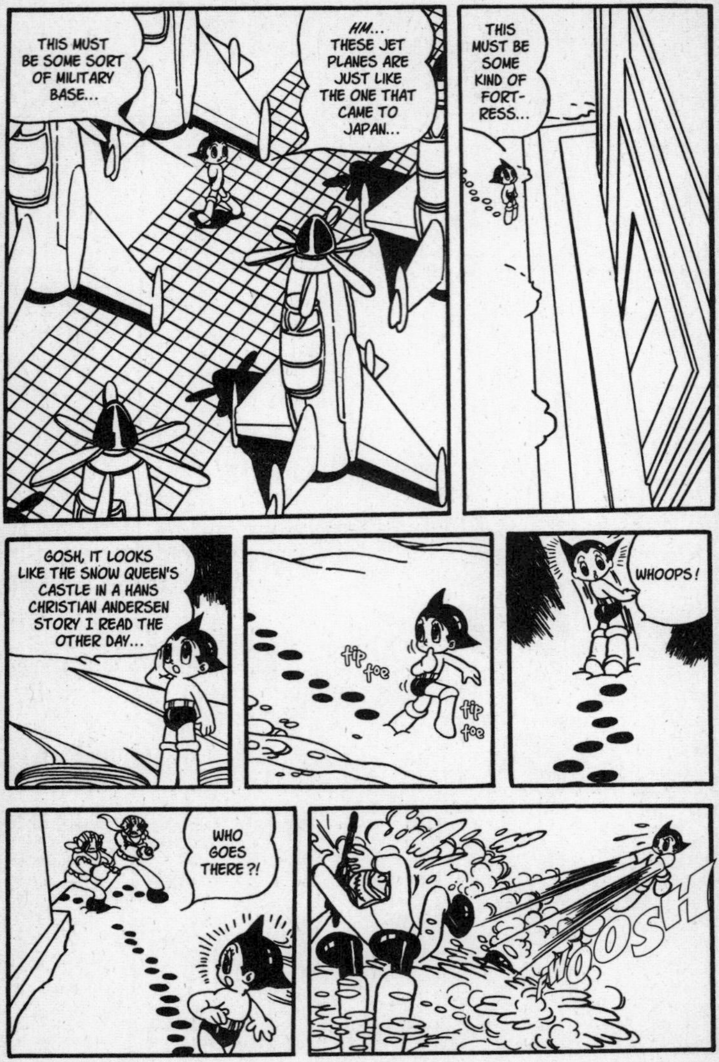
THIS MUST BE SOME SORT OF MILITARY BASE...
HM... THESE JET PLANES ARE JUST LIKE THE ONE THAT CAME TO JAPAN...
THIS MUST BE SOME KIND OF FORT-RESS...
GOSH, IT LOOKS LIKE THE SNOW QUEEN'S CASTLE IN A HANS CHRISTIAN ANDERSEN STORY I READ THE OTHER DAY...
tip toe
tip toe
WHOOPS!
WHO GOES THERE?!
FWOOSH

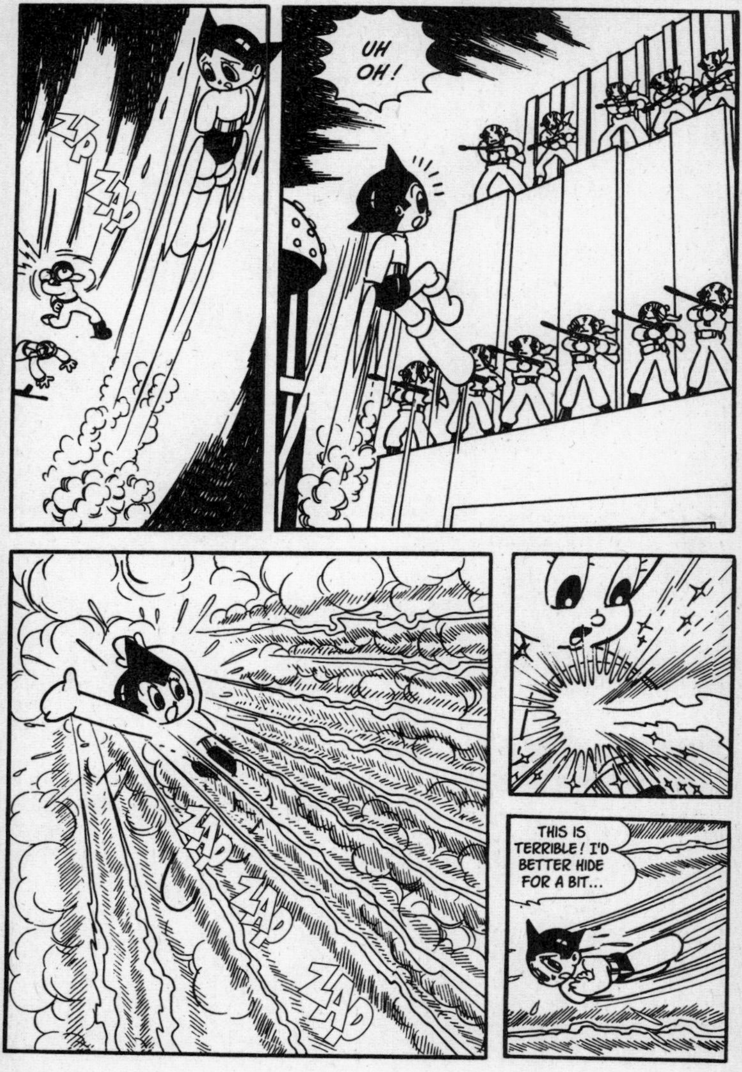
ZIP
ZAP
UH OH!
ZAP
ZAP
ZAP
THIS IS TERRIBLE! I'D BETTER HIDE FOR A BIT...

I WONDER WHO THOSE MEN ARE? SEEMS LIKE THEY REALLY KNOW ROBOTS' WEAK POINTS. I'D BETTER BE CAREFUL...

VRROOM VROOOM

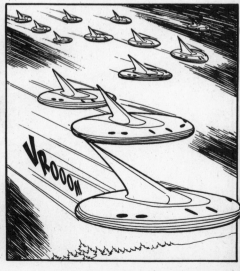

VROOOM

THAT'S ODD. I HEAR THE SOUND OF ROCKET ENGINES...

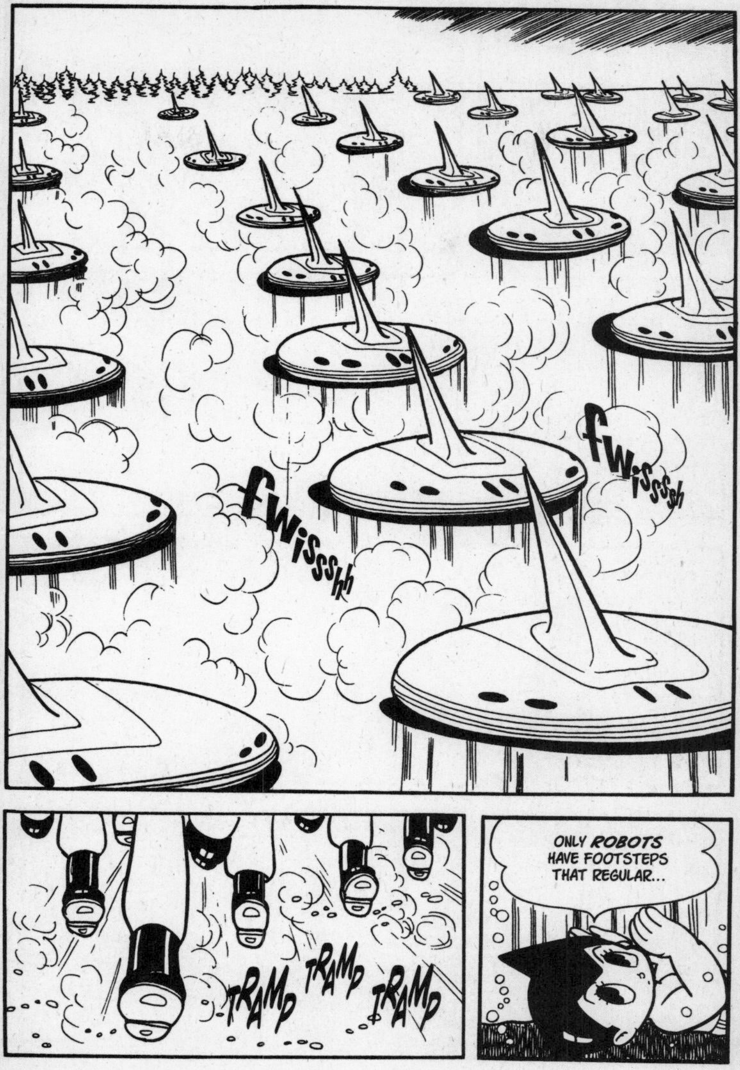

fwisssh
fwisssh
TRAMP TRAMP TRAMP
ONLY ROBOTS HAVE FOOTSTEPS THAT REGULAR...

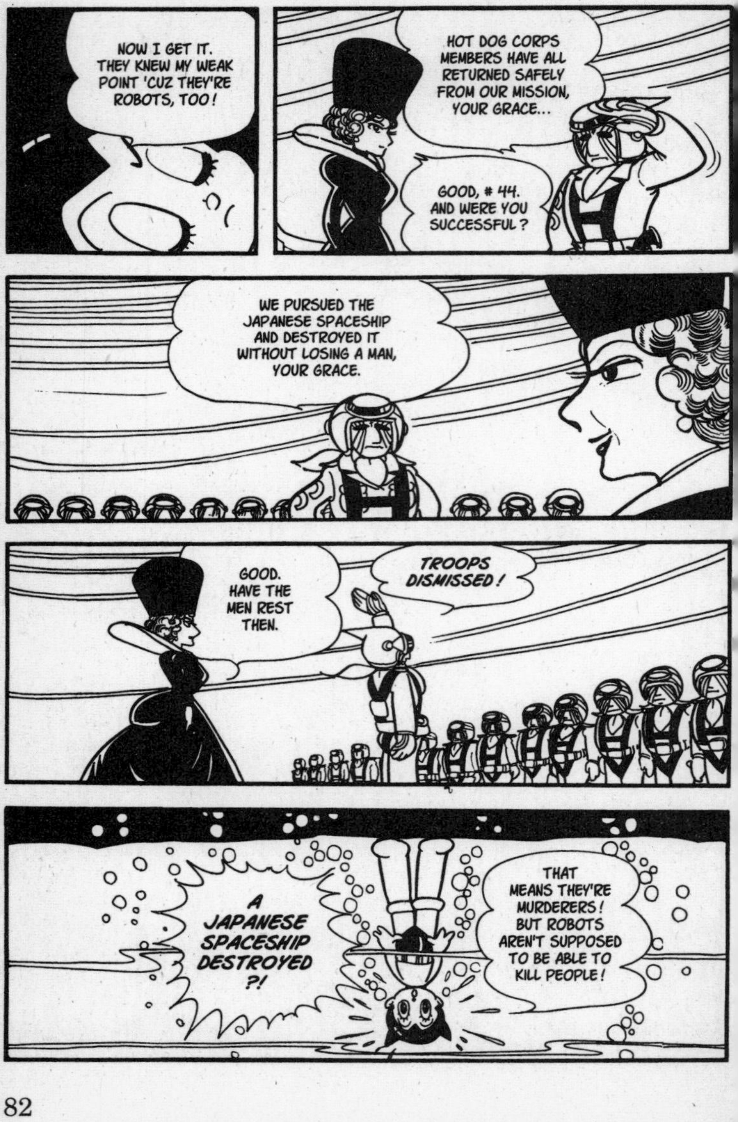
NOW I GET IT. THEY KNEW MY WEAK POINT 'CUZ THEY'RE ROBOTS, TOO!
HOT DOG CORPS MEMBERS HAVE ALL RETURNED SAFELY FROM OUR MISSION, YOUR GRACE...
GOOD, # 44. AND WERE YOU SUCCESSFUL?
WE PURSUED THE JAPANESE SPACESHIP AND DESTROYED IT WITHOUT LOSING A MAN, YOUR GRACE.
GOOD. HAVE THE MEN REST THEN.
TROOPS DISMISSED!
A JAPANESE SPACESHIP DESTROYED ?!
THAT MEANS THEY'RE MURDERERS! BUT ROBOTS AREN'T SUPPOSED TO BE ABLE TO KILL PEOPLE!

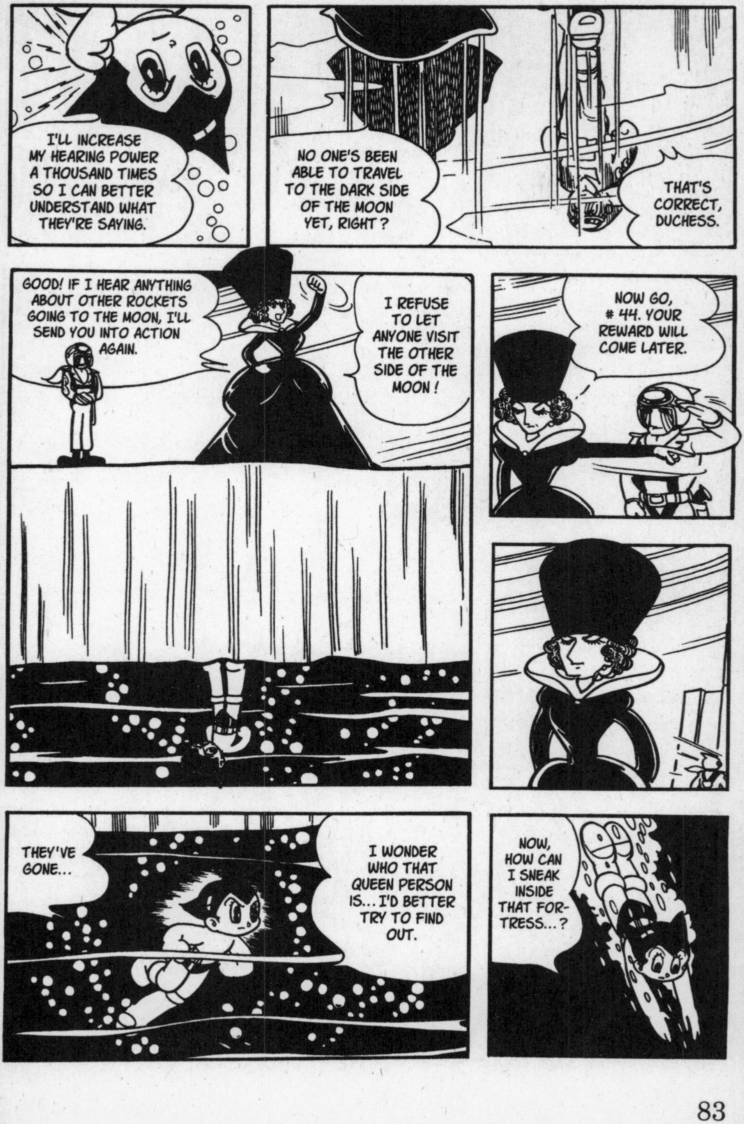
I'LL INCREASE MY HEARING POWER A THOUSAND TIMES SO I CAN BETTER UNDERSTAND WHAT THEY'RE SAYING.
NO ONE'S BEEN ABLE TO TRAVEL TO THE DARK SIDE OF THE MOON YET, RIGHT?
THAT'S CORRECT, DUCHESS.
GOOD! IF I HEAR ANYTHING ABOUT OTHER ROCKETS GOING TO THE MOON, I'LL SEND YOU INTO ACTION AGAIN.
I REFUSE TO LET ANYONE VISIT THE OTHER SIDE OF THE MOON!
NOW GO, # 44. YOUR REWARD WILL COME LATER.
THEY'VE GONE...
I WONDER WHO THAT QUEEN PERSON IS... I'D BETTER TRY TO FIND OUT.
NOW, HOW CAN I SNEAK INSIDE THAT FORTRESS...?

HMM...
THESE HOLES IN THE ICE ARE FOR FISHING...
I KNOW JUST WHAT TO DO.
AND HERE'S JUST WHAT I NEED.
CHOMP

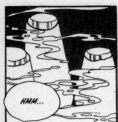

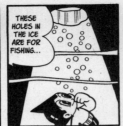

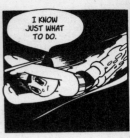

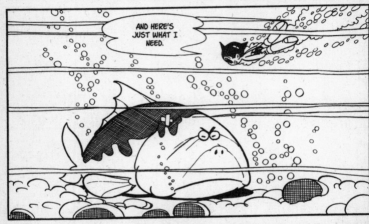

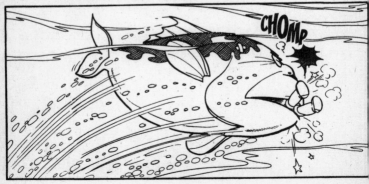

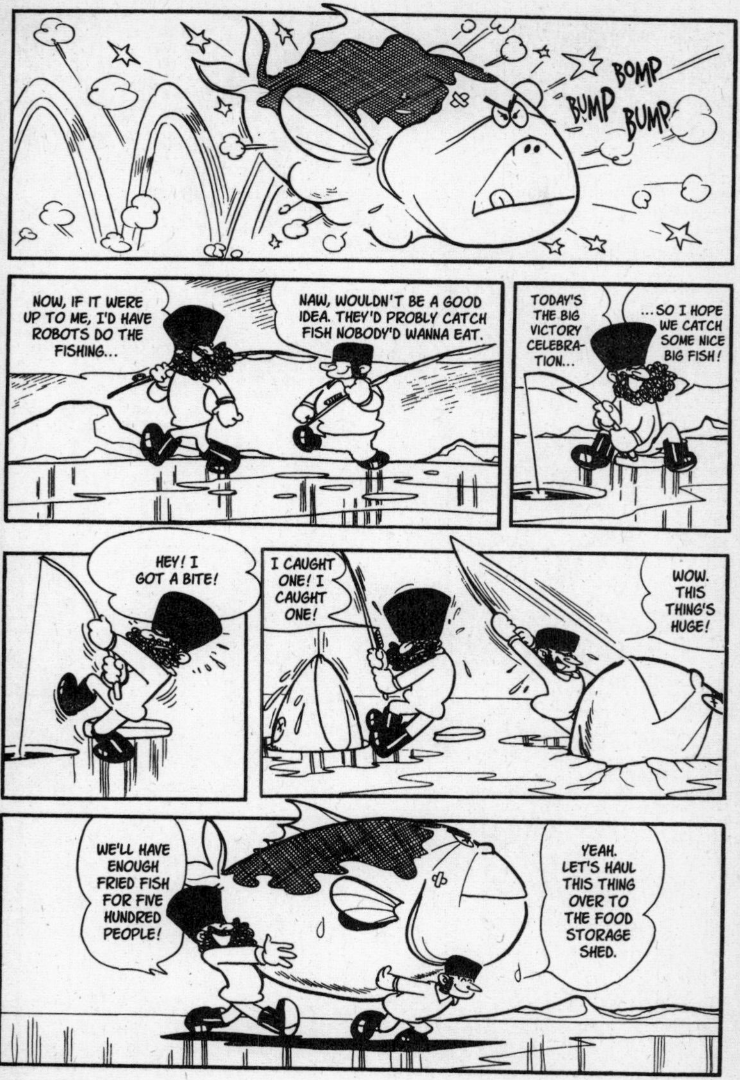
BOMP
BUMP
BUMP
NOW, IF IT WERE UP TO ME, I'D HAVE ROBOTS DO THE FISHING...
NAW, WOULDN'T BE A GOOD IDEA. THEY'D PROBLY CATCH FISH NOBODY'D WANNA EAT.
TODAY'S THE BIG VICTORY CELEBRA-TION...
...SO I HOPE WE CATCH SOME NICE BIG FISH!
HEY! I GOT A BITE!
I CAUGHT ONE! I CAUGHT ONE!
WOW. THIS THING'S HUGE!
WE'LL HAVE ENOUGH FRIED FISH FOR FIVE HUNDRED PEOPLE!
YEAH. LET'S HAUL THIS THING OVER TO THE FOOD STORAGE SHED.

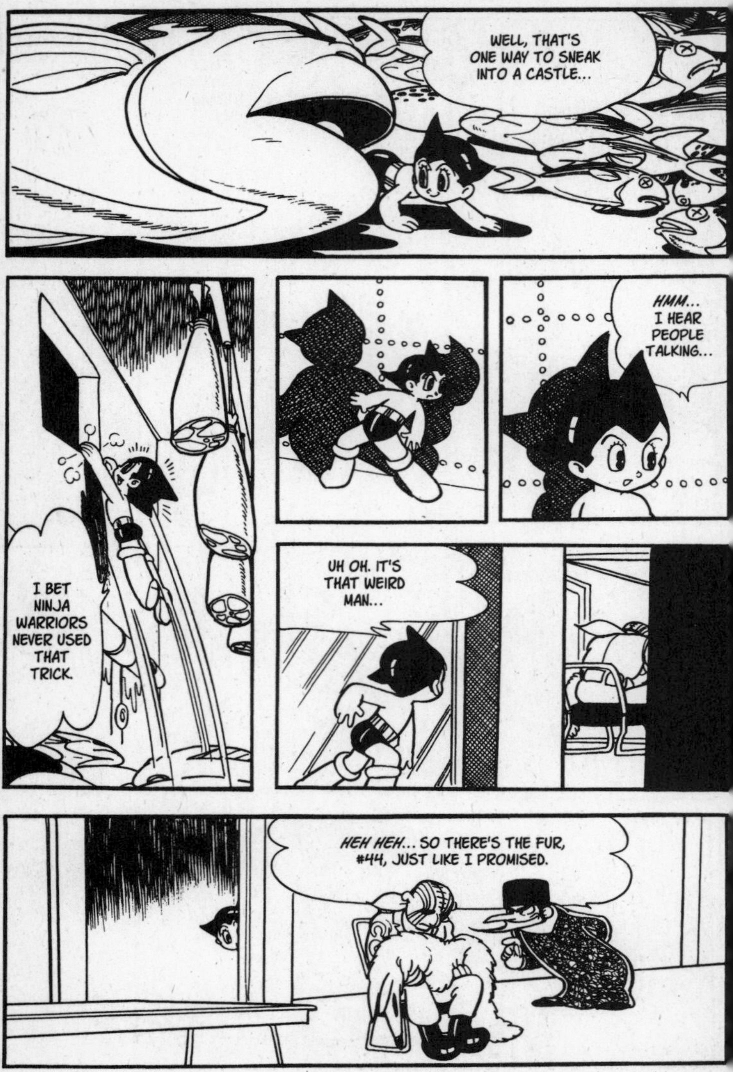
WELL, THAT'S ONE WAY TO SNEAK INTO A CASTLE...
I BET NINJA WARRIORS NEVER USED THAT TRICK.
HMM... I HEAR PEOPLE TALKING...
UH OH. IT'S THAT WEIRD MAN...
HEH HEH... SO THERE'S THE FUR, #44, JUST LIKE I PROMISED.

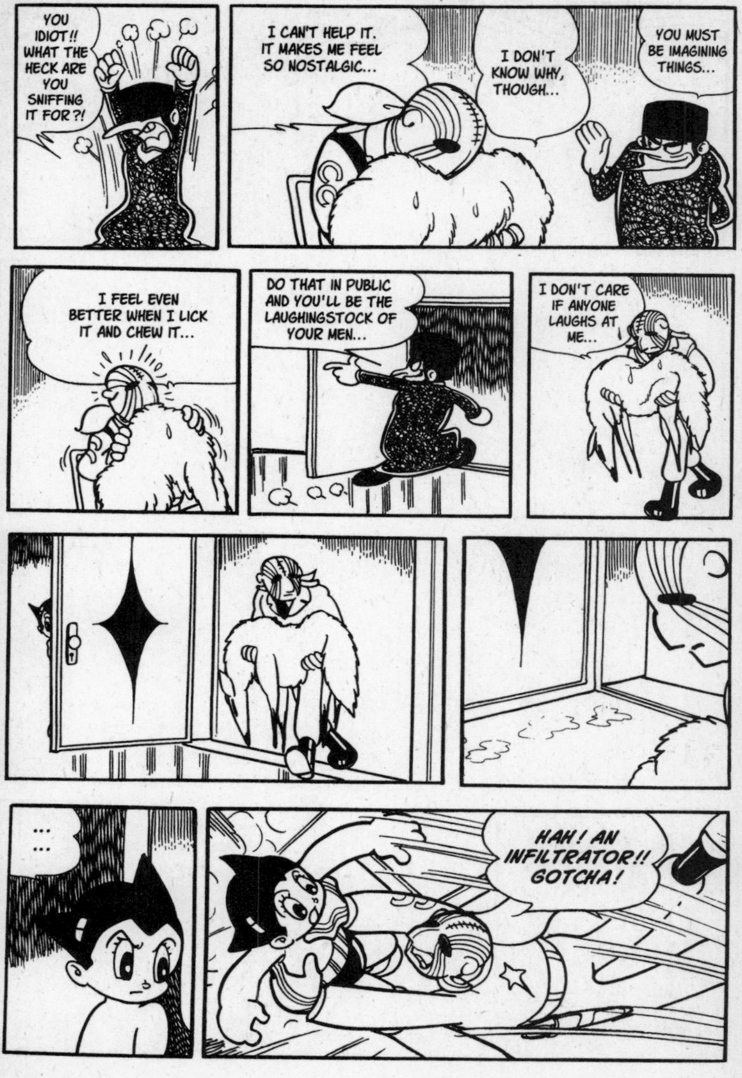

YOU IDIOT!! WHAT THE HECK ARE YOU SNIFFING IT FOR?!
I CAN'T HELP IT. IT MAKES ME FEEL SO NOSTALGIC...
I DON'T KNOW WHY, THOUGH...
YOU MUST BE IMAGINING THINGS...
I FEEL EVEN BETTER WHEN I LICK IT AND CHEW IT...
DO THAT IN PUBLIC AND YOU'LL BE THE LAUGHINGSTOCK OF YOUR MEN...
I DON'T CARE IF ANYONE LAUGHS AT ME...
...
...
HAH! AN INFILTRATOR!! GOTCHA!

DRAT !! SPOTTED ME, EH ?
YOU'VE GOT A LOT OF NERVE, SNEAKING IN HERE, KID !
BUT NOW I'M GONNA TEAR YOUR HEAD OFF...
OH NO YOU WON'T !
I'VE GOT SOME WEAPONS YOU DON'T KNOW ABOUT !
HA HA... THAT'S CHILD'S PLAY TO ME, KID.
MY TURN NEXT !
ZAP
RATS...!
TIME TO GET SERIOUS !

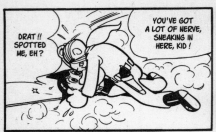

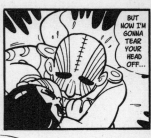

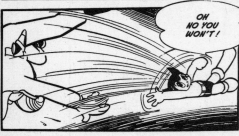

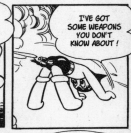

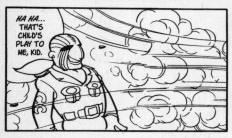

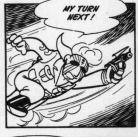

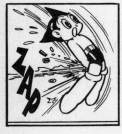

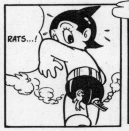

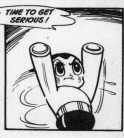

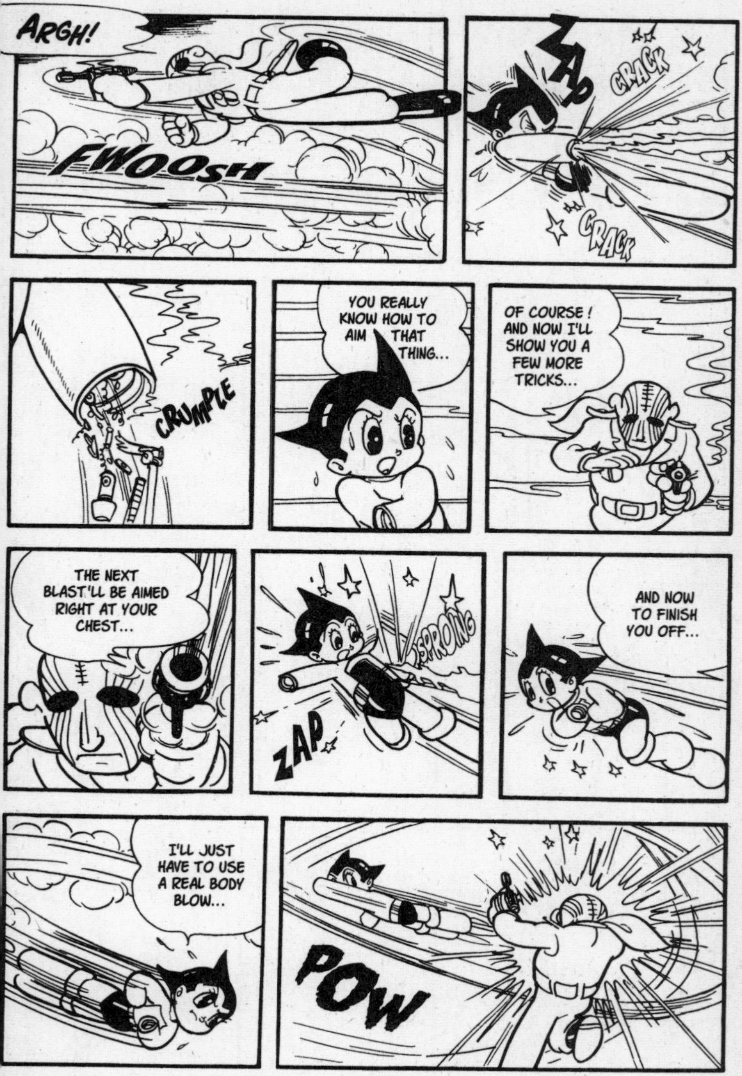
ARGH!
FWOOSH
ZAP
CRACK
CRACK
CRUMPLE
YOU REALLY KNOW HOW TO AIM THAT THING...
OF COURSE! AND NOW I'LL SHOW YOU A FEW MORE TRICKS...
THE NEXT BLAST'LL BE AIMED RIGHT AT YOUR CHEST...
SPROING
ZAP
AND NOW TO FINISH YOU OFF...
I'LL JUST HAVE TO USE A REAL BODY BLOW...
POW

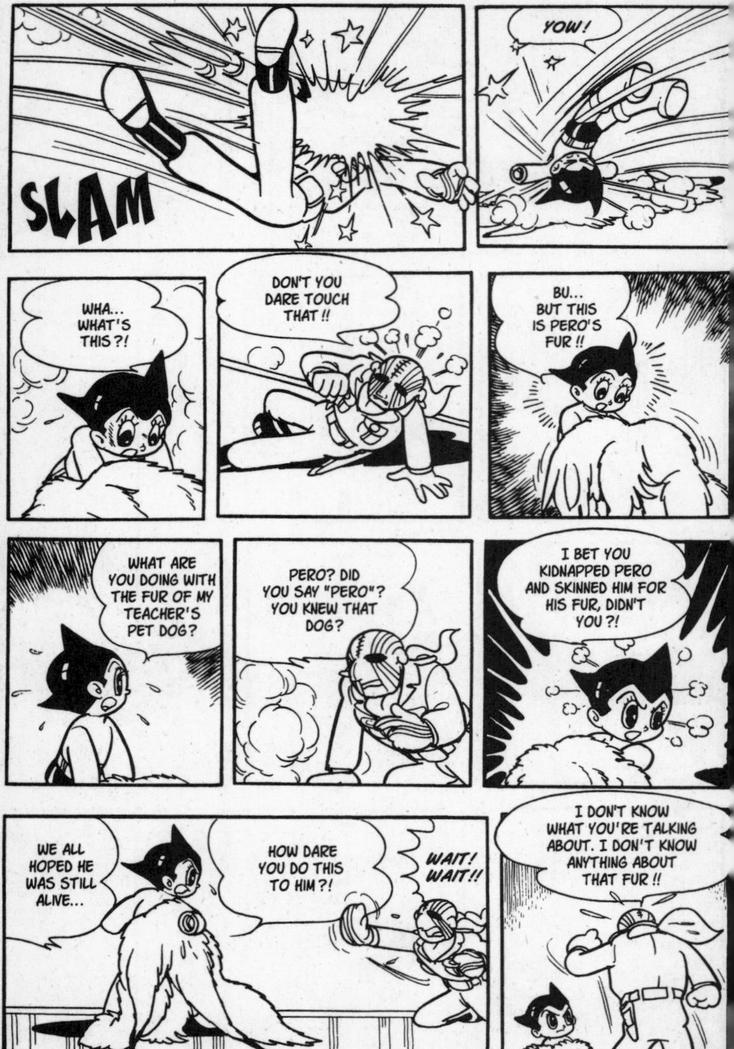
SLAM
YOW!
WHA... WHAT'S THIS?!
DON'T YOU DARE TOUCH THAT!!
BU... BUT THIS IS PERO'S FUR!!
WHAT ARE YOU DOING WITH THE FUR OF MY TEACHER'S PET DOG?
PERO? DID YOU SAY "PERO"? YOU KNEW THAT DOG?
I BET YOU KIDNAPPED PERO AND SKINNED HIM FOR HIS FUR, DIDN'T YOU?!
WE ALL HOPED HE WAS STILL ALIVE...
HOW DARE YOU DO THIS TO HIM?!
WAIT! WAIT!!
I DON'T KNOW WHAT YOU'RE TALKING ABOUT. I DON'T KNOW ANYTHING ABOUT THAT FUR!!

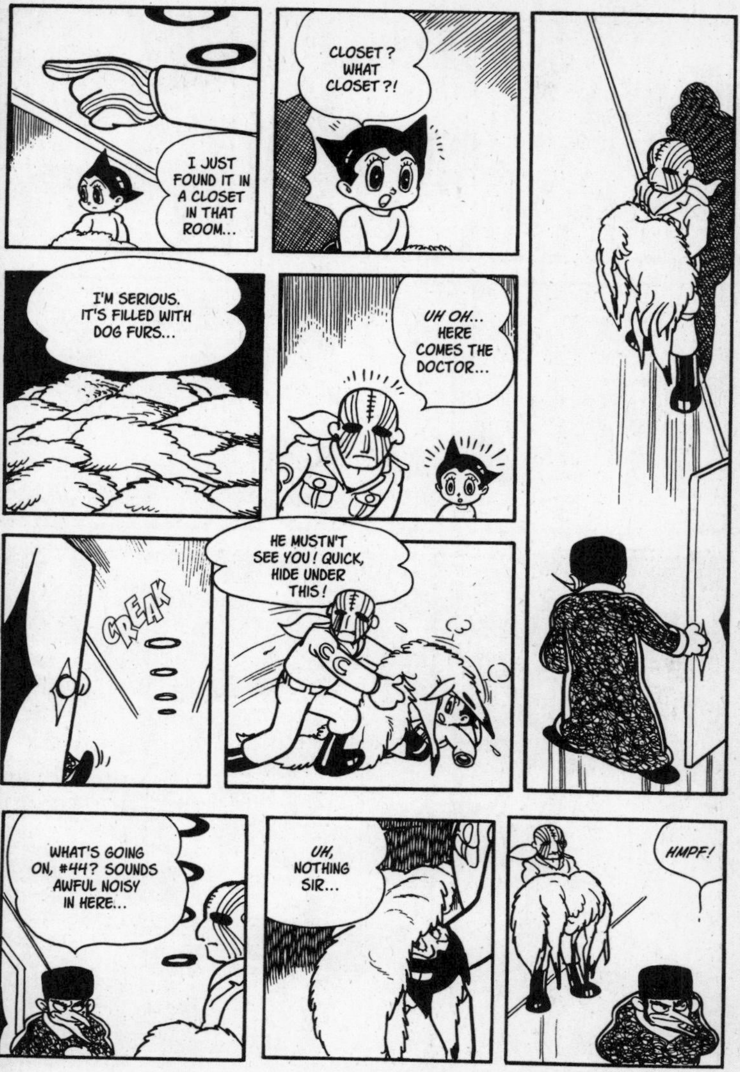
I JUST FOUND IT IN A CLOSET IN THAT ROOM...
CLOSET? WHAT CLOSET?!
I'M SERIOUS. IT'S FILLED WITH DOG FURS...
UH OH... HERE COMES THE DOCTOR...
CREAK
HE MUSTN'T SEE YOU! QUICK, HIDE UNDER THIS!
WHAT'S GOING ON, #44? SOUNDS AWFUL NOISY IN HERE...
UH, NOTHING SIR...
HMPF!

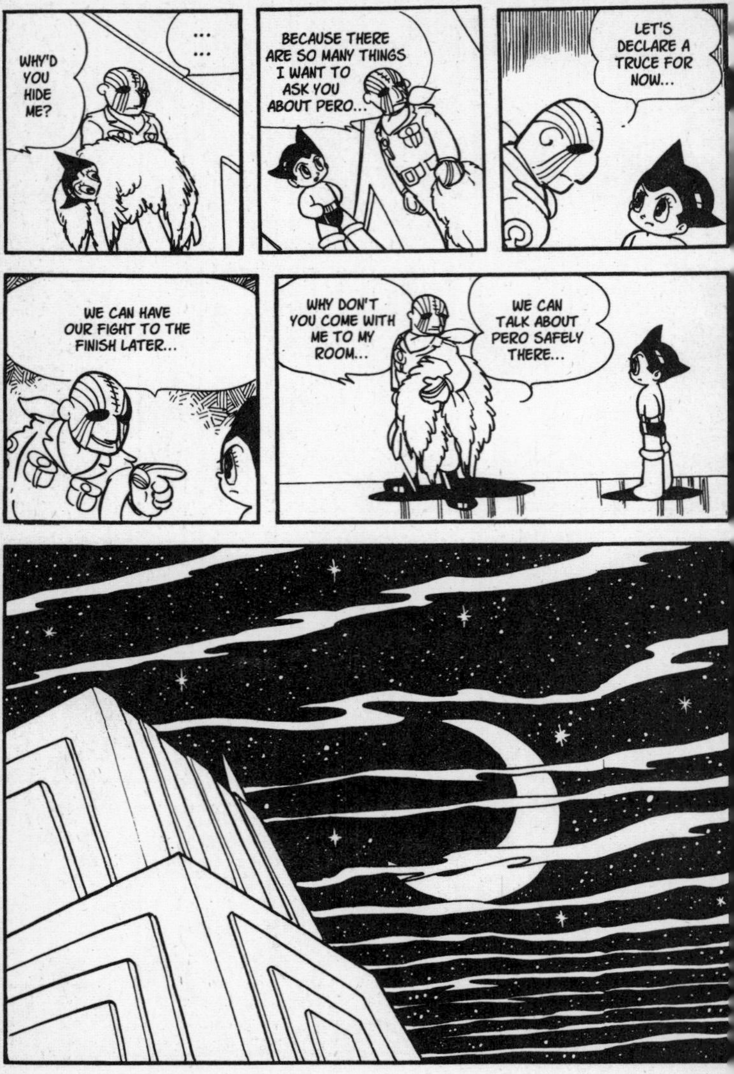
WHY'D YOU HIDE ME?
...
...
BECAUSE THERE ARE SO MANY THINGS I WANT TO ASK YOU ABOUT PERO...
LET'S DECLARE A TRUCE FOR NOW...
WE CAN HAVE OUR FIGHT TO THE FINISH LATER...
WHY DON'T YOU COME WITH ME TO MY ROOM...
WE CAN TALK ABOUT PERO SAFELY THERE...

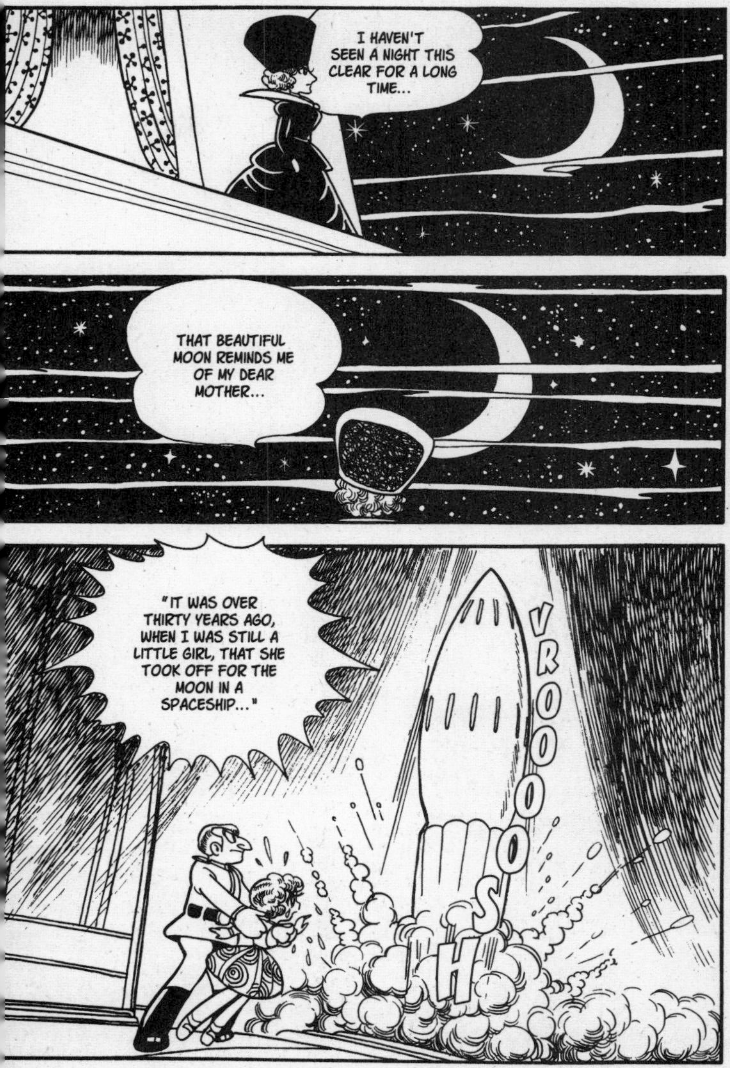
I HAVEN'T SEEN A NIGHT THIS CLEAR FOR A LONG TIME...
THAT BEAUTIFUL MOON REMINDS ME OF MY DEAR MOTHER...
"IT WAS OVER THIRTY YEARS AGO, WHEN I WAS STILL A LITTLE GIRL, THAT SHE TOOK OFF FOR THE MOON IN A SPACESHIP..."
VROOOOOOSH

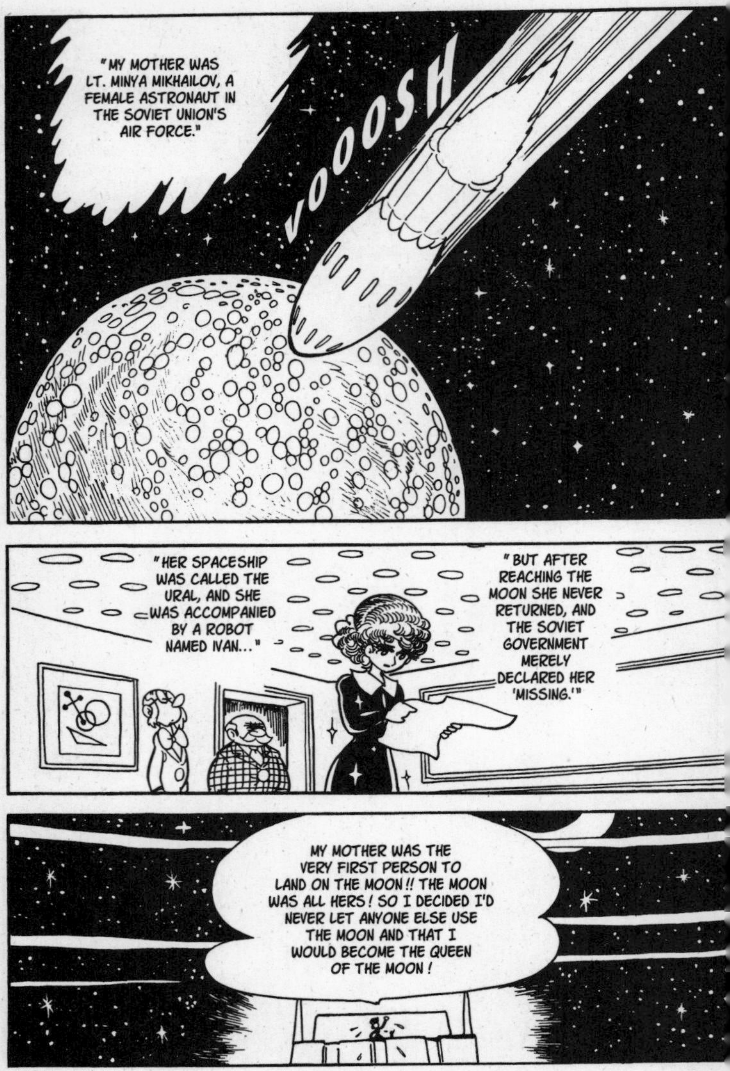
"MY MOTHER WAS LT. MINYA MIKHAILOV, A FEMALE ASTRONAUT IN THE SOVIET UNION'S AIR FORCE."
VOOOSH
"HER SPACESHIP WAS CALLED THE URAL, AND SHE WAS ACCOMPANIED BY A ROBOT NAMED IVAN..."
"BUT AFTER REACHING THE MOON SHE NEVER RETURNED, AND THE SOVIET GOVERNMENT MERELY DECLARED HER 'MISSING.'"
MY MOTHER WAS THE VERY FIRST PERSON TO LAND ON THE MOON!! THE MOON WAS ALL HERS! SO I DECIDED I'D NEVER LET ANYONE ELSE USE THE MOON AND THAT I WOULD BECOME THE QUEEN OF THE MOON!

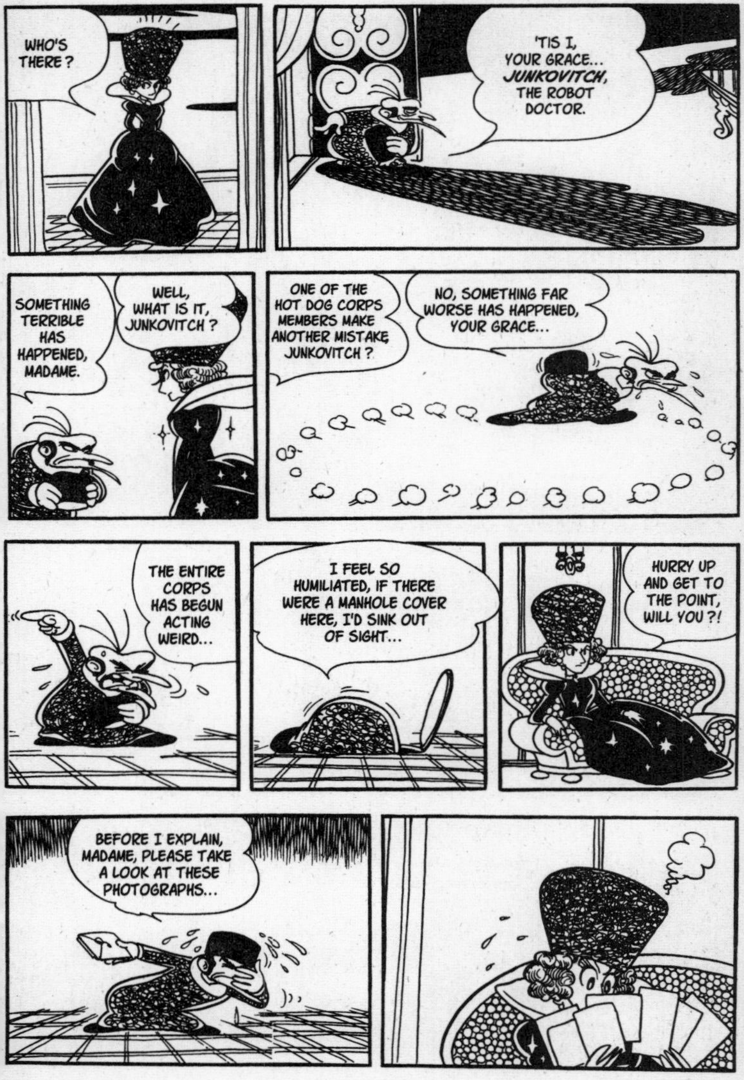
WHO'S THERE?
'TIS I, YOUR GRACE... JUNKOVITCH, THE ROBOT DOCTOR.
SOMETHING TERRIBLE HAS HAPPENED, MADAME.
WELL, WHAT IS IT, JUNKOVITCH?
ONE OF THE HOT DOG CORPS MEMBERS MAKE ANOTHER MISTAKE, JUNKOVITCH?
NO, SOMETHING FAR WORSE HAS HAPPENED, YOUR GRACE...
THE ENTIRE CORPS HAS BEGUN ACTING WEIRD...
I FEEL SO HUMILIATED, IF THERE WERE A MANHOLE COVER HERE, I'D SINK OUT OF SIGHT...
HURRY UP AND GET TO THE POINT, WILL YOU?!
BEFORE I EXPLAIN, MADAME, PLEASE TAKE A LOOK AT THESE PHOTOGRAPHS...

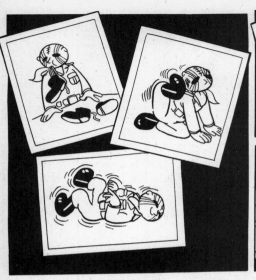

AS YOU KNOW, THE HOT DOG MODEL ROBOT IS REALLY A *CYBORG DOG*... THEY'RE DOGS I TURNED INTO ROBOTS...

WELL, THEY'RE CERTAINLY ACTING LIKE DOGS IN THESE PICTURES!

INDEED, YOUR GRACE, THEY ARE...

WHY DIDN'T YOU MAKE THEM TOTAL ROBOTS IN THE FIRST PLACE?

BECAUSE, MADAME, IF I HAD THEY WOULDN'T HAVE MADE GOOD SOLDIERS...

AS YOU KNOW, ROBOTS CAN'T FIGHT HUMANS...

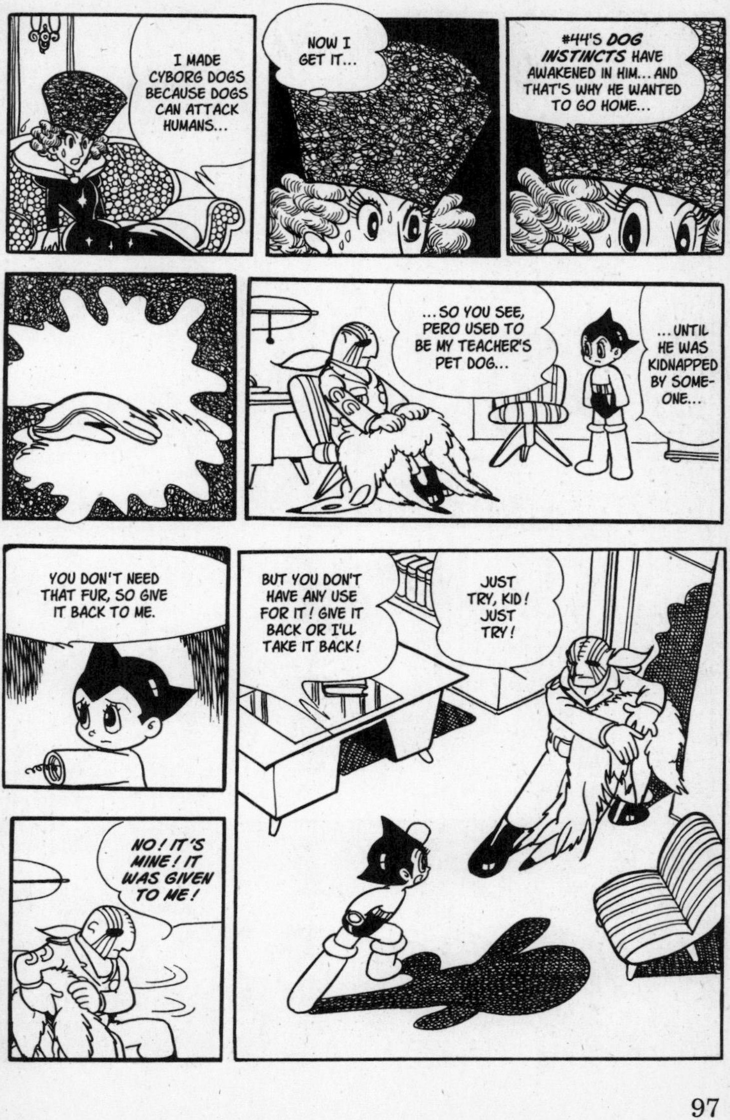
I MADE CYBORG DOGS BECAUSE DOGS CAN ATTACK HUMANS...
NOW I GET IT...
#44'S *DOG INSTINCTS* HAVE AWAKENED IN HIM... AND THAT'S WHY HE WANTED TO GO HOME...
...SO YOU SEE, PERO USED TO BE MY TEACHER'S PET DOG...
...UNTIL HE WAS KIDNAPPED BY SOME-ONE...
YOU DON'T NEED THAT FUR, SO GIVE IT BACK TO ME.
NO! IT'S MINE! IT WAS GIVEN TO ME!
BUT YOU DON'T HAVE ANY USE FOR IT! GIVE IT BACK OR I'LL TAKE IT BACK!
JUST TRY, KID! JUST TRY!

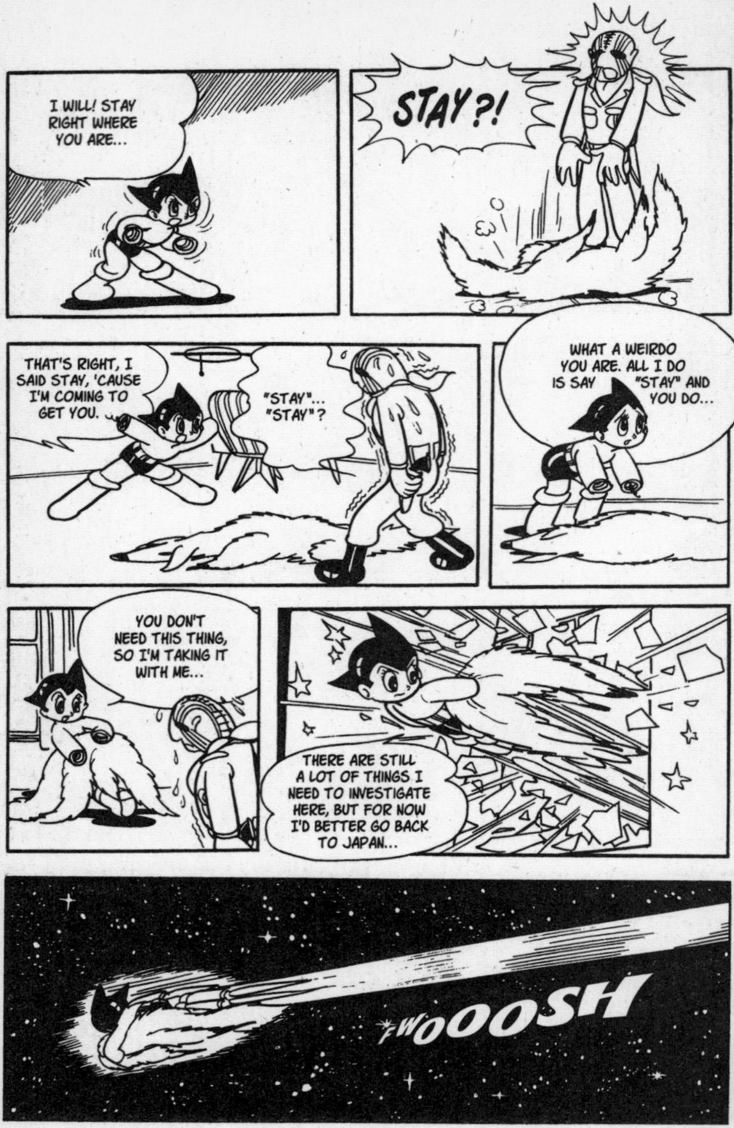
I WILL! STAY RIGHT WHERE YOU ARE...
STAY?!
THAT'S RIGHT, I SAID STAY, 'CAUSE I'M COMING TO GET YOU.
"STAY"... "STAY"?
WHAT A WEIRDO YOU ARE. ALL I DO IS SAY "STAY" AND YOU DO...
YOU DON'T NEED THIS THING, SO I'M TAKING IT WITH ME...
THERE ARE STILL A LOT OF THINGS I NEED TO INVESTIGATE HERE, BUT FOR NOW I'D BETTER GO BACK TO JAPAN...
FWOOOSH

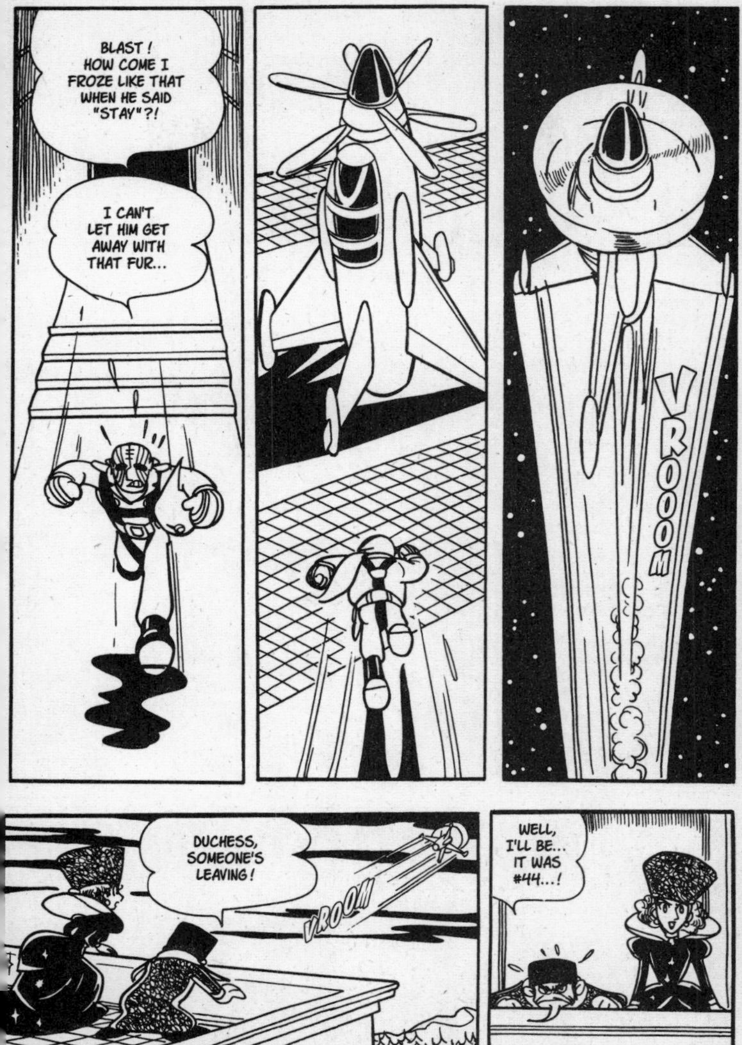
BLAST ! HOW COME I FROZE LIKE THAT WHEN HE SAID "STAY"?!
I CAN'T LET HIM GET AWAY WITH THAT FUR...
VROOOOM
DUCHESS, SOMEONE'S LEAVING !
VROOM
WELL, I'LL BE... IT WAS #44...!

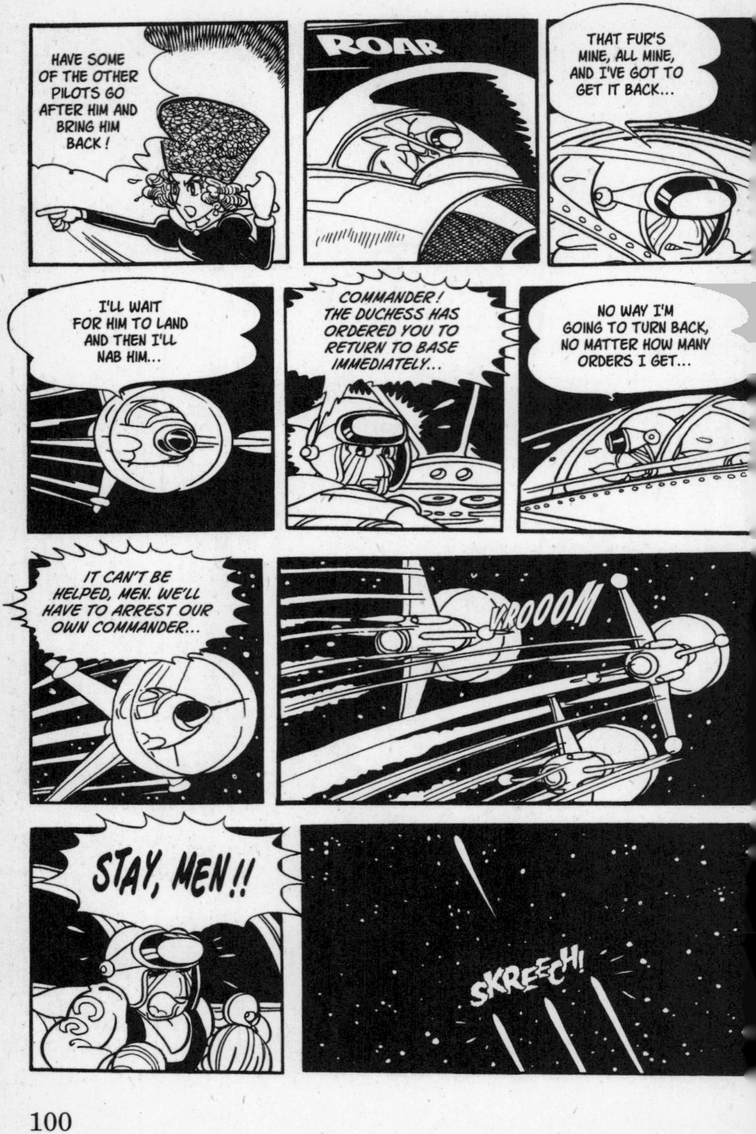
HAVE SOME OF THE OTHER PILOTS GO AFTER HIM AND BRING HIM BACK!
ROAR
THAT FUR'S MINE, ALL MINE, AND I'VE GOT TO GET IT BACK...
I'LL WAIT FOR HIM TO LAND AND THEN I'LL NAB HIM...
COMMANDER! THE DUCHESS HAS ORDERED YOU TO RETURN TO BASE IMMEDIATELY...
NO WAY I'M GOING TO TURN BACK, NO MATTER HOW MANY ORDERS I GET...
IT CAN'T BE HELPED, MEN. WE'LL HAVE TO ARREST OUR OWN COMMANDER...
VROOOM
STAY, MEN!!
SKREECH!

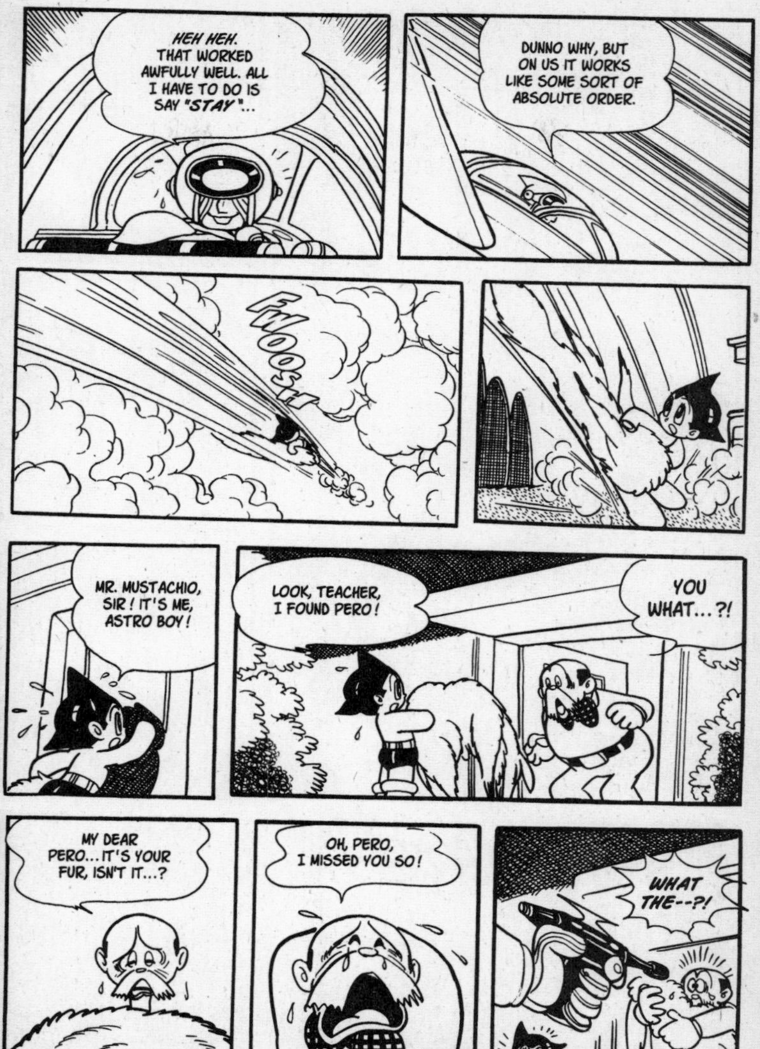
HEH HEH. THAT WORKED AWFULLY WELL. ALL I HAVE TO DO IS SAY "STAY"...
DUNNO WHY, BUT ON US IT WORKS LIKE SOME SORT OF ABSOLUTE ORDER.
FWOOSH
MR. MUSTACHIO, SIR! IT'S ME, ASTRO BOY!
LOOK, TEACHER, I FOUND PERO!
YOU WHAT...?!
MY DEAR PERO... IT'S YOUR FUR, ISN'T IT...?
OH, PERO, I MISSED YOU SO!
WHAT THE--?!

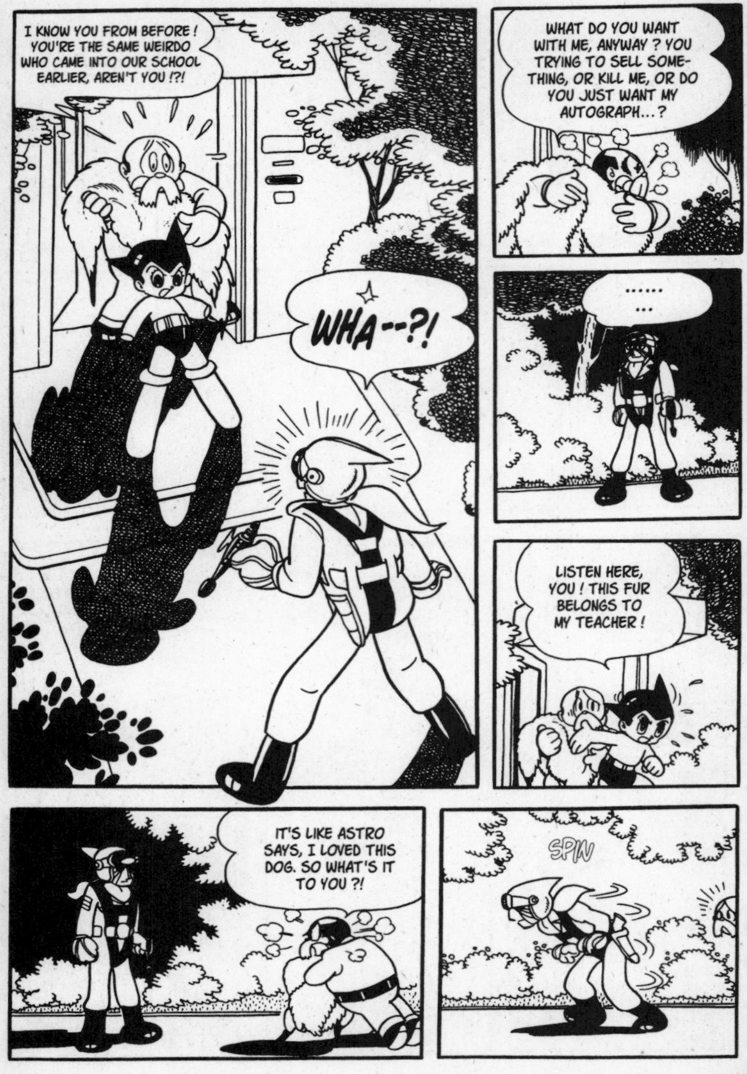
I KNOW YOU FROM BEFORE! YOU'RE THE SAME WEIRDO WHO CAME INTO OUR SCHOOL EARLIER, AREN'T YOU!?!
WHA--?!
WHAT DO YOU WANT WITH ME, ANYWAY? YOU TRYING TO SELL SOMETHING, OR KILL ME, OR DO YOU JUST WANT MY AUTOGRAPH...?
....
LISTEN HERE, YOU! THIS FUR BELONGS TO MY TEACHER!
IT'S LIKE ASTRO SAYS, I LOVED THIS DOG. SO WHAT'S IT TO YOU?!
SPIN

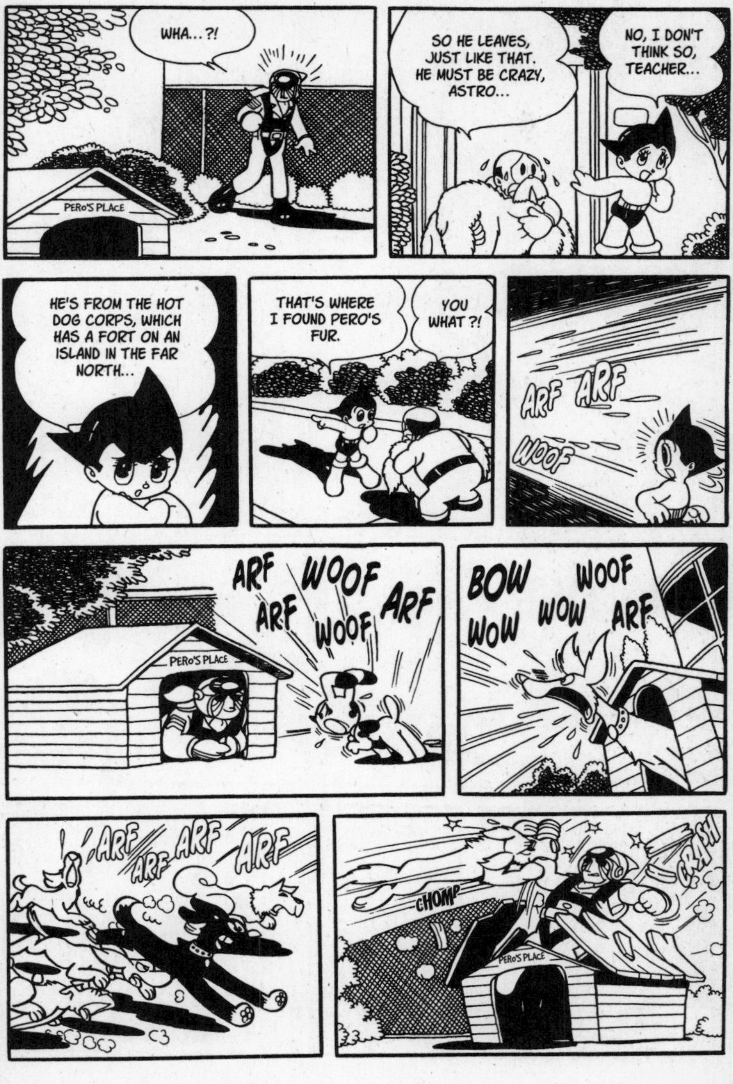
WHA...?!
PERO'S PLACE
SO HE LEAVES, JUST LIKE THAT. HE MUST BE CRAZY, ASTRO...
NO, I DON'T THINK SO, TEACHER...
HE'S FROM THE HOT DOG CORPS, WHICH HAS A FORT ON AN ISLAND IN THE FAR NORTH...
THAT'S WHERE I FOUND PERO'S FUR.
YOU WHAT?!
ARF ARF
WOOF
ARF WOOF
ARF WOOF ARF
PERO'S PLACE
BOW WOOF
WOW WOW ARF
ARF ARF ARF ARF
CHOMP
CRASH
PERO'S PLACE

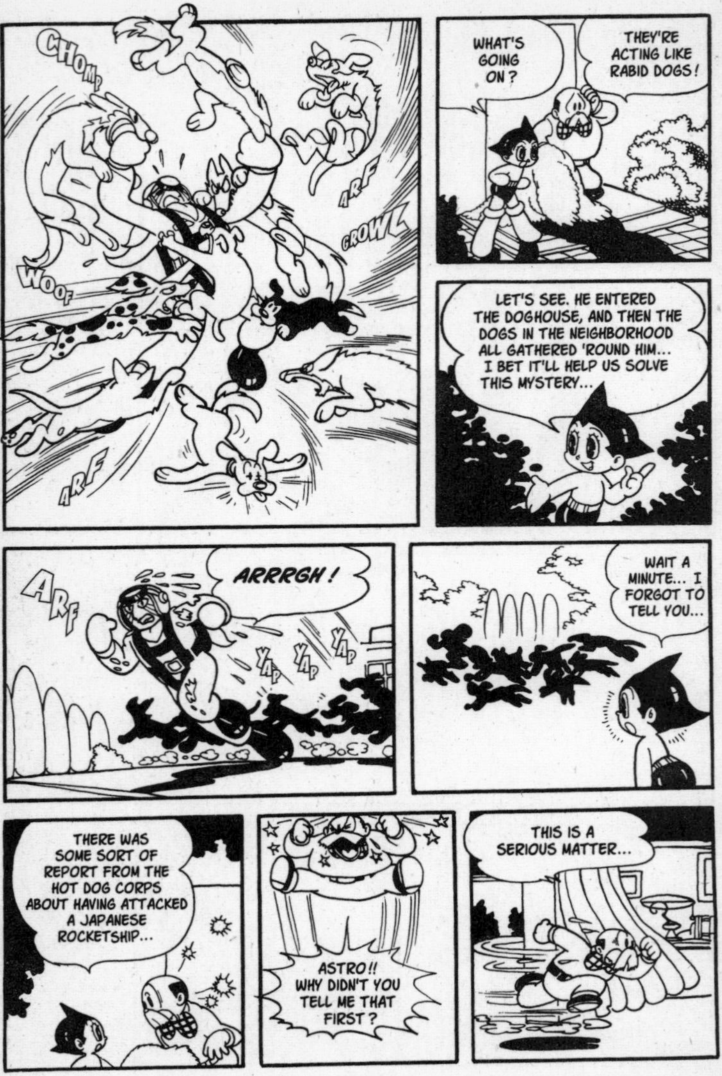
CHOMP
ARF
GROWL
WOOF
ARF
WHAT'S GOING ON?
THEY'RE ACTING LIKE RABID DOGS!
LET'S SEE. HE ENTERED THE DOGHOUSE, AND THEN THE DOGS IN THE NEIGHBORHOOD ALL GATHERED 'ROUND HIM... I BET IT'LL HELP US SOLVE THIS MYSTERY...
ARF
ARRRGH!
YAP
YAP
YAP
WAIT A MINUTE... I FORGOT TO TELL YOU...
THERE WAS SOME SORT OF REPORT FROM THE HOT DOG CORPS ABOUT HAVING ATTACKED A JAPANESE ROCKETSHIP...
ASTRO!! WHY DIDN'T YOU TELL ME THAT FIRST?
THIS IS A SERIOUS MATTER...

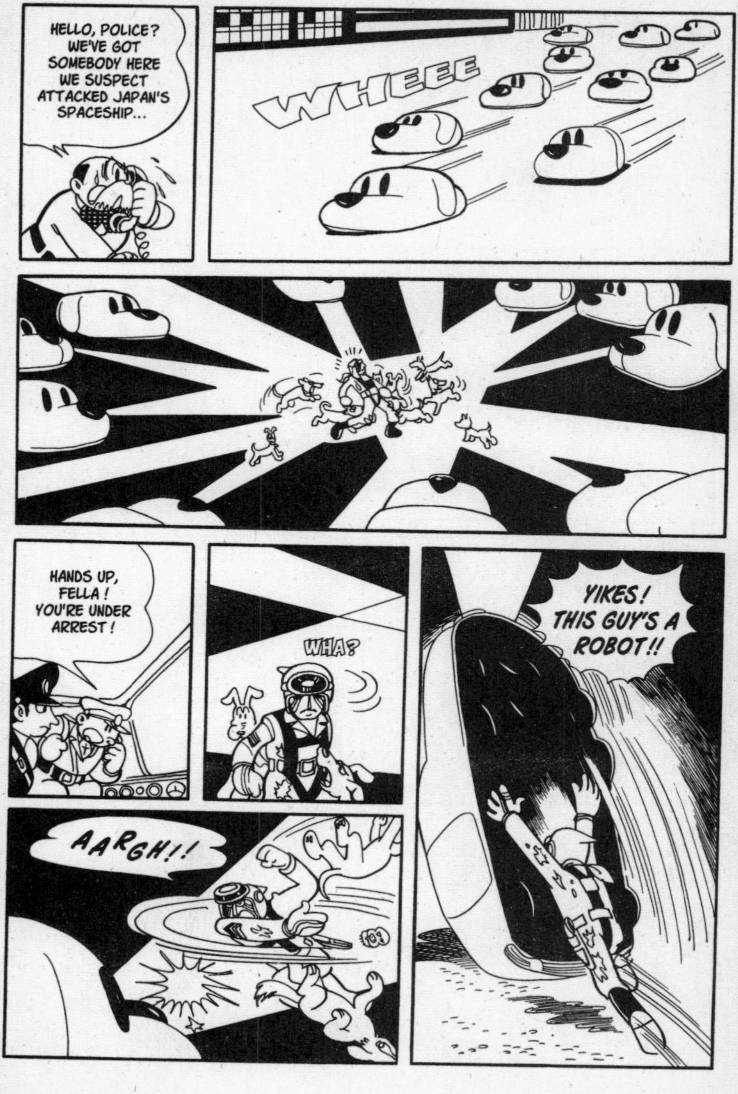
HELLO, POLICE? WE'VE GOT SOMEBODY HERE WE SUSPECT ATTACKED JAPAN'S SPACESHIP...
WHEEE
HANDS UP, FELLA! YOU'RE UNDER ARREST!
WHA?
YIKES! THIS GUY'S A ROBOT!!
AARGH!!

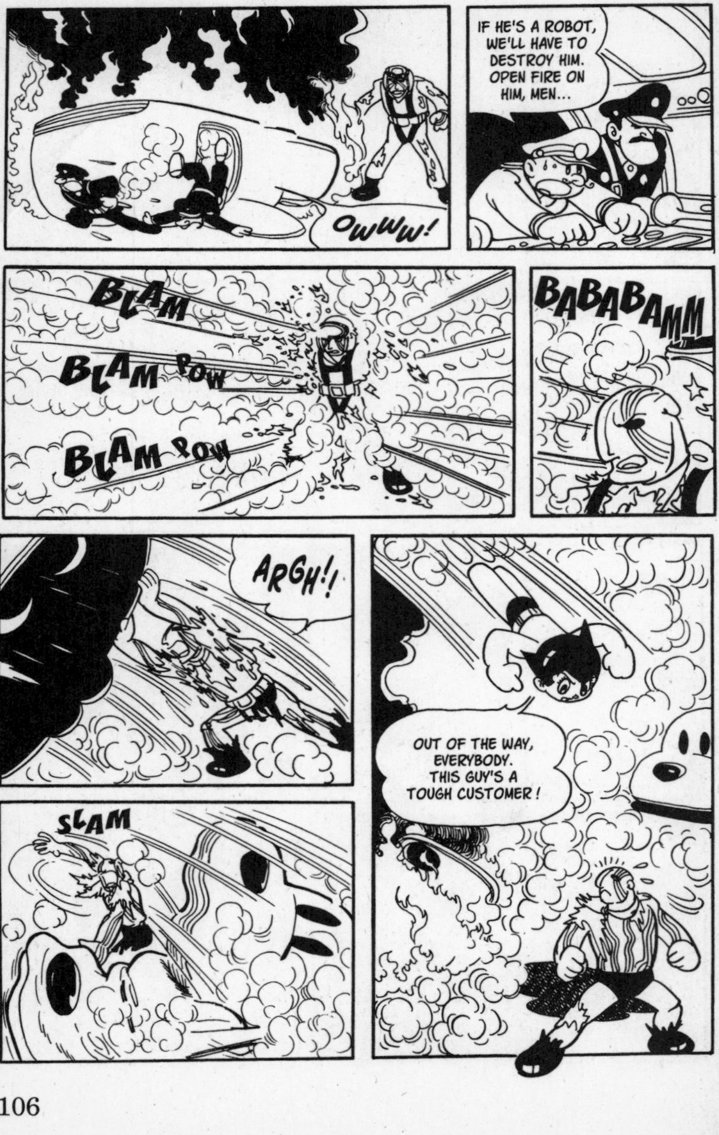
OWWW!
IF HE'S A ROBOT, WE'LL HAVE TO DESTROY HIM. OPEN FIRE ON HIM, MEN...
BLAM
BLAM POW
BLAM POW
BABABAMM
ARGH!!
OUT OF THE WAY, EVERYBODY. THIS GUY'S A TOUGH CUSTOMER!
SLAM

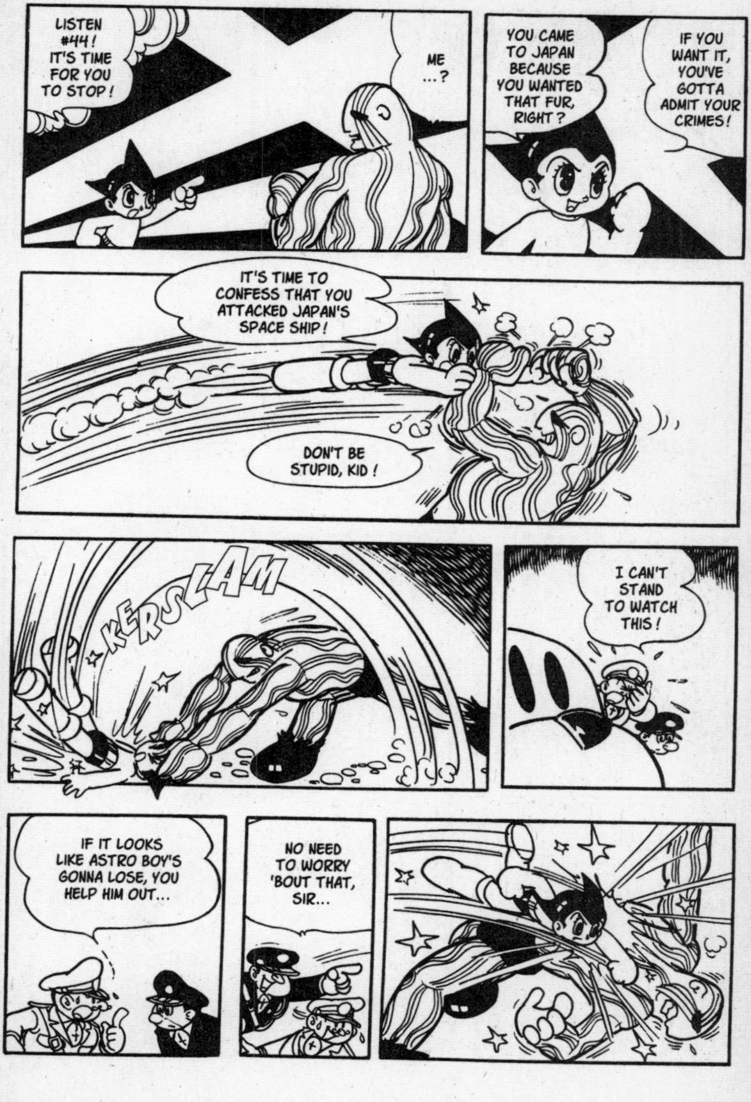
LISTEN #44! IT'S TIME FOR YOU TO STOP!
ME ...?
YOU CAME TO JAPAN BECAUSE YOU WANTED THAT FUR, RIGHT?
IF YOU WANT IT, YOU'VE GOTTA ADMIT YOUR CRIMES!
IT'S TIME TO CONFESS THAT YOU ATTACKED JAPAN'S SPACE SHIP!
DON'T BE STUPID, KID!
KERSLAM
I CAN'T STAND TO WATCH THIS!
IF IT LOOKS LIKE ASTRO BOY'S GONNA LOSE, YOU HELP HIM OUT...
NO NEED TO WORRY 'BOUT THAT, SIR...

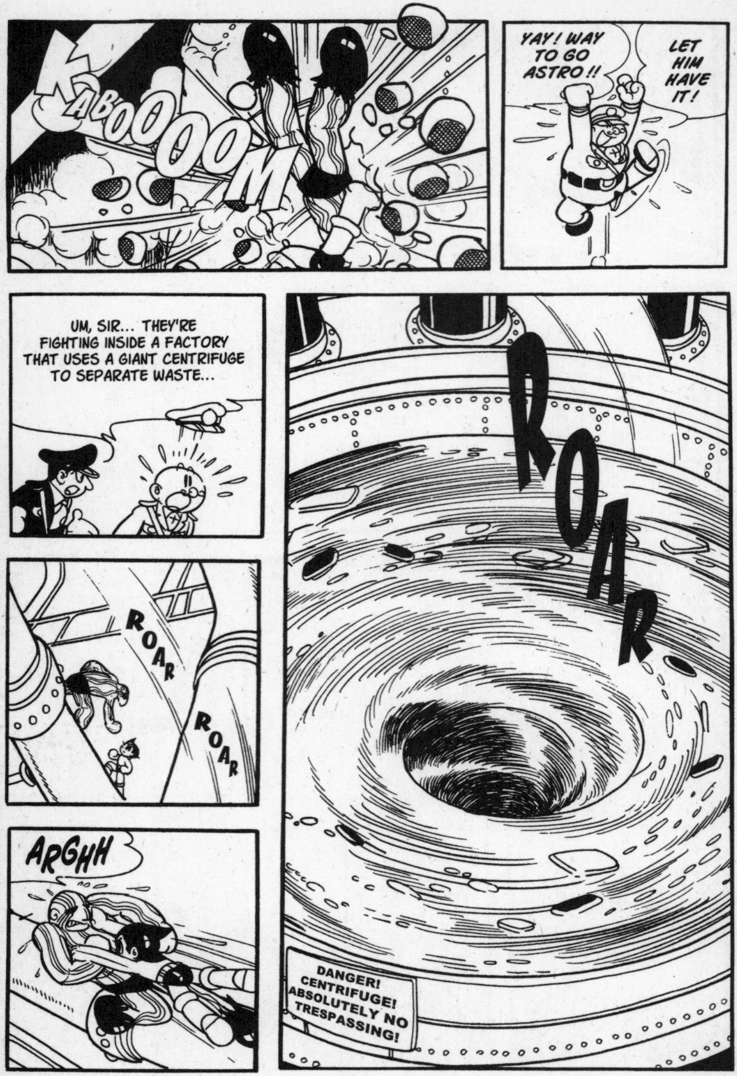
KABOOOOOM
YAY! WAY TO GO ASTRO!!
LET HIM HAVE IT!
UM, SIR... THEY'RE FIGHTING INSIDE A FACTORY THAT USES A GIANT CENTRIFUGE TO SEPARATE WASTE...
ROAR
ROAR
ARGHH
ROAR
DANGER! CENTRIFUGE! ABSOLUTELY NO TRESPASSING!

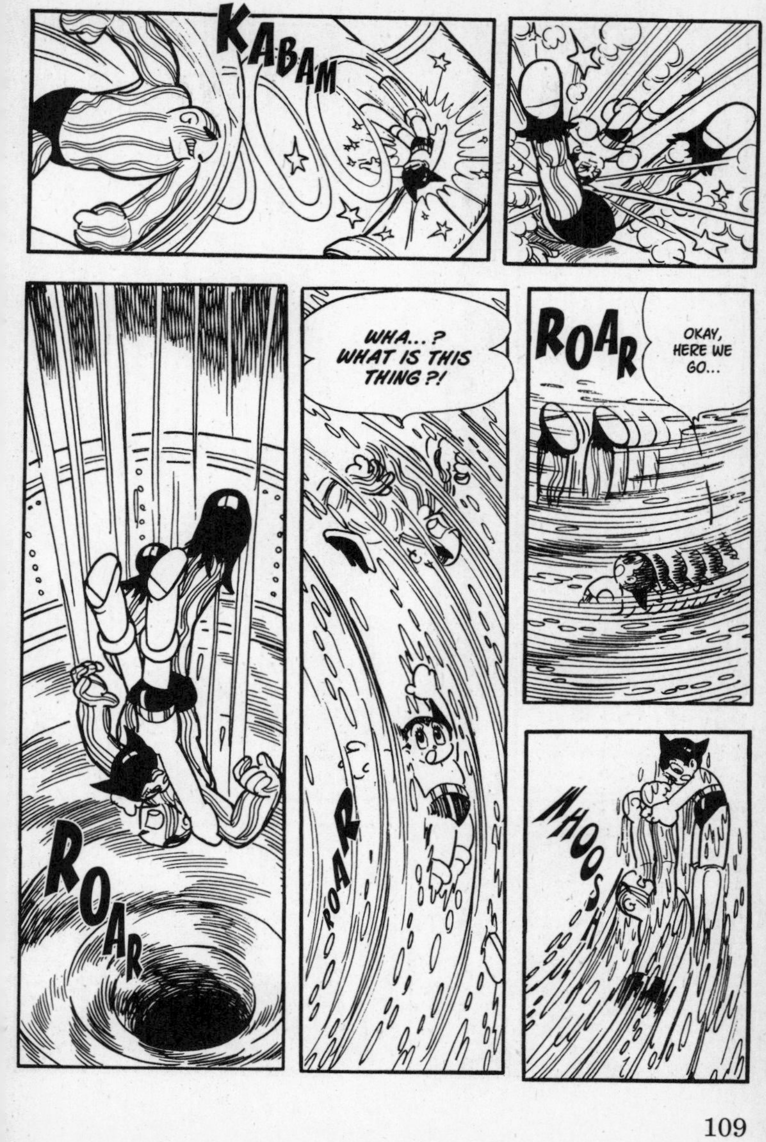
KABAM
ROAR
WHA...? WHAT IS THIS THING?!
ROAR
ROAR
OKAY, HERE WE GO...
WHOOSH

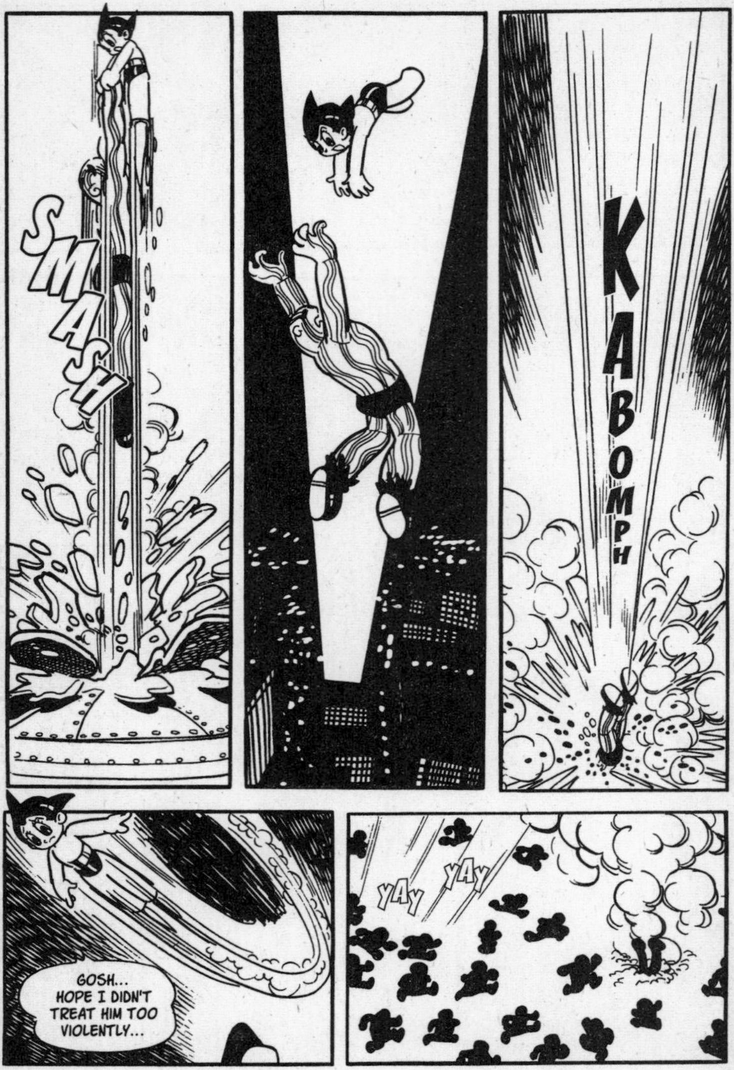
SMASH
KABOOMPH
GOSH... HOPE I DIDN'T TREAT HIM TOO VIOLENTLY...
YAY
YAY

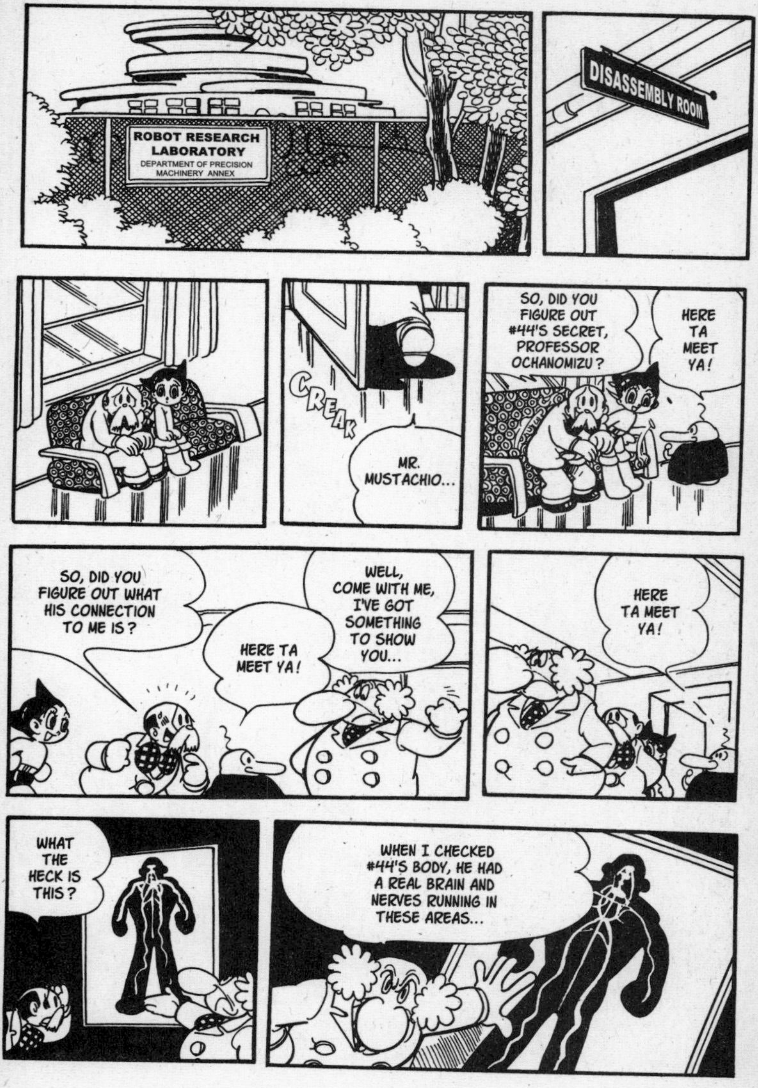
ROBOT RESEARCH LABORATORY
DEPARTMENT OF PRECISION MACHINERY ANNEX
DISASSEMBLY ROOM
CREAK
MR. MUSTACHIO...
SO, DID YOU FIGURE OUT #44'S SECRET, PROFESSOR OCHANOMIZU?
HERE TA MEET YA!
SO, DID YOU FIGURE OUT WHAT HIS CONNECTION TO ME IS?
HERE TA MEET YA!
WELL, COME WITH ME, I'VE GOT SOMETHING TO SHOW YOU...
HERE TA MEET YA!
WHAT THE HECK IS THIS?
WHEN I CHECKED #44'S BODY, HE HAD A REAL BRAIN AND NERVES RUNNING IN THESE AREAS...

HA HA HA! A REAL NERVOUS SYSTEM IN A ROBOT'S BODY?

HA HAH! YOU MUST BE JOKING!!

THIS IS NO LAUGHING MATTER, MUSTACHIO.

I'M TRYING TO BE SERIOUS.

WHAT WE HAVE HERE IS A CASE OF AN EXTREME CYBORG...

?

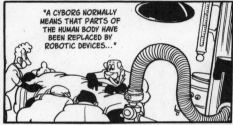

"A CYBORG NORMALLY MEANS THAT PARTS OF THE HUMAN BODY HAVE BEEN REPLACED BY ROBOTIC DEVICES..."

"CYBORGS BECAME NECESSARY BECAUSE ON MANY WORLDS IN OUTER SPACE HUMANS CAN'T SURVIVE, EVEN WITH SPACE SUITS..."

112

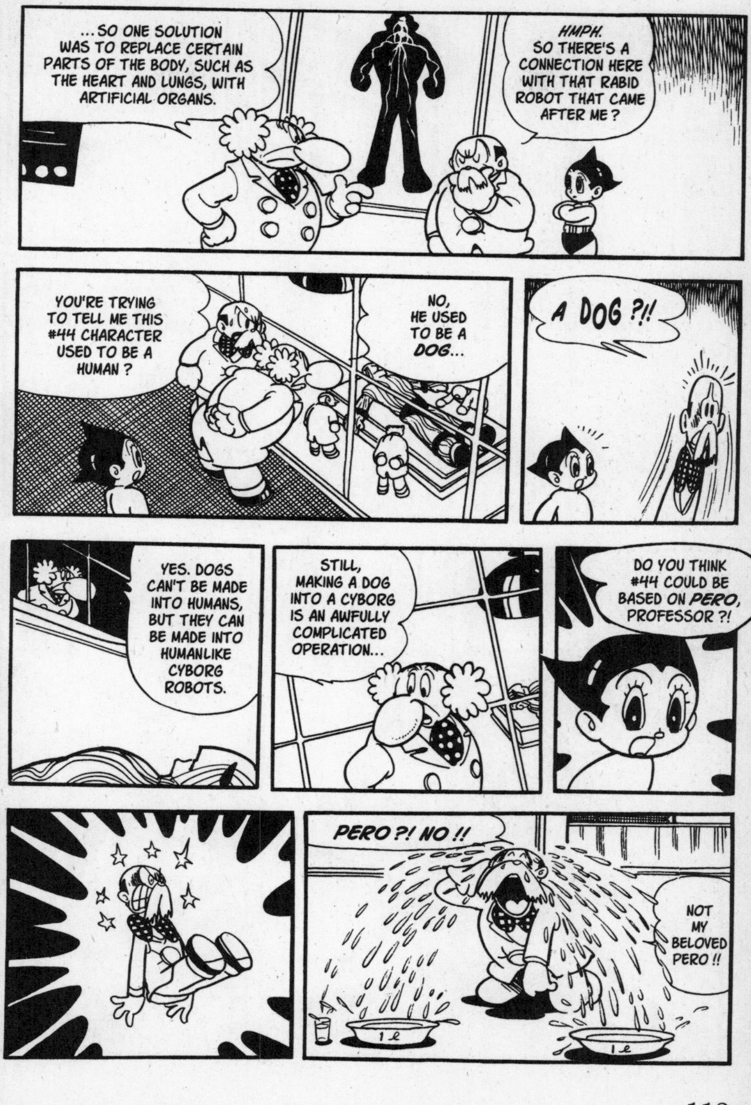
...SO ONE SOLUTION WAS TO REPLACE CERTAIN PARTS OF THE BODY, SUCH AS THE HEART AND LUNGS, WITH ARTIFICIAL ORGANS.
HMPH. SO THERE'S A CONNECTION HERE WITH THAT RABID ROBOT THAT CAME AFTER ME?
YOU'RE TRYING TO TELL ME THIS #44 CHARACTER USED TO BE A HUMAN?
NO, HE USED TO BE A DOG...
A DOG?!!
YES. DOGS CAN'T BE MADE INTO HUMANS, BUT THEY CAN BE MADE INTO HUMANLIKE CYBORG ROBOTS.
STILL, MAKING A DOG INTO A CYBORG IS AN AWFULLY COMPLICATED OPERATION...
DO YOU THINK #44 COULD BE BASED ON PERO, PROFESSOR?!
PERO?! NO!!
NOT MY BELOVED PERO!!

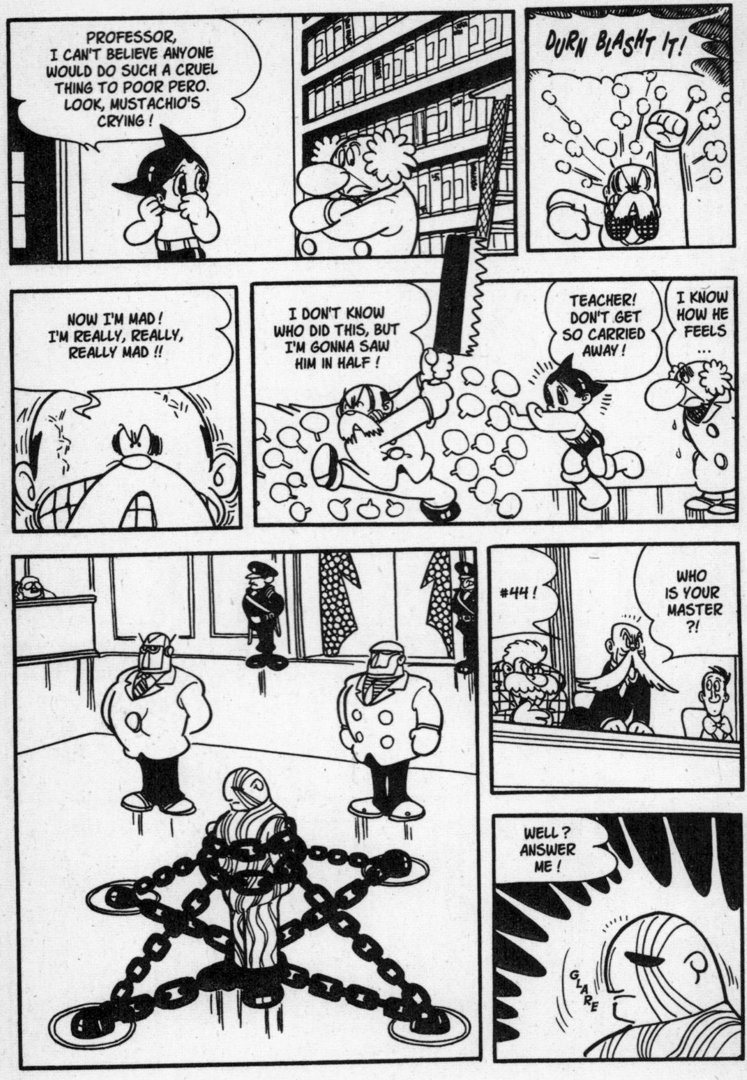
PROFESSOR, I CAN'T BELIEVE ANYONE WOULD DO SUCH A CRUEL THING TO POOR PERO. LOOK, MUSTACHIO'S CRYING !
DURN BLASHT IT!
NOW I'M MAD ! I'M REALLY, REALLY, REALLY MAD !!
I DON'T KNOW WHO DID THIS, BUT I'M GONNA SAW HIM IN HALF !
TEACHER! DON'T GET SO CARRIED AWAY !
I KNOW HOW HE FEELS ...
#44 !
WHO IS YOUR MASTER ?!
WELL ? ANSWER ME !
GLARE

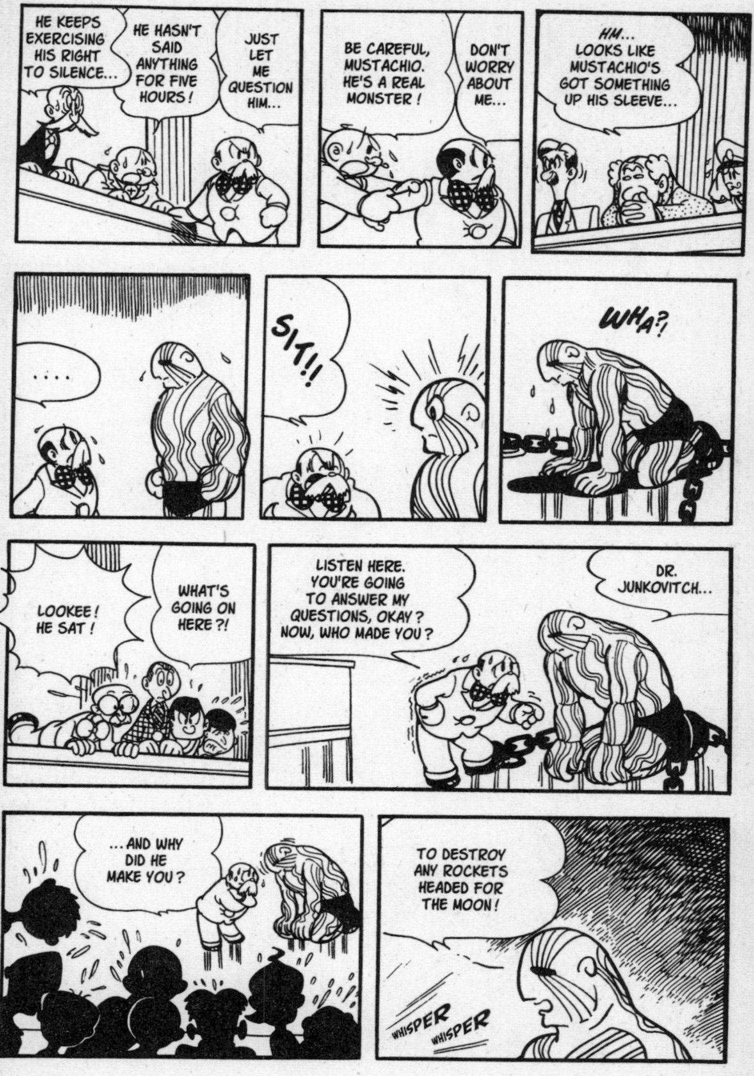
HE KEEPS EXERCISING HIS RIGHT TO SILENCE...
HE HASN'T SAID ANYTHING FOR FIVE HOURS!
JUST LET ME QUESTION HIM...
BE CAREFUL, MUSTACHIO. HE'S A REAL MONSTER!
DON'T WORRY ABOUT ME...
HM... LOOKS LIKE MUSTACHIO'S GOT SOMETHING UP HIS SLEEVE...
....
SIT!!
WHA?!
LOOKEE! HE SAT!
WHAT'S GOING ON HERE?!
LISTEN HERE. YOU'RE GOING TO ANSWER MY QUESTIONS, OKAY? NOW, WHO MADE YOU?
DR. JUNKOVITCH...
...AND WHY DID HE MAKE YOU?
TO DESTROY ANY ROCKETS HEADED FOR THE MOON!
WHISPER
WHISPER

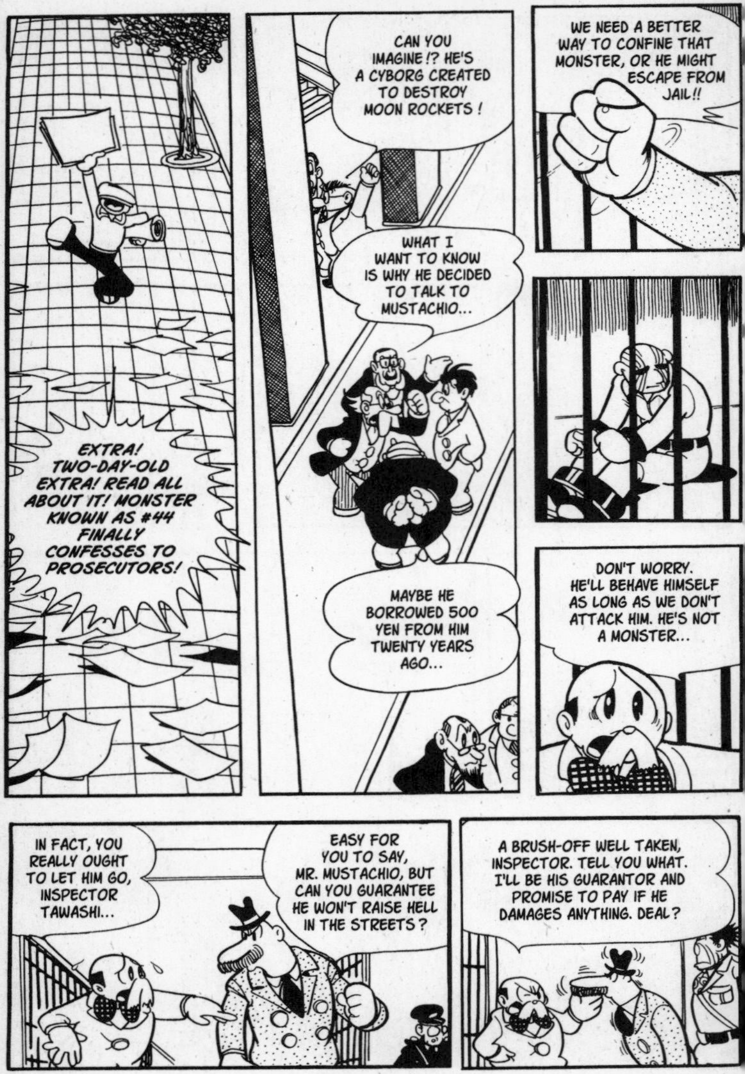
EXTRA! TWO-DAY-OLD EXTRA! READ ALL ABOUT IT! MONSTER KNOWN AS #44 FINALLY CONFESSES TO PROSECUTORS!
CAN YOU IMAGINE!? HE'S A CYBORG CREATED TO DESTROY MOON ROCKETS!
WHAT I WANT TO KNOW IS WHY HE DECIDED TO TALK TO MUSTACHIO...
MAYBE HE BORROWED 500 YEN FROM HIM TWENTY YEARS AGO...
WE NEED A BETTER WAY TO CONFINE THAT MONSTER, OR HE MIGHT ESCAPE FROM JAIL!!
DON'T WORRY. HE'LL BEHAVE HIMSELF AS LONG AS WE DON'T ATTACK HIM. HE'S NOT A MONSTER...
IN FACT, YOU REALLY OUGHT TO LET HIM GO, INSPECTOR TAWASHI...
EASY FOR YOU TO SAY, MR. MUSTACHIO, BUT CAN YOU GUARANTEE HE WON'T RAISE HELL IN THE STREETS?
A BRUSH-OFF WELL TAKEN, INSPECTOR. TELL YOU WHAT. I'LL BE HIS GUARANTOR AND PROMISE TO PAY IF HE DAMAGES ANYTHING. DEAL?

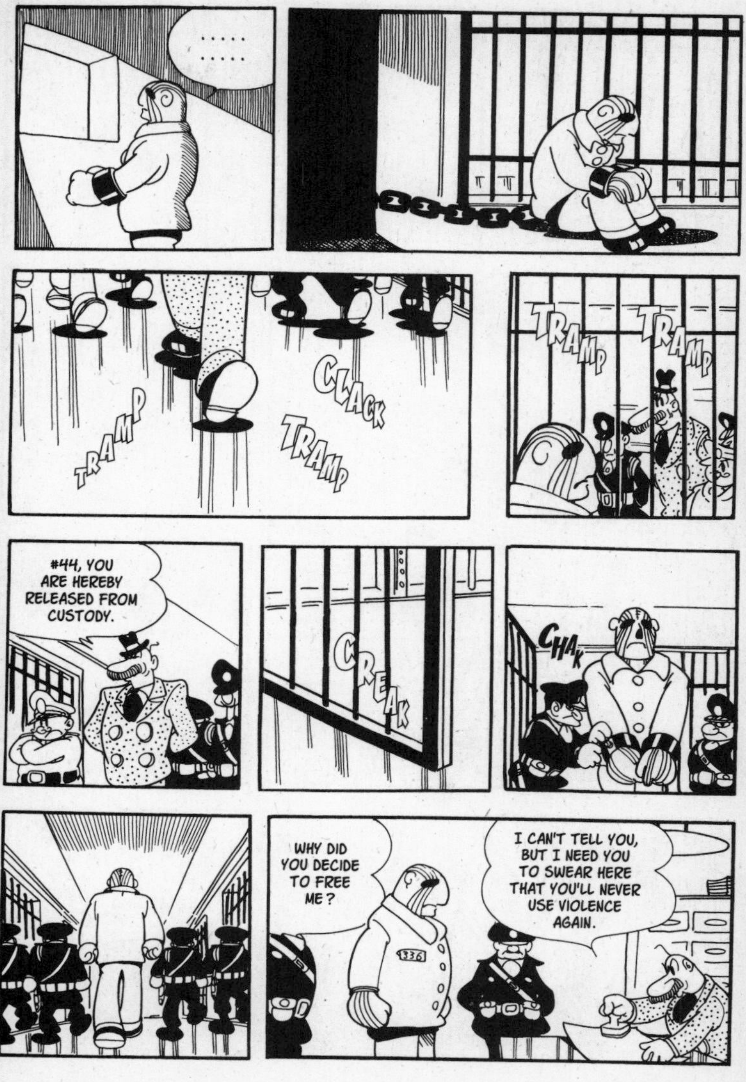
......
......
TRAMP
CLACK
TRAMP
TRAMP
TRAMP
#44, YOU ARE HEREBY RELEASED FROM CUSTODY.
CREAK
CHAK
WHY DID YOU DECIDE TO FREE ME?
I CAN'T TELL YOU, BUT I NEED YOU TO SWEAR HERE THAT YOU'LL NEVER USE VIOLENCE AGAIN.
1336

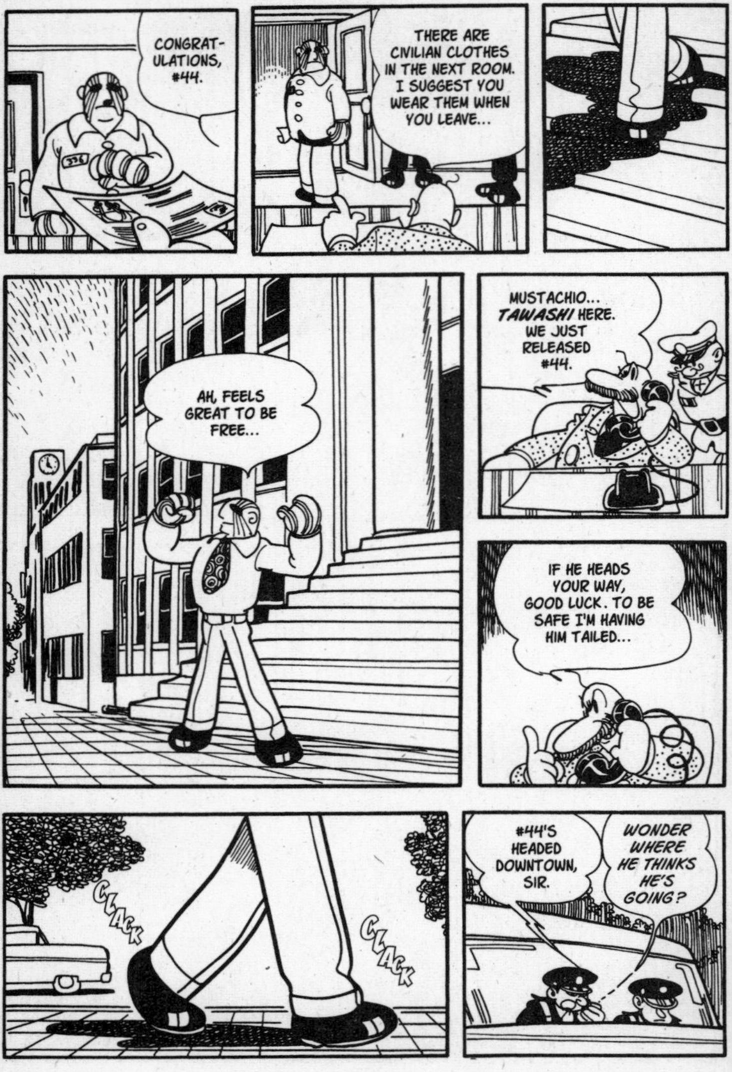
CONGRAT-ULATIONS, #44.
THERE ARE CIVILIAN CLOTHES IN THE NEXT ROOM. I SUGGEST YOU WEAR THEM WHEN YOU LEAVE...
AH, FEELS GREAT TO BE FREE...
MUSTACHIO... *TAWASHI* HERE. WE JUST RELEASED #44.
IF HE HEADS YOUR WAY, GOOD LUCK. TO BE SAFE I'M HAVING HIM TAILED...
CLACK
CLACK
#44'S HEADED DOWNTOWN, SIR.
WONDER WHERE HE THINKS HE'S GOING?

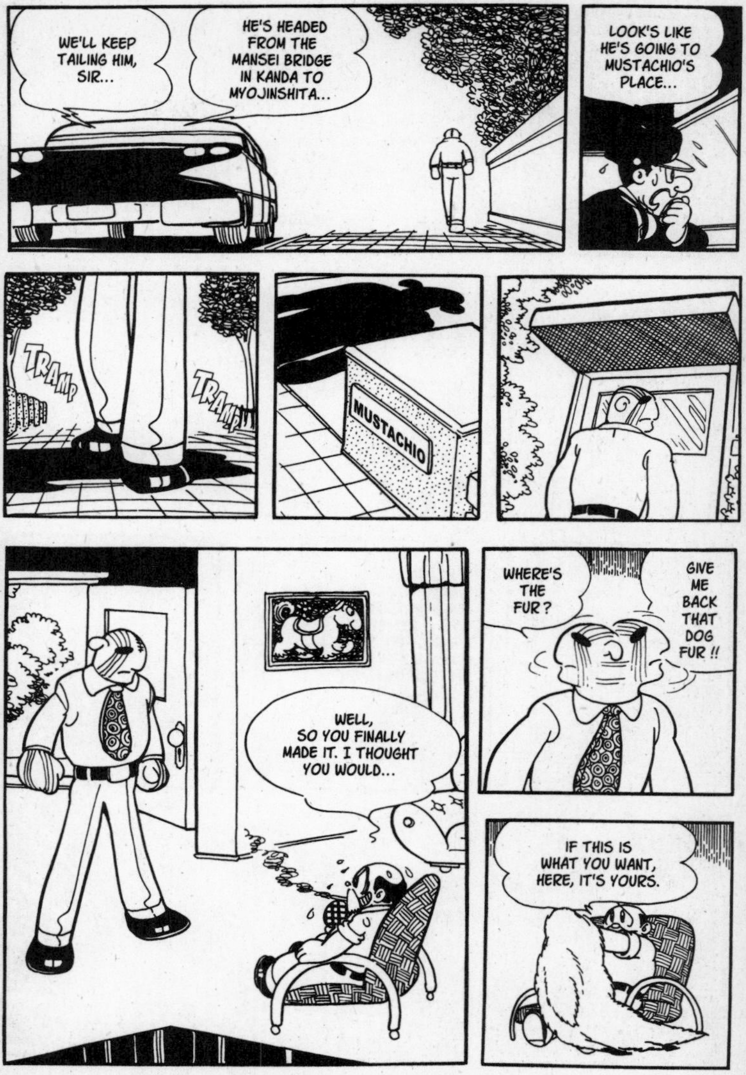
WE'LL KEEP TAILING HIM, SIR...
HE'S HEADED FROM THE MANSEI BRIDGE IN KANDA TO MYOJINSHITA...
LOOK'S LIKE HE'S GOING TO MUSTACHIO'S PLACE...
TRAMP
TRAMP
MUSTACHIO
WELL, SO YOU FINALLY MADE IT. I THOUGHT YOU WOULD...
WHERE'S THE FUR?
GIVE ME BACK THAT DOG FUR !!
IF THIS IS WHAT YOU WANT, HERE, IT'S YOURS.

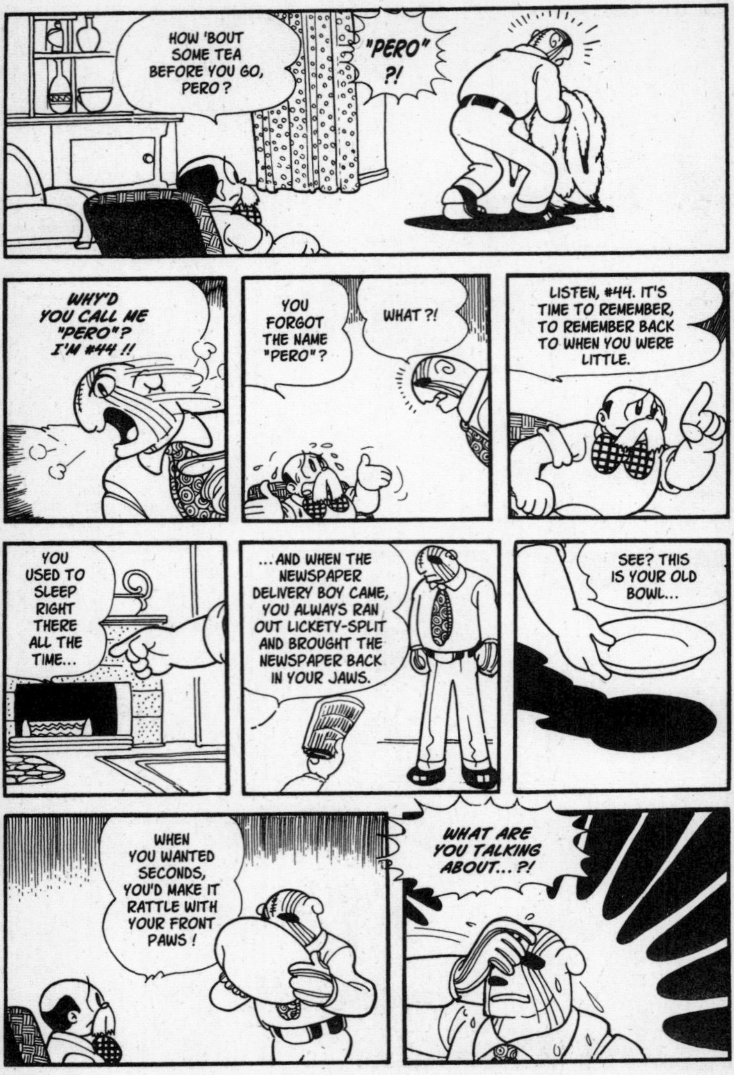
HOW 'BOUT SOME TEA BEFORE YOU GO, PERO ?
"PERO" ?!
WHY'D YOU CALL ME "PERO"? I'M #44 !!
YOU FORGOT THE NAME "PERO"?
WHAT ?!
LISTEN, #44. IT'S TIME TO REMEMBER, TO REMEMBER BACK TO WHEN YOU WERE LITTLE.
YOU USED TO SLEEP RIGHT THERE ALL THE TIME...
...AND WHEN THE NEWSPAPER DELIVERY BOY CAME, YOU ALWAYS RAN OUT LICKETY-SPLIT AND BROUGHT THE NEWSPAPER BACK IN YOUR JAWS.
SEE? THIS IS YOUR OLD BOWL...
WHEN YOU WANTED SECONDS, YOU'D MAKE IT RATTLE WITH YOUR FRONT PAWS !
WHAT ARE YOU TALKING ABOUT...?!

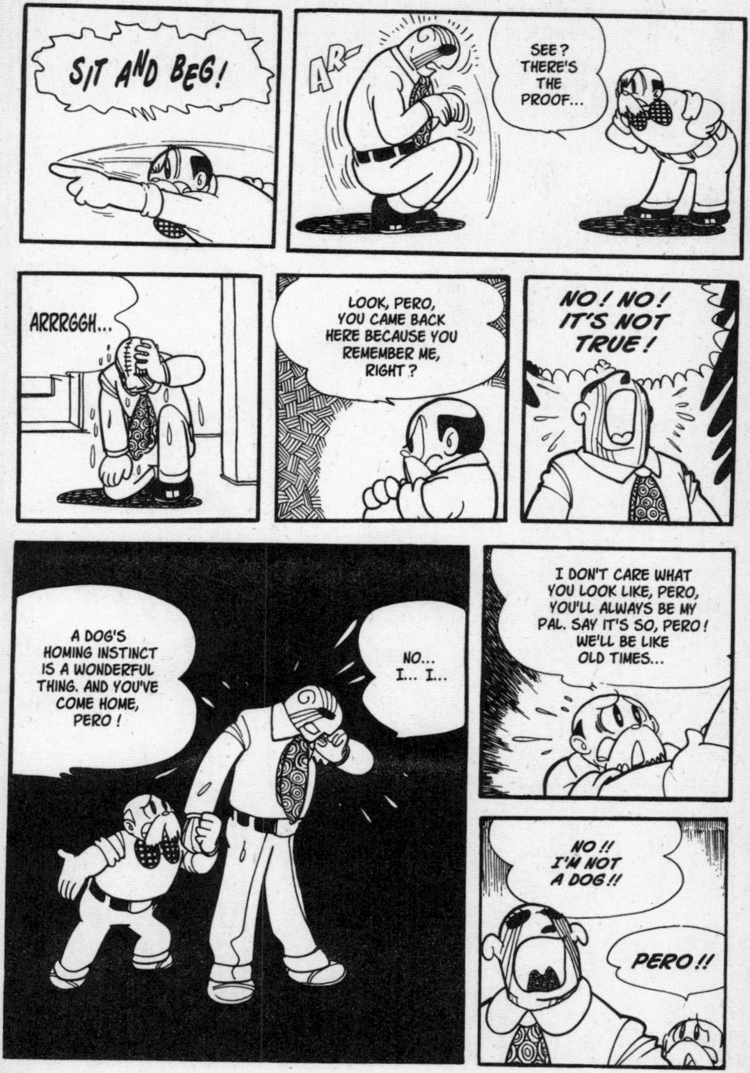
SIT AND BEG!
AR-
SEE? THERE'S THE PROOF...
ARRRGGH...
LOOK, PERO, YOU CAME BACK HERE BECAUSE YOU REMEMBER ME, RIGHT?
NO! NO! IT'S NOT TRUE!
A DOG'S HOMING INSTINCT IS A WONDERFUL THING. AND YOU'VE COME HOME, PERO!
NO... I... I...
I DON'T CARE WHAT YOU LOOK LIKE, PERO, YOU'LL ALWAYS BE MY PAL. SAY IT'S SO, PERO! WE'LL BE LIKE OLD TIMES...
NO!! I'M NOT A DOG!!
PERO!!

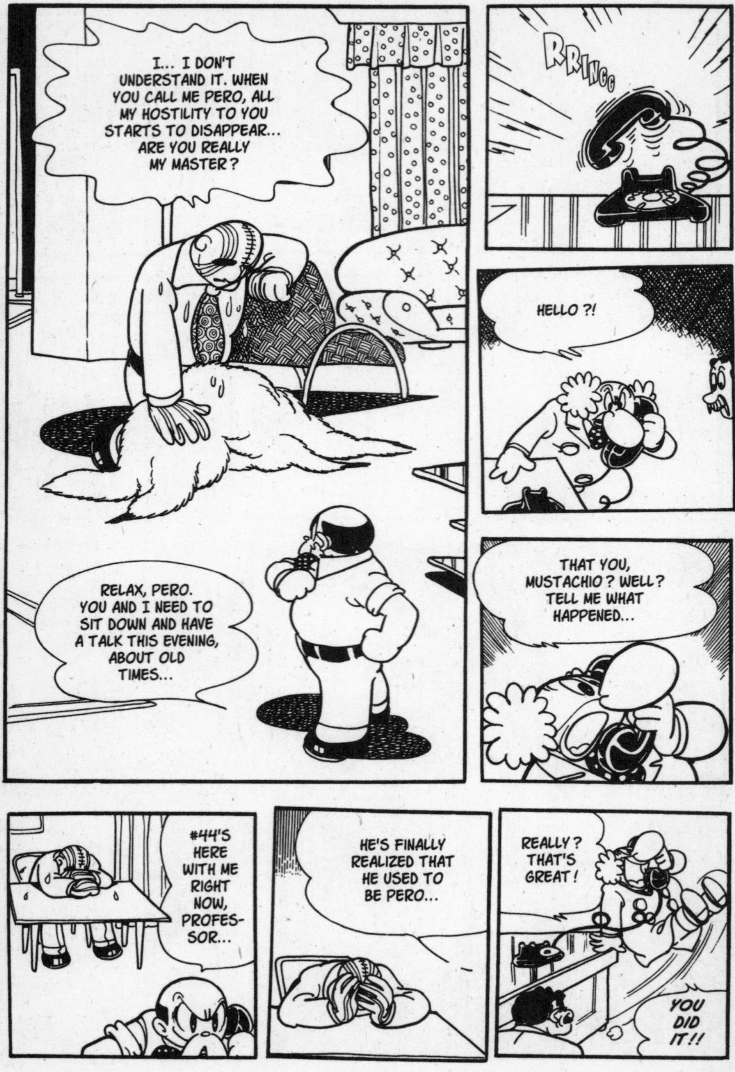
I... I DON'T UNDERSTAND IT. WHEN YOU CALL ME PERO, ALL MY HOSTILITY TO YOU STARTS TO DISAPPEAR... ARE YOU REALLY MY MASTER?
RELAX, PERO. YOU AND I NEED TO SIT DOWN AND HAVE A TALK THIS EVENING, ABOUT OLD TIMES...
RRINGG
HELLO ?!
THAT YOU, MUSTACHIO? WELL? TELL ME WHAT HAPPENED...
#44'S HERE WITH ME RIGHT NOW, PROFES-SOR...
HE'S FINALLY REALIZED THAT HE USED TO BE PERO...
REALLY? THAT'S GREAT!
YOU DID IT!!

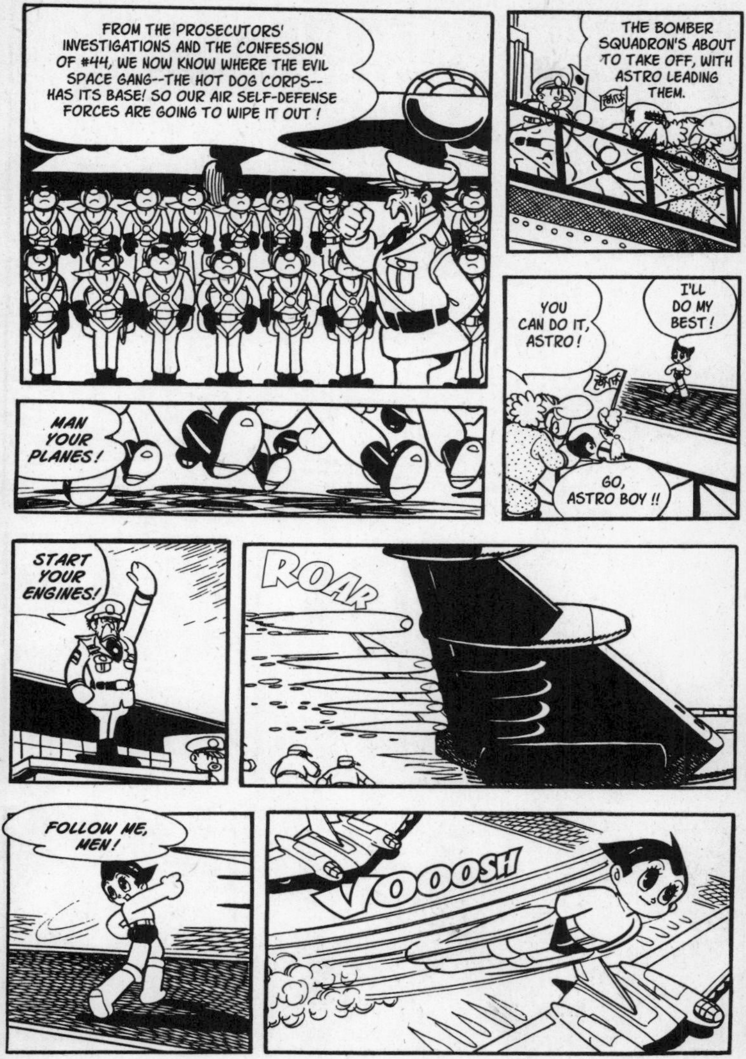
FROM THE PROSECUTORS' INVESTIGATIONS AND THE CONFESSION OF #44, WE NOW KNOW WHERE THE EVIL SPACE GANG--THE HOT DOG CORPS--HAS ITS BASE! SO OUR AIR SELF-DEFENSE FORCES ARE GOING TO WIPE IT OUT !
THE BOMBER SQUADRON'S ABOUT TO TAKE OFF, WITH ASTRO LEADING THEM.
MAN YOUR PLANES !
YOU CAN DO IT, ASTRO !
I'LL DO MY BEST !
GO, ASTRO BOY !!
START YOUR ENGINES!
ROAR
FOLLOW ME, MEN !
VOOOSH

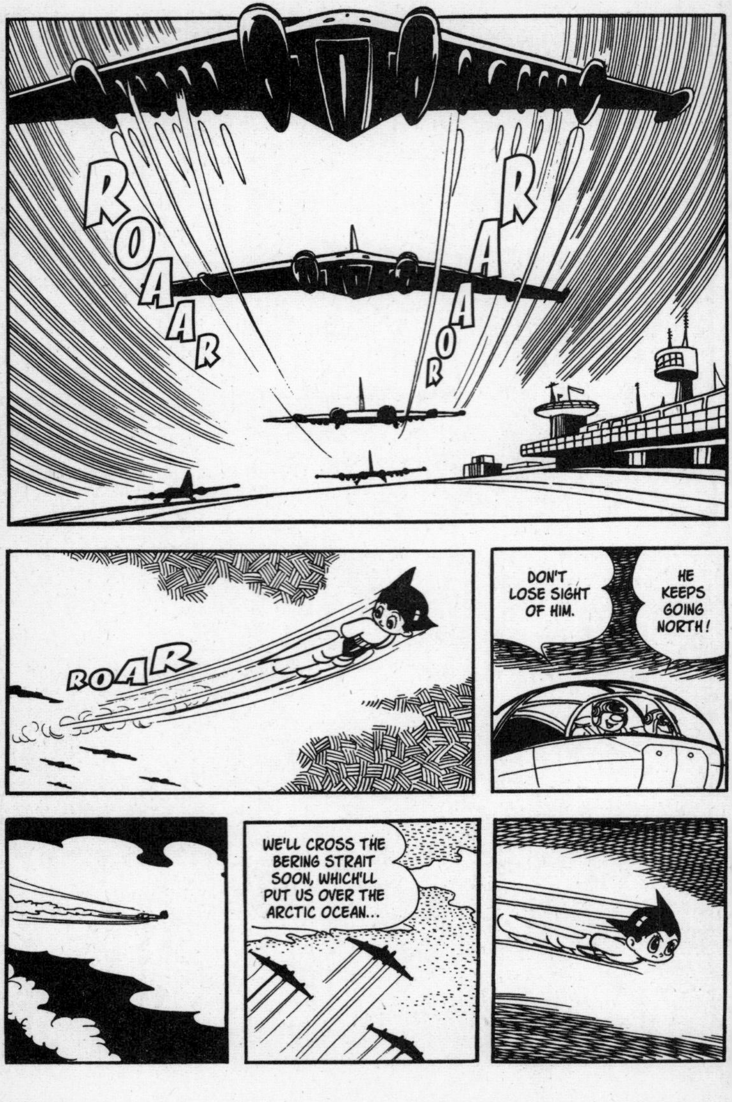
ROAAR
ROAAR
ROAR
DON'T LOSE SIGHT OF HIM.
HE KEEPS GOING NORTH!
WE'LL CROSS THE BERING STRAIT SOON, WHICH'LL PUT US OVER THE ARCTIC OCEAN...

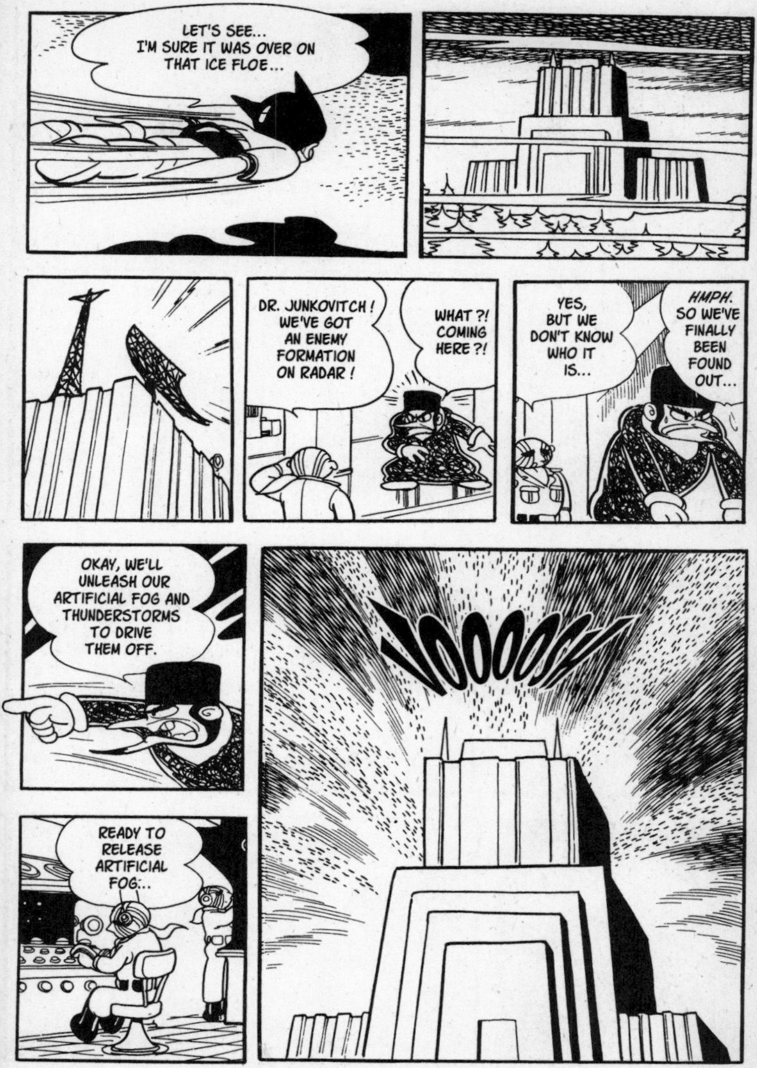
LET'S SEE... I'M SURE IT WAS OVER ON THAT ICE FLOE...
DR. JUNKOVITCH! WE'VE GOT AN ENEMY FORMATION ON RADAR!
WHAT?! COMING HERE?!
YES, BUT WE DON'T KNOW WHO IT IS...
HMPH. SO WE'VE FINALLY BEEN FOUND OUT...
OKAY, WE'LL UNLEASH OUR ARTIFICIAL FOG AND THUNDERSTORMS TO DRIVE THEM OFF.
READY TO RELEASE ARTIFICIAL FOG...
VOOOOSH

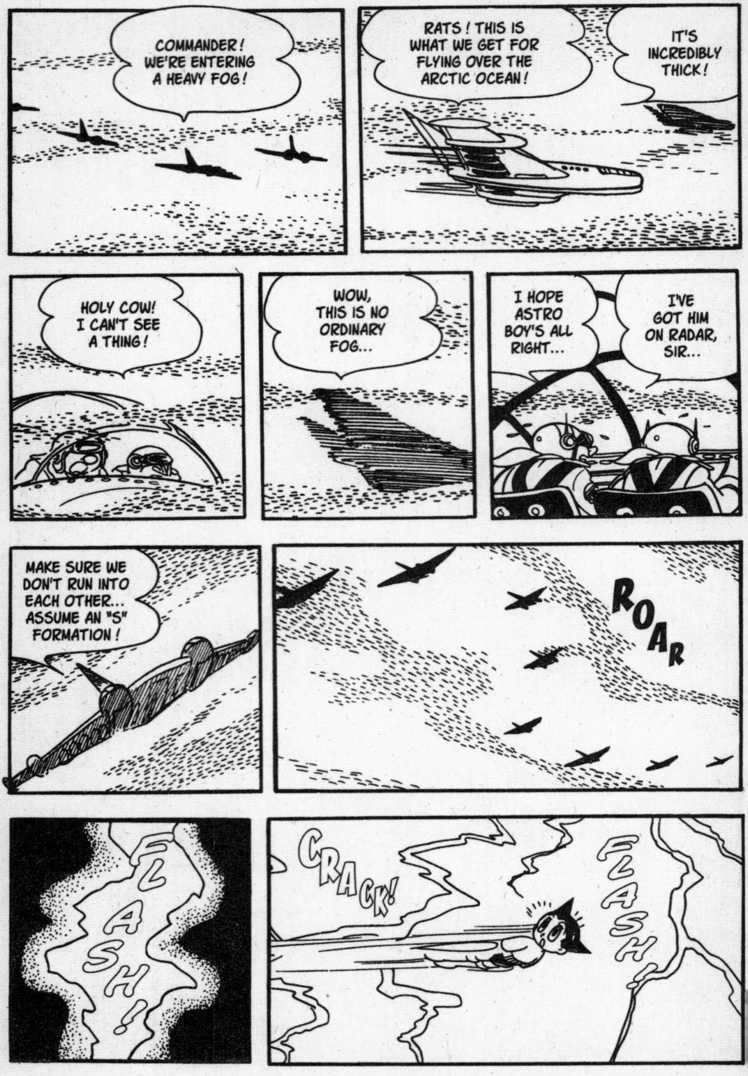
COMMANDER! WE'RE ENTERING A HEAVY FOG!
RATS! THIS IS WHAT WE GET FOR FLYING OVER THE ARCTIC OCEAN!
IT'S INCREDIBLY THICK!
HOLY COW! I CAN'T SEE A THING!
WOW, THIS IS NO ORDINARY FOG...
I HOPE ASTRO BOY'S ALL RIGHT...
I'VE GOT HIM ON RADAR, SIR...
MAKE SURE WE DON'T RUN INTO EACH OTHER... ASSUME AN "S" FORMATION!
ROAR
FLASH!
CRACK!
FLASH!

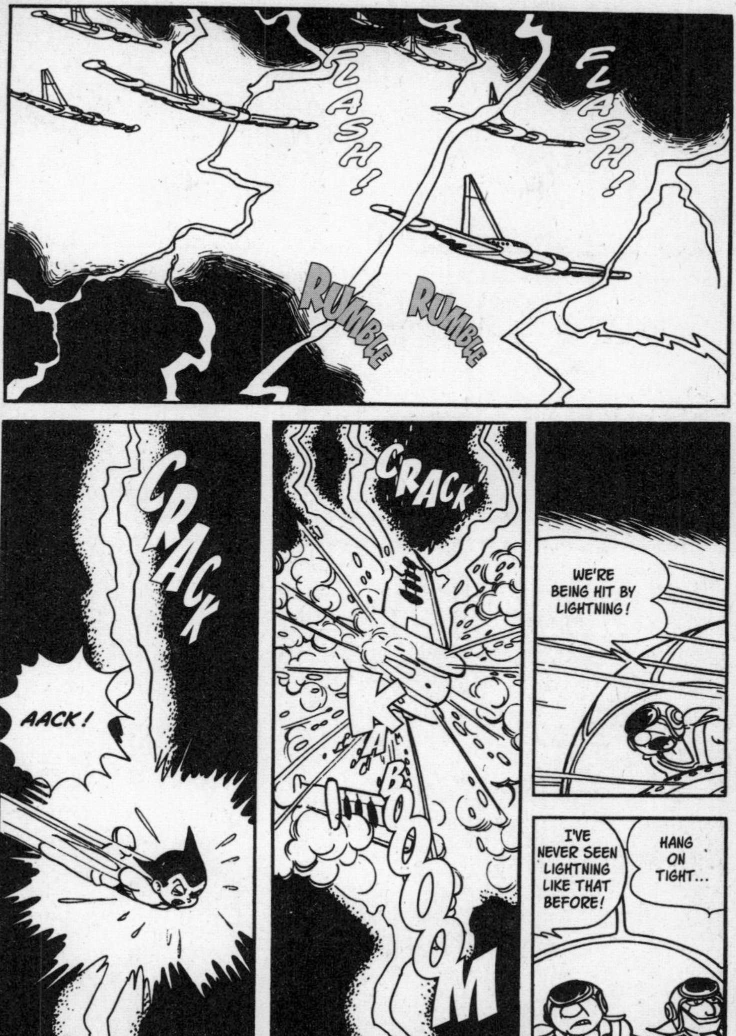

FLASH!
FLASH!
RUMBLE
RUMBLE
CRACK
AACK!
CRACK
KA-BOOOOOM
WE'RE BEING HIT BY LIGHTNING!
I'VE NEVER SEEN LIGHTNING LIKE THAT BEFORE!
HANG ON TIGHT...

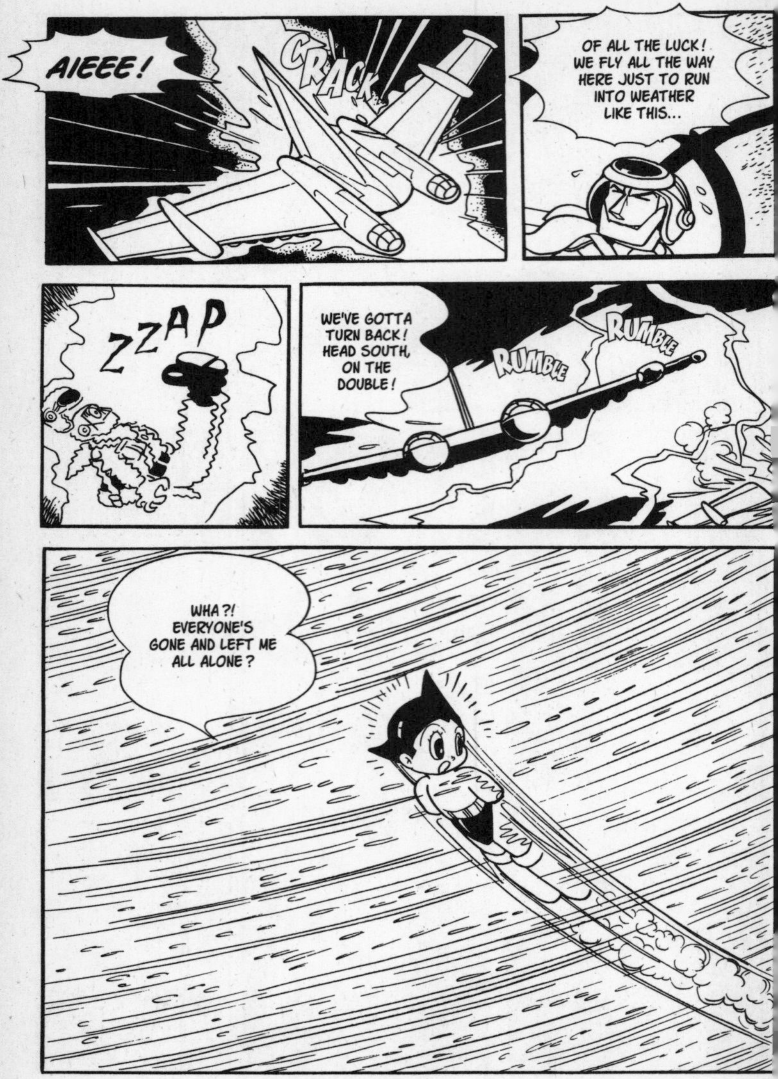
AIEEE!
CRACK
OF ALL THE LUCK! WE FLY ALL THE WAY HERE JUST TO RUN INTO WEATHER LIKE THIS...
ZZAP
WE'VE GOTTA TURN BACK! HEAD SOUTH, ON THE DOUBLE!
RUMBLE
RUMBLE
WHA?! EVERYONE'S GONE AND LEFT ME ALL ALONE?

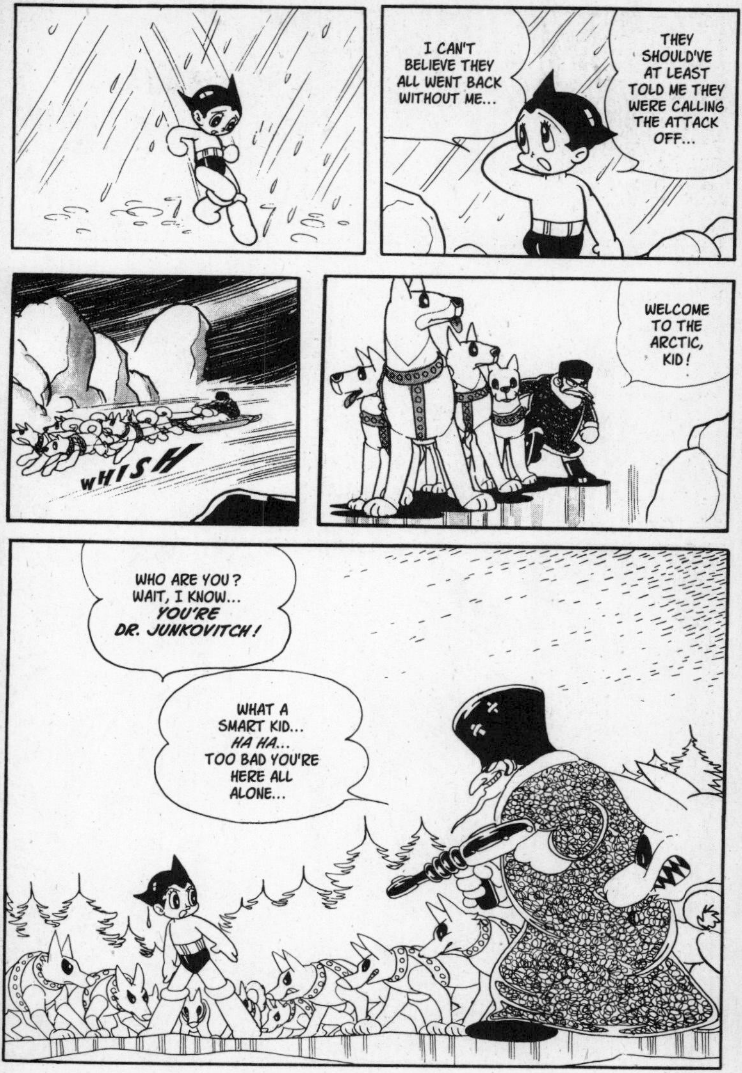
I CAN'T BELIEVE THEY ALL WENT BACK WITHOUT ME...
THEY SHOULD'VE AT LEAST TOLD ME THEY WERE CALLING THE ATTACK OFF...
WHISH
WELCOME TO THE ARCTIC, KID!
WHO ARE YOU? WAIT, I KNOW... *YOU'RE DR. JUNKOVITCH!*
WHAT A SMART KID... *HA HA...* TOO BAD YOU'RE HERE ALL ALONE...

QUITE THE DAREDEVIL, AREN'T YOU, COMING HERE TO ATTACK OUR FORTRESS BY YOURSELF...

BUT EVERYONE ELSE WENT HOME...

HEH HEH HEH. JUST LIKE THEY WERE SUPPOSED TO. OUR ARTIFICIAL FOG WORKED PERFECTLY...

SO THAT WAS IT... I THOUGHT THERE WAS SOMETHING ODD ABOUT IT...

BUT YOU'LL NEVER GET ME THAT EASILY, JUNKOVITCH !

WHAT THE --!?

FLIP

WHADDAYOU THINK YOU'RE DOING !? AIEEE !

HA HA HA ! THIS'LL TEACH YOU TO LET YOUR GUARD DOWN !

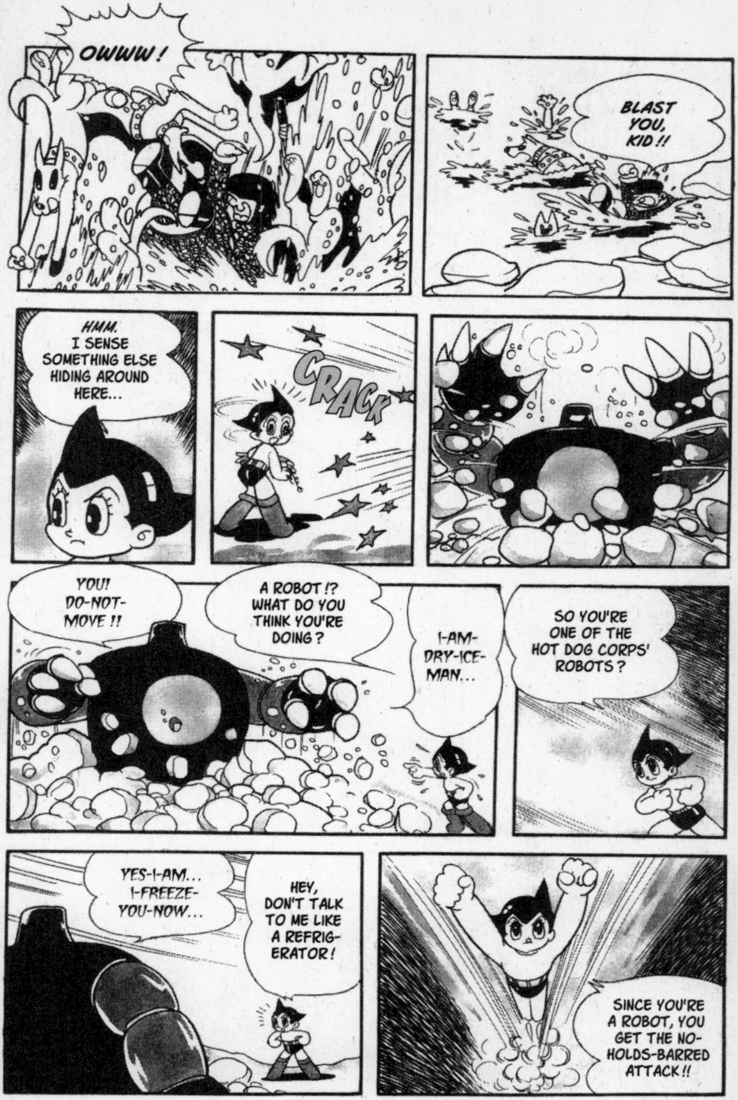
OWWW!
BLAST YOU, KID!!
HMM. I SENSE SOMETHING ELSE HIDING AROUND HERE...
CRACK
YOU! DO-NOT-MOVE!!
A ROBOT!? WHAT DO YOU THINK YOU'RE DOING?
I-AM-DRY-ICE-MAN...
SO YOU'RE ONE OF THE HOT DOG CORPS' ROBOTS?
YES-I-AM... I-FREEZE-YOU-NOW...
HEY, DON'T TALK TO ME LIKE A REFRIG-ERATOR!
SINCE YOU'RE A ROBOT, YOU GET THE NO-HOLDS-BARRED ATTACK!!

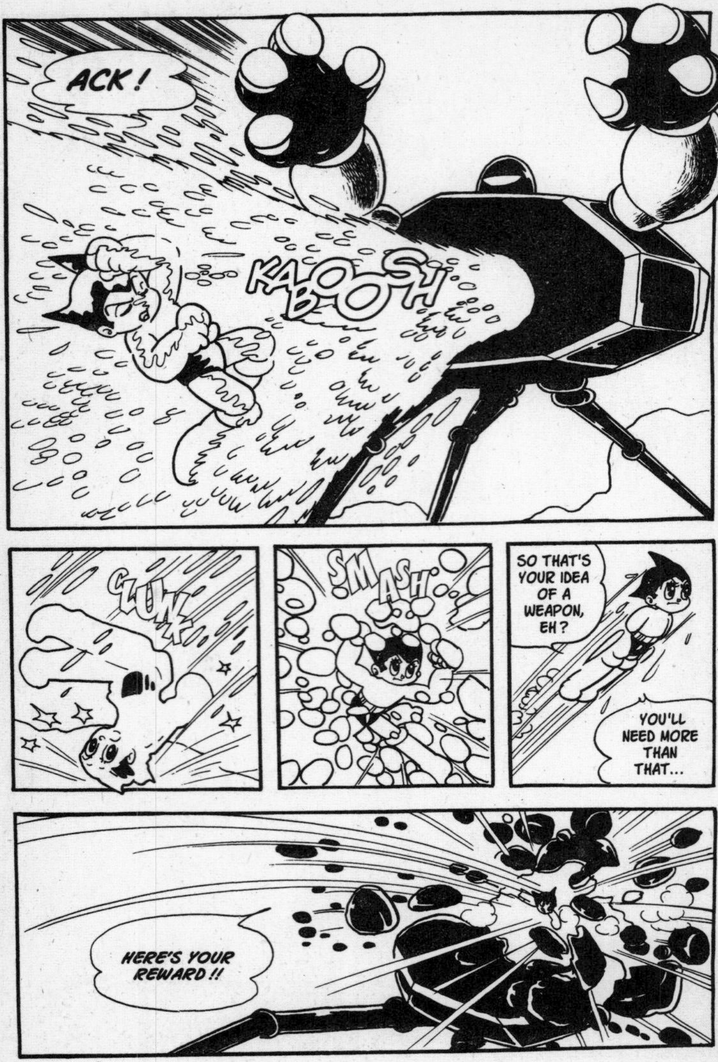
ACK!
KABOOSH
CLUNK
SMASH
SO THAT'S YOUR IDEA OF A WEAPON, EH?
YOU'LL NEED MORE THAN THAT...
HERE'S YOUR REWARD!!

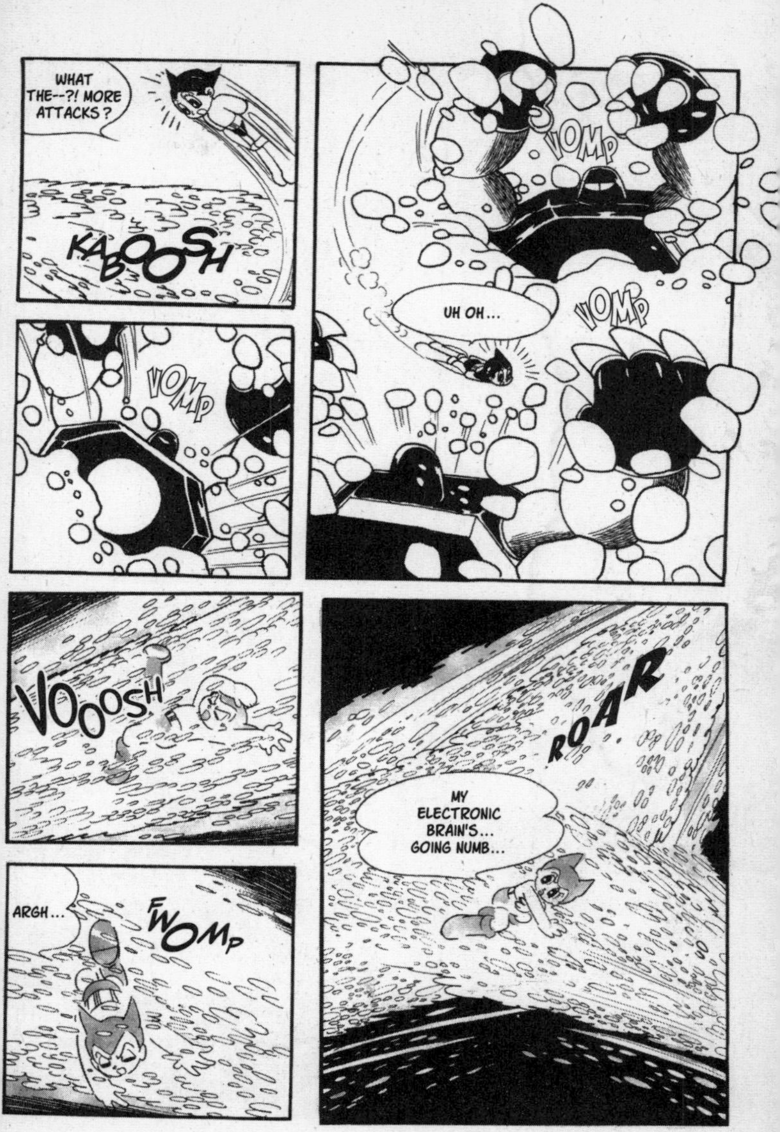
WHAT THE--?! MORE ATTACKS?
KABOOSH
VOMP
UH OH...
VOMP
VOMP
VOOOSH
ROAR
MY ELECTRONIC BRAIN'S... GOING NUMB...
ARGH...
FWOMP

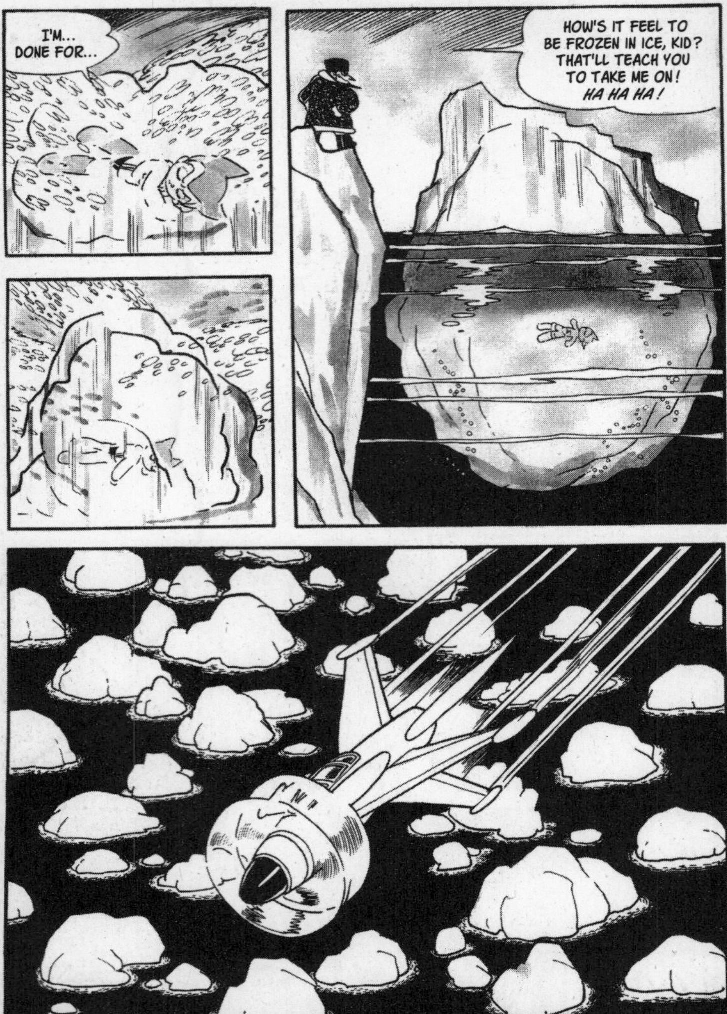
I'M... DONE FOR...
HOW'S IT FEEL TO BE FROZEN IN ICE, KID? THAT'LL TEACH YOU TO TAKE ME ON! HA HA HA!

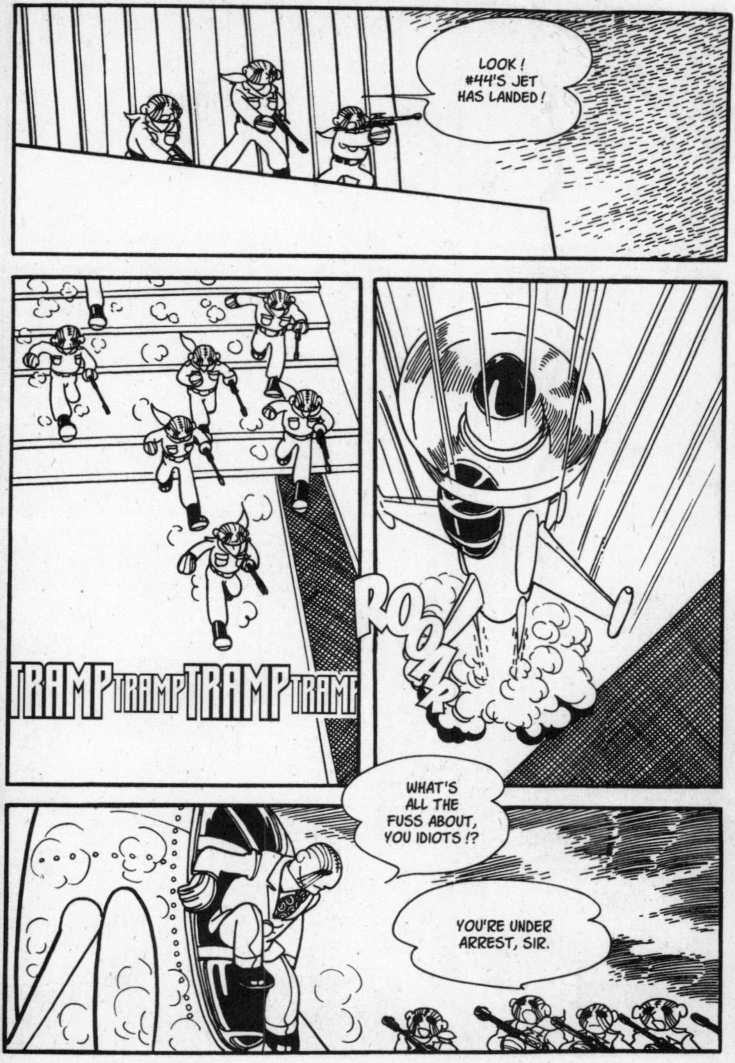
LOOK! #44'S JET HAS LANDED!
TRAMP TRAMP TRAMP TRAMP
ROOAR
WHAT'S ALL THE FUSS ABOUT, YOU IDIOTS!?
YOU'RE UNDER ARREST, SIR.

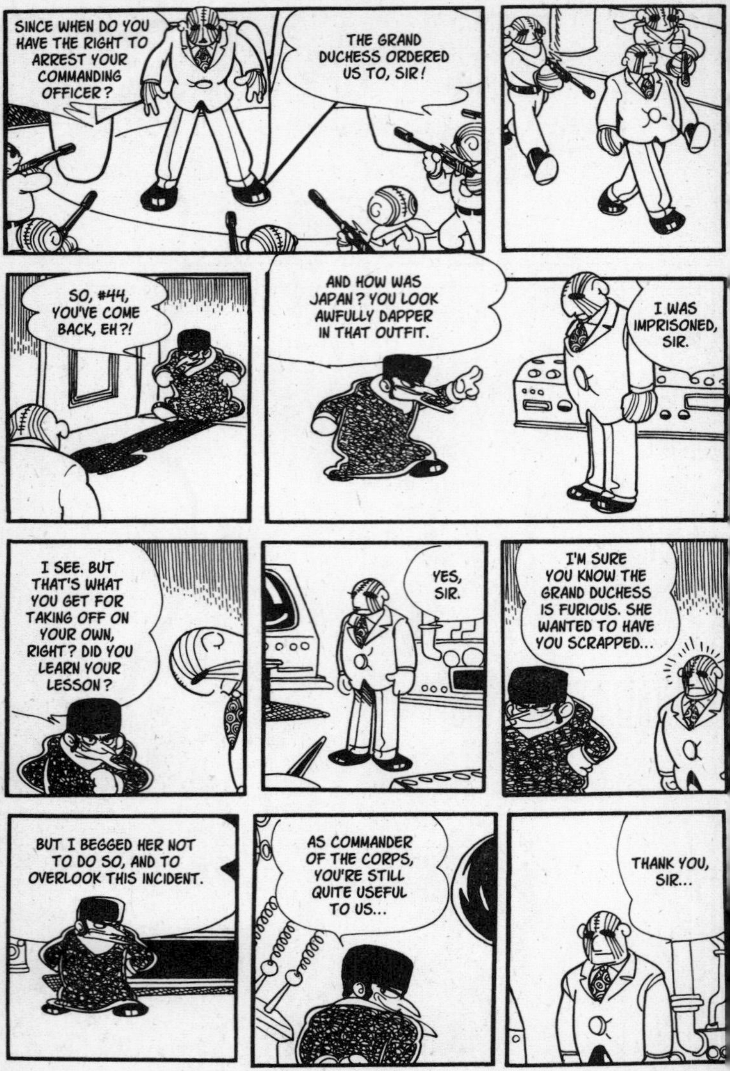
SINCE WHEN DO YOU HAVE THE RIGHT TO ARREST YOUR COMMANDING OFFICER?
THE GRAND DUCHESS ORDERED US TO, SIR!
SO, #44, YOU'VE COME BACK, EH?!
AND HOW WAS JAPAN? YOU LOOK AWFULLY DAPPER IN THAT OUTFIT.
I WAS IMPRISONED, SIR.
I SEE. BUT THAT'S WHAT YOU GET FOR TAKING OFF ON YOUR OWN, RIGHT? DID YOU LEARN YOUR LESSON?
YES, SIR.
I'M SURE YOU KNOW THE GRAND DUCHESS IS FURIOUS. SHE WANTED TO HAVE YOU SCRAPPED...
BUT I BEGGED HER NOT TO DO SO, AND TO OVERLOOK THIS INCIDENT.
AS COMMANDER OF THE CORPS, YOU'RE STILL QUITE USEFUL TO US...
THANK YOU, SIR...

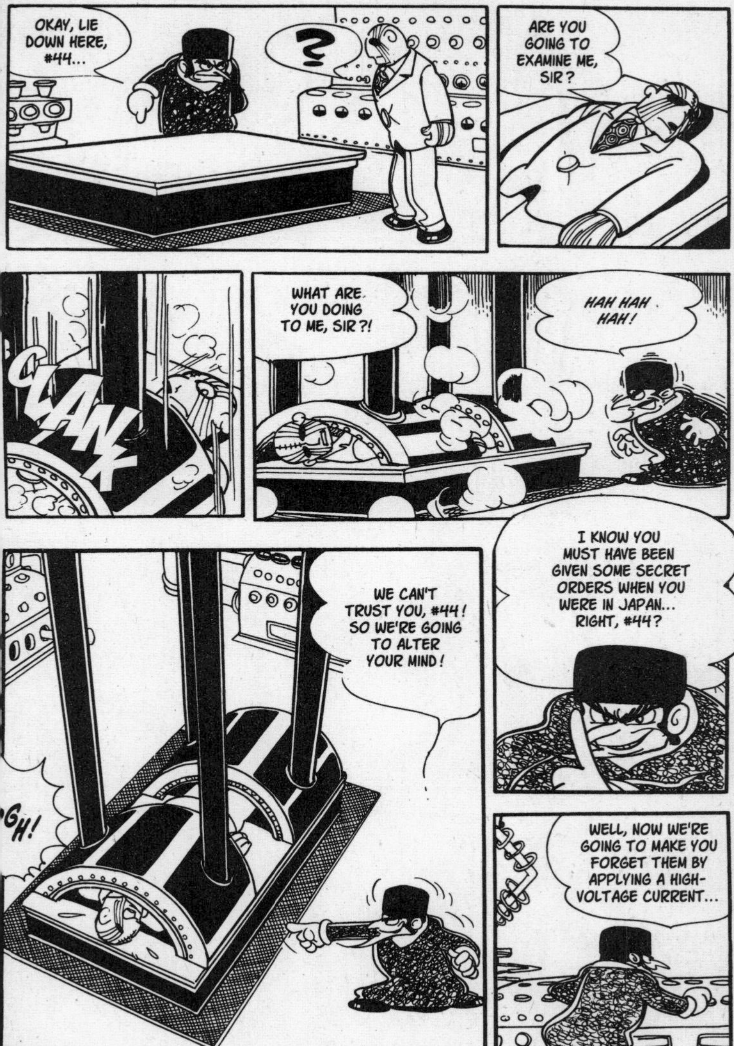
OKAY, LIE DOWN HERE, #44...
?
ARE YOU GOING TO EXAMINE ME, SIR?
CLANK
WHAT ARE YOU DOING TO ME, SIR?!
HAH HAH HAH!
WE CAN'T TRUST YOU, #44! SO WE'RE GOING TO ALTER YOUR MIND!
I KNOW YOU MUST HAVE BEEN GIVEN SOME SECRET ORDERS WHEN YOU WERE IN JAPAN... RIGHT, #44?
WELL, NOW WE'RE GOING TO MAKE YOU FORGET THEM BY APPLYING A HIGH-VOLTAGE CURRENT...

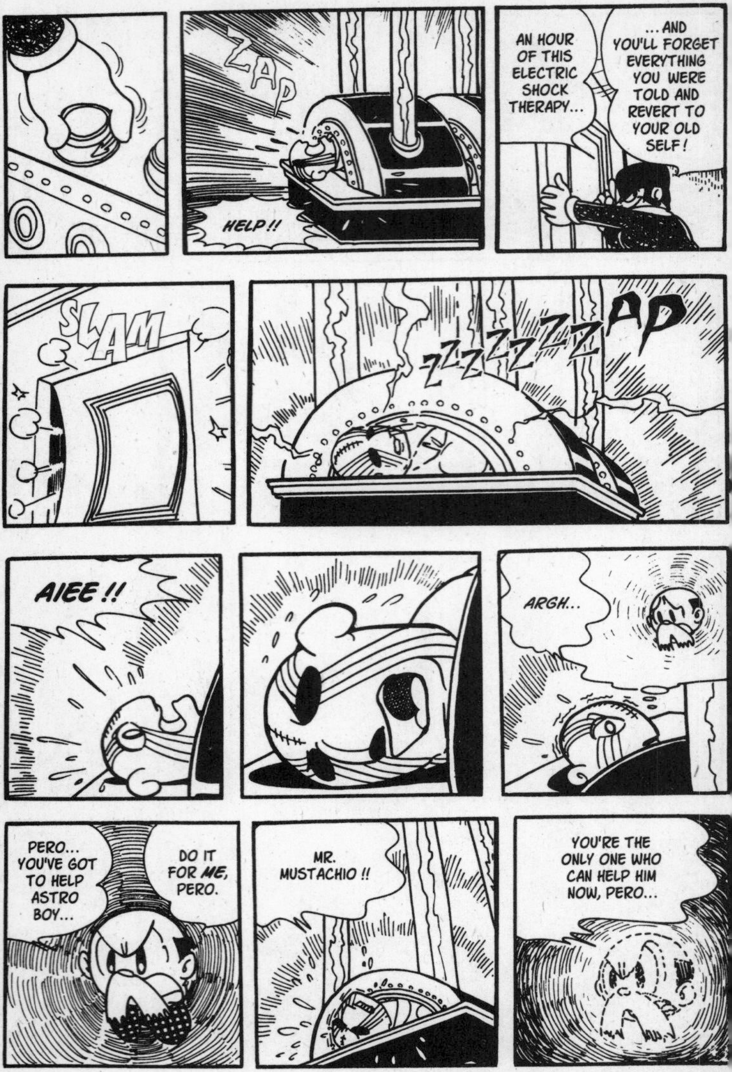

ZAP
HELP!!
AN HOUR OF THIS ELECTRIC SHOCK THERAPY...
...AND YOU'LL FORGET EVERYTHING YOU WERE TOLD AND REVERT TO YOUR OLD SELF!
SLAM
ZZZZZZZZAP
AIEE!!
ARGH...
PERO... YOU'VE GOT TO HELP ASTRO BOY...
DO IT FOR ME, PERO.
MR. MUSTACHIO!!
YOU'RE THE ONLY ONE WHO CAN HELP HIM NOW, PERO...

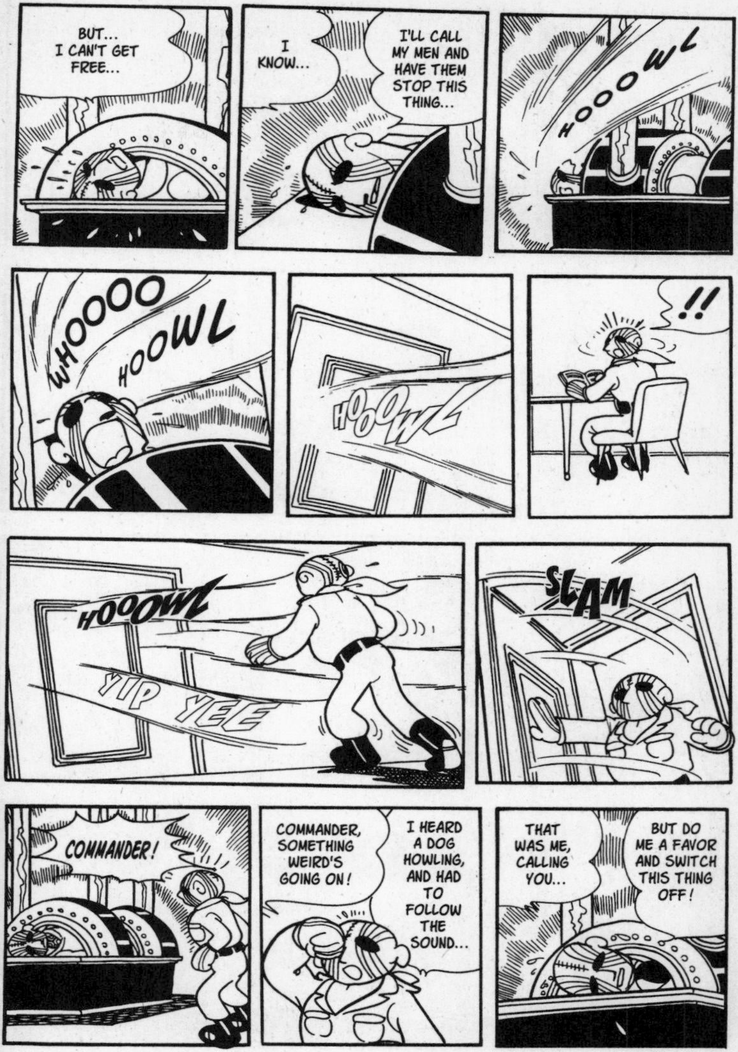

BUT... I CAN'T GET FREE...
I KNOW...
I'LL CALL MY MEN AND HAVE THEM STOP THIS THING...
HOOOOWL
WHOOOO
HOOWL
HOOOWL
!!
HOOOWL
YIP
YEE
SLAM
COMMANDER!
COMMANDER, SOMETHING WEIRD'S GOING ON!
I HEARD A DOG HOWLING, AND HAD TO FOLLOW THE SOUND...
THAT WAS ME, CALLING YOU...
BUT DO ME A FAVOR AND SWITCH THIS THING OFF!

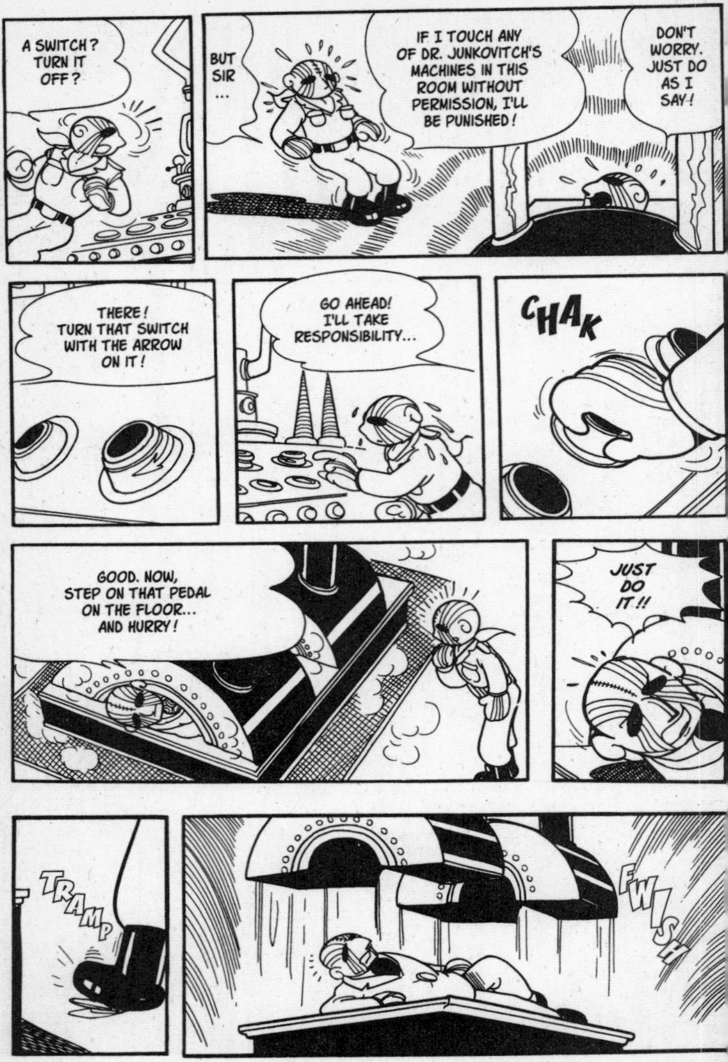
A SWITCH? TURN IT OFF?
BUT SIR ...
IF I TOUCH ANY OF DR. JUNKOVITCH'S MACHINES IN THIS ROOM WITHOUT PERMISSION, I'LL BE PUNISHED!
DON'T WORRY. JUST DO AS I SAY!
THERE! TURN THAT SWITCH WITH THE ARROW ON IT!
GO AHEAD! I'LL TAKE RESPONSIBILITY...
CHAK
GOOD. NOW, STEP ON THAT PEDAL ON THE FLOOR... AND HURRY!
JUST DO IT!!
TRAMP
FWISH

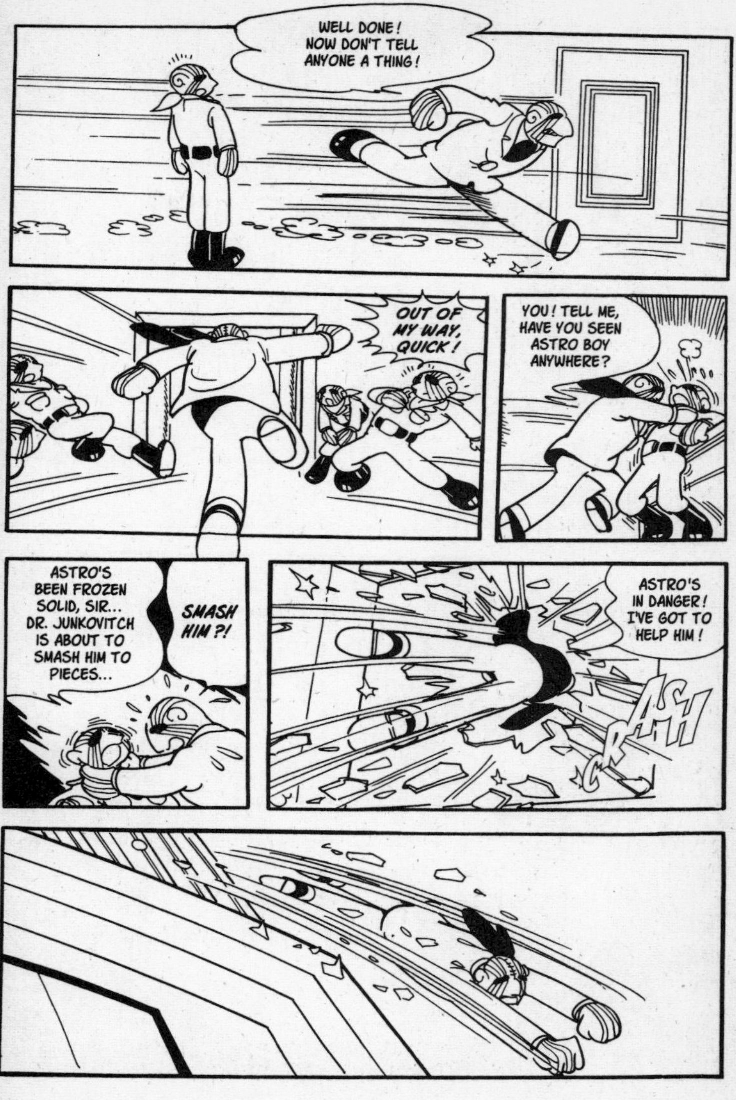
WELL DONE! NOW DON'T TELL ANYONE A THING!
OUT OF MY WAY, QUICK!
YOU! TELL ME, HAVE YOU SEEN ASTRO BOY ANYWHERE?
ASTRO'S BEEN FROZEN SOLID, SIR... DR. JUNKOVITCH IS ABOUT TO SMASH HIM TO PIECES...
SMASH HIM?!
ASTRO'S IN DANGER! I'VE GOT TO HELP HIM!
CRASH

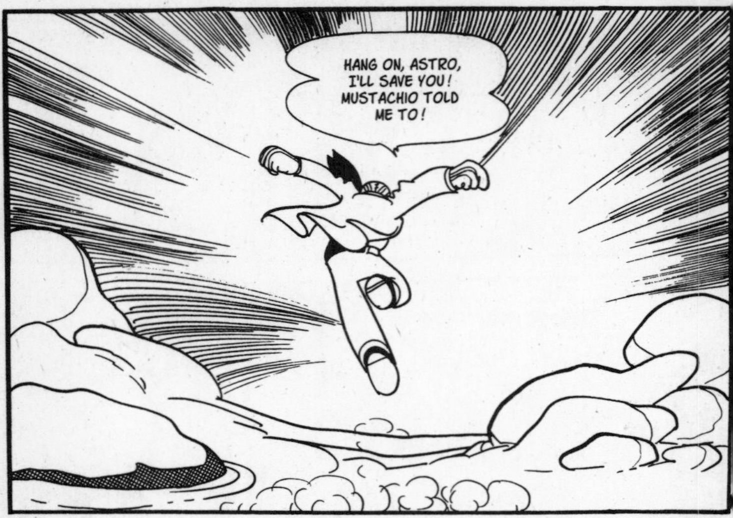
HANG ON, ASTRO, I'LL SAVE YOU! MUSTACHIO TOLD ME TO!
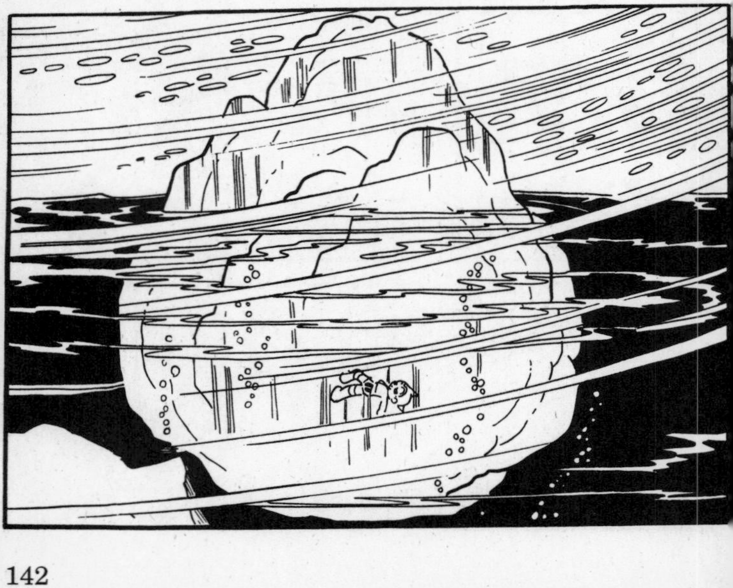

A FRIEND IN #44

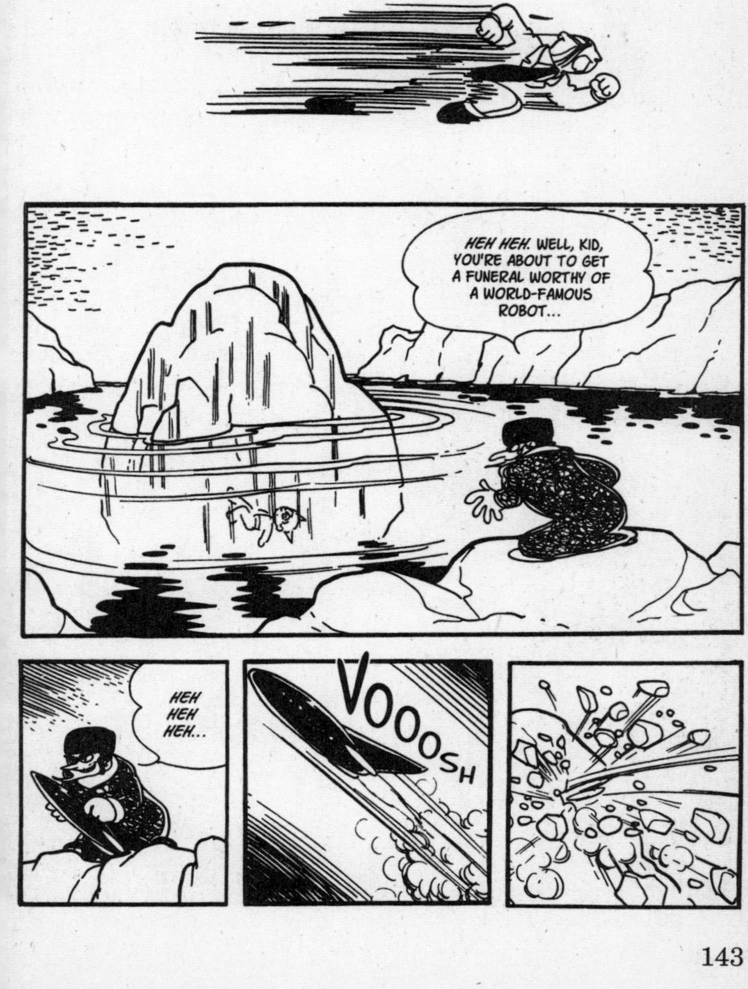

HEH HEH. WELL, KID, YOU'RE ABOUT TO GET A FUNERAL WORTHY OF A WORLD-FAMOUS ROBOT...
HEH HEH HEH...
VOOOOSH

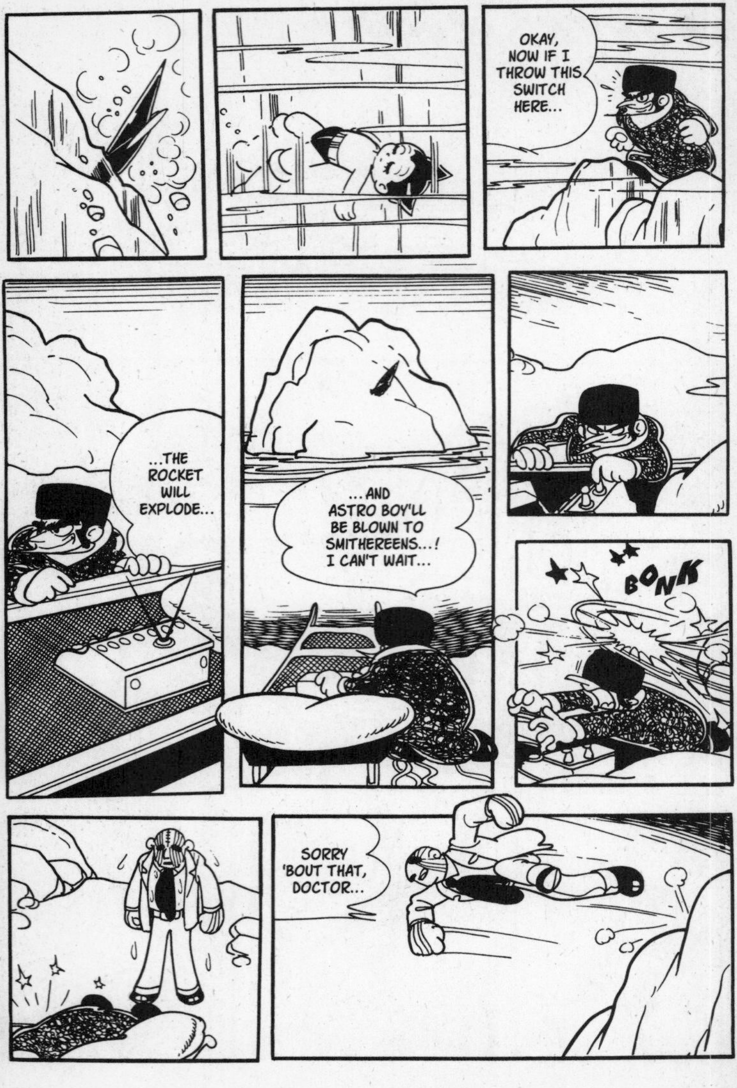
OKAY, NOW IF I THROW THIS SWITCH HERE...
...THE ROCKET WILL EXPLODE...
...AND ASTRO BOY'LL BE BLOWN TO SMITHEREENS...! I CAN'T WAIT...
BONK
SORRY 'BOUT THAT, DOCTOR...

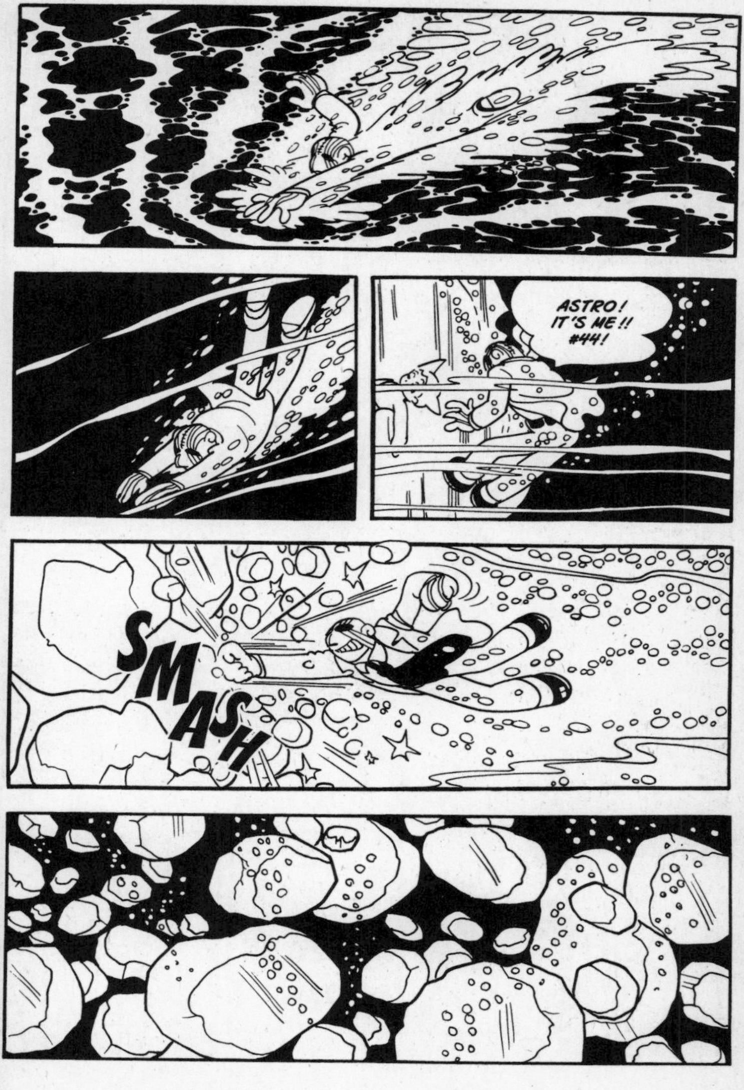
ASTRO! IT'S ME!! #44!
SMASH

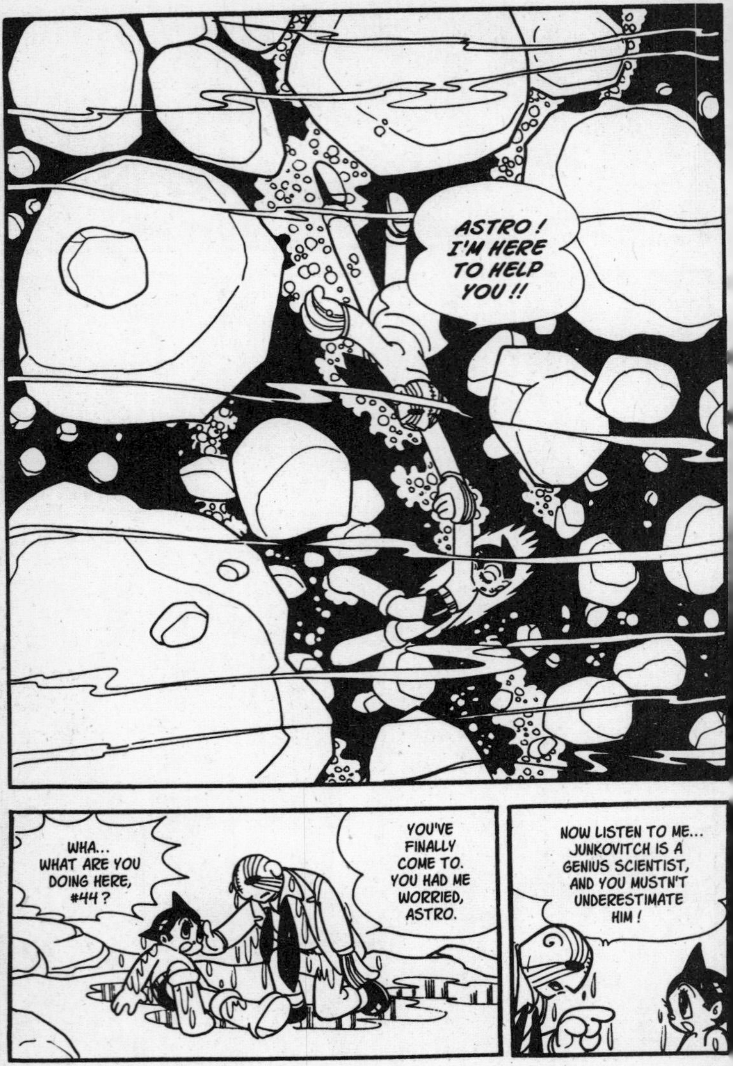
ASTRO! I'M HERE TO HELP YOU!!
WHA... WHAT ARE YOU DOING HERE, #44?
YOU'VE FINALLY COME TO. YOU HAD ME WORRIED, ASTRO.
NOW LISTEN TO ME... JUNKOVITCH IS A GENIUS SCIENTIST, AND YOU MUSTN'T UNDERESTIMATE HIM!

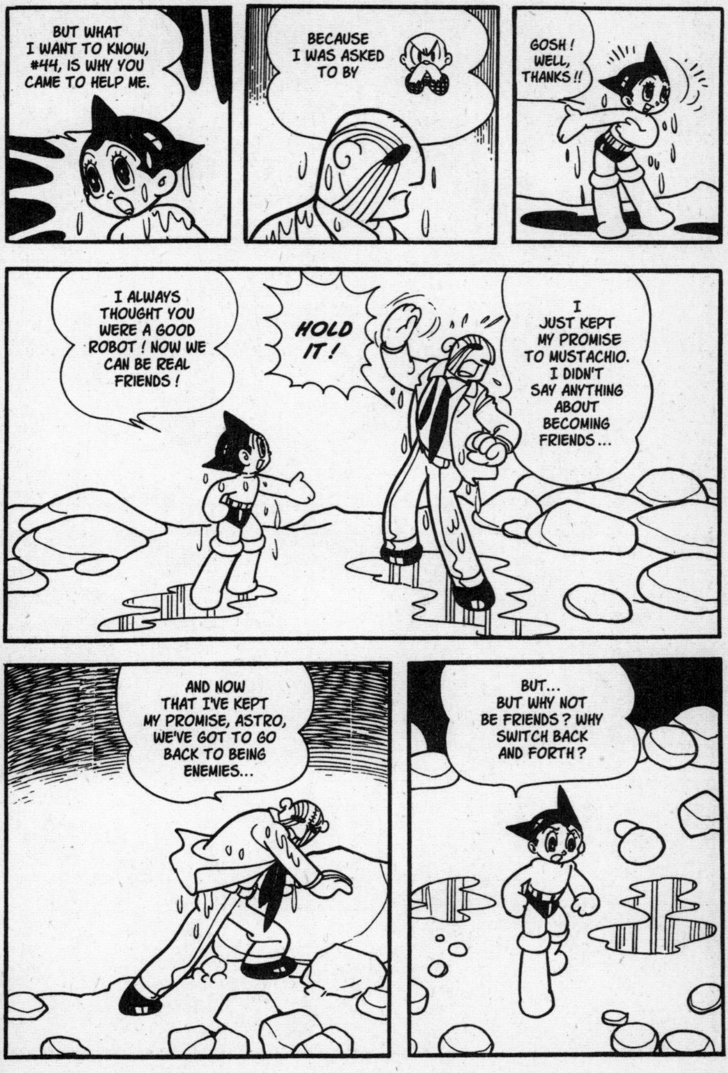
BUT WHAT I WANT TO KNOW, #44, IS WHY YOU CAME TO HELP ME.
BECAUSE I WAS ASKED TO BY
GOSH! WELL, THANKS!!
I ALWAYS THOUGHT YOU WERE A GOOD ROBOT! NOW WE CAN BE REAL FRIENDS!
HOLD IT!
I JUST KEPT MY PROMISE TO MUSTACHIO. I DIDN'T SAY ANYTHING ABOUT BECOMING FRIENDS...
AND NOW THAT I'VE KEPT MY PROMISE, ASTRO, WE'VE GOT TO GO BACK TO BEING ENEMIES...
BUT... BUT WHY NOT BE FRIENDS? WHY SWITCH BACK AND FORTH?

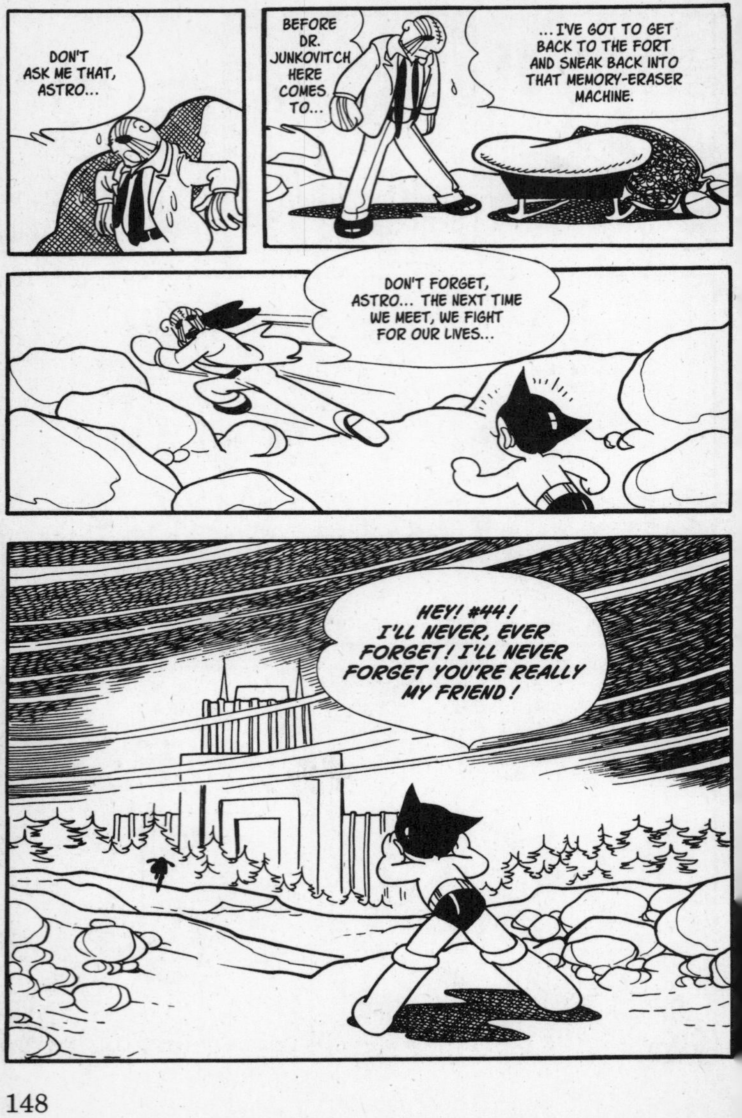
DON'T ASK ME THAT, ASTRO...
BEFORE DR. JUNKOVITCH HERE COMES TO...
...I'VE GOT TO GET BACK TO THE FORT AND SNEAK BACK INTO THAT MEMORY-ERASER MACHINE.
DON'T FORGET, ASTRO... THE NEXT TIME WE MEET, WE FIGHT FOR OUR LIVES...
HEY! #44! I'LL NEVER, EVER FORGET! I'LL NEVER FORGET YOU'RE REALLY MY FRIEND!

A SHOWDOWN IN SPACE

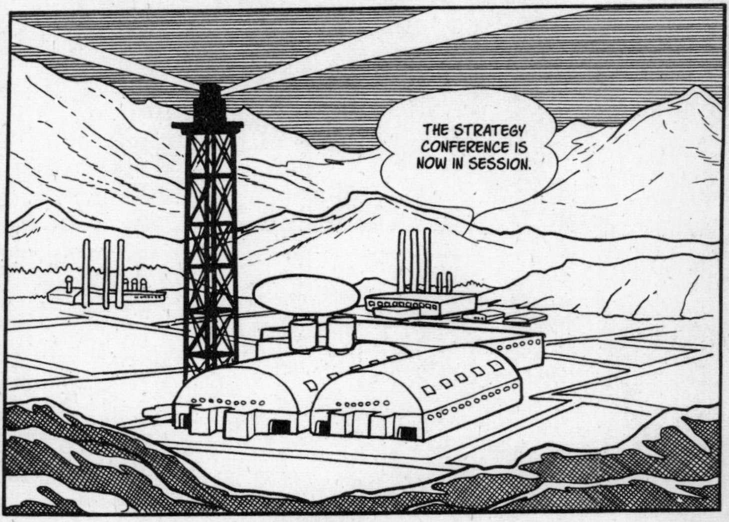
THE STRATEGY CONFERENCE IS NOW IN SESSION.

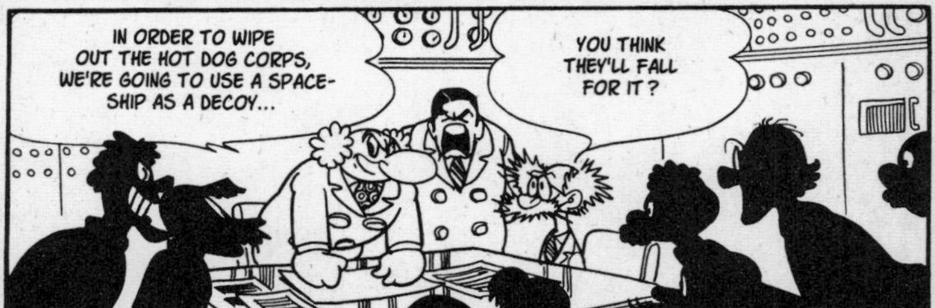
IN ORDER TO WIPE OUT THE HOT DOG CORPS, WE'RE GOING TO USE A SPACE-SHIP AS A DECOY...
YOU THINK THEY'LL FALL FOR IT?

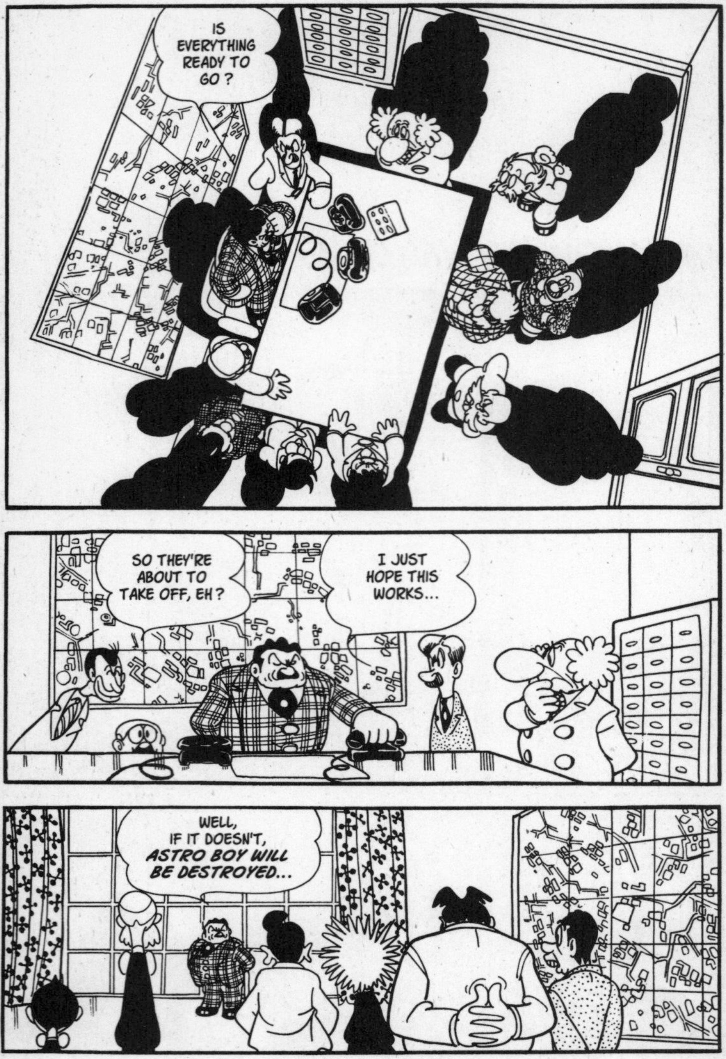
IS EVERYTHING READY TO GO ?
SO THEY'RE ABOUT TO TAKE OFF, EH ?
I JUST HOPE THIS WORKS...
WELL, IF IT DOESN'T, *ASTRO BOY WILL BE DESTROYED...*

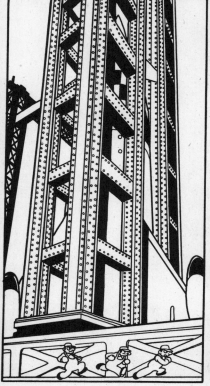

LOOK, ASTRO'S HERE!

YOU ALL READY TO GO, ASTRO?

YES, PROFESSOR.

SORRY TO ASK YOU TO DO THIS RIGHT AFTER COMING BACK FROM THE ARCTIC, BUT WE NEED YOU...

YOU'RE THE ONLY ONE WHO CAN MAKE THIS PLAN WORK.

151

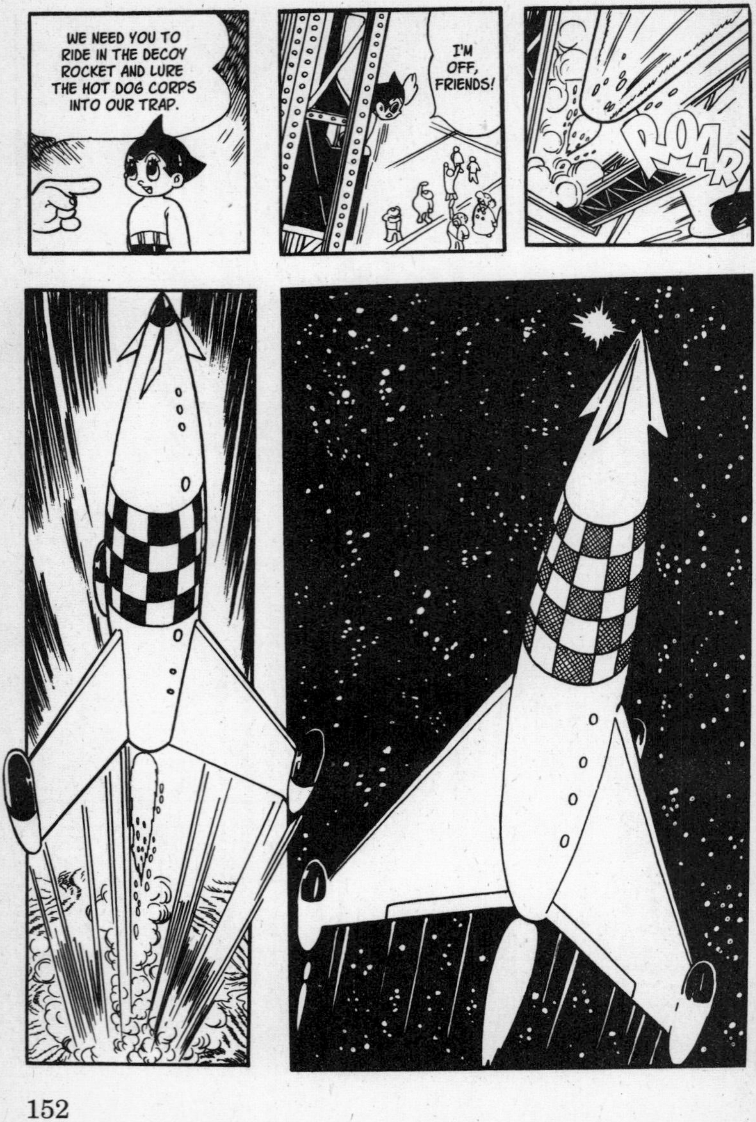
WE NEED YOU TO RIDE IN THE DECOY ROCKET AND LURE THE HOT DOG CORPS INTO OUR TRAP.
I'M OFF, FRIENDS!
ROAR

EVERYTHING OKAY, ASTRO?

BUZZ BUZZ

NO PROBLEMS YET, PROFESSOR.

...EXCEPT ONE FLY WAS FLATTENED BY THE ACCELERATION...

WATCH THE WARNING LAMPS CAREFULLY. THEY'LL LIGHT UP WHEN THE ENEMY'S NEARING...

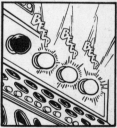

BEEP BEEP BEEP

PROFESSOR! LOOKS LIKE THE ENEMY'S DETECTED THE SHIP!

THEY'RE REALLY COMING, EH? WE'RE DEPENDING ON YOU ASTRO!

153

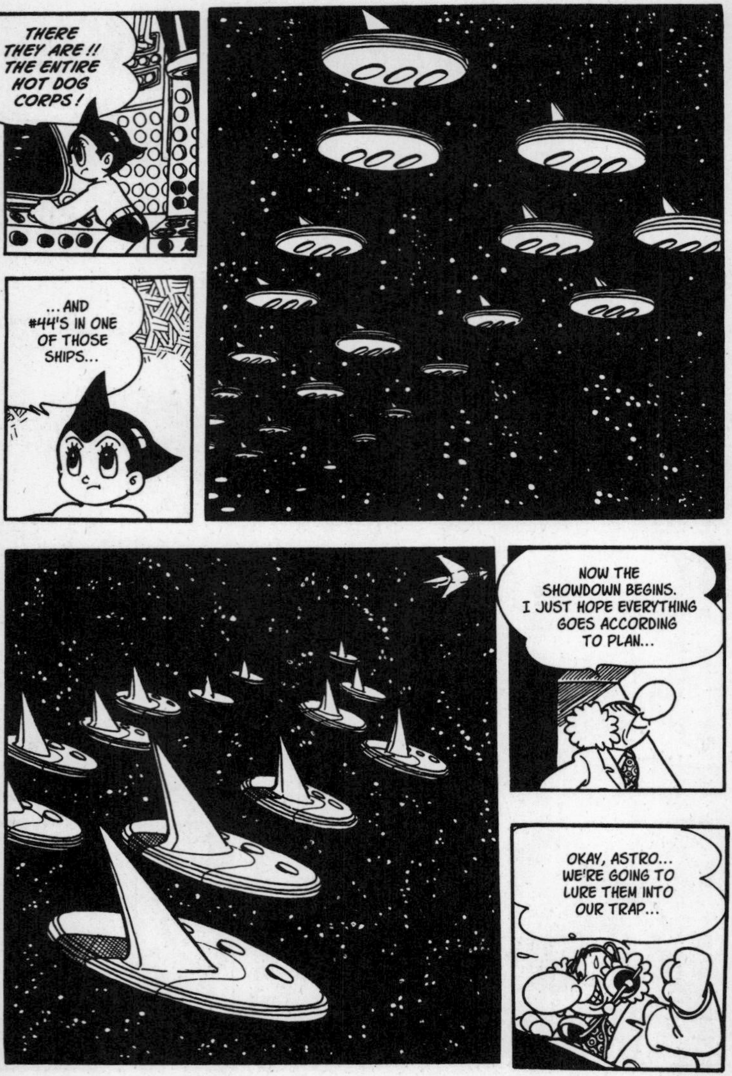
THERE THEY ARE !! THE ENTIRE HOT DOG CORPS !
... AND #44'S IN ONE OF THOSE SHIPS...
NOW THE SHOWDOWN BEGINS. I JUST HOPE EVERYTHING GOES ACCORDING TO PLAN...
OKAY, ASTRO... WE'RE GOING TO LURE THEM INTO OUR TRAP...

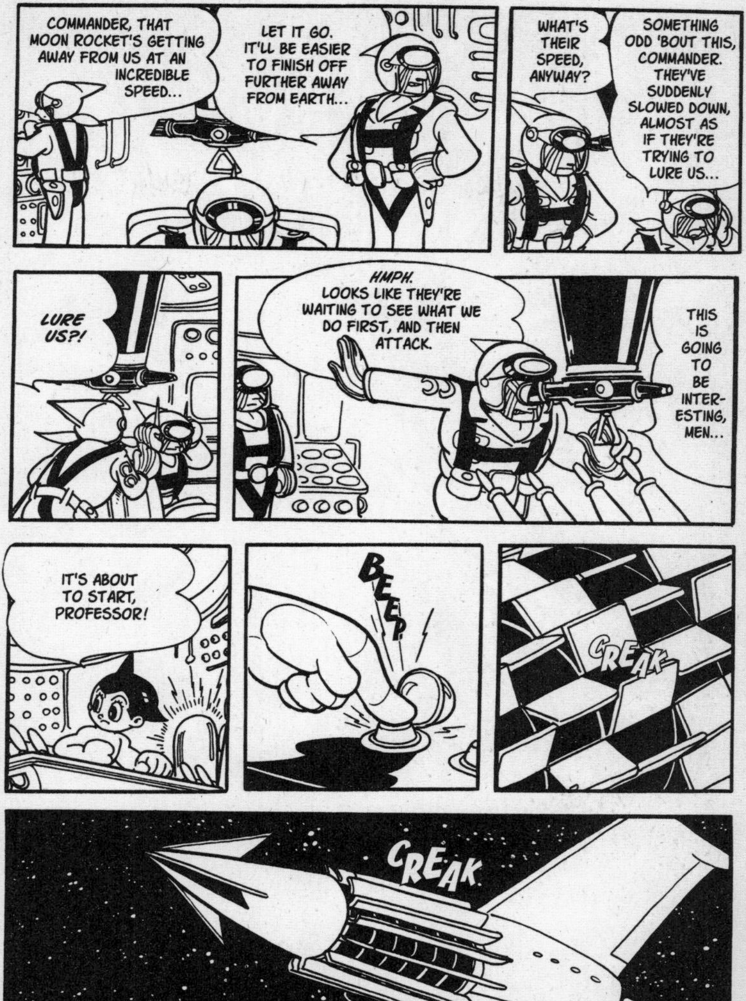
COMMANDER, THAT MOON ROCKET'S GETTING AWAY FROM US AT AN INCREDIBLE SPEED...
LET IT GO. IT'LL BE EASIER TO FINISH OFF FURTHER AWAY FROM EARTH...
WHAT'S THEIR SPEED, ANYWAY?
SOMETHING ODD 'BOUT THIS, COMMANDER. THEY'VE SUDDENLY SLOWED DOWN, ALMOST AS IF THEY'RE TRYING TO LURE US...
LURE US?!
HMPH. LOOKS LIKE THEY'RE WAITING TO SEE WHAT WE DO FIRST, AND THEN ATTACK.
THIS IS GOING TO BE INTER-ESTING, MEN...
IT'S ABOUT TO START, PROFESSOR!
BEEP
CREAK
CREAK

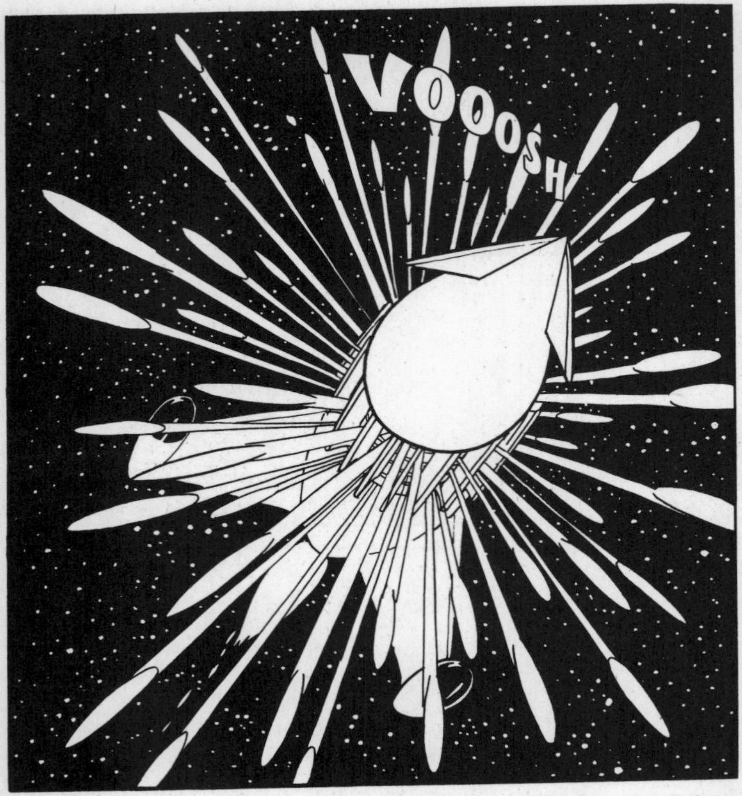
VOOOSH

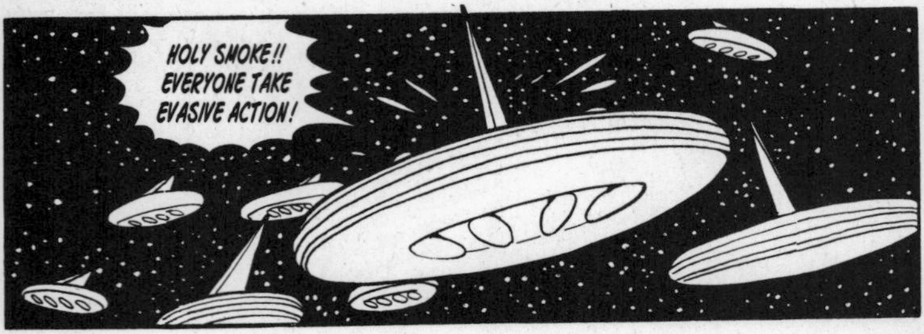
HOLY SMOKE!! EVERYONE TAKE EVASIVE ACTION!

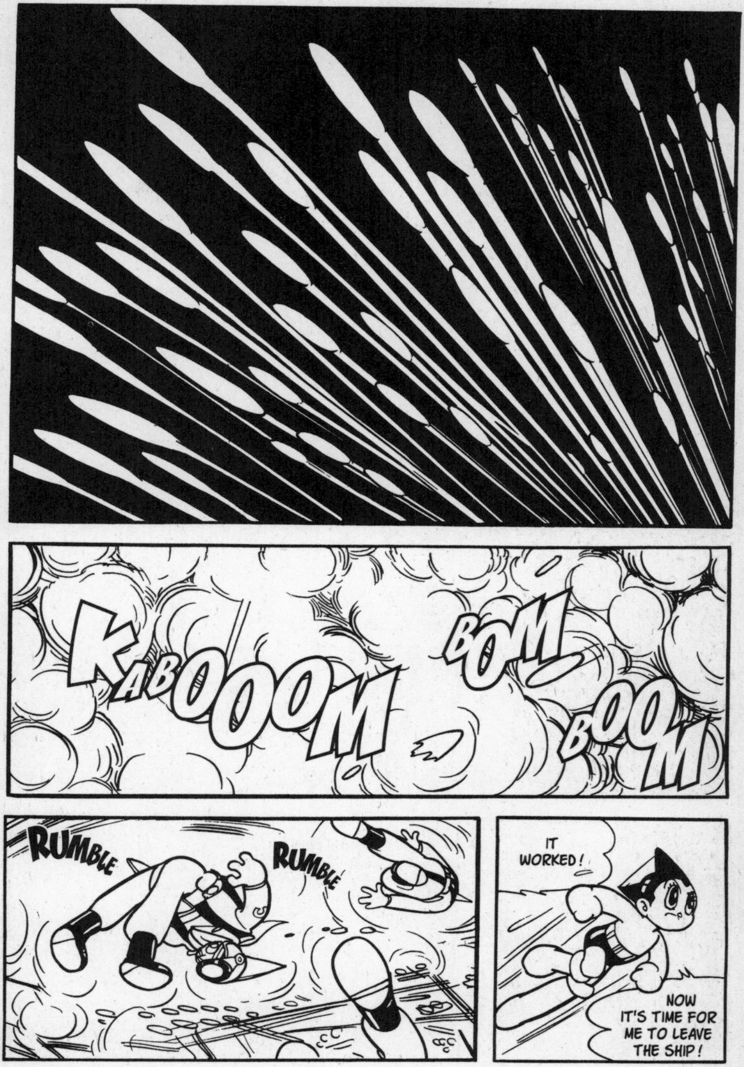
KABOOOOM
BOM
BOOM
RUMBLE
RUMBLE
IT WORKED!
NOW IT'S TIME FOR ME TO LEAVE THE SHIP!

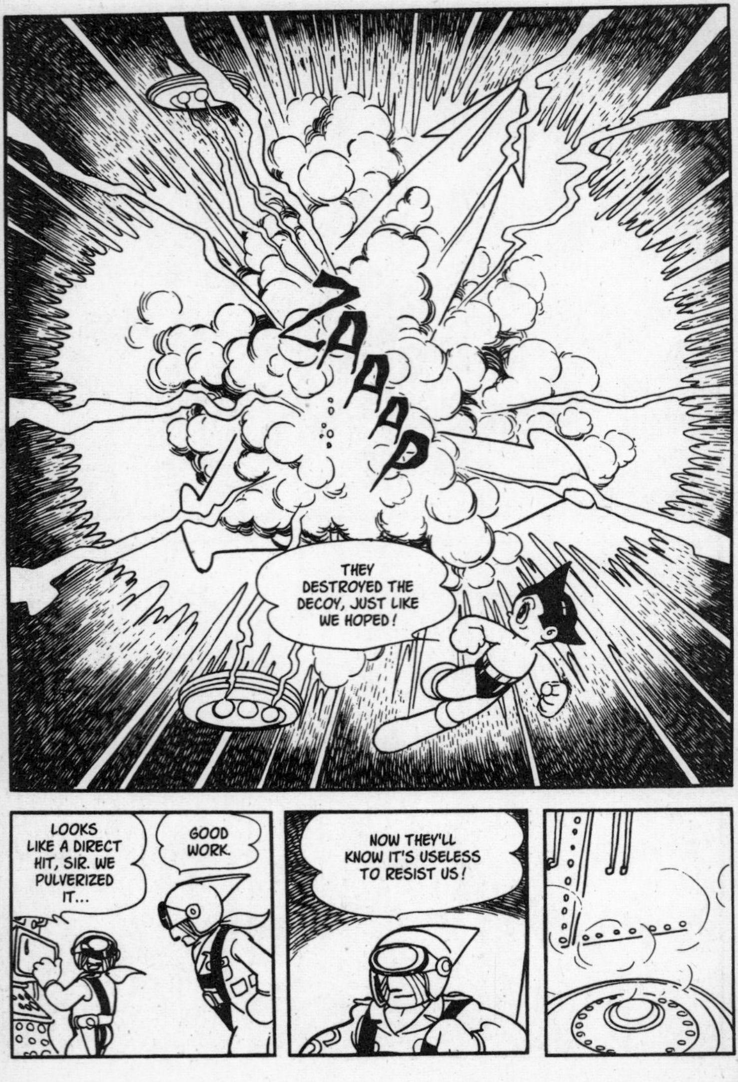
ZAAAP
THEY DESTROYED THE DECOY, JUST LIKE WE HOPED!
LOOKS LIKE A DIRECT HIT, SIR. WE PULVERIZED IT...
GOOD WORK.
NOW THEY'LL KNOW IT'S USELESS TO RESIST US!

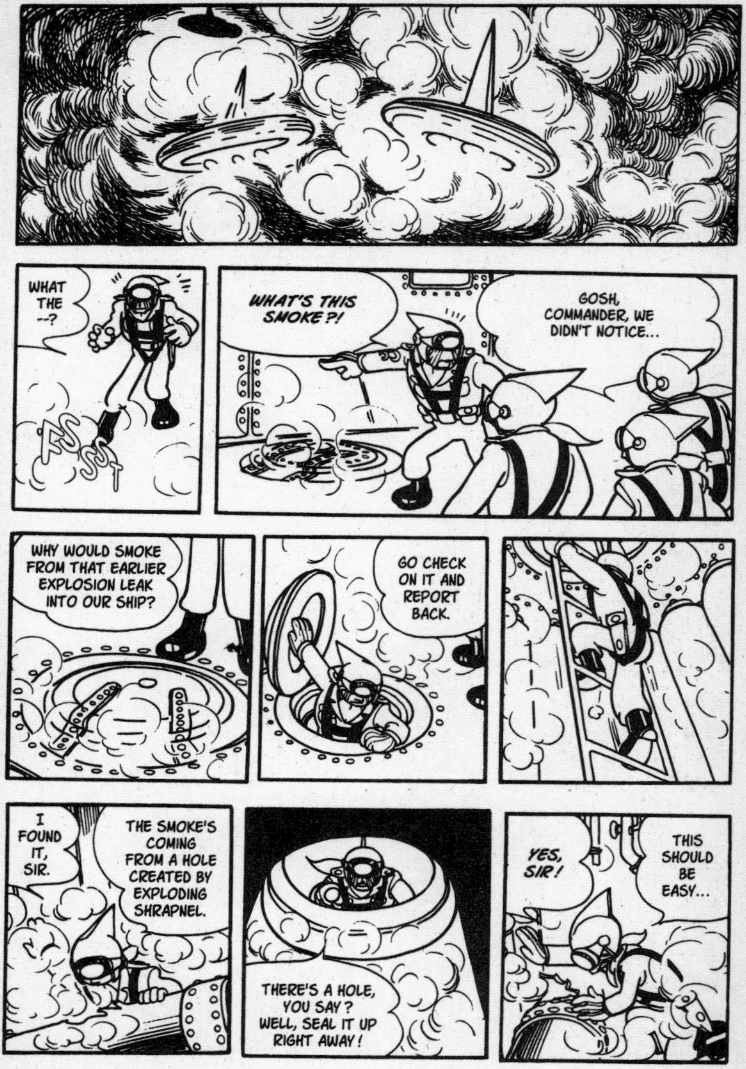
WHAT THE --?
FSSST
WHAT'S THIS SMOKE?!
GOSH, COMMANDER, WE DIDN'T NOTICE...
WHY WOULD SMOKE FROM THAT EARLIER EXPLOSION LEAK INTO OUR SHIP?
GO CHECK ON IT AND REPORT BACK.
I FOUND IT, SIR.
THE SMOKE'S COMING FROM A HOLE CREATED BY EXPLODING SHRAPNEL.
THERE'S A HOLE, YOU SAY? WELL, SEAL IT UP RIGHT AWAY!
YES, SIR!
THIS SHOULD BE EASY...

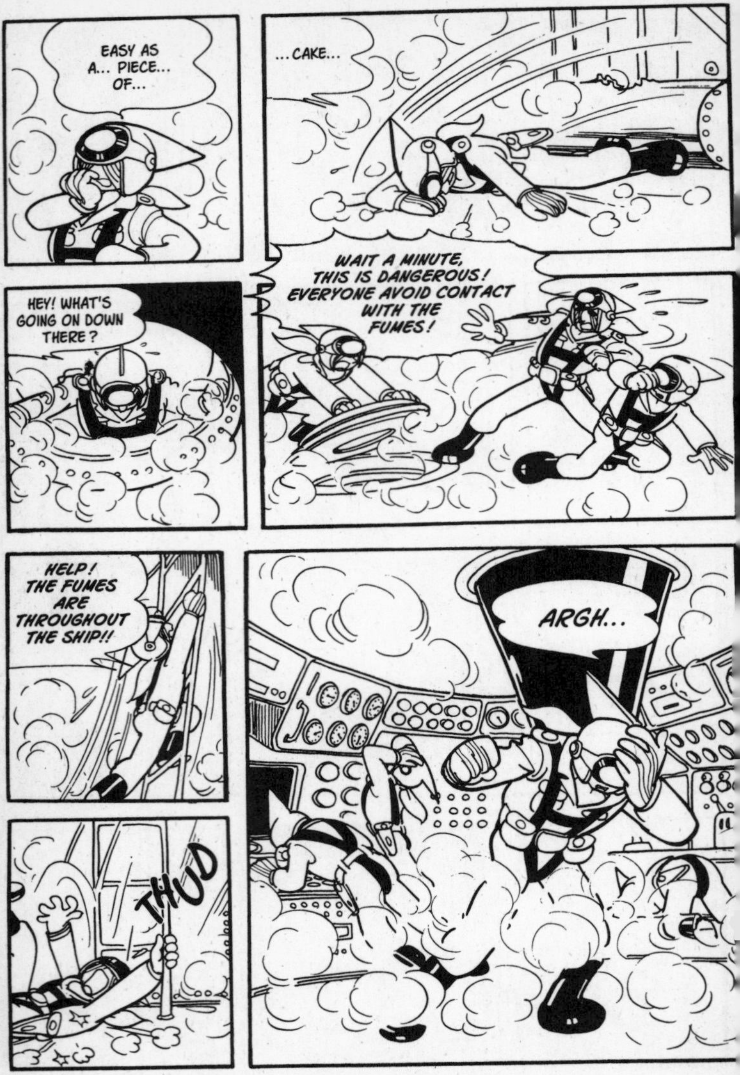
EASY AS A... PIECE... OF...
...CAKE...
HEY! WHAT'S GOING ON DOWN THERE?
WAIT A MINUTE, THIS IS DANGEROUS! EVERYONE AVOID CONTACT WITH THE FUMES!
HELP! THE FUMES ARE THROUGHOUT THE SHIP!!
THUD
ARGH...

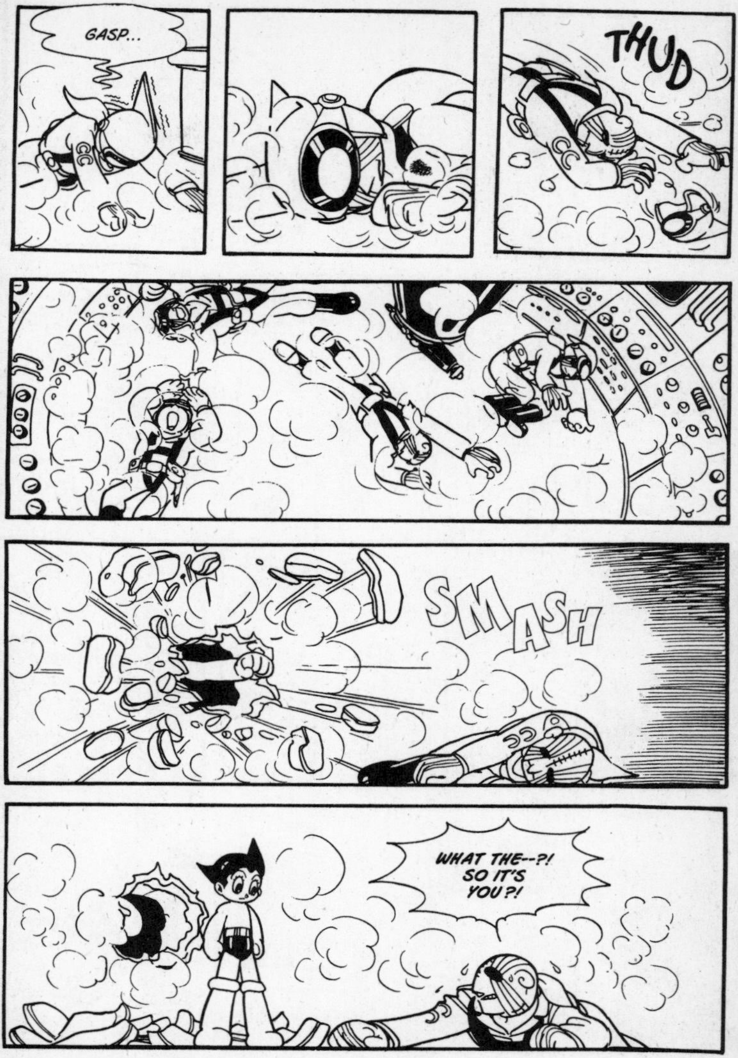
GASP...
THUD
SMASH
WHAT THE--?! SO IT'S YOU?!

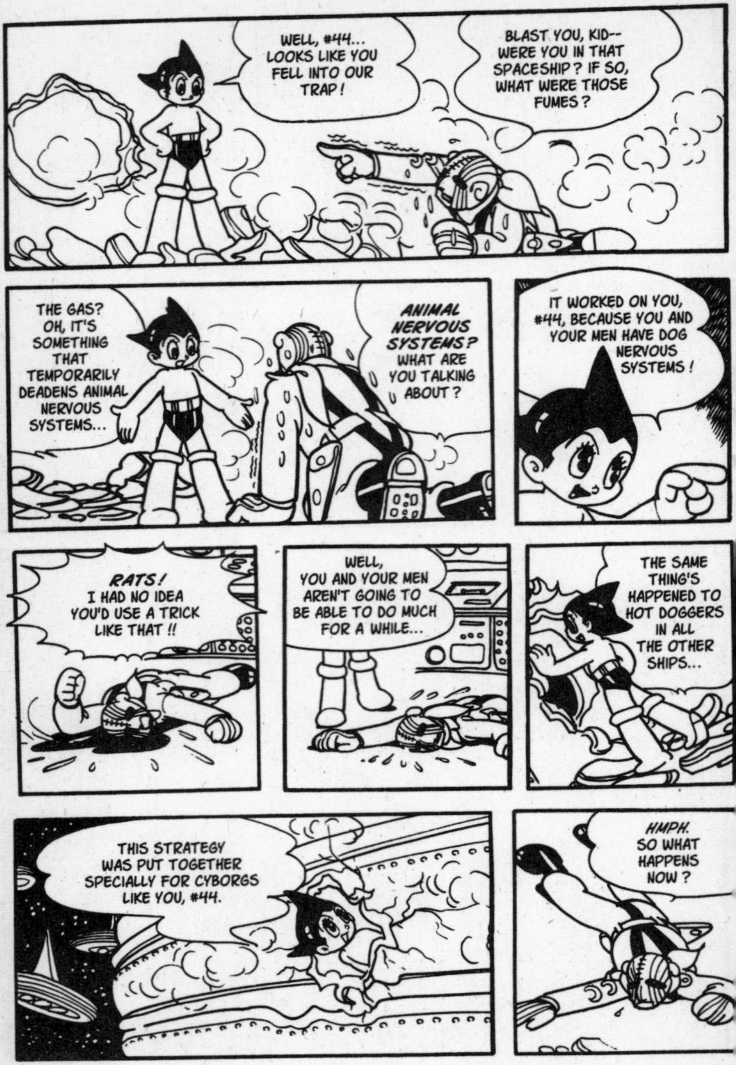
WELL, #44... LOOKS LIKE YOU FELL INTO OUR TRAP!
BLAST YOU, KID-- WERE YOU IN THAT SPACESHIP? IF SO, WHAT WERE THOSE FUMES?
THE GAS? OH, IT'S SOMETHING THAT TEMPORARILY DEADENS ANIMAL NERVOUS SYSTEMS...
ANIMAL NERVOUS SYSTEMS? WHAT ARE YOU TALKING ABOUT?
IT WORKED ON YOU, #44, BECAUSE YOU AND YOUR MEN HAVE DOG NERVOUS SYSTEMS!
RATS! I HAD NO IDEA YOU'D USE A TRICK LIKE THAT!!
WELL, YOU AND YOUR MEN AREN'T GOING TO BE ABLE TO DO MUCH FOR A WHILE...
THE SAME THING'S HAPPENED TO HOT DOGGERS IN ALL THE OTHER SHIPS...
THIS STRATEGY WAS PUT TOGETHER SPECIALLY FOR CYBORGS LIKE YOU, #44.
HMPH. SO WHAT HAPPENS NOW?

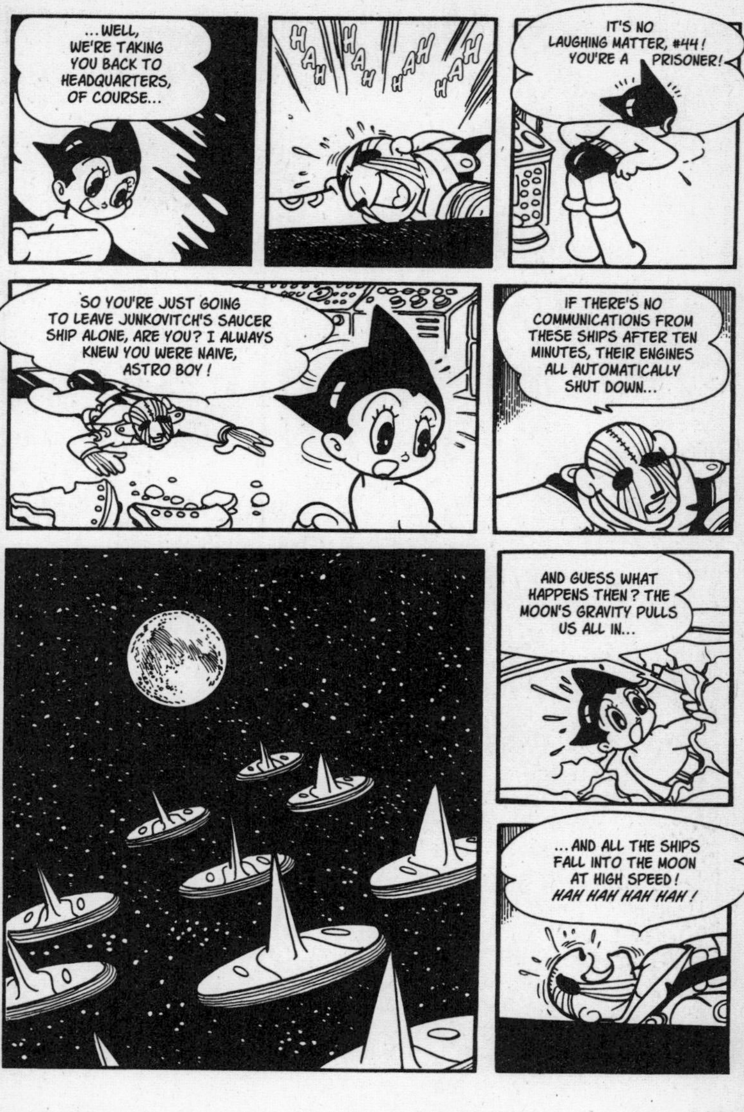
...WELL, WE'RE TAKING YOU BACK TO HEADQUARTERS, OF COURSE...
HAH HAH HAH HAH HAH
IT'S NO LAUGHING MATTER, #44! YOU'RE A PRISONER!
SO YOU'RE JUST GOING TO LEAVE JUNKOVITCH'S SAUCER SHIP ALONE, ARE YOU? I ALWAYS KNEW YOU WERE NAIVE, ASTRO BOY!
IF THERE'S NO COMMUNICATIONS FROM THESE SHIPS AFTER TEN MINUTES, THEIR ENGINES ALL AUTOMATICALLY SHUT DOWN...
AND GUESS WHAT HAPPENS THEN? THE MOON'S GRAVITY PULLS US ALL IN...
...AND ALL THE SHIPS FALL INTO THE MOON AT HIGH SPEED! *HAH HAH HAH HAH!*

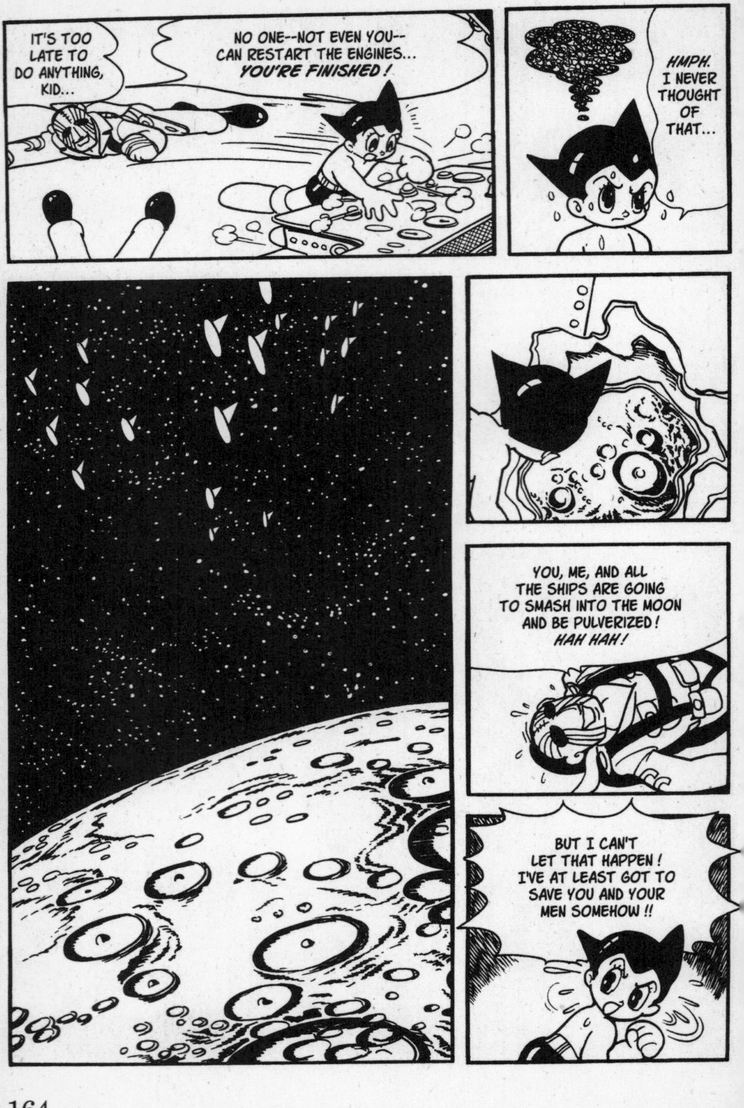
IT'S TOO LATE TO DO ANYTHING, KID...
NO ONE--NOT EVEN YOU--CAN RESTART THE ENGINES... YOU'RE FINISHED!
HMPH. I NEVER THOUGHT OF THAT...
YOU, ME, AND ALL THE SHIPS ARE GOING TO SMASH INTO THE MOON AND BE PULVERIZED! HAH HAH!
BUT I CAN'T LET THAT HAPPEN! I'VE AT LEAST GOT TO SAVE YOU AND YOUR MEN SOMEHOW!!

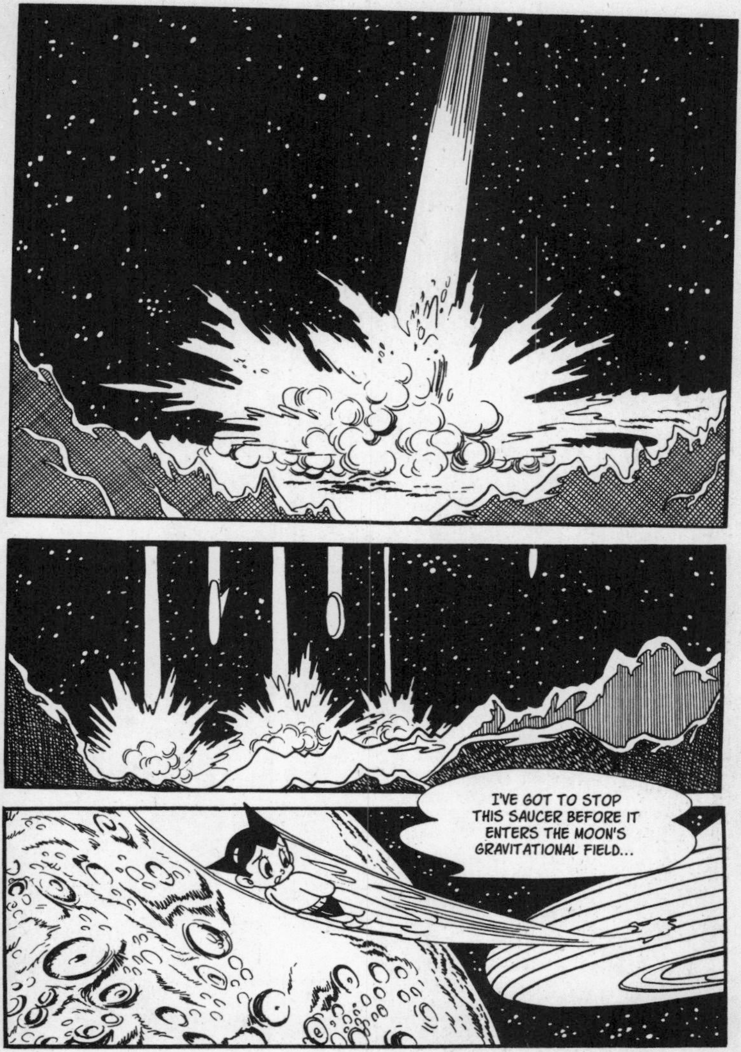
I'VE GOT TO STOP THIS SAUCER BEFORE IT ENTERS THE MOON'S GRAVITATIONAL FIELD...

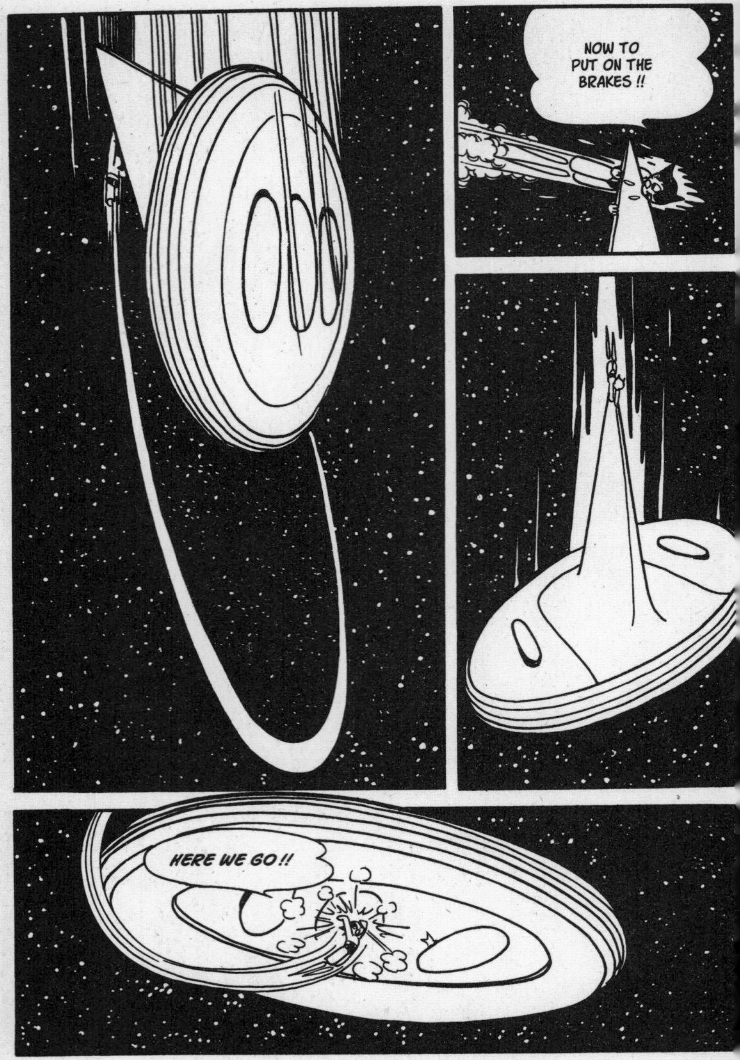
NOW TO PUT ON THE BRAKES !!
HERE WE GO !!

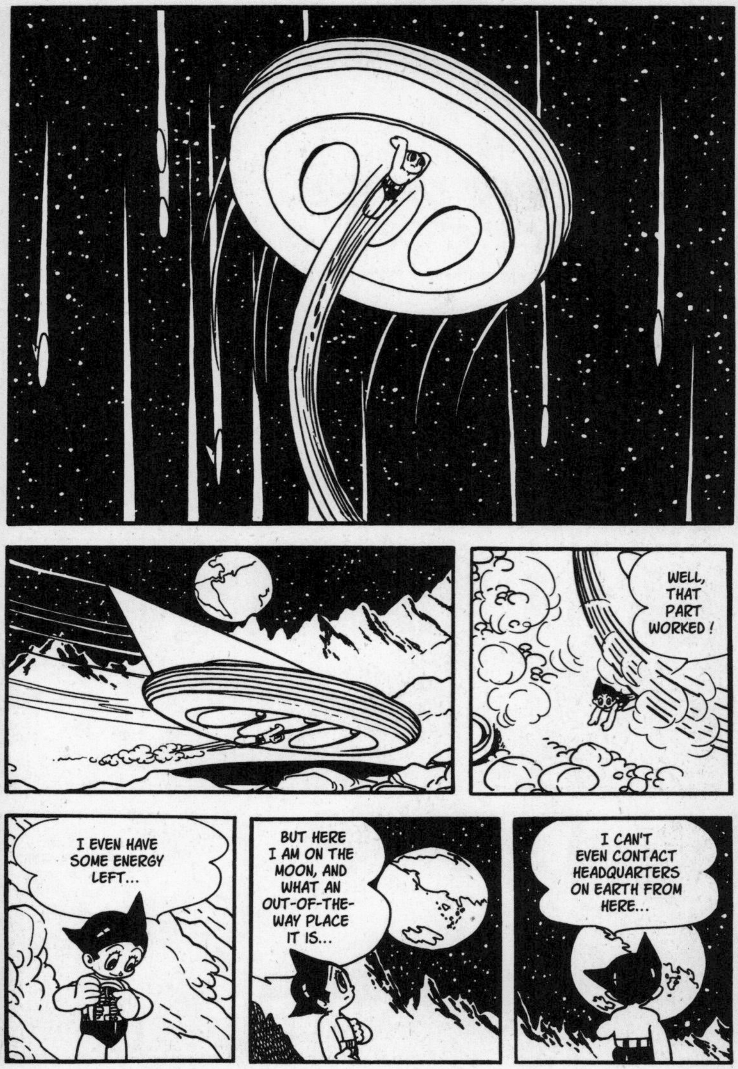
WELL, THAT PART WORKED!
I EVEN HAVE SOME ENERGY LEFT...
BUT HERE I AM ON THE MOON, AND WHAT AN OUT-OF-THE-WAY PLACE IT IS...
I CAN'T EVEN CONTACT HEADQUARTERS ON EARTH FROM HERE...

THE SECRET OF THE MOON'S CRATERS

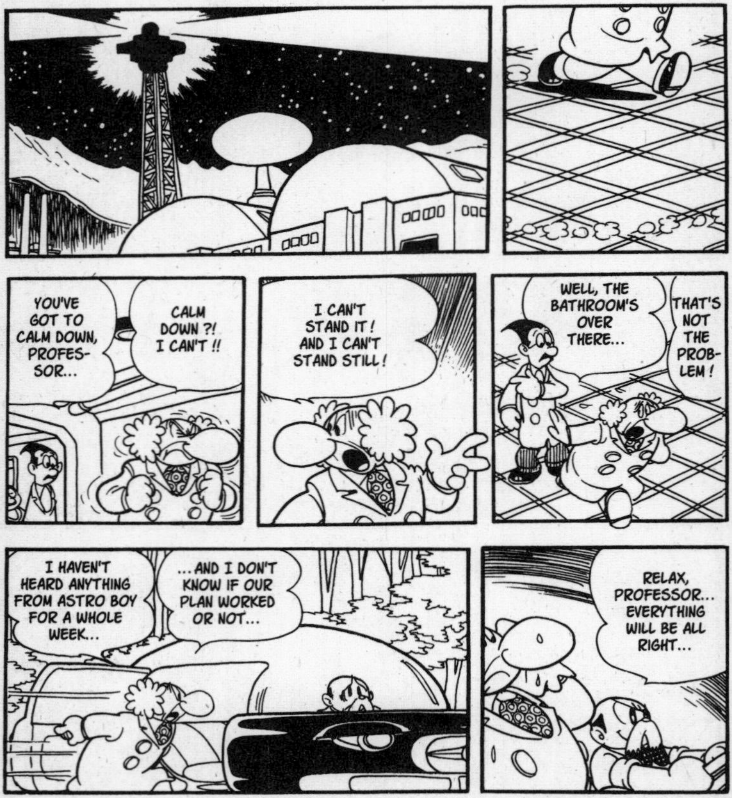
YOU'VE GOT TO CALM DOWN, PROFES-SOR...
CALM DOWN ?! I CAN'T !!
I CAN'T STAND IT ! AND I CAN'T STAND STILL !
WELL, THE BATHROOM'S OVER THERE...
THAT'S NOT THE PROB-LEM !
I HAVEN'T HEARD ANYTHING FROM ASTRO BOY FOR A WHOLE WEEK...
...AND I DON'T KNOW IF OUR PLAN WORKED OR NOT...
RELAX, PROFESSOR... EVERYTHING WILL BE ALL RIGHT...

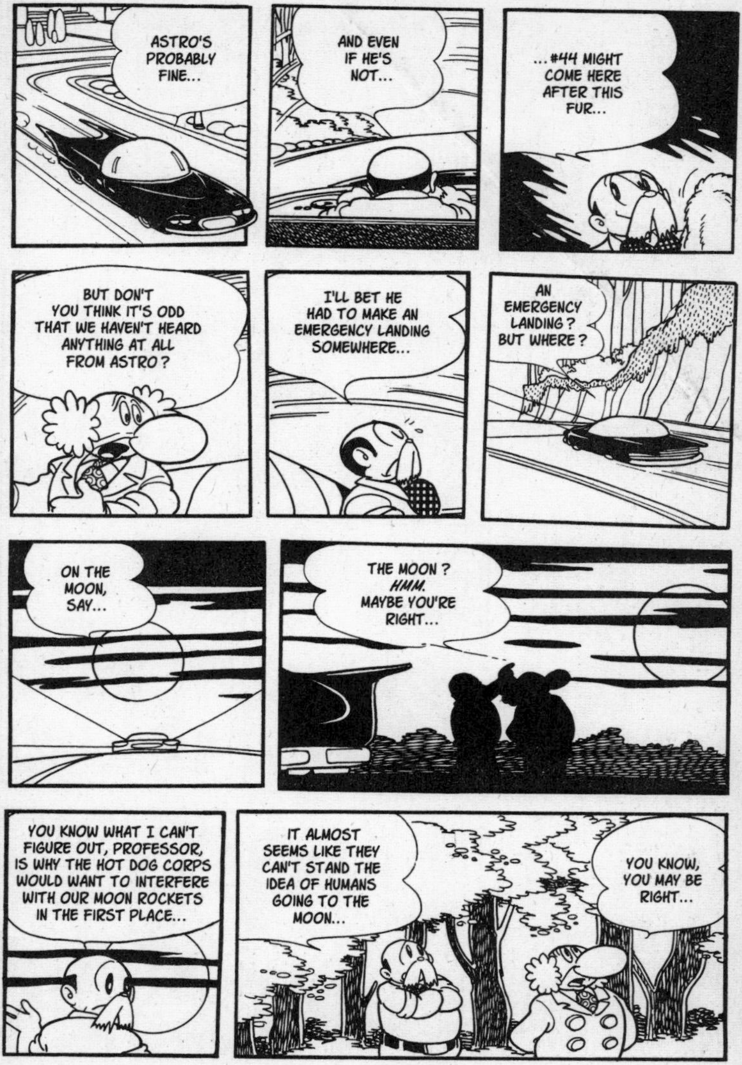
ASTRO'S PROBABLY FINE...
AND EVEN IF HE'S NOT...
...#44 MIGHT COME HERE AFTER THIS FUR...
BUT DON'T YOU THINK IT'S ODD THAT WE HAVEN'T HEARD ANYTHING AT ALL FROM ASTRO?
I'LL BET HE HAD TO MAKE AN EMERGENCY LANDING SOMEWHERE...
AN EMERGENCY LANDING? BUT WHERE?
ON THE MOON, SAY...
THE MOON? HMM. MAYBE YOU'RE RIGHT...
YOU KNOW WHAT I CAN'T FIGURE OUT, PROFESSOR, IS WHY THE HOT DOG CORPS WOULD WANT TO INTERFERE WITH OUR MOON ROCKETS IN THE FIRST PLACE...
IT ALMOST SEEMS LIKE THEY CAN'T STAND THE IDEA OF HUMANS GOING TO THE MOON...
YOU KNOW, YOU MAY BE RIGHT...

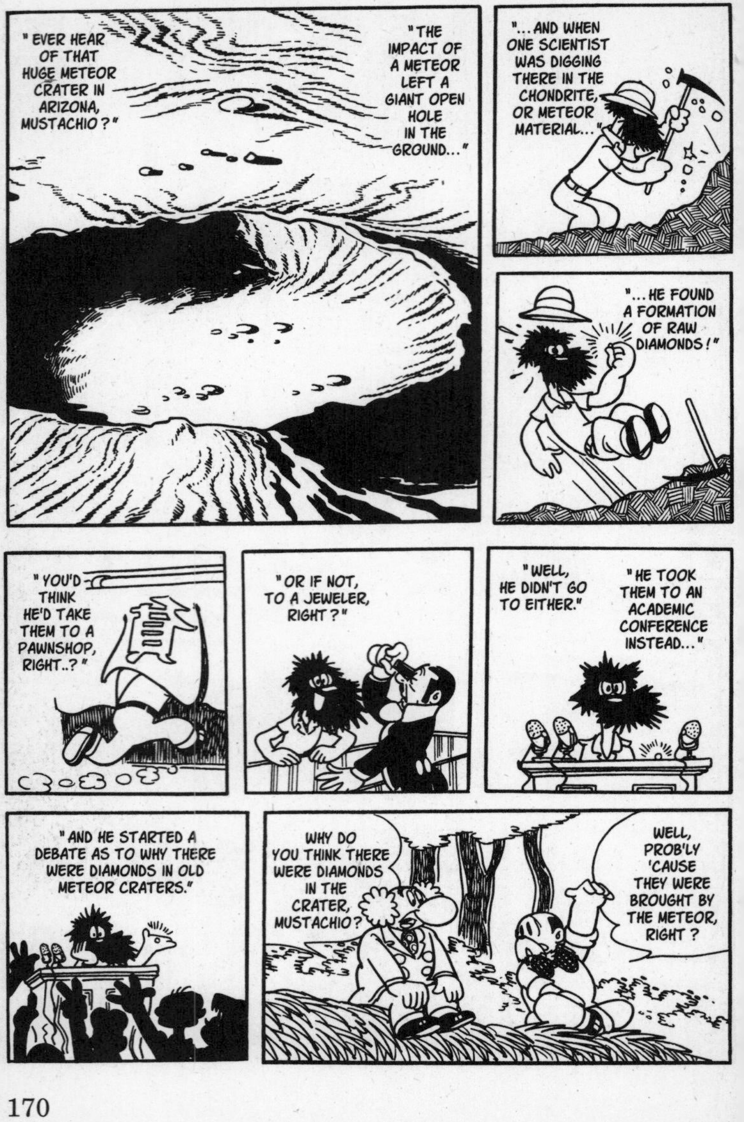
"EVER HEAR OF THAT HUGE METEOR CRATER IN ARIZONA, MUSTACHIO?"
"THE IMPACT OF A METEOR LEFT A GIANT OPEN HOLE IN THE GROUND..."
"...AND WHEN ONE SCIENTIST WAS DIGGING THERE IN THE CHONDRITE, OR METEOR MATERIAL..."
"...HE FOUND A FORMATION OF RAW DIAMONDS!"
"YOU'D THINK HE'D TAKE THEM TO A PAWNSHOP, RIGHT..?"
"OR IF NOT, TO A JEWELER, RIGHT?"
"WELL, HE DIDN'T GO TO EITHER."
"HE TOOK THEM TO AN ACADEMIC CONFERENCE INSTEAD..."
"AND HE STARTED A DEBATE AS TO WHY THERE WERE DIAMONDS IN OLD METEOR CRATERS."
WHY DO YOU THINK THERE WERE DIAMONDS IN THE CRATER, MUSTACHIO?
WELL, PROB'LY 'CAUSE THEY WERE BROUGHT BY THE METEOR, RIGHT?

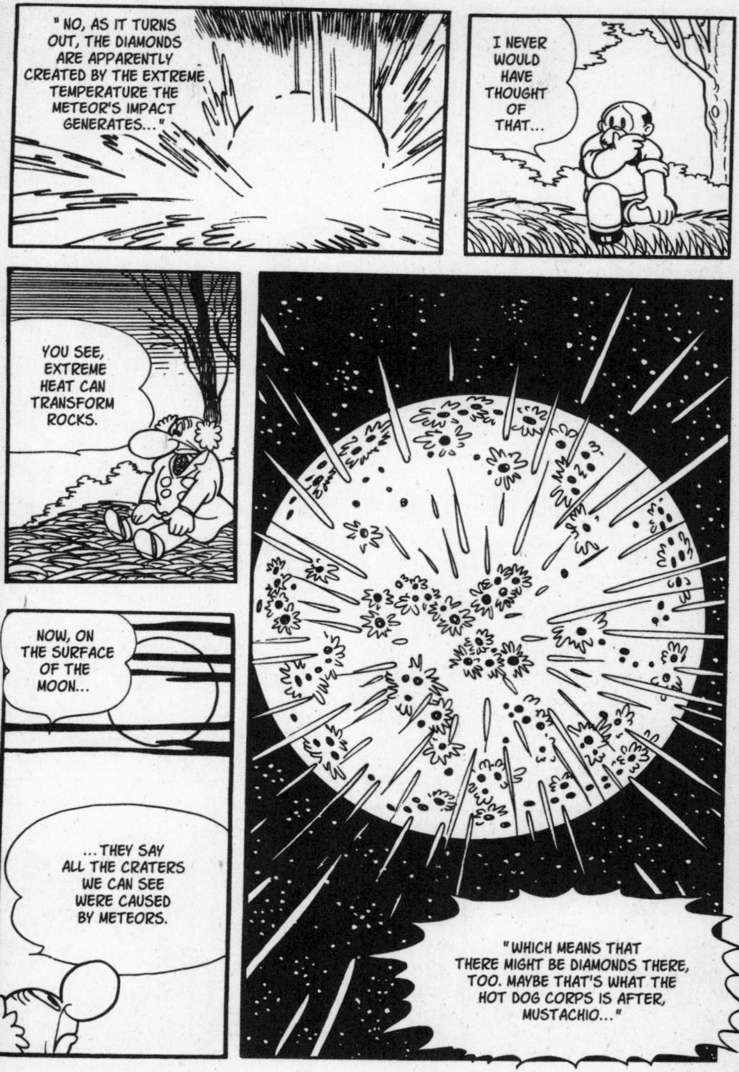
" NO, AS IT TURNS OUT, THE DIAMONDS ARE APPARENTLY CREATED BY THE EXTREME TEMPERATURE THE METEOR'S IMPACT GENERATES..."
I NEVER WOULD HAVE THOUGHT OF THAT...
YOU SEE, EXTREME HEAT CAN TRANSFORM ROCKS.
NOW, ON THE SURFACE OF THE MOON...
...THEY SAY ALL THE CRATERS WE CAN SEE WERE CAUSED BY METEORS.
"WHICH MEANS THAT THERE MIGHT BE DIAMONDS THERE, TOO. MAYBE THAT'S WHAT THE HOT DOG CORPS IS AFTER, MUSTACHIO..."

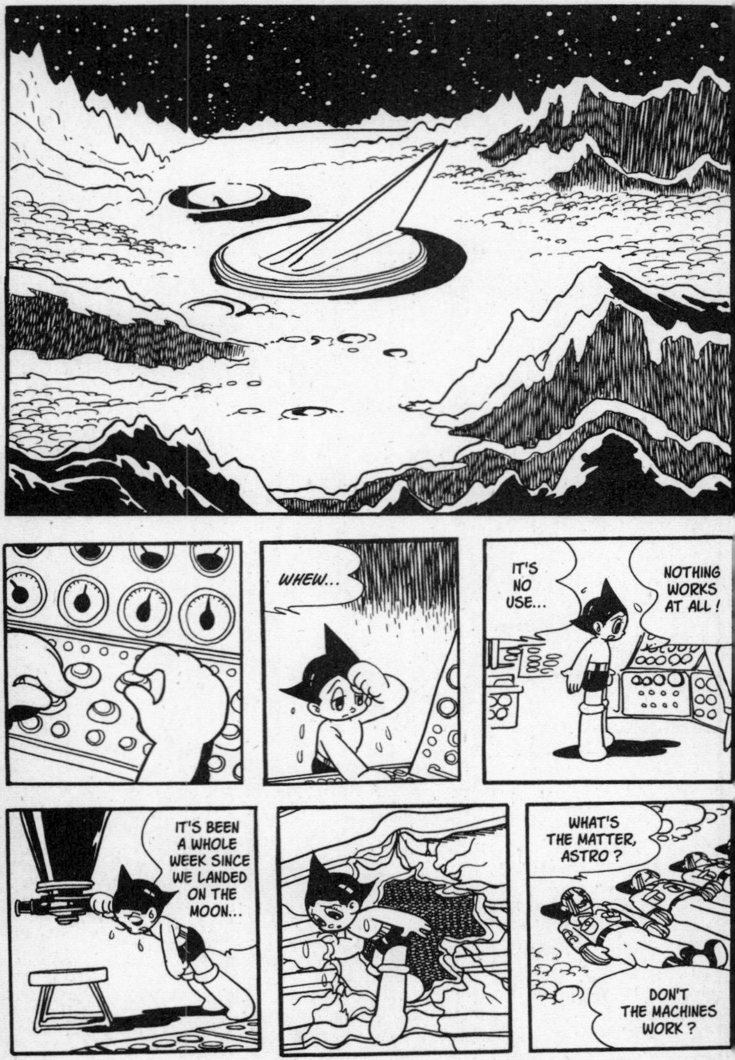
WHEW...
IT'S NO USE...
NOTHING WORKS AT ALL !
IT'S BEEN A WHOLE WEEK SINCE WE LANDED ON THE MOON...
WHAT'S THE MATTER, ASTRO ?
DON'T THE MACHINES WORK ?

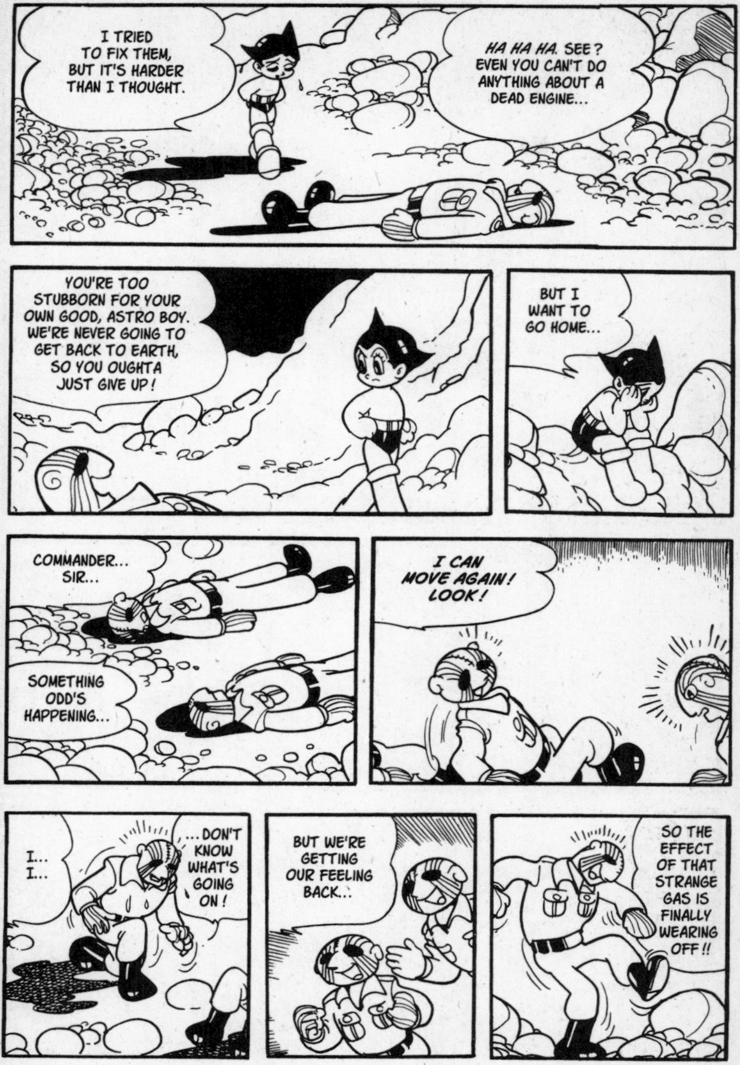
I TRIED TO FIX THEM, BUT IT'S HARDER THAN I THOUGHT.
HA HA HA. SEE? EVEN YOU CAN'T DO ANYTHING ABOUT A DEAD ENGINE...
YOU'RE TOO STUBBORN FOR YOUR OWN GOOD, ASTRO BOY. WE'RE NEVER GOING TO GET BACK TO EARTH, SO YOU OUGHTA JUST GIVE UP!
BUT I WANT TO GO HOME...
COMMANDER... SIR...
SOMETHING ODD'S HAPPENING...
I CAN MOVE AGAIN! LOOK!
I... I...
...DON'T KNOW WHAT'S GOING ON!
BUT WE'RE GETTING OUR FEELING BACK...
SO THE EFFECT OF THAT STRANGE GAS IS FINALLY WEARING OFF!!

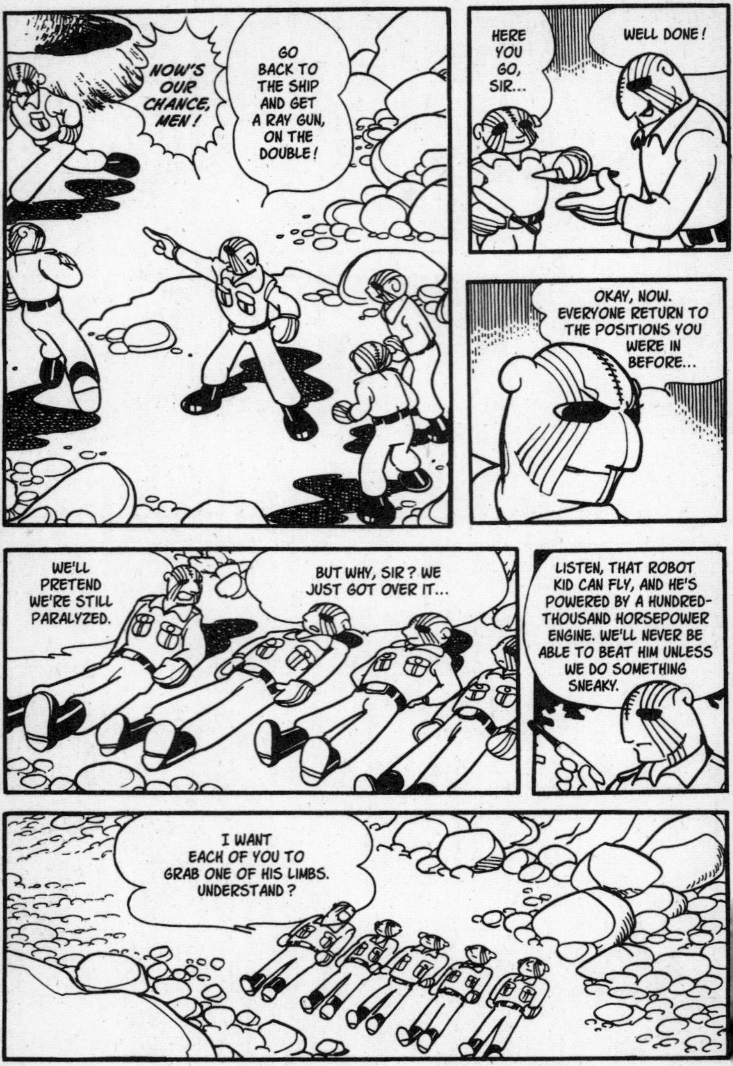
NOW'S OUR CHANCE, MEN!
GO BACK TO THE SHIP AND GET A RAY GUN, ON THE DOUBLE!
HERE YOU GO, SIR...
WELL DONE!
OKAY, NOW. EVERYONE RETURN TO THE POSITIONS YOU WERE IN BEFORE...
WE'LL PRETEND WE'RE STILL PARALYZED.
BUT WHY, SIR? WE JUST GOT OVER IT...
LISTEN, THAT ROBOT KID CAN FLY, AND HE'S POWERED BY A HUNDRED-THOUSAND HORSEPOWER ENGINE. WE'LL NEVER BE ABLE TO BEAT HIM UNLESS WE DO SOMETHING SNEAKY.
I WANT EACH OF YOU TO GRAB ONE OF HIS LIMBS. UNDERSTAND?

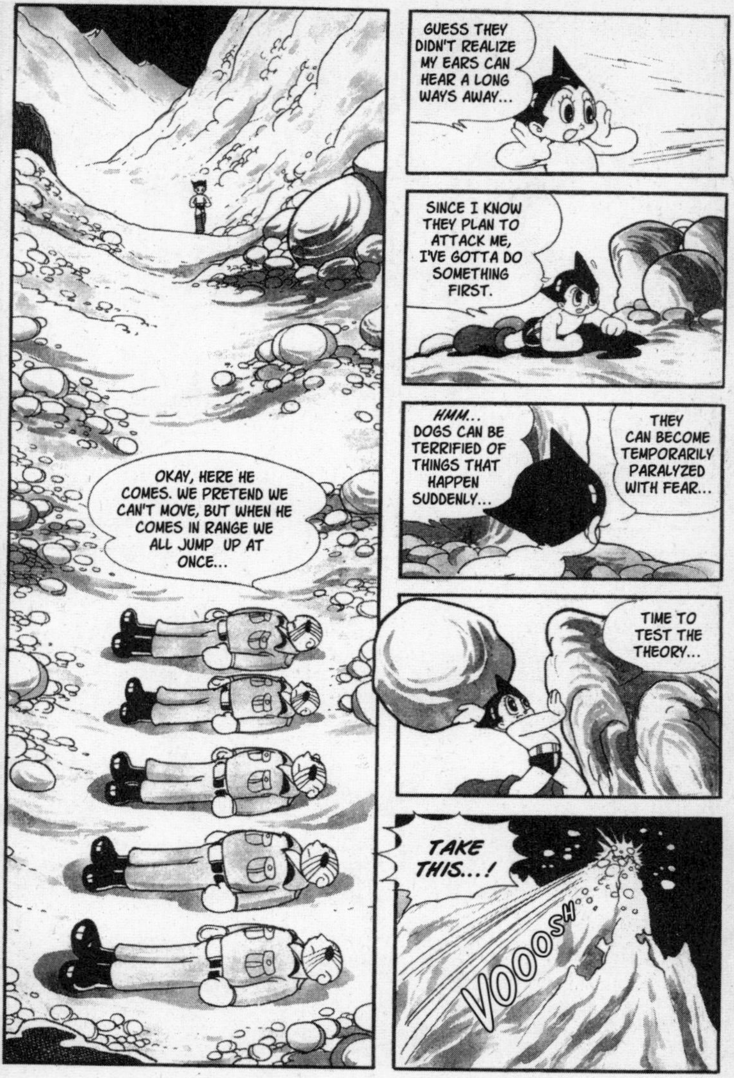
OKAY, HERE HE COMES. WE PRETEND WE CAN'T MOVE, BUT WHEN HE COMES IN RANGE WE ALL JUMP UP AT ONCE...
GUESS THEY DIDN'T REALIZE MY EARS CAN HEAR A LONG WAYS AWAY...
SINCE I KNOW THEY PLAN TO ATTACK ME, I'VE GOTTA DO SOMETHING FIRST.
HMM... DOGS CAN BE TERRIFIED OF THINGS THAT HAPPEN SUDDENLY...
THEY CAN BECOME TEMPORARILY PARALYZED WITH FEAR...
TIME TO TEST THE THEORY...
TAKE THIS...!
VOOOOSH

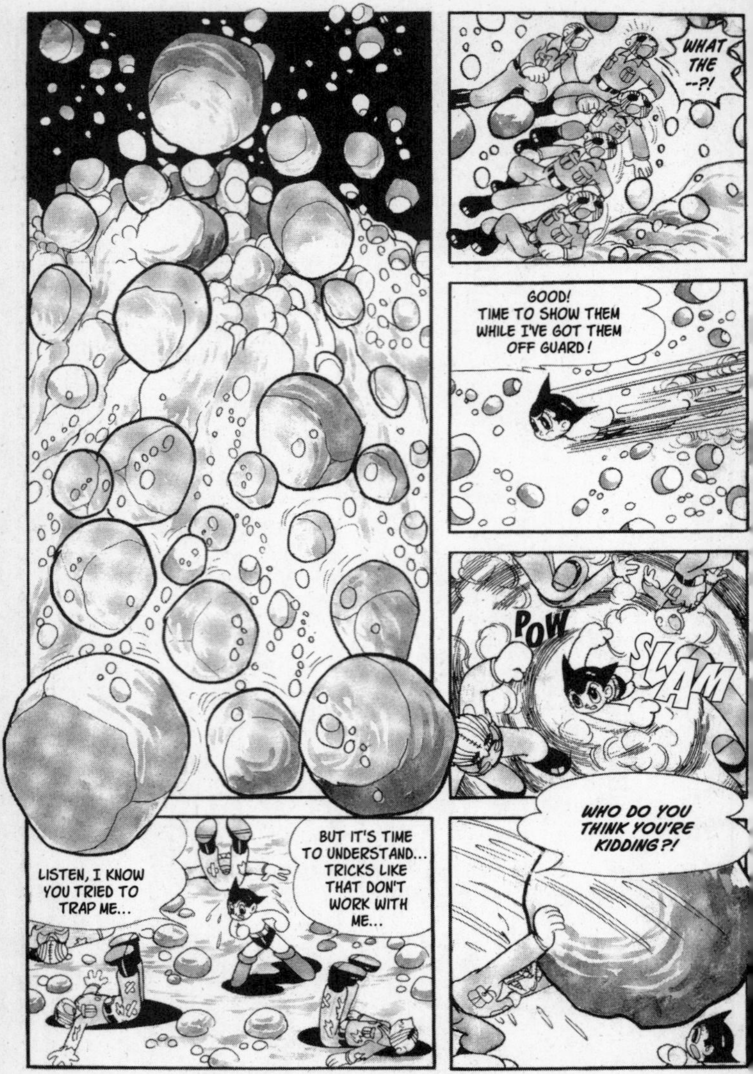
WHAT THE --?!
GOOD! TIME TO SHOW THEM WHILE I'VE GOT THEM OFF GUARD!
POW
SLAM
LISTEN, I KNOW YOU TRIED TO TRAP ME...
BUT IT'S TIME TO UNDERSTAND... TRICKS LIKE THAT DON'T WORK WITH ME...
WHO DO YOU THINK YOU'RE KIDDING?!

VOOOSh

TAKE THIS !!

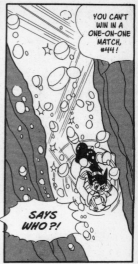

YOU CAN'T WIN IN A ONE-ON-ONE MATCH, #44 !

SAYS WHO ?!

LOOK !!

HEY, WAIT A MINUTE...

LOOKS LIKE WE'VE FALLEN INTO A DEEP VALLEY...

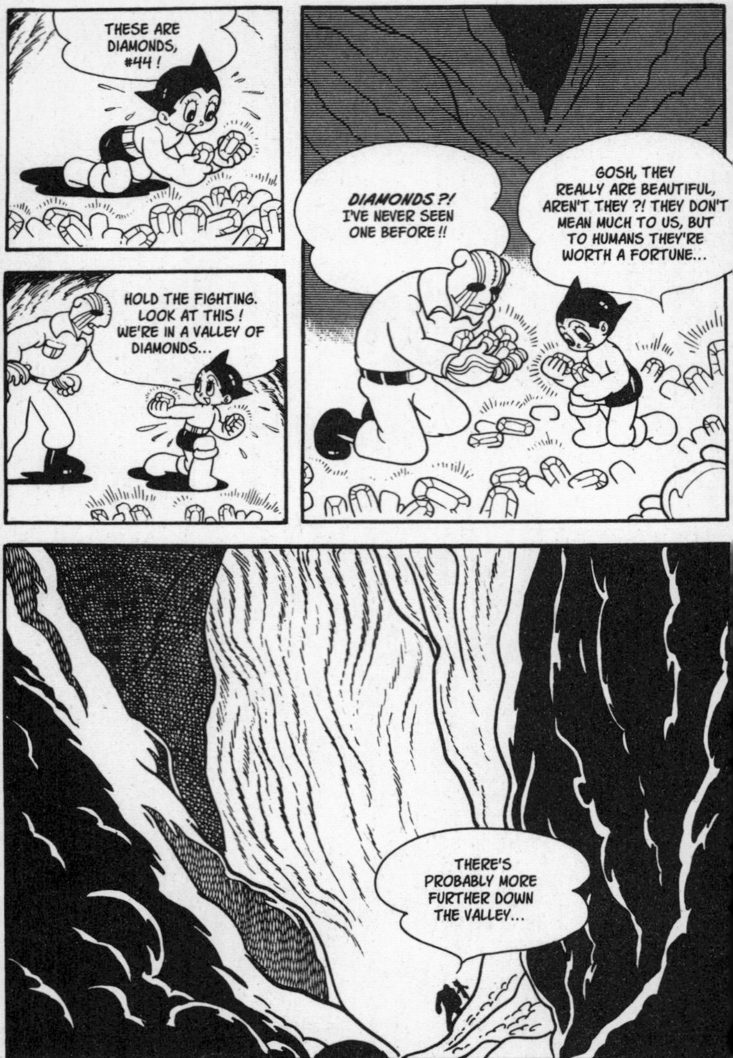
THESE ARE DIAMONDS, #44 !
HOLD THE FIGHTING. LOOK AT THIS ! WE'RE IN A VALLEY OF DIAMONDS...
DIAMONDS ?! I'VE NEVER SEEN ONE BEFORE !!
GOSH, THEY REALLY ARE BEAUTIFUL, AREN'T THEY ?! THEY DON'T MEAN MUCH TO US, BUT TO HUMANS THEY'RE WORTH A FORTUNE...
THERE'S PROBABLY MORE FURTHER DOWN THE VALLEY...

A DEAD CITY ON THE MOON

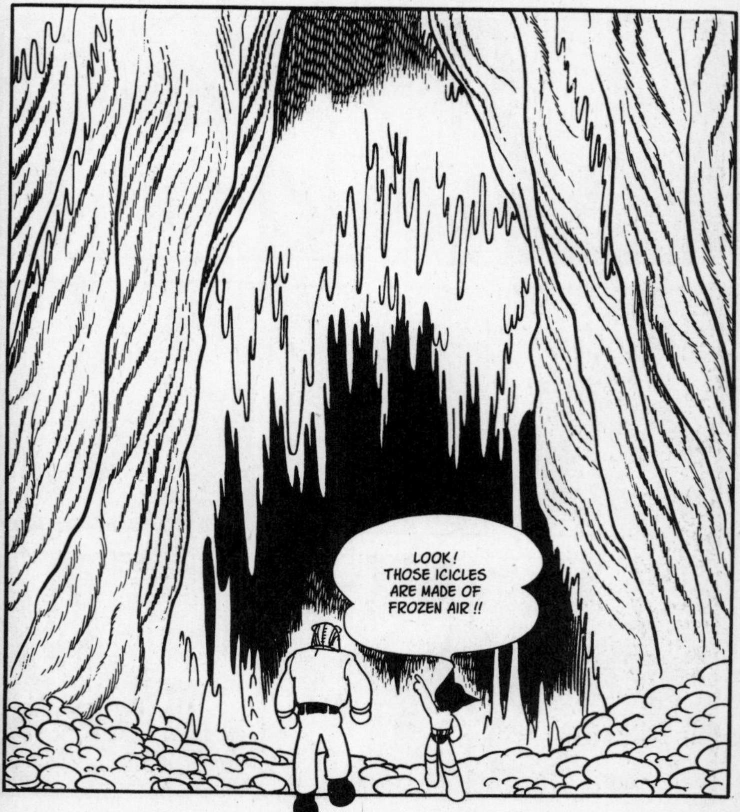
LOOK! THOSE ICICLES ARE MADE OF FROZEN AIR!!

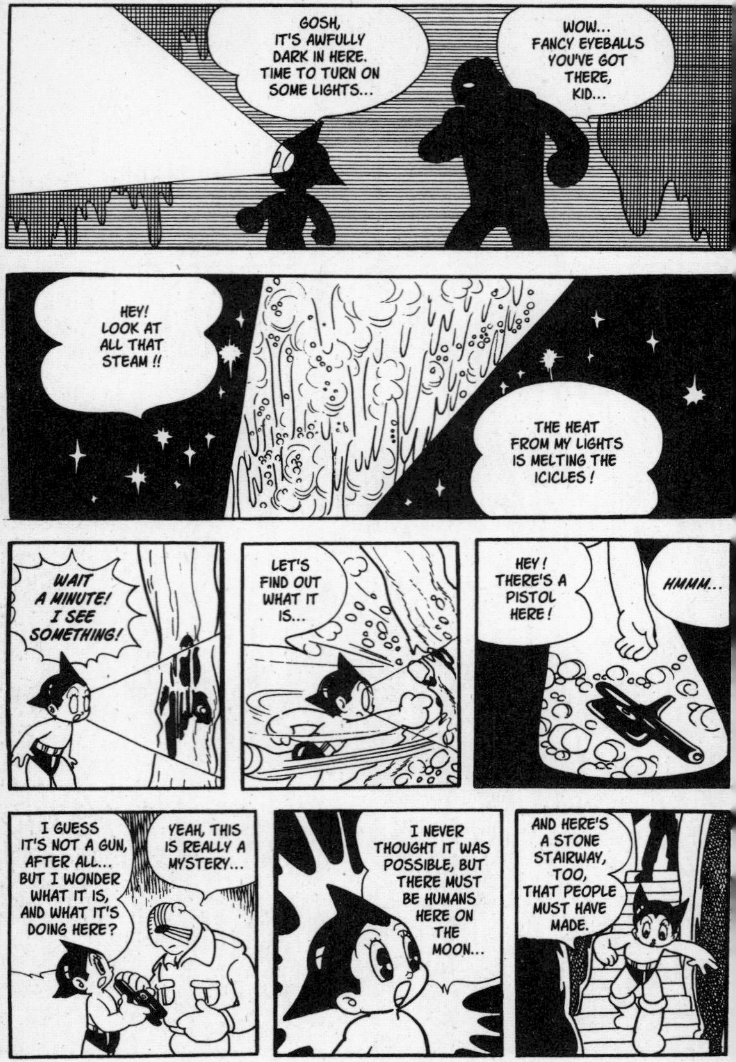
GOSH, IT'S AWFULLY DARK IN HERE. TIME TO TURN ON SOME LIGHTS...
WOW... FANCY EYEBALLS YOU'VE GOT THERE, KID...
HEY! LOOK AT ALL THAT STEAM !!
THE HEAT FROM MY LIGHTS IS MELTING THE ICICLES !
WAIT A MINUTE! I SEE SOMETHING!
LET'S FIND OUT WHAT IT IS...
HEY ! THERE'S A PISTOL HERE !
HMMM...
I GUESS IT'S NOT A GUN, AFTER ALL... BUT I WONDER WHAT IT IS, AND WHAT IT'S DOING HERE?
YEAH, THIS IS REALLY A MYSTERY...
I NEVER THOUGHT IT WAS POSSIBLE, BUT THERE MUST BE HUMANS HERE ON THE MOON...
AND HERE'S A STONE STAIRWAY, TOO, THAT PEOPLE MUST HAVE MADE.

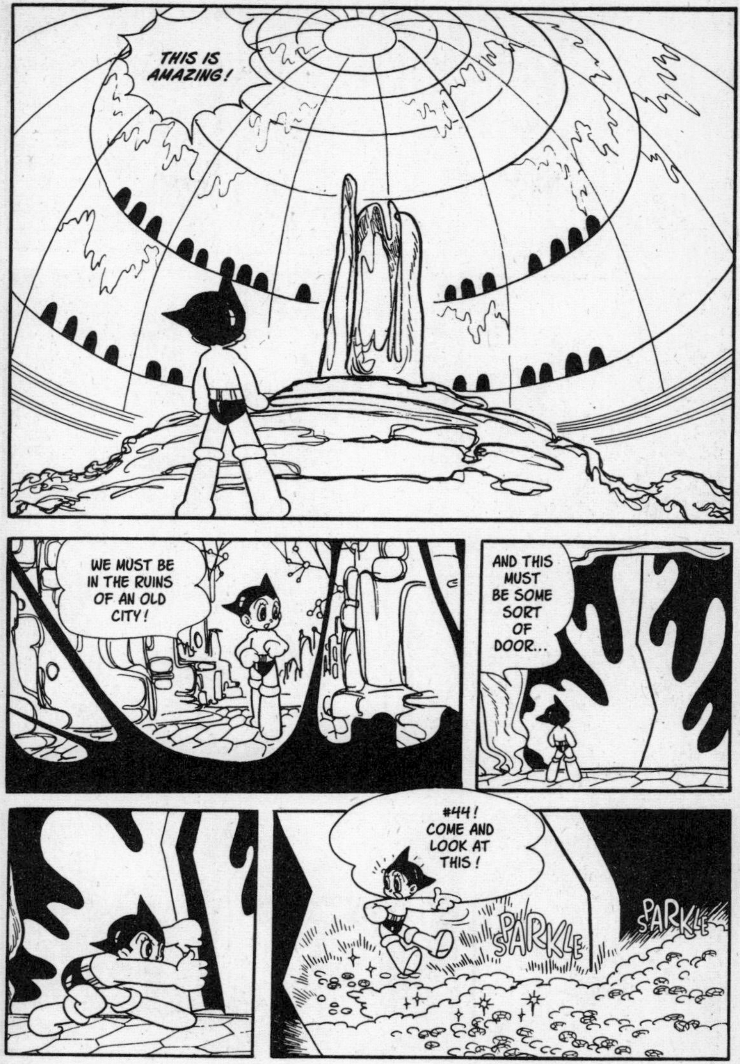
THIS IS AMAZING!
WE MUST BE IN THE RUINS OF AN OLD CITY!
AND THIS MUST BE SOME SORT OF DOOR...
#44! COME AND LOOK AT THIS!
SPARKLE
SPARKLE

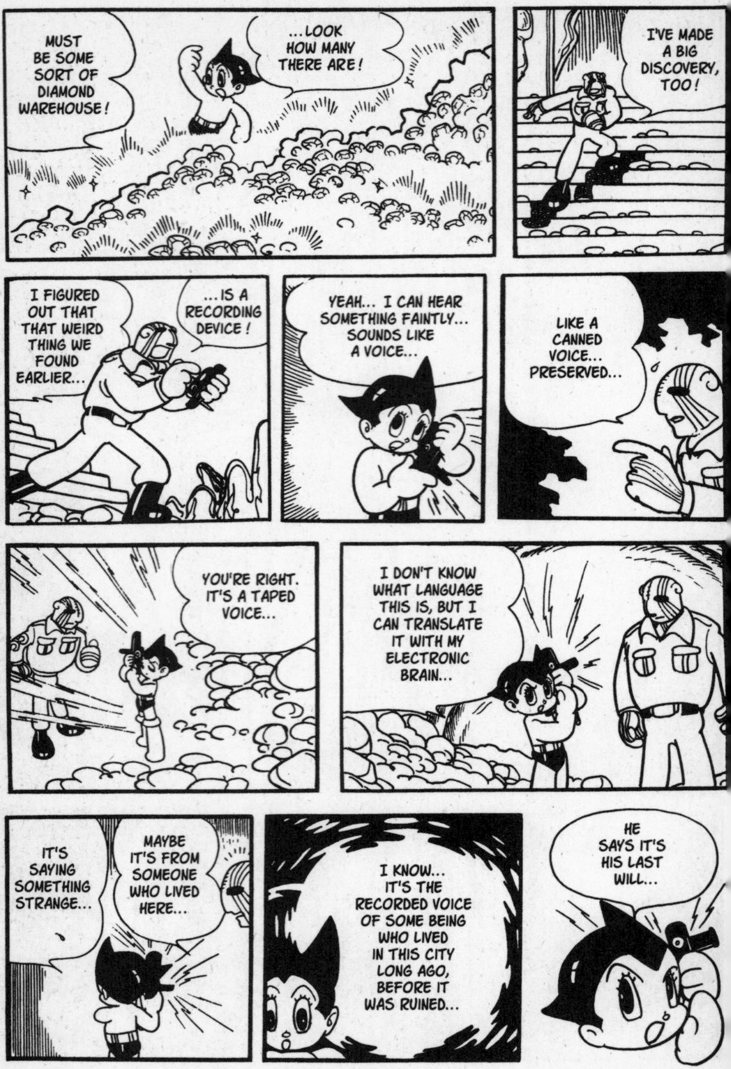
MUST BE SOME SORT OF DIAMOND WAREHOUSE!
...LOOK HOW MANY THERE ARE!
I'VE MADE A BIG DISCOVERY, TOO!
I FIGURED OUT THAT THAT WEIRD THING WE FOUND EARLIER...
...IS A RECORDING DEVICE!
YEAH... I CAN HEAR SOMETHING FAINTLY... SOUNDS LIKE A VOICE...
LIKE A CANNED VOICE... PRESERVED...
YOU'RE RIGHT. IT'S A TAPED VOICE...
I DON'T KNOW WHAT LANGUAGE THIS IS, BUT I CAN TRANSLATE IT WITH MY ELECTRONIC BRAIN...
IT'S SAYING SOMETHING STRANGE...
MAYBE IT'S FROM SOMEONE WHO LIVED HERE...
I KNOW... IT'S THE RECORDED VOICE OF SOME BEING WHO LIVED IN THIS CITY LONG AGO, BEFORE IT WAS RUINED...
HE SAYS IT'S HIS LAST WILL...

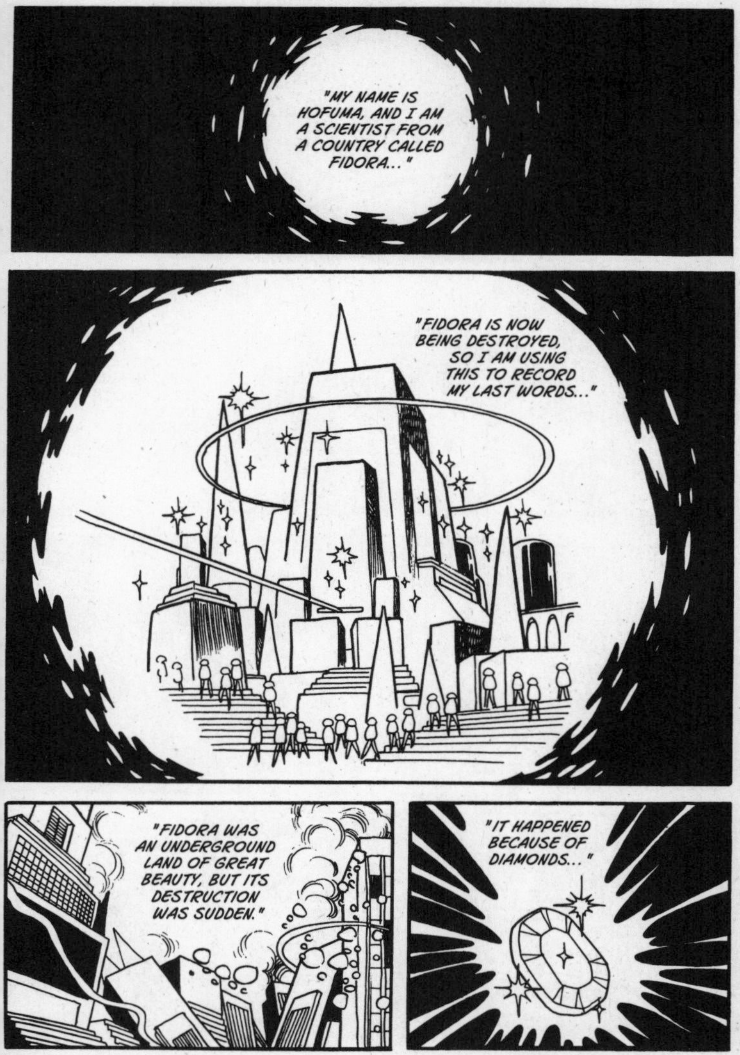
"MY NAME IS HOFUMA, AND I AM A SCIENTIST FROM A COUNTRY CALLED FIDORA..."
"FIDORA IS NOW BEING DESTROYED, SO I AM USING THIS TO RECORD MY LAST WORDS..."
"FIDORA WAS AN UNDERGROUND LAND OF GREAT BEAUTY, BUT ITS DESTRUCTION WAS SUDDEN."
"IT HAPPENED BECAUSE OF DIAMONDS..."

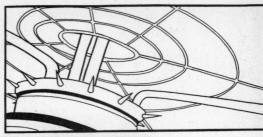

"WE USED DIAMONDS AS OUR CURRENCY, AND WE WANTED MORE AND MORE OF THEM. EVENTUALLY WE DISCOVERED A WAY TO MAKE ARTIFICIAL DIAMONDS..."

"WE KNEW WE COULD USE A GRAVITY GENERATOR TO ATTRACT METEORS TO THE MOON..."

"...AND WE KNEW THAT WHEN THEY STRUCK THE SURFACE THE EXPLOSION WOULD CREATE DIAMONDS..."

"I WAS ORDERED BY THE GOVERNMENT TO TEST THIS THEORY..."

"IT MIGHT HAVE WORKED WITH A FEW METEORS, BUT TO OUR HORROR, THOUSANDS OF THEM RAINED DOWN ON THE MOON'S SURFACE LIKE A HAIL STORM..."

"WE HAD BEEN TOO GREEDY... BY THE TIME WE REALIZED THAT WE SHOULD NEVER HAVE RUN THE EXPERIMENT, IT WAS TOO LATE..."

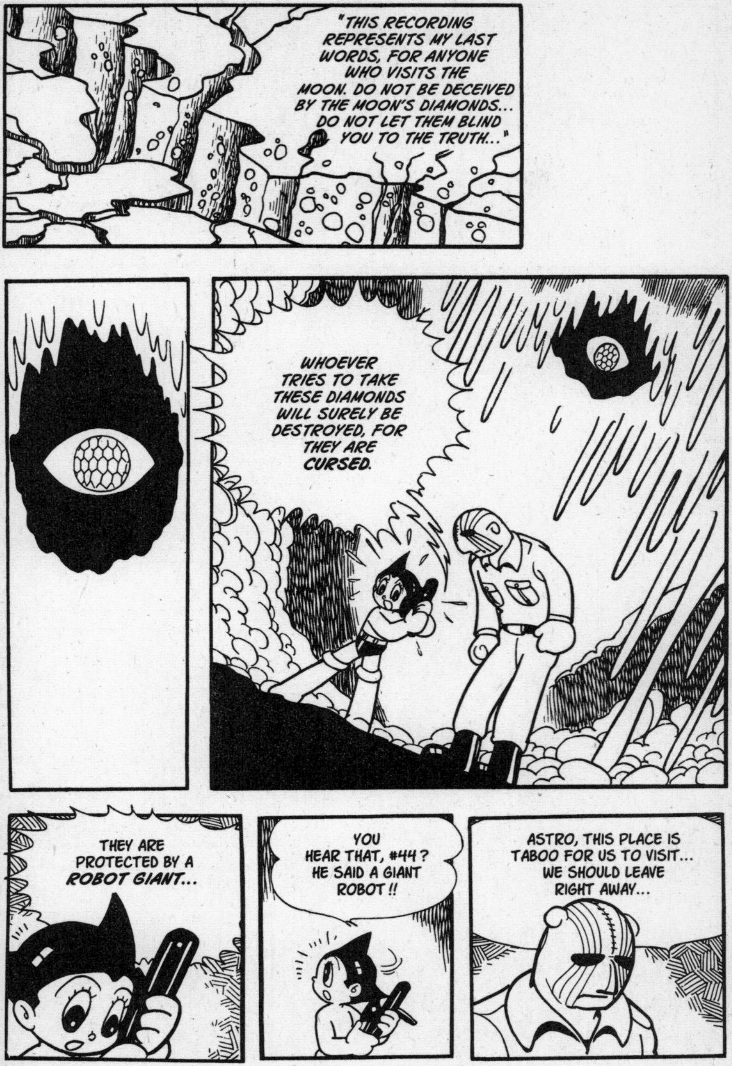
"THIS RECORDING REPRESENTS MY LAST WORDS, FOR ANYONE WHO VISITS THE MOON. DO NOT BE DECEIVED BY THE MOON'S DIAMONDS... DO NOT LET THEM BLIND YOU TO THE TRUTH..."
WHOEVER TRIES TO TAKE THESE DIAMONDS WILL SURELY BE DESTROYED, FOR THEY ARE CURSED.
THEY ARE PROTECTED BY A ROBOT GIANT...
YOU HEAR THAT, #44? HE SAID A GIANT ROBOT!!
ASTRO, THIS PLACE IS TABOO FOR US TO VISIT... WE SHOULD LEAVE RIGHT AWAY...

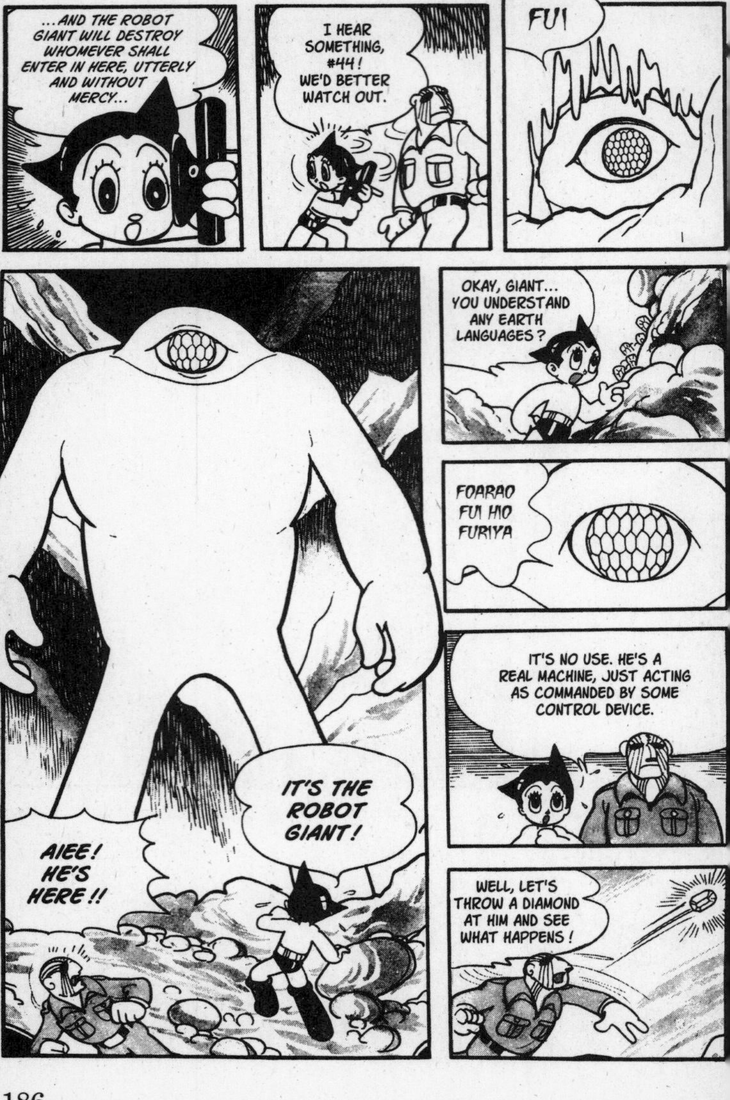
...AND THE ROBOT GIANT WILL DESTROY WHOMEVER SHALL ENTER IN HERE, UTTERLY AND WITHOUT MERCY...
I HEAR SOMETHING, #44! WE'D BETTER WATCH OUT.
FUI
IT'S THE ROBOT GIANT!
AIEE! HE'S HERE!!
OKAY, GIANT... YOU UNDERSTAND ANY EARTH LANGUAGES?
FOARAO FUI HIO FURIYA
IT'S NO USE. HE'S A REAL MACHINE, JUST ACTING AS COMMANDED BY SOME CONTROL DEVICE.
WELL, LET'S THROW A DIAMOND AT HIM AND SEE WHAT HAPPENS!

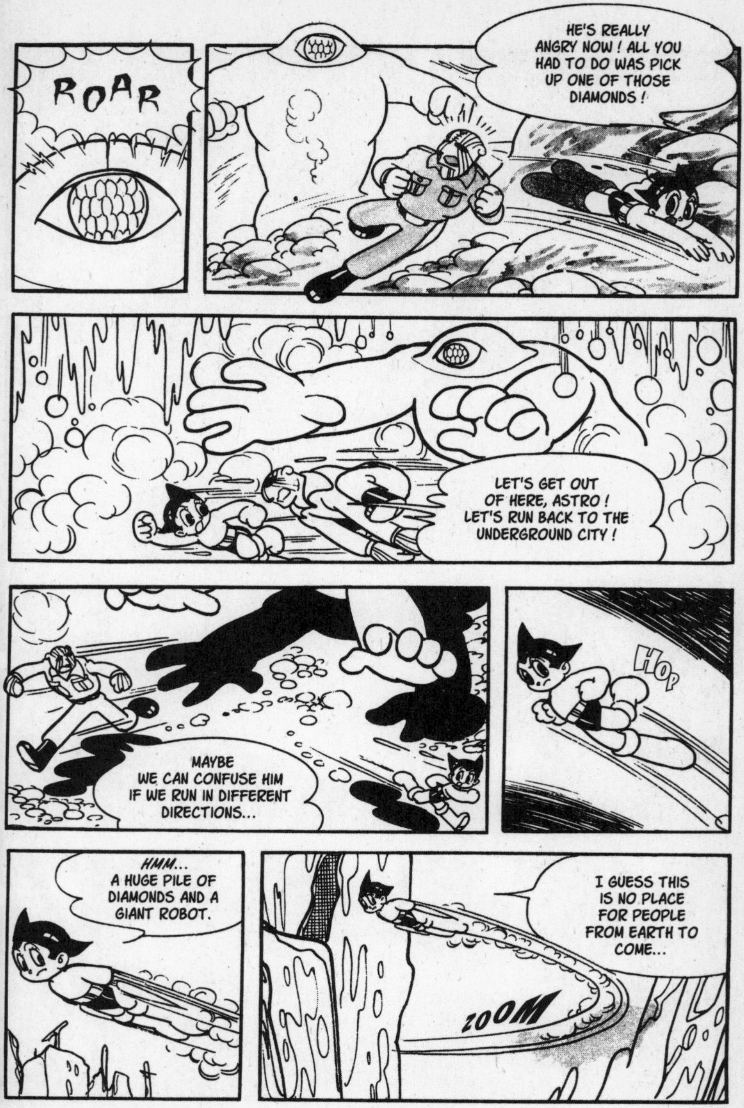
ROAR
HE'S REALLY ANGRY NOW! ALL YOU HAD TO DO WAS PICK UP ONE OF THOSE DIAMONDS!
LET'S GET OUT OF HERE, ASTRO! LET'S RUN BACK TO THE UNDERGROUND CITY!
MAYBE WE CAN CONFUSE HIM IF WE RUN IN DIFFERENT DIRECTIONS...
HOP
HMM... A HUGE PILE OF DIAMONDS AND A GIANT ROBOT.
I GUESS THIS IS NO PLACE FOR PEOPLE FROM EARTH TO COME...
ZOOM

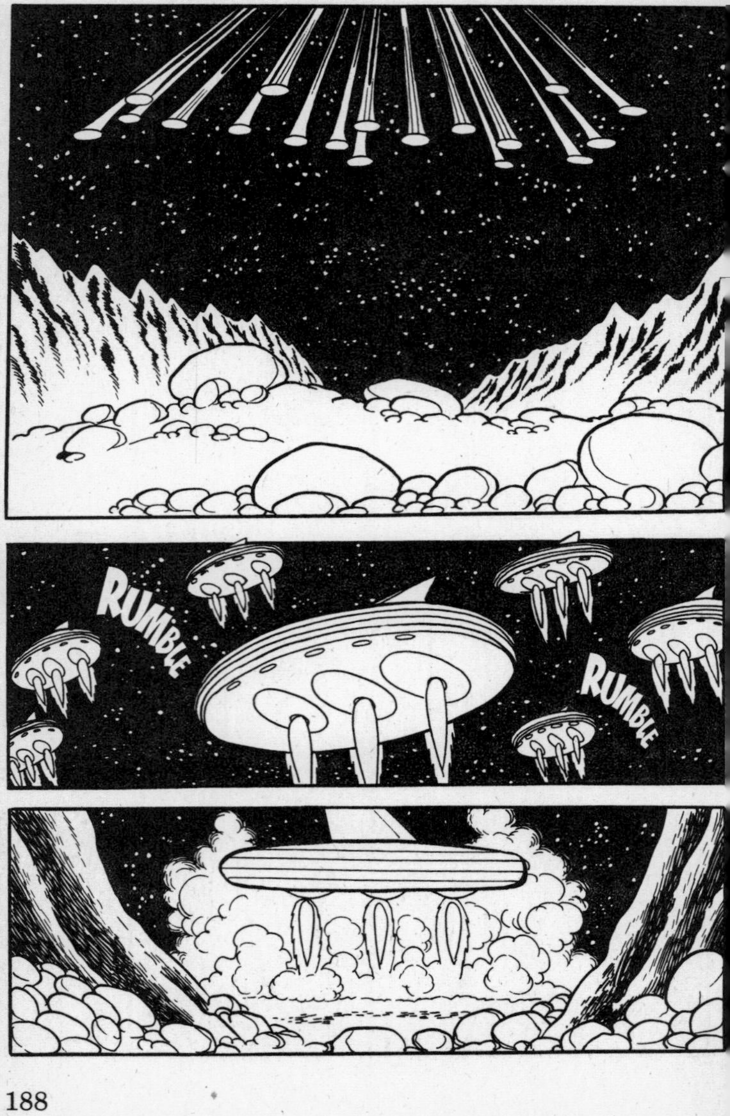
RUMBLE
RUMBLE

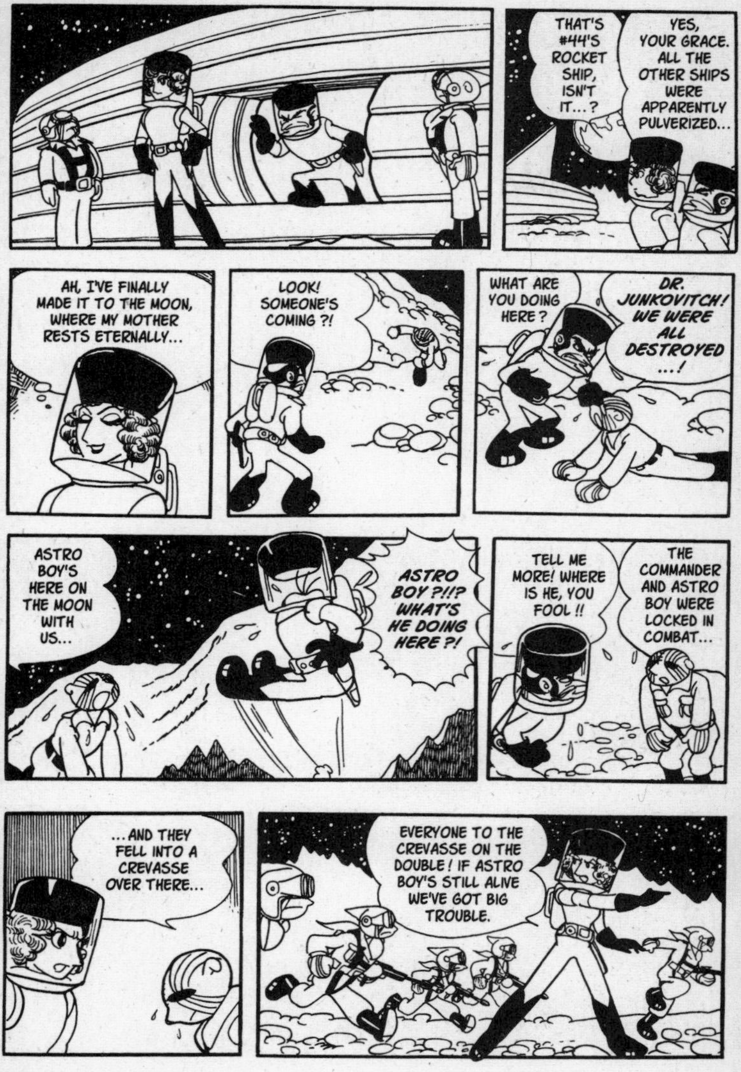
THAT'S #44'S ROCKET SHIP, ISN'T IT...?
YES, YOUR GRACE. ALL THE OTHER SHIPS WERE APPARENTLY PULVERIZED...
AH, I'VE FINALLY MADE IT TO THE MOON, WHERE MY MOTHER RESTS ETERNALLY...
LOOK! SOMEONE'S COMING ?!
WHAT ARE YOU DOING HERE?
DR. JUNKOVITCH! WE WERE ALL DESTROYED ...!
ASTRO BOY'S HERE ON THE MOON WITH US...
ASTRO BOY ?!!? WHAT'S HE DOING HERE ?!
TELL ME MORE! WHERE IS HE, YOU FOOL !!
THE COMMANDER AND ASTRO BOY WERE LOCKED IN COMBAT...
...AND THEY FELL INTO A CREVASSE OVER THERE...
EVERYONE TO THE CREVASSE ON THE DOUBLE! IF ASTRO BOY'S STILL ALIVE WE'VE GOT BIG TROUBLE.

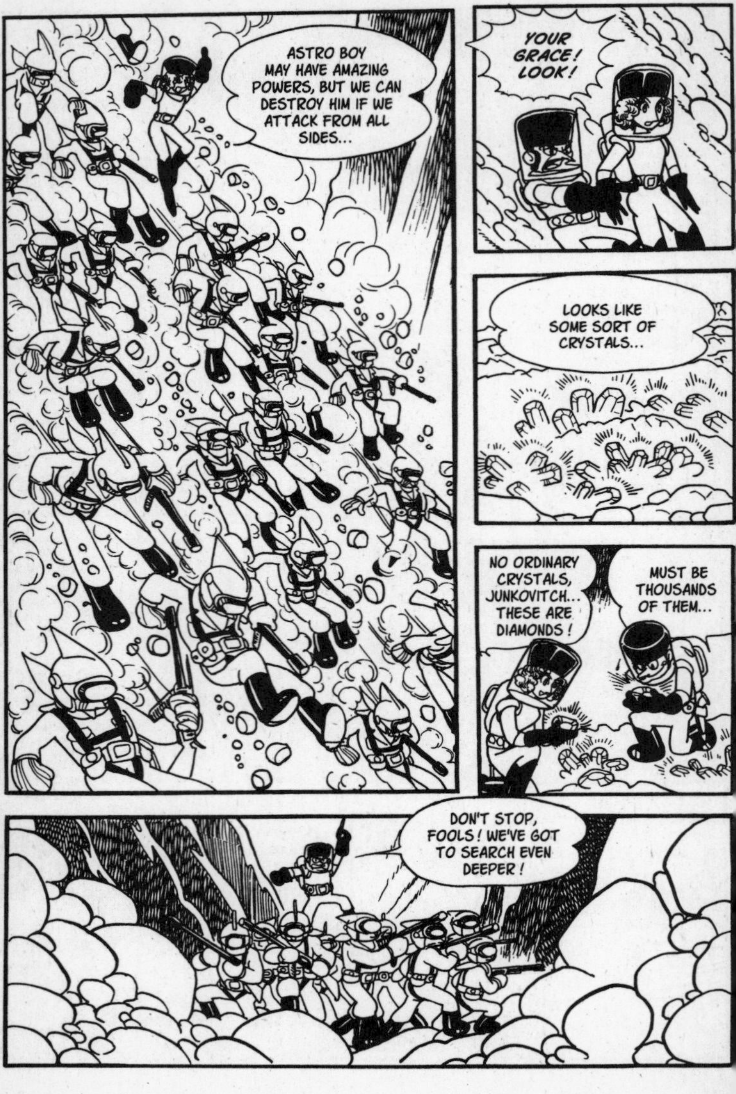
ASTRO BOY MAY HAVE AMAZING POWERS, BUT WE CAN DESTROY HIM IF WE ATTACK FROM ALL SIDES...
YOUR GRACE! LOOK!
LOOKS LIKE SOME SORT OF CRYSTALS...
NO ORDINARY CRYSTALS, JUNKOVITCH... THESE ARE DIAMONDS!
MUST BE THOUSANDS OF THEM...
DON'T STOP, FOOLS! WE'VE GOT TO SEARCH EVEN DEEPER!

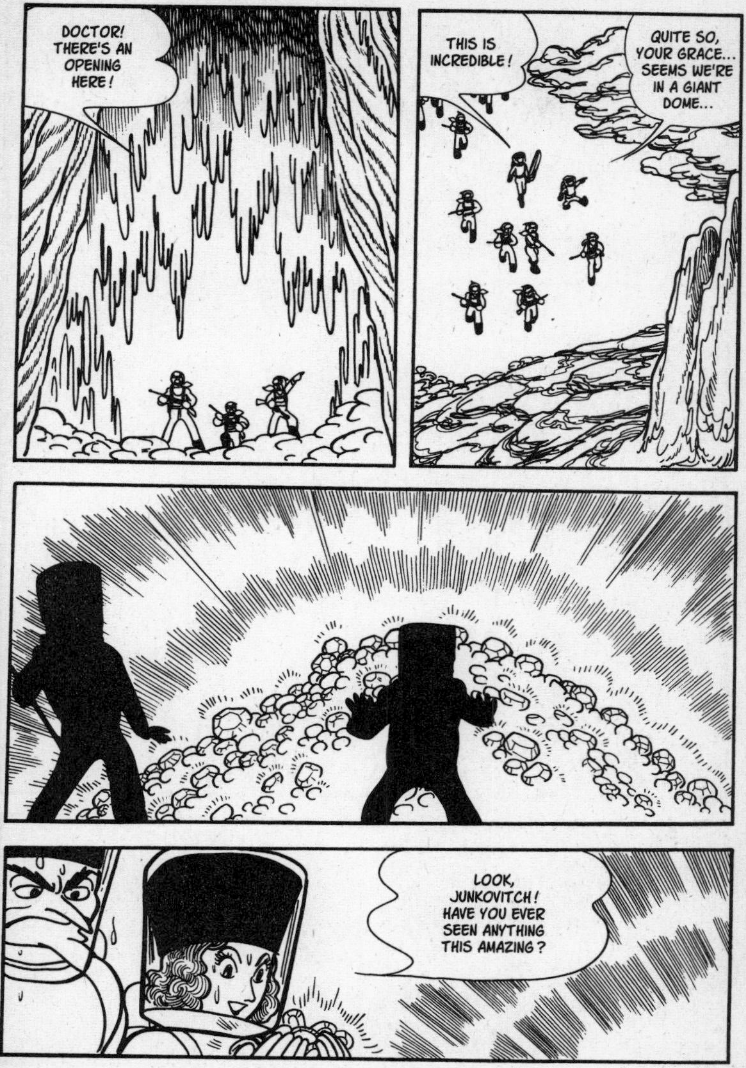
DOCTOR! THERE'S AN OPENING HERE!
THIS IS INCREDIBLE!
QUITE SO, YOUR GRACE... SEEMS WE'RE IN A GIANT DOME...
LOOK, JUNKOVITCH! HAVE YOU EVER SEEN ANYTHING THIS AMAZING?

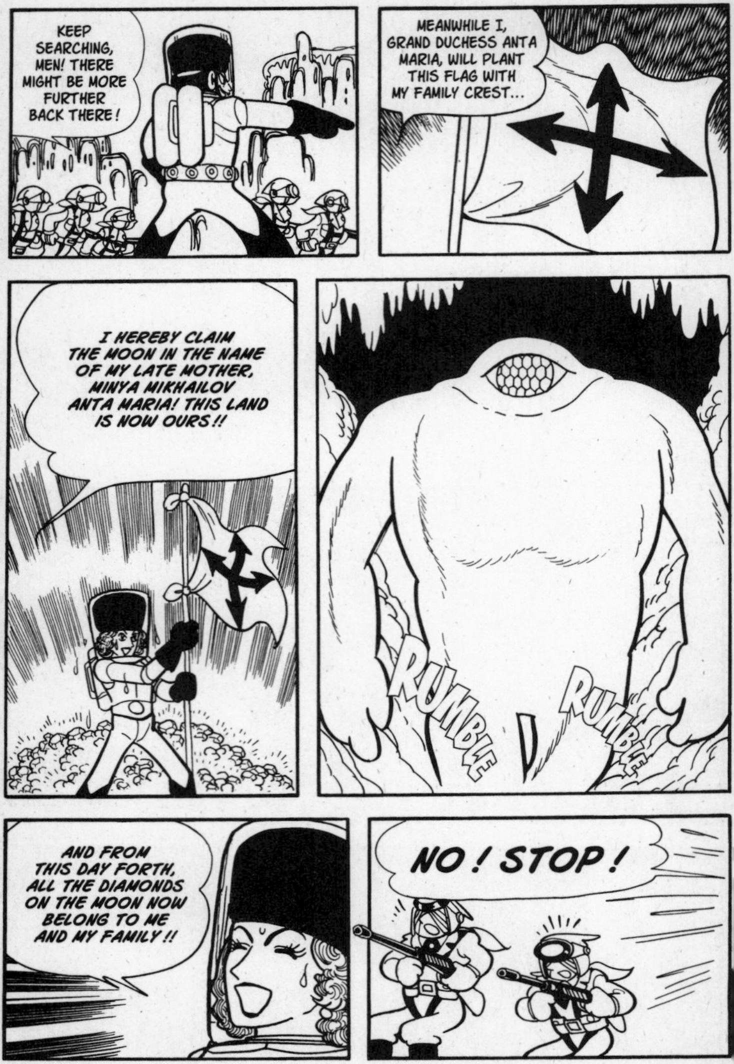
KEEP SEARCHING, MEN! THERE MIGHT BE MORE FURTHER BACK THERE!
MEANWHILE I, GRAND DUCHESS ANTA MARIA, WILL PLANT THIS FLAG WITH MY FAMILY CREST...
I HEREBY CLAIM THE MOON IN THE NAME OF MY LATE MOTHER, MINYA MIKHAILOV ANTA MARIA! THIS LAND IS NOW OURS!!
RUMBLE
RUMBLE
AND FROM THIS DAY FORTH, ALL THE DIAMONDS ON THE MOON NOW BELONG TO ME AND MY FAMILY!!
NO! STOP!

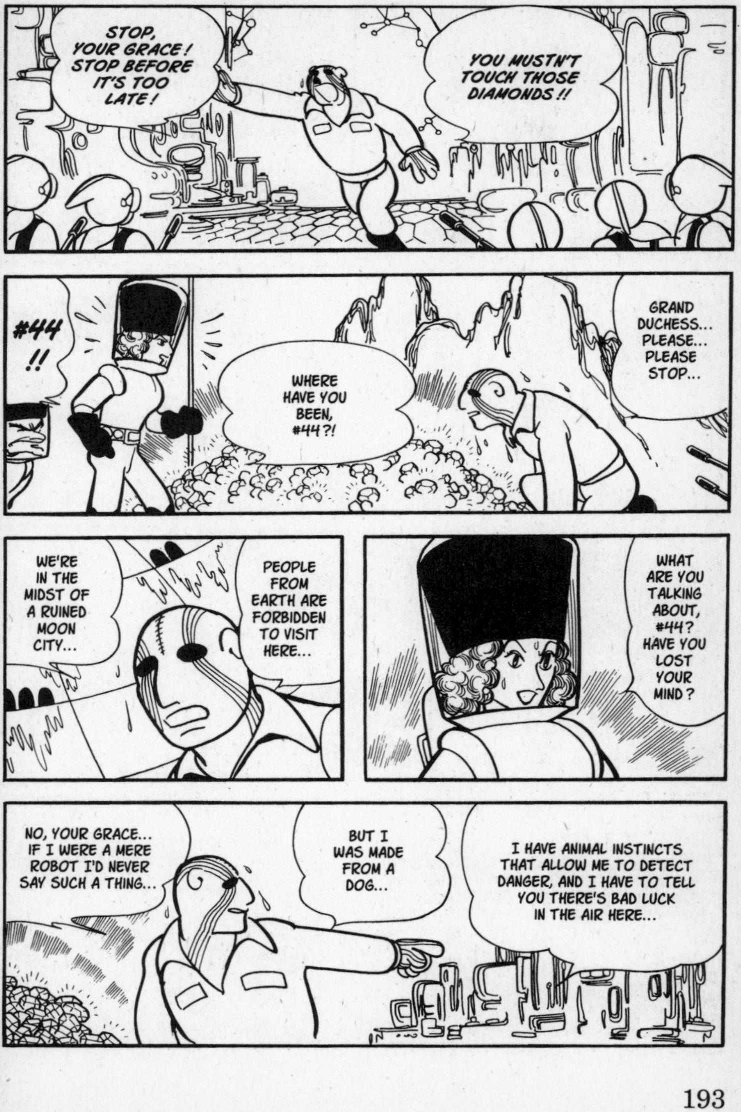
STOP, YOUR GRACE! STOP BEFORE IT'S TOO LATE!
YOU MUSTN'T TOUCH THOSE DIAMONDS!!
#44 !!
WHERE HAVE YOU BEEN, #44?!
GRAND DUCHESS... PLEASE... PLEASE STOP...
WE'RE IN THE MIDST OF A RUINED MOON CITY...
PEOPLE FROM EARTH ARE FORBIDDEN TO VISIT HERE...
WHAT ARE YOU TALKING ABOUT, #44? HAVE YOU LOST YOUR MIND?
NO, YOUR GRACE... IF I WERE A MERE ROBOT I'D NEVER SAY SUCH A THING...
BUT I WAS MADE FROM A DOG...
I HAVE ANIMAL INSTINCTS THAT ALLOW ME TO DETECT DANGER, AND I HAVE TO TELL YOU THERE'S BAD LUCK IN THE AIR HERE...

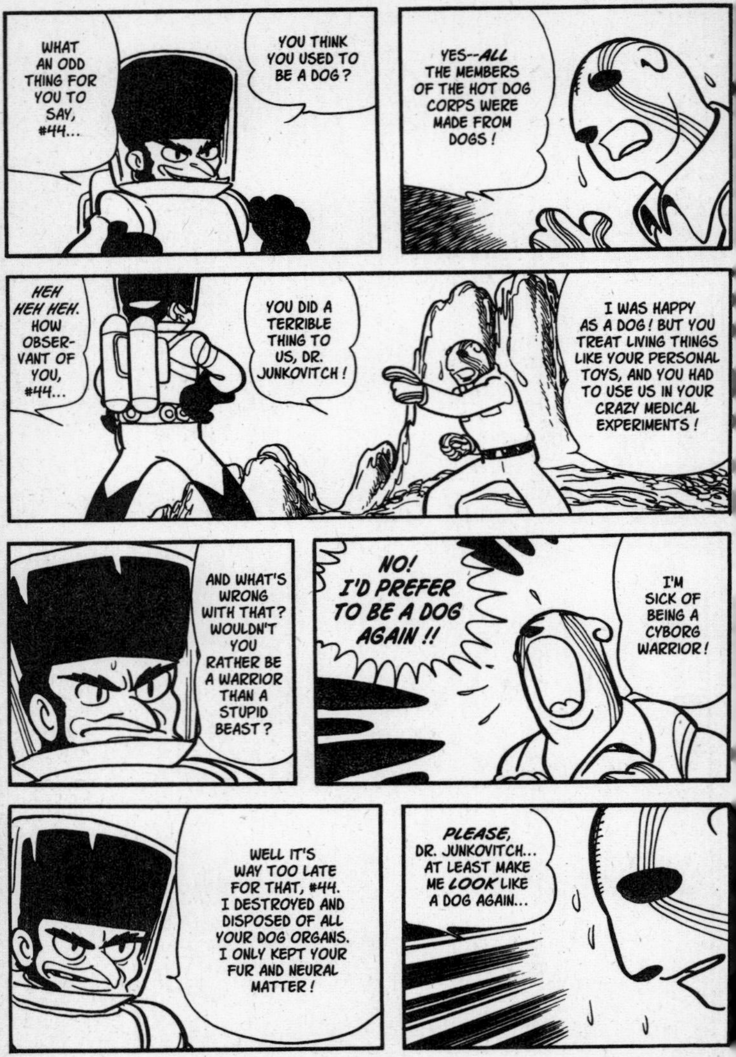
WHAT AN ODD THING FOR YOU TO SAY, #44...
YOU THINK YOU USED TO BE A DOG?
YES--**ALL** THE MEMBERS OF THE HOT DOG CORPS WERE MADE FROM DOGS!
HEH HEH HEH. HOW OBSER-VANT OF YOU, #44...
YOU DID A TERRIBLE THING TO US, DR. JUNKOVITCH!
I WAS HAPPY AS A DOG! BUT YOU TREAT LIVING THINGS LIKE YOUR PERSONAL TOYS, AND YOU HAD TO USE US IN YOUR CRAZY MEDICAL EXPERIMENTS!
AND WHAT'S WRONG WITH THAT? WOULDN'T YOU RATHER BE A WARRIOR THAN A STUPID BEAST?
NO! I'D PREFER TO BE A DOG AGAIN!!
I'M SICK OF BEING A CYBORG WARRIOR!
WELL IT'S WAY TOO LATE FOR THAT, #44. I DESTROYED AND DISPOSED OF ALL YOUR DOG ORGANS. I ONLY KEPT YOUR FUR AND NEURAL MATTER!
PLEASE, DR. JUNKOVITCH... AT LEAST MAKE ME **LOOK** LIKE A DOG AGAIN...

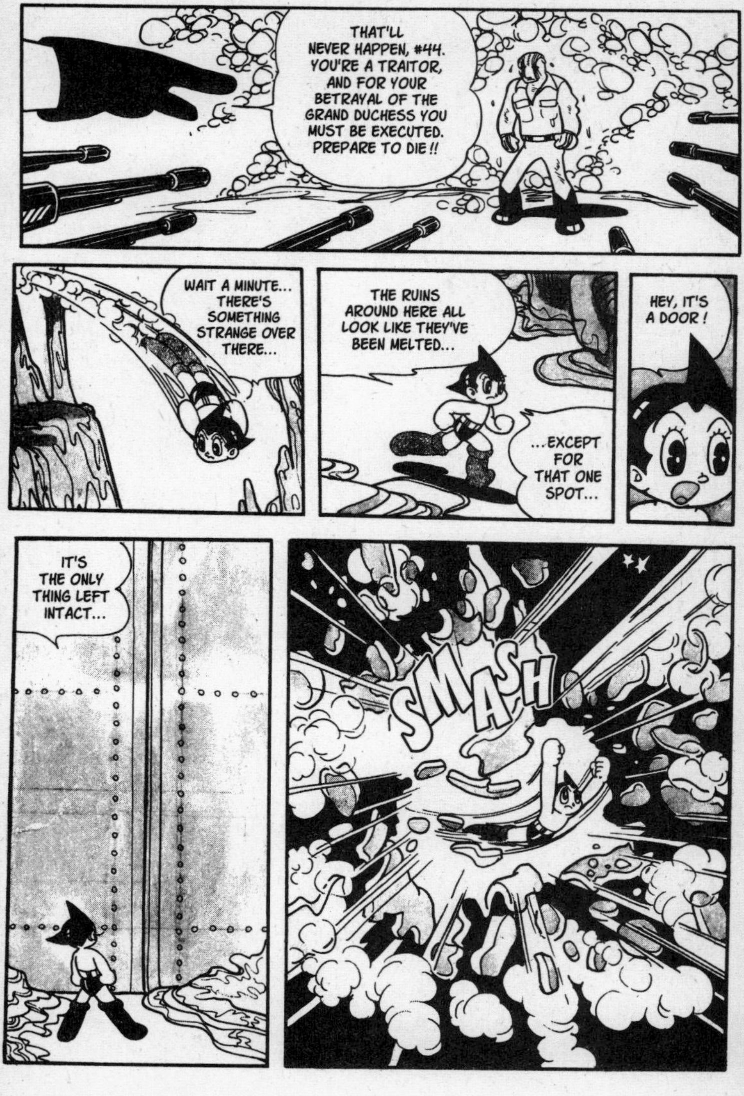
THAT'LL NEVER HAPPEN, #44. YOU'RE A TRAITOR, AND FOR YOUR BETRAYAL OF THE GRAND DUCHESS YOU MUST BE EXECUTED. PREPARE TO DIE!!
WAIT A MINUTE... THERE'S SOMETHING STRANGE OVER THERE...
THE RUINS AROUND HERE ALL LOOK LIKE THEY'VE BEEN MELTED...
...EXCEPT FOR THAT ONE SPOT...
HEY, IT'S A DOOR!
IT'S THE ONLY THING LEFT INTACT...
SMASH

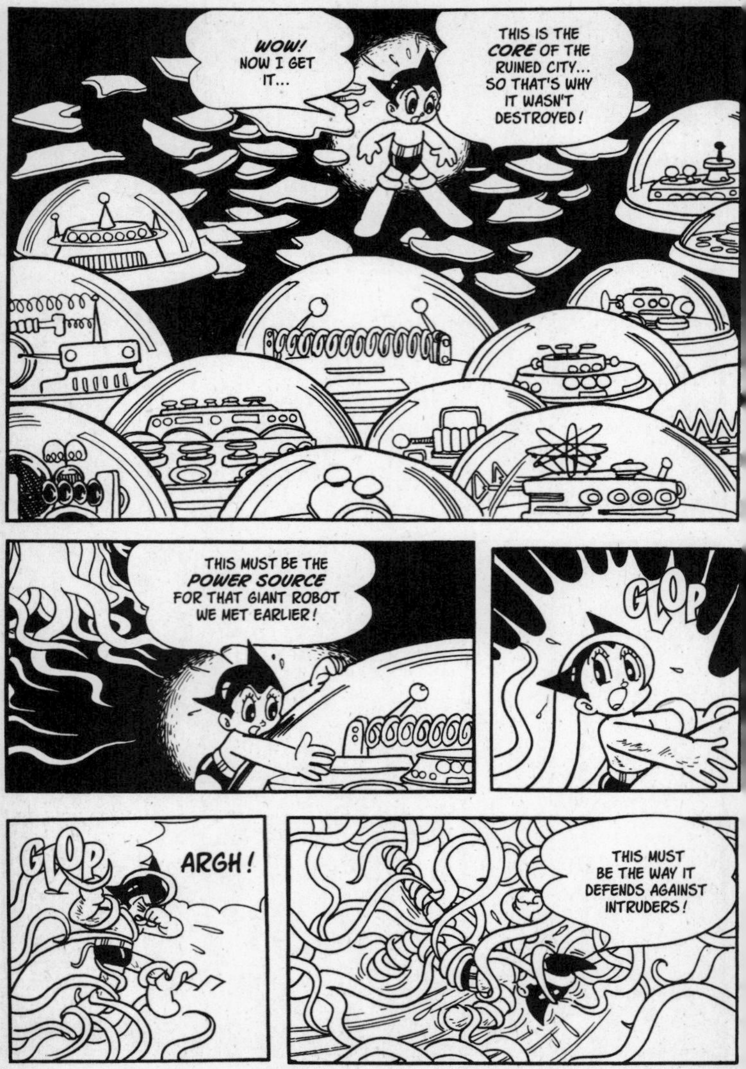
WOW! NOW I GET IT...
THIS IS THE CORE OF THE RUINED CITY... SO THAT'S WHY IT WASN'T DESTROYED!
THIS MUST BE THE POWER SOURCE FOR THAT GIANT ROBOT WE MET EARLIER!
GLOP
GLOP
ARGH!
THIS MUST BE THE WAY IT DEFENDS AGAINST INTRUDERS!

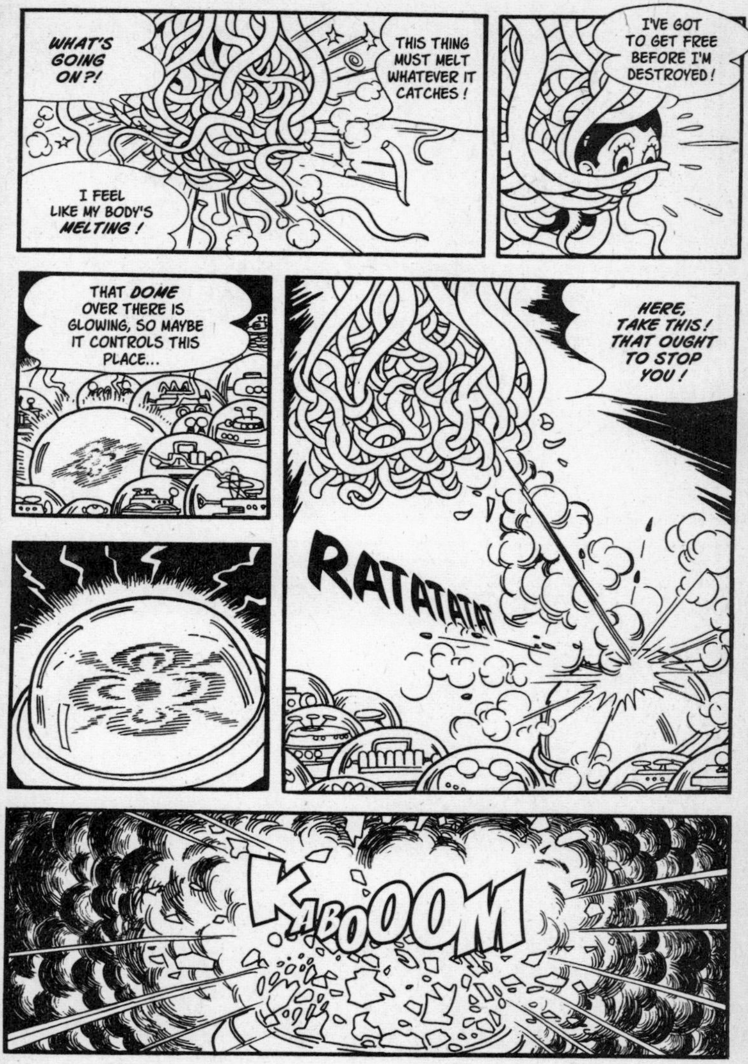
WHAT'S GOING ON?!
THIS THING MUST MELT WHATEVER IT CATCHES!
I FEEL LIKE MY BODY'S MELTING!
I'VE GOT TO GET FREE BEFORE I'M DESTROYED!
THAT DOME OVER THERE IS GLOWING, SO MAYBE IT CONTROLS THIS PLACE...
HERE, TAKE THIS! THAT OUGHT TO STOP YOU!
RATATATAT
KABOOOOM

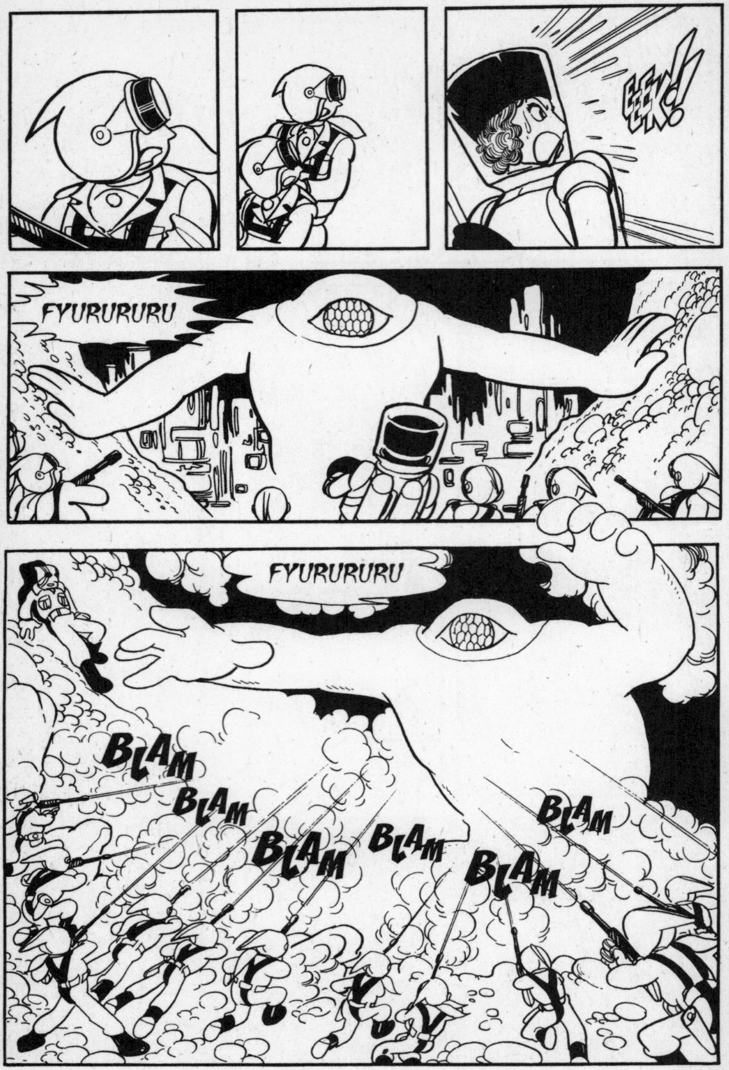
EEEK!!
FYURURURU
FYURURURU
BLAM
BLAM
BLAM
BLAM
BLAM
BLAM

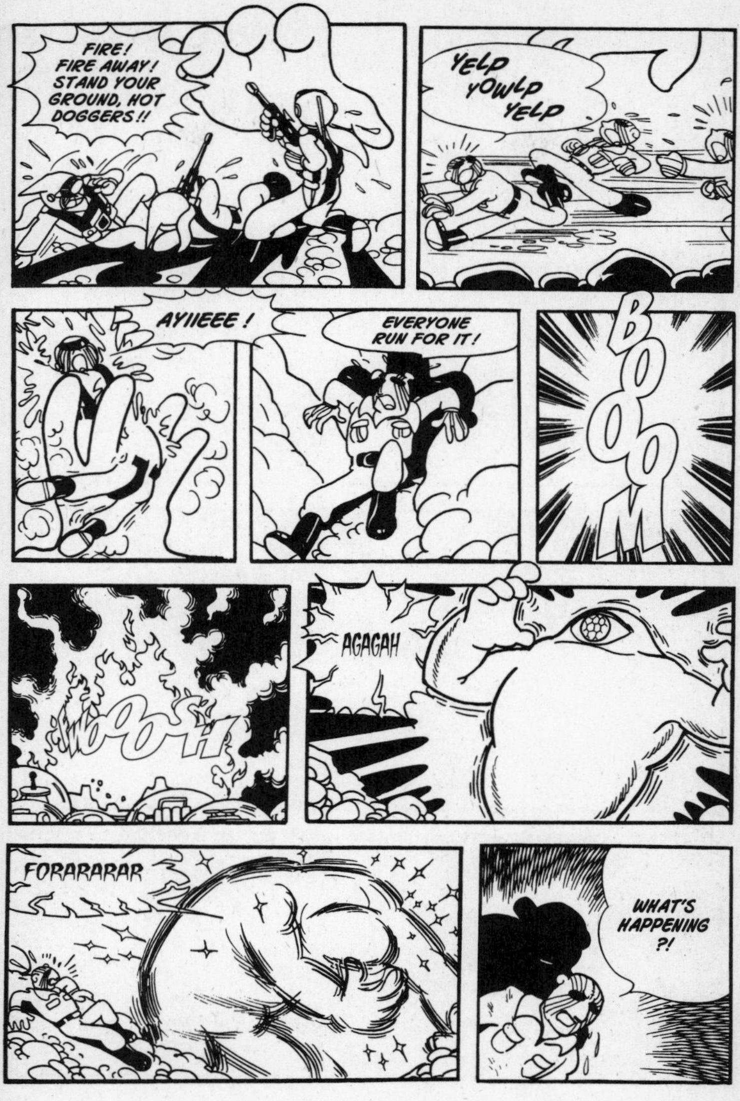
FIRE! FIRE AWAY! STAND YOUR GROUND, HOT DOGGERS!!
YELP YOWLP YELP
AYIIEEE!
EVERYONE RUN FOR IT!
BOOOOM
WOOSH
AGAGAH
FORARARAR
WHAT'S HAPPENING ?!

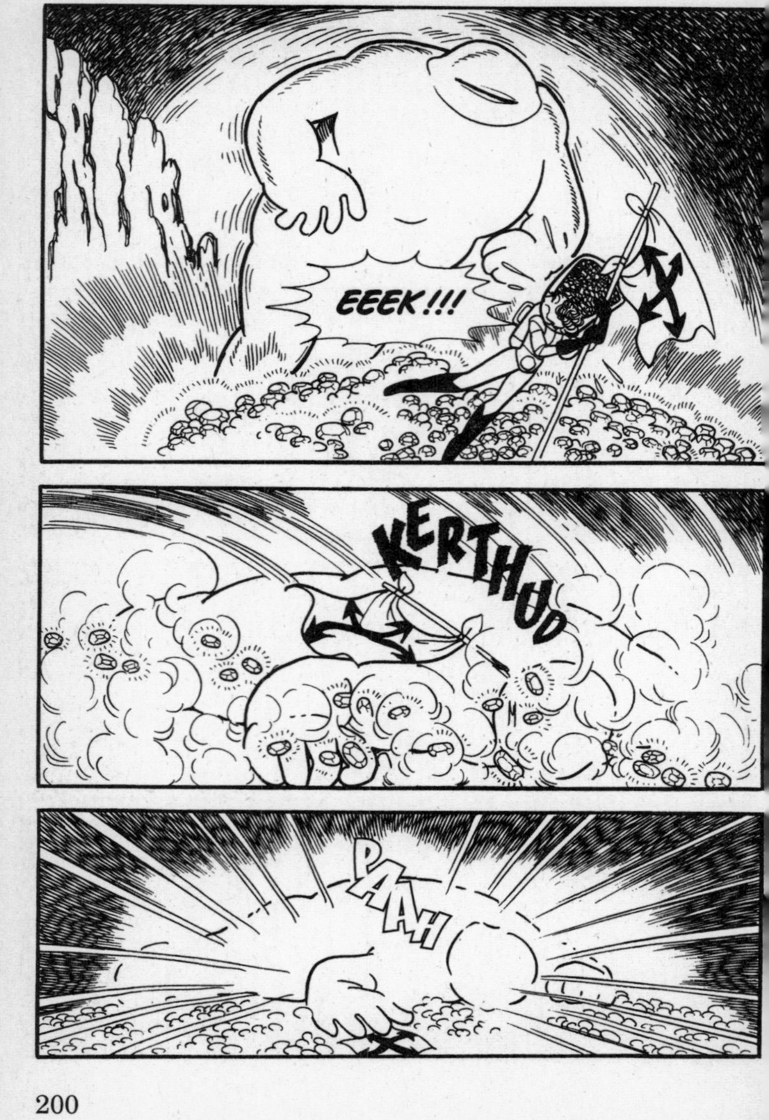
EEEK!!!
KERTHUD
PAAAH

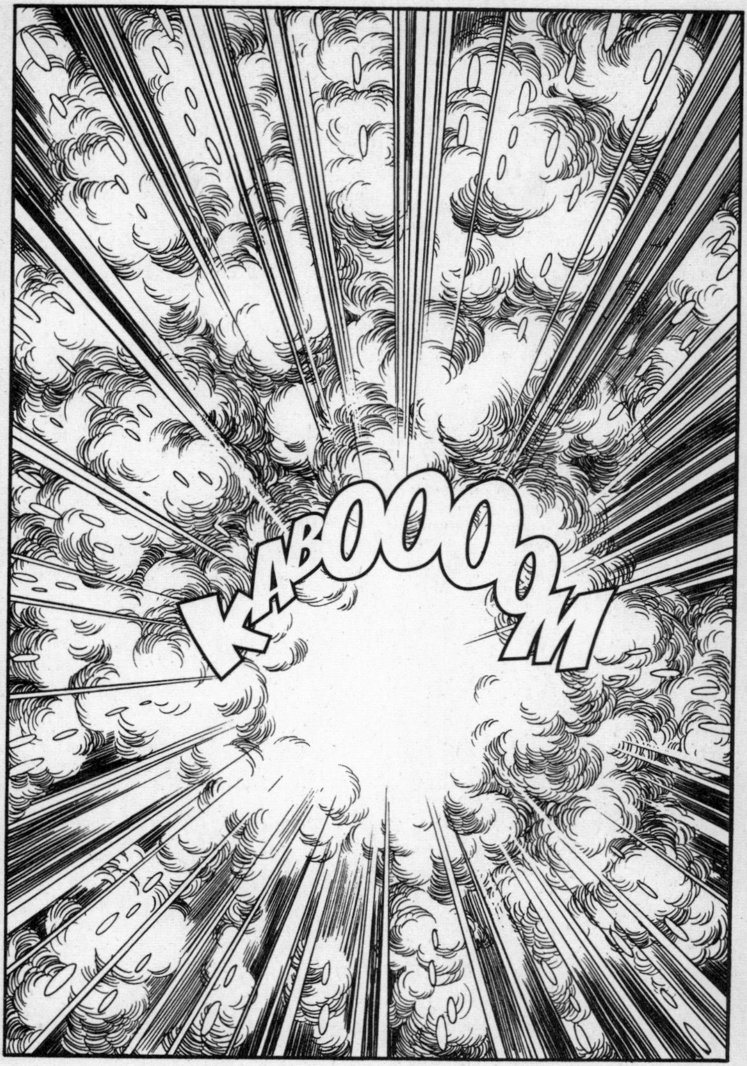
KABOOOOOM

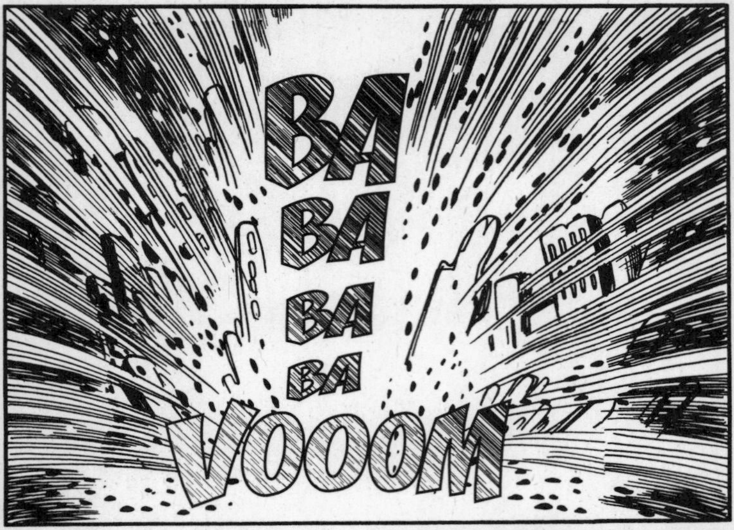
BA
BA
BA
BA
VOOOM

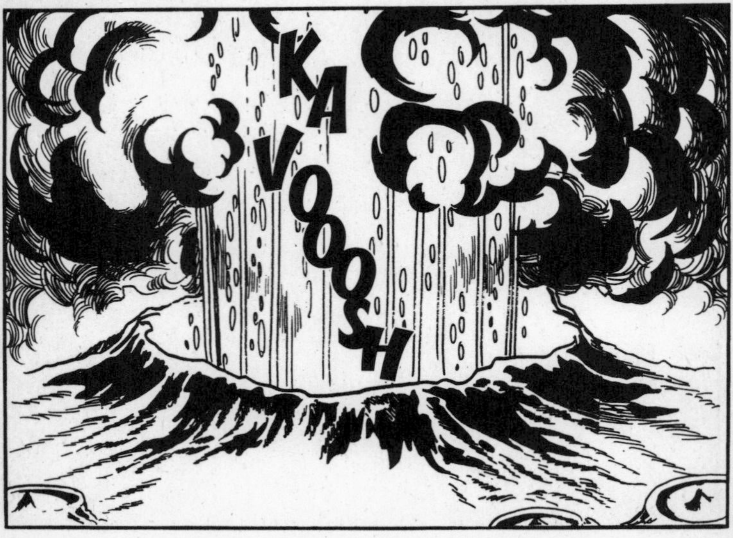
KA
VOOOSH

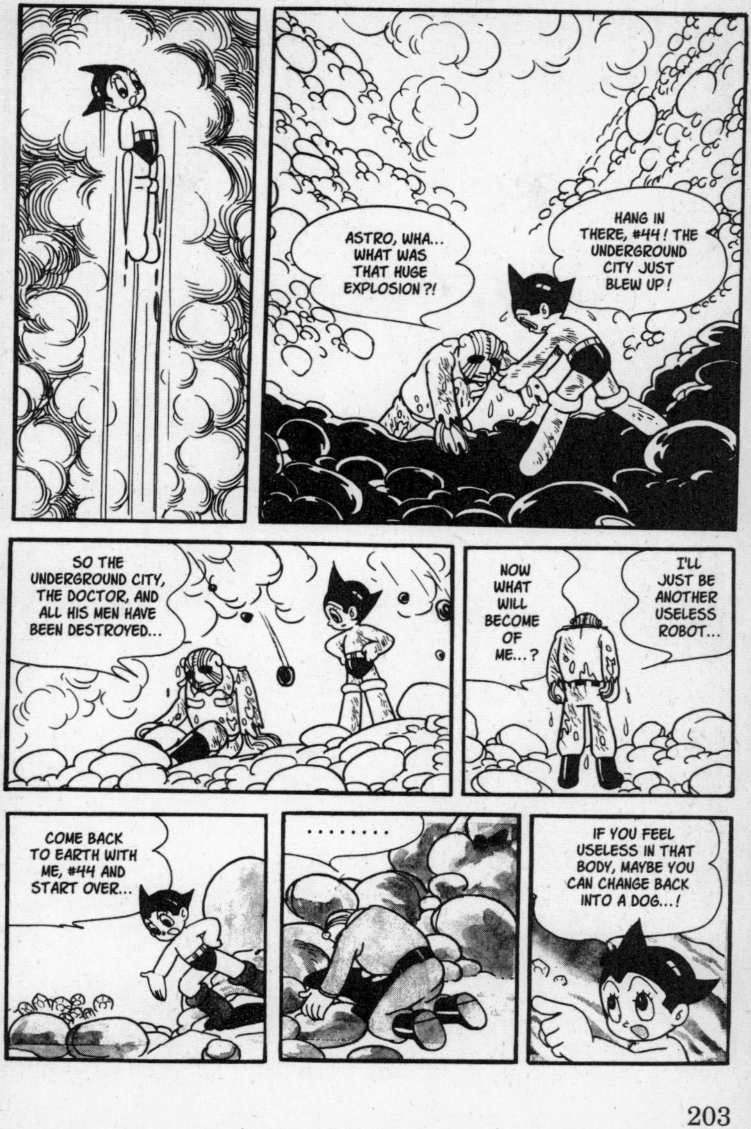
ASTRO, WHA... WHAT WAS THAT HUGE EXPLOSION?!
HANG IN THERE, #44! THE UNDERGROUND CITY JUST BLEW UP!
SO THE UNDERGROUND CITY, THE DOCTOR, AND ALL HIS MEN HAVE BEEN DESTROYED...
NOW WHAT WILL BECOME OF ME...?
I'LL JUST BE ANOTHER USELESS ROBOT...
COME BACK TO EARTH WITH ME, #44 AND START OVER...
....
IF YOU FEEL USELESS IN THAT BODY, MAYBE YOU CAN CHANGE BACK INTO A DOG...!

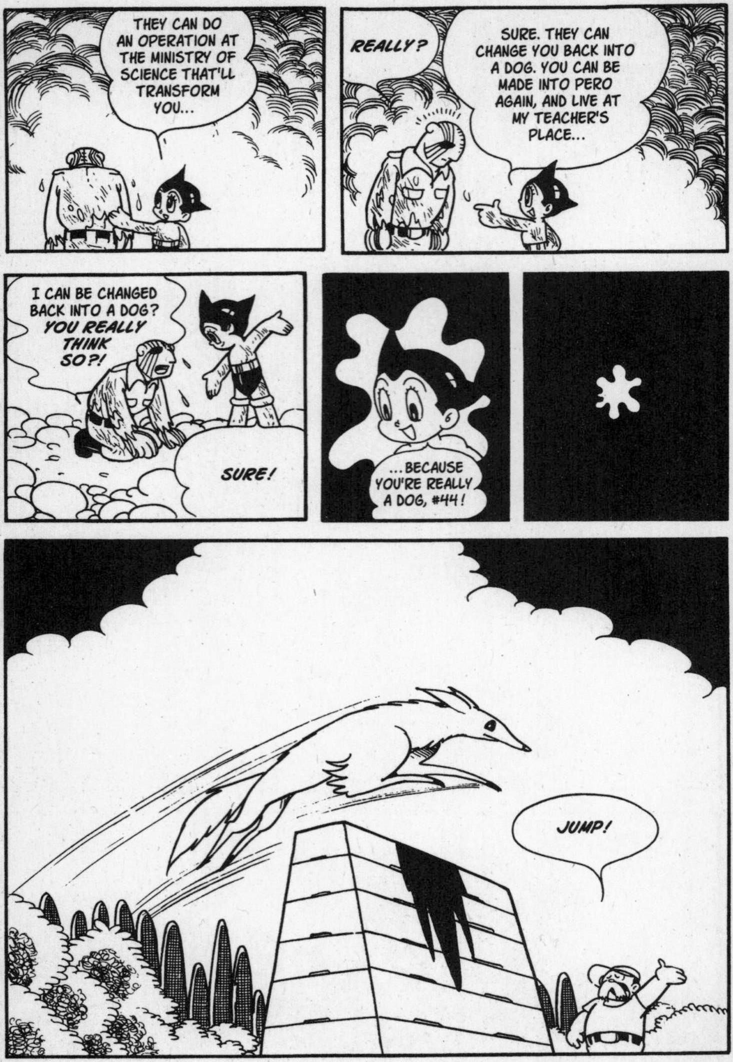
THEY CAN DO AN OPERATION AT THE MINISTRY OF SCIENCE THAT'LL TRANSFORM YOU...
REALLY?
SURE. THEY CAN CHANGE YOU BACK INTO A DOG. YOU CAN BE MADE INTO PERO AGAIN, AND LIVE AT MY TEACHER'S PLACE...
I CAN BE CHANGED BACK INTO A DOG? YOU REALLY THINK SO?!
SURE!
...BECAUSE YOU'RE REALLY A DOG, #44!
JUMP!

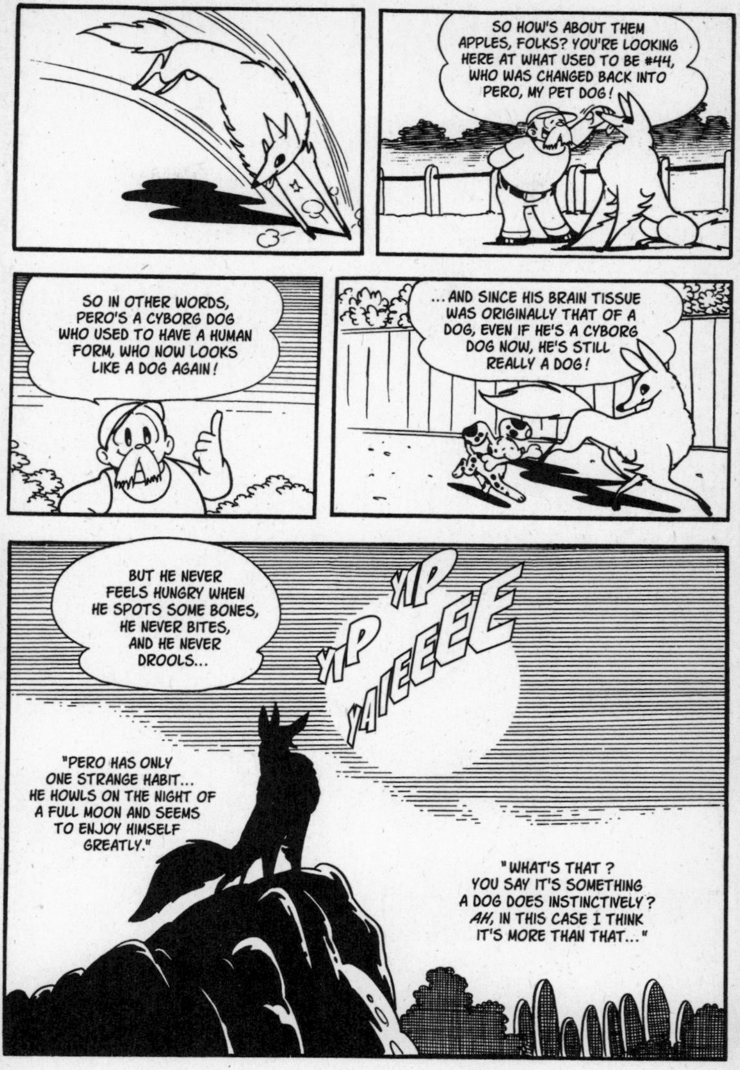

SO HOW'S ABOUT THEM APPLES, FOLKS? YOU'RE LOOKING HERE AT WHAT USED TO BE #44, WHO WAS CHANGED BACK INTO PERO, MY PET DOG!
SO IN OTHER WORDS, PERO'S A CYBORG DOG WHO USED TO HAVE A HUMAN FORM, WHO NOW LOOKS LIKE A DOG AGAIN!
...AND SINCE HIS BRAIN TISSUE WAS ORIGINALLY THAT OF A DOG, EVEN IF HE'S A CYBORG DOG NOW, HE'S STILL REALLY A DOG!
BUT HE NEVER FEELS HUNGRY WHEN HE SPOTS SOME BONES, HE NEVER BITES, AND HE NEVER DROOLS...
YIP YIP YAIEEEEE
"PERO HAS ONLY ONE STRANGE HABIT... HE HOWLS ON THE NIGHT OF A FULL MOON AND SEEMS TO ENJOY HIMSELF GREATLY."
"WHAT'S THAT? YOU SAY IT'S SOMETHING A DOG DOES INSTINCTIVELY? AH, IN THIS CASE I THINK IT'S MORE THAN THAT..."

PLANT PEOPLE

First published in the special expanded 1961
New Year's Day edition of *Shonen* magazine.

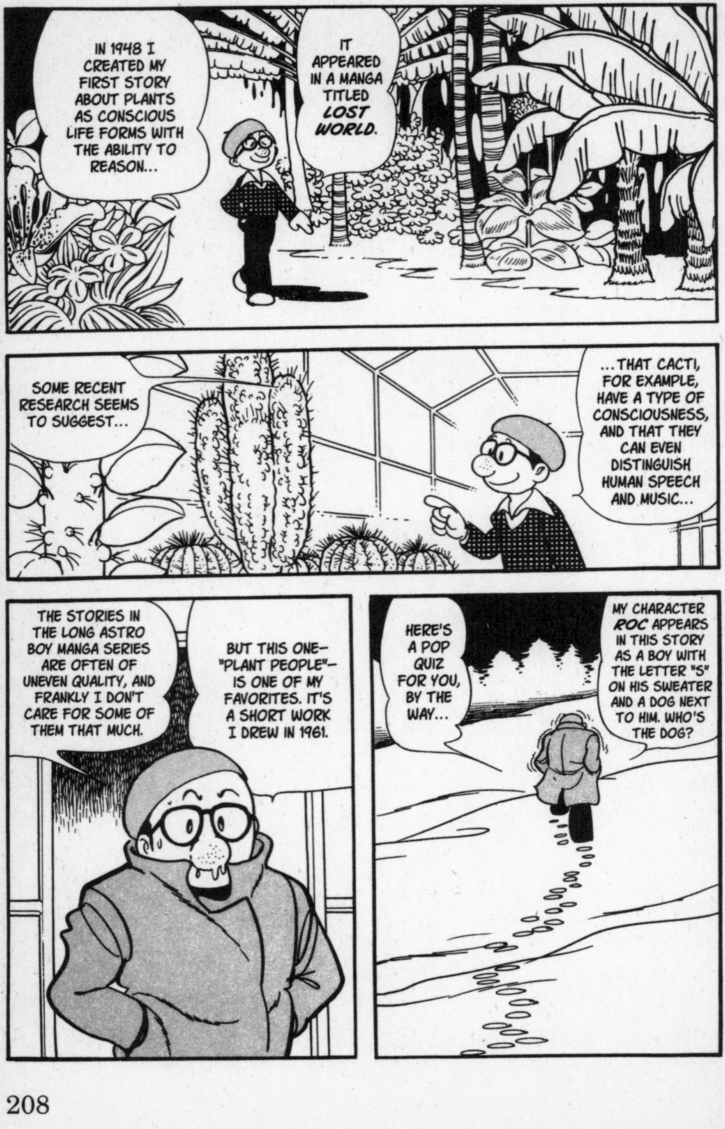
IN 1948 I CREATED MY FIRST STORY ABOUT PLANTS AS CONSCIOUS LIFE FORMS WITH THE ABILITY TO REASON...
IT APPEARED IN A MANGA TITLED *LOST WORLD*.
SOME RECENT RESEARCH SEEMS TO SUGGEST...
...THAT CACTI, FOR EXAMPLE, HAVE A TYPE OF CONSCIOUSNESS, AND THAT THEY CAN EVEN DISTINGUISH HUMAN SPEECH AND MUSIC...
THE STORIES IN THE LONG ASTRO BOY MANGA SERIES ARE OFTEN OF UNEVEN QUALITY, AND FRANKLY I DON'T CARE FOR SOME OF THEM THAT MUCH.
BUT THIS ONE—"PLANT PEOPLE"—IS ONE OF MY FAVORITES. IT'S A SHORT WORK I DREW IN 1961.
HERE'S A POP QUIZ FOR YOU, BY THE WAY...
MY CHARACTER *ROC* APPEARS IN THIS STORY AS A BOY WITH THE LETTER "S" ON HIS SWEATER AND A DOG NEXT TO HIM. WHO'S THE DOG?

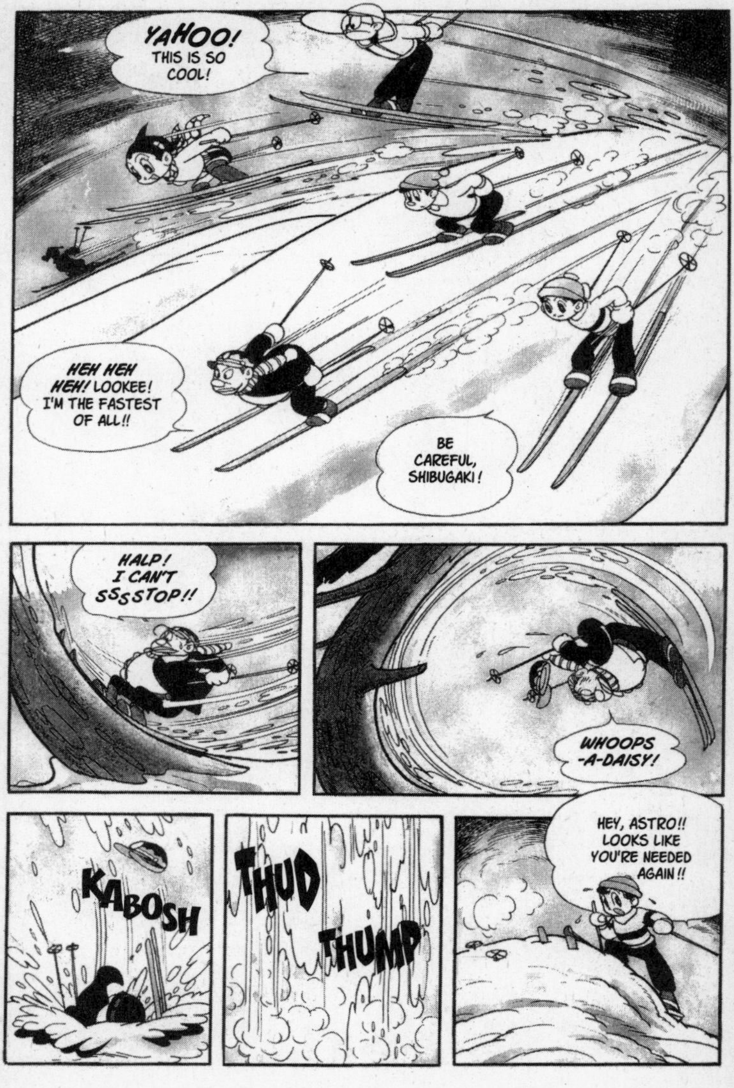
YAHOO! THIS IS SO COOL!
HEH HEH HEH! LOOKEE! I'M THE FASTEST OF ALL!!
BE CAREFUL, SHIBUGAKI!
HALP! I CAN'T SSSSTOP!!
WHOOPS -A-DAISY!
KABOSH
THUD
THUMP
HEY, ASTRO!! LOOKS LIKE YOU'RE NEEDED AGAIN!!

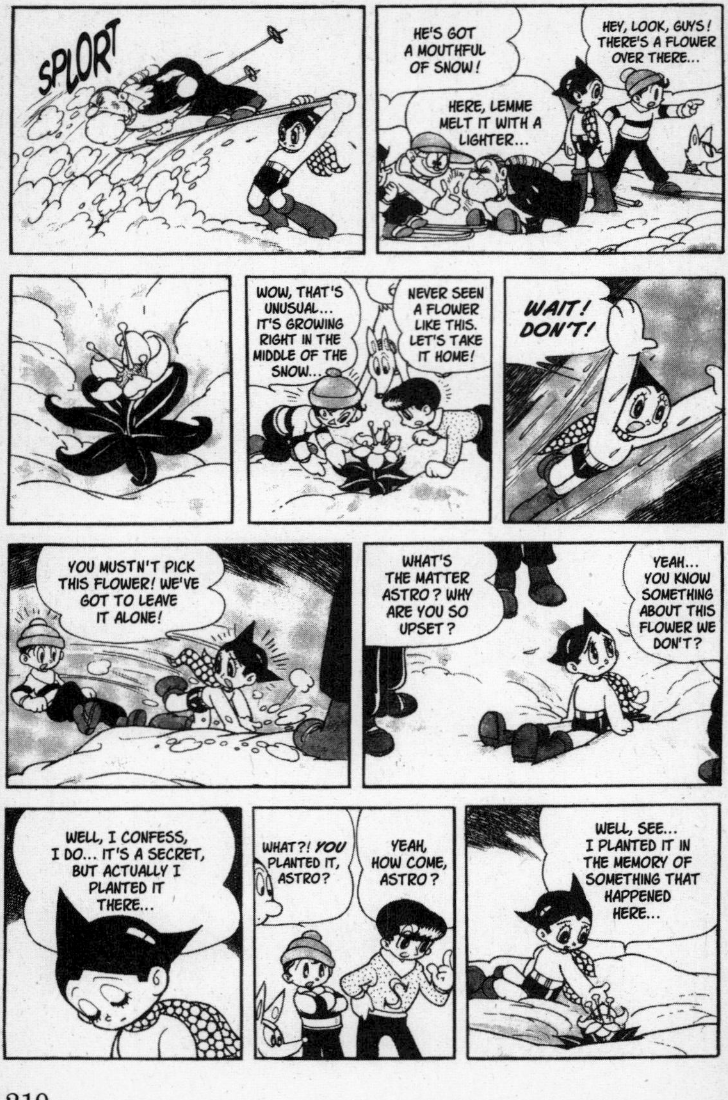

SPLORT
HE'S GOT A MOUTHFUL OF SNOW!
HEY, LOOK, GUYS! THERE'S A FLOWER OVER THERE...
HERE, LEMME MELT IT WITH A LIGHTER...
WOW, THAT'S UNUSUAL... IT'S GROWING RIGHT IN THE MIDDLE OF THE SNOW...
NEVER SEEN A FLOWER LIKE THIS. LET'S TAKE IT HOME!
WAIT! DON'T!
YOU MUSTN'T PICK THIS FLOWER! WE'VE GOT TO LEAVE IT ALONE!
WHAT'S THE MATTER ASTRO? WHY ARE YOU SO UPSET?
YEAH... YOU KNOW SOMETHING ABOUT THIS FLOWER WE DON'T?
WELL, I CONFESS, I DO... IT'S A SECRET, BUT ACTUALLY I PLANTED IT THERE...
WHAT?! YOU PLANTED IT, ASTRO?
YEAH, HOW COME, ASTRO?
WELL, SEE... I PLANTED IT IN THE MEMORY OF SOMETHING THAT HAPPENED HERE...

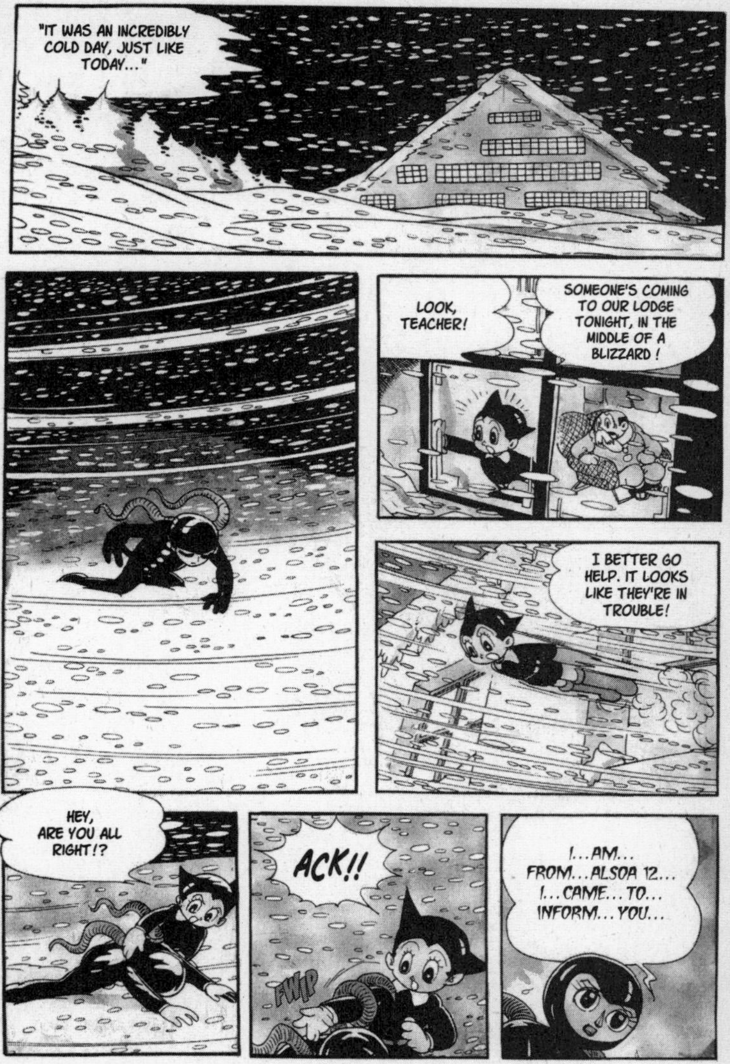
"IT WAS AN INCREDIBLY COLD DAY, JUST LIKE TODAY..."
LOOK, TEACHER!
SOMEONE'S COMING TO OUR LODGE TONIGHT, IN THE MIDDLE OF A BLIZZARD!
I BETTER GO HELP. IT LOOKS LIKE THEY'RE IN TROUBLE!
HEY, ARE YOU ALL RIGHT!?
ACK!!
FWIP
I...AM... FROM...ALSOA 12... I...CAME...TO... INFORM...YOU...

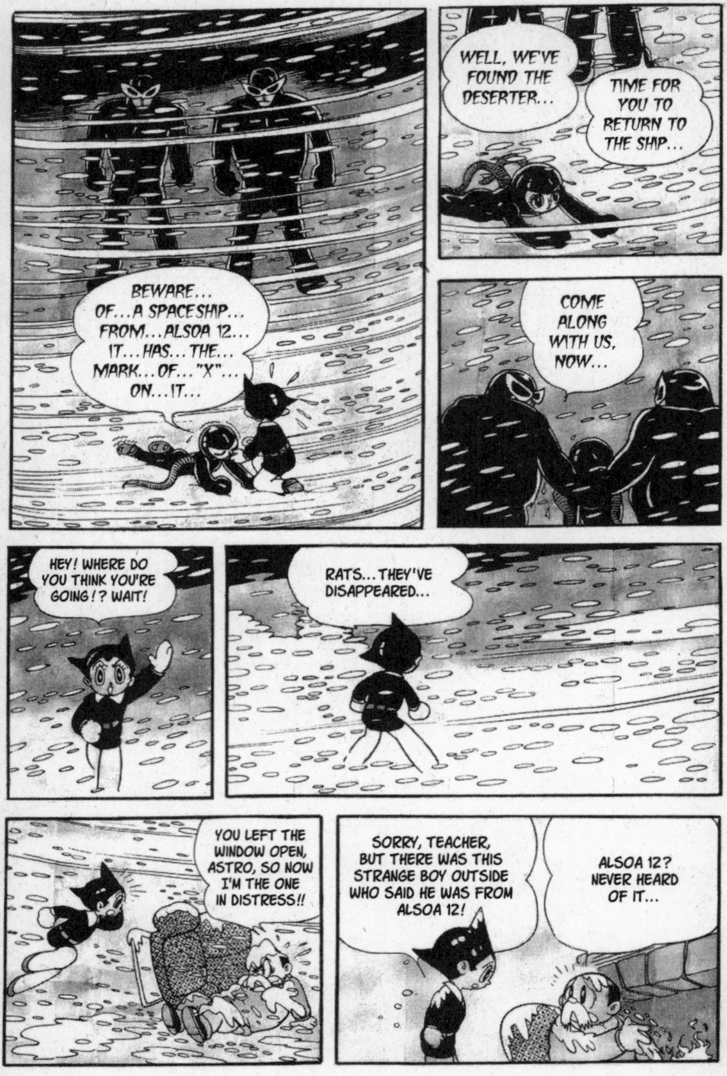
BEWARE... OF...A SPACESHIP... FROM...ALSOA 12... IT...HAS...THE... MARK...OF..."X"... ON...IT...
WELL, WE'VE FOUND THE DESERTER...
TIME FOR YOU TO RETURN TO THE SHIP...
COME ALONG WITH US, NOW...
HEY! WHERE DO YOU THINK YOU'RE GOING!? WAIT!
RATS...THEY'VE DISAPPEARED...
YOU LEFT THE WINDOW OPEN, ASTRO, SO NOW I'M THE ONE IN DISTRESS!!
SORRY, TEACHER, BUT THERE WAS THIS STRANGE BOY OUTSIDE WHO SAID HE WAS FROM ALSOA 12!
ALSOA 12? NEVER HEARD OF IT...

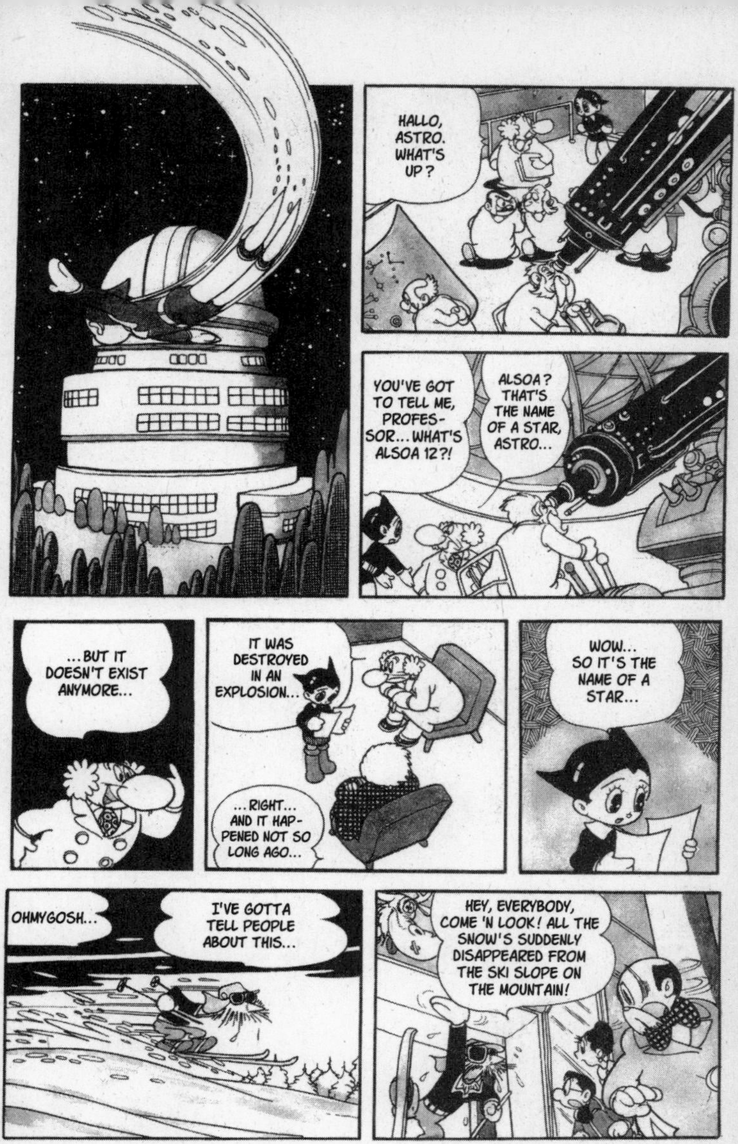
HALLO, ASTRO. WHAT'S UP?
YOU'VE GOT TO TELL ME, PROFES-SOR... WHAT'S ALSOA 12?!
ALSOA? THAT'S THE NAME OF A STAR, ASTRO...
...BUT IT DOESN'T EXIST ANYMORE...
IT WAS DESTROYED IN AN EXPLOSION...
...RIGHT... AND IT HAP-PENED NOT SO LONG AGO...
WOW... SO IT'S THE NAME OF A STAR...
OHMYGOSH...
I'VE GOTTA TELL PEOPLE ABOUT THIS...
HEY, EVERYBODY, COME 'N LOOK! ALL THE SNOW'S SUDDENLY DISAPPEARED FROM THE SKI SLOPE ON THE MOUNTAIN!

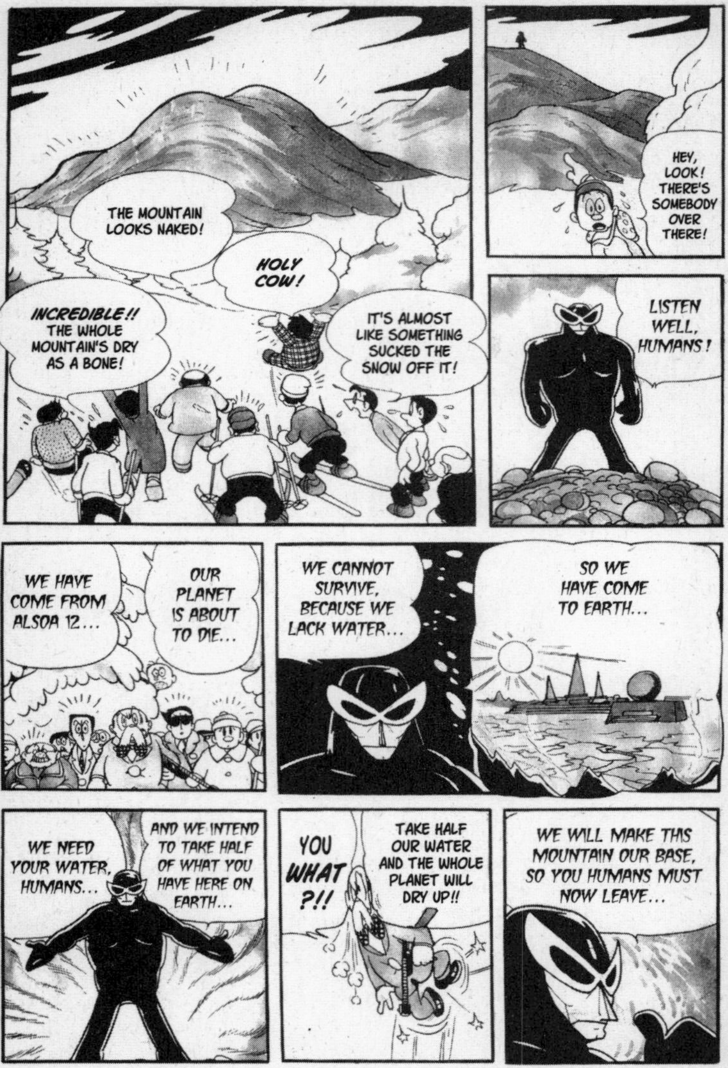
THE MOUNTAIN LOOKS NAKED!
HOLY COW!
INCREDIBLE!! THE WHOLE MOUNTAIN'S DRY AS A BONE!
IT'S ALMOST LIKE SOMETHING SUCKED THE SNOW OFF IT!
HEY, LOOK! THERE'S SOMEBODY OVER THERE!
LISTEN WELL, HUMANS!
WE HAVE COME FROM ALSOA 12…
OUR PLANET IS ABOUT TO DIE…
WE CANNOT SURVIVE, BECAUSE WE LACK WATER…
SO WE HAVE COME TO EARTH…
WE NEED YOUR WATER, HUMANS…
AND WE INTEND TO TAKE HALF OF WHAT YOU HAVE HERE ON EARTH…
YOU WHAT?!!
TAKE HALF OUR WATER AND THE WHOLE PLANET WILL DRY UP!!
WE WILL MAKE THIS MOUNTAIN OUR BASE, SO YOU HUMANS MUST NOW LEAVE…

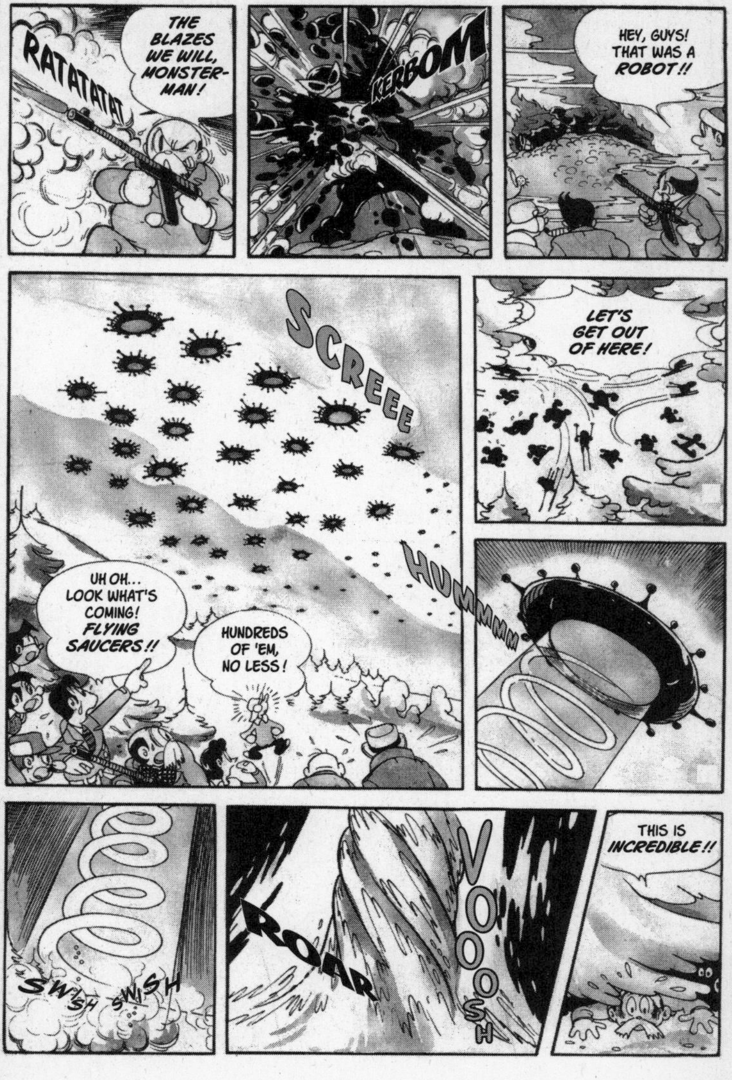
RATATATAT
THE BLAZES WE WILL, MONSTER-MAN!
KERBOM
HEY, GUYS! THAT WAS A ROBOT!!
SCREEEE
UH OH... LOOK WHAT'S COMING! FLYING SAUCERS!!
HUNDREDS OF 'EM, NO LESS!
HUMMMMM
LET'S GET OUT OF HERE!
SWISH SWISH
ROAR
VOOOOSH
THIS IS INCREDIBLE!!

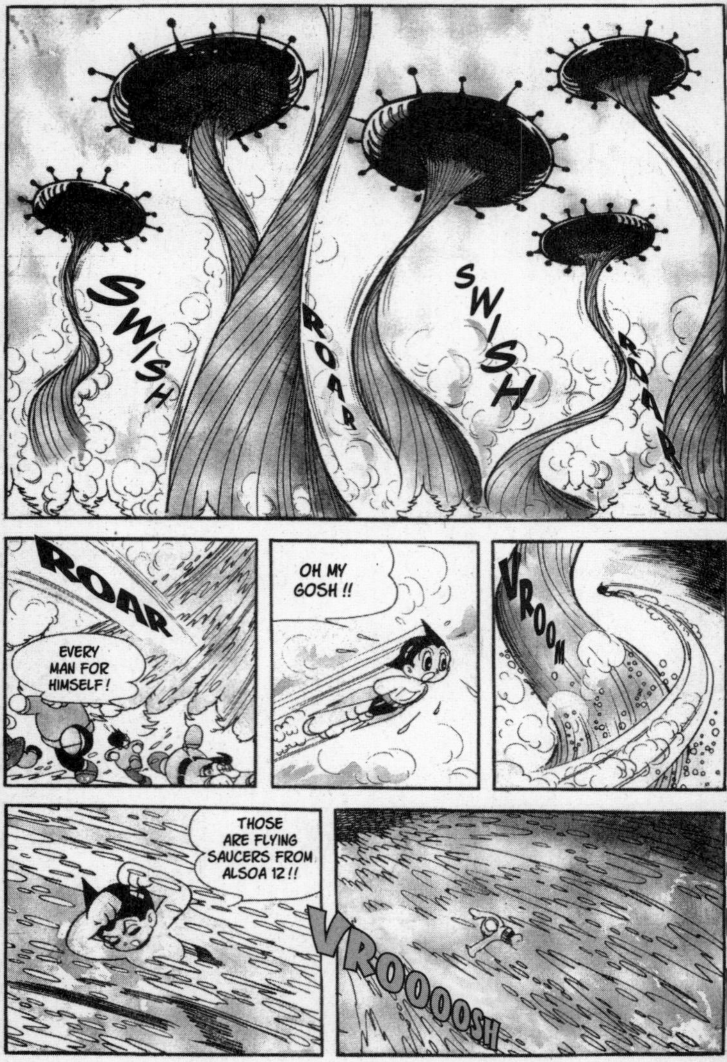
SWISH
ROAR
SWISH
ROAR
ROAR
EVERY MAN FOR HIMSELF!
OH MY GOSH!!
VROOM
THOSE ARE FLYING SAUCERS FROM ALSOA 12!!
VROOOOOSH

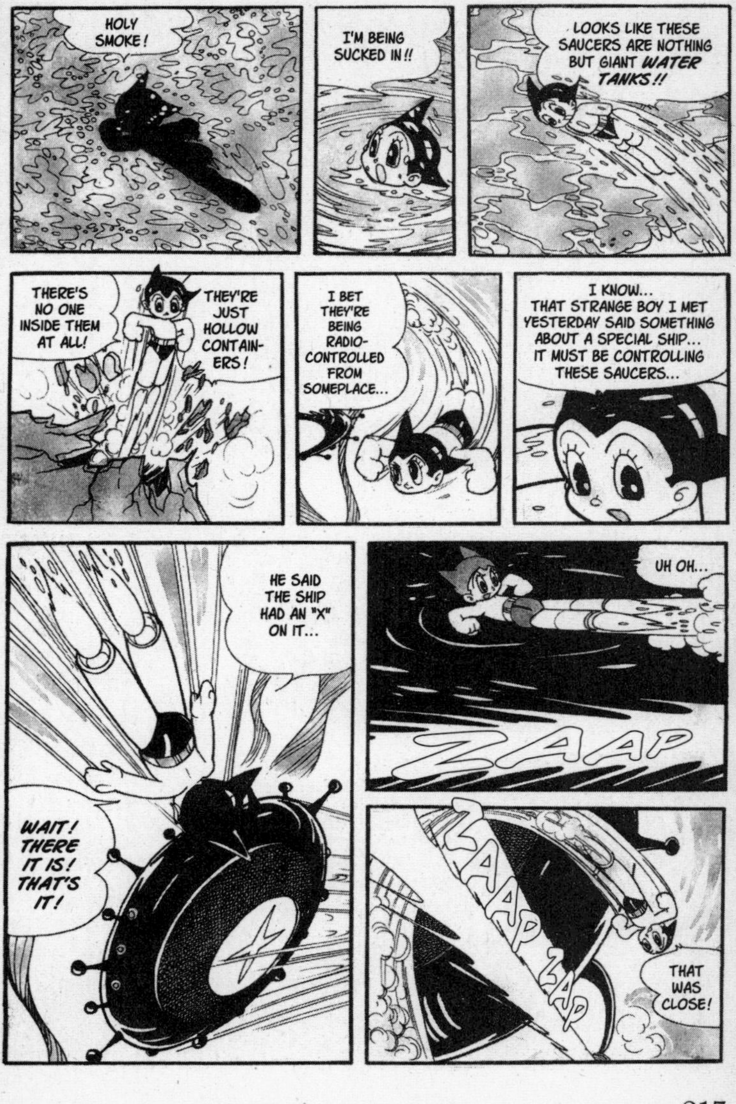
HOLY SMOKE!
I'M BEING SUCKED IN!!
LOOKS LIKE THESE SAUCERS ARE NOTHING BUT GIANT *WATER TANKS!!*
THERE'S NO ONE INSIDE THEM AT ALL!
THEY'RE JUST HOLLOW CONTAIN-ERS!
I BET THEY'RE BEING RADIO-CONTROLLED FROM SOMEPLACE...
I KNOW... THAT STRANGE BOY I MET YESTERDAY SAID SOMETHING ABOUT A SPECIAL SHIP... IT MUST BE CONTROLLING THESE SAUCERS...
HE SAID THE SHIP HAD AN "X" ON IT...
WAIT! THERE IT IS! THAT'S IT!
UH OH...
ZAAP
ZAAP
ZAAP
THAT WAS CLOSE!

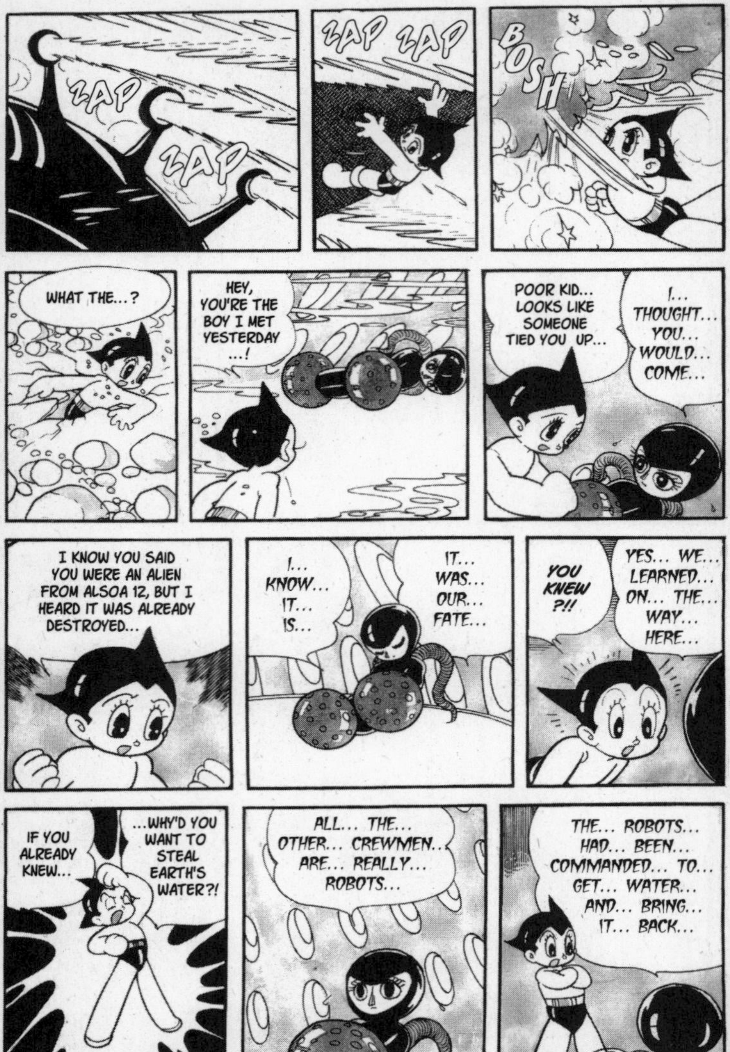
ZAP
ZAP
ZAP ZAP
BOSH
WHAT THE...?
HEY, YOU'RE THE BOY I MET YESTERDAY ...!
POOR KID... LOOKS LIKE SOMEONE TIED YOU UP...
I... THOUGHT... YOU... WOULD... COME...
I KNOW YOU SAID YOU WERE AN ALIEN FROM ALSOA 12, BUT I HEARD IT WAS ALREADY DESTROYED...
I... KNOW... IT... IS...
IT... WAS... OUR... FATE...
YOU KNEW ?!!
YES... WE... LEARNED... ON... THE... WAY... HERE...
IF YOU ALREADY KNEW...
...WHY'D YOU WANT TO STEAL EARTH'S WATER?!
ALL... THE... OTHER... CREWMEN... ARE... REALLY... ROBOTS...
THE... ROBOTS... HAD... BEEN... COMMANDED... TO... GET... WATER... AND... BRING... IT... BACK...

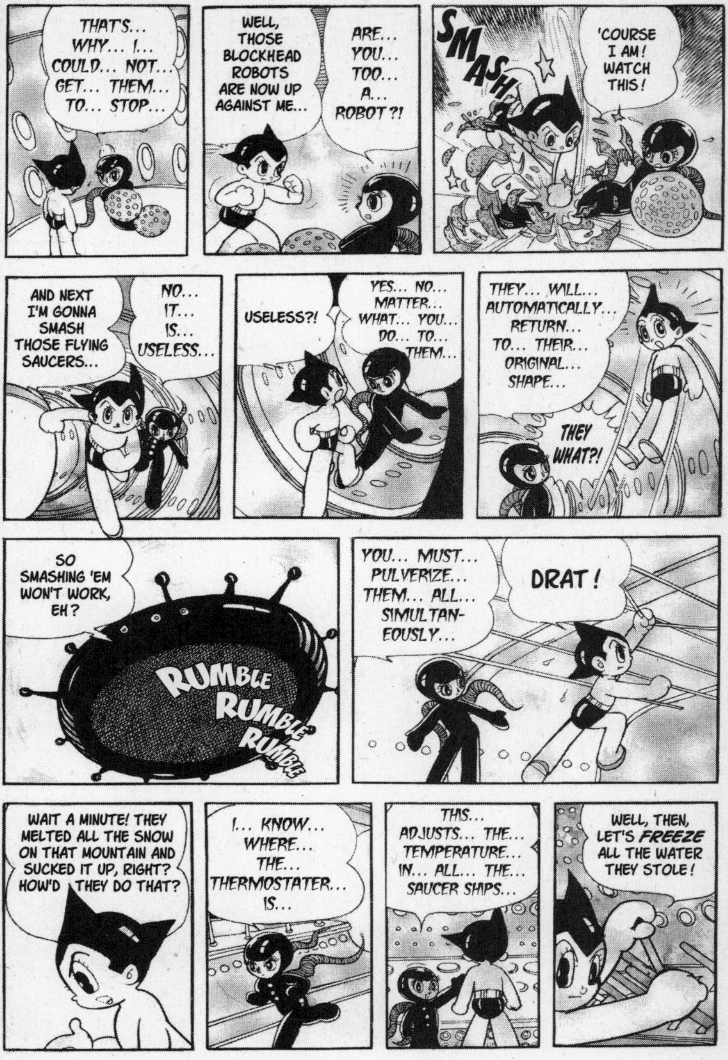
THAT'S... WHY... I... COULD... NOT... GET... THEM... TO... STOP...
WELL, THOSE BLOCKHEAD ROBOTS ARE NOW UP AGAINST ME...
ARE... YOU... TOO... A... ROBOT?!
SMASH
'COURSE I AM! WATCH THIS!
AND NEXT I'M GONNA SMASH THOSE FLYING SAUCERS...
NO... IT... IS... USELESS...
USELESS?!
YES... NO... MATTER... WHAT... YOU... DO... TO... THEM...
THEY... WILL... AUTOMATICALLY... RETURN... TO... THEIR... ORIGINAL... SHAPE...
THEY WHAT?!
SO SMASHING 'EM WON'T WORK, EH?
RUMBLE RUMBLE RUMBLE
YOU... MUST... PULVERIZE... THEM... ALL... SIMULTAN-EOUSLY...
DRAT!
WAIT A MINUTE! THEY MELTED ALL THE SNOW ON THAT MOUNTAIN AND SUCKED IT UP, RIGHT? HOW'D THEY DO THAT?
I... KNOW... WHERE... THE... THERMOSTATER... IS...
THIS... ADJUSTS... THE... TEMPERATURE... IN... ALL... THE... SAUCER SHIPS...
WELL, THEN, LET'S *FREEZE* ALL THE WATER THEY STOLE!

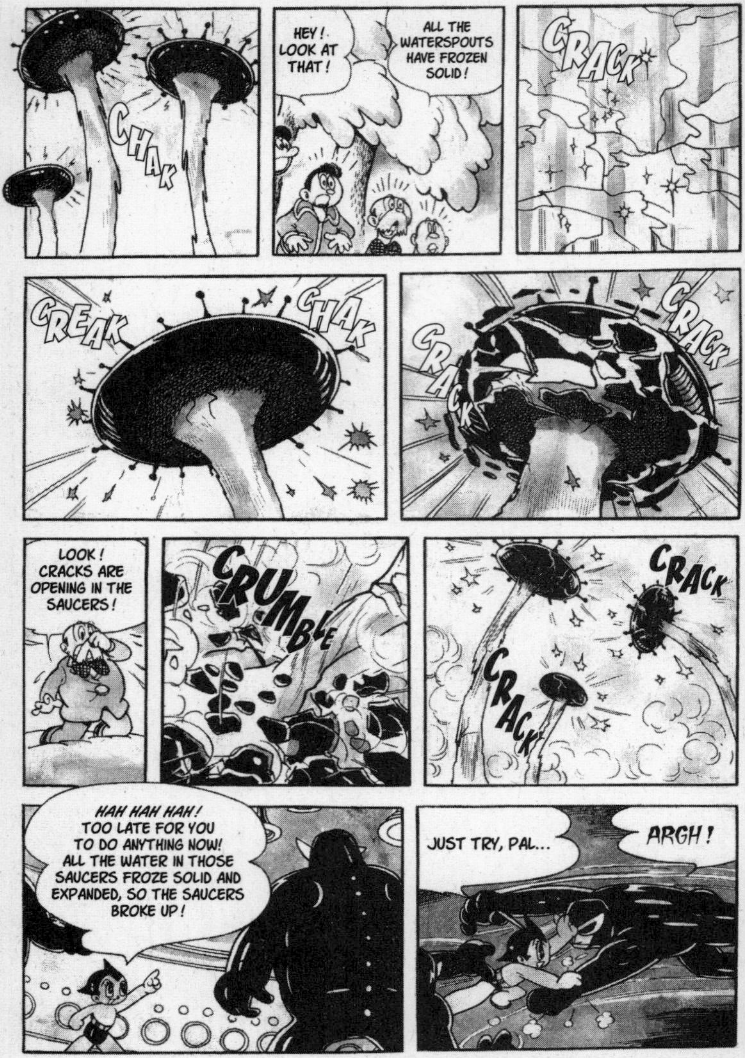
CHAK
HEY! LOOK AT THAT!
ALL THE WATERSPOUTS HAVE FROZEN SOLID!
CRACK
CREAK
CHAK
CRACK
CRACK
LOOK! CRACKS ARE OPENING IN THE SAUCERS!
CRUMBLE
CRACK
CRACK
HAH HAH HAH! TOO LATE FOR YOU TO DO ANYTHING NOW! ALL THE WATER IN THOSE SAUCERS FROZE SOLID AND EXPANDED, SO THE SAUCERS BROKE UP!
JUST TRY, PAL...
ARGH!

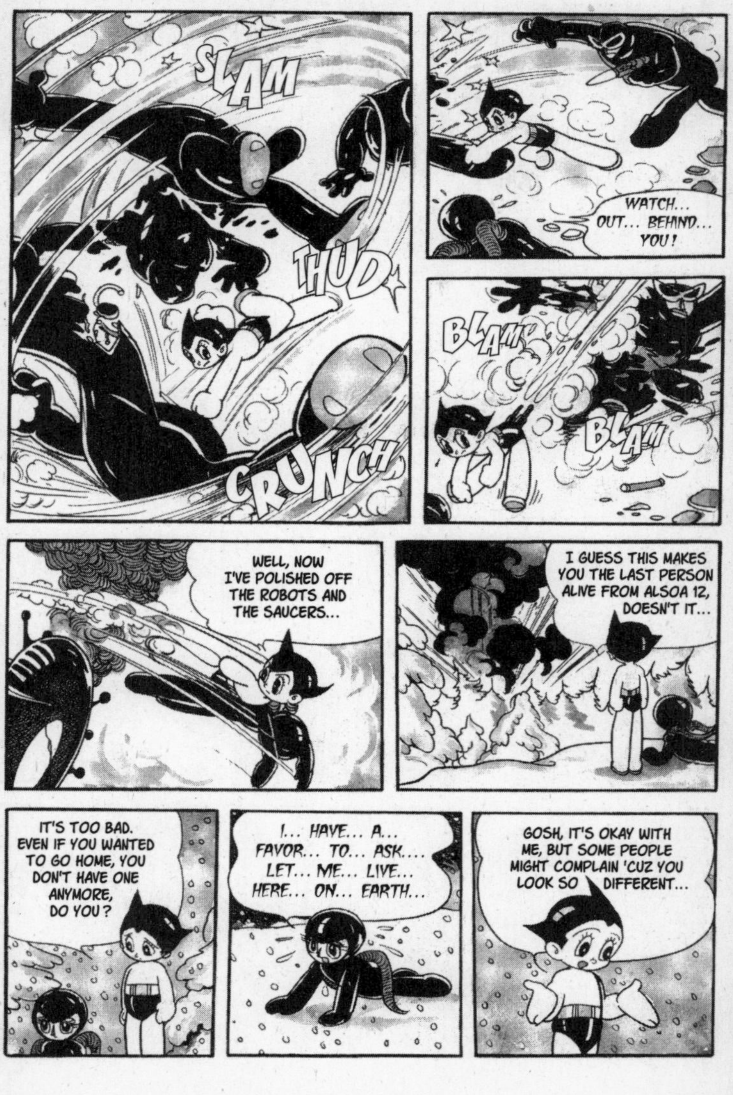
SLAM
THUD
CRUNCH
WATCH... OUT... BEHIND... YOU!
BLAM
BLAM
WELL, NOW I'VE POLISHED OFF THE ROBOTS AND THE SAUCERS...
I GUESS THIS MAKES YOU THE LAST PERSON ALIVE FROM ALSOA 12, DOESN'T IT...
IT'S TOO BAD. EVEN IF YOU WANTED TO GO HOME, YOU DON'T HAVE ONE ANYMORE, DO YOU?
I... HAVE... A... FAVOR... TO... ASK.... LET... ME... LIVE... HERE... ON... EARTH...
GOSH, IT'S OKAY WITH ME, BUT SOME PEOPLE MIGHT COMPLAIN 'CUZ YOU LOOK SO DIFFERENT...

AH... BUT... MY... PEOPLE... KNOW... HOW... TO... LIVE... HERE... AND... NOT... BE... CONSPICUOUS...

WHAT'S HAPPENING?

YOUR BACK HAS SPLIT OPEN AND I CAN SEE YOUR INSIDES!!

THIS IS PLANT MATTER!! COVERED BY A SHELL!!

THAT MEANS PEOPLE ON ALSOA WERE PLANTS!!

"SO I CAREFULLY PUT THE PLANT IN A LITTLE HOLE IN THE GROUND..."

...AND IT TURNED INTO THIS FLOWER...

HEY, GUYS... LET'S GO HOME. WE'LL LET THE BOY FROM ALSOA BLOOM HERE FOREVER...

BUT IN THIS SNOW-STORM WE'LL FORGET WHERE IT WAS...

IT'S BETTER THAT WAY...

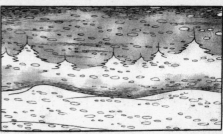

222

HIS HIGHNESS DEADCROSS

First serialized between September and
December 1960 in *Shonen* magazine.

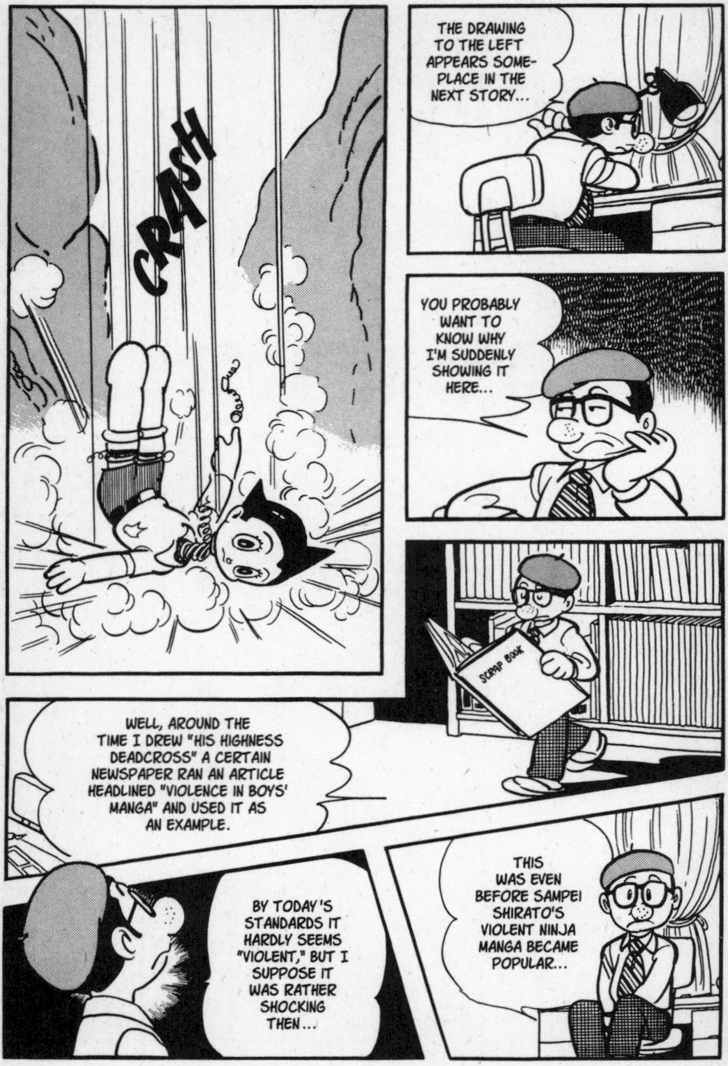
CRASH
THE DRAWING TO THE LEFT APPEARS SOME-PLACE IN THE NEXT STORY...
YOU PROBABLY WANT TO KNOW WHY I'M SUDDENLY SHOWING IT HERE...
SCRAP BOOK
WELL, AROUND THE TIME I DREW "HIS HIGHNESS DEADCROSS" A CERTAIN NEWSPAPER RAN AN ARTICLE HEADLINED "VIOLENCE IN BOYS' MANGA" AND USED IT AS AN EXAMPLE.
BY TODAY'S STANDARDS IT HARDLY SEEMS "VIOLENT," BUT I SUPPOSE IT WAS RATHER SHOCKING THEN...
THIS WAS EVEN BEFORE SAMPEI SHIRATO'S VIOLENT NINJA MANGA BECAME POPULAR...

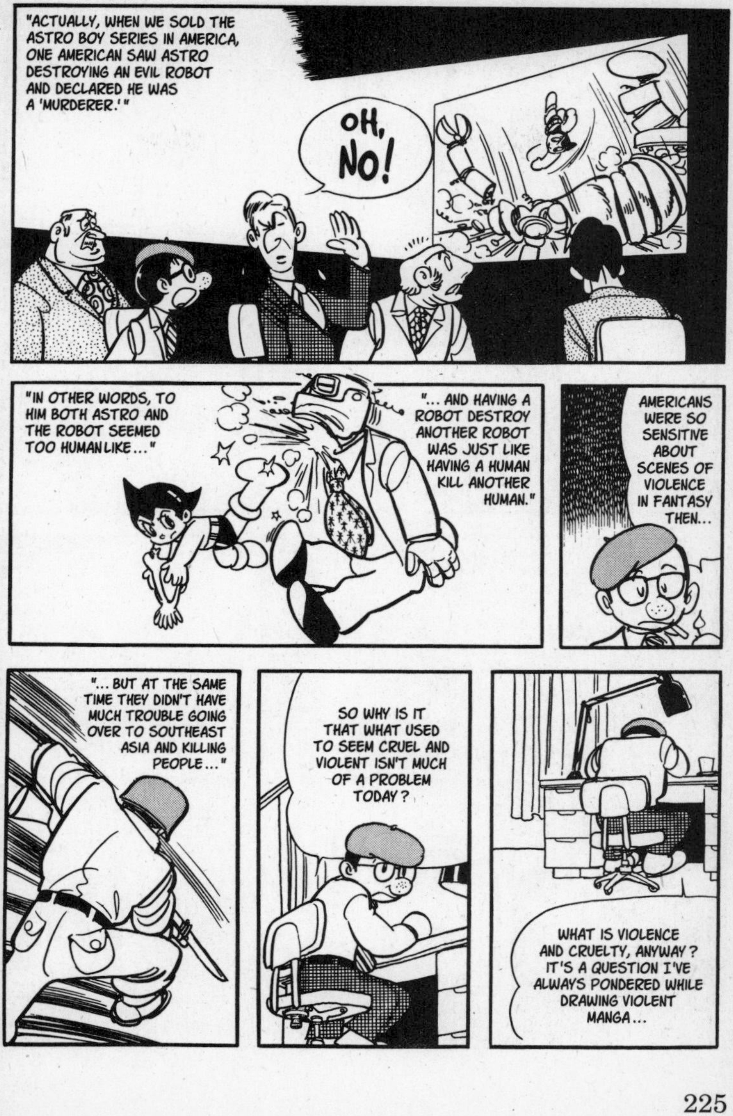
"ACTUALLY, WHEN WE SOLD THE ASTRO BOY SERIES IN AMERICA, ONE AMERICAN SAW ASTRO DESTROYING AN EVIL ROBOT AND DECLARED HE WAS A 'MURDERER.'"
OH, NO!
"IN OTHER WORDS, TO HIM BOTH ASTRO AND THE ROBOT SEEMED TOO HUMANLIKE..."
"... AND HAVING A ROBOT DESTROY ANOTHER ROBOT WAS JUST LIKE HAVING A HUMAN KILL ANOTHER HUMAN."
AMERICANS WERE SO SENSITIVE ABOUT SCENES OF VIOLENCE IN FANTASY THEN...
"... BUT AT THE SAME TIME THEY DIDN'T HAVE MUCH TROUBLE GOING OVER TO SOUTHEAST ASIA AND KILLING PEOPLE..."
SO WHY IS IT THAT WHAT USED TO SEEM CRUEL AND VIOLENT ISN'T MUCH OF A PROBLEM TODAY?
WHAT IS VIOLENCE AND CRUELTY, ANYWAY? IT'S A QUESTION I'VE ALWAYS PONDERED WHILE DRAWING VIOLENT MANGA...

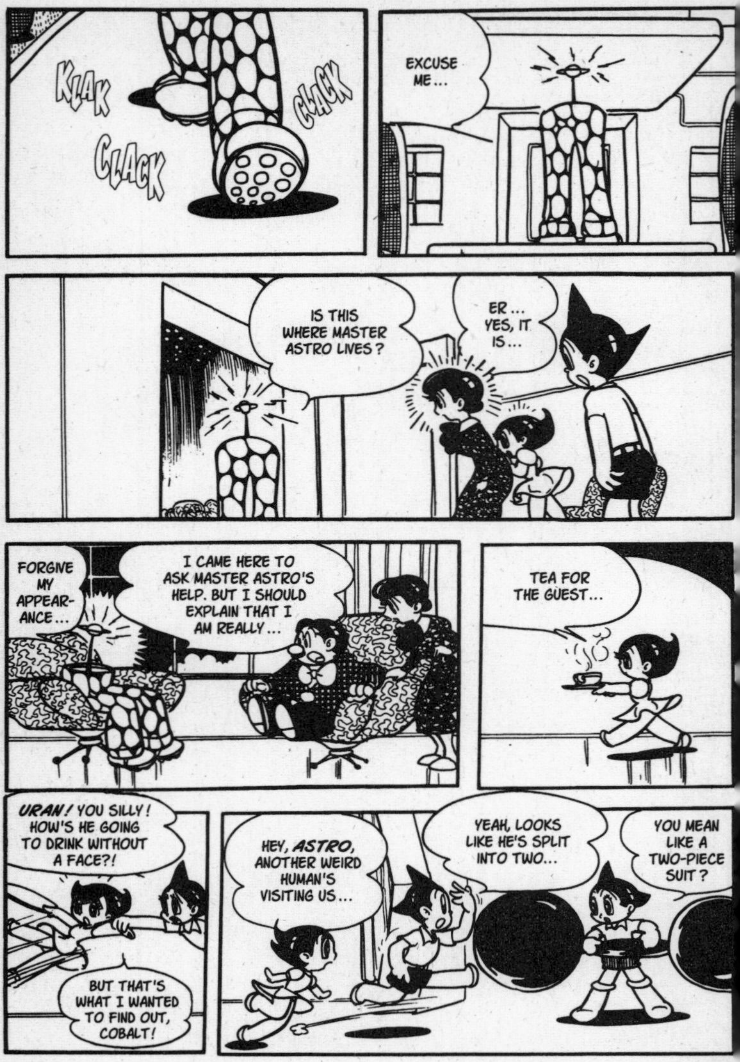
KLAK
CLACK
CLACK
EXCUSE ME...
IS THIS WHERE MASTER ASTRO LIVES?
ER... YES, IT IS...
FORGIVE MY APPEAR-ANCE...
I CAME HERE TO ASK MASTER ASTRO'S HELP. BUT I SHOULD EXPLAIN THAT I AM REALLY...
TEA FOR THE GUEST...
URAN! YOU SILLY! HOW'S HE GOING TO DRINK WITHOUT A FACE?!
BUT THAT'S WHAT I WANTED TO FIND OUT, COBALT!
HEY, ASTRO, ANOTHER WEIRD HUMAN'S VISITING US...
YEAH, LOOKS LIKE HE'S SPLIT INTO TWO...
YOU MEAN LIKE A TWO-PIECE SUIT?

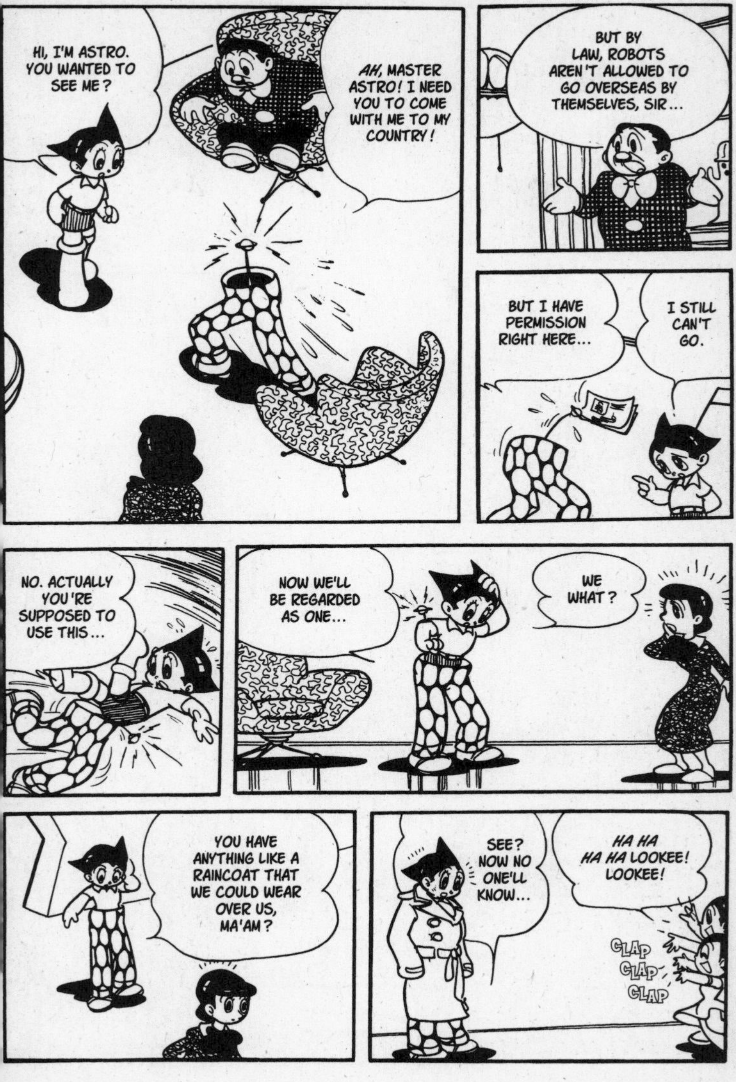
HI, I'M ASTRO. YOU WANTED TO SEE ME?
AH, MASTER ASTRO! I NEED YOU TO COME WITH ME TO MY COUNTRY!
BUT BY LAW, ROBOTS AREN'T ALLOWED TO GO OVERSEAS BY THEMSELVES, SIR...
BUT I HAVE PERMISSION RIGHT HERE...
I STILL CAN'T GO.
NO. ACTUALLY YOU'RE SUPPOSED TO USE THIS...
NOW WE'LL BE REGARDED AS ONE...
WE WHAT?
YOU HAVE ANYTHING LIKE A RAINCOAT THAT WE COULD WEAR OVER US, MA'AM?
SEE? NOW NO ONE'LL KNOW...
HA HA HA HA LOOKEE! LOOKEE!
CLAP
CLAP
CLAP

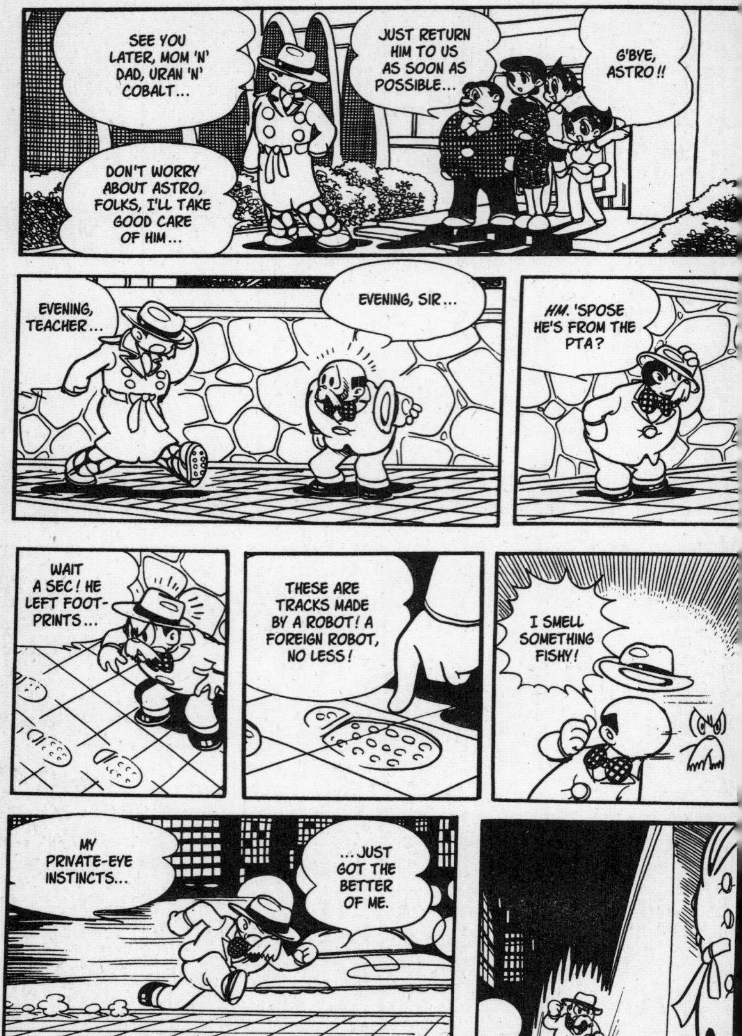
SEE YOU LATER, MOM 'N' DAD, URAN 'N' COBALT...
DON'T WORRY ABOUT ASTRO, FOLKS, I'LL TAKE GOOD CARE OF HIM...
JUST RETURN HIM TO US AS SOON AS POSSIBLE...
G'BYE, ASTRO!!
EVENING, TEACHER...
EVENING, SIR...
HM. 'SPOSE HE'S FROM THE PTA?
WAIT A SEC! HE LEFT FOOT-PRINTS...
THESE ARE TRACKS MADE BY A ROBOT! A FOREIGN ROBOT, NO LESS!
I SMELL SOMETHING FISHY!
MY PRIVATE-EYE INSTINCTS...
...JUST GOT THE BETTER OF ME.

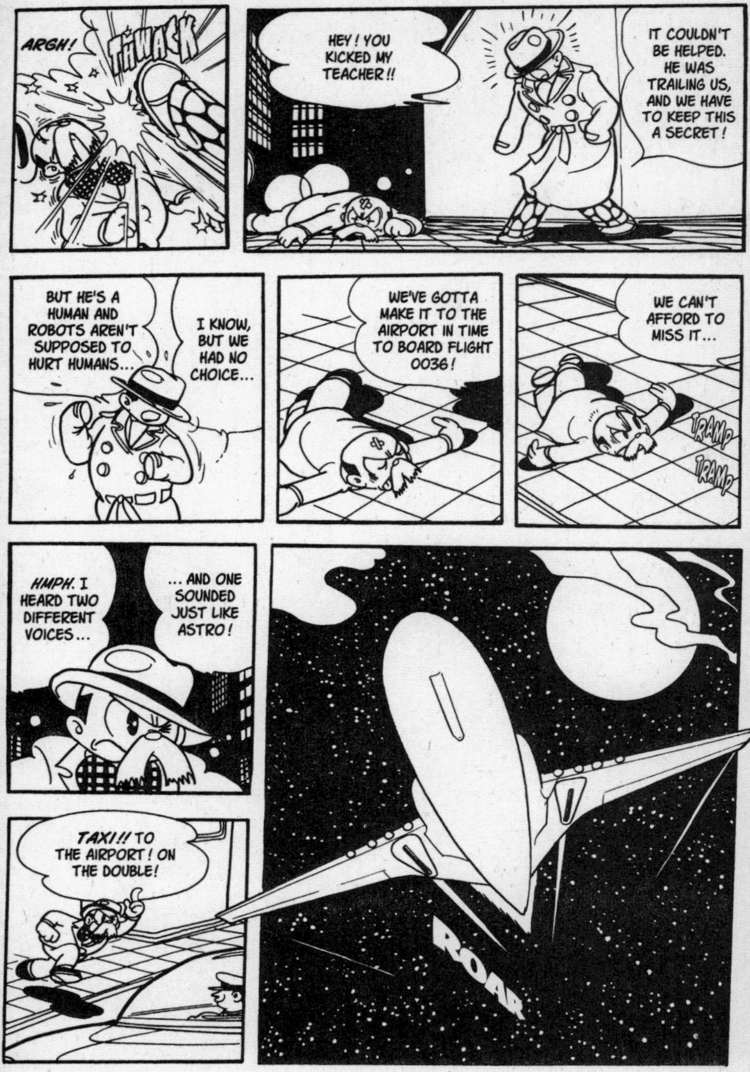
ARGH!
THWACK
HEY! YOU KICKED MY TEACHER!!
IT COULDN'T BE HELPED. HE WAS TRAILING US, AND WE HAVE TO KEEP THIS A SECRET!
BUT HE'S A HUMAN AND ROBOTS AREN'T SUPPOSED TO HURT HUMANS...
I KNOW, BUT WE HAD NO CHOICE...
WE'VE GOTTA MAKE IT TO THE AIRPORT IN TIME TO BOARD FLIGHT 0036!
WE CAN'T AFFORD TO MISS IT...
TRAMP
TRAMP
HMPH. I HEARD TWO DIFFERENT VOICES...
... AND ONE SOUNDED JUST LIKE ASTRO!
TAXI!! TO THE AIRPORT! ON THE DOUBLE!
ROAR

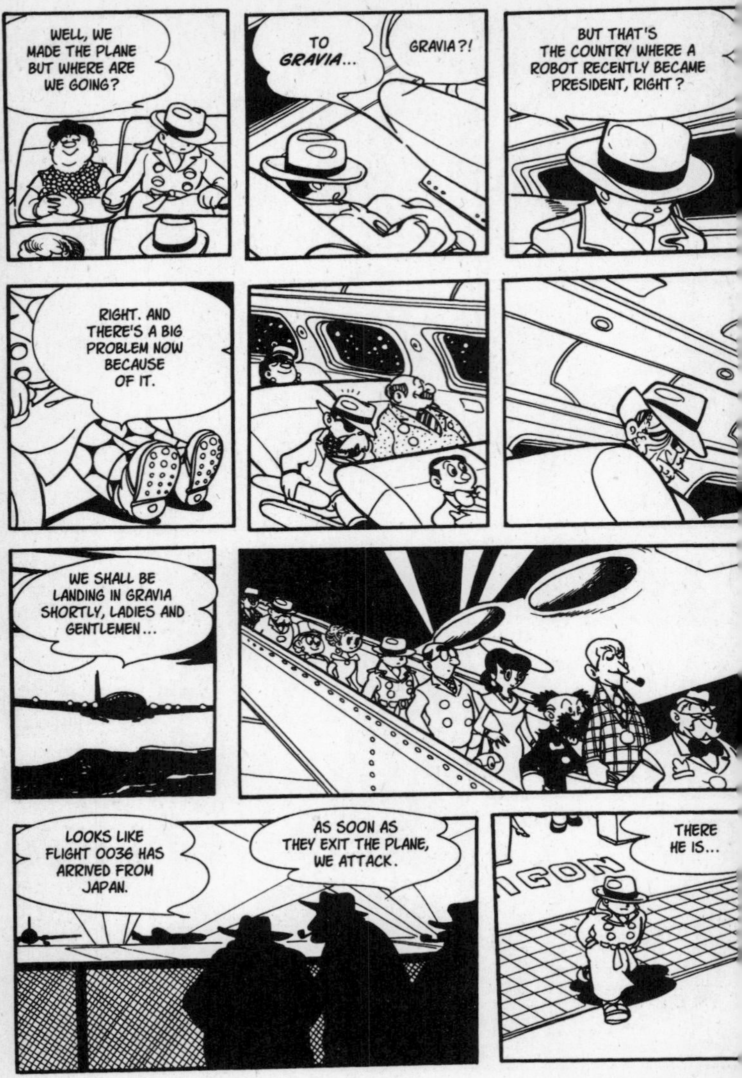

WELL, WE MADE THE PLANE BUT WHERE ARE WE GOING?
TO GRAVIA...
GRAVIA?!
BUT THAT'S THE COUNTRY WHERE A ROBOT RECENTLY BECAME PRESIDENT, RIGHT?
RIGHT. AND THERE'S A BIG PROBLEM NOW BECAUSE OF IT.
WE SHALL BE LANDING IN GRAVIA SHORTLY, LADIES AND GENTLEMEN...
LOOKS LIKE FLIGHT 0036 HAS ARRIVED FROM JAPAN.
AS SOON AS THEY EXIT THE PLANE, WE ATTACK.
ICON
THERE HE IS...

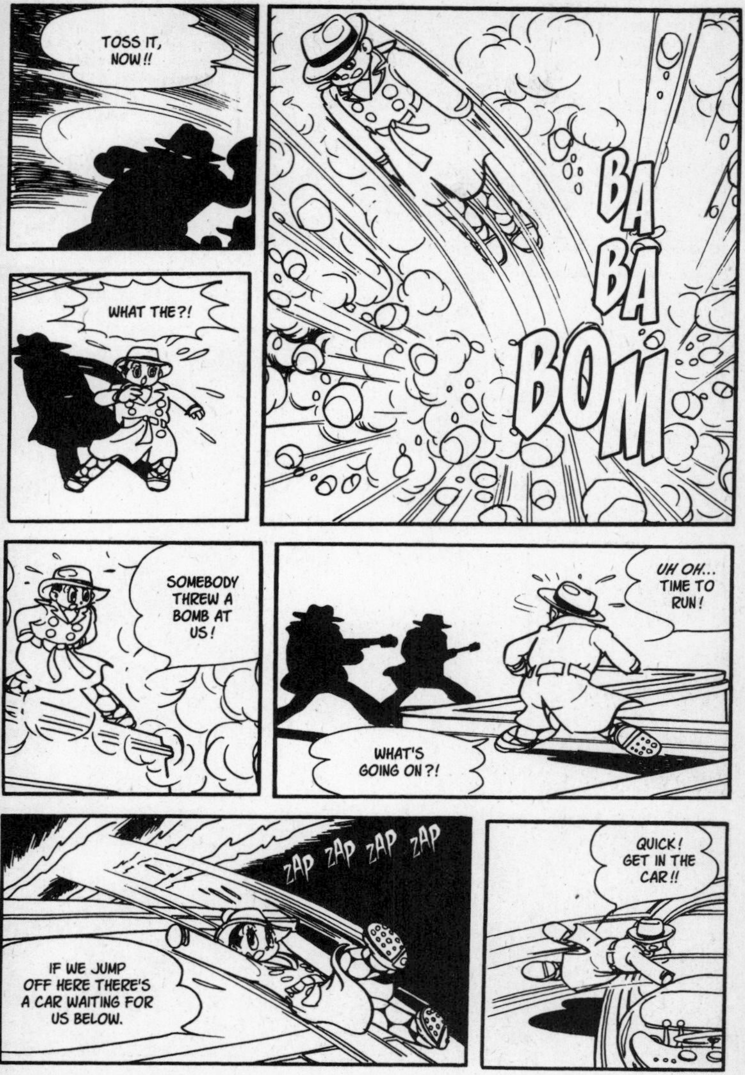
TOSS IT, NOW!!
BA BA BOM
WHAT THE?!
SOMEBODY THREW A BOMB AT US!
UH OH... TIME TO RUN!
WHAT'S GOING ON?!
ZAP ZAP ZAP ZAP
IF WE JUMP OFF HERE THERE'S A CAR WAITING FOR US BELOW.
QUICK! GET IN THE CAR!!

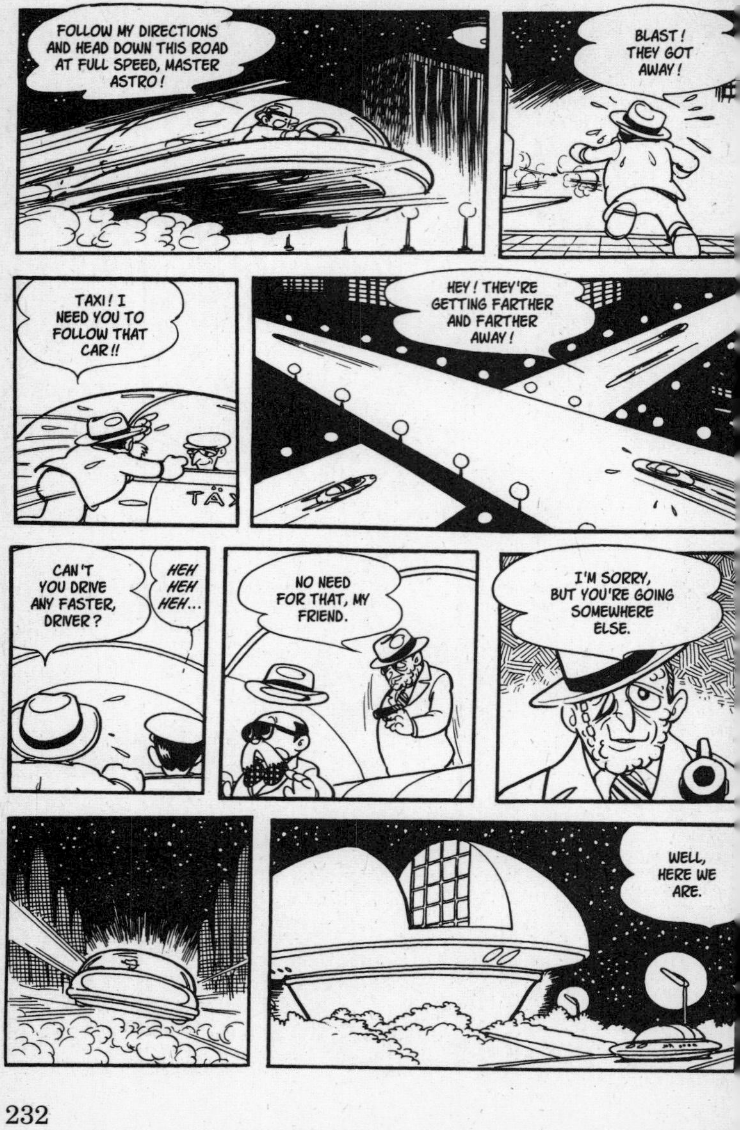
FOLLOW MY DIRECTIONS AND HEAD DOWN THIS ROAD AT FULL SPEED, MASTER ASTRO!
BLAST! THEY GOT AWAY!
TAXI! I NEED YOU TO FOLLOW THAT CAR!!
TÄX
HEY! THEY'RE GETTING FARTHER AND FARTHER AWAY!
CAN'T YOU DRIVE ANY FASTER, DRIVER?
HEH HEH HEH...
NO NEED FOR THAT, MY FRIEND.
I'M SORRY, BUT YOU'RE GOING SOMEWHERE ELSE.
WELL, HERE WE ARE.

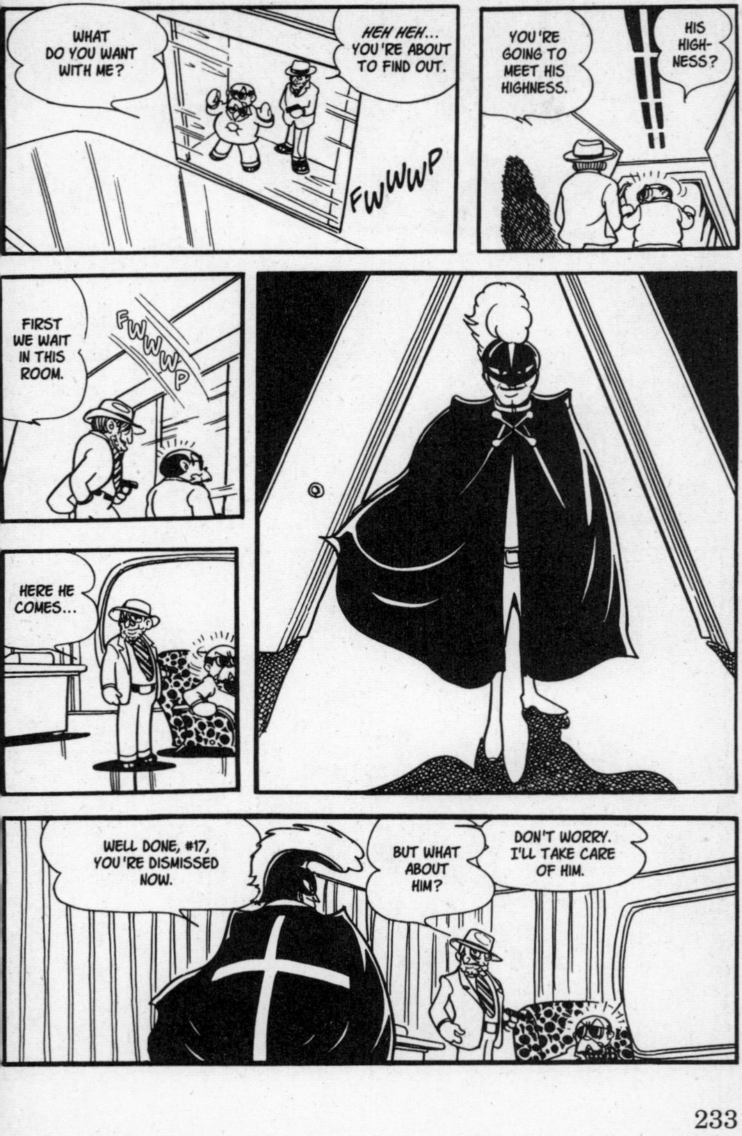
WHAT DO YOU WANT WITH ME?
HEH HEH... YOU'RE ABOUT TO FIND OUT.
FWWWP
YOU'RE GOING TO MEET HIS HIGHNESS.
HIS HIGH-NESS?
FIRST WE WAIT IN THIS ROOM.
FWWWP
HERE HE COMES...
WELL DONE, #17, YOU'RE DISMISSED NOW.
BUT WHAT ABOUT HIM?
DON'T WORRY. I'LL TAKE CARE OF HIM.

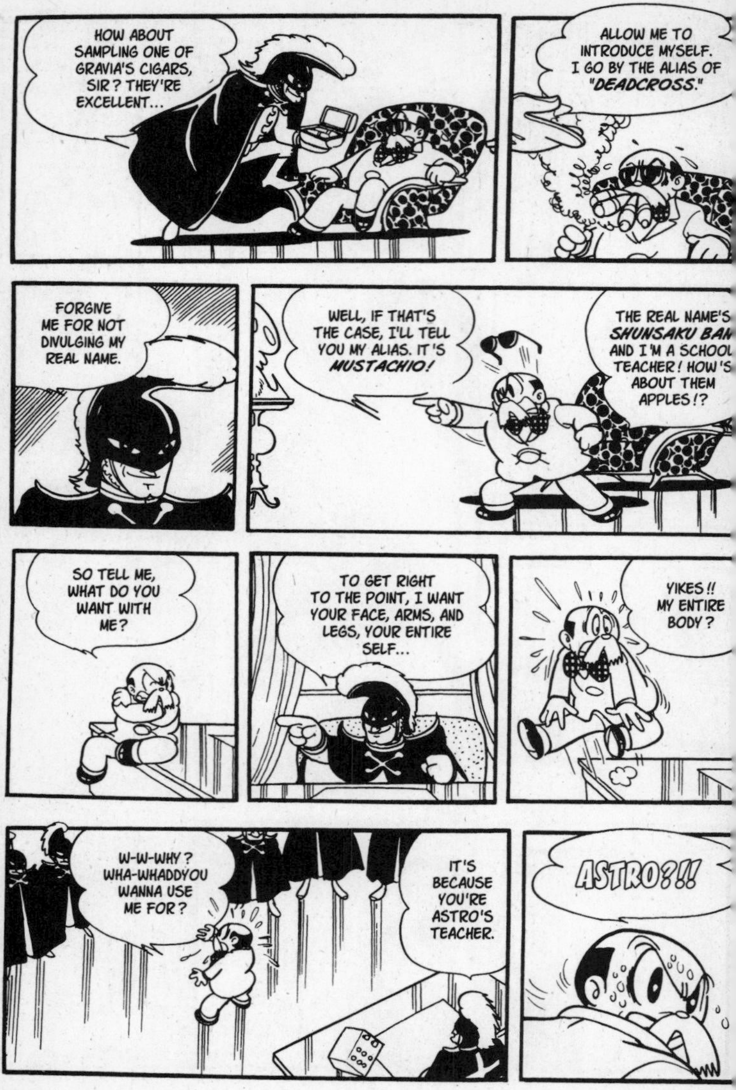
HOW ABOUT SAMPLING ONE OF GRAVIA'S CIGARS, SIR? THEY'RE EXCELLENT...
ALLOW ME TO INTRODUCE MYSELF. I GO BY THE ALIAS OF "DEADCROSS."
FORGIVE ME FOR NOT DIVULGING MY REAL NAME.
WELL, IF THAT'S THE CASE, I'LL TELL YOU MY ALIAS. IT'S MUSTACHIO!
THE REAL NAME'S SHUNSAKU BAN AND I'M A SCHOOL TEACHER! HOW'S ABOUT THEM APPLES!?
SO TELL ME, WHAT DO YOU WANT WITH ME?
TO GET RIGHT TO THE POINT, I WANT YOUR FACE, ARMS, AND LEGS, YOUR ENTIRE SELF...
YIKES!! MY ENTIRE BODY?
W-W-WHY? WHA-WHADDYOU WANNA USE ME FOR?
IT'S BECAUSE YOU'RE ASTRO'S TEACHER.
ASTRO?!!

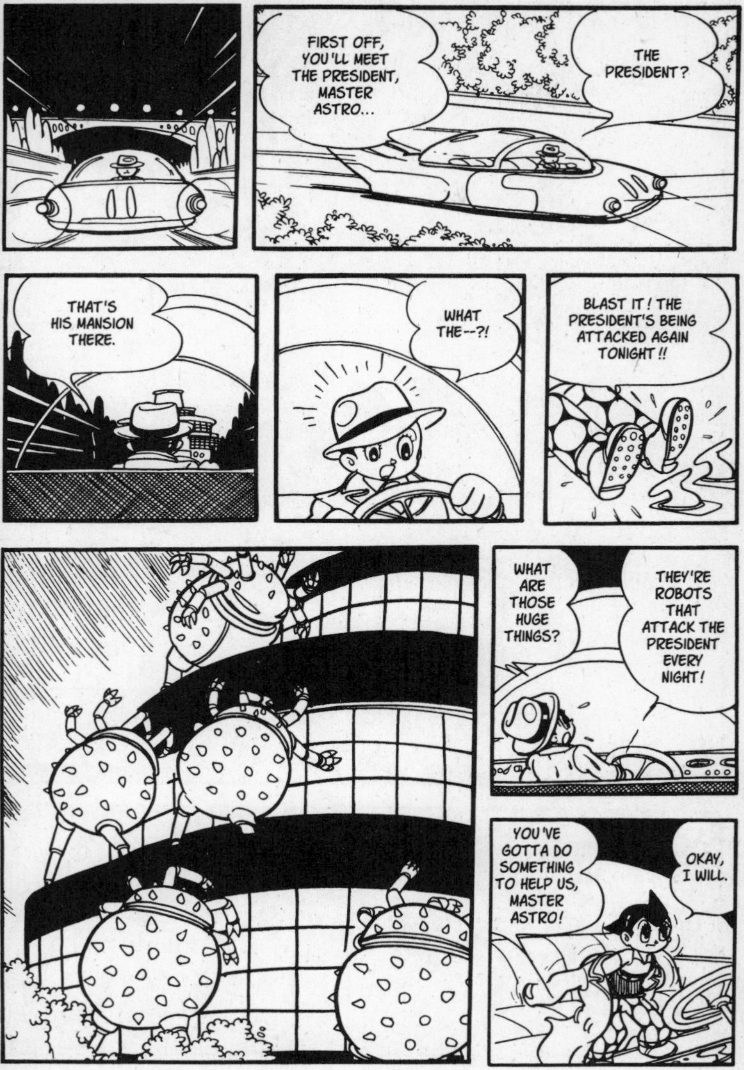
FIRST OFF, YOU'LL MEET THE PRESIDENT, MASTER ASTRO...
THE PRESIDENT?
THAT'S HIS MANSION THERE.
WHAT THE--?!
BLAST IT! THE PRESIDENT'S BEING ATTACKED AGAIN TONIGHT!!
WHAT ARE THOSE HUGE THINGS?
THEY'RE ROBOTS THAT ATTACK THE PRESIDENT EVERY NIGHT!
YOU'VE GOTTA DO SOMETHING TO HELP US, MASTER ASTRO!
OKAY, I WILL.

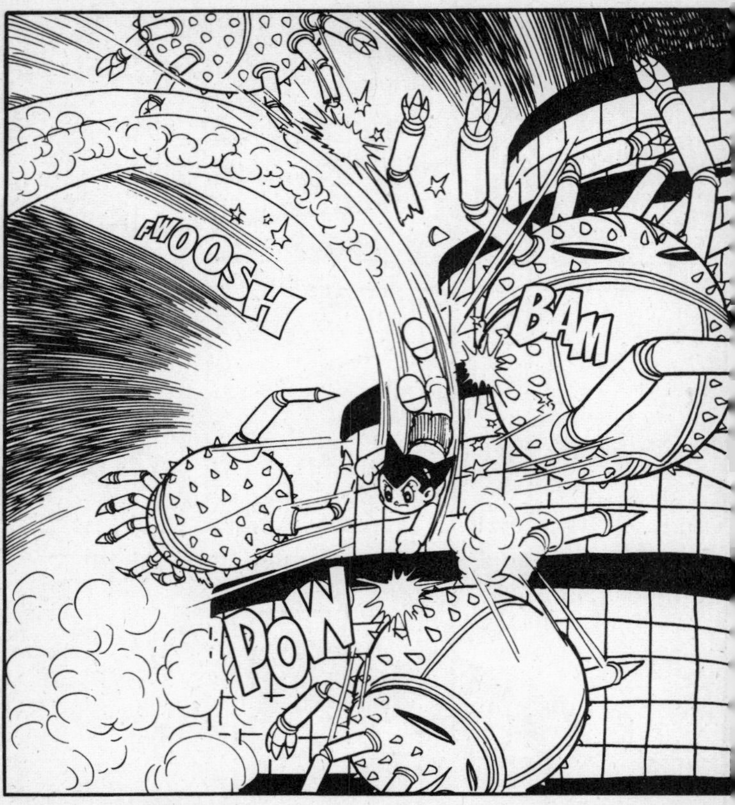
FWOOSH
BAM
POW
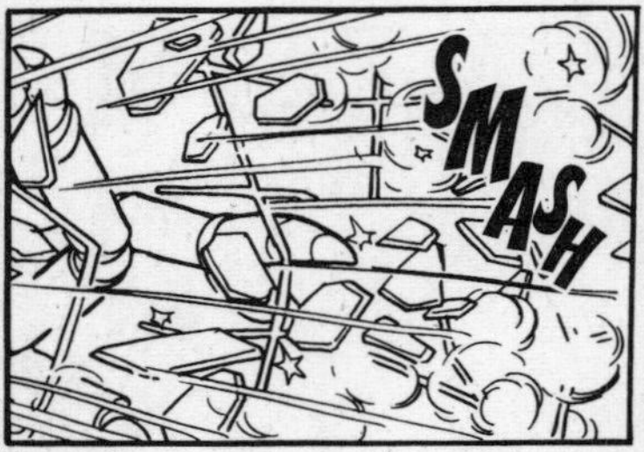
SMASH
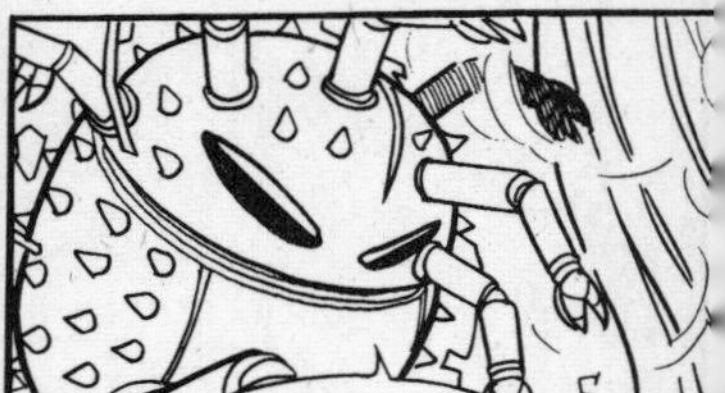
HYU HYU
HYU HYU

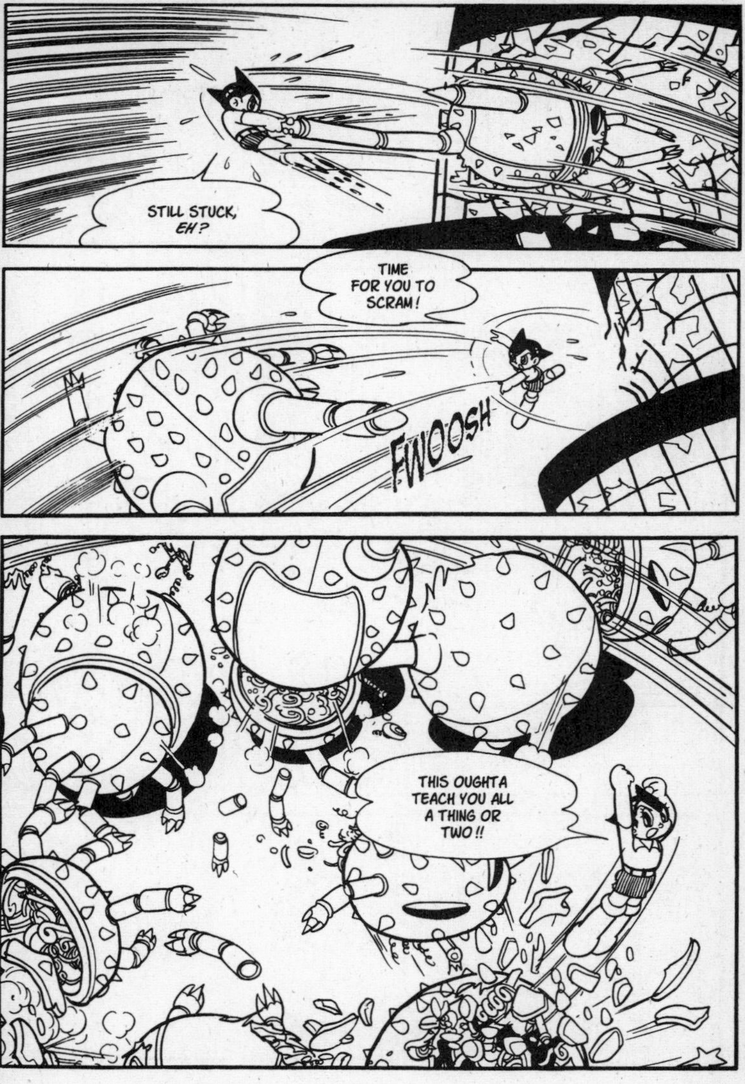
STILL STUCK, EH?
TIME FOR YOU TO SCRAM!
FWOOSH
THIS OUGHTA TEACH YOU ALL A THING OR TWO!!

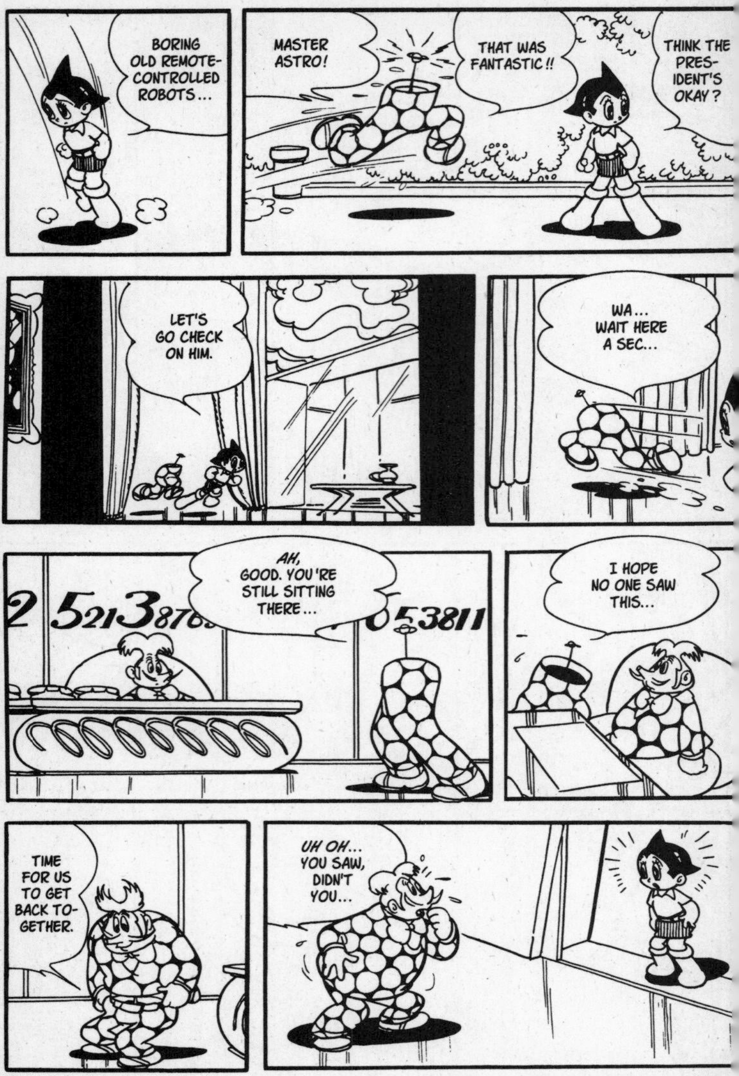
BORING OLD REMOTE-CONTROLLED ROBOTS...
MASTER ASTRO!
THAT WAS FANTASTIC!!
THINK THE PRES-IDENT'S OKAY?
LET'S GO CHECK ON HIM.
WA... WAIT HERE A SEC...
AH, GOOD. YOU'RE STILL SITTING THERE...
I HOPE NO ONE SAW THIS...
TIME FOR US TO GET BACK TO-GETHER.
UH OH... YOU SAW, DIDN'T YOU...

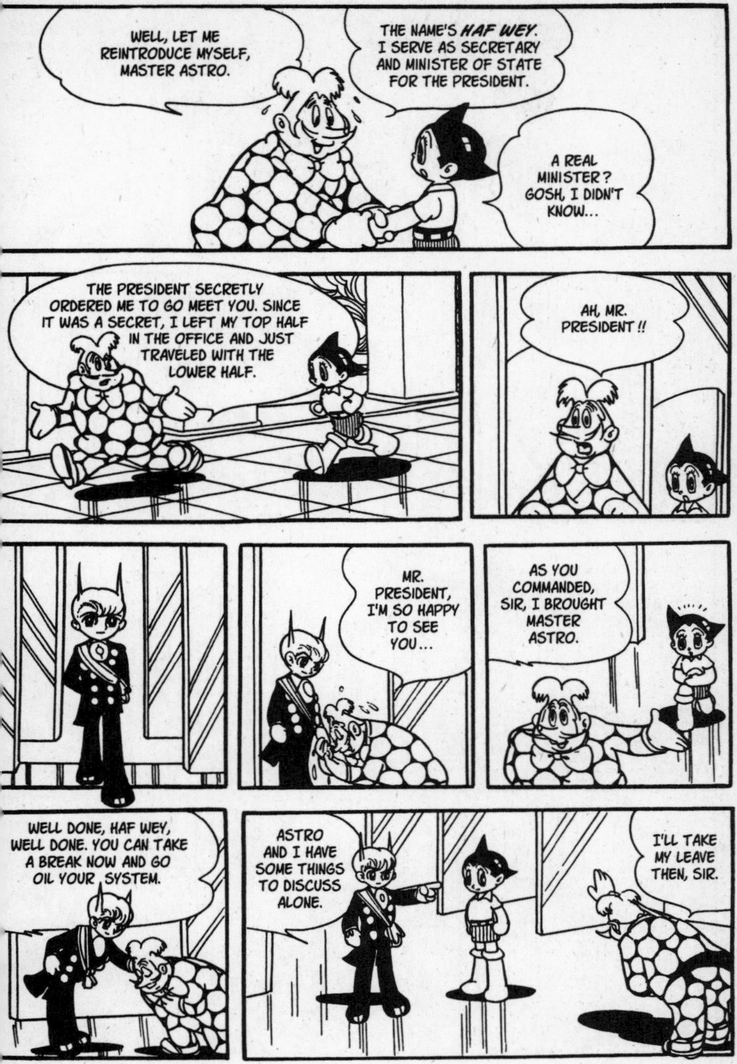
WELL, LET ME REINTRODUCE MYSELF, MASTER ASTRO.
THE NAME'S ***HAF WEY***. I SERVE AS SECRETARY AND MINISTER OF STATE FOR THE PRESIDENT.
A REAL MINISTER? GOSH, I DIDN'T KNOW...
THE PRESIDENT SECRETLY ORDERED ME TO GO MEET YOU. SINCE IT WAS A SECRET, I LEFT MY TOP HALF IN THE OFFICE AND JUST TRAVELED WITH THE LOWER HALF.
AH, MR. PRESIDENT!!
MR. PRESIDENT, I'M SO HAPPY TO SEE YOU...
AS YOU COMMANDED, SIR, I BROUGHT MASTER ASTRO.
WELL DONE, HAF WEY, WELL DONE. YOU CAN TAKE A BREAK NOW AND GO OIL YOUR SYSTEM.
ASTRO AND I HAVE SOME THINGS TO DISCUSS ALONE.
I'LL TAKE MY LEAVE THEN, SIR.

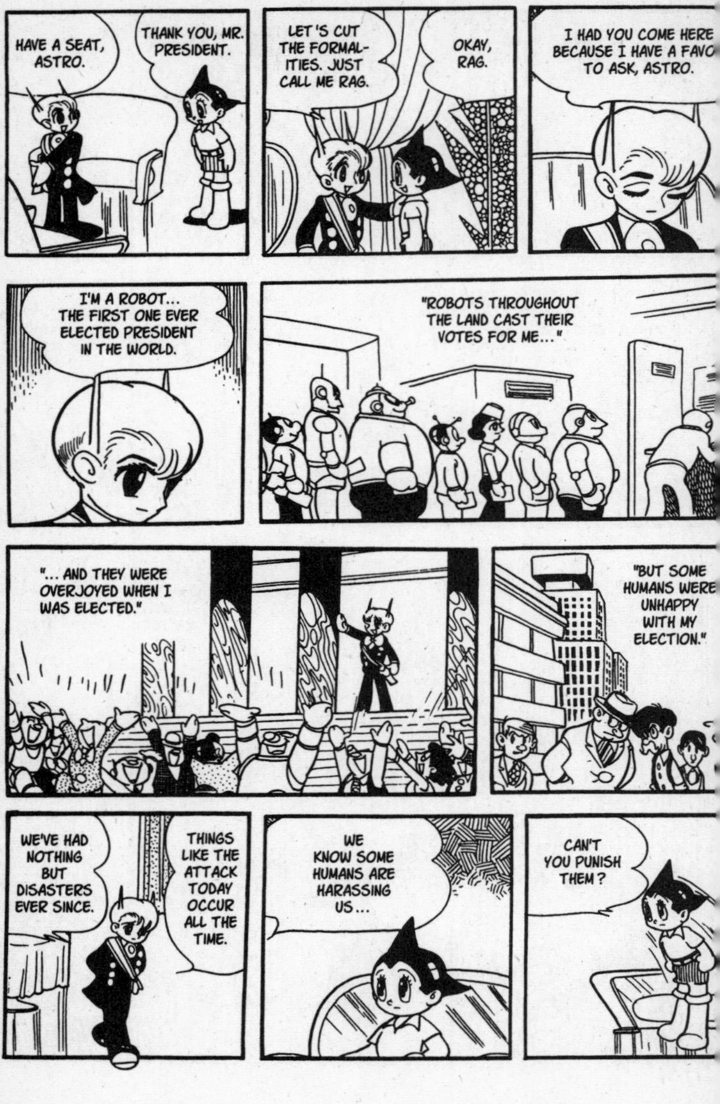
HAVE A SEAT, ASTRO.
THANK YOU, MR. PRESIDENT.
LET'S CUT THE FORMALITIES. JUST CALL ME RAG.
OKAY, RAG.
I HAD YOU COME HERE BECAUSE I HAVE A FAVO TO ASK, ASTRO.
I'M A ROBOT... THE FIRST ONE EVER ELECTED PRESIDENT IN THE WORLD.
"ROBOTS THROUGHOUT THE LAND CAST THEIR VOTES FOR ME..."
"... AND THEY WERE OVERJOYED WHEN I WAS ELECTED."
"BUT SOME HUMANS WERE UNHAPPY WITH MY ELECTION."
WE'VE HAD NOTHING BUT DISASTERS EVER SINCE.
THINGS LIKE THE ATTACK TODAY OCCUR ALL THE TIME.
WE KNOW SOME HUMANS ARE HARASSING US...
CAN'T YOU PUNISH THEM?

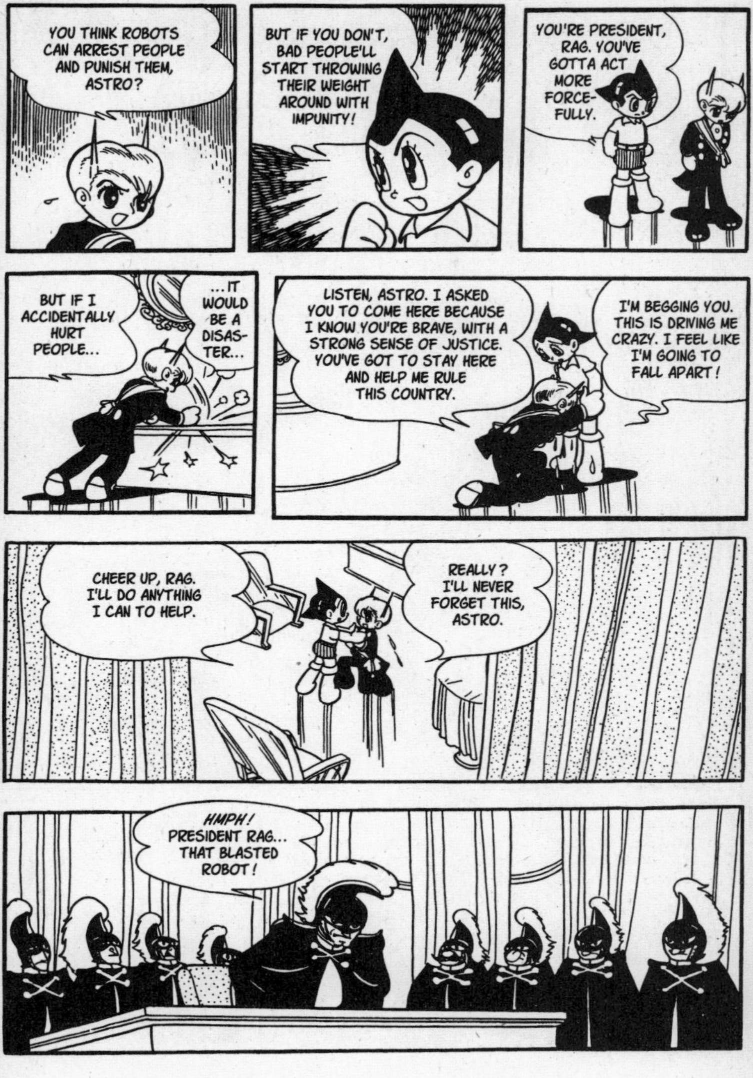
YOU THINK ROBOTS CAN ARREST PEOPLE AND PUNISH THEM, ASTRO?
BUT IF YOU DON'T, BAD PEOPLE'LL START THROWING THEIR WEIGHT AROUND WITH IMPUNITY!
YOU'RE PRESIDENT, RAG. YOU'VE GOTTA ACT MORE FORCE-FULLY.
BUT IF I ACCIDENTALLY HURT PEOPLE...
...IT WOULD BE A DISAS-TER...
LISTEN, ASTRO. I ASKED YOU TO COME HERE BECAUSE I KNOW YOU'RE BRAVE, WITH A STRONG SENSE OF JUSTICE. YOU'VE GOT TO STAY HERE AND HELP ME RULE THIS COUNTRY.
I'M BEGGING YOU. THIS IS DRIVING ME CRAZY. I FEEL LIKE I'M GOING TO FALL APART!
CHEER UP, RAG. I'LL DO ANYTHING I CAN TO HELP.
REALLY? I'LL NEVER FORGET THIS, ASTRO.
HMPH! PRESIDENT RAG... THAT BLASTED ROBOT!

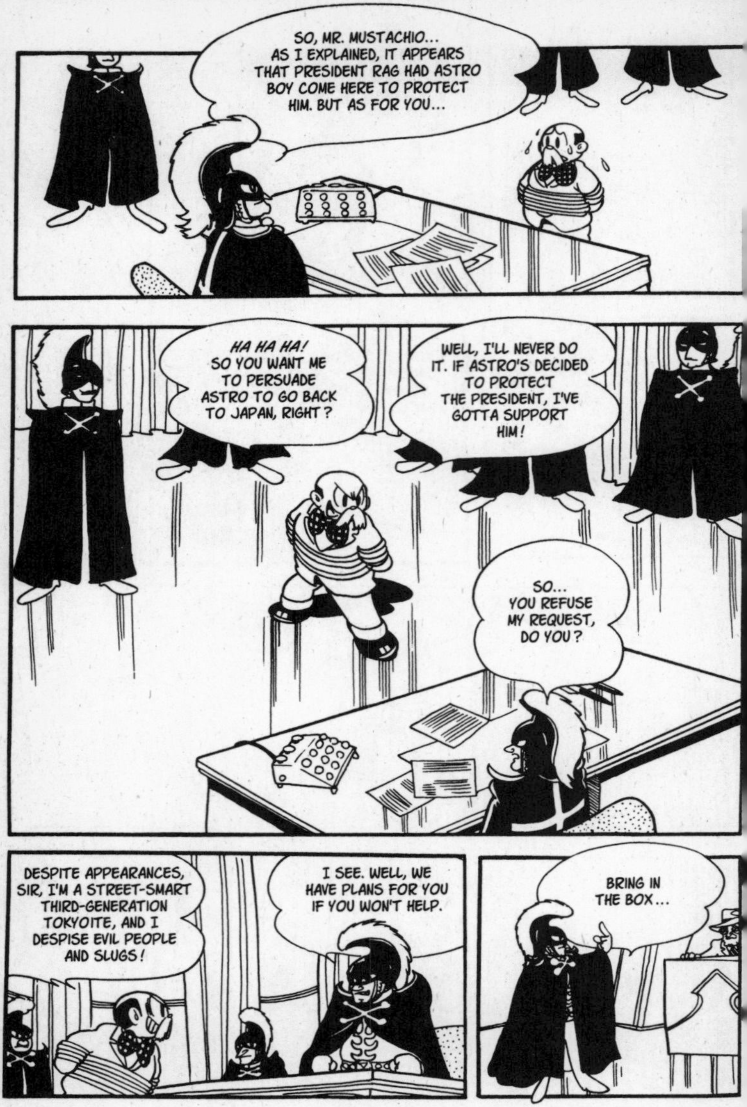
SO, MR. MUSTACHIO... AS I EXPLAINED, IT APPEARS THAT PRESIDENT RAG HAD ASTRO BOY COME HERE TO PROTECT HIM. BUT AS FOR YOU...
HA HA HA! SO YOU WANT ME TO PERSUADE ASTRO TO GO BACK TO JAPAN, RIGHT?
WELL, I'LL NEVER DO IT. IF ASTRO'S DECIDED TO PROTECT THE PRESIDENT, I'VE GOTTA SUPPORT HIM!
SO... YOU REFUSE MY REQUEST, DO YOU?
DESPITE APPEARANCES, SIR, I'M A STREET-SMART THIRD-GENERATION TOKYOITE, AND I DESPISE EVIL PEOPLE AND SLUGS!
I SEE. WELL, WE HAVE PLANS FOR YOU IF YOU WON'T HELP.
BRING IN THE BOX...

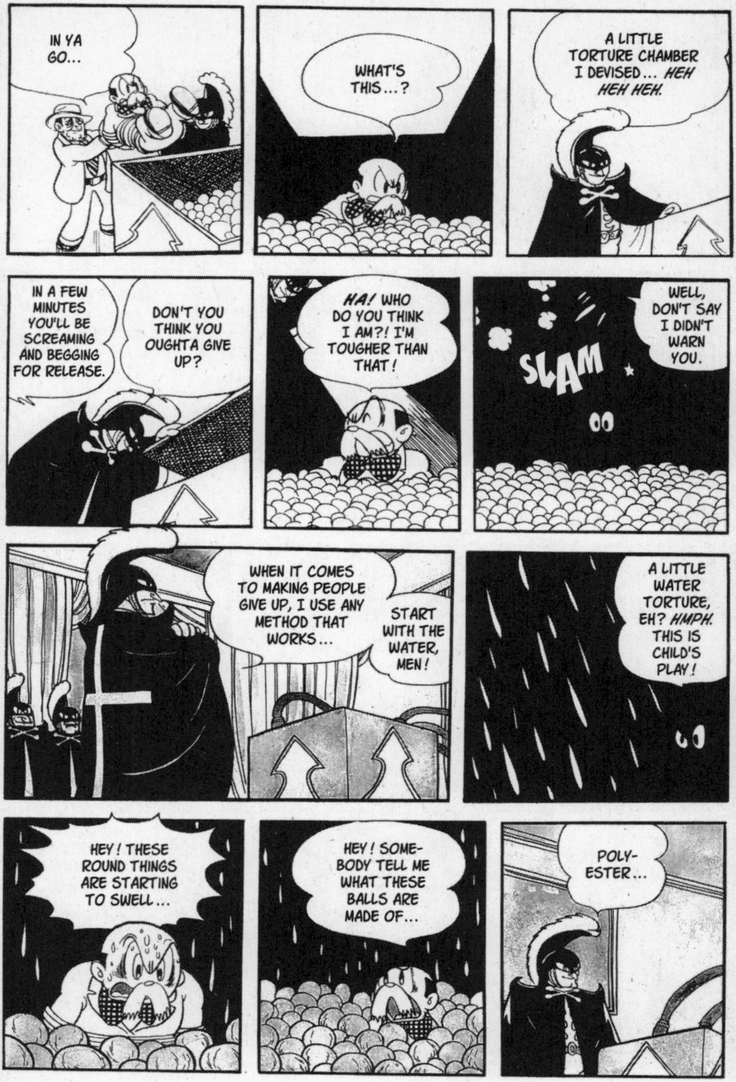
IN YA GO...
WHAT'S THIS...?
A LITTLE TORTURE CHAMBER I DEVISED... *HEH HEH HEH.*
IN A FEW MINUTES YOU'LL BE SCREAMING AND BEGGING FOR RELEASE.
DON'T YOU THINK YOU OUGHTA GIVE UP?
HA! WHO DO YOU THINK I AM?! I'M TOUGHER THAN THAT!
SLAM
WELL, DON'T SAY I DIDN'T WARN YOU.
WHEN IT COMES TO MAKING PEOPLE GIVE UP, I USE ANY METHOD THAT WORKS...
START WITH THE WATER, MEN!
A LITTLE WATER TORTURE, EH? *HMPH.* THIS IS CHILD'S PLAY!
HEY! THESE ROUND THINGS ARE STARTING TO SWELL...
HEY! SOME-BODY TELL ME WHAT THESE BALLS ARE MADE OF...
POLY-ESTER...

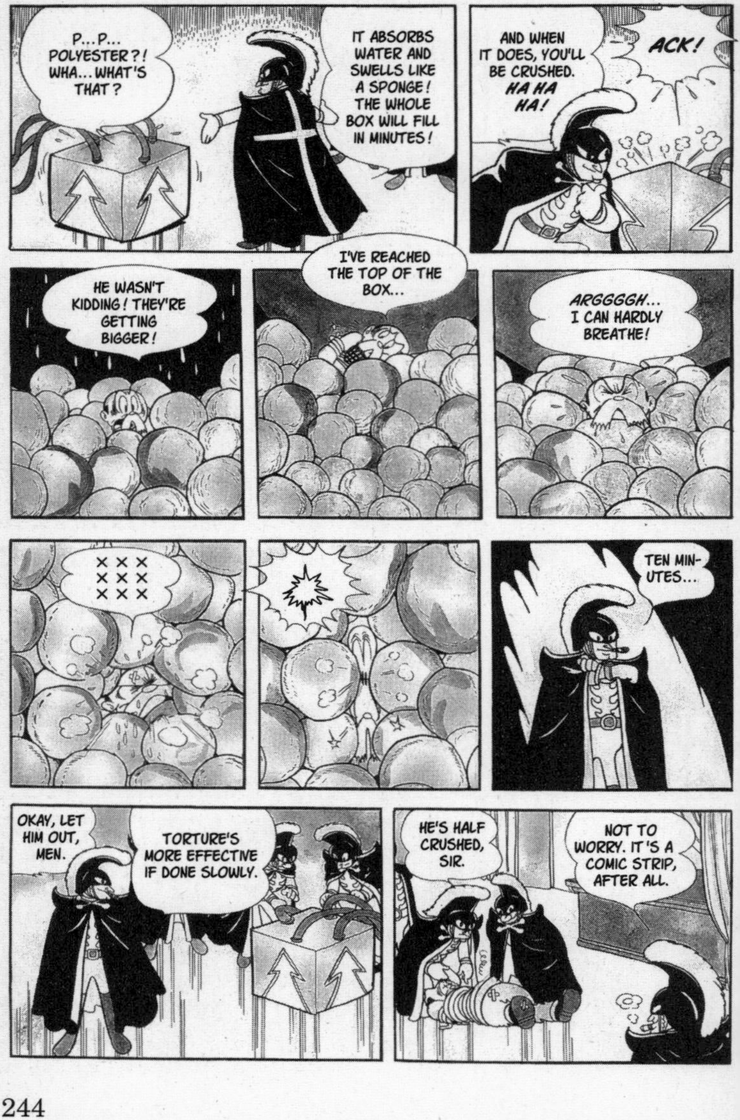
P... P... POLYESTER?! WHA... WHAT'S THAT?
IT ABSORBS WATER AND SWELLS LIKE A SPONGE! THE WHOLE BOX WILL FILL IN MINUTES!
AND WHEN IT DOES, YOU'LL BE CRUSHED. HA HA HA!
ACK!
HE WASN'T KIDDING! THEY'RE GETTING BIGGER!
I'VE REACHED THE TOP OF THE BOX...
ARGGGGH... I CAN HARDLY BREATHE!
× × × × × × × × ×
TEN MIN-UTES...
OKAY, LET HIM OUT, MEN.
TORTURE'S MORE EFFECTIVE IF DONE SLOWLY.
HE'S HALF CRUSHED, SIR.
NOT TO WORRY. IT'S A COMIC STRIP, AFTER ALL.

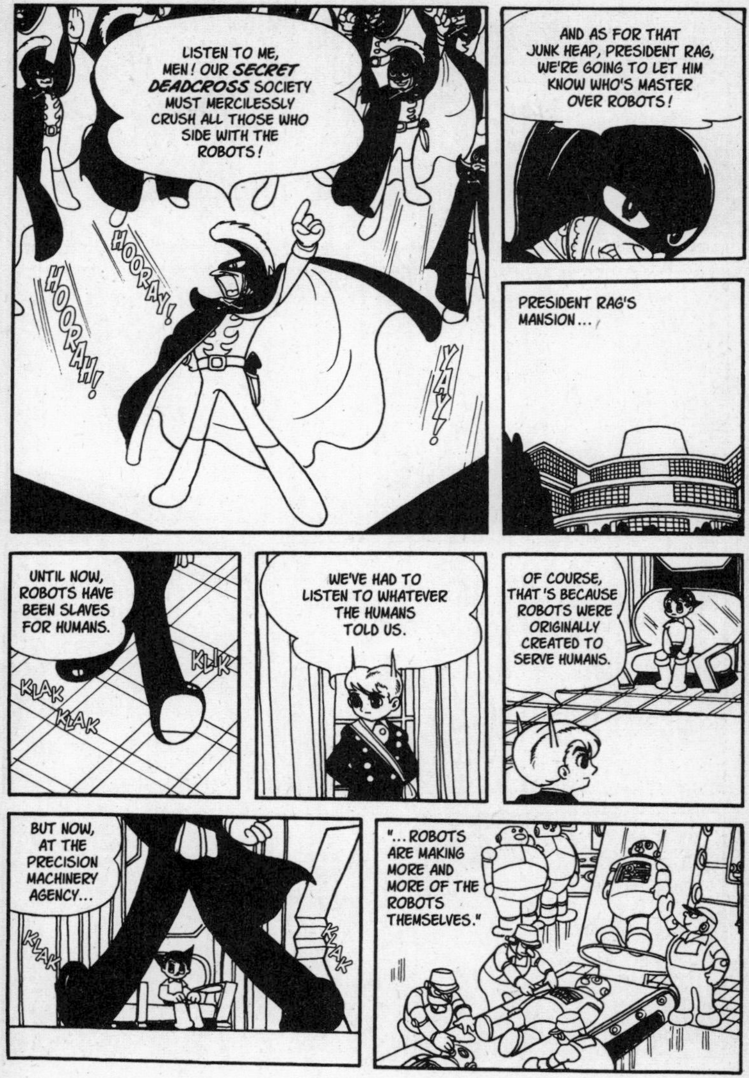
LISTEN TO ME, MEN! OUR SECRET DEADCROSS SOCIETY MUST MERCILESSLY CRUSH ALL THOSE WHO SIDE WITH THE ROBOTS!
HOORAY!
HOORAH!
YAY!
AND AS FOR THAT JUNK HEAP, PRESIDENT RAG, WE'RE GOING TO LET HIM KNOW WHO'S MASTER OVER ROBOTS!
PRESIDENT RAG'S MANSION...
UNTIL NOW, ROBOTS HAVE BEEN SLAVES FOR HUMANS.
KLIK
KLAK
KLAK
WE'VE HAD TO LISTEN TO WHATEVER THE HUMANS TOLD US.
OF COURSE, THAT'S BECAUSE ROBOTS WERE ORIGINALLY CREATED TO SERVE HUMANS.
BUT NOW, AT THE PRECISION MACHINERY AGENCY...
KLAK
KLAK
"...ROBOTS ARE MAKING MORE AND MORE OF THE ROBOTS THEMSELVES."

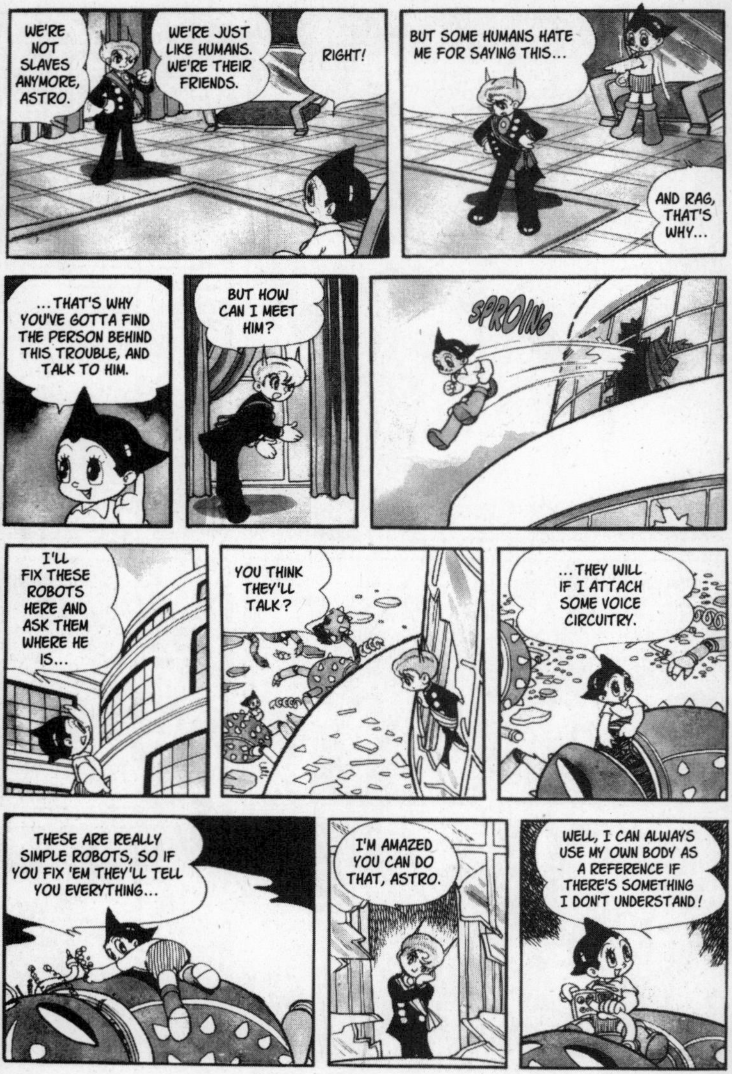
WE'RE NOT SLAVES ANYMORE, ASTRO.
WE'RE JUST LIKE HUMANS. WE'RE THEIR FRIENDS.
RIGHT!
BUT SOME HUMANS HATE ME FOR SAYING THIS...
AND RAG, THAT'S WHY...
...THAT'S WHY YOU'VE GOTTA FIND THE PERSON BEHIND THIS TROUBLE, AND TALK TO HIM.
BUT HOW CAN I MEET HIM?
SPROING
I'LL FIX THESE ROBOTS HERE AND ASK THEM WHERE HE IS...
YOU THINK THEY'LL TALK?
...THEY WILL IF I ATTACH SOME VOICE CIRCUITRY.
THESE ARE REALLY SIMPLE ROBOTS, SO IF YOU FIX 'EM THEY'LL TELL YOU EVERYTHING...
I'M AMAZED YOU CAN DO THAT, ASTRO.
WELL, I CAN ALWAYS USE MY OWN BODY AS A REFERENCE IF THERE'S SOMETHING I DON'T UNDERSTAND!

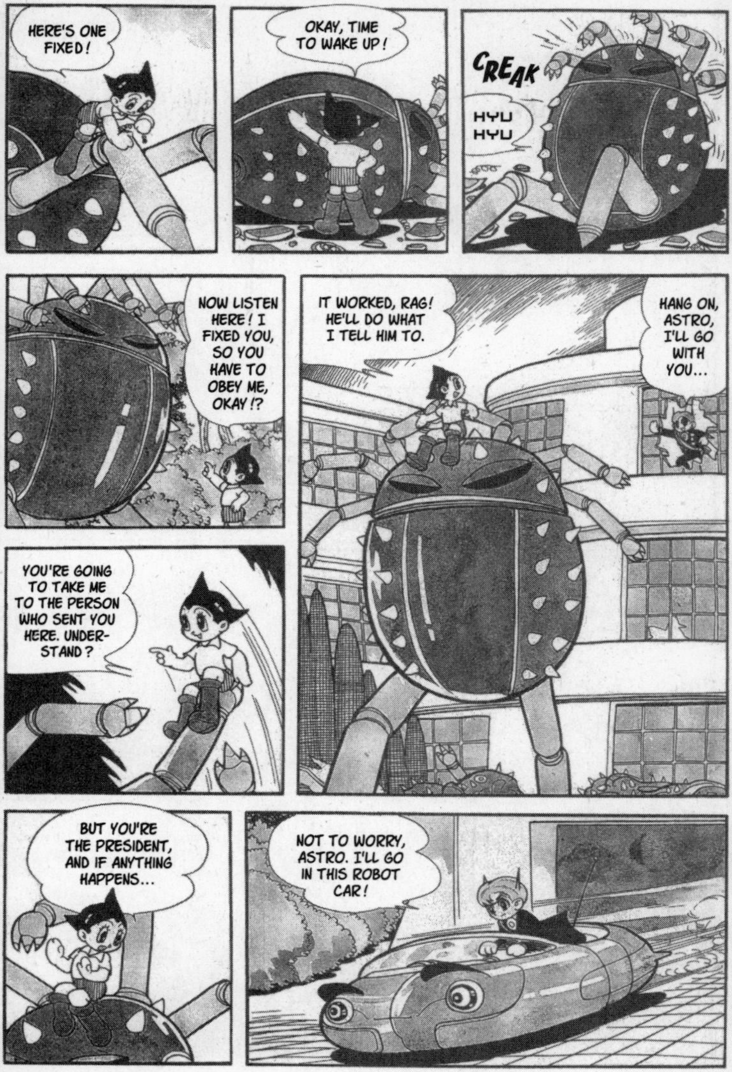
HERE'S ONE FIXED!
OKAY, TIME TO WAKE UP!
CREAK
HYU HYU
NOW LISTEN HERE! I FIXED YOU, SO YOU HAVE TO OBEY ME, OKAY!?
IT WORKED, RAG! HE'LL DO WHAT I TELL HIM TO.
HANG ON, ASTRO, I'LL GO WITH YOU...
YOU'RE GOING TO TAKE ME TO THE PERSON WHO SENT YOU HERE. UNDER-STAND?
BUT YOU'RE THE PRESIDENT, AND IF ANYTHING HAPPENS...
NOT TO WORRY, ASTRO. I'LL GO IN THIS ROBOT CAR!

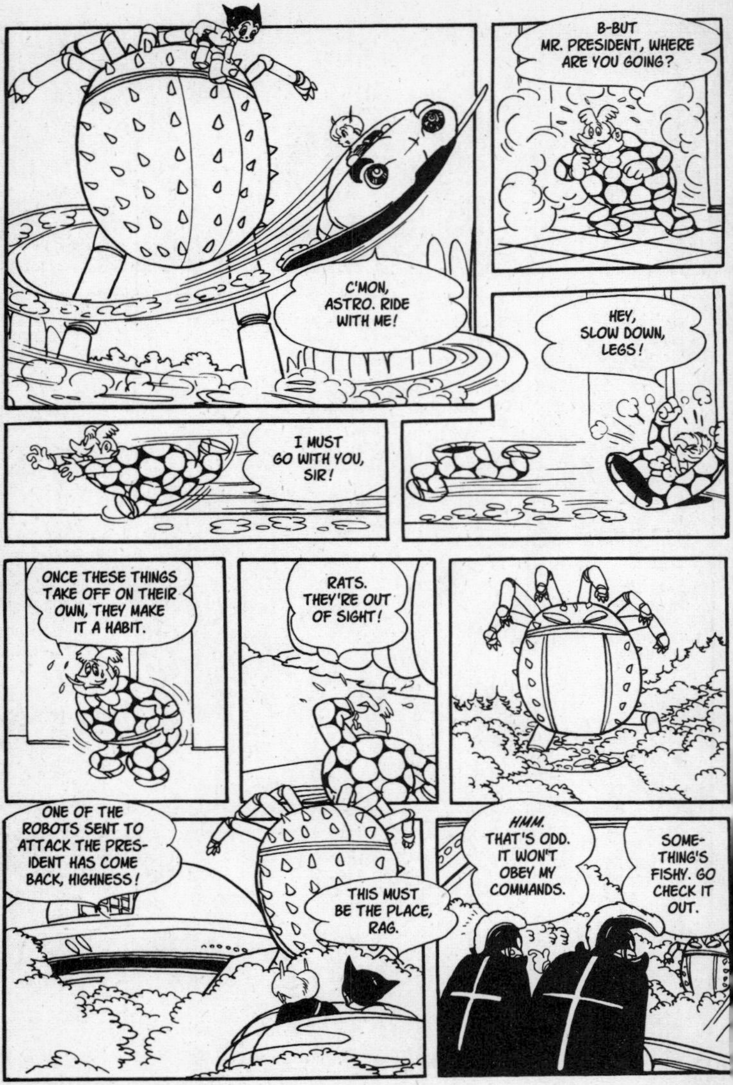

C'MON, ASTRO. RIDE WITH ME!
B-BUT MR. PRESIDENT, WHERE ARE YOU GOING?
I MUST GO WITH YOU, SIR!
HEY, SLOW DOWN, LEGS!
ONCE THESE THINGS TAKE OFF ON THEIR OWN, THEY MAKE IT A HABIT.
RATS. THEY'RE OUT OF SIGHT!
ONE OF THE ROBOTS SENT TO ATTACK THE PRES-IDENT HAS COME BACK, HIGHNESS!
THIS MUST BE THE PLACE, RAG.
HMM. THAT'S ODD. IT WON'T OBEY MY COMMANDS.
SOME-THING'S FISHY. GO CHECK IT OUT.

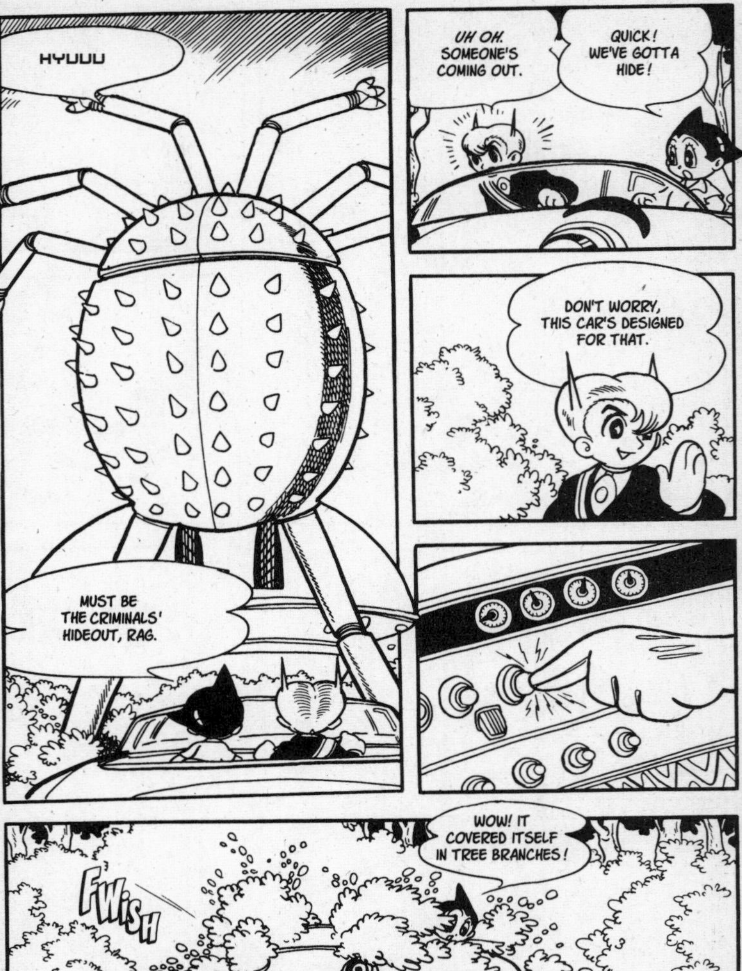
HYUUU
MUST BE THE CRIMINALS' HIDEOUT, RAG.
UH OH. SOMEONE'S COMING OUT.
QUICK! WE'VE GOTTA HIDE!
DON'T WORRY, THIS CAR'S DESIGNED FOR THAT.
FWISH
WOW! IT COVERED ITSELF IN TREE BRANCHES!

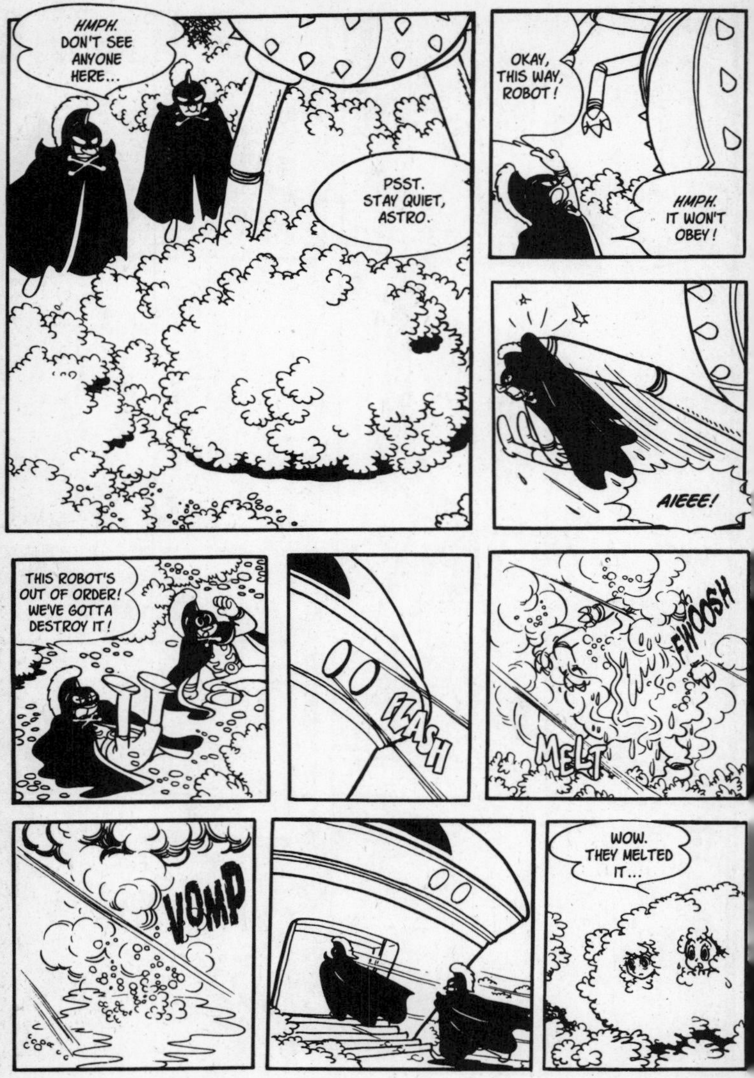
HMPH. DON'T SEE ANYONE HERE...
PSST. STAY QUIET, ASTRO.
OKAY, THIS WAY, ROBOT!
HMPH. IT WON'T OBEY!
AIEEE!
THIS ROBOT'S OUT OF ORDER! WE'VE GOTTA DESTROY IT!
FLASH
FWOOSH
MELT
VOMP
WOW. THEY MELTED IT...

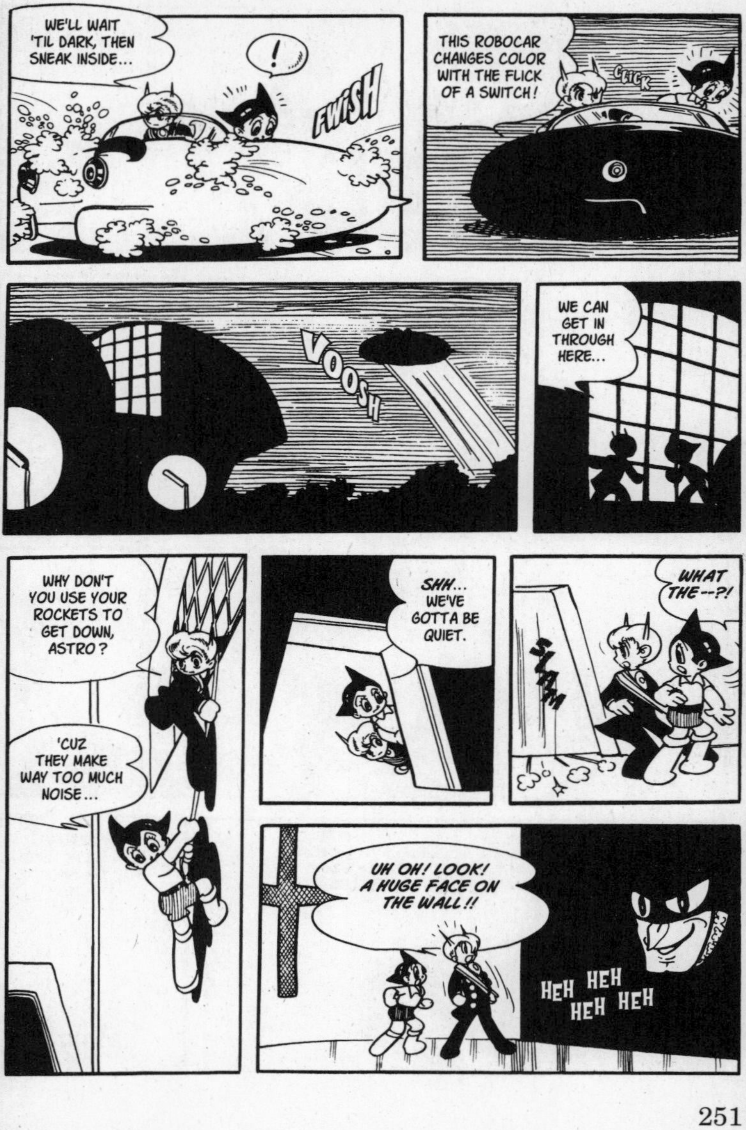

WE'LL WAIT 'TIL DARK, THEN SNEAK INSIDE...
!
FWISH
THIS ROBOCAR CHANGES COLOR WITH THE FLICK OF A SWITCH!
CLICK
VOOSH
WE CAN GET IN THROUGH HERE...
WHY DON'T YOU USE YOUR ROCKETS TO GET DOWN, ASTRO?
'CUZ THEY MAKE WAY TOO MUCH NOISE...
SHH... WE'VE GOTTA BE QUIET.
WHAT THE--?!
SLAM
UH OH! LOOK! A HUGE FACE ON THE WALL!!
HEH HEH HEH HEH

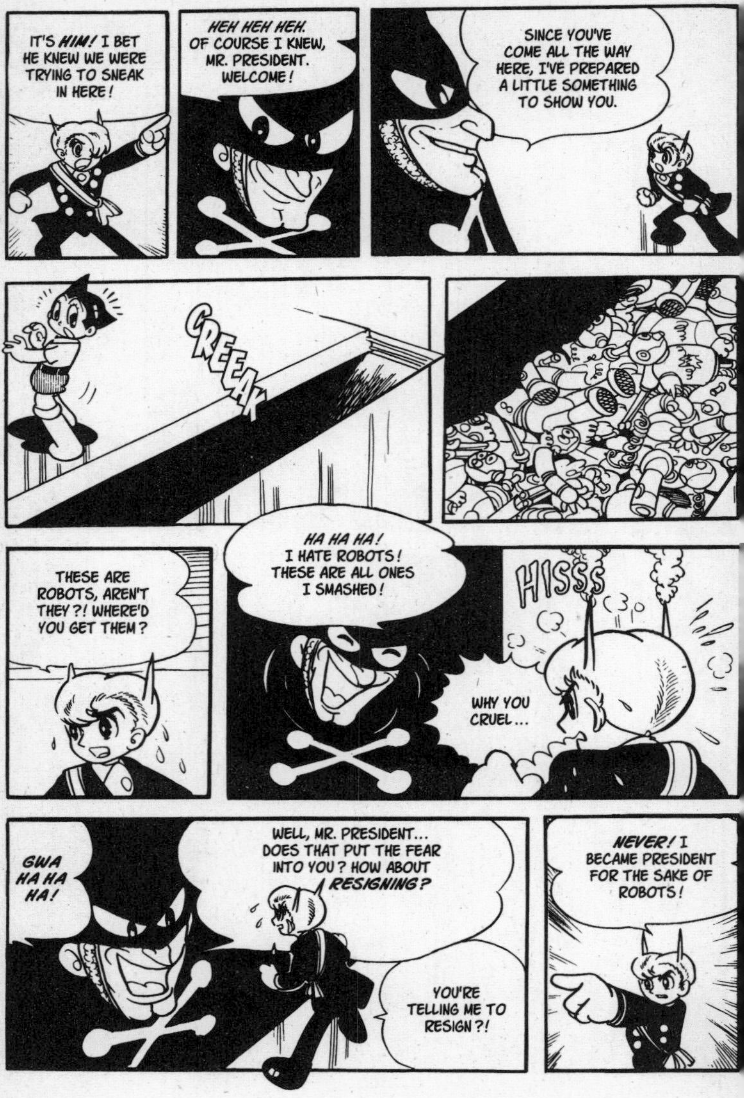
IT'S HIM! I BET HE KNEW WE WERE TRYING TO SNEAK IN HERE!
HEH HEH HEH. OF COURSE I KNEW, MR. PRESIDENT. WELCOME!
SINCE YOU'VE COME ALL THE WAY HERE, I'VE PREPARED A LITTLE SOMETHING TO SHOW YOU.
CREEEAK
THESE ARE ROBOTS, AREN'T THEY?! WHERE'D YOU GET THEM?
HA HA HA! I HATE ROBOTS! THESE ARE ALL ONES I SMASHED!
HISSS
WHY YOU CRUEL...
GWA HA HA HA!
WELL, MR. PRESIDENT... DOES THAT PUT THE FEAR INTO YOU? HOW ABOUT RESIGNING?
YOU'RE TELLING ME TO RESIGN?!
NEVER! I BECAME PRESIDENT FOR THE SAKE OF ROBOTS!

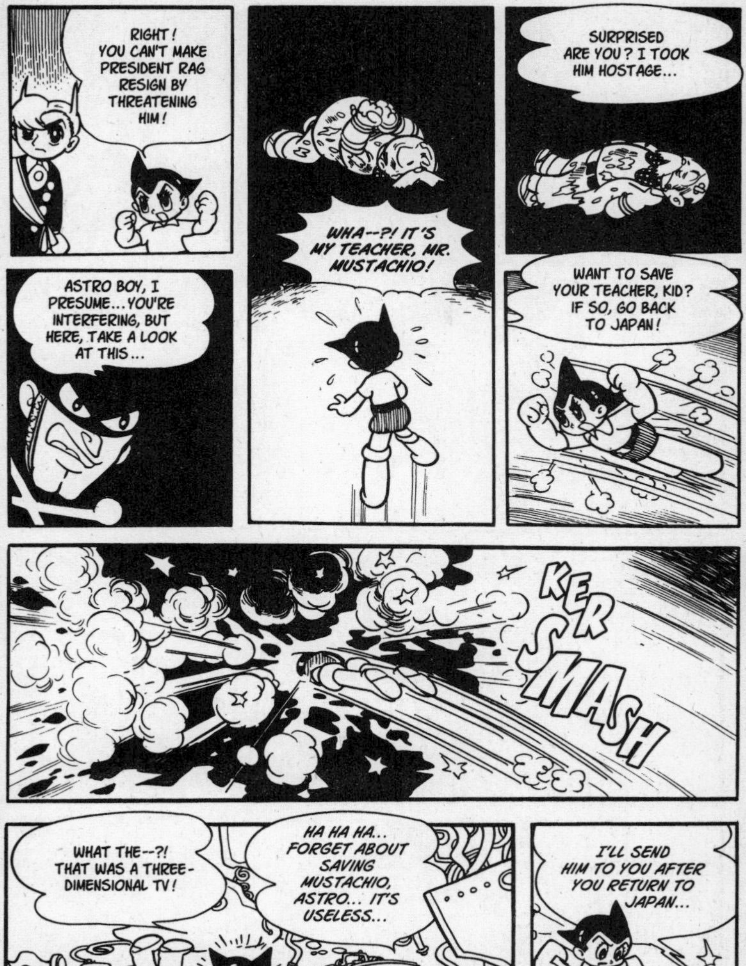

RIGHT! YOU CAN'T MAKE PRESIDENT RAG RESIGN BY THREATENING HIM!
WHA--?! IT'S MY TEACHER, MR. MUSTACHIO!
SURPRISED ARE YOU? I TOOK HIM HOSTAGE...
ASTRO BOY, I PRESUME...YOU'RE INTERFERING, BUT HERE, TAKE A LOOK AT THIS...
WANT TO SAVE YOUR TEACHER, KID? IF SO, GO BACK TO JAPAN!
KER SMASH
WHAT THE--?! THAT WAS A THREE-DIMENSIONAL TV!
HA HA HA... FORGET ABOUT SAVING MUSTACHIO, ASTRO... IT'S USELESS...
I'LL SEND HIM TO YOU AFTER YOU RETURN TO JAPAN...

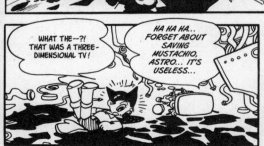

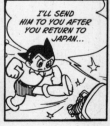

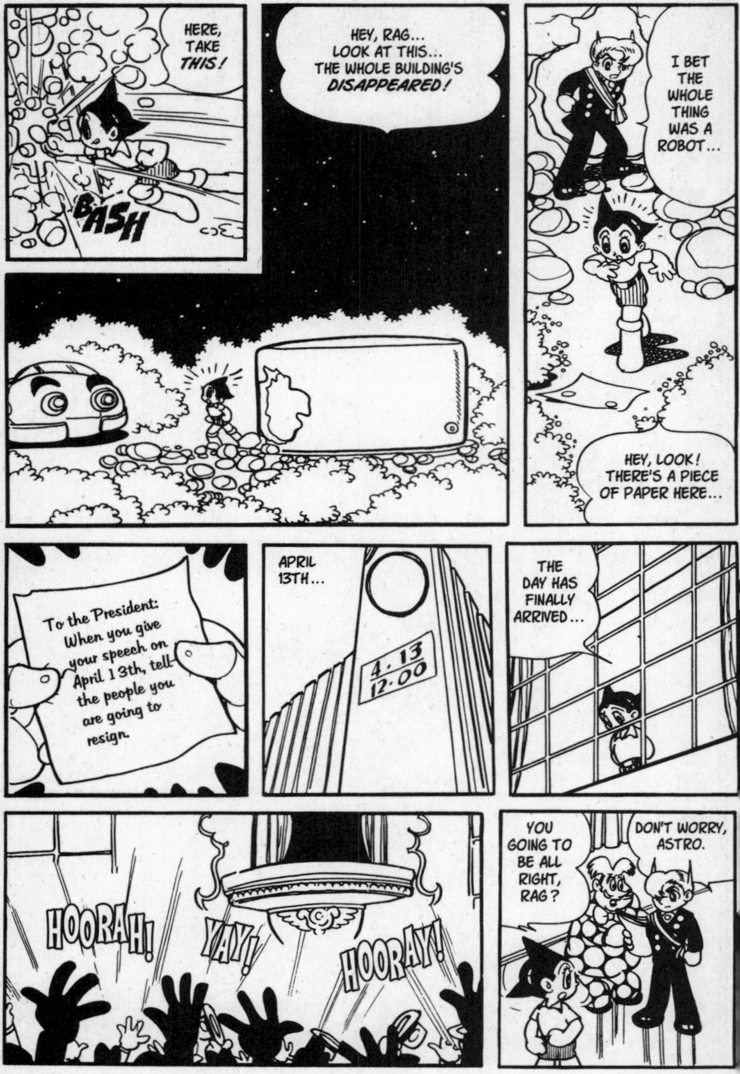
HERE, TAKE THIS!
BASH
HEY, RAG... LOOK AT THIS... THE WHOLE BUILDING'S DISAPPEARED!
I BET THE WHOLE THING WAS A ROBOT...
HEY, LOOK! THERE'S A PIECE OF PAPER HERE...
To the President: When you give your speech on April 13th, tell the people you are going to resign.
APRIL 13TH...
4.13 12.00
THE DAY HAS FINALLY ARRIVED...
HOORAH!
YAY!
HOORAY!
YOU GOING TO BE ALL RIGHT, RAG?
DON'T WORRY, ASTRO.

LOOK AT ALL THE PEOPLE WHO'VE GATHERED TO HEAR ME!

BUT THERE'LL BE SOME OF THE DEADCROSS GANG AMONG THEM, RAG...

RAH RAH YAY YAY

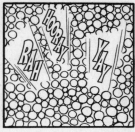

HOORAY! RAH YAY

CITIZENS OF GRAVIA, PRESIDENT RAG IS ABOUT TO MAKE A SPEECH!

THERE'S GREAT ANTICIPATION OVER WHAT THE FIRST ROBOT PRESIDENT WILL SAY...

OVER FIFTY THOUSAND PEOPLE ARE HERE TODAY!

SO IT'S FINALLY SPEECH TIME...

HOW GOES IT, #17?

HE'S ABOUT TO START...

WONDER WHAT HE'S GOING TO SAY?

WELL, IF HE DOESN'T SAY WHAT WE WANT...

...YOU KNOW WHAT TO DO.

DON'T WORRY, I'M READY...

LADIES AND GENTLEMEN! THE PRESIDENT HAS APPEARED ON THE BALCONY!

YAY YAY YAY

YAY YAY YAY BANZAI!!

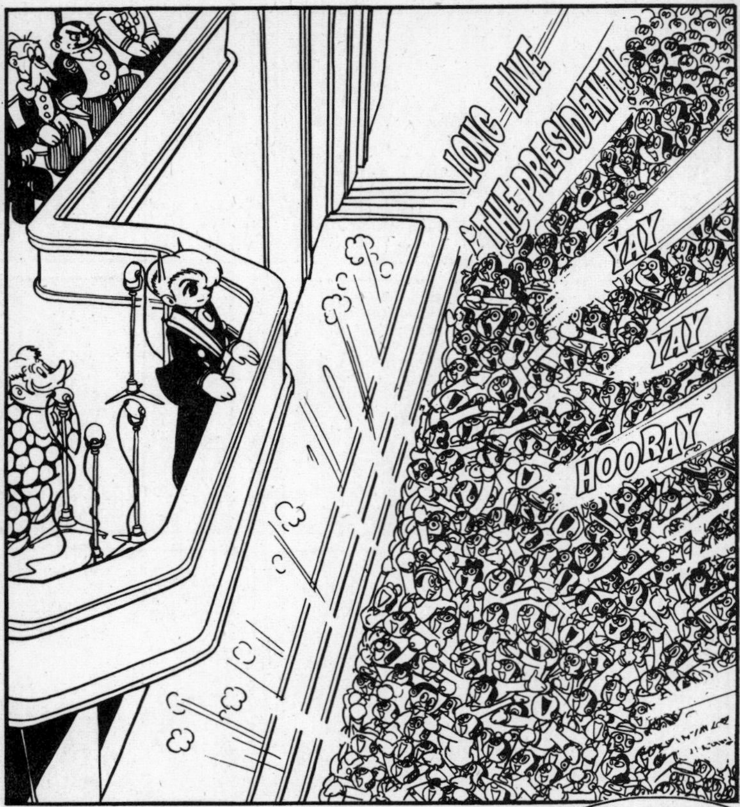
LONG LIVE THE PRESIDENT!
YAY
YAY
HOORAY
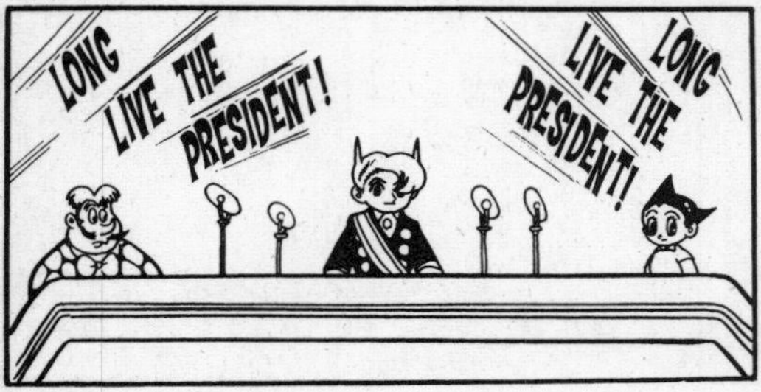
LONG LIVE THE PRESIDENT!
LONG LIVE THE PRESIDENT!
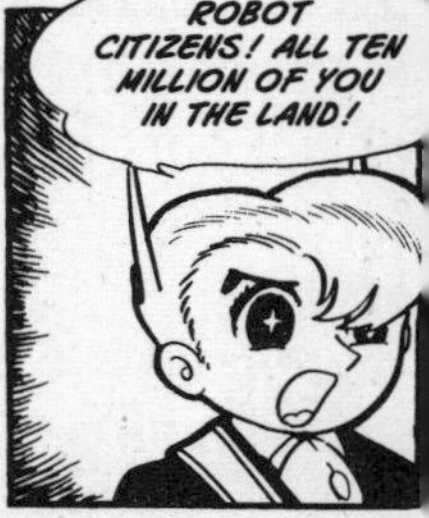
ROBOT CITIZENS! ALL TEN MILLION OF YOU IN THE LAND!

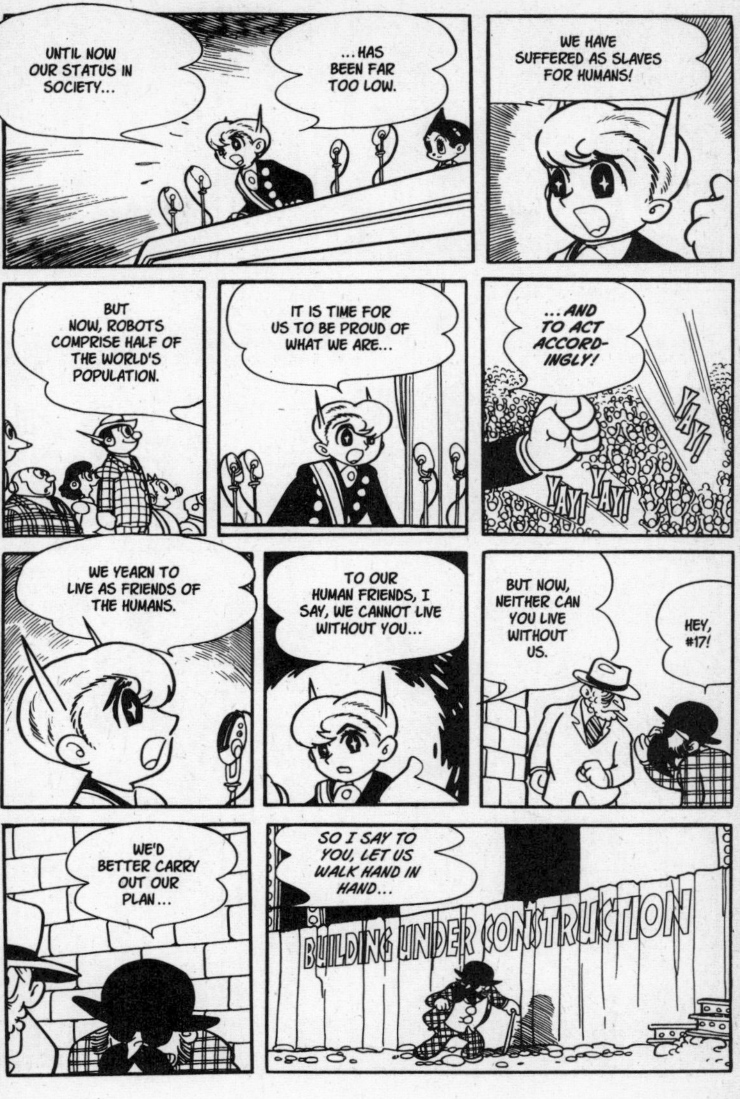
UNTIL NOW OUR STATUS IN SOCIETY...
...HAS BEEN FAR TOO LOW.
WE HAVE SUFFERED AS SLAVES FOR HUMANS!
BUT NOW, ROBOTS COMPRISE HALF OF THE WORLD'S POPULATION.
IT IS TIME FOR US TO BE PROUD OF WHAT WE ARE...
...AND TO ACT ACCORDINGLY!
YAY!
YAY!
YAY!
WE YEARN TO LIVE AS FRIENDS OF THE HUMANS.
TO OUR HUMAN FRIENDS, I SAY, WE CANNOT LIVE WITHOUT YOU...
BUT NOW, NEITHER CAN YOU LIVE WITHOUT US.
HEY, #17!
WE'D BETTER CARRY OUT OUR PLAN...
SO I SAY TO YOU, LET US WALK HAND IN HAND...
BUILDING UNDER CONSTRUCTION

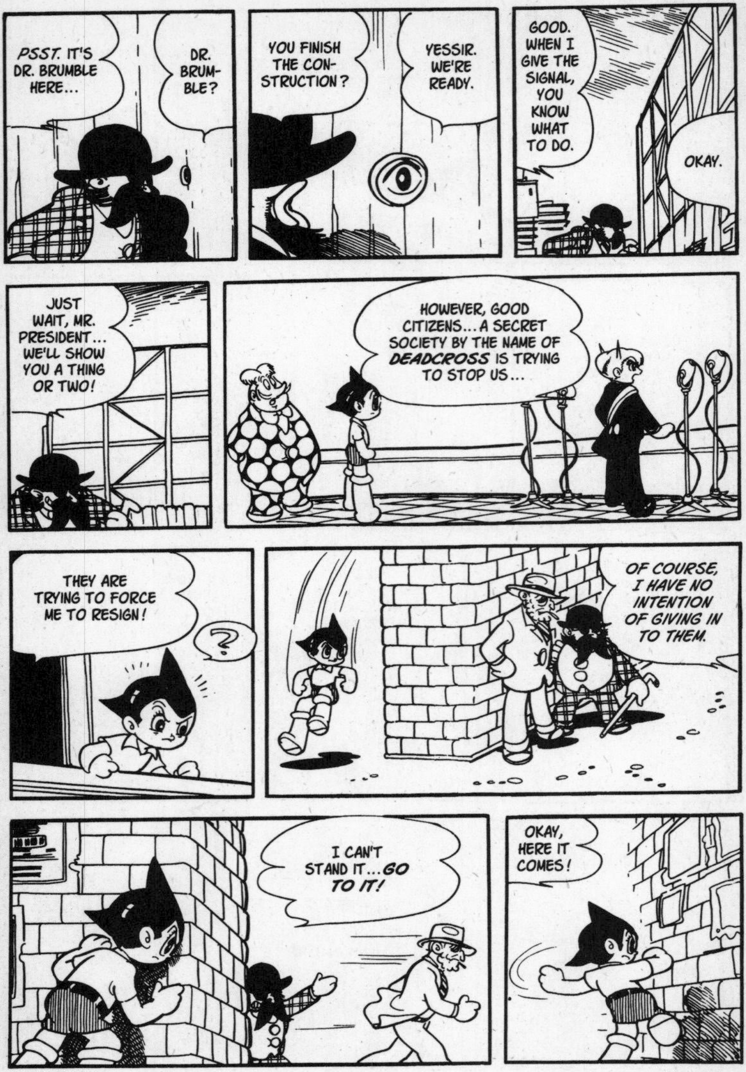
PSST. IT'S DR. BRUMBLE HERE...
DR. BRUMBLE?
YOU FINISH THE CONSTRUCTION?
YESSIR. WE'RE READY.
GOOD. WHEN I GIVE THE SIGNAL, YOU KNOW WHAT TO DO.
OKAY.
JUST WAIT, MR. PRESIDENT... WE'LL SHOW YOU A THING OR TWO!
HOWEVER, GOOD CITIZENS... A SECRET SOCIETY BY THE NAME OF DEADCROSS IS TRYING TO STOP US...
THEY ARE TRYING TO FORCE ME TO RESIGN!
?
OF COURSE, I HAVE NO INTENTION OF GIVING IN TO THEM.
I CAN'T STAND IT... GO TO IT!
OKAY, HERE IT COMES!

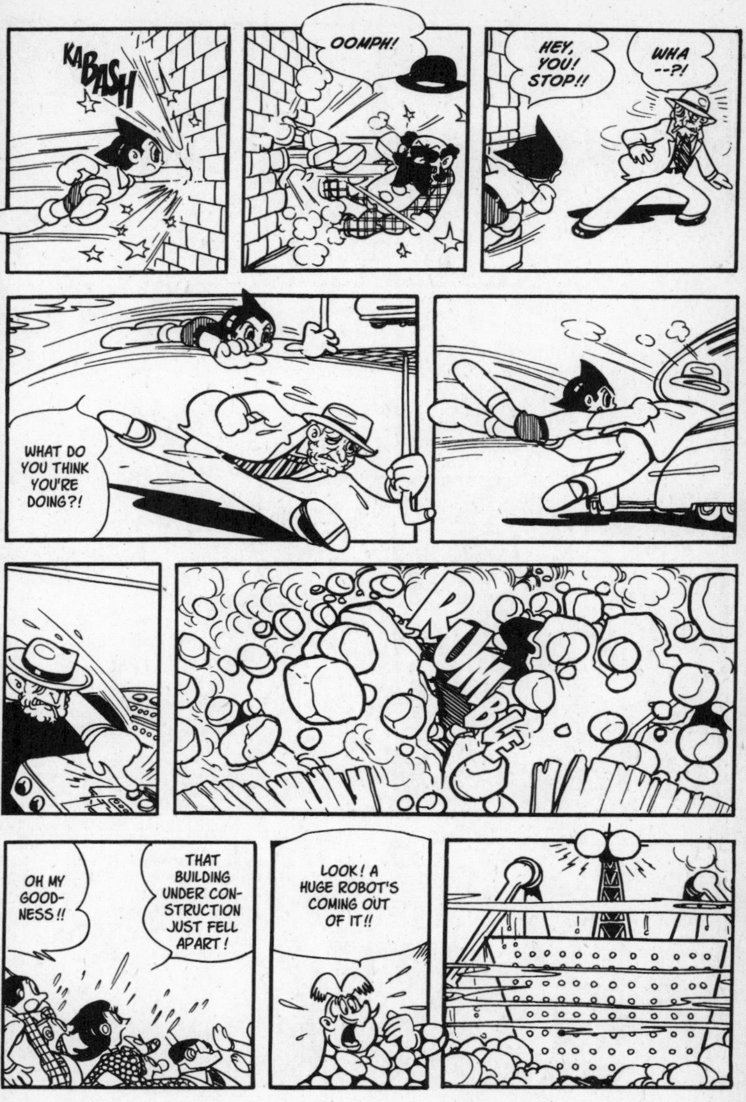
KABASH
OOMPH!
HEY, YOU! STOP!!
WHA --?!
WHAT DO YOU THINK YOU'RE DOING?!
RUMBLE
OH MY GOOD-NESS!!
THAT BUILDING UNDER CON-STRUCTION JUST FELL APART!
LOOK! A HUGE ROBOT'S COMING OUT OF IT!!

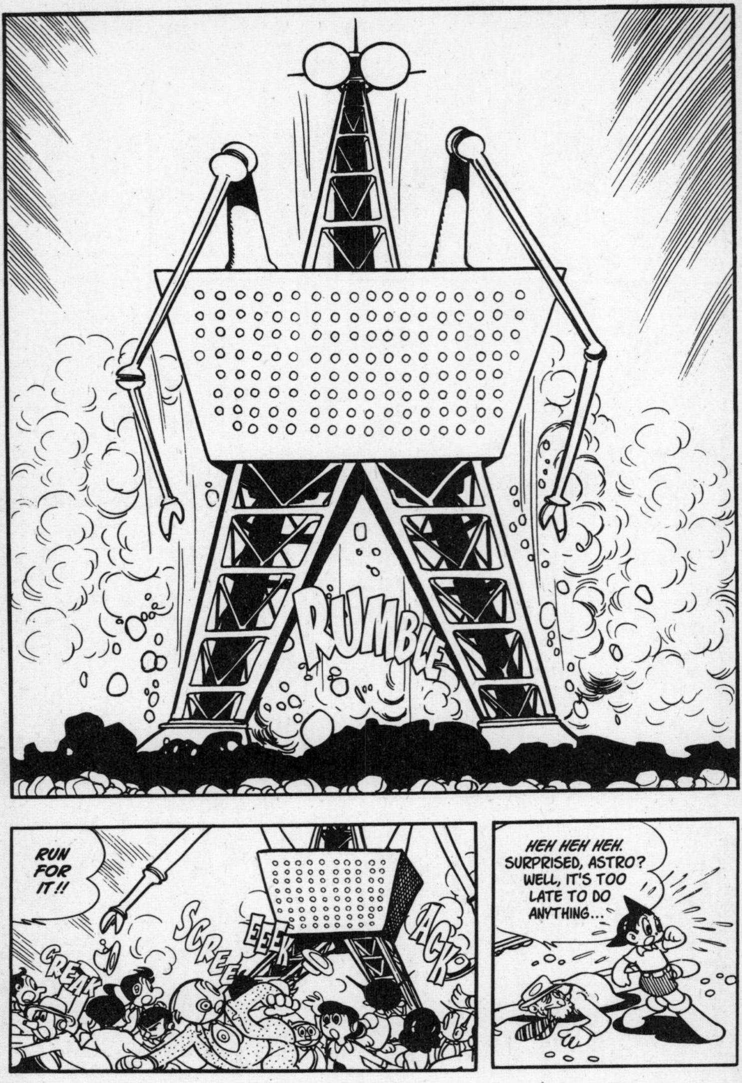
RUMBLE
RUN FOR IT!!
CREAK
SCREE
EEEK
ACK
HEH HEH HEH. SURPRISED, ASTRO? WELL, IT'S TOO LATE TO DO ANYTHING...

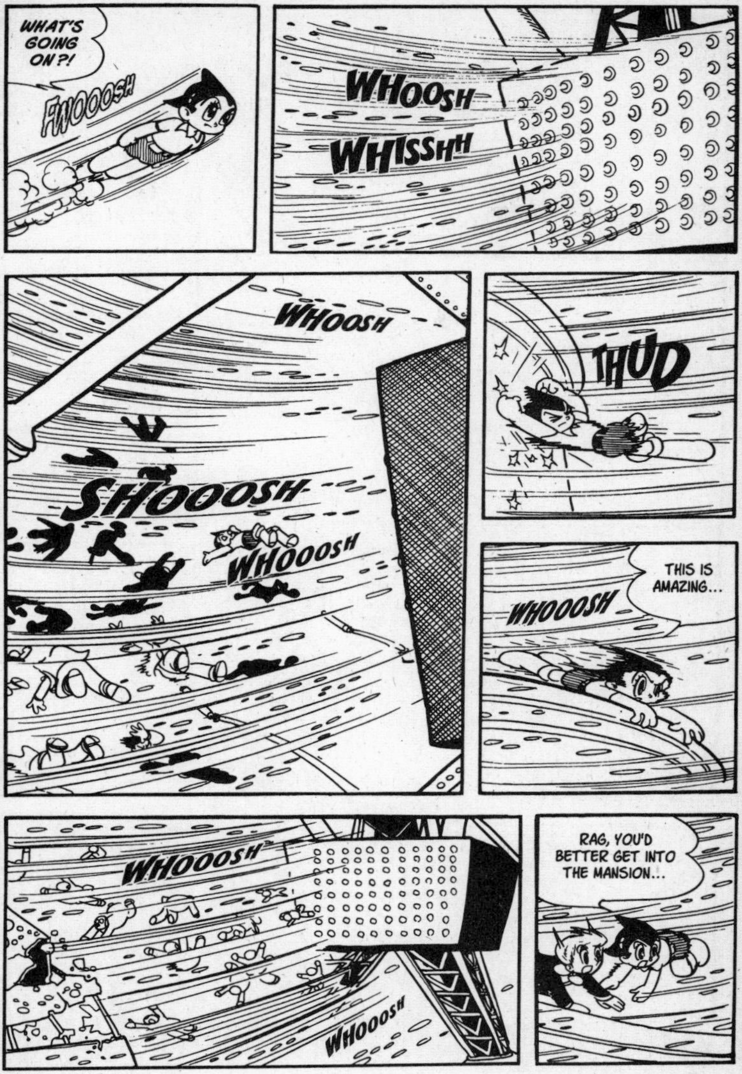
WHAT'S GOING ON?!
FWOOOSH
WHOOSH
WHISSHH
WHOOSH
SHOOOOSH
WHOOOSH
THUD
WHOOOSH
THIS IS AMAZING...
WHOOOSH
WHOOOSH
RAG, YOU'D BETTER GET INTO THE MANSION...

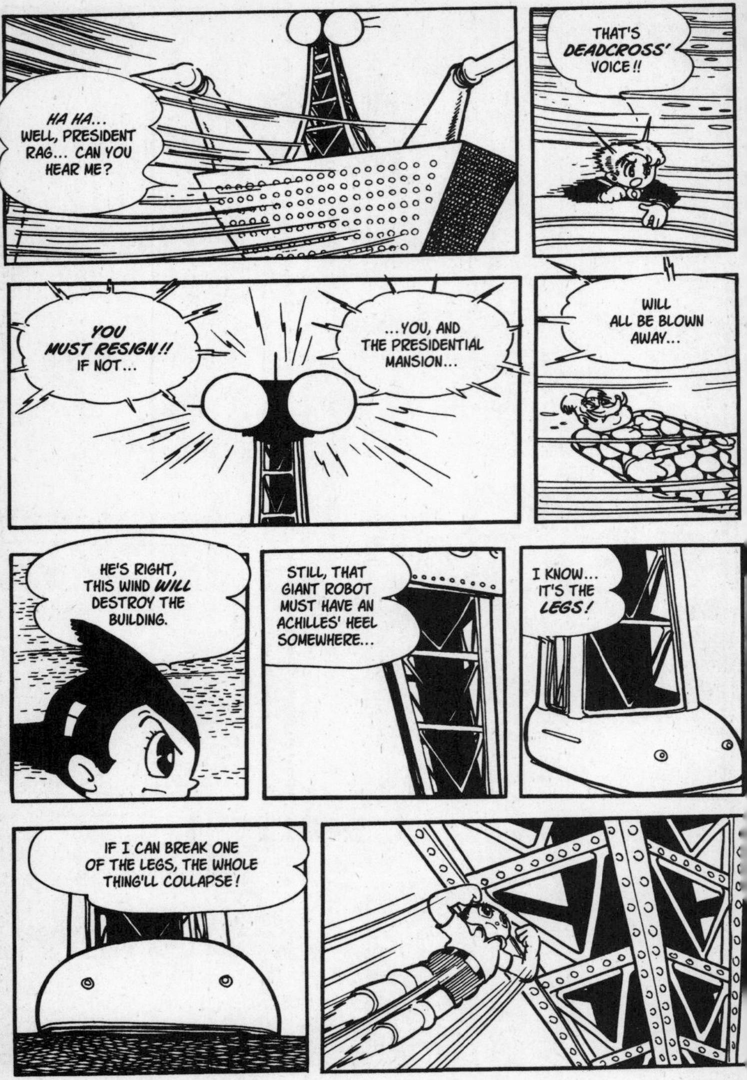
HA HA... WELL, PRESIDENT RAG... CAN YOU HEAR ME?
THAT'S DEADCROSS' VOICE!!
YOU MUST RESIGN!! IF NOT...
...YOU, AND THE PRESIDENTIAL MANSION...
WILL ALL BE BLOWN AWAY...
HE'S RIGHT, THIS WIND WILL DESTROY THE BUILDING.
STILL, THAT GIANT ROBOT MUST HAVE AN ACHILLES' HEEL SOMEWHERE...
I KNOW... IT'S THE LEGS!
IF I CAN BREAK ONE OF THE LEGS, THE WHOLE THING'LL COLLAPSE!

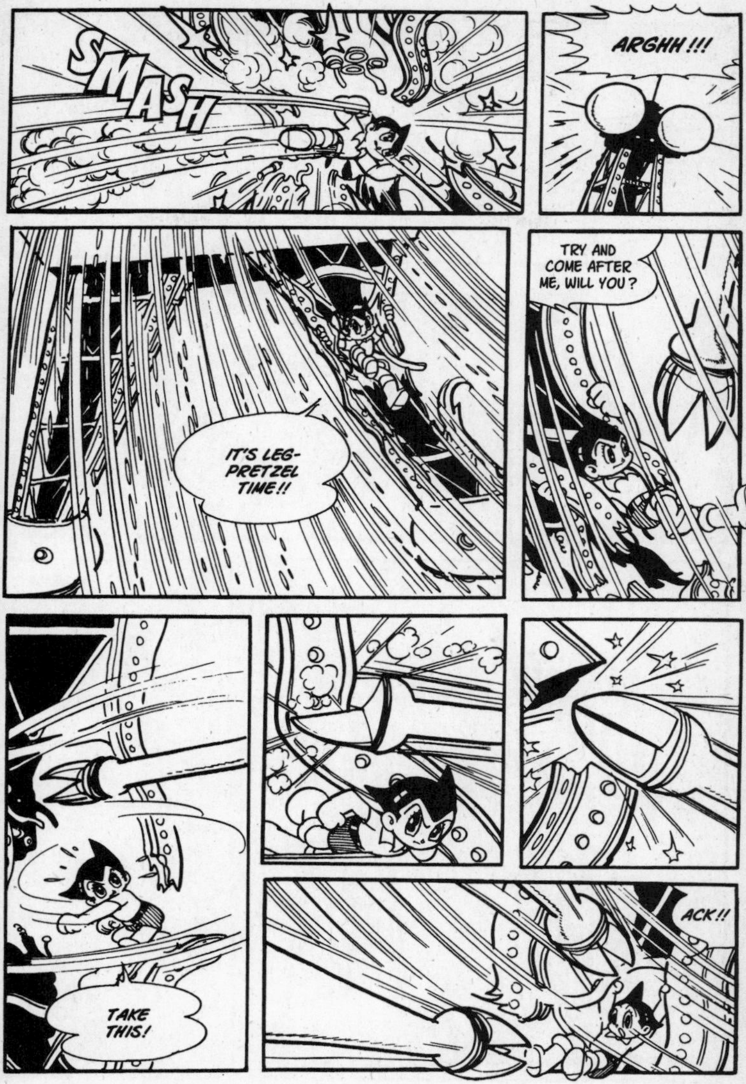
SMASH
ARGHH!!!
IT'S LEG-PRETZEL TIME!!
TRY AND COME AFTER ME, WILL YOU?
TAKE THIS!
ACK!!

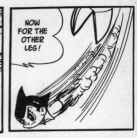
NOW FOR THE OTHER LEG!

KACHANK

CHANG

WHOOOOSHH

VOOOOM

HOORAY! HE BLASTED OFF UNDER HIS OWN WIND POWER!

MASTER ASTRO! THE PRESIDENT...

264

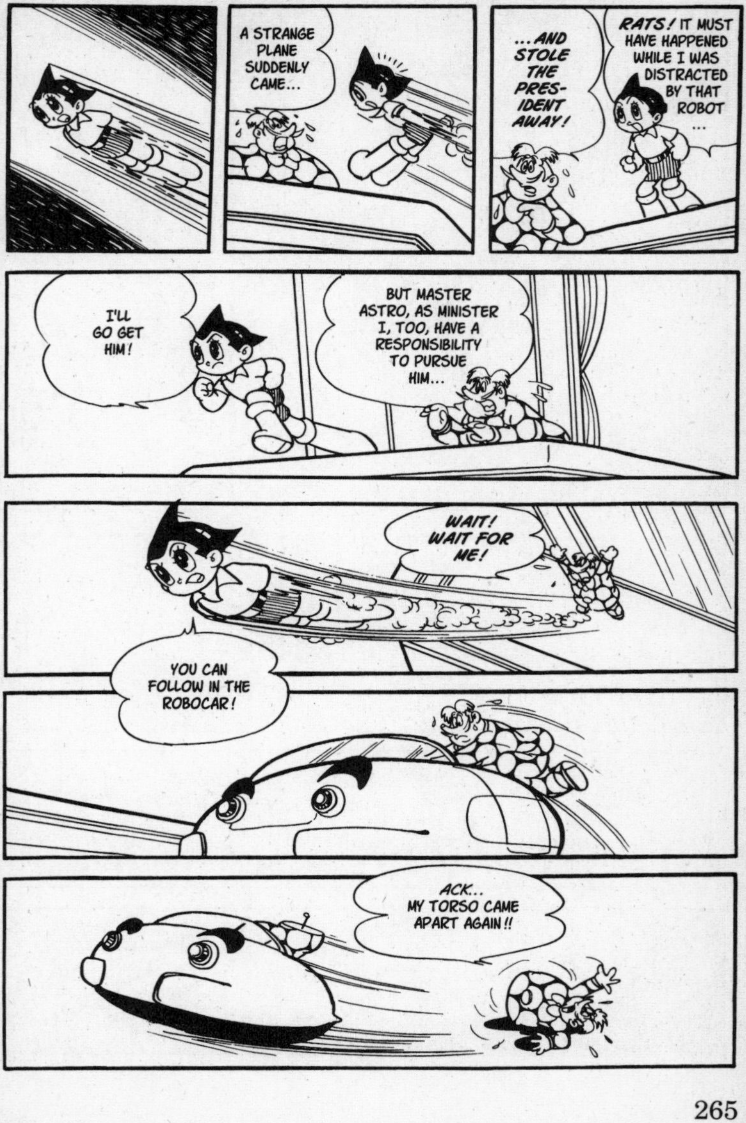
A STRANGE PLANE SUDDENLY CAME...
...AND STOLE THE PRES-IDENT AWAY!
RATS! IT MUST HAVE HAPPENED WHILE I WAS DISTRACTED BY THAT ROBOT ...
I'LL GO GET HIM!
BUT MASTER ASTRO, AS MINISTER I, TOO, HAVE A RESPONSIBILITY TO PURSUE HIM...
WAIT! WAIT FOR ME!
YOU CAN FOLLOW IN THE ROBOCAR!
ACK... MY TORSO CAME APART AGAIN!!

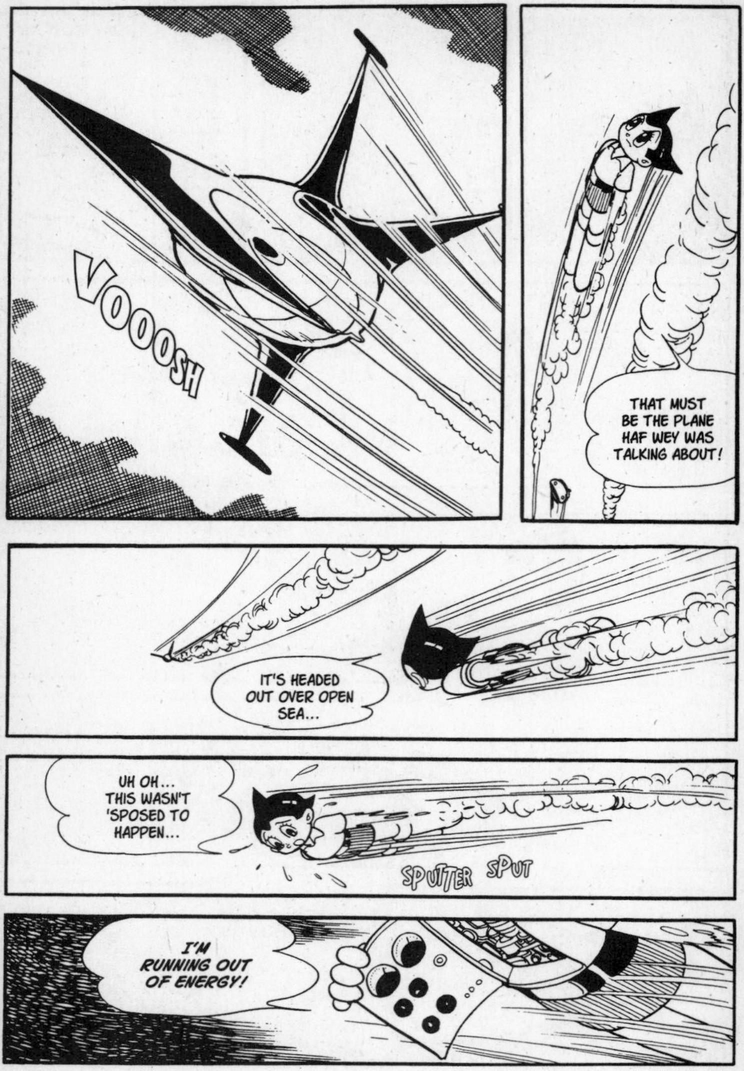
VOOOSH
THAT MUST BE THE PLANE HAF WEY WAS TALKING ABOUT!
IT'S HEADED OUT OVER OPEN SEA...
UH OH... THIS WASN'T 'SPOSED TO HAPPEN...
SPUTTER SPUT
I'M RUNNING OUT OF ENERGY!

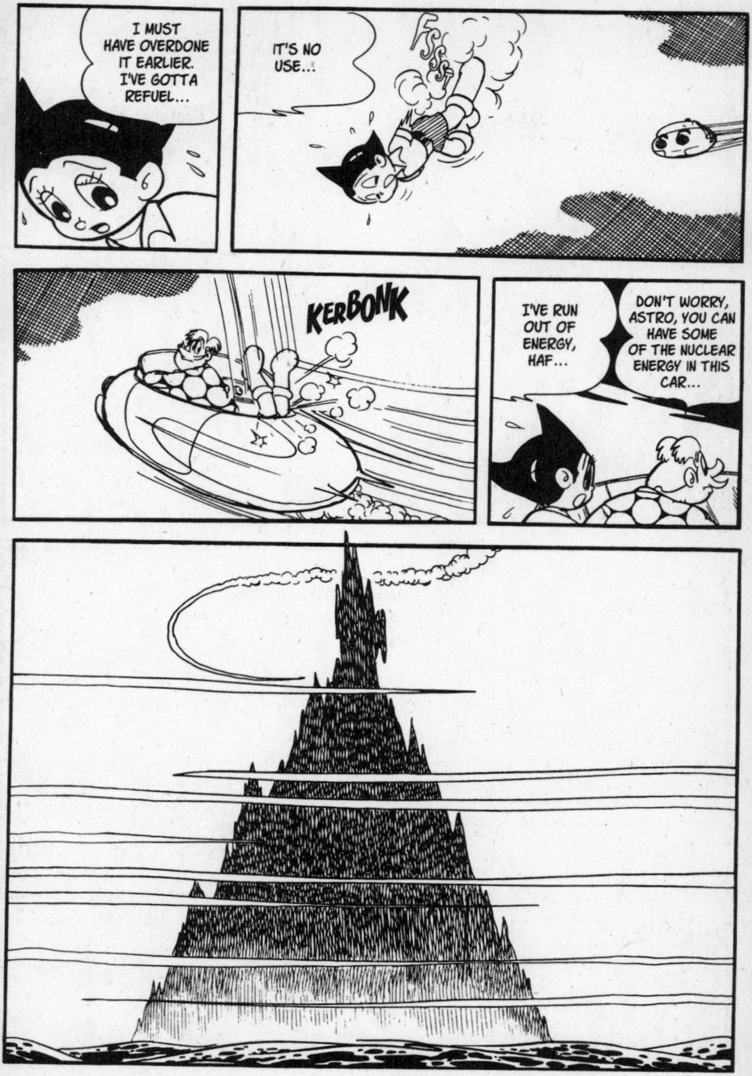
I MUST HAVE OVERDONE IT EARLIER. I'VE GOTTA REFUEL...
IT'S NO USE...!
KERBONK
I'VE RUN OUT OF ENERGY, HAF...
DON'T WORRY, ASTRO, YOU CAN HAVE SOME OF THE NUCLEAR ENERGY IN THIS CAR...

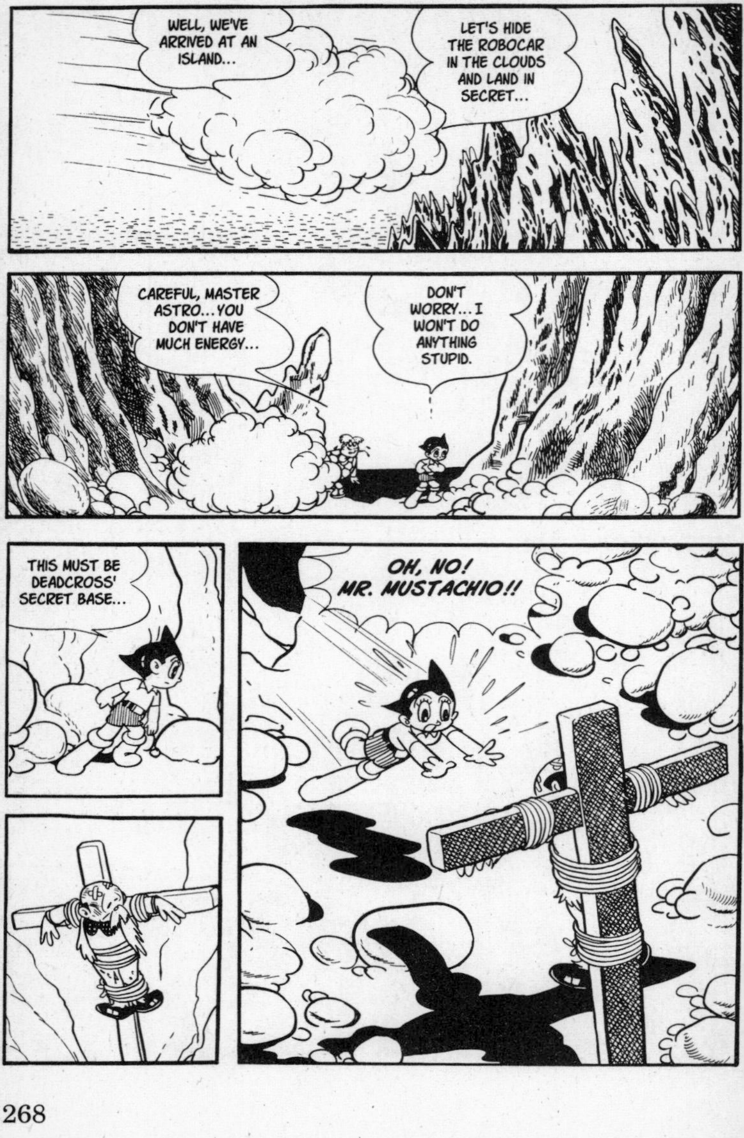
WELL, WE'VE ARRIVED AT AN ISLAND...
LET'S HIDE THE ROBOCAR IN THE CLOUDS AND LAND IN SECRET...
CAREFUL, MASTER ASTRO...YOU DON'T HAVE MUCH ENERGY...
DON'T WORRY...I WON'T DO ANYTHING STUPID.
THIS MUST BE DEADCROSS' SECRET BASE...
OH, NO! MR. MUSTACHIO!!

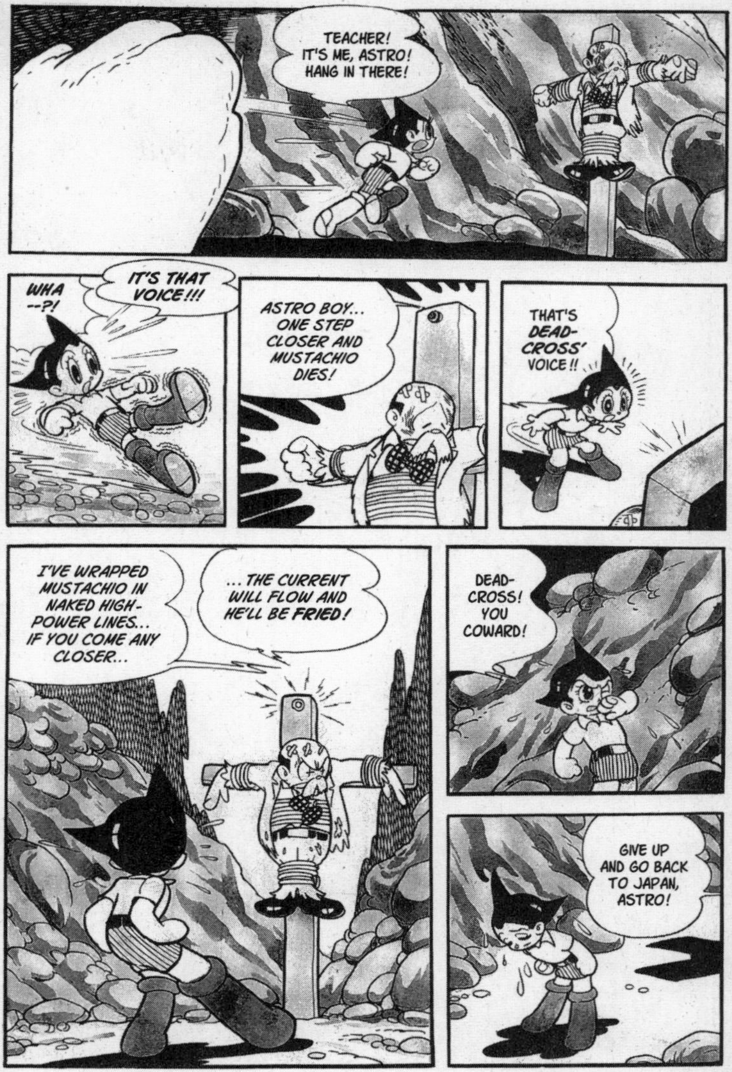
TEACHER! IT'S ME, ASTRO! HANG IN THERE!
WHA --?!
IT'S THAT VOICE!!!
ASTRO BOY... ONE STEP CLOSER AND MUSTACHIO DIES!
THAT'S DEAD-CROSS' VOICE!!
I'VE WRAPPED MUSTACHIO IN NAKED HIGH-POWER LINES... IF YOU COME ANY CLOSER...
...THE CURRENT WILL FLOW AND HE'LL BE FRIED!
DEAD-CROSS! YOU COWARD!
GIVE UP AND GO BACK TO JAPAN, ASTRO!

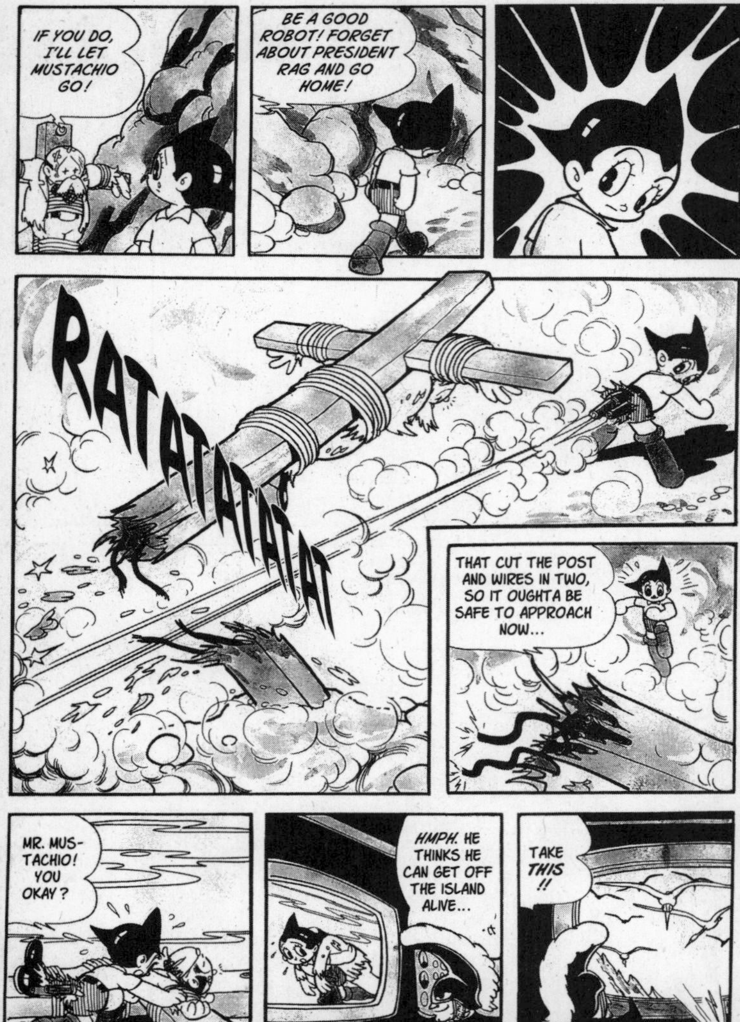
IF YOU DO, I'LL LET MUSTACHIO GO!
BE A GOOD ROBOT! FORGET ABOUT PRESIDENT RAG AND GO HOME!
RATATATATATAT
THAT CUT THE POST AND WIRES IN TWO, SO IT OUGHTA BE SAFE TO APPROACH NOW...
MR. MUS-TACHIO! YOU OKAY?
HMPH. HE THINKS HE CAN GET OFF THE ISLAND ALIVE...
TAKE THIS!!

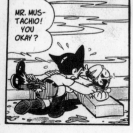

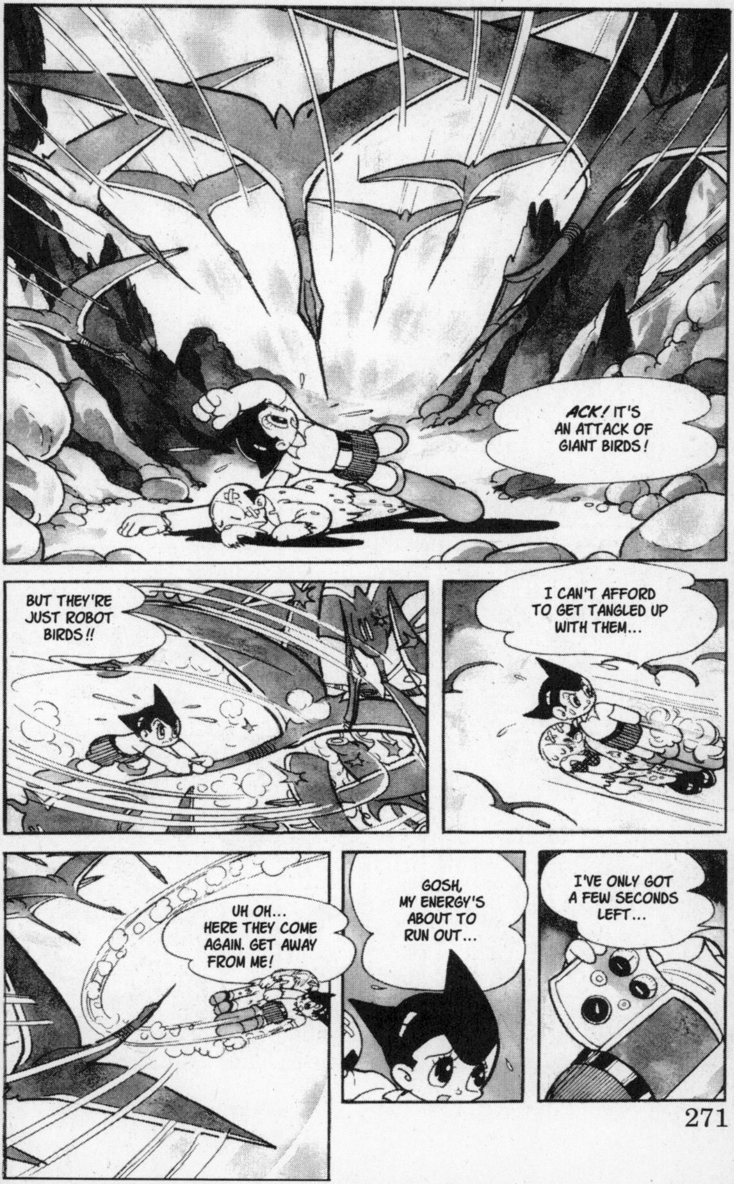
ACK! IT'S AN ATTACK OF GIANT BIRDS!
BUT THEY'RE JUST ROBOT BIRDS!!
I CAN'T AFFORD TO GET TANGLED UP WITH THEM...
UH OH... HERE THEY COME AGAIN. GET AWAY FROM ME!
GOSH, MY ENERGY'S ABOUT TO RUN OUT...
I'VE ONLY GOT A FEW SECONDS LEFT...

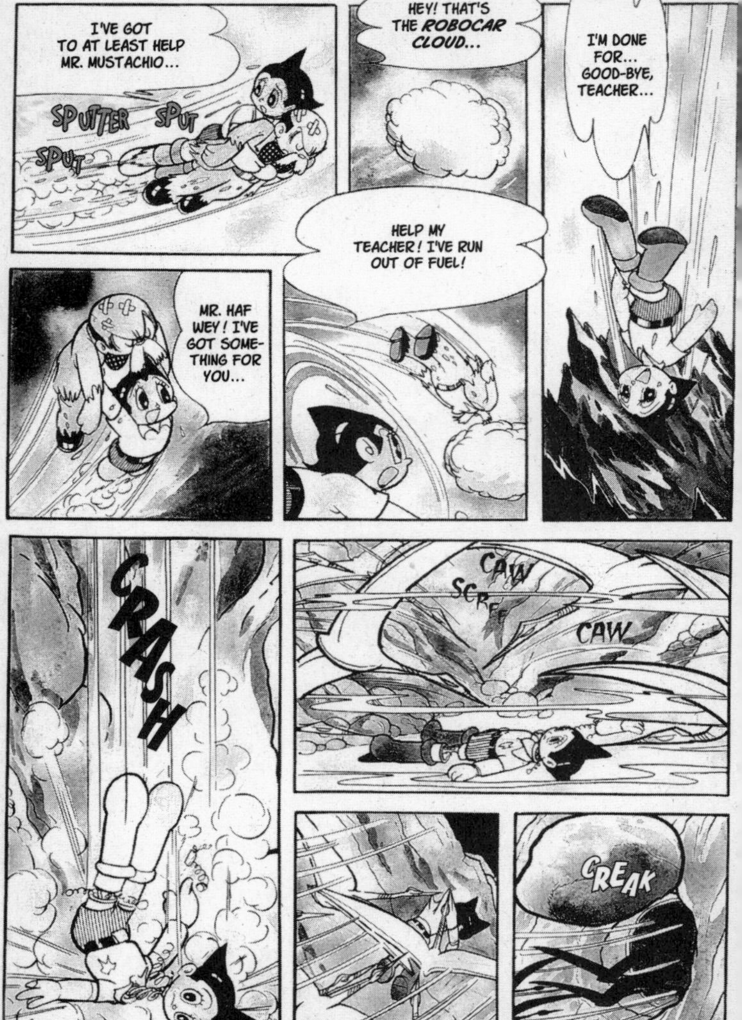
I'VE GOT TO AT LEAST HELP MR. MUSTACHIO...
SPUTTER
SPUT
SPUT
HEY! THAT'S THE ROBOCAR CLOUD...
MR. HAF WEY! I'VE GOT SOMETHING FOR YOU...
HELP MY TEACHER! I'VE RUN OUT OF FUEL!
I'M DONE FOR... GOOD-BYE, TEACHER...
CRASH
CAW
SCRE
CAW
CREAK

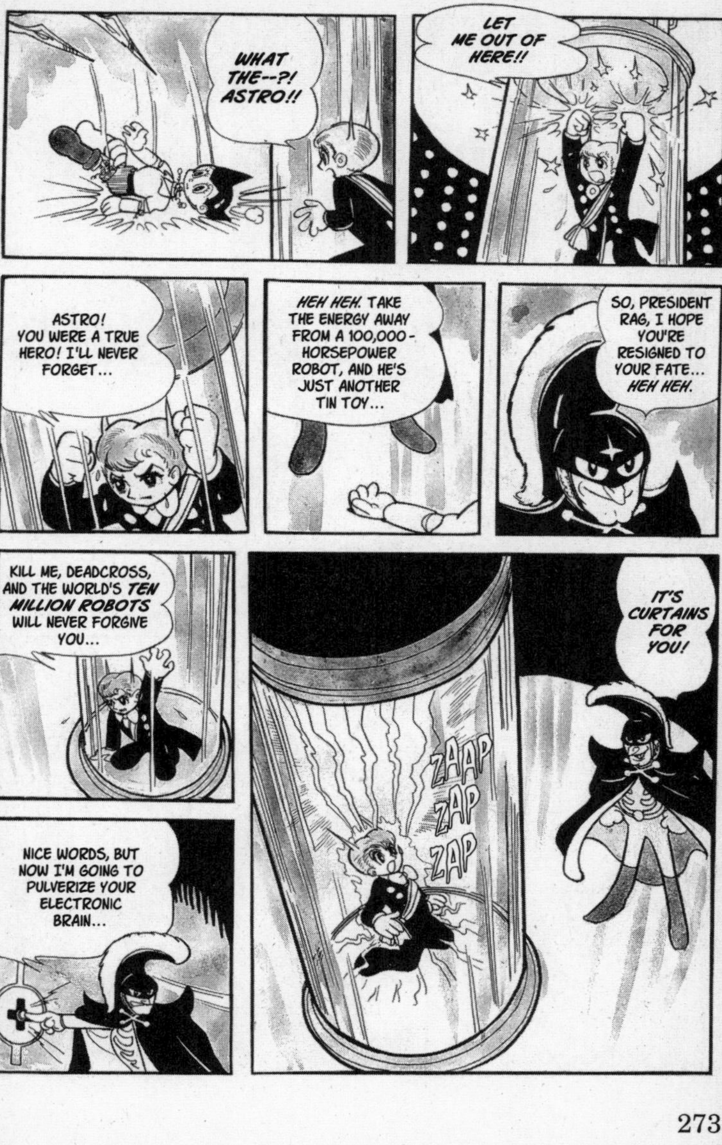
WHAT THE--?! ASTRO!!
LET ME OUT OF HERE!!
ASTRO! YOU WERE A TRUE HERO! I'LL NEVER FORGET...
HEH HEH. TAKE THE ENERGY AWAY FROM A 100,000-HORSEPOWER ROBOT, AND HE'S JUST ANOTHER TIN TOY...
SO, PRESIDENT RAG, I HOPE YOU'RE RESIGNED TO YOUR FATE... *HEH HEH.*
KILL ME, DEADCROSS, AND THE WORLD'S *TEN MILLION ROBOTS* WILL NEVER FORGIVE YOU...
NICE WORDS, BUT NOW I'M GOING TO PULVERIZE YOUR ELECTRONIC BRAIN...
IT'S CURTAINS FOR YOU!
ZAAP ZAP ZAP

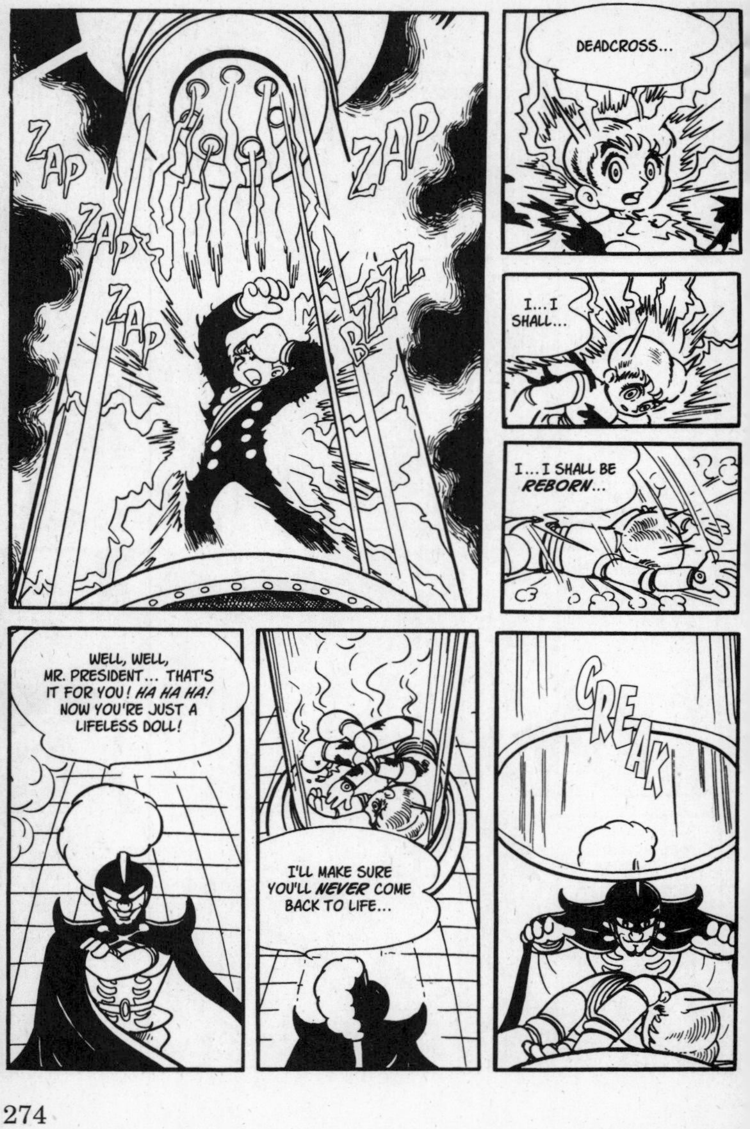
ZAP
ZAP
ZAP
ZAP
BZZZZ
DEADCROSS...
I... I SHALL...
I... I SHALL BE *REBORN*...
WELL, WELL, MR. PRESIDENT... THAT'S IT FOR YOU! *HA HA HA!* NOW YOU'RE JUST A LIFELESS DOLL!
I'LL MAKE SURE YOU'LL *NEVER* COME BACK TO LIFE...
CREAK

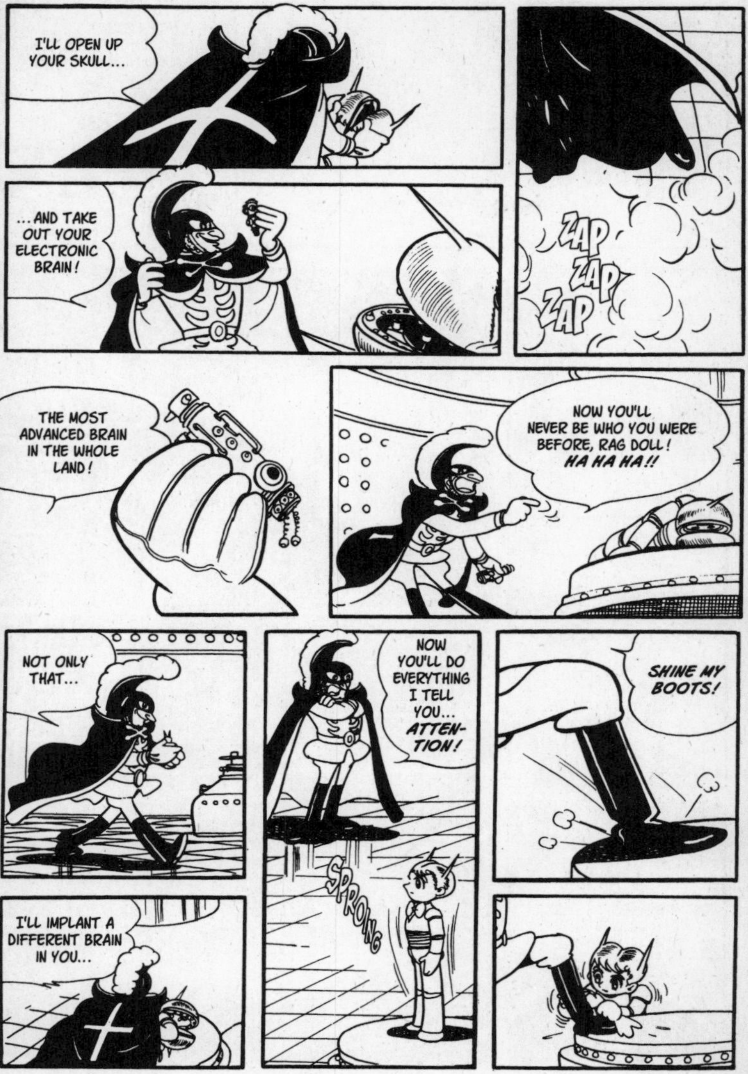
I'LL OPEN UP YOUR SKULL...
...AND TAKE OUT YOUR ELECTRONIC BRAIN!
ZAP
ZAP
ZAP
THE MOST ADVANCED BRAIN IN THE WHOLE LAND!
NOW YOU'LL NEVER BE WHO YOU WERE BEFORE, RAG DOLL! HA HA HA!!
NOT ONLY THAT...
I'LL IMPLANT A DIFFERENT BRAIN IN YOU...
NOW YOU'LL DO EVERYTHING I TELL YOU... ATTEN-TION!
SPROING
SHINE MY BOOTS!

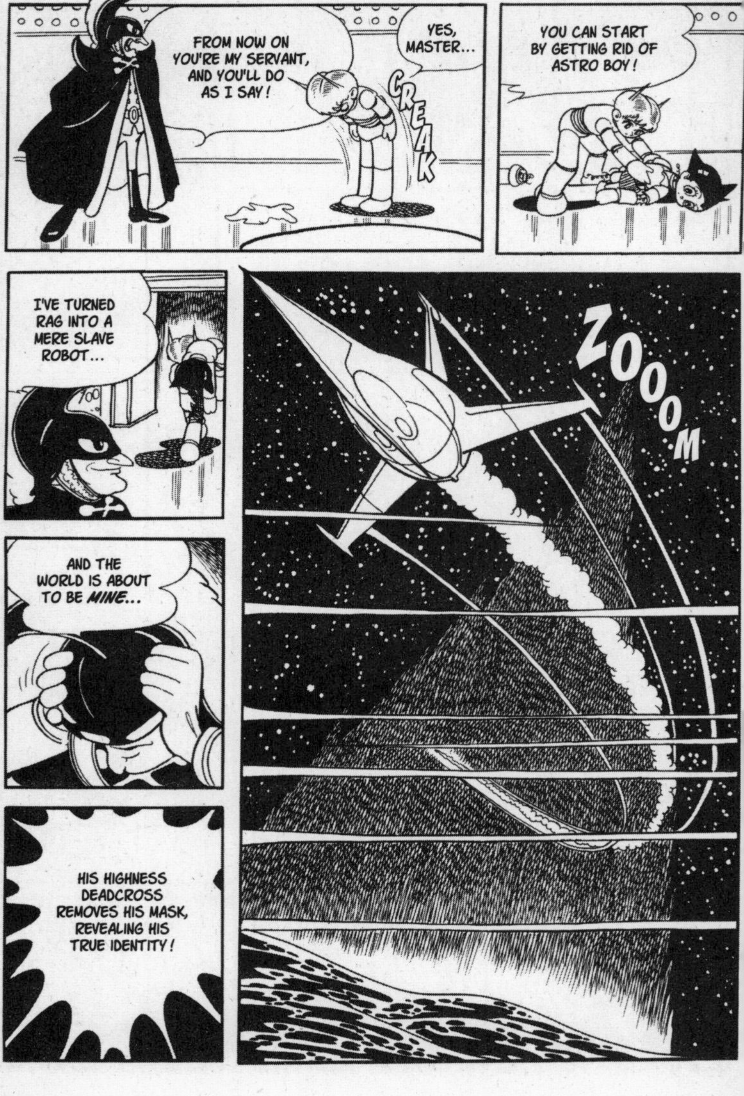
FROM NOW ON YOU'RE MY SERVANT, AND YOU'LL DO AS I SAY!
YES, MASTER...
CREAK
YOU CAN START BY GETTING RID OF ASTRO BOY!
I'VE TURNED RAG INTO A MERE SLAVE ROBOT...
AND THE WORLD IS ABOUT TO BE *MINE*...
HIS HIGHNESS DEADCROSS REMOVES HIS MASK, REVEALING HIS TRUE IDENTITY!
ZOOOOM

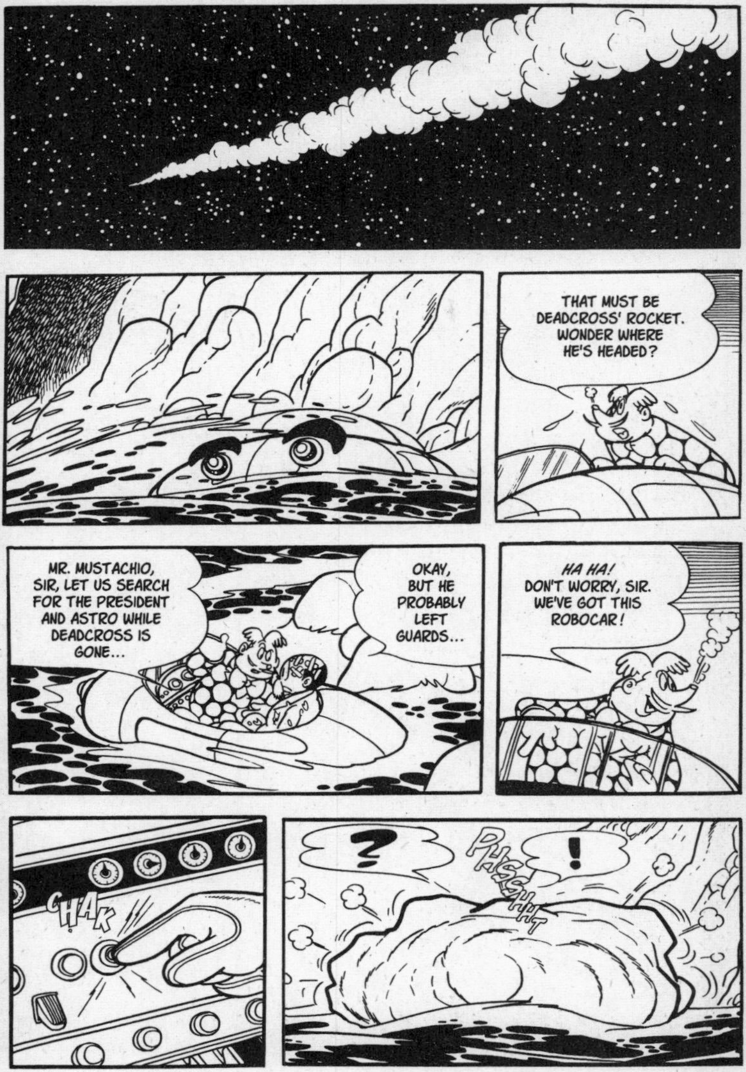
THAT MUST BE DEADCROSS' ROCKET. WONDER WHERE HE'S HEADED?
MR. MUSTACHIO, SIR, LET US SEARCH FOR THE PRESIDENT AND ASTRO WHILE DEADCROSS IS GONE...
OKAY, BUT HE PROBABLY LEFT GUARDS...
HA HA! DON'T WORRY, SIR. WE'VE GOT THIS ROBOCAR!
CHAK
?
PHSSHHT
!

WHAT'S GOING ON?! THE CAR LOOKS LIKE PUFFY ROCK CANDY!

THE ROBO-CAR CAN CAMOUFLAGE ITSELF LIKE THE ROCK WALL, SIR!

I'VE SEEN ROCKS FALL OFF CLIFFS, BUT I'VE NEVER HEARD OF ONE CRAWLING UP...

SHH, SIR...

HERE COME SOME ROBO BIRDS!

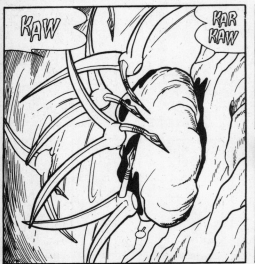

KAW

KAR KAW

PECK PECK

HACK PECK

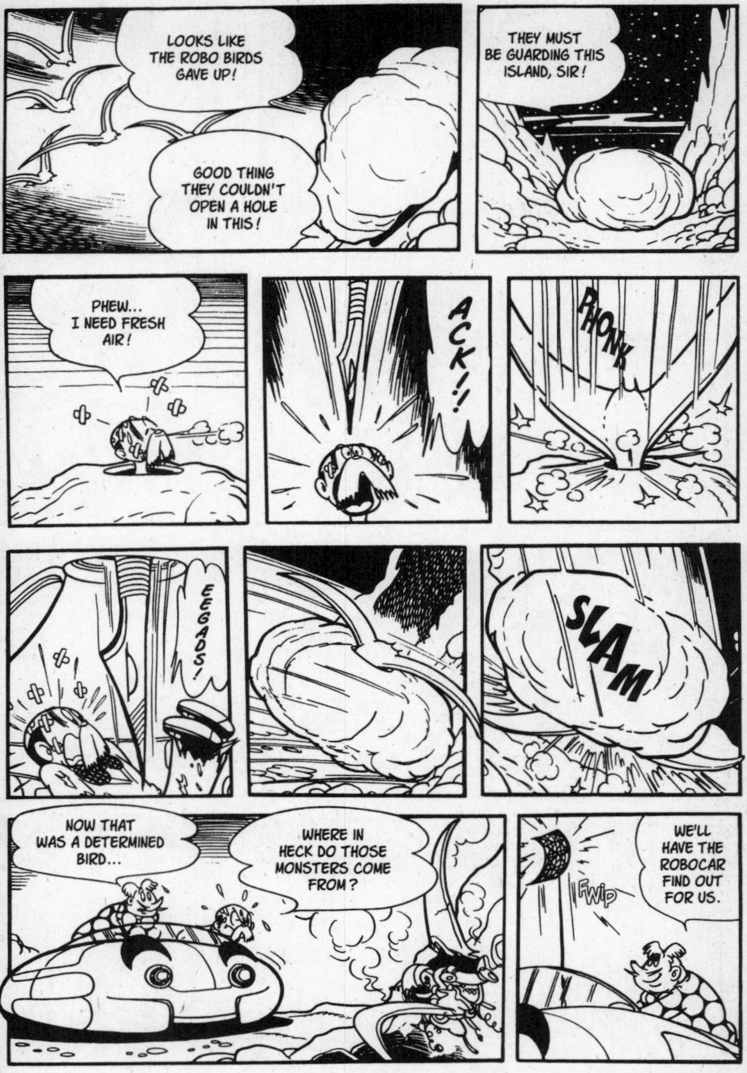
LOOKS LIKE THE ROBO BIRDS GAVE UP!
GOOD THING THEY COULDN'T OPEN A HOLE IN THIS!
THEY MUST BE GUARDING THIS ISLAND, SIR!
PHEW... I NEED FRESH AIR!
ACK!!
PHONK
EEGADS!
SLAM
NOW THAT WAS A DETERMINED BIRD...
WHERE IN HECK DO THOSE MONSTERS COME FROM?
FWIP
WE'LL HAVE THE ROBOCAR FIND OUT FOR US.

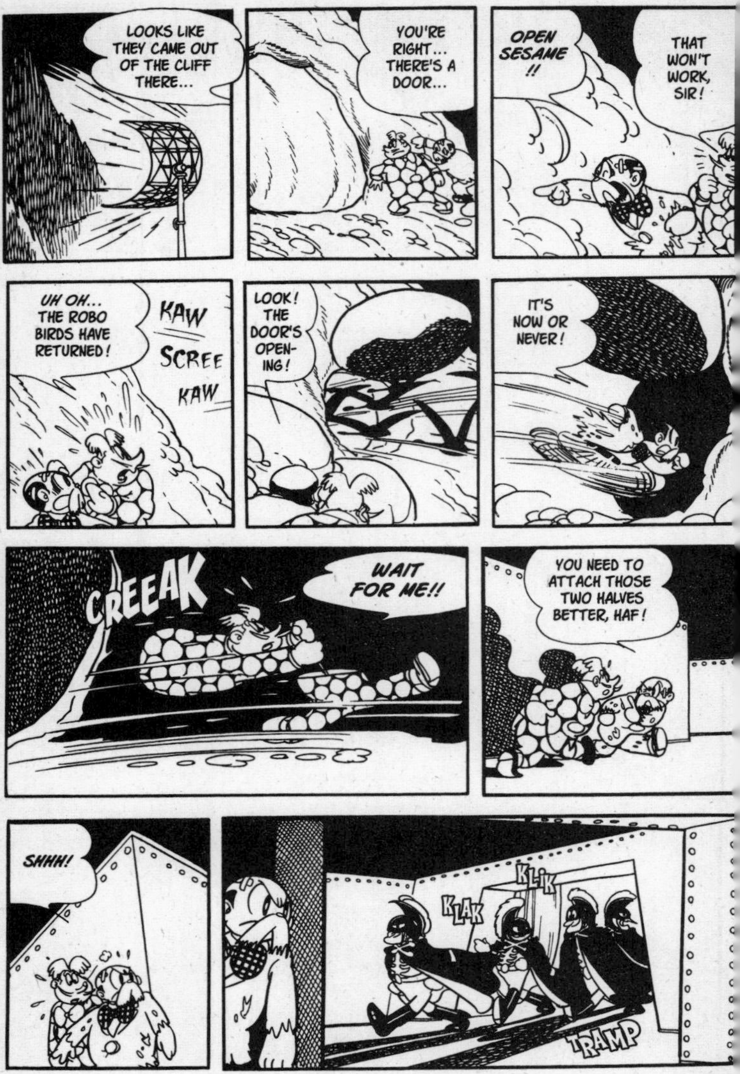
LOOKS LIKE THEY CAME OUT OF THE CLIFF THERE...
YOU'RE RIGHT... THERE'S A DOOR...
OPEN SESAME !!
THAT WON'T WORK, SIR !
UH OH... THE ROBO BIRDS HAVE RETURNED !
KAW
SCREE
KAW
LOOK! THE DOOR'S OPEN-ING !
IT'S NOW OR NEVER !
CREEAK
WAIT FOR ME!!
YOU NEED TO ATTACH THOSE TWO HALVES BETTER, HAF !
SHHH!
KLIK
KLAK
TRAMP

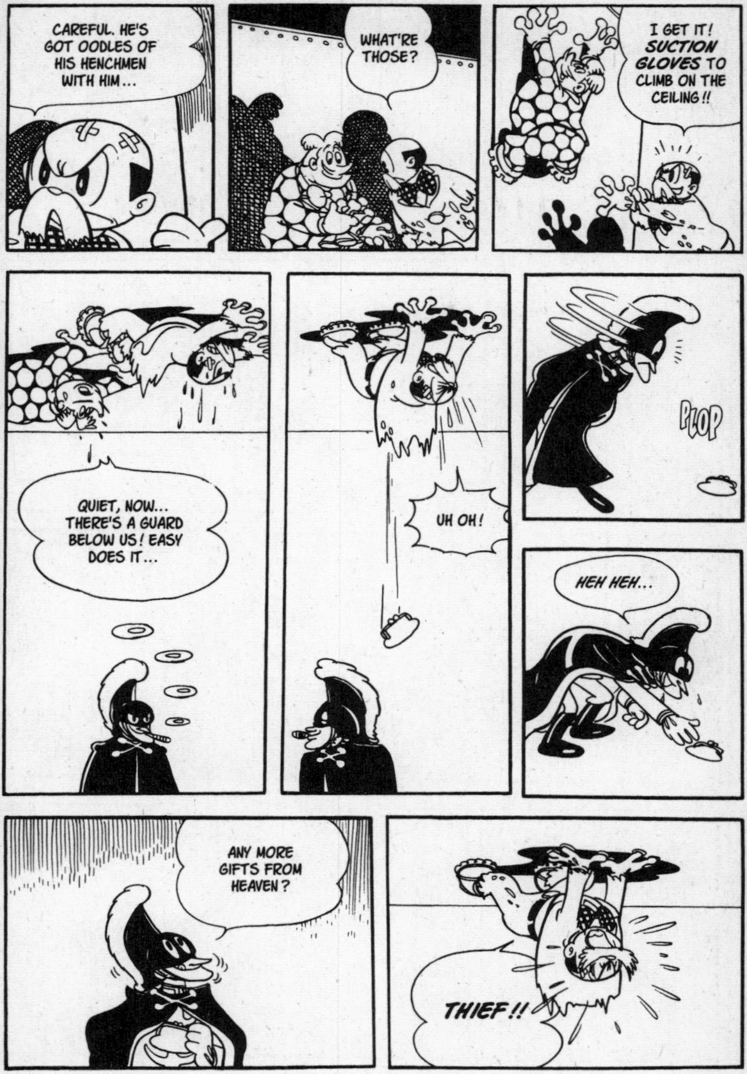
CAREFUL. HE'S GOT OODLES OF HIS HENCHMEN WITH HIM...
WHAT'RE THOSE?
I GET IT! SUCTION GLOVES TO CLIMB ON THE CEILING!!
QUIET, NOW... THERE'S A GUARD BELOW US! EASY DOES IT...
UH OH!
PLOP
HEH HEH...
ANY MORE GIFTS FROM HEAVEN?
THIEF!!

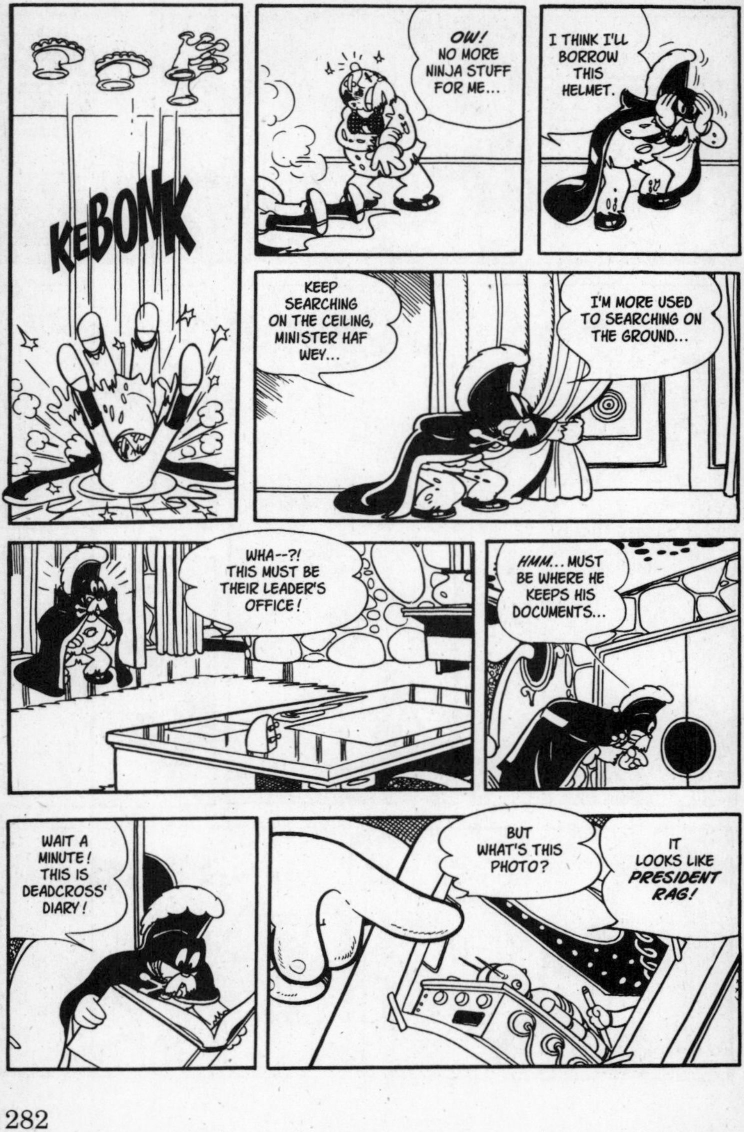

KEBONK
OW! NO MORE NINJA STUFF FOR ME...
I THINK I'LL BORROW THIS HELMET.
KEEP SEARCHING ON THE CEILING, MINISTER HAF WEY...
I'M MORE USED TO SEARCHING ON THE GROUND...
WHA--?! THIS MUST BE THEIR LEADER'S OFFICE!
HMM... MUST BE WHERE HE KEEPS HIS DOCUMENTS...
WAIT A MINUTE! THIS IS DEADCROSS' DIARY!
BUT WHAT'S THIS PHOTO?
IT LOOKS LIKE PRESIDENT RAG!

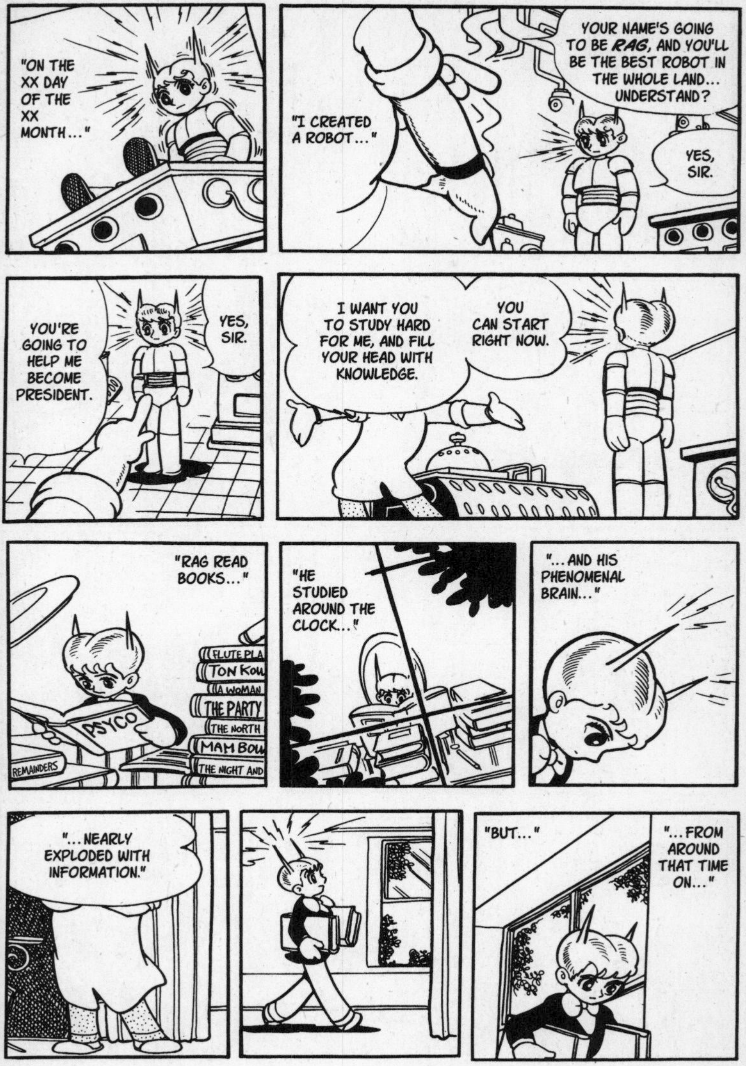
"ON THE XX DAY OF THE XX MONTH..."
"I CREATED A ROBOT..."
YOUR NAME'S GOING TO BE *RAG*, AND YOU'LL BE THE BEST ROBOT IN THE WHOLE LAND... UNDERSTAND?
YES, SIR.
YOU'RE GOING TO HELP ME BECOME PRESIDENT.
YES, SIR.
I WANT YOU TO STUDY HARD FOR ME, AND FILL YOUR HEAD WITH KNOWLEDGE.
YOU CAN START RIGHT NOW.
"RAG READ BOOKS..."
FLUTE PLA
TON KOW
A WOMAN
THE PARTY
PSYCO
THE NORTH
MAM BOW
REMAINDERS
THE NIGHT AND
"HE STUDIED AROUND THE CLOCK..."
"...AND HIS PHENOMENAL BRAIN..."
"...NEARLY EXPLODED WITH INFORMATION."
"BUT..."
"...FROM AROUND THAT TIME ON..."

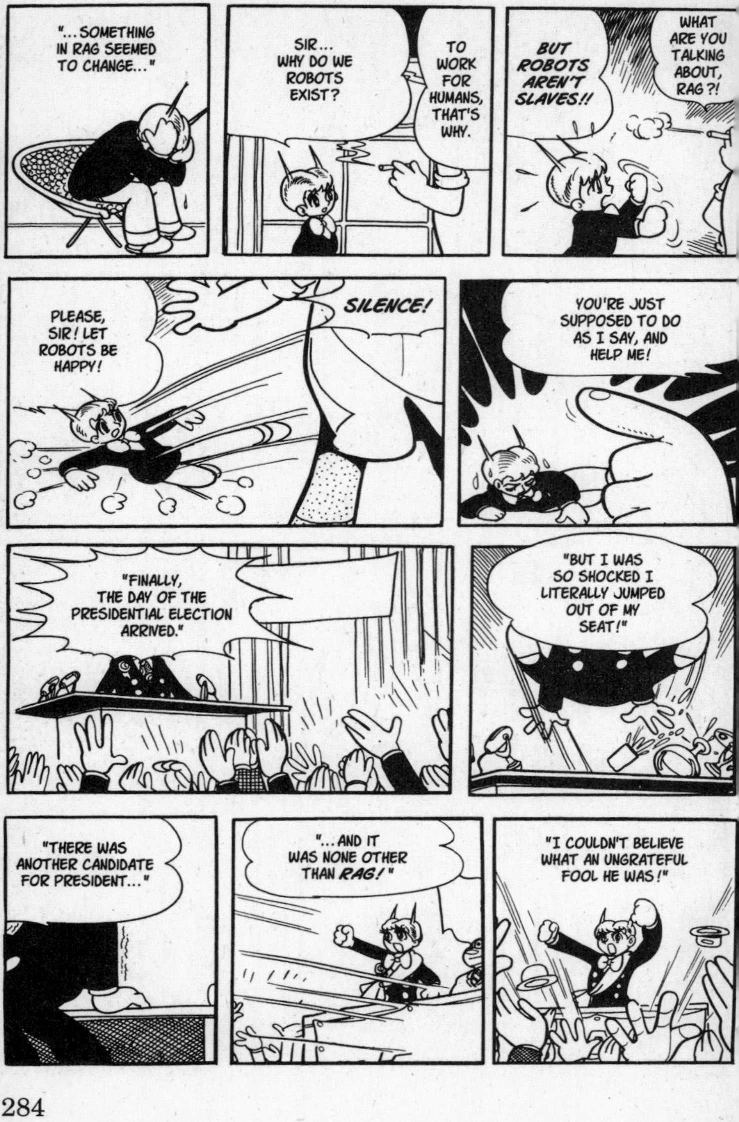
"...SOMETHING IN RAG SEEMED TO CHANGE..."
SIR... WHY DO WE ROBOTS EXIST?
TO WORK FOR HUMANS, THAT'S WHY.
BUT ROBOTS AREN'T SLAVES!!
WHAT ARE YOU TALKING ABOUT, RAG?!
PLEASE, SIR! LET ROBOTS BE HAPPY!
SILENCE!
YOU'RE JUST SUPPOSED TO DO AS I SAY, AND HELP ME!
"FINALLY, THE DAY OF THE PRESIDENTIAL ELECTION ARRIVED."
"BUT I WAS SO SHOCKED I LITERALLY JUMPED OUT OF MY SEAT!"
"THERE WAS ANOTHER CANDIDATE FOR PRESIDENT..."
"...AND IT WAS NONE OTHER THAN RAG!"
"I COULDN'T BELIEVE WHAT AN UNGRATEFUL FOOL HE WAS!"

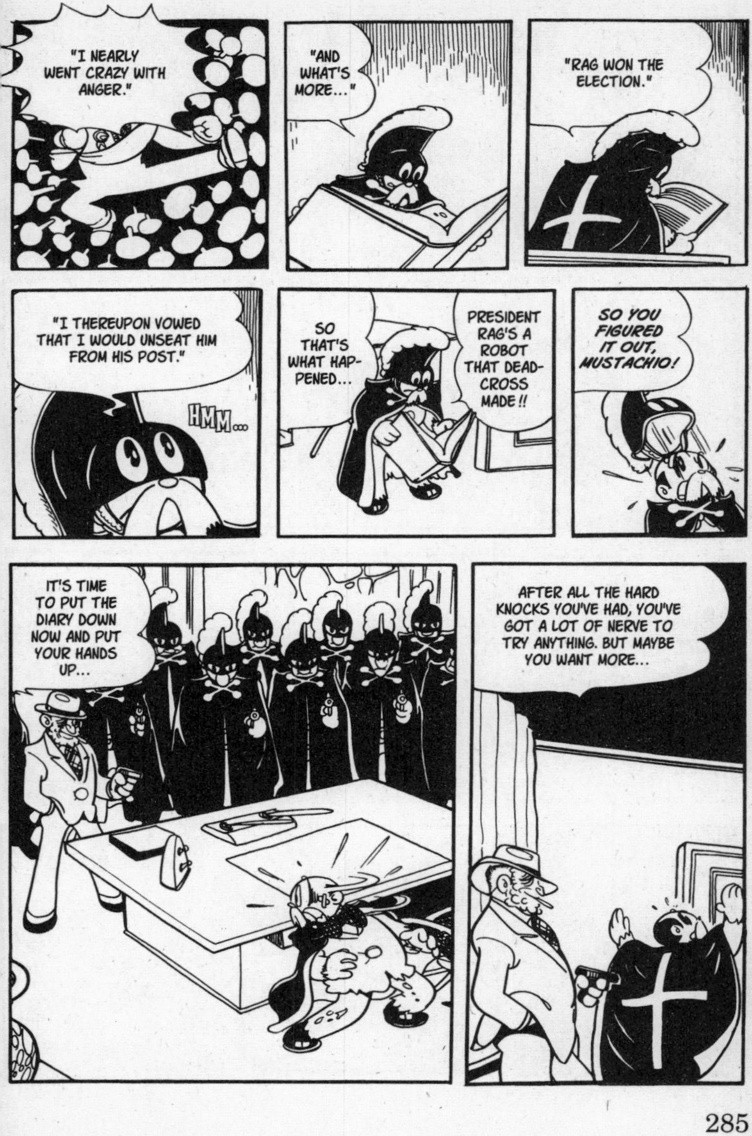
"I NEARLY WENT CRAZY WITH ANGER."
"AND WHAT'S MORE..."
"RAG WON THE ELECTION."
"I THEREUPON VOWED THAT I WOULD UNSEAT HIM FROM HIS POST."
HMM...
SO THAT'S WHAT HAP-PENED...
PRESIDENT RAG'S A ROBOT THAT DEAD-CROSS MADE!!
SO YOU FIGURED IT OUT, MUSTACHIO!
IT'S TIME TO PUT THE DIARY DOWN NOW AND PUT YOUR HANDS UP...
AFTER ALL THE HARD KNOCKS YOU'VE HAD, YOU'VE GOT A LOT OF NERVE TO TRY ANYTHING. BUT MAYBE YOU WANT MORE...

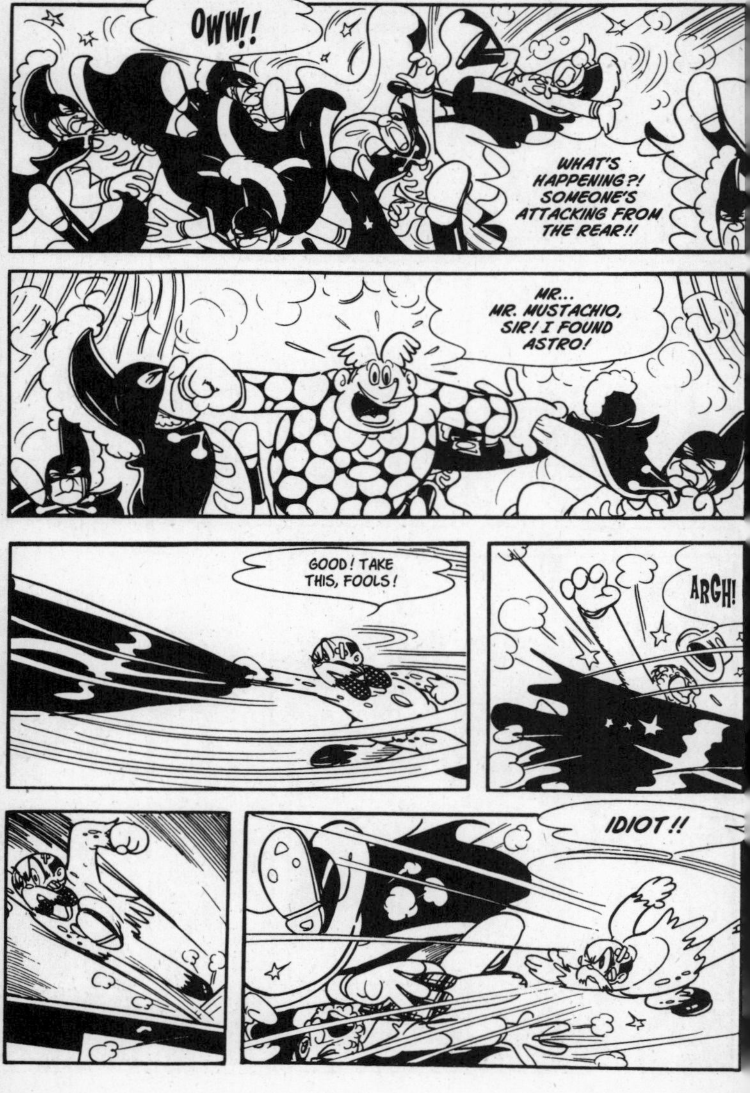
OWW!!
WHAT'S HAPPENING?! SOMEONE'S ATTACKING FROM THE REAR!!
MR... MR. MUSTACHIO, SIR! I FOUND ASTRO!
GOOD! TAKE THIS, FOOLS!
ARGH!
IDIOT!!

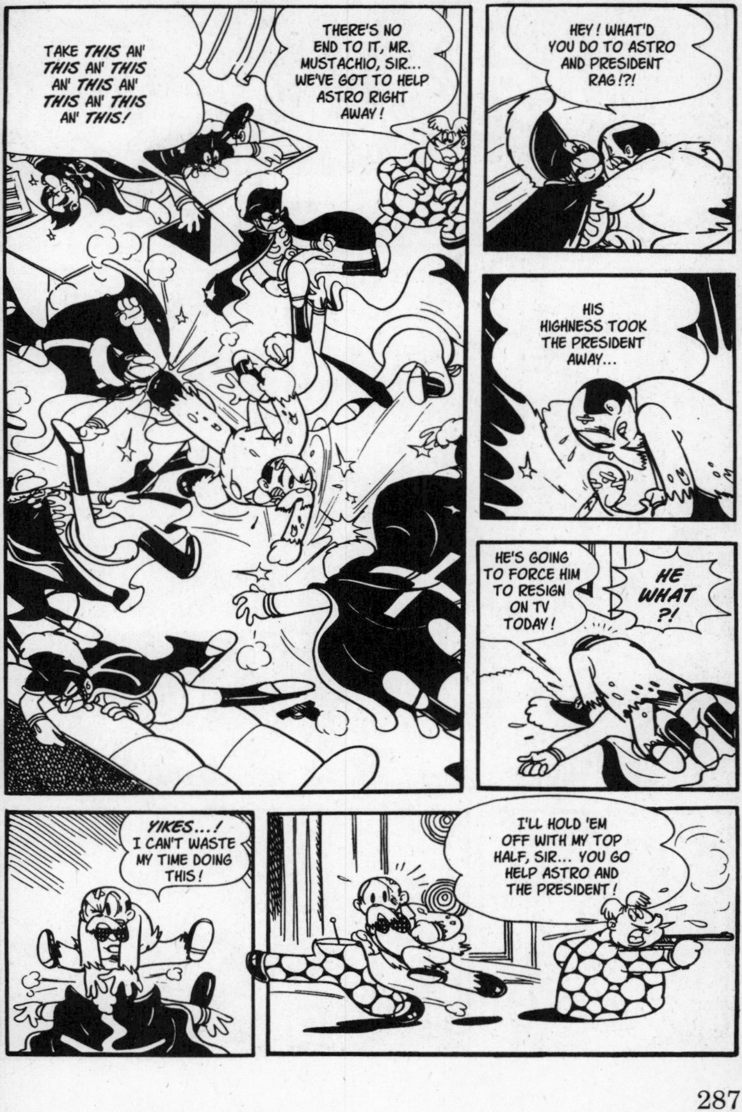
TAKE THIS AN' THIS AN' THIS AN' THIS AN' THIS AN' THIS AN' THIS!
THERE'S NO END TO IT, MR. MUSTACHIO, SIR... WE'VE GOT TO HELP ASTRO RIGHT AWAY!
HEY! WHAT'D YOU DO TO ASTRO AND PRESIDENT RAG!?!
HIS HIGHNESS TOOK THE PRESIDENT AWAY...
HE'S GOING TO FORCE HIM TO RESIGN ON TV TODAY!
HE WHAT ?!
YIKES...! I CAN'T WASTE MY TIME DOING THIS!
I'LL HOLD 'EM OFF WITH MY TOP HALF, SIR... YOU GO HELP ASTRO AND THE PRESIDENT!

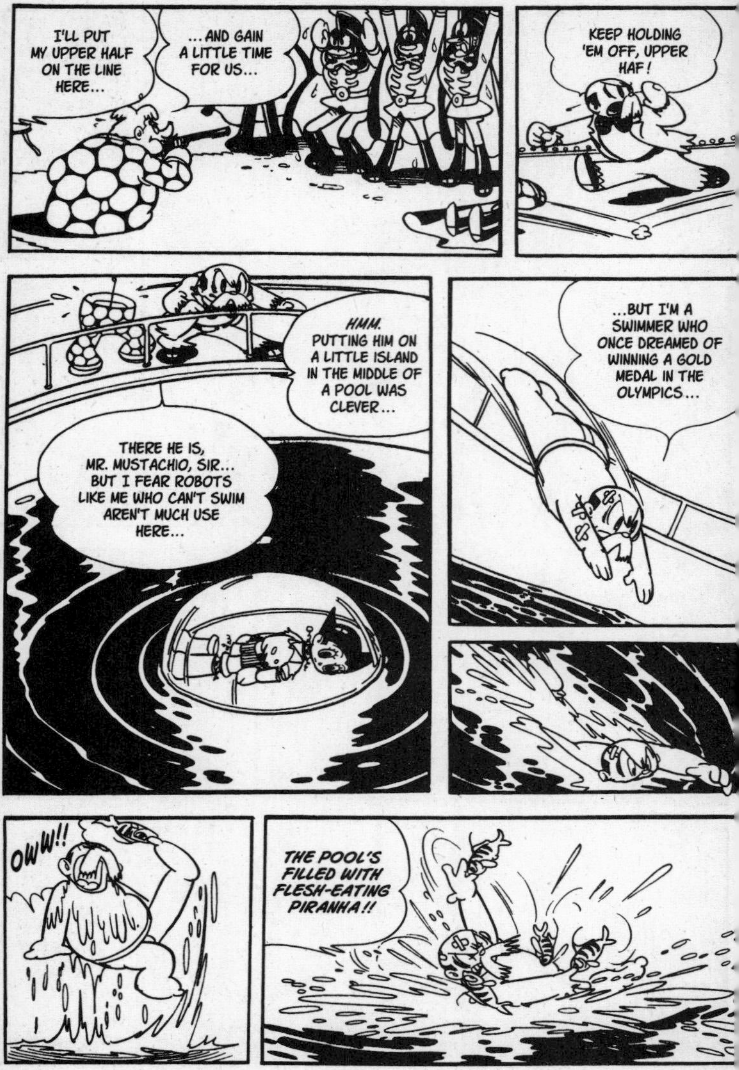
I'LL PUT MY UPPER HALF ON THE LINE HERE...
...AND GAIN A LITTLE TIME FOR US...
KEEP HOLDING 'EM OFF, UPPER HAF!
HMM. PUTTING HIM ON A LITTLE ISLAND IN THE MIDDLE OF A POOL WAS CLEVER...
THERE HE IS, MR. MUSTACHIO, SIR... BUT I FEAR ROBOTS LIKE ME WHO CAN'T SWIM AREN'T MUCH USE HERE...
...BUT I'M A SWIMMER WHO ONCE DREAMED OF WINNING A GOLD MEDAL IN THE OLYMPICS...
OWW!!
THE POOL'S FILLED WITH FLESH-EATING PIRANHA!!

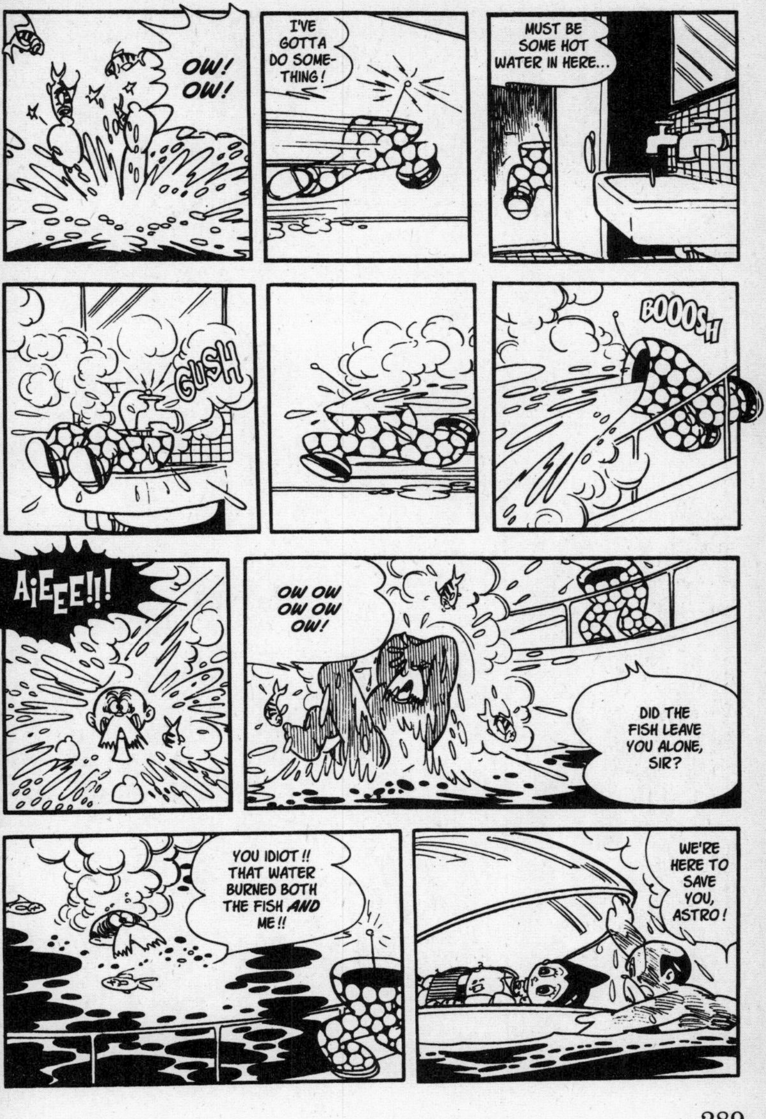
OW! OW!
I'VE GOTTA DO SOME-THING!
MUST BE SOME HOT WATER IN HERE...
GUSH
BOOOSH
AiEEE!!!
OW OW OW OW OW!
DID THE FISH LEAVE YOU ALONE, SIR?
YOU IDIOT!! THAT WATER BURNED BOTH THE FISH AND ME!!
WE'RE HERE TO SAVE YOU, ASTRO!

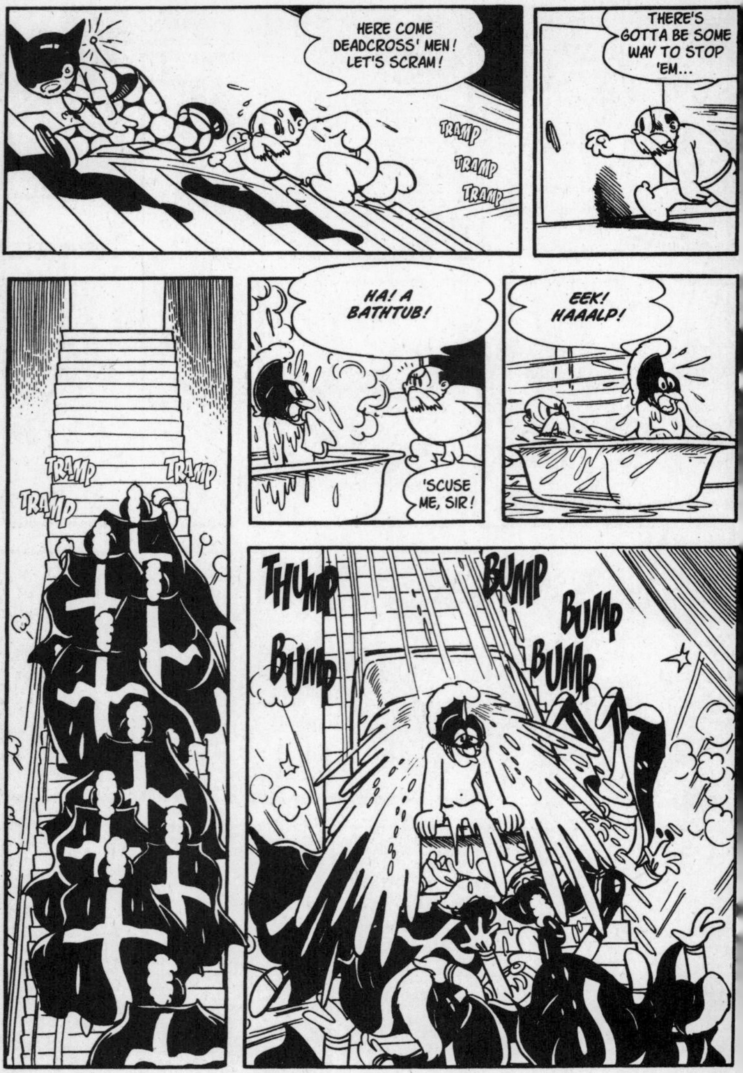
HERE COME DEADCROSS' MEN! LET'S SCRAM!
TRAMP
TRAMP
TRAMP
THERE'S GOTTA BE SOME WAY TO STOP 'EM...
TRAMP
TRAMP
TRAMP
HA! A BATHTUB!
'SCUSE ME, SIR!
EEK! HAAALP!
THUMP
BUMP
BUMP
BUMP
BUMP

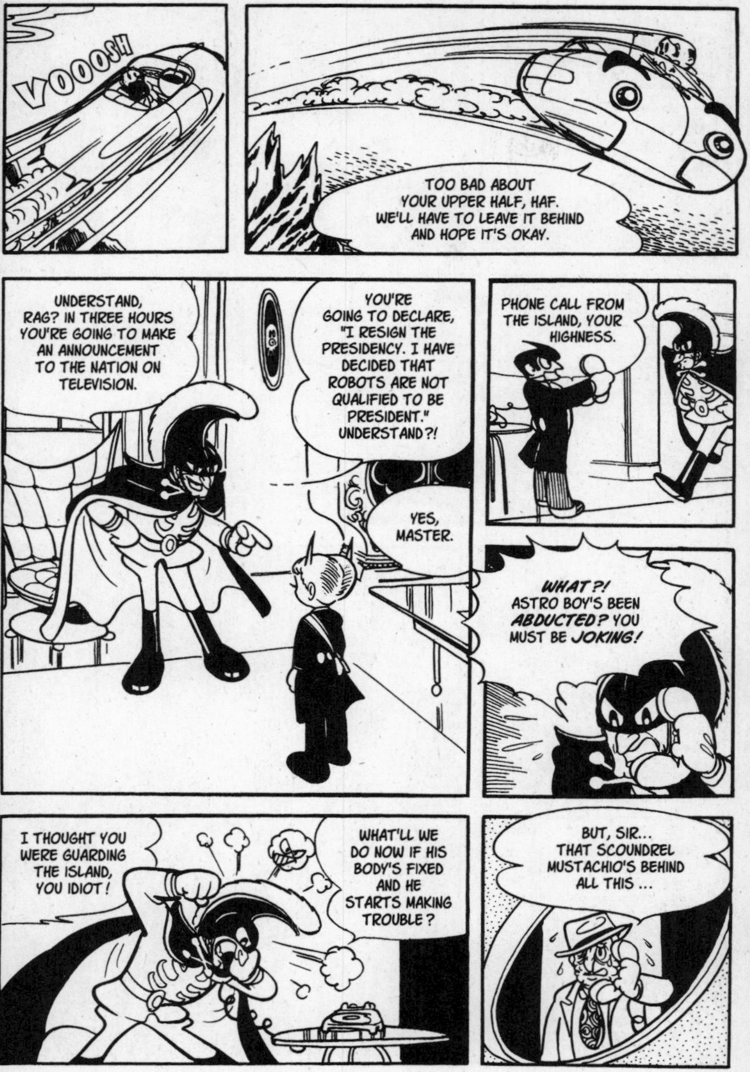
VOOOSH
TOO BAD ABOUT YOUR UPPER HALF, HAF. WE'LL HAVE TO LEAVE IT BEHIND AND HOPE IT'S OKAY.
UNDERSTAND, RAG? IN THREE HOURS YOU'RE GOING TO MAKE AN ANNOUNCEMENT TO THE NATION ON TELEVISION.
YOU'RE GOING TO DECLARE, "I RESIGN THE PRESIDENCY. I HAVE DECIDED THAT ROBOTS ARE NOT QUALIFIED TO BE PRESIDENT." UNDERSTAND?!
YES, MASTER.
PHONE CALL FROM THE ISLAND, YOUR HIGHNESS.
WHAT?! ASTRO BOY'S BEEN ABDUCTED? YOU MUST BE JOKING!
I THOUGHT YOU WERE GUARDING THE ISLAND, YOU IDIOT!
WHAT'LL WE DO NOW IF HIS BODY'S FIXED AND HE STARTS MAKING TROUBLE?
BUT, SIR... THAT SCOUNDREL MUSTACHIO'S BEHIND ALL THIS ...

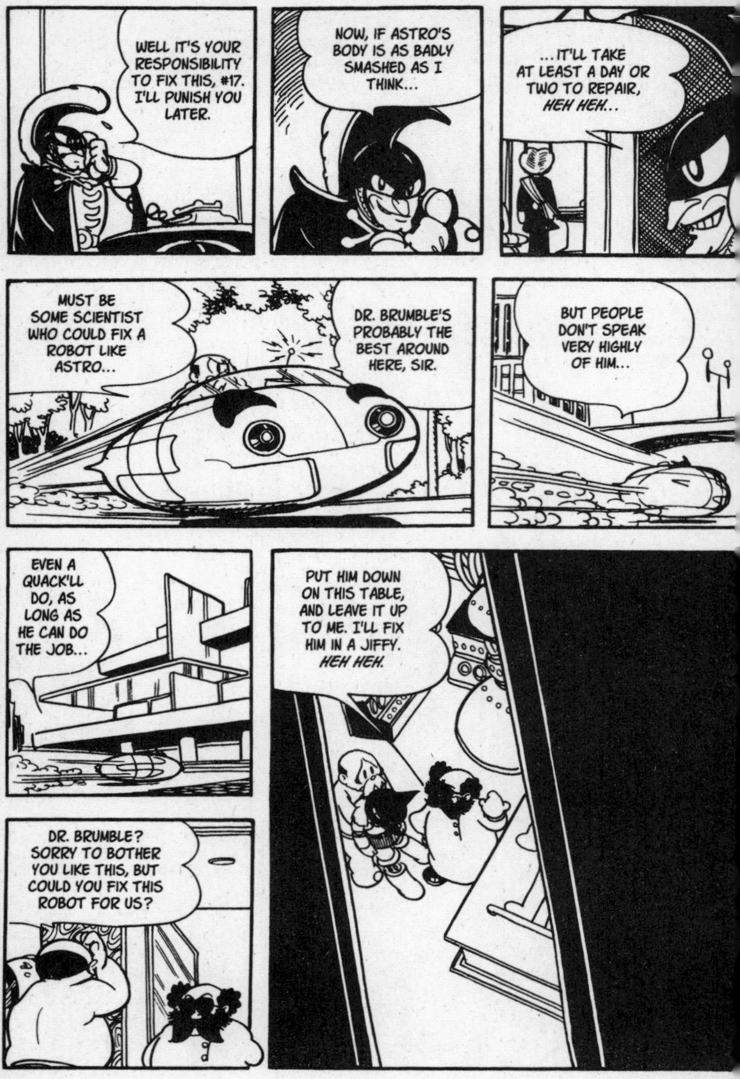
WELL IT'S YOUR RESPONSIBILITY TO FIX THIS, #17. I'LL PUNISH YOU LATER.
NOW, IF ASTRO'S BODY IS AS BADLY SMASHED AS I THINK...
...IT'LL TAKE AT LEAST A DAY OR TWO TO REPAIR, *HEH HEH...*
MUST BE SOME SCIENTIST WHO COULD FIX A ROBOT LIKE ASTRO...
DR. BRUMBLE'S PROBABLY THE BEST AROUND HERE, SIR.
BUT PEOPLE DON'T SPEAK VERY HIGHLY OF HIM...
EVEN A QUACK'LL DO, AS LONG AS HE CAN DO THE JOB...
DR. BRUMBLE? SORRY TO BOTHER YOU LIKE THIS, BUT COULD YOU FIX THIS ROBOT FOR US?
PUT HIM DOWN ON THIS TABLE, AND LEAVE IT UP TO ME. I'LL FIX HIM IN A JIFFY. *HEH HEH.*

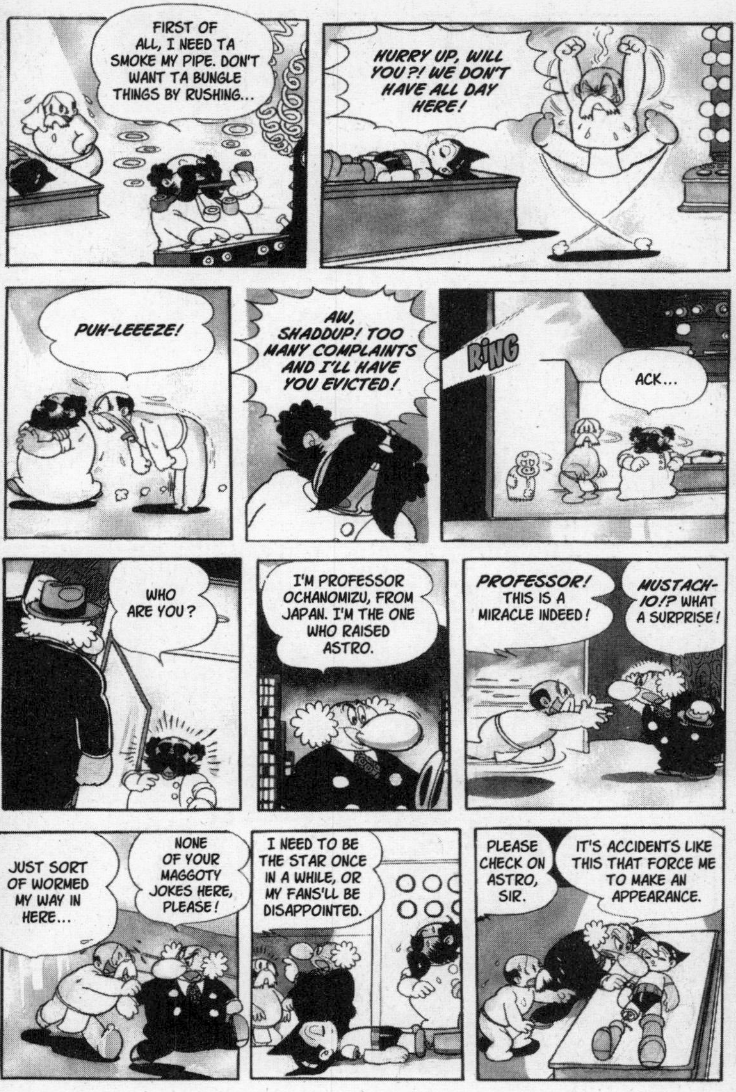
FIRST OF ALL, I NEED TA SMOKE MY PIPE. DON'T WANT TA BUNGLE THINGS BY RUSHING...
HURRY UP, WILL YOU?! WE DON'T HAVE ALL DAY HERE!
PUH-LEEEZE!
AW, SHADDUP! TOO MANY COMPLAINTS AND I'LL HAVE YOU EVICTED!
RING
ACK...
WHO ARE YOU?
I'M PROFESSOR OCHANOMIZU, FROM JAPAN. I'M THE ONE WHO RAISED ASTRO.
PROFESSOR! THIS IS A MIRACLE INDEED!
MUSTACHIO!? WHAT A SURPRISE!
JUST SORT OF WORMED MY WAY IN HERE...
NONE OF YOUR MAGGOTY JOKES HERE, PLEASE!
I NEED TO BE THE STAR ONCE IN A WHILE, OR MY FANS'LL BE DISAPPOINTED.
PLEASE CHECK ON ASTRO, SIR.
IT'S ACCIDENTS LIKE THIS THAT FORCE ME TO MAKE AN APPEARANCE.

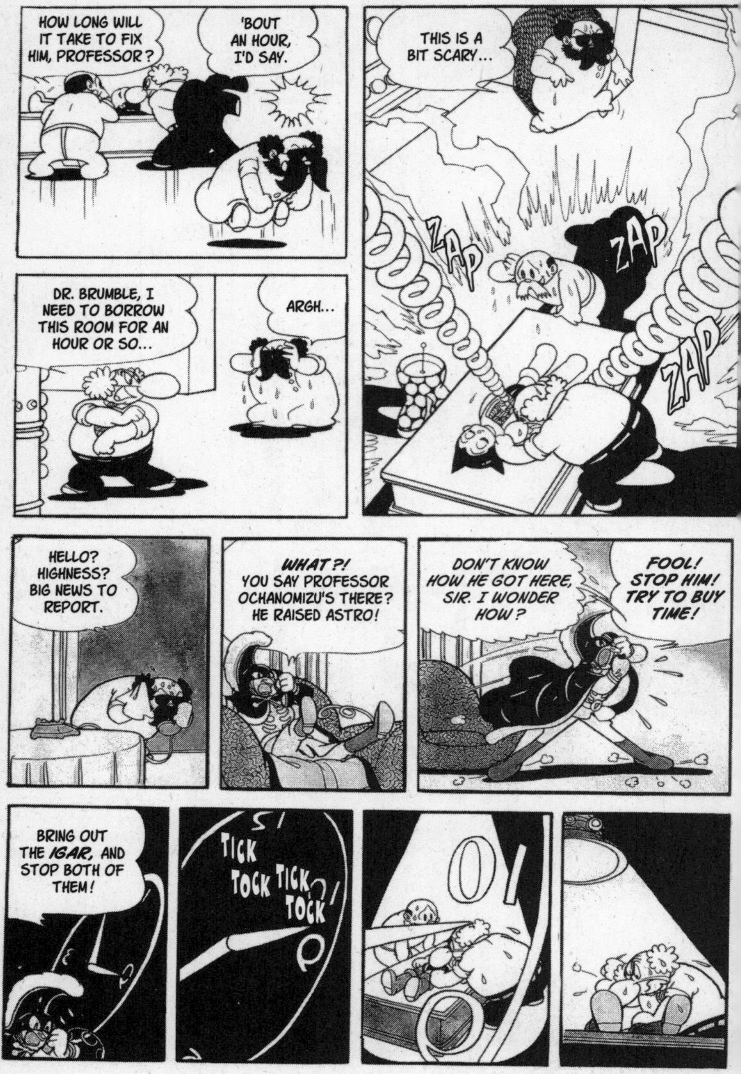
HOW LONG WILL IT TAKE TO FIX HIM, PROFESSOR?
'BOUT AN HOUR, I'D SAY.
THIS IS A BIT SCARY...
ZAP
ZAP
ZAP
DR. BRUMBLE, I NEED TO BORROW THIS ROOM FOR AN HOUR OR SO...
ARGH...
HELLO? HIGHNESS? BIG NEWS TO REPORT.
WHAT?! YOU SAY PROFESSOR OCHANOMIZU'S THERE? HE RAISED ASTRO!
DON'T KNOW HOW HE GOT HERE, SIR. I WONDER HOW?
FOOL! STOP HIM! TRY TO BUY TIME!
BRING OUT THE IGAR, AND STOP BOTH OF THEM!
TICK TOCK TICK TOCK

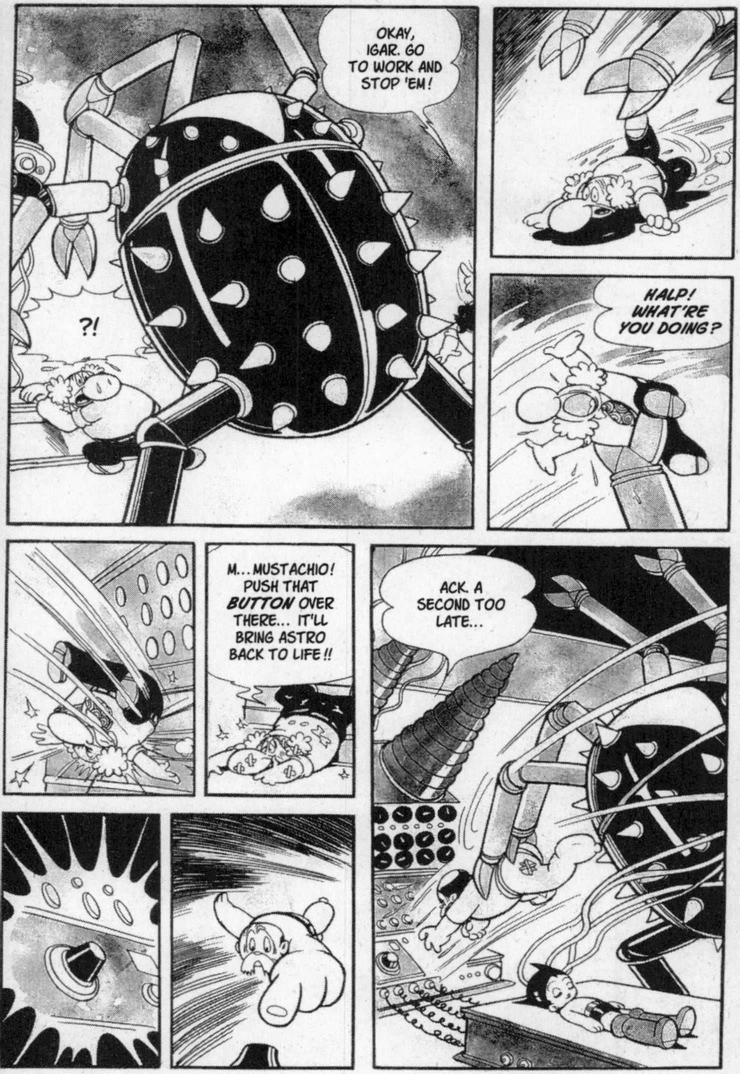
OKAY, IGAR. GO TO WORK AND STOP 'EM!
?!
HALP! WHAT'RE YOU DOING?
M... MUSTACHIO! PUSH THAT **BUTTON** OVER THERE... IT'LL BRING ASTRO BACK TO LIFE!!
ACK. A SECOND TOO LATE...

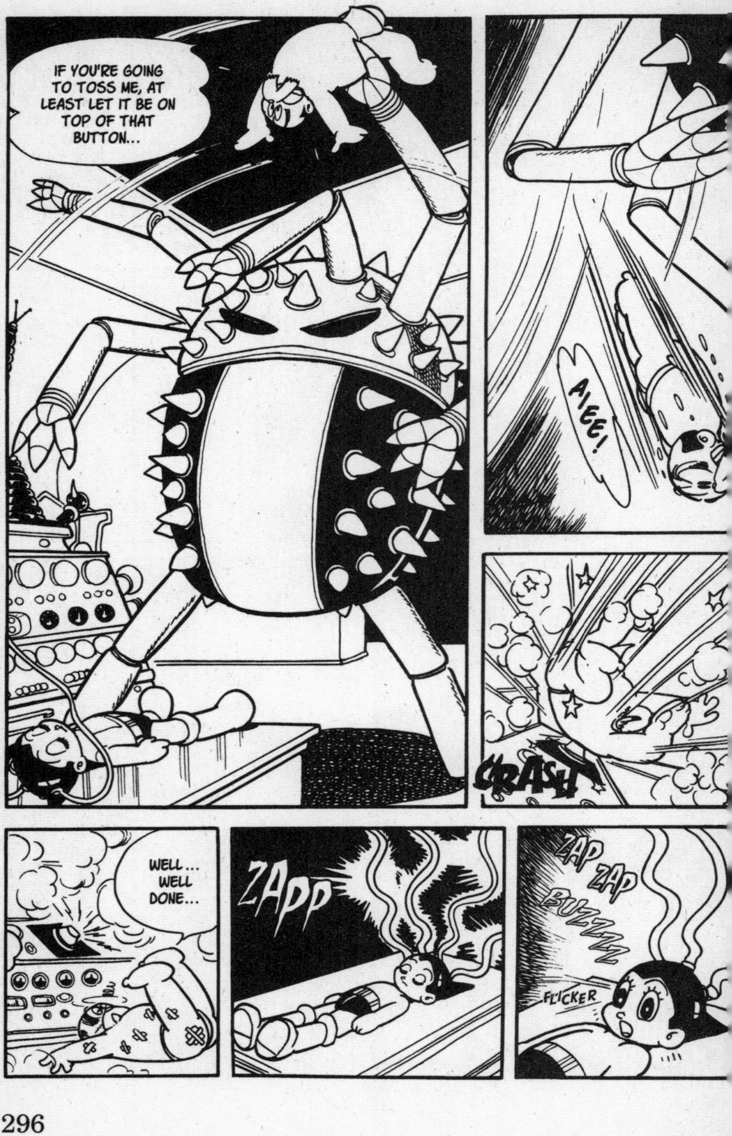

IF YOU'RE GOING TO TOSS ME, AT LEAST LET IT BE ON TOP OF THAT BUTTON...
AIEE!
CRASH
WELL... WELL DONE...
ZAPP
ZAP ZAP
BUZZZZ
FLICKER

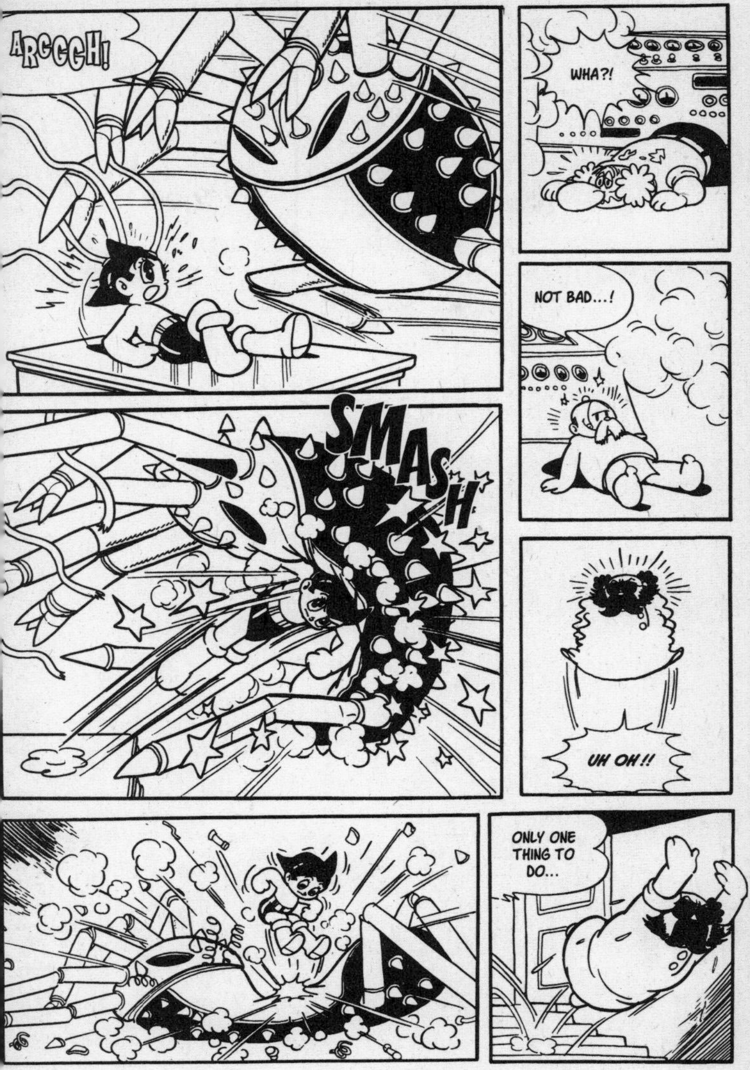
ARGGGH!
WHA?!
NOT BAD...!
SMASH
UH OH!!
ONLY ONE THING TO DO...

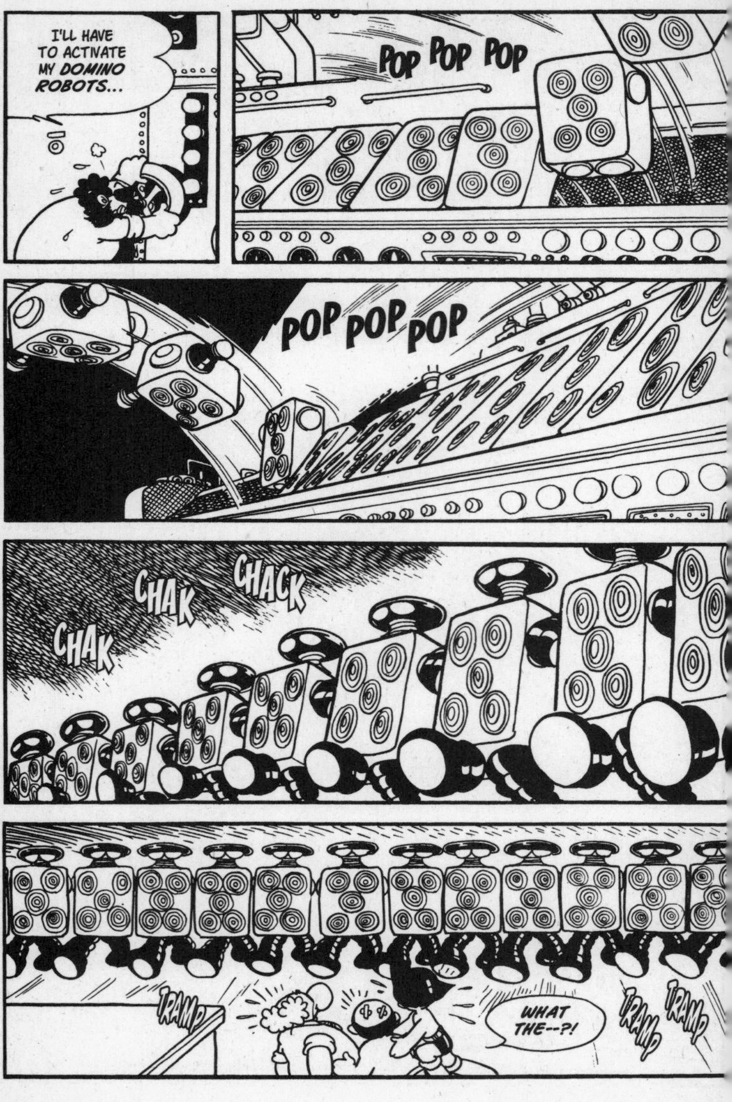

I'LL HAVE TO ACTIVATE MY DOMINO ROBOTS...
POP POP POP
POP POP POP
CHAK
CHAK
CHACK
TRAMP
WHAT THE--?!
TRAMP
TRAMP

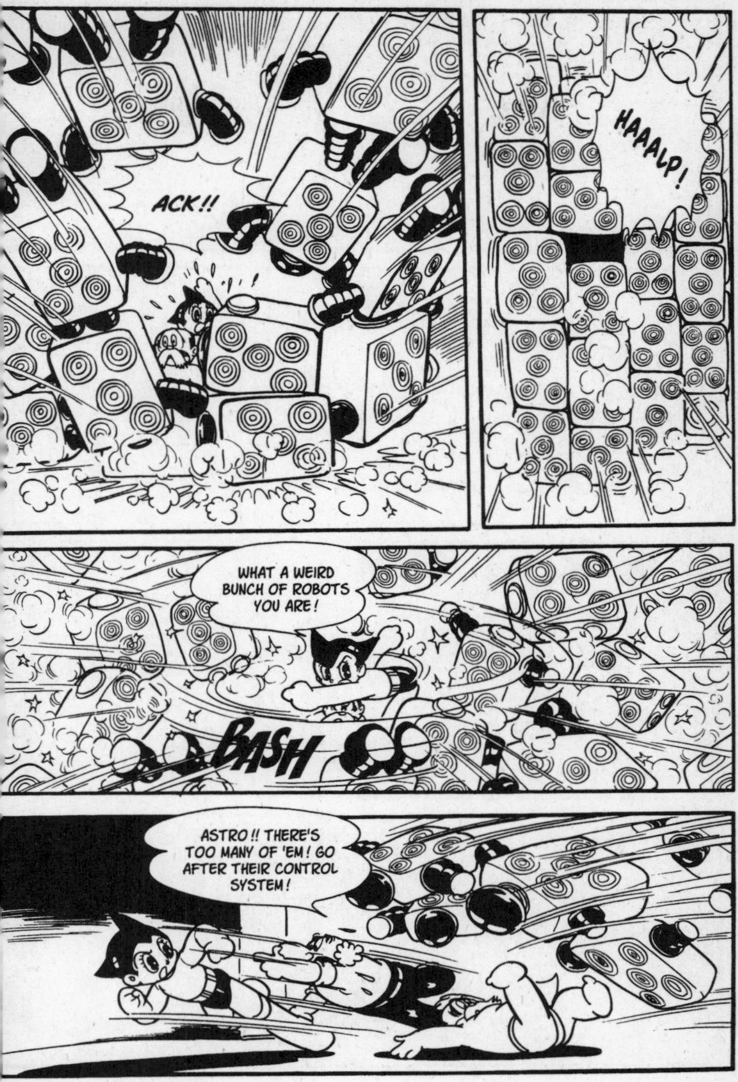
ACK!!
HAAALP!
WHAT A WEIRD BUNCH OF ROBOTS YOU ARE!
BASH
ASTRO!! THERE'S TOO MANY OF 'EM! GO AFTER THEIR CONTROL SYSTEM!

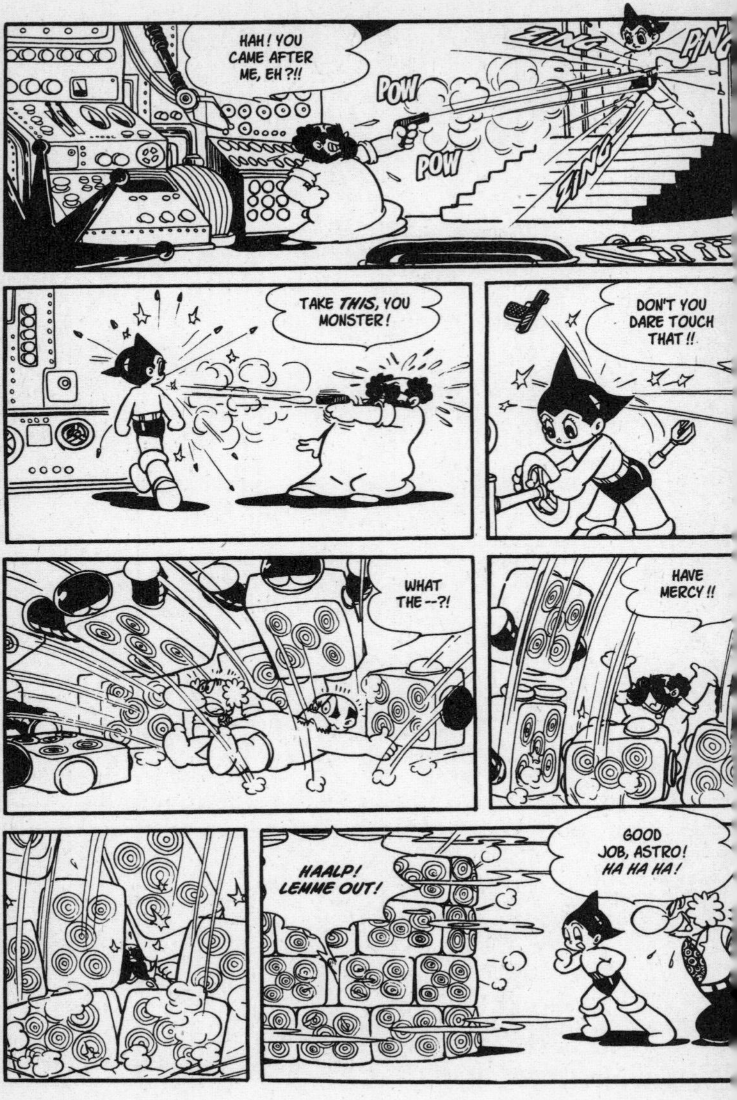

HAH! YOU CAME AFTER ME, EH?!!
ZING
PING
POW
POW
ZING
TAKE THIS, YOU MONSTER!
DON'T YOU DARE TOUCH THAT!!
WHAT THE--?!
HAVE MERCY!!
HAALP! LEMME OUT!
GOOD JOB, ASTRO! HA HA HA!

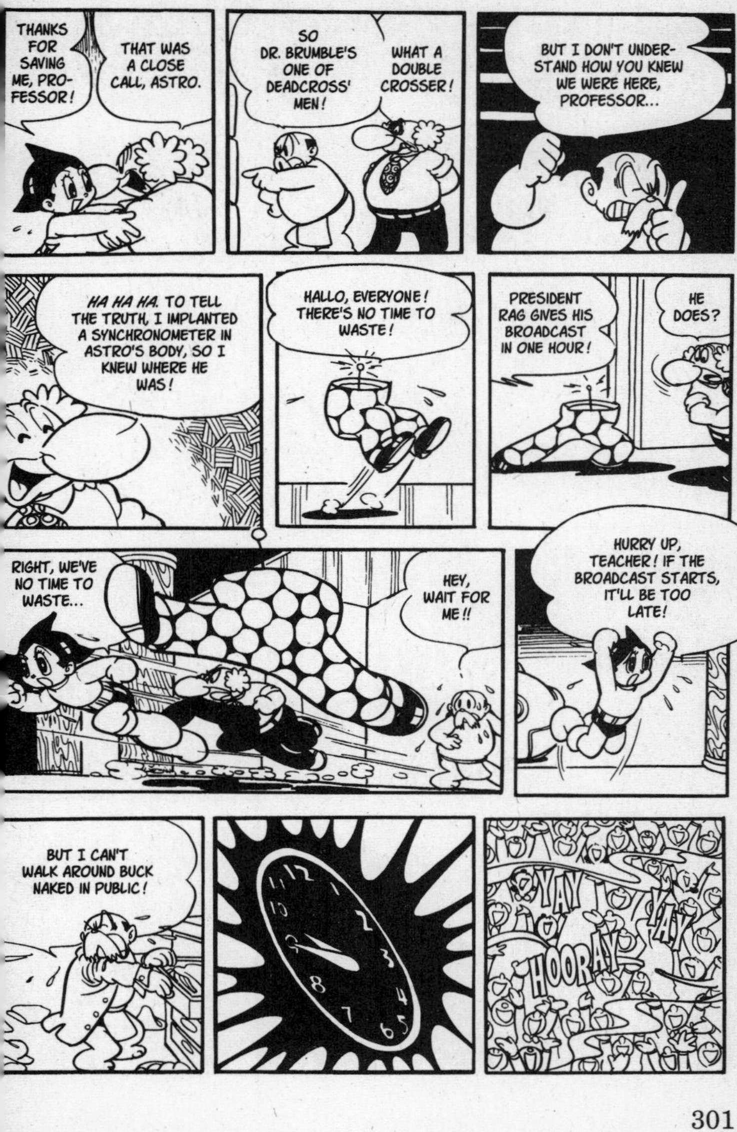

THANKS FOR SAVING ME, PRO-FESSOR!
THAT WAS A CLOSE CALL, ASTRO.
SO DR. BRUMBLE'S ONE OF DEADCROSS' MEN!
WHAT A DOUBLE CROSSER!
BUT I DON'T UNDER-STAND HOW YOU KNEW WE WERE HERE, PROFESSOR...
HA HA HA. TO TELL THE TRUTH, I IMPLANTED A SYNCHRONOMETER IN ASTRO'S BODY, SO I KNEW WHERE HE WAS!
HALLO, EVERYONE! THERE'S NO TIME TO WASTE!
PRESIDENT RAG GIVES HIS BROADCAST IN ONE HOUR!
HE DOES?
RIGHT, WE'VE NO TIME TO WASTE...
HEY, WAIT FOR ME!!
HURRY UP, TEACHER! IF THE BROADCAST STARTS, IT'LL BE TOO LATE!
BUT I CAN'T WALK AROUND BUCK NAKED IN PUBLIC!
YAY
YAY
HOORAY

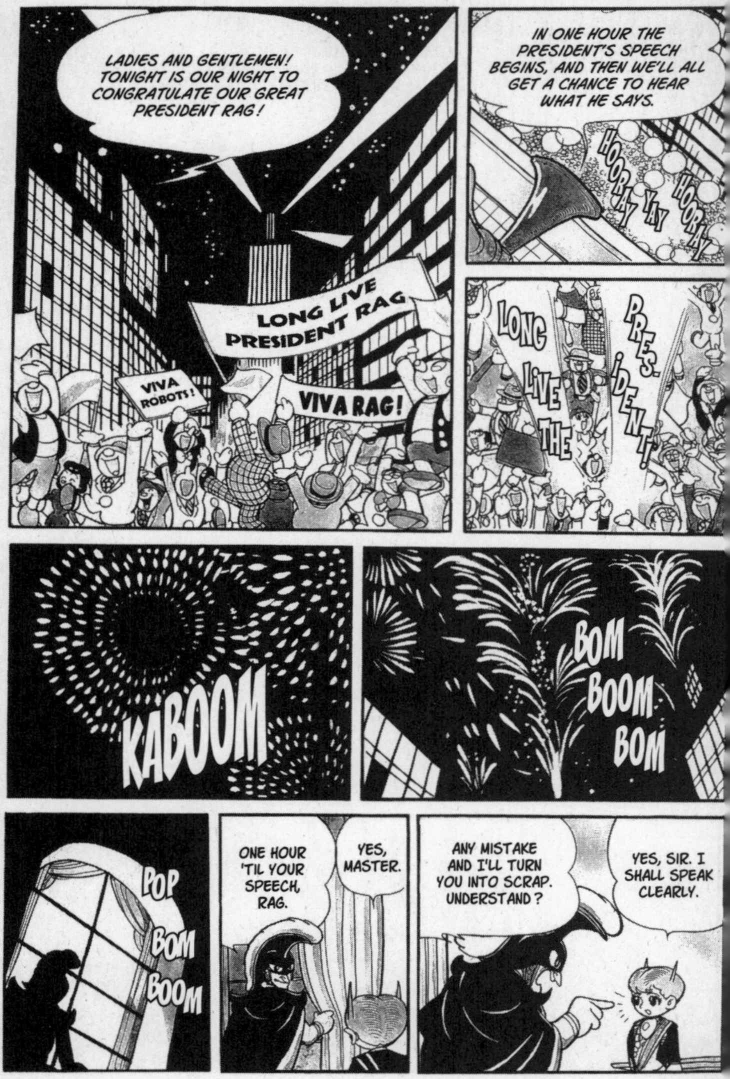
LADIES AND GENTLEMEN! TONIGHT IS OUR NIGHT TO CONGRATULATE OUR GREAT PRESIDENT RAG!
LONG LIVE PRESIDENT RAG
VIVA ROBOTS!
VIVA RAG!
IN ONE HOUR THE PRESIDENT'S SPEECH BEGINS, AND THEN WE'LL ALL GET A CHANCE TO HEAR WHAT HE SAYS.
HOORAY YAY HOORAY
LONG LIVE THE PRES-IDENT!
KABOOM
BOM BOOM BOM
POP BOM BOOM
ONE HOUR 'TIL YOUR SPEECH, RAG.
YES, MASTER.
ANY MISTAKE AND I'LL TURN YOU INTO SCRAP. UNDERSTAND?
YES, SIR. I SHALL SPEAK CLEARLY.

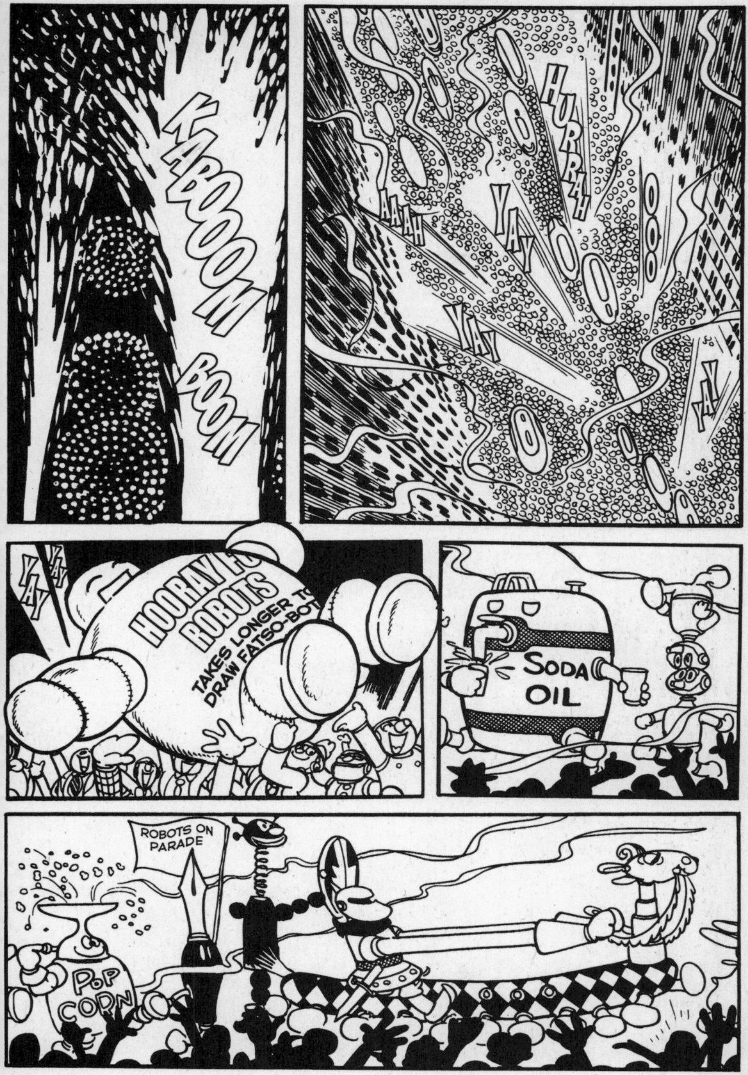
KABOOOM
BOOM
HURRAH
AAAH
YAY
YAY
YAY
YAY
YAY
HOORAY FO
ROBOTS
TAKES LONGER T
DRAW FATSO-BOT
SODA
OIL
ROBOTS ON PARADE
POP CORN

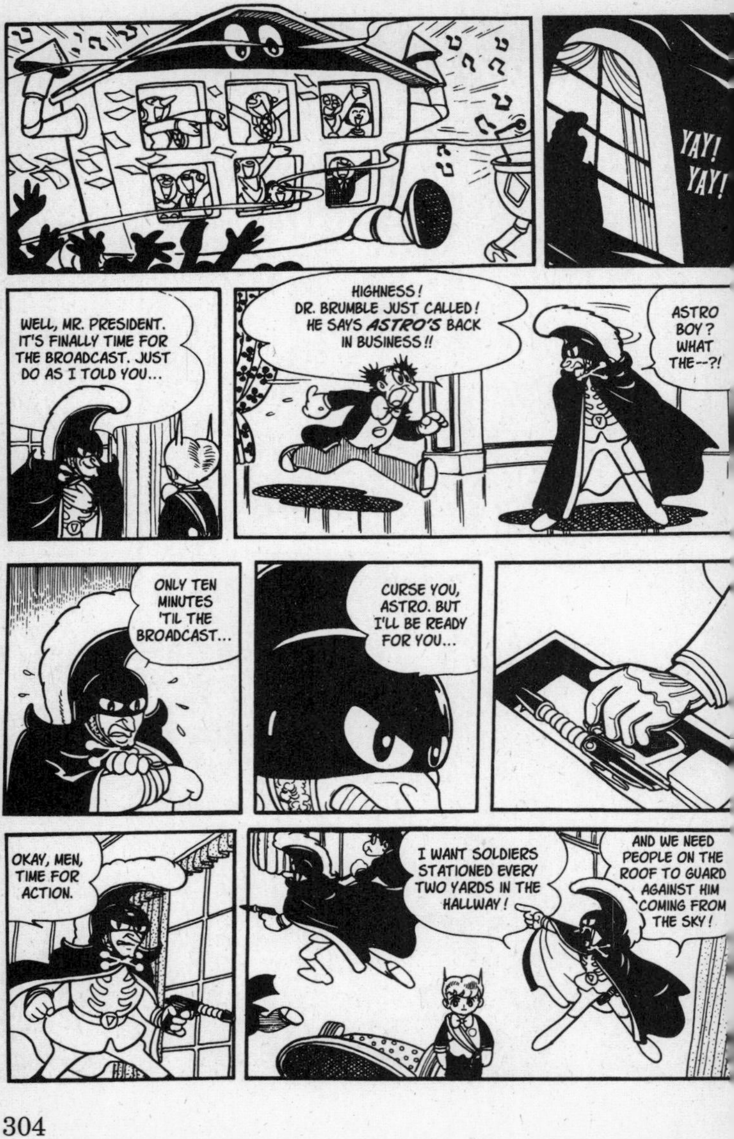
YAY! YAY!
WELL, MR. PRESIDENT. IT'S FINALLY TIME FOR THE BROADCAST. JUST DO AS I TOLD YOU...
HIGHNESS! DR. BRUMBLE JUST CALLED! HE SAYS ASTRO'S BACK IN BUSINESS!!
ASTRO BOY? WHAT THE--?!
ONLY TEN MINUTES 'TIL THE BROADCAST...
CURSE YOU, ASTRO. BUT I'LL BE READY FOR YOU...
OKAY, MEN, TIME FOR ACTION.
I WANT SOLDIERS STATIONED EVERY TWO YARDS IN THE HALLWAY!
AND WE NEED PEOPLE ON THE ROOF TO GUARD AGAINST HIM COMING FROM THE SKY!

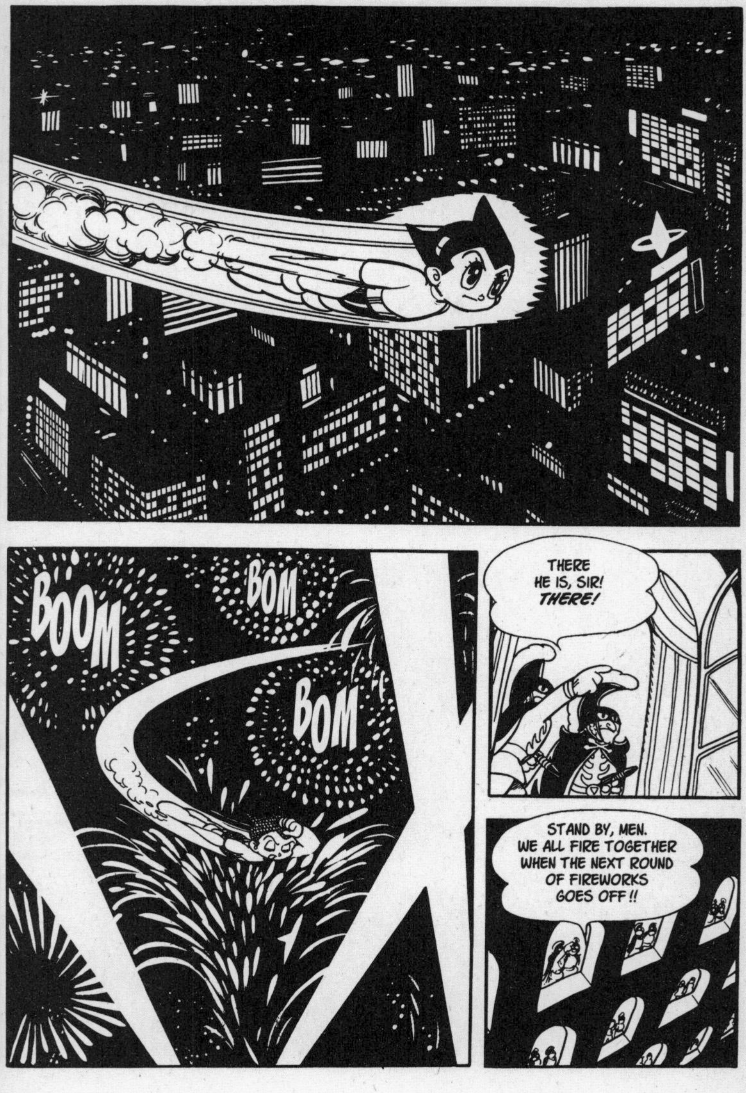
BOOM
BOM
BOM
THERE HE IS, SIR! THERE!
STAND BY, MEN. WE ALL FIRE TOGETHER WHEN THE NEXT ROUND OF FIREWORKS GOES OFF !!

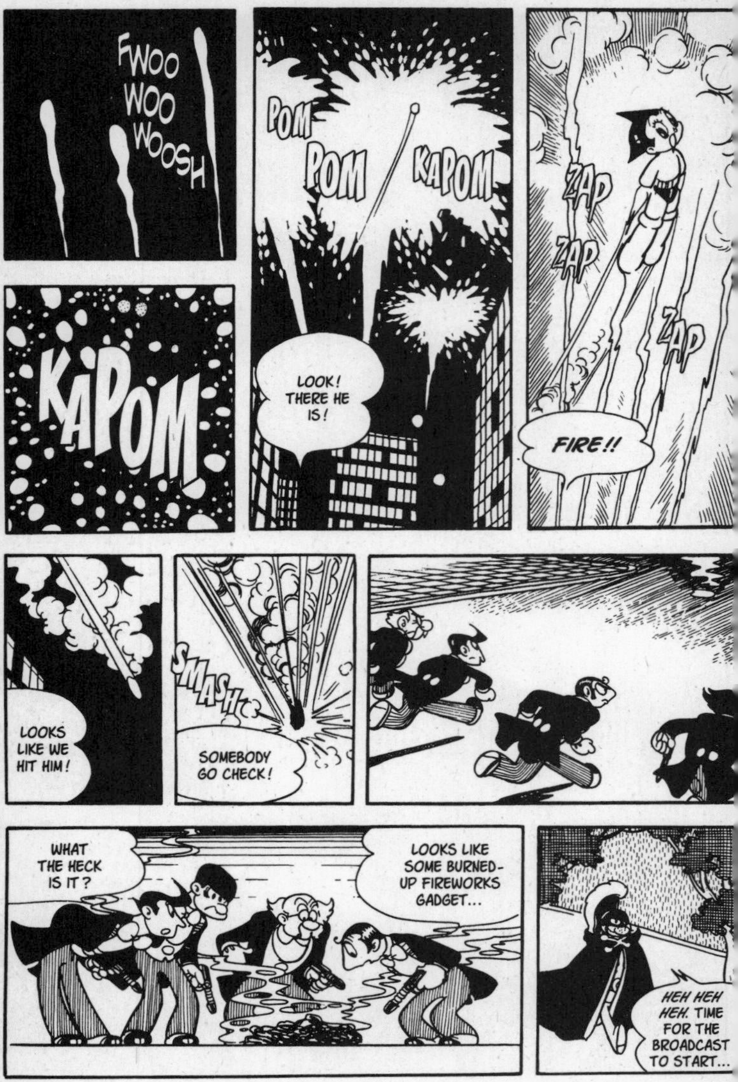
FWOO
WOO
WOOSH
POM
POM
KAPOM
ZAP
ZAP
ZAP
KAPOM
LOOK! THERE HE IS!
FIRE!!
LOOKS LIKE WE HIT HIM!
SMASH
SOMEBODY GO CHECK!
WHAT THE HECK IS IT?
LOOKS LIKE SOME BURNED-UP FIREWORKS GADGET...
HEH HEH HEH. TIME FOR THE BROADCAST TO START...

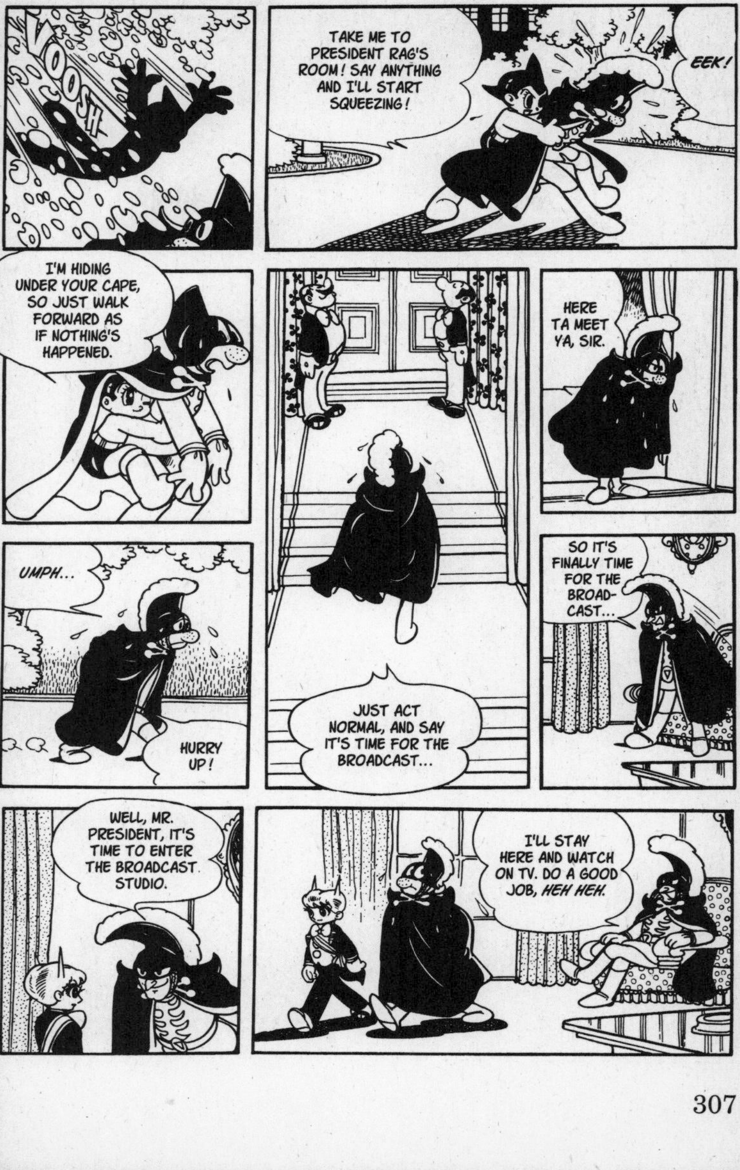
VOOSH
TAKE ME TO PRESIDENT RAG'S ROOM! SAY ANYTHING AND I'LL START SQUEEZING!
EEK!
I'M HIDING UNDER YOUR CAPE, SO JUST WALK FORWARD AS IF NOTHING'S HAPPENED.
JUST ACT NORMAL, AND SAY IT'S TIME FOR THE BROADCAST...
HERE TA MEET YA, SIR.
UMPH...
HURRY UP!
SO IT'S FINALLY TIME FOR THE BROAD-CAST...
WELL, MR. PRESIDENT, IT'S TIME TO ENTER THE BROADCAST STUDIO.
I'LL STAY HERE AND WATCH ON TV. DO A GOOD JOB, HEH HEH.

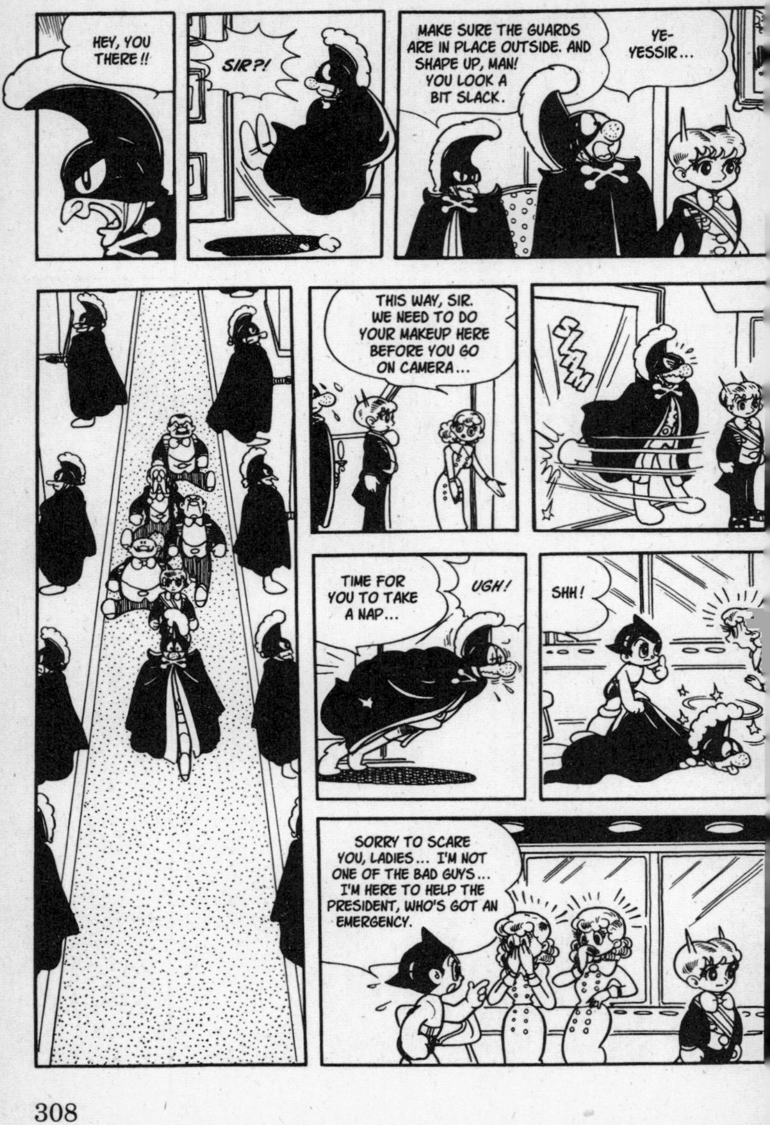
HEY, YOU THERE!!
SIR?!
MAKE SURE THE GUARDS ARE IN PLACE OUTSIDE. AND SHAPE UP, MAN! YOU LOOK A BIT SLACK.
YE- YESSIR...
THIS WAY, SIR. WE NEED TO DO YOUR MAKEUP HERE BEFORE YOU GO ON CAMERA...
SLAM
TIME FOR YOU TO TAKE A NAP...
UGH!
SHH!
SORRY TO SCARE YOU, LADIES... I'M NOT ONE OF THE BAD GUYS... I'M HERE TO HELP THE PRESIDENT, WHO'S GOT AN EMERGENCY.

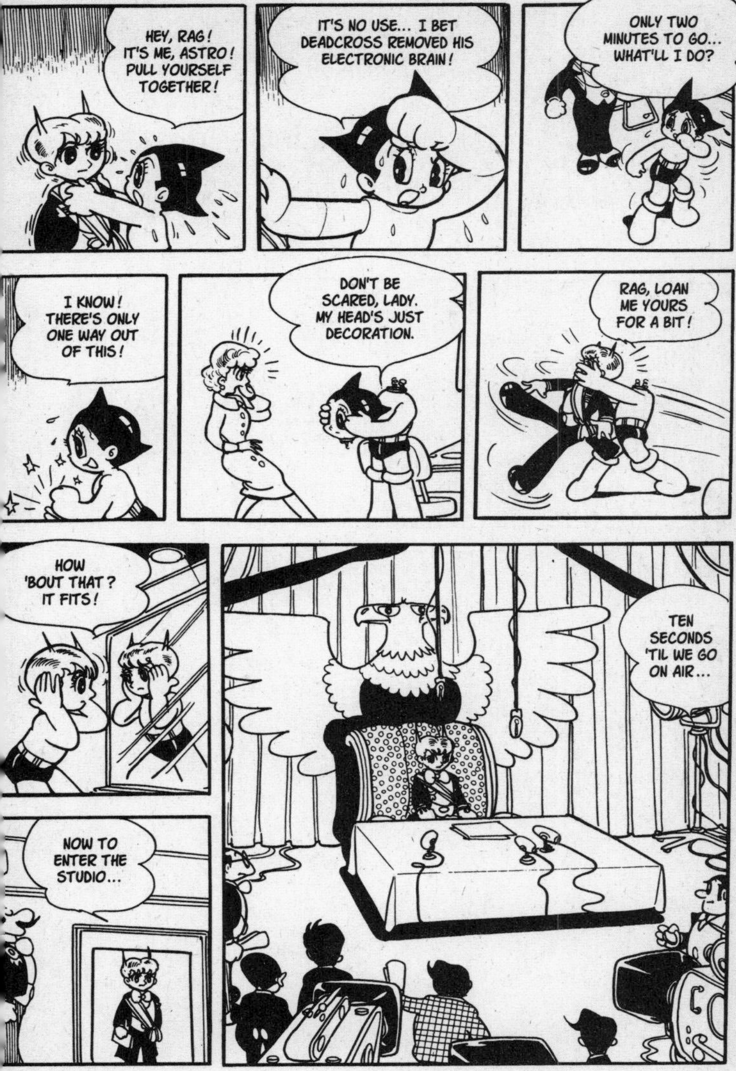

HEY, RAG! IT'S ME, ASTRO! PULL YOURSELF TOGETHER!
IT'S NO USE... I BET DEADCROSS REMOVED HIS ELECTRONIC BRAIN!
ONLY TWO MINUTES TO GO... WHAT'LL I DO?
I KNOW! THERE'S ONLY ONE WAY OUT OF THIS!
DON'T BE SCARED, LADY. MY HEAD'S JUST DECORATION.
RAG, LOAN ME YOURS FOR A BIT!
HOW 'BOUT THAT? IT FITS!
NOW TO ENTER THE STUDIO...
TEN SECONDS 'TIL WE GO ON AIR...

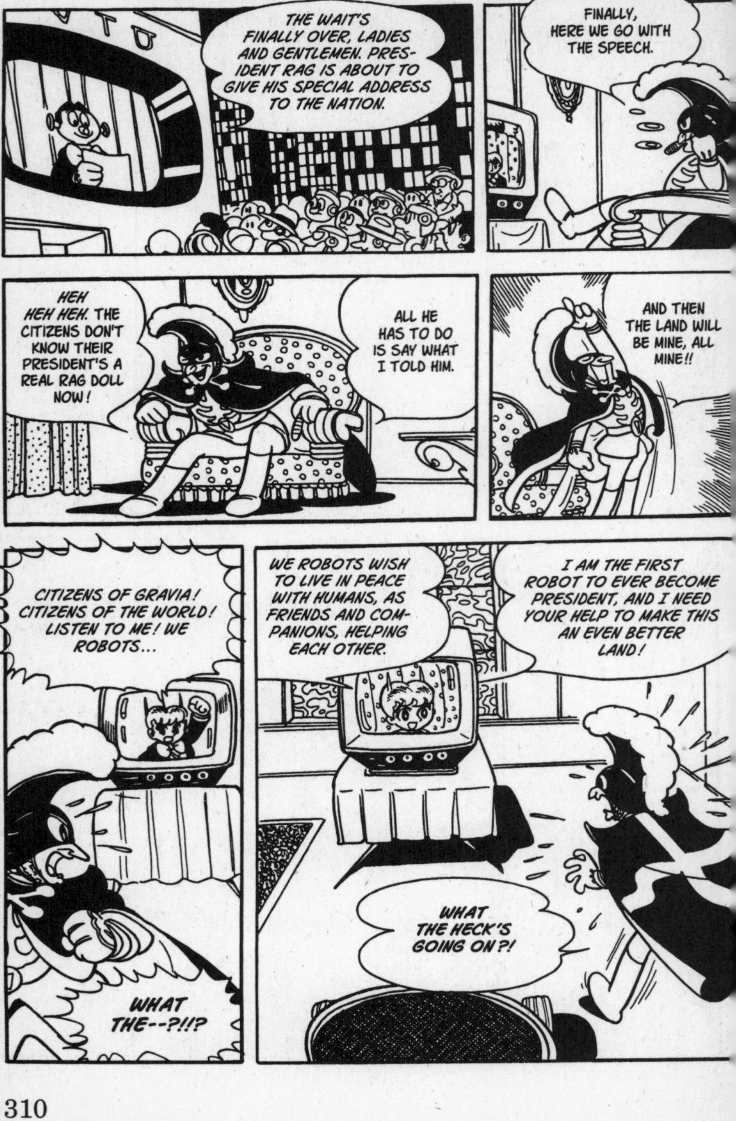
THE WAIT'S FINALLY OVER, LADIES AND GENTLEMEN. PRESIDENT RAG IS ABOUT TO GIVE HIS SPECIAL ADDRESS TO THE NATION.
FINALLY, HERE WE GO WITH THE SPEECH.
HEH HEH HEH. THE CITIZENS DON'T KNOW THEIR PRESIDENT'S A REAL RAG DOLL NOW!
ALL HE HAS TO DO IS SAY WHAT I TOLD HIM.
AND THEN THE LAND WILL BE MINE, ALL MINE!!
CITIZENS OF GRAVIA! CITIZENS OF THE WORLD! LISTEN TO ME! WE ROBOTS...
WHAT THE--?!!?
WE ROBOTS WISH TO LIVE IN PEACE WITH HUMANS, AS FRIENDS AND COMPANIONS, HELPING EACH OTHER.
I AM THE FIRST ROBOT TO EVER BECOME PRESIDENT, AND I NEED YOUR HELP TO MAKE THIS AN EVEN BETTER LAND!
WHAT THE HECK'S GOING ON?!

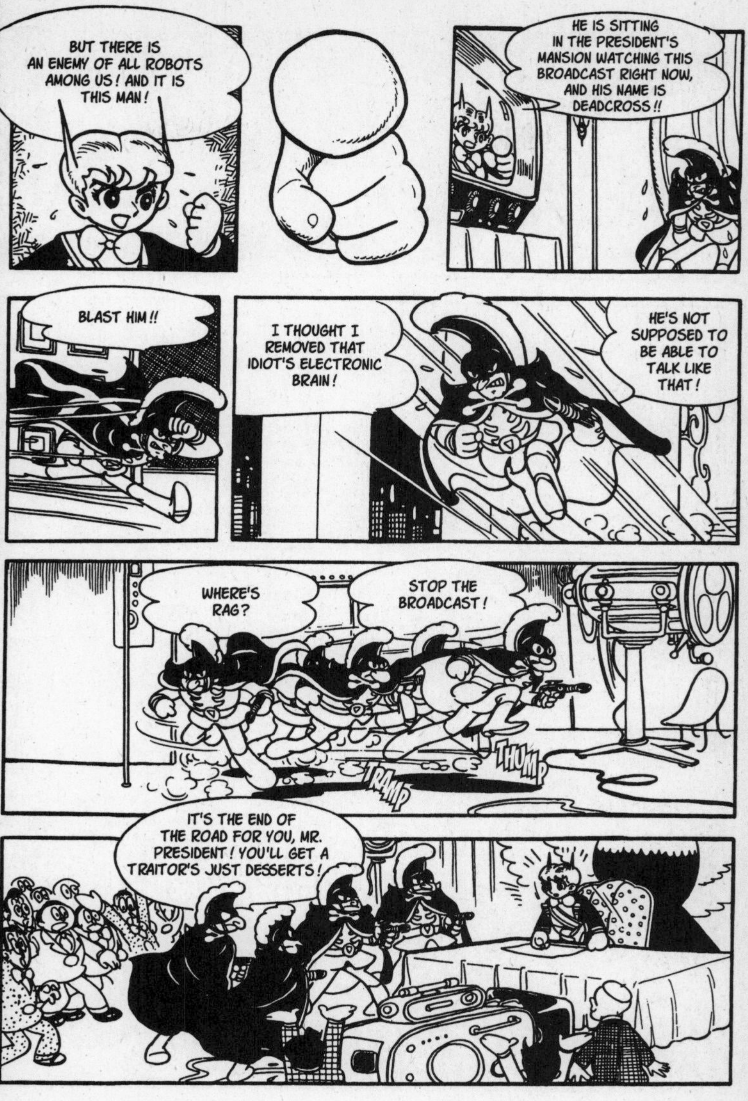
BUT THERE IS AN ENEMY OF ALL ROBOTS AMONG US! AND IT IS THIS MAN!
HE IS SITTING IN THE PRESIDENT'S MANSION WATCHING THIS BROADCAST RIGHT NOW, AND HIS NAME IS DEADCROSS!!
BLAST HIM!!
I THOUGHT I REMOVED THAT IDIOT'S ELECTRONIC BRAIN!
HE'S NOT SUPPOSED TO BE ABLE TO TALK LIKE THAT!
WHERE'S RAG?
STOP THE BROADCAST!
TRAMP
THUMP
IT'S THE END OF THE ROAD FOR YOU, MR. PRESIDENT! YOU'LL GET A TRAITOR'S JUST DESSERTS!

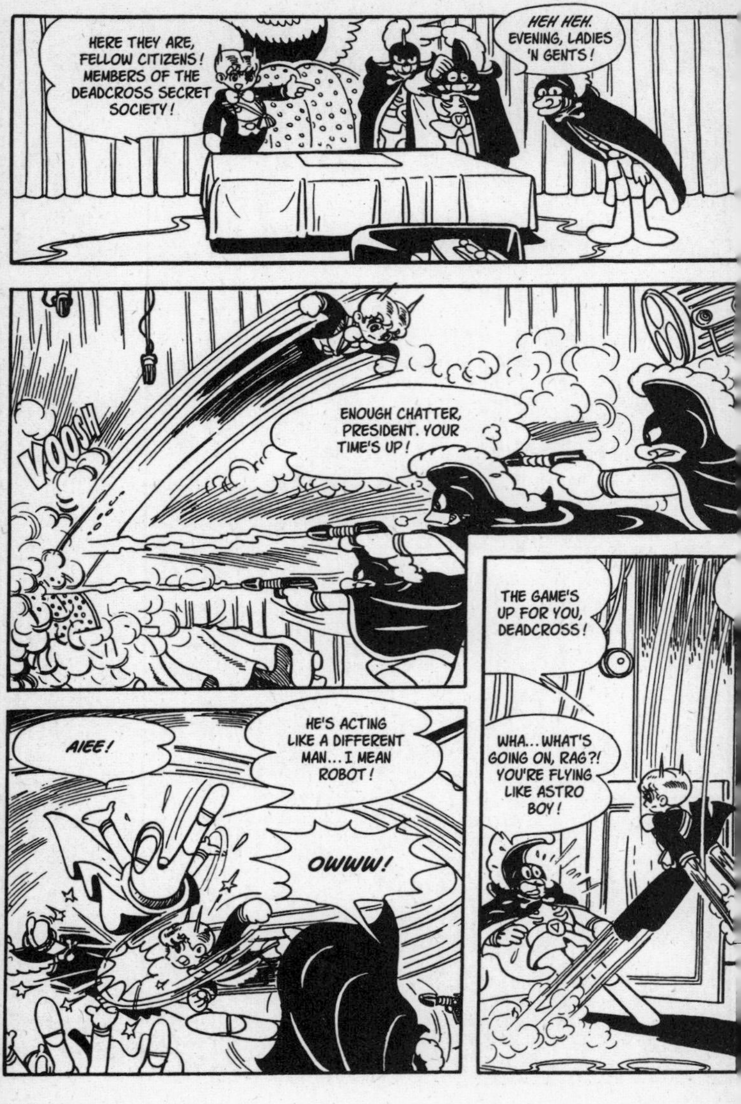
HERE THEY ARE, FELLOW CITIZENS! MEMBERS OF THE DEADCROSS SECRET SOCIETY!
HEH HEH. EVENING, LADIES 'N GENTS!
VOOSH
ENOUGH CHATTER, PRESIDENT. YOUR TIME'S UP!
THE GAME'S UP FOR YOU, DEADCROSS!
AIEE!
HE'S ACTING LIKE A DIFFERENT MAN... I MEAN ROBOT!
OWWW!
WHA... WHAT'S GOING ON, RAG?! YOU'RE FLYING LIKE ASTRO BOY!

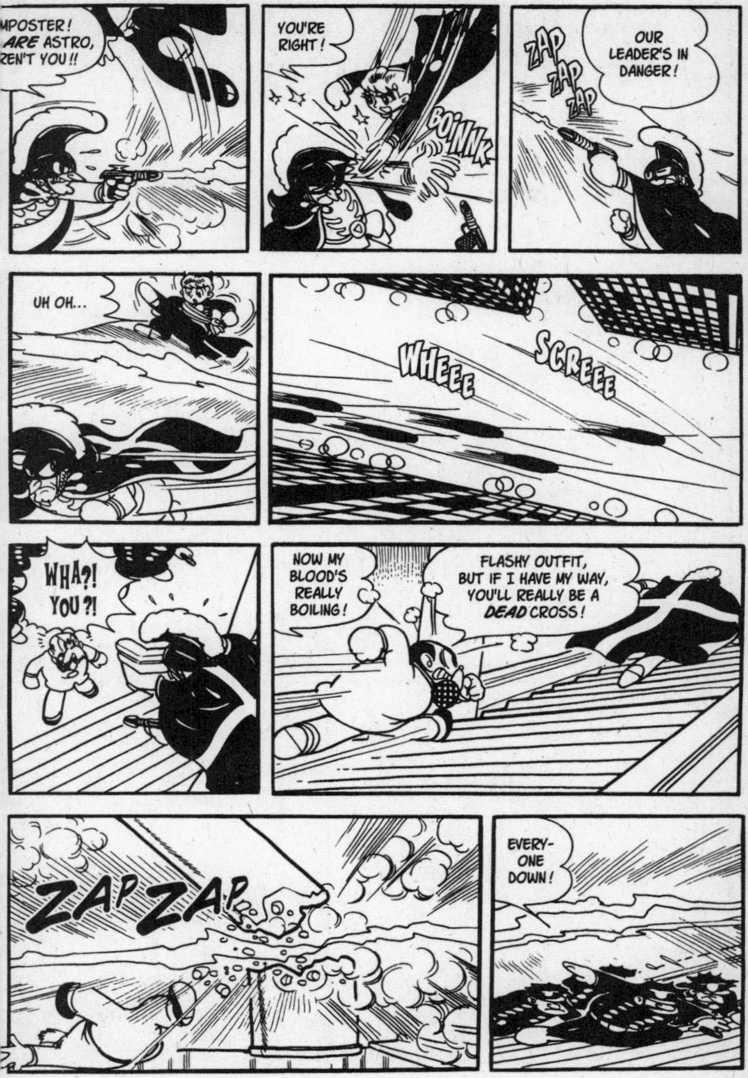
MPOSTER! ARE ASTRO, ZEN'T YOU!!
YOU'RE RIGHT!
BOINNK
ZAP ZAP ZAP
OUR LEADER'S IN DANGER!
UH OH...
WHEEE
SCREEE
WHA?! YOU?!
NOW MY BLOOD'S REALLY BOILING!
FLASHY OUTFIT, BUT IF I HAVE MY WAY, YOU'LL REALLY BE A DEAD CROSS!
ZAP ZAP
EVERY-ONE DOWN!

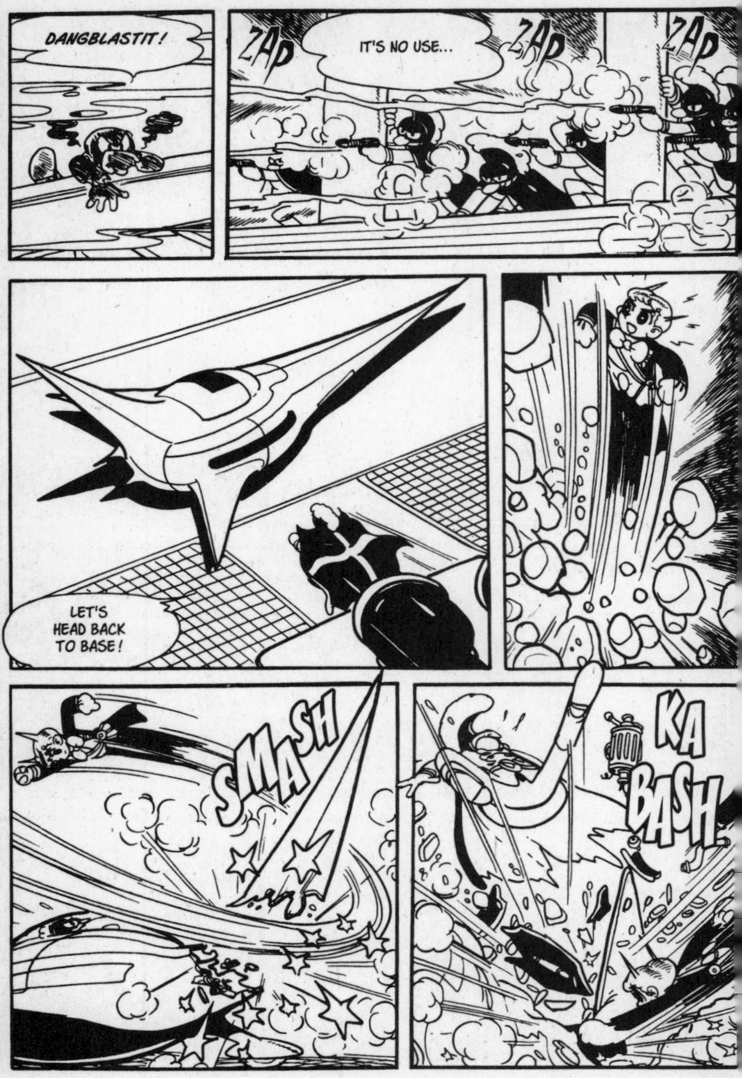
DANGBLASTIT!
ZAP
IT'S NO USE...
ZAP
ZAP
LET'S HEAD BACK TO BASE!
SMASH
KA BASH

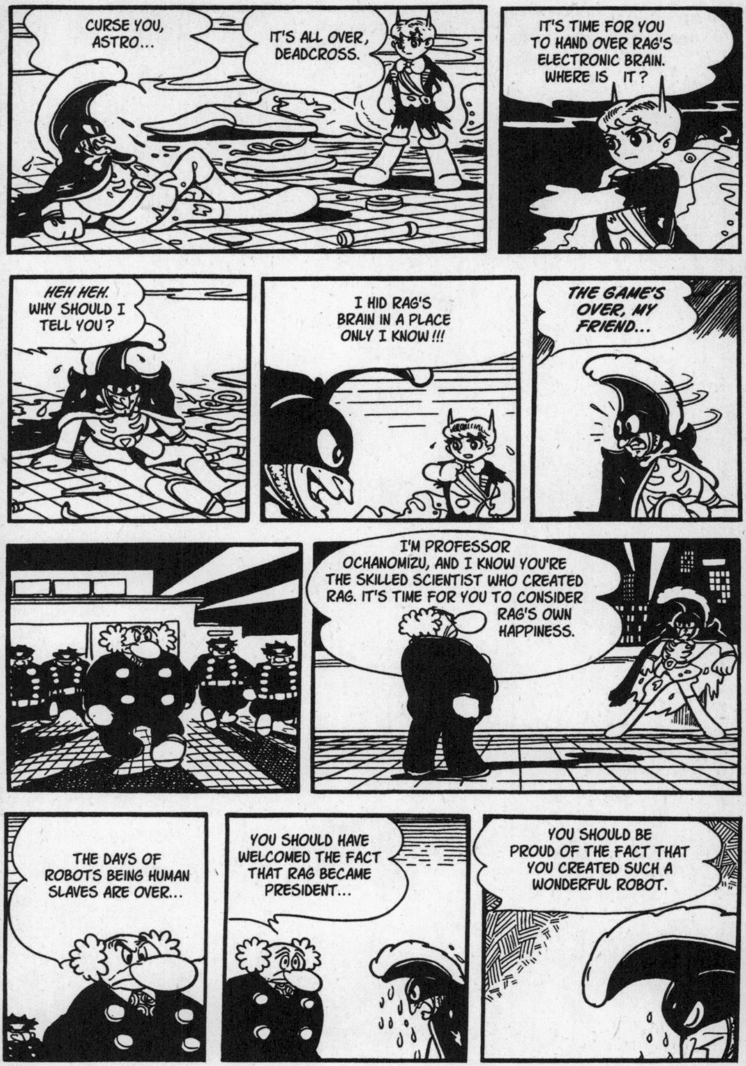
CURSE YOU, ASTRO...
IT'S ALL OVER, DEADCROSS.
IT'S TIME FOR YOU TO HAND OVER RAG'S ELECTRONIC BRAIN. WHERE IS IT?
HEH HEH. WHY SHOULD I TELL YOU?
I HID RAG'S BRAIN IN A PLACE ONLY I KNOW!!!
THE GAME'S OVER, MY FRIEND...
I'M PROFESSOR OCHANOMIZU, AND I KNOW YOU'RE THE SKILLED SCIENTIST WHO CREATED RAG. IT'S TIME FOR YOU TO CONSIDER RAG'S OWN HAPPINESS.
THE DAYS OF ROBOTS BEING HUMAN SLAVES ARE OVER...
YOU SHOULD HAVE WELCOMED THE FACT THAT RAG BECAME PRESIDENT...
YOU SHOULD BE PROUD OF THE FACT THAT YOU CREATED SUCH A WONDERFUL ROBOT.

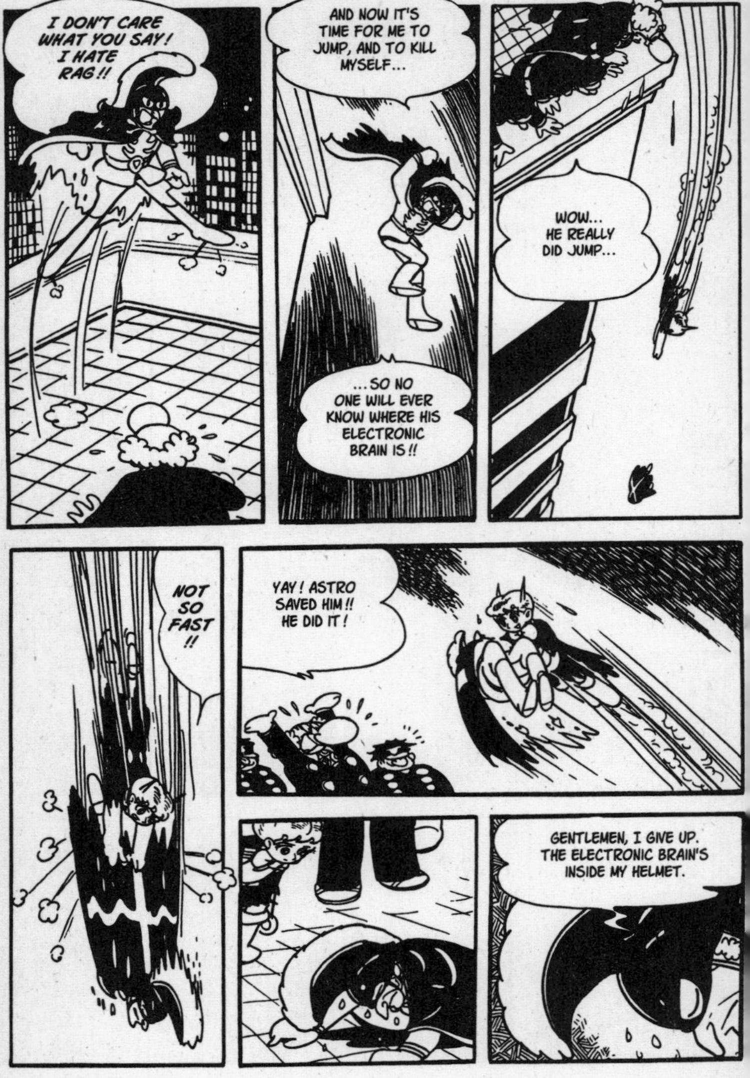
I DON'T CARE WHAT YOU SAY! I HATE RAG!!
AND NOW IT'S TIME FOR ME TO JUMP, AND TO KILL MYSELF...
...SO NO ONE WILL EVER KNOW WHERE HIS ELECTRONIC BRAIN IS!!
WOW... HE REALLY DID JUMP...
NOT SO FAST!!
YAY! ASTRO SAVED HIM!! HE DID IT!
GENTLEMEN, I GIVE UP. THE ELECTRONIC BRAIN'S INSIDE MY HELMET.

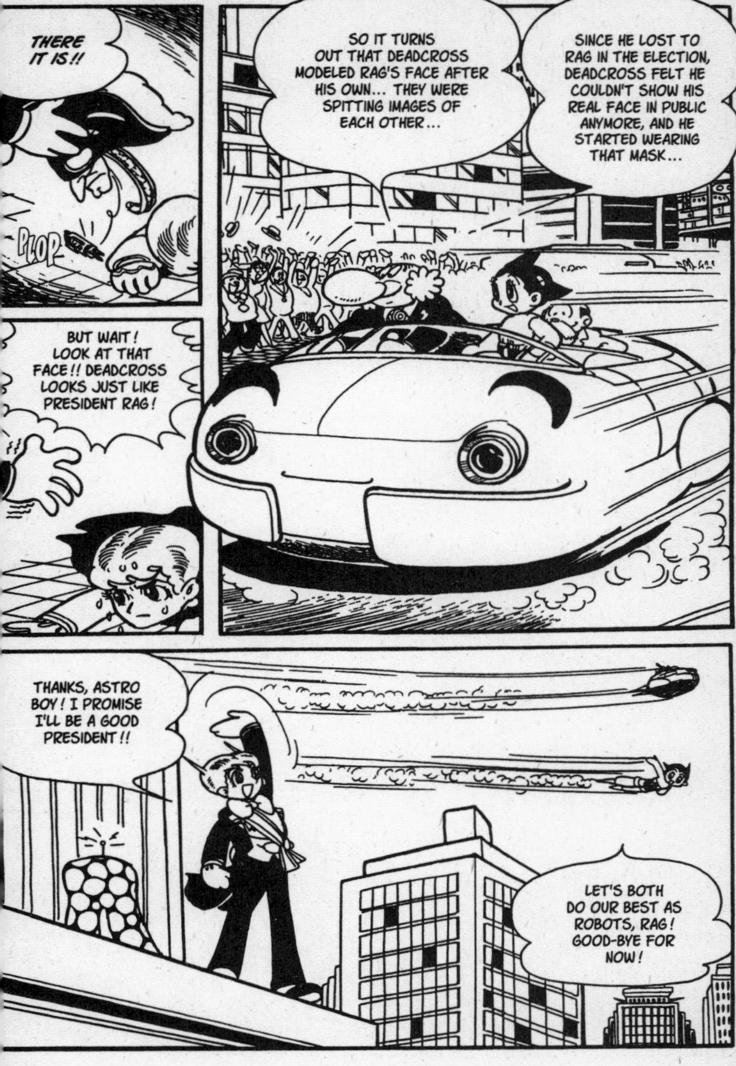

THERE IT IS!!
PLOP
BUT WAIT! LOOK AT THAT FACE!! DEADCROSS LOOKS JUST LIKE PRESIDENT RAG!
SO IT TURNS OUT THAT DEADCROSS MODELED RAG'S FACE AFTER HIS OWN... THEY WERE SPITTING IMAGES OF EACH OTHER...
SINCE HE LOST TO RAG IN THE ELECTION, DEADCROSS FELT HE COULDN'T SHOW HIS REAL FACE IN PUBLIC ANYMORE, AND HE STARTED WEARING THAT MASK...
THANKS, ASTRO BOY! I PROMISE I'LL BE A GOOD PRESIDENT!!
LET'S BOTH DO OUR BEST AS ROBOTS, RAG! GOOD-BYE FOR NOW!

THE THIRD
MAGICIAN

Originally serialized between October 1961
and January 1962 in *Shonen* magazine.

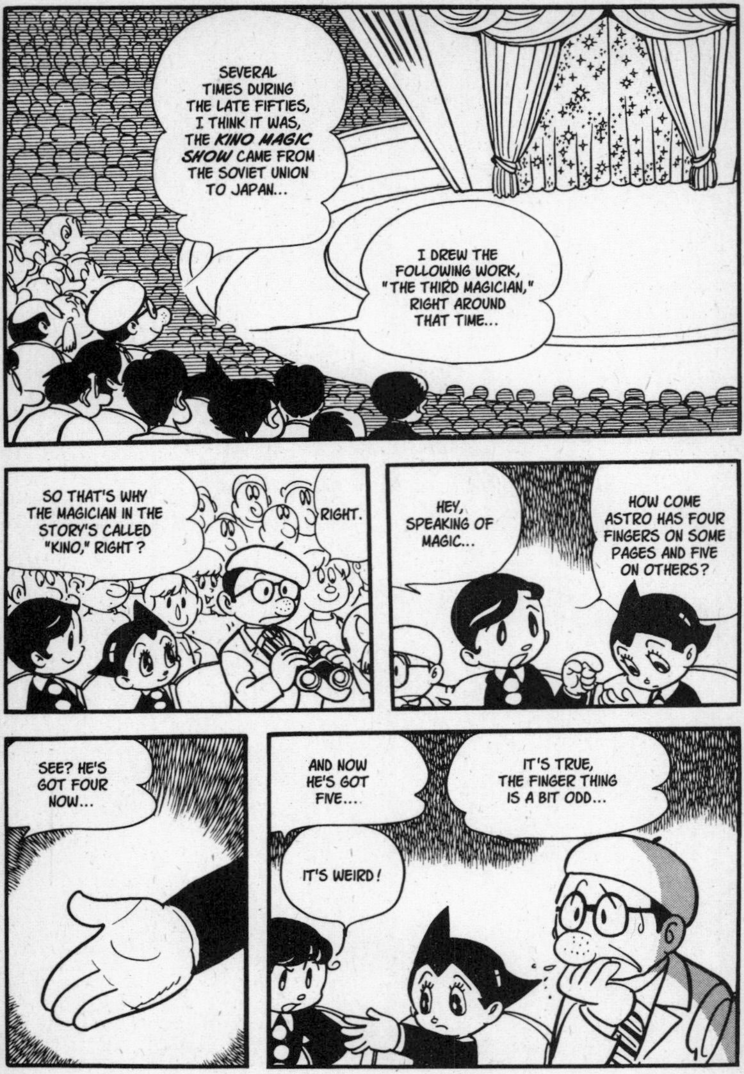
SEVERAL TIMES DURING THE LATE FIFTIES, I THINK IT WAS, THE *KINO MAGIC SHOW* CAME FROM THE SOVIET UNION TO JAPAN...
I DREW THE FOLLOWING WORK, "THE THIRD MAGICIAN," RIGHT AROUND THAT TIME...
SO THAT'S WHY THE MAGICIAN IN THE STORY'S CALLED "KINO," RIGHT?
RIGHT.
HEY, SPEAKING OF MAGIC...
HOW COME ASTRO HAS FOUR FINGERS ON SOME PAGES AND FIVE ON OTHERS?
SEE? HE'S GOT FOUR NOW...
AND NOW HE'S GOT FIVE....
IT'S TRUE, THE FINGER THING IS A BIT ODD...
IT'S WEIRD!

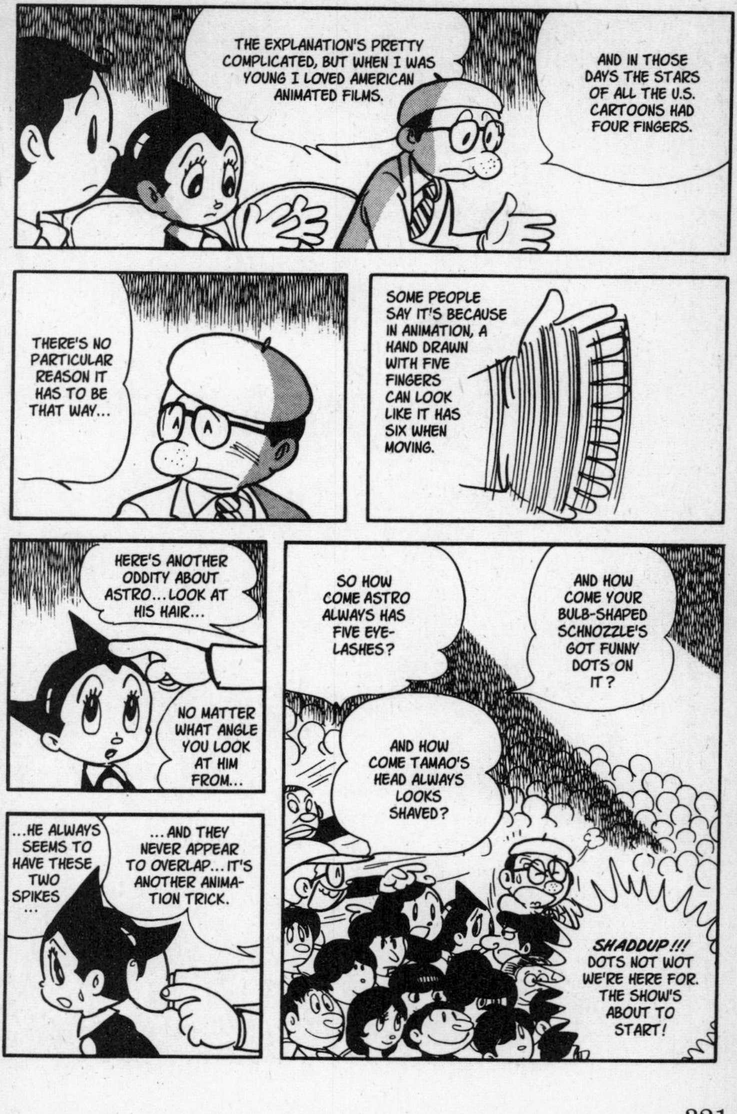
THE EXPLANATION'S PRETTY COMPLICATED, BUT WHEN I WAS YOUNG I LOVED AMERICAN ANIMATED FILMS.
AND IN THOSE DAYS THE STARS OF ALL THE U.S. CARTOONS HAD FOUR FINGERS.
THERE'S NO PARTICULAR REASON IT HAS TO BE THAT WAY...
SOME PEOPLE SAY IT'S BECAUSE IN ANIMATION, A HAND DRAWN WITH FIVE FINGERS CAN LOOK LIKE IT HAS SIX WHEN MOVING.
HERE'S ANOTHER ODDITY ABOUT ASTRO...LOOK AT HIS HAIR...
NO MATTER WHAT ANGLE YOU LOOK AT HIM FROM...
SO HOW COME ASTRO ALWAYS HAS FIVE EYE-LASHES?
AND HOW COME YOUR BULB-SHAPED SCHNOZZLE'S GOT FUNNY DOTS ON IT?
AND HOW COME TAMAO'S HEAD ALWAYS LOOKS SHAVED?
SHADDUP!!! DOTS NOT WOT WE'RE HERE FOR. THE SHOW'S ABOUT TO START!
...HE ALWAYS SEEMS TO HAVE THESE TWO SPIKES ...
...AND THEY NEVER APPEAR TO OVERLAP...IT'S ANOTHER ANIMA-TION TRICK.

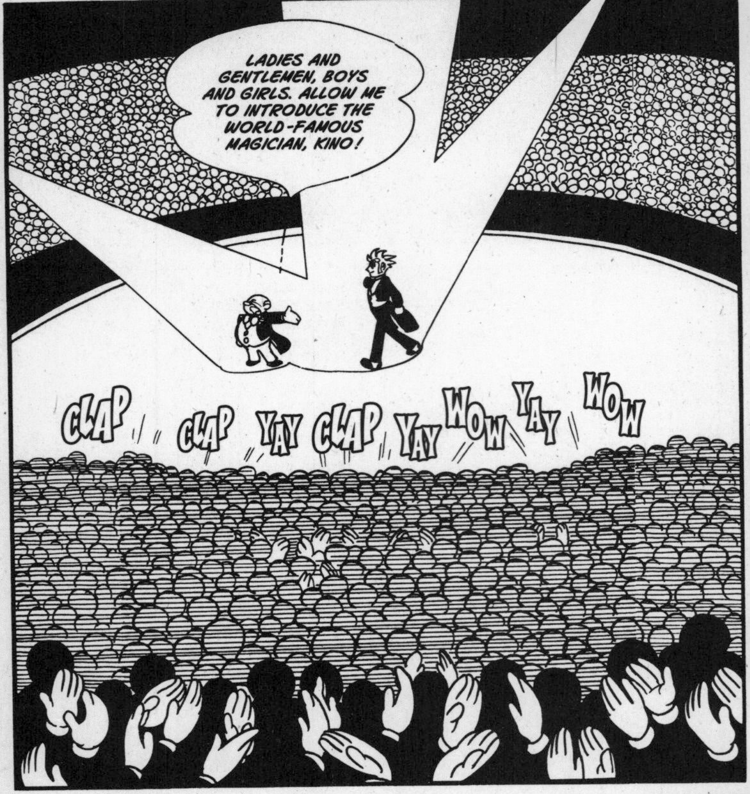
LADIES AND GENTLEMEN, BOYS AND GIRLS. ALLOW ME TO INTRODUCE THE WORLD-FAMOUS MAGICIAN, KINO!
CLAP
CLAP
YAY
CLAP
YAY
WOW
YAY
WOW

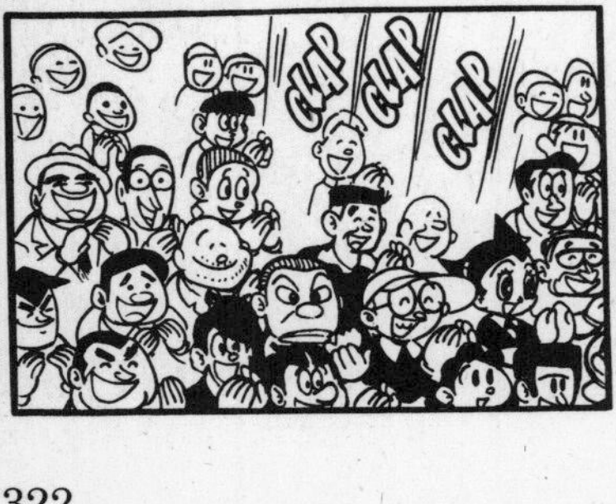
CLAP
CLAP
CLAP

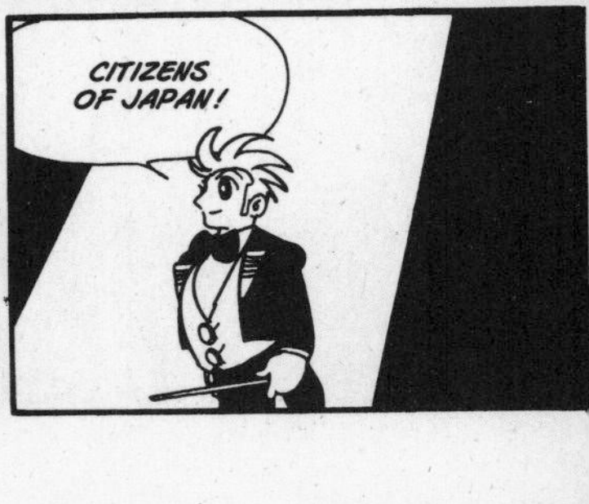
CITIZENS OF JAPAN!

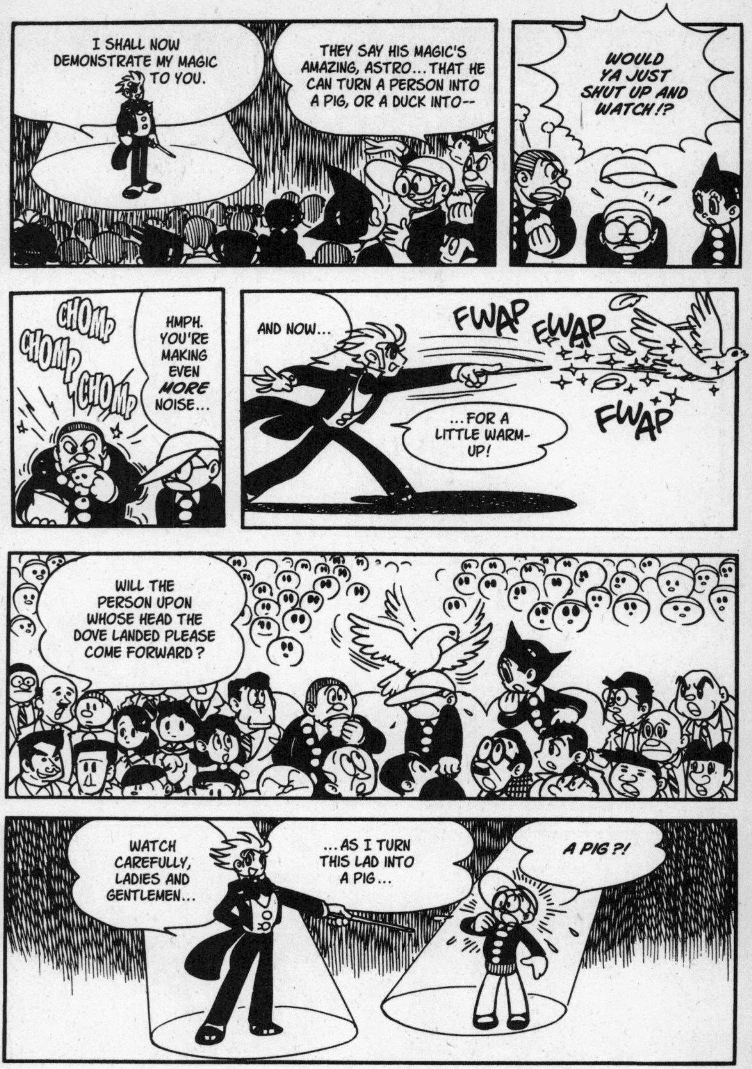
I SHALL NOW DEMONSTRATE MY MAGIC TO YOU.
THEY SAY HIS MAGIC'S AMAZING, ASTRO... THAT HE CAN TURN A PERSON INTO A PIG, OR A DUCK INTO--
WOULD YA JUST SHUT UP AND WATCH!?
CHOMP CHOMP CHOMP
HMPH. YOU'RE MAKING EVEN MORE NOISE...
AND NOW...
FWAP FWAP
...FOR A LITTLE WARM-UP!
FWAP
WILL THE PERSON UPON WHOSE HEAD THE DOVE LANDED PLEASE COME FORWARD?
WATCH CAREFULLY, LADIES AND GENTLEMEN...
...AS I TURN THIS LAD INTO A PIG...
A PIG?!

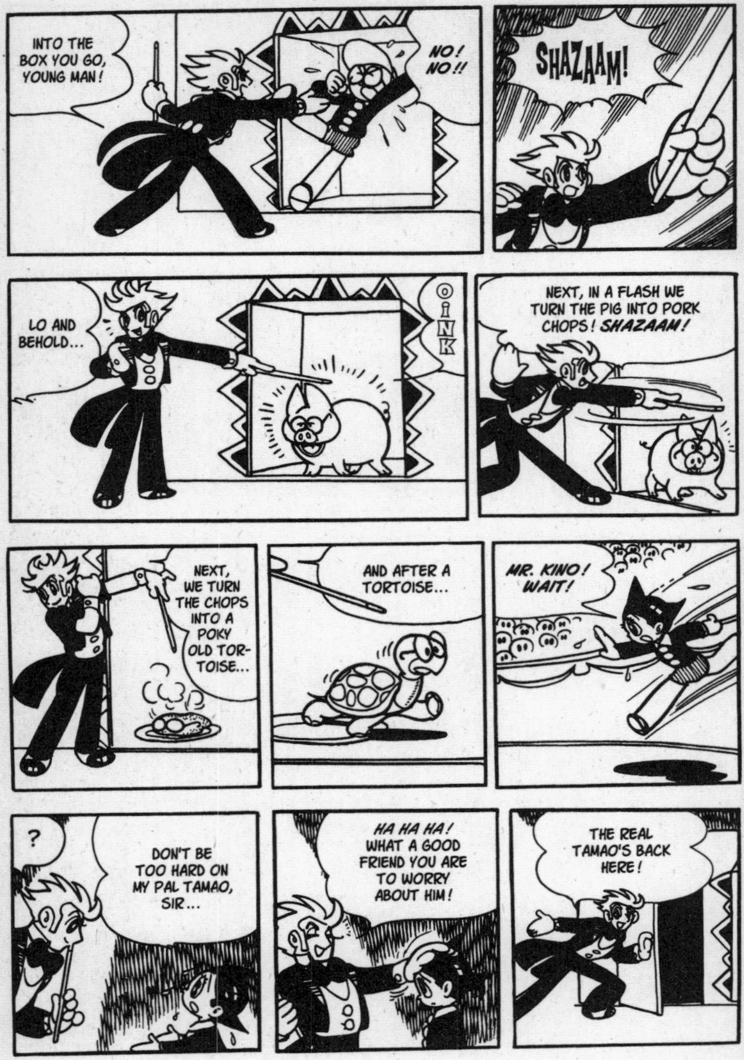

INTO THE BOX YOU GO, YOUNG MAN!
NO! NO!!
SHAZAAM!
LO AND BEHOLD...
OINK
NEXT, IN A FLASH WE TURN THE PIG INTO PORK CHOPS! SHAZAAM!
NEXT, WE TURN THE CHOPS INTO A POKY OLD TOR-TOISE...
AND AFTER A TORTOISE...
MR. KINO! WAIT!
?
DON'T BE TOO HARD ON MY PAL TAMAO, SIR...
HA HA HA! WHAT A GOOD FRIEND YOU ARE TO WORRY ABOUT HIM!
THE REAL TAMAO'S BACK HERE!

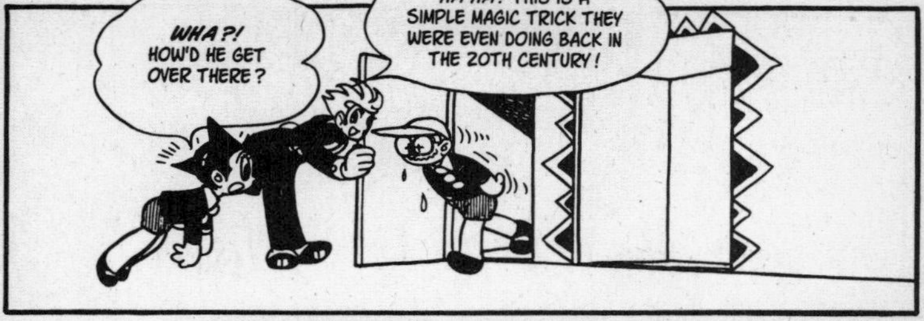
WHA?! HOW'D HE GET OVER THERE?
HA HA! THIS IS A SIMPLE MAGIC TRICK THEY WERE EVEN DOING BACK IN THE 20TH CENTURY!

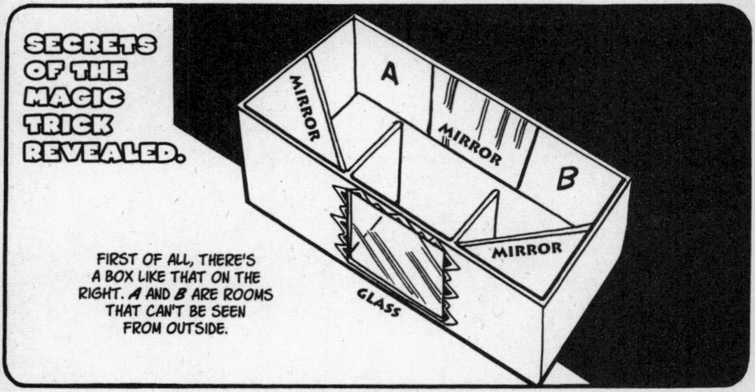
SECRETS OF THE MAGIC TRICK REVEALED.
A
MIRROR
MIRROR
B
MIRROR
GLASS
FIRST OF ALL, THERE'S A BOX LIKE THAT ON THE RIGHT. A AND B ARE ROOMS THAT CAN'T BE SEEN FROM OUTSIDE.

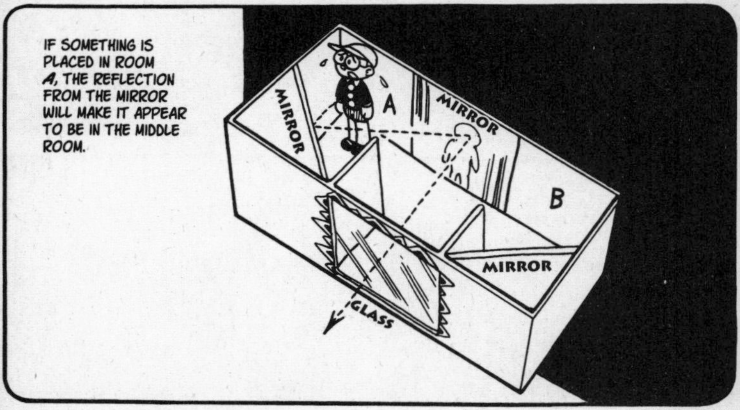
IF SOMETHING IS PLACED IN ROOM A, THE REFLECTION FROM THE MIRROR WILL MAKE IT APPEAR TO BE IN THE MIDDLE ROOM.
MIRROR
A
MIRROR
B
MIRROR
GLASS

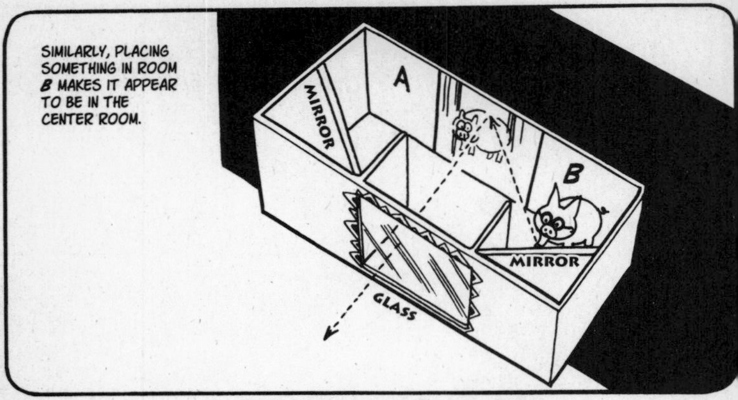
SIMILARLY, PLACING SOMETHING IN ROOM B MAKES IT APPEAR TO BE IN THE CENTER ROOM.
A
B
MIRROR
MIRROR
GLASS

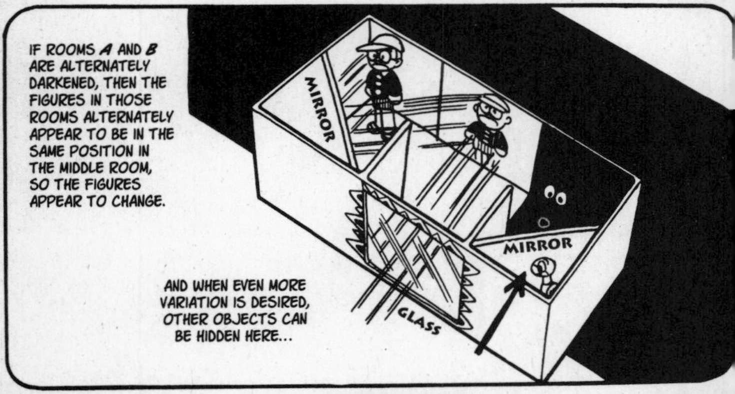
IF ROOMS A AND B ARE ALTERNATELY DARKENED, THEN THE FIGURES IN THOSE ROOMS ALTERNATELY APPEAR TO BE IN THE SAME POSITION IN THE MIDDLE ROOM, SO THE FIGURES APPEAR TO CHANGE.
MIRROR
MIRROR
AND WHEN EVEN MORE VARIATION IS DESIRED, OTHER OBJECTS CAN BE HIDDEN HERE...
GLASS

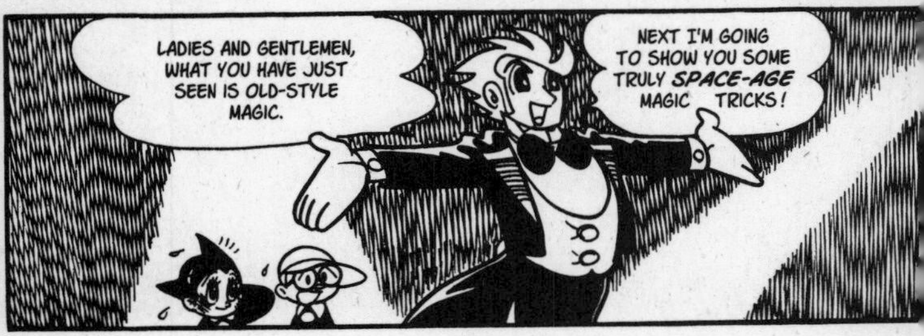
LADIES AND GENTLEMEN, WHAT YOU HAVE JUST SEEN IS OLD-STYLE MAGIC.
NEXT I'M GOING TO SHOW YOU SOME TRULY SPACE-AGE MAGIC TRICKS!

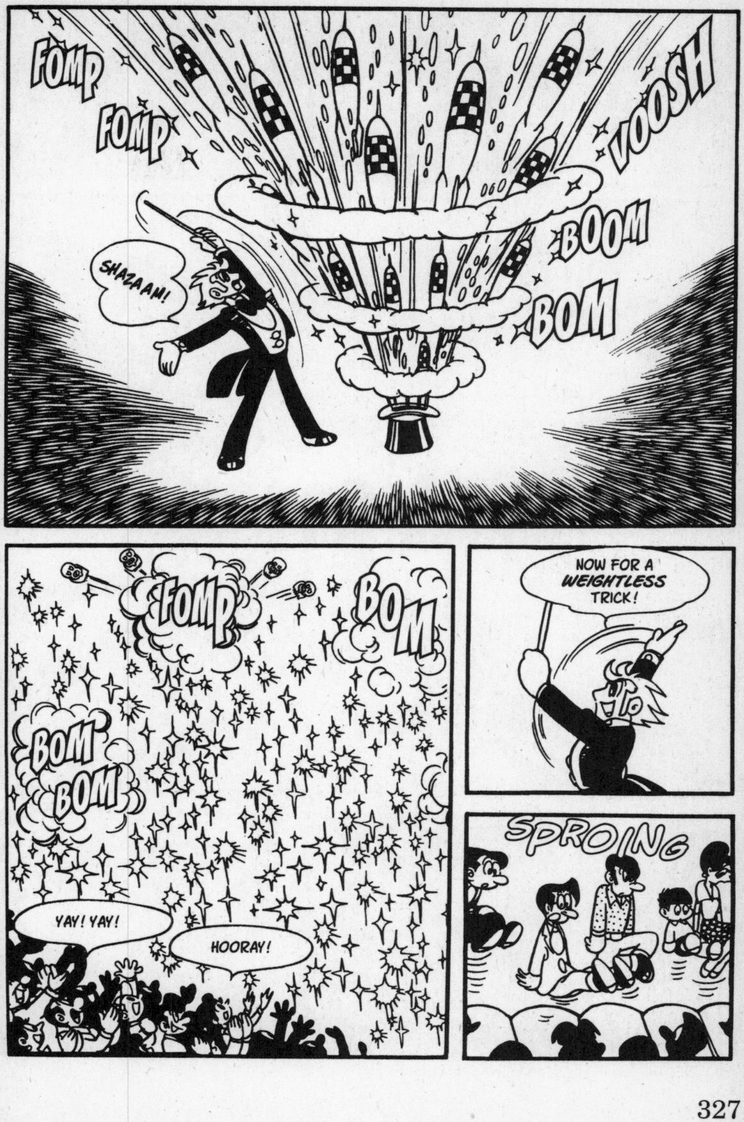

FOMP
FOMP
VOOSH
SHAZAAM!
BOOM
BOM
FOMP
BOM
BOM
BOM
YAY! YAY!
HOORAY!
NOW FOR A *WEIGHTLESS* TRICK!
SPROING

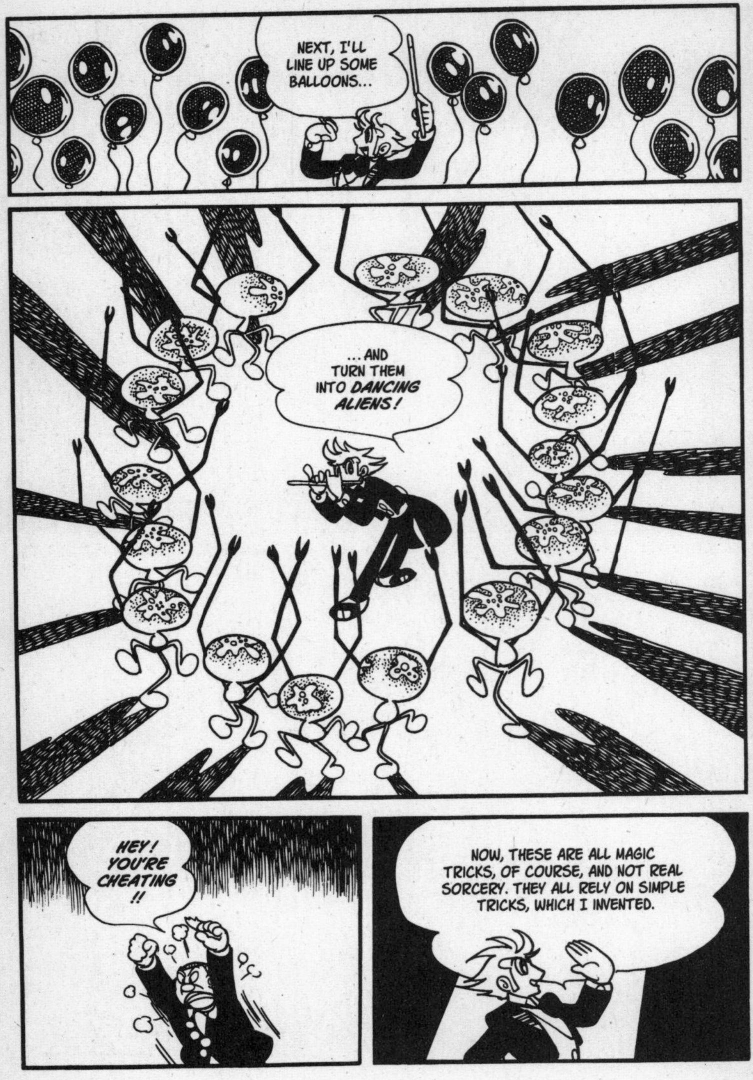
NEXT, I'LL LINE UP SOME BALLOONS...
...AND TURN THEM INTO DANCING ALIENS!
HEY! YOU'RE CHEATING!!
NOW, THESE ARE ALL MAGIC TRICKS, OF COURSE, AND NOT REAL SORCERY. THEY ALL RELY ON SIMPLE TRICKS, WHICH I INVENTED.

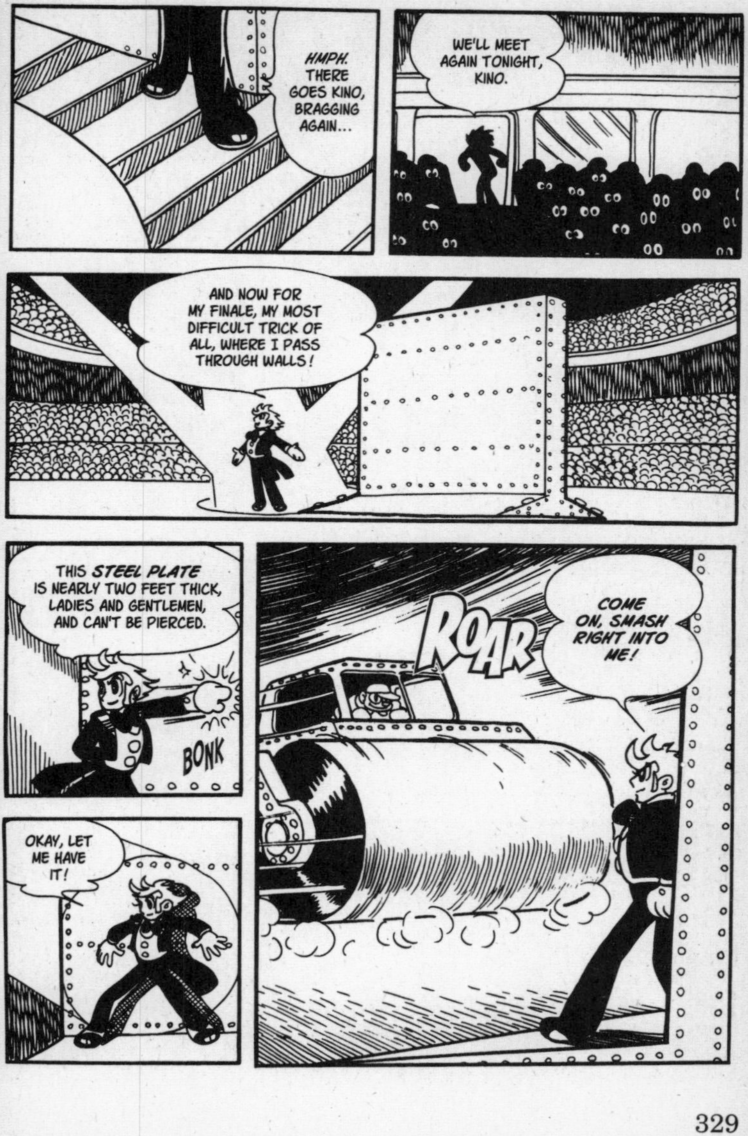
HMPH. THERE GOES KINO, BRAGGING AGAIN...
WE'LL MEET AGAIN TONIGHT, KINO.
AND NOW FOR MY FINALE, MY MOST DIFFICULT TRICK OF ALL, WHERE I PASS THROUGH WALLS!
THIS STEEL PLATE IS NEARLY TWO FEET THICK, LADIES AND GENTLEMEN, AND CAN'T BE PIERCED.
BONK
OKAY, LET ME HAVE IT!
ROAR
COME ON, SMASH RIGHT INTO ME!

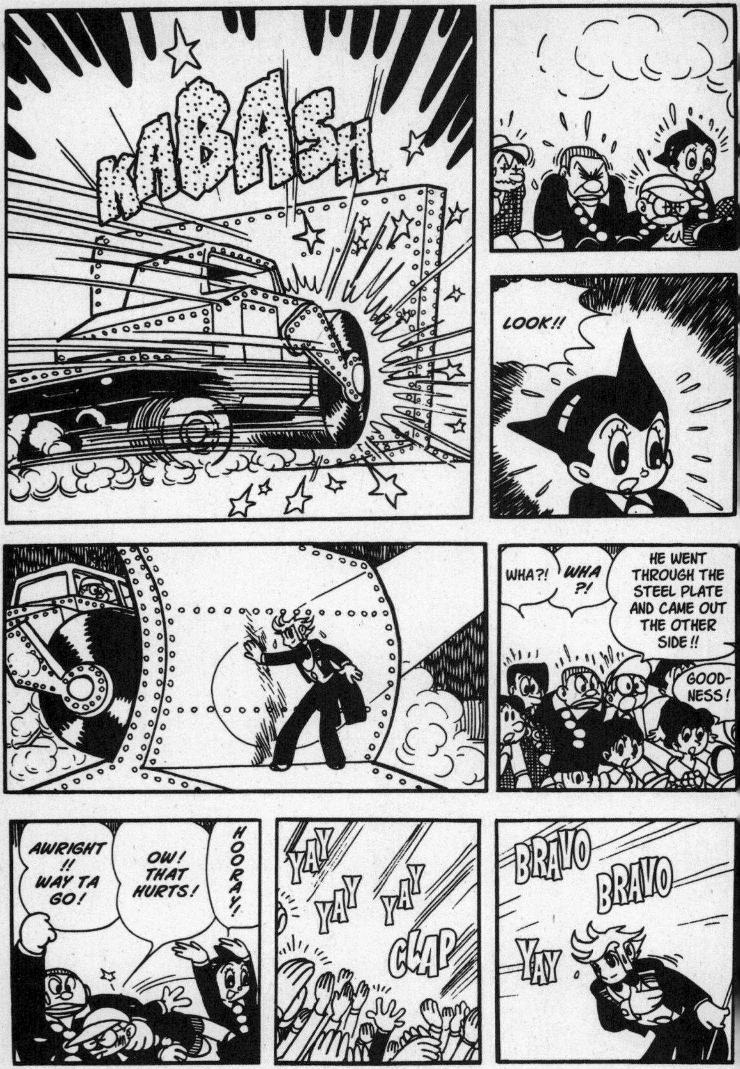
KABASH
LOOK!!
WHA?!
WHA ?!
HE WENT THROUGH THE STEEL PLATE AND CAME OUT THE OTHER SIDE!!
GOODNESS!
AWRIGHT!! WAY TA GO!
OW! THAT HURTS!
HOORAY!!
YAY
YAY
YAY
CLAP
BRAVO
BRAVO
YAY

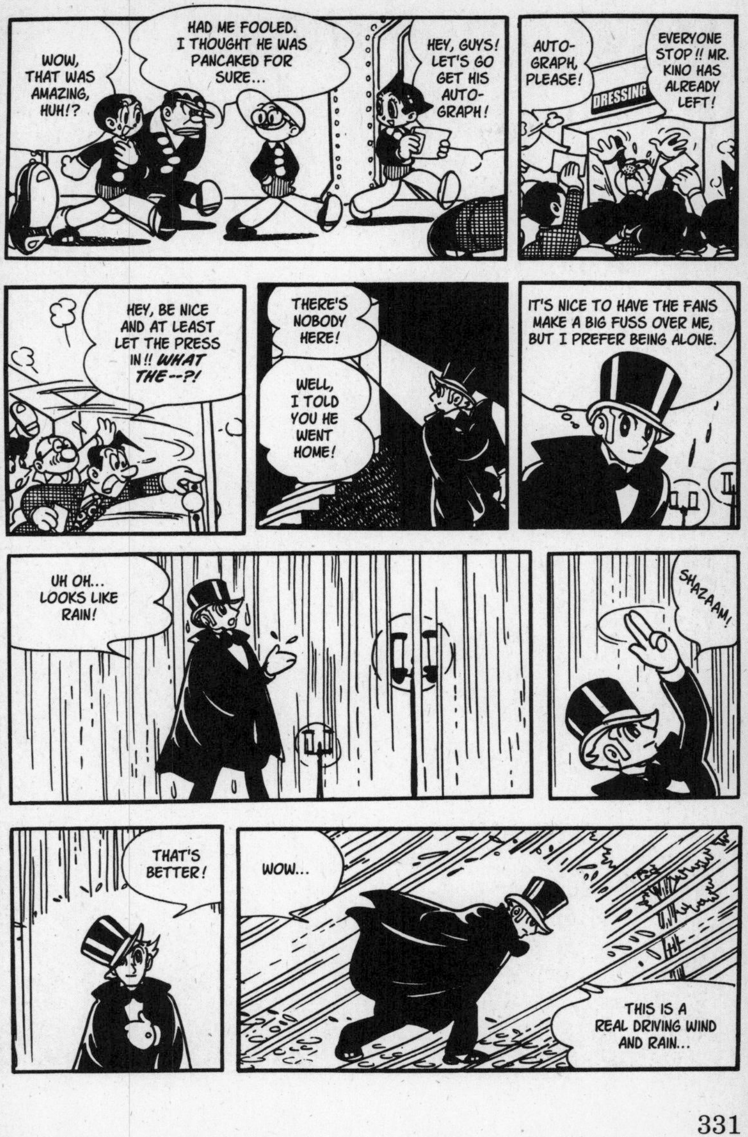
WOW, THAT WAS AMAZING, HUH!?
HAD ME FOOLED. I THOUGHT HE WAS PANCAKED FOR SURE...
HEY, GUYS! LET'S GO GET HIS AUTO-GRAPH!
AUTO-GRAPH, PLEASE!
DRESSING
EVERYONE STOP!! MR. KINO HAS ALREADY LEFT!
HEY, BE NICE AND AT LEAST LET THE PRESS IN!! WHAT THE--?!
THERE'S NOBODY HERE!
WELL, I TOLD YOU HE WENT HOME!
IT'S NICE TO HAVE THE FANS MAKE A BIG FUSS OVER ME, BUT I PREFER BEING ALONE.
UH OH... LOOKS LIKE RAIN!
SHAZAAM!
THAT'S BETTER!
WOW...
THIS IS A REAL DRIVING WIND AND RAIN...

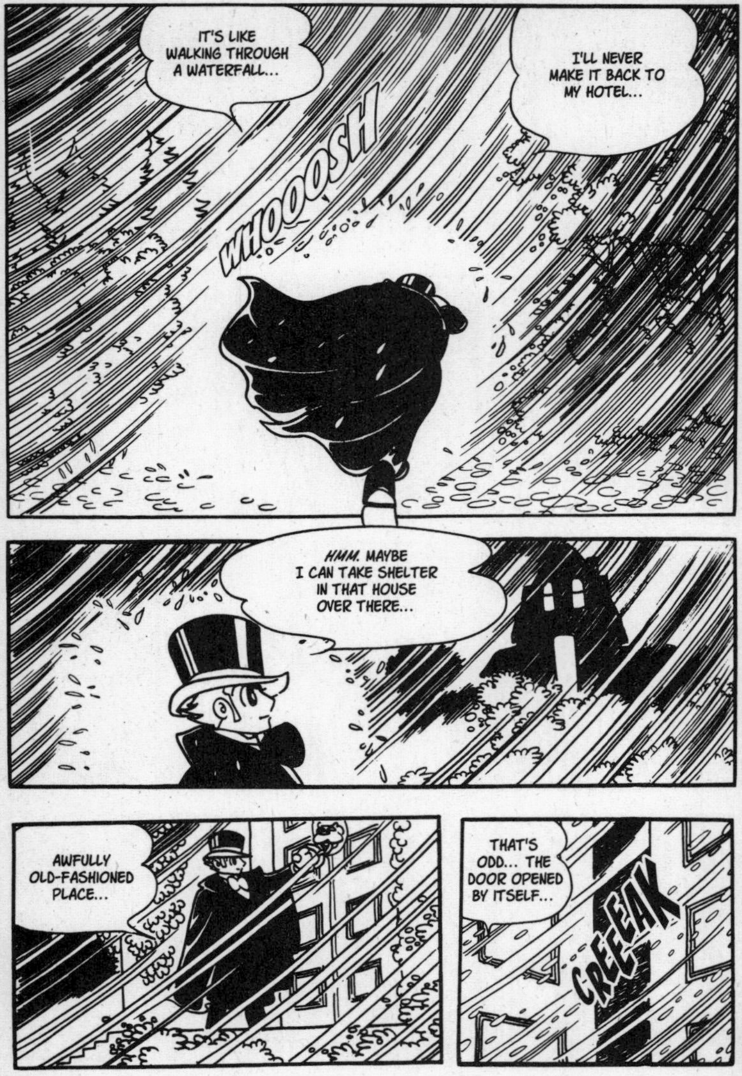
IT'S LIKE WALKING THROUGH A WATERFALL...
I'LL NEVER MAKE IT BACK TO MY HOTEL...
WHOOOSH
HMM. MAYBE I CAN TAKE SHELTER IN THAT HOUSE OVER THERE...
AWFULLY OLD-FASHIONED PLACE...
THAT'S ODD... THE DOOR OPENED BY ITSELF...
CREEEAK

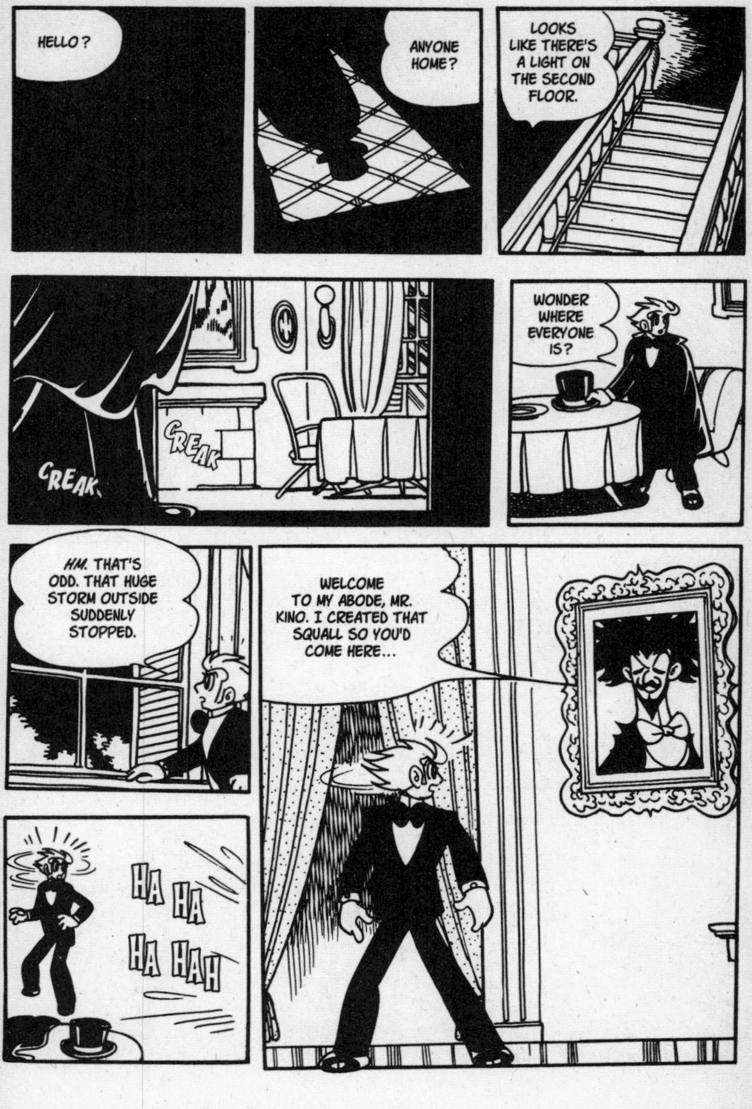

HELLO?
ANYONE HOME?
LOOKS LIKE THERE'S A LIGHT ON THE SECOND FLOOR.
CREAK
CREAK
WONDER WHERE EVERYONE IS?
HM. THAT'S ODD. THAT HUGE STORM OUTSIDE SUDDENLY STOPPED.
WELCOME TO MY ABODE, MR. KINO. I CREATED THAT SQUALL SO YOU'D COME HERE...
HA HA HA HAH

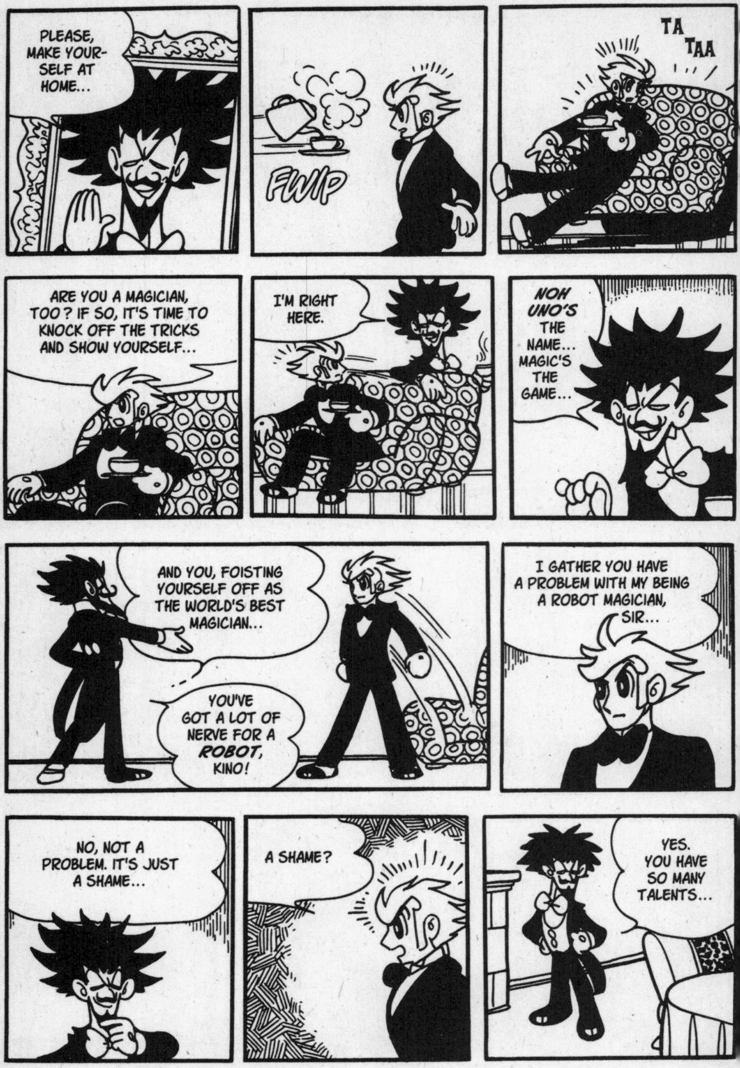
PLEASE, MAKE YOURSELF AT HOME...
FWIP
TA TAA
ARE YOU A MAGICIAN, TOO? IF SO, IT'S TIME TO KNOCK OFF THE TRICKS AND SHOW YOURSELF...
I'M RIGHT HERE.
NOH UNO'S THE NAME... MAGIC'S THE GAME...
AND YOU, FOISTING YOURSELF OFF AS THE WORLD'S BEST MAGICIAN...
YOU'VE GOT A LOT OF NERVE FOR A ROBOT, KINO!
I GATHER YOU HAVE A PROBLEM WITH MY BEING A ROBOT MAGICIAN, SIR...
NO, NOT A PROBLEM. IT'S JUST A SHAME...
A SHAME?
YES. YOU HAVE SO MANY TALENTS...

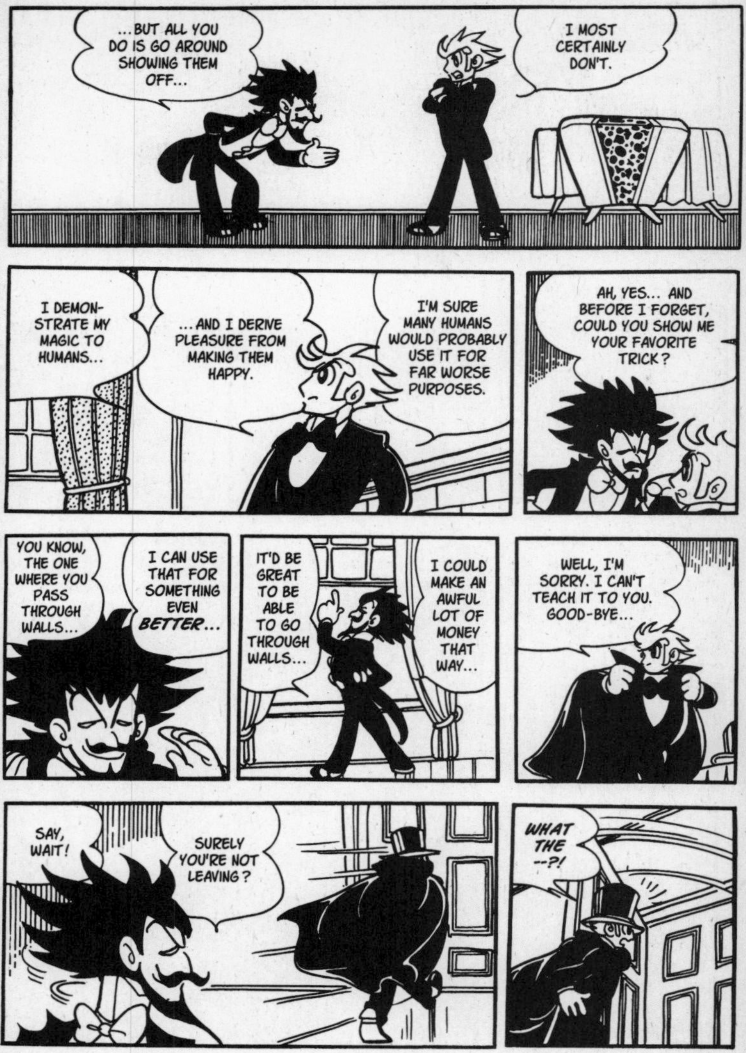
...BUT ALL YOU DO IS GO AROUND SHOWING THEM OFF...
I MOST CERTAINLY DON'T.
I DEMON-STRATE MY MAGIC TO HUMANS...
...AND I DERIVE PLEASURE FROM MAKING THEM HAPPY.
I'M SURE MANY HUMANS WOULD PROBABLY USE IT FOR FAR WORSE PURPOSES.
AH, YES... AND BEFORE I FORGET, COULD YOU SHOW ME YOUR FAVORITE TRICK?
YOU KNOW, THE ONE WHERE YOU PASS THROUGH WALLS...
I CAN USE THAT FOR SOMETHING EVEN *BETTER*...
IT'D BE GREAT TO BE ABLE TO GO THROUGH WALLS...
I COULD MAKE AN AWFUL LOT OF MONEY THAT WAY...
WELL, I'M SORRY. I CAN'T TEACH IT TO YOU. GOOD-BYE...
SAY, WAIT!
SURELY YOU'RE NOT LEAVING?
WHAT THE --?!

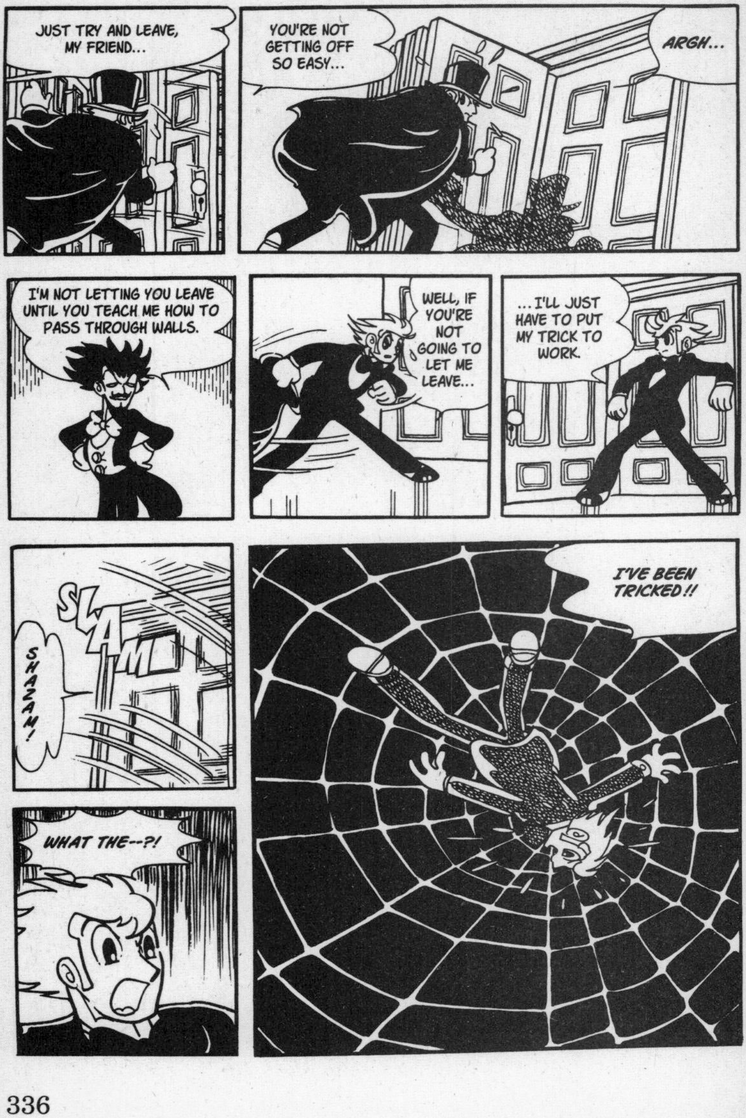

JUST TRY AND LEAVE, MY FRIEND...
YOU'RE NOT GETTING OFF SO EASY...
ARGH...
I'M NOT LETTING YOU LEAVE UNTIL YOU TEACH ME HOW TO PASS THROUGH WALLS.
WELL, IF YOU'RE NOT GOING TO LET ME LEAVE...
...I'LL JUST HAVE TO PUT MY TRICK TO WORK.
SHAZAM!
SLAM
WHAT THE--?!
I'VE BEEN TRICKED!!

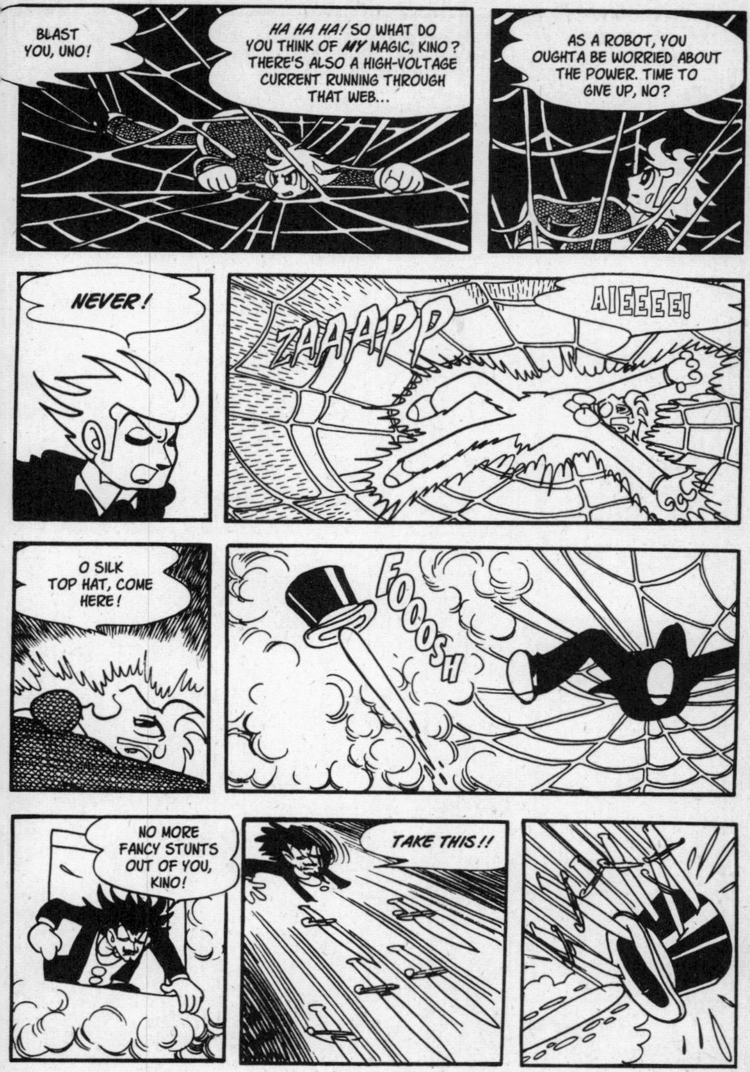
BLAST YOU, UNO!
HA HA HA! SO WHAT DO YOU THINK OF MY MAGIC, KINO? THERE'S ALSO A HIGH-VOLTAGE CURRENT RUNNING THROUGH THAT WEB...
AS A ROBOT, YOU OUGHTA BE WORRIED ABOUT THE POWER. TIME TO GIVE UP, NO?
NEVER!
ZAAAPP
AIEEEEE!
O SILK TOP HAT, COME HERE!
FOOOOSH
NO MORE FANCY STUNTS OUT OF YOU, KINO!
TAKE THIS!!

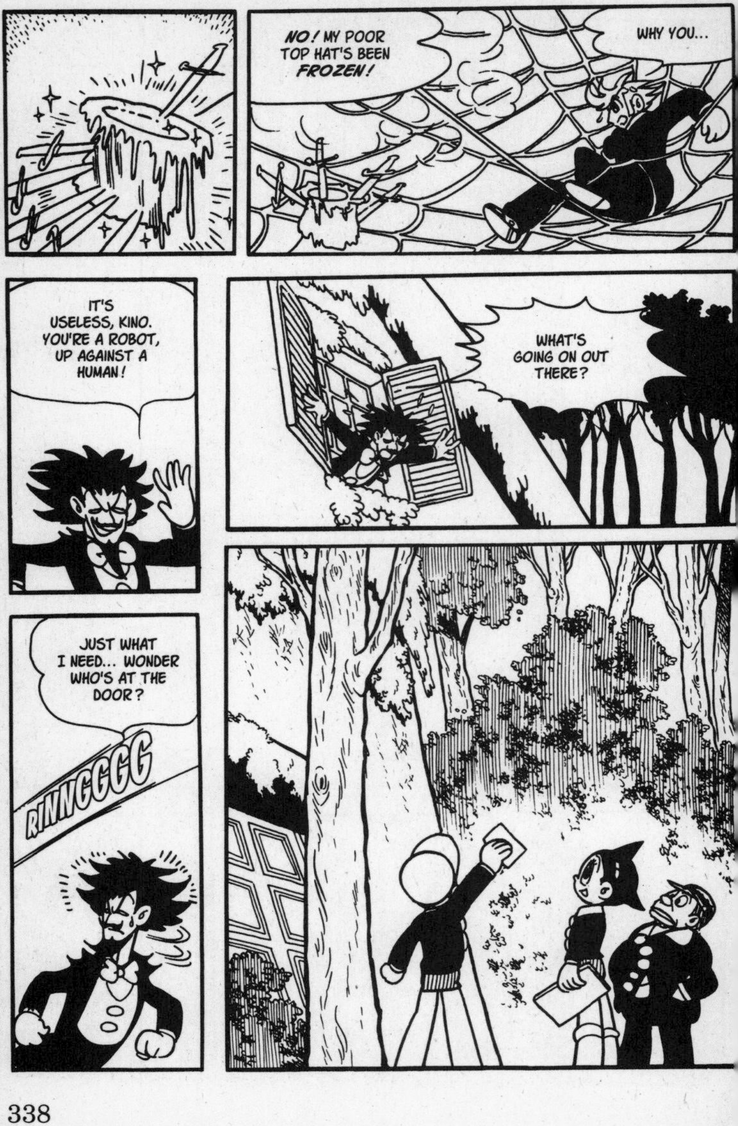
NO! MY POOR TOP HAT'S BEEN FROZEN!
WHY YOU...
IT'S USELESS, KINO. YOU'RE A ROBOT, UP AGAINST A HUMAN!
WHAT'S GOING ON OUT THERE?
JUST WHAT I NEED... WONDER WHO'S AT THE DOOR?
RINNGGGG

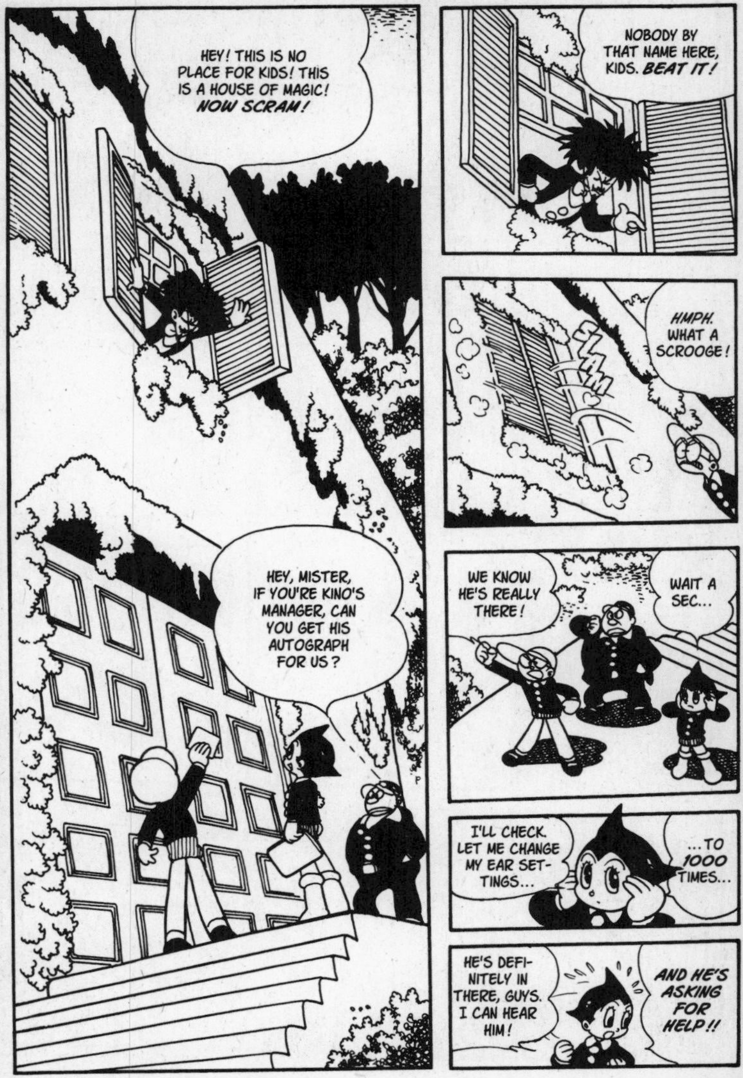
HEY! THIS IS NO PLACE FOR KIDS! THIS IS A HOUSE OF MAGIC! *NOW SCRAM!*
HEY, MISTER, IF YOU'RE KINO'S MANAGER, CAN YOU GET HIS AUTOGRAPH FOR US?
NOBODY BY THAT NAME HERE, KIDS. *BEAT IT!*
SLAM
HMPH. WHAT A SCROOGE!
WE KNOW HE'S REALLY THERE!
WAIT A SEC...
I'LL CHECK. LET ME CHANGE MY EAR SET-TINGS...
...TO *1000* TIMES...
HE'S DEFI-NITELY IN THERE, GUYS. I CAN HEAR HIM!
AND HE'S ASKING FOR HELP!!

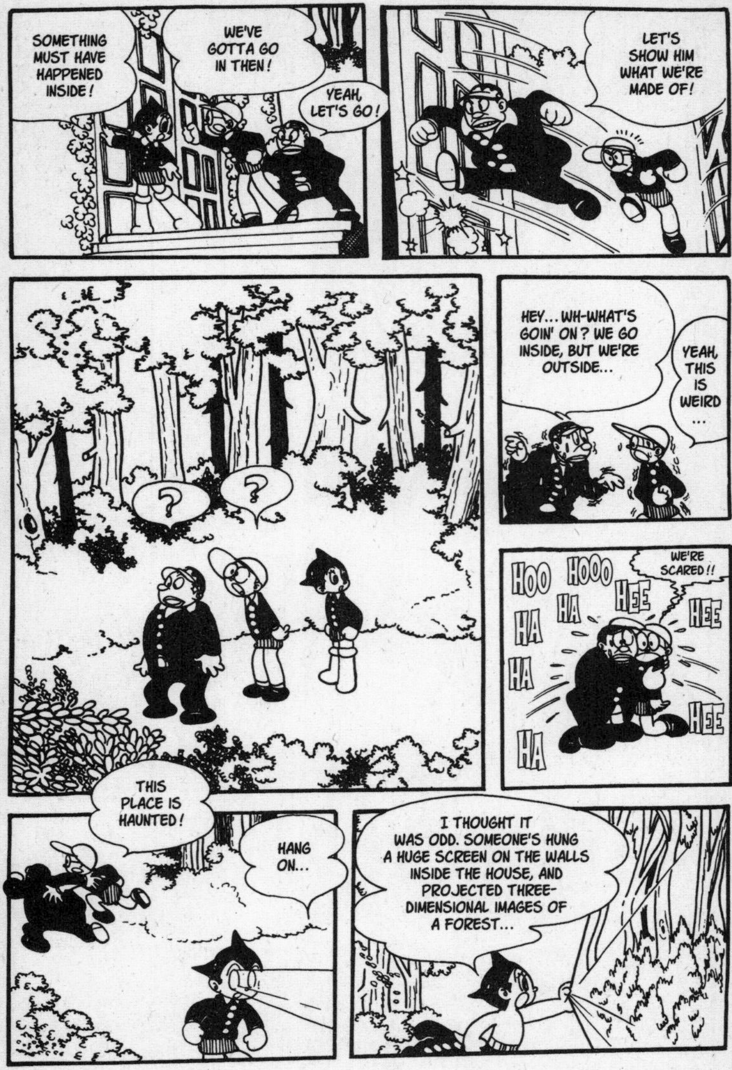
SOMETHING MUST HAVE HAPPENED INSIDE!
WE'VE GOTTA GO IN THEN!
YEAH, LET'S GO!
LET'S SHOW HIM WHAT WE'RE MADE OF!
?
?
HEY... WH-WHAT'S GOIN' ON? WE GO INSIDE, BUT WE'RE OUTSIDE...
YEAH, THIS IS WEIRD ...
HOO HOOO HA HEE HA HA HEE HA HEE
WE'RE SCARED!!
THIS PLACE IS HAUNTED!
HANG ON...
I THOUGHT IT WAS ODD. SOMEONE'S HUNG A HUGE SCREEN ON THE WALLS INSIDE THE HOUSE, AND PROJECTED THREE-DIMENSIONAL IMAGES OF A FOREST...

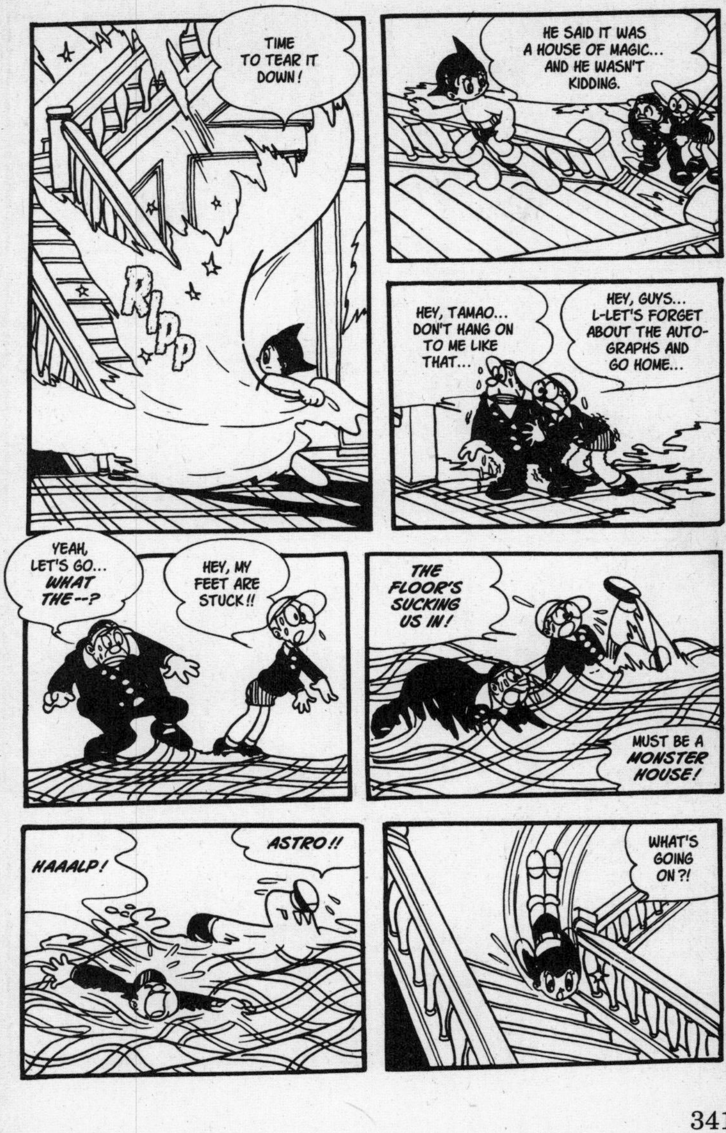
TIME TO TEAR IT DOWN!
RIPP
HE SAID IT WAS A HOUSE OF MAGIC... AND HE WASN'T KIDDING.
HEY, TAMAO... DON'T HANG ON TO ME LIKE THAT...
HEY, GUYS... L-LET'S FORGET ABOUT THE AUTO-GRAPHS AND GO HOME...
YEAH, LET'S GO... WHAT THE--?
HEY, MY FEET ARE STUCK!!
THE FLOOR'S SUCKING US IN!
MUST BE A MONSTER HOUSE!
HAAALP!
ASTRO!!
WHAT'S GOING ON?!

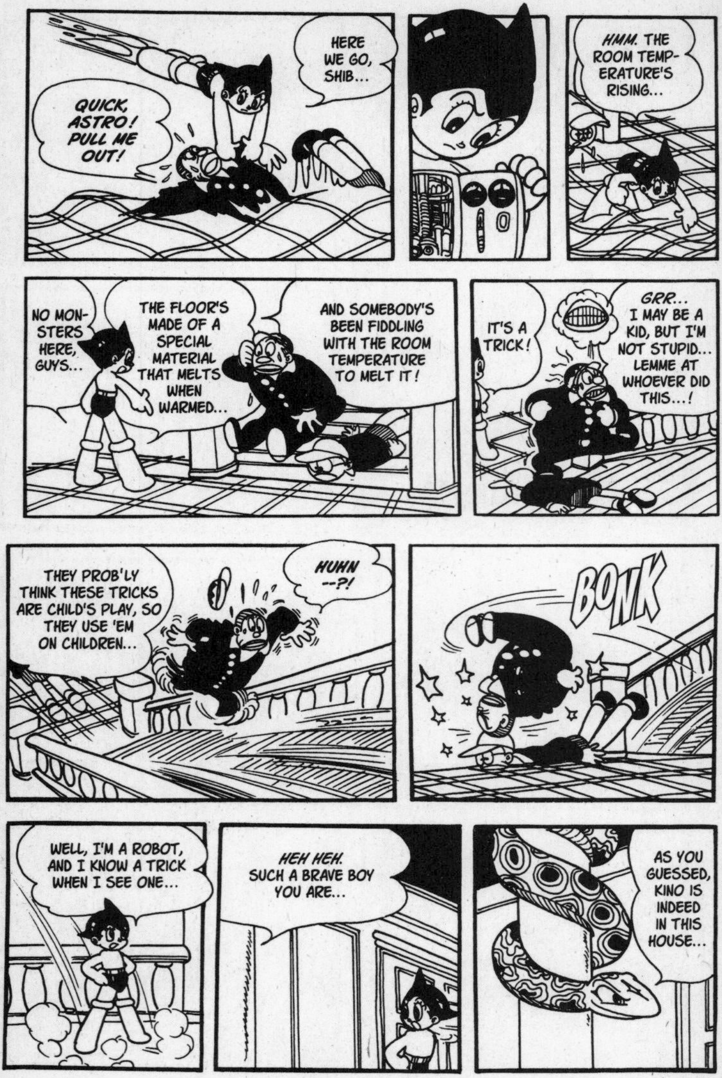
QUICK, ASTRO! PULL ME OUT!
HERE WE GO, SHIB...
HMM. THE ROOM TEMPERATURE'S RISING...
NO MONSTERS HERE, GUYS...
THE FLOOR'S MADE OF A SPECIAL MATERIAL THAT MELTS WHEN WARMED...
AND SOMEBODY'S BEEN FIDDLING WITH THE ROOM TEMPERATURE TO MELT IT!
IT'S A TRICK!
GRR... I MAY BE A KID, BUT I'M NOT STUPID... LEMME AT WHOEVER DID THIS...!
THEY PROB'LY THINK THESE TRICKS ARE CHILD'S PLAY, SO THEY USE 'EM ON CHILDREN...
HUHN --?!
BONK
WELL, I'M A ROBOT, AND I KNOW A TRICK WHEN I SEE ONE...
HEH HEH. SUCH A BRAVE BOY YOU ARE...
AS YOU GUESSED, KINO IS INDEED IN THIS HOUSE...

AND ME? I'M NOH UNO, AND I LIVE HERE.

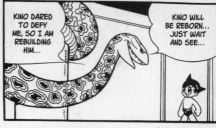

KINO DARED TO DEFY ME, SO I AM REBUILDING HIM...

KINO WILL BE REBORN... JUST WAIT AND SEE...

I SHALL TRANSFORM HIM FROM A MAGICIAN INTO A WORLD-CLASS THIEF. *HA HA HA HA!*

HA HA HA HA--

RATS! WHERE'S HE BROAD-CASTING FROM!?

MR. KINO!!

WHAT THE --?!

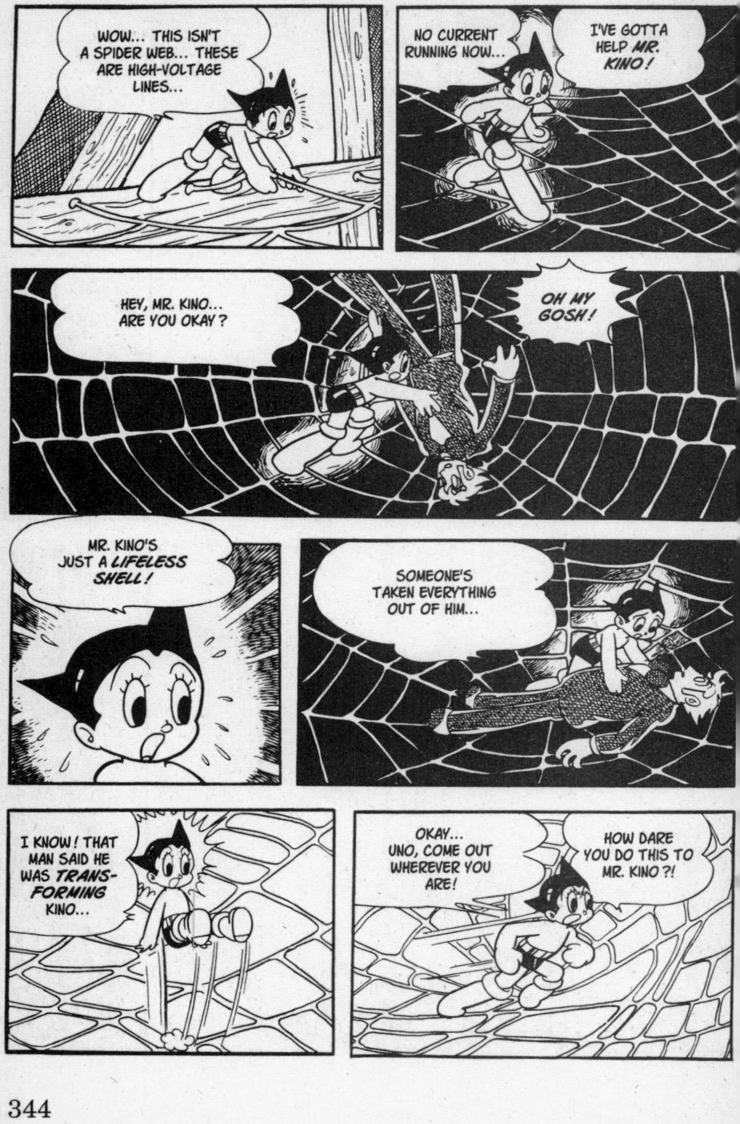
WOW... THIS ISN'T A SPIDER WEB... THESE ARE HIGH-VOLTAGE LINES...
NO CURRENT RUNNING NOW...
I'VE GOTTA HELP MR. KINO!
HEY, MR. KINO... ARE YOU OKAY?
OH MY GOSH!
MR. KINO'S JUST A LIFELESS SHELL!
SOMEONE'S TAKEN EVERYTHING OUT OF HIM...
I KNOW! THAT MAN SAID HE WAS TRANS-FORMING KINO...
OKAY... UNO, COME OUT WHEREVER YOU ARE!
HOW DARE YOU DO THIS TO MR. KINO?!

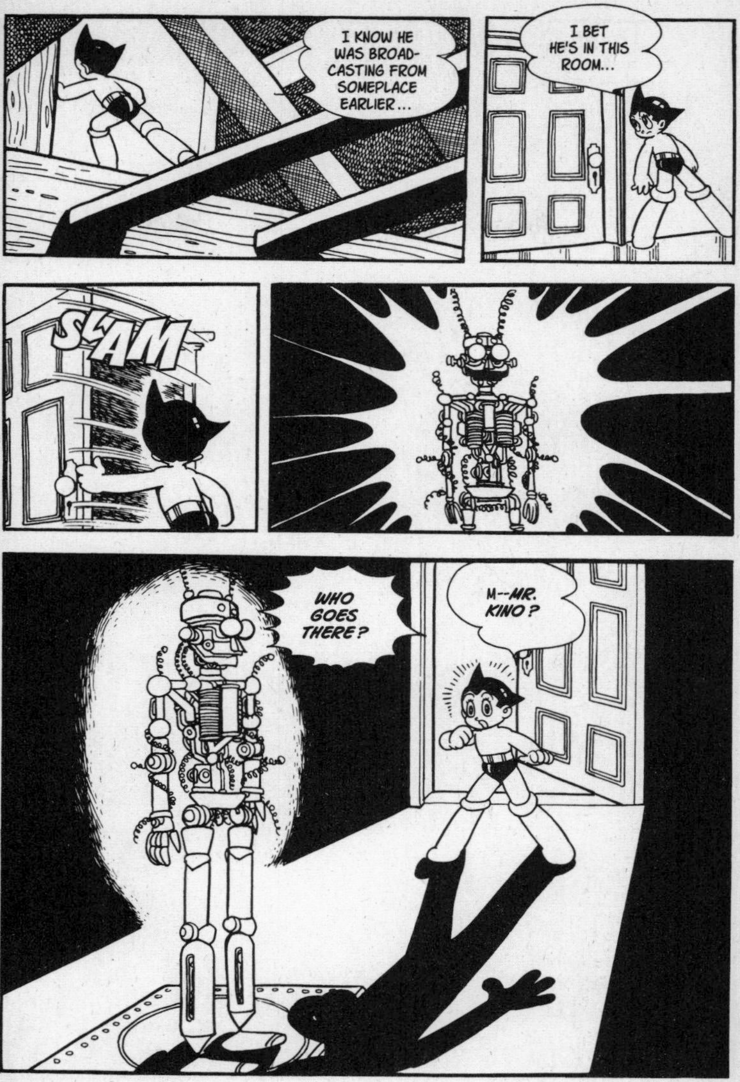
I KNOW HE WAS BROAD-CASTING FROM SOMEPLACE EARLIER...
I BET HE'S IN THIS ROOM...
SLAM
WHO GOES THERE?
M--MR. KINO?

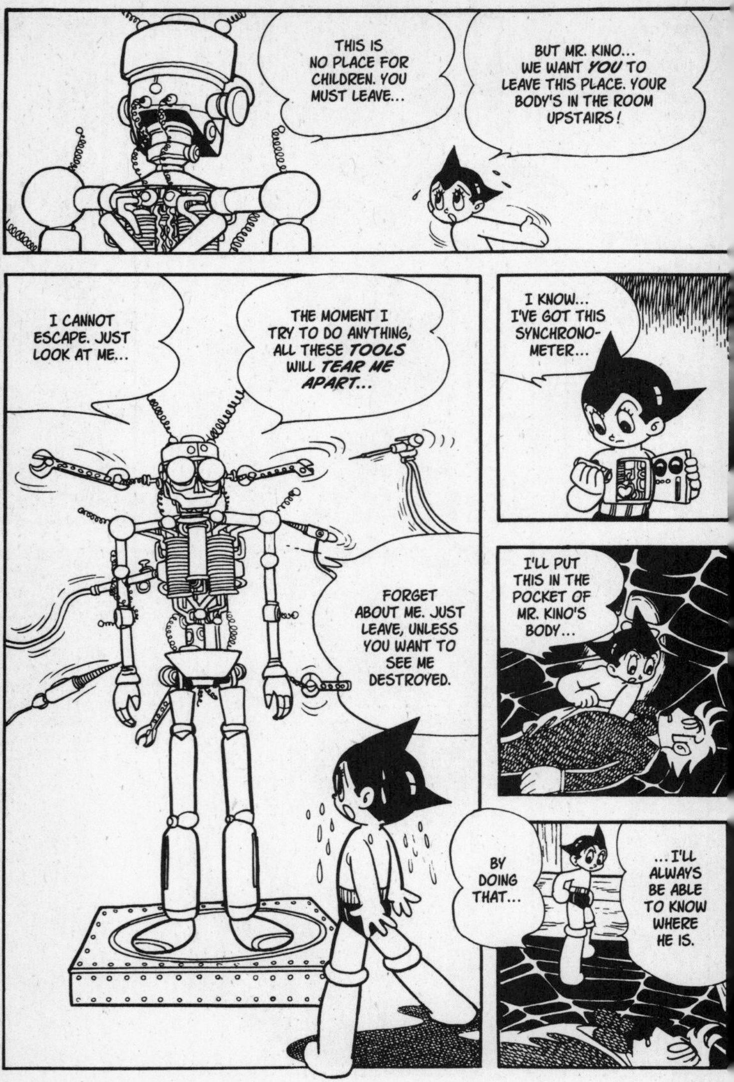
THIS IS NO PLACE FOR CHILDREN. YOU MUST LEAVE...
BUT MR. KINO... WE WANT *YOU* TO LEAVE THIS PLACE. YOUR BODY'S IN THE ROOM UPSTAIRS!
I CANNOT ESCAPE. JUST LOOK AT ME...
THE MOMENT I TRY TO DO ANYTHING, ALL THESE *TOOLS* WILL *TEAR ME APART*...
FORGET ABOUT ME. JUST LEAVE, UNLESS YOU WANT TO SEE ME DESTROYED.
I KNOW... I'VE GOT THIS SYNCHRONO-METER...
I'LL PUT THIS IN THE POCKET OF MR. KINO'S BODY...
BY DOING THAT...
...I'LL ALWAYS BE ABLE TO KNOW WHERE HE IS.

TWO OR THREE DAYS LATER PEOPLE THROUGHOUT TOKYO WERE SHOCKED TO READ IN THE NEWSPAPER THE WORDS, "CITIZENS! I AM KINO, THE WORLD'S TOP MAGICIAN, AND I HAVE COME TO JAPAN. I AM GOING TO DEMONSTRATE A MAGIC TRICK THAT WILL SHOCK YOU!"

"ON THE TWENTIETH OF OCTOBER, AT EXACTLY MIDNIGHT, YOU WILL SEE ME STEAL ONE HUNDRED CLASSIC WORKS OF ART FROM THE NATIONAL ART MUSEUM."

347

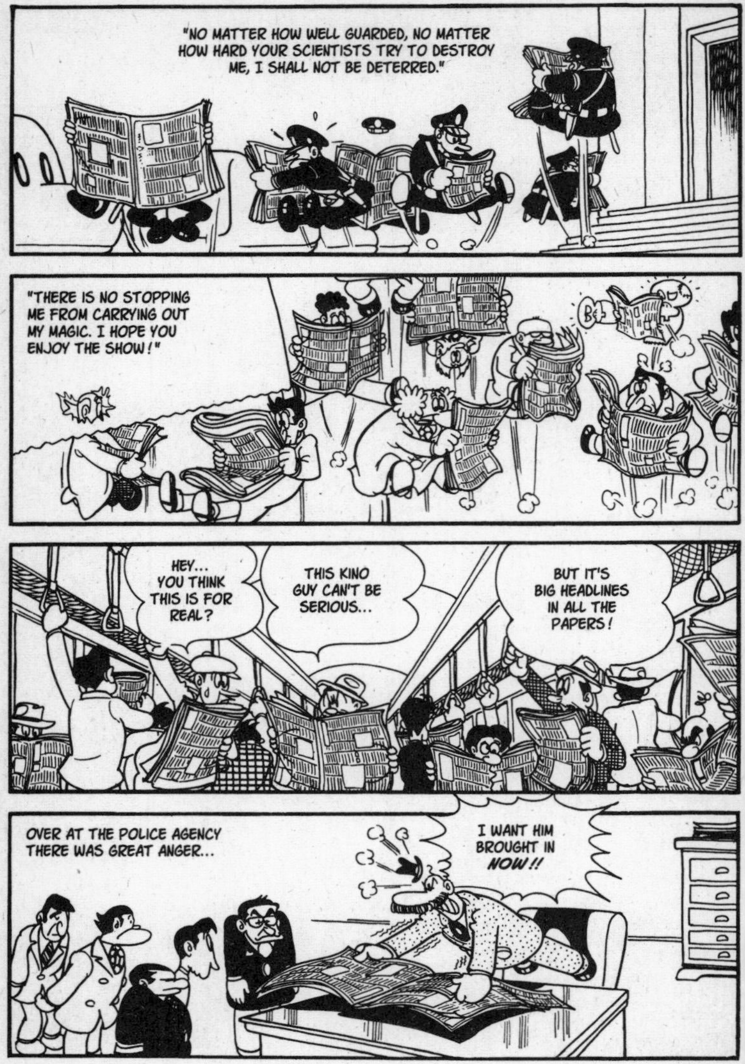
"NO MATTER HOW WELL GUARDED, NO MATTER HOW HARD YOUR SCIENTISTS TRY TO DESTROY ME, I SHALL NOT BE DETERRED."
"THERE IS NO STOPPING ME FROM CARRYING OUT MY MAGIC. I HOPE YOU ENJOY THE SHOW!"
HEY... YOU THINK THIS IS FOR REAL?
THIS KINO GUY CAN'T BE SERIOUS...
BUT IT'S BIG HEADLINES IN ALL THE PAPERS!
OVER AT THE POLICE AGENCY THERE WAS GREAT ANGER...
I WANT HIM BROUGHT IN *NOW!!*

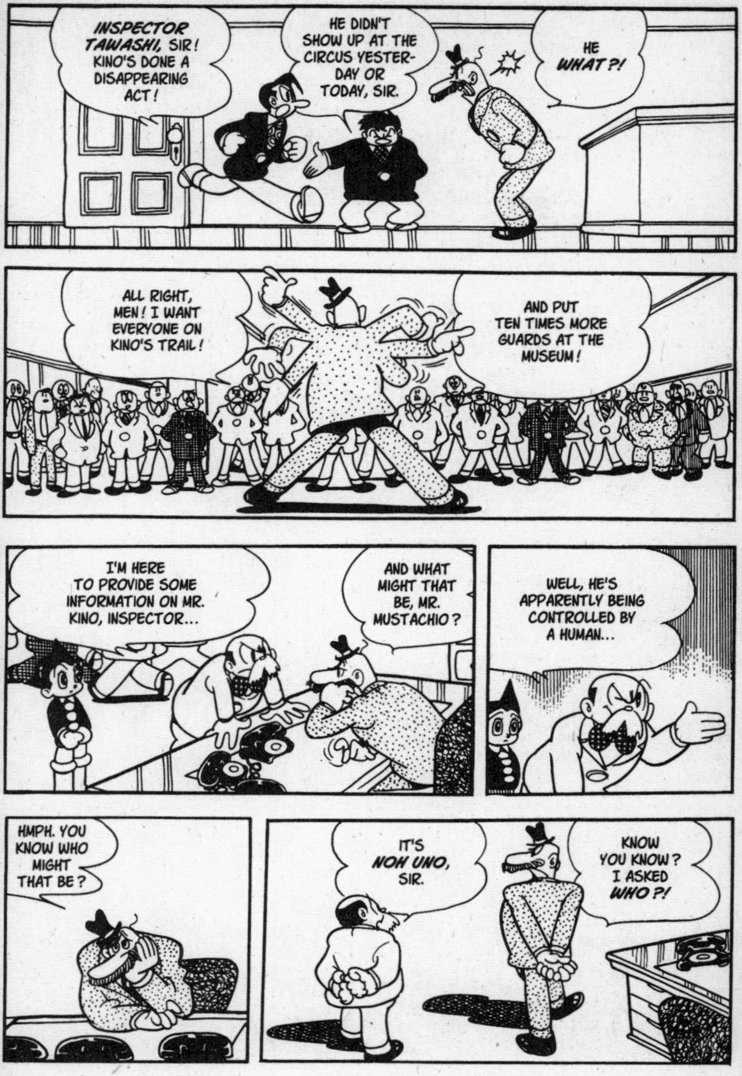
INSPECTOR TAWASHI, SIR! KINO'S DONE A DISAPPEARING ACT!
HE DIDN'T SHOW UP AT THE CIRCUS YESTER-DAY OR TODAY, SIR.
HE WHAT?!
ALL RIGHT, MEN! I WANT EVERYONE ON KINO'S TRAIL!
AND PUT TEN TIMES MORE GUARDS AT THE MUSEUM!
I'M HERE TO PROVIDE SOME INFORMATION ON MR. KINO, INSPECTOR...
AND WHAT MIGHT THAT BE, MR. MUSTACHIO?
WELL, HE'S APPARENTLY BEING CONTROLLED BY A HUMAN...
HMPH. YOU KNOW WHO MIGHT THAT BE?
IT'S NOH UNO, SIR.
KNOW YOU KNOW? I ASKED WHO?!

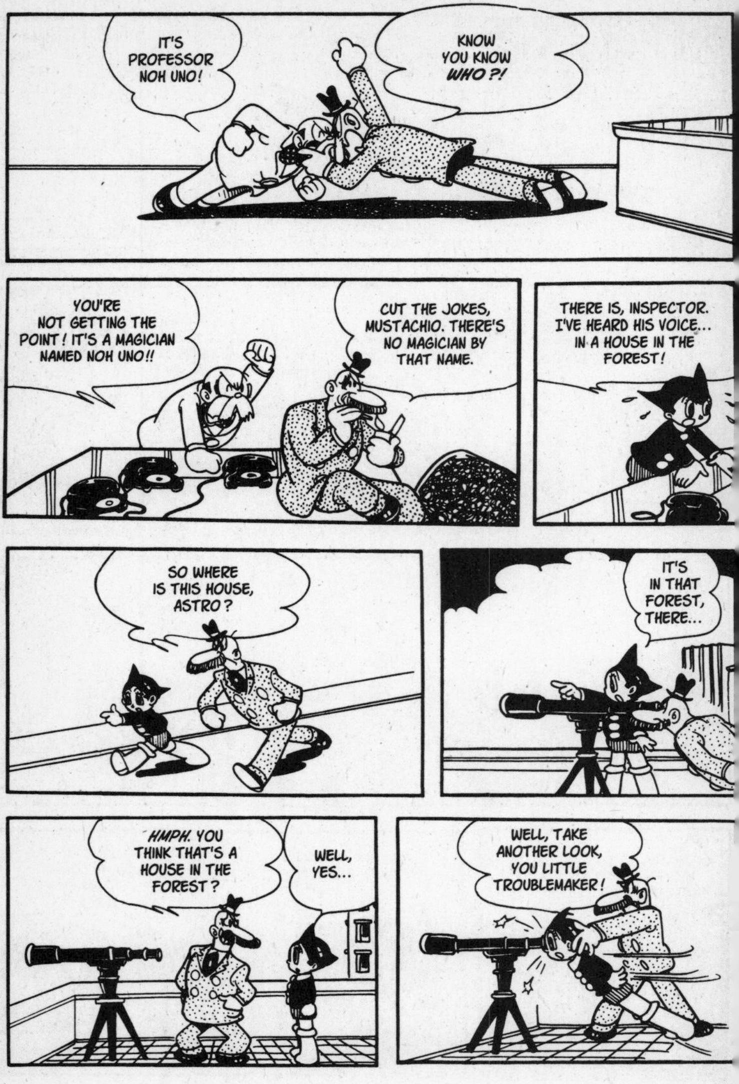
IT'S PROFESSOR NOH UNO!
KNOW YOU KNOW *WHO?!*
YOU'RE NOT GETTING THE POINT! IT'S A MAGICIAN NAMED NOH UNO!!
CUT THE JOKES, MUSTACHIO. THERE'S NO MAGICIAN BY THAT NAME.
THERE IS, INSPECTOR. I'VE HEARD HIS VOICE... IN A HOUSE IN THE FOREST!
SO WHERE IS THIS HOUSE, ASTRO?
IT'S IN THAT FOREST, THERE...
HMPH. YOU THINK THAT'S A HOUSE IN THE FOREST?
WELL, YES...
WELL, TAKE ANOTHER LOOK, YOU LITTLE TROUBLEMAKER!

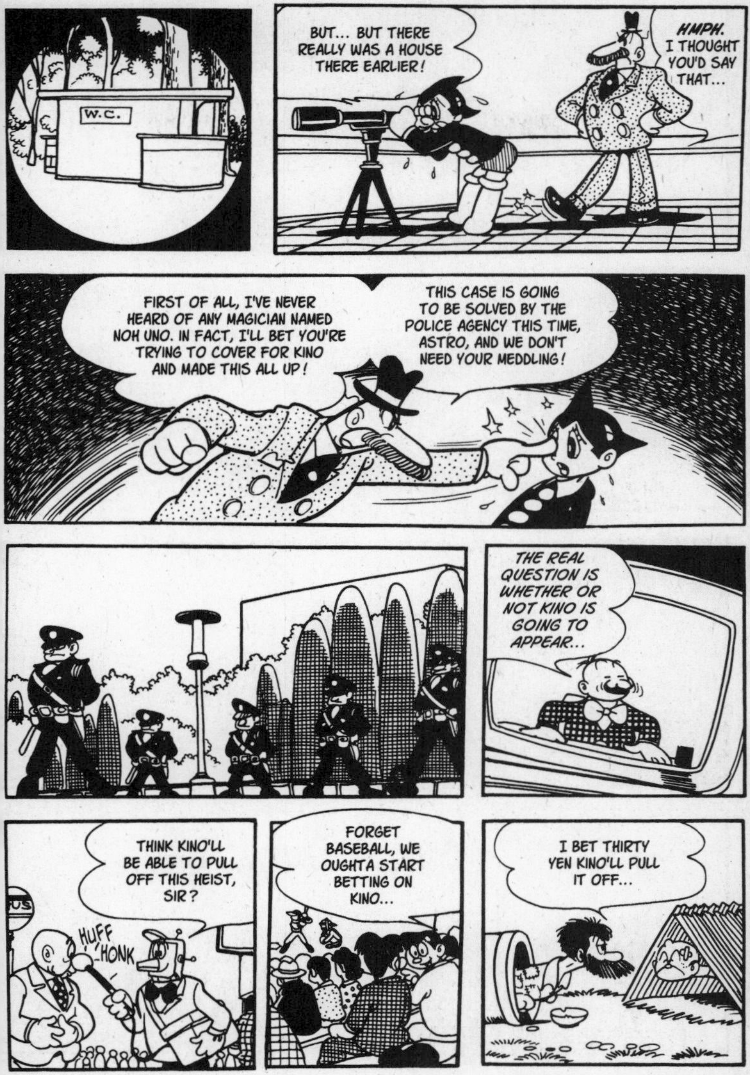
W.C.
BUT... BUT THERE REALLY WAS A HOUSE THERE EARLIER!
HMPH. I THOUGHT YOU'D SAY THAT...
FIRST OF ALL, I'VE NEVER HEARD OF ANY MAGICIAN NAMED NOH UNO. IN FACT, I'LL BET YOU'RE TRYING TO COVER FOR KINO AND MADE THIS ALL UP!
THIS CASE IS GOING TO BE SOLVED BY THE POLICE AGENCY THIS TIME, ASTRO, AND WE DON'T NEED YOUR MEDDLING!
THE REAL QUESTION IS WHETHER OR NOT KINO IS GOING TO APPEAR...
THINK KINO'LL BE ABLE TO PULL OFF THIS HEIST, SIR?
HUFF
HONK
FORGET BASEBALL, WE OUGHTA START BETTING ON KINO...
I BET THIRTY YEN KINO'LL PULL IT OFF...

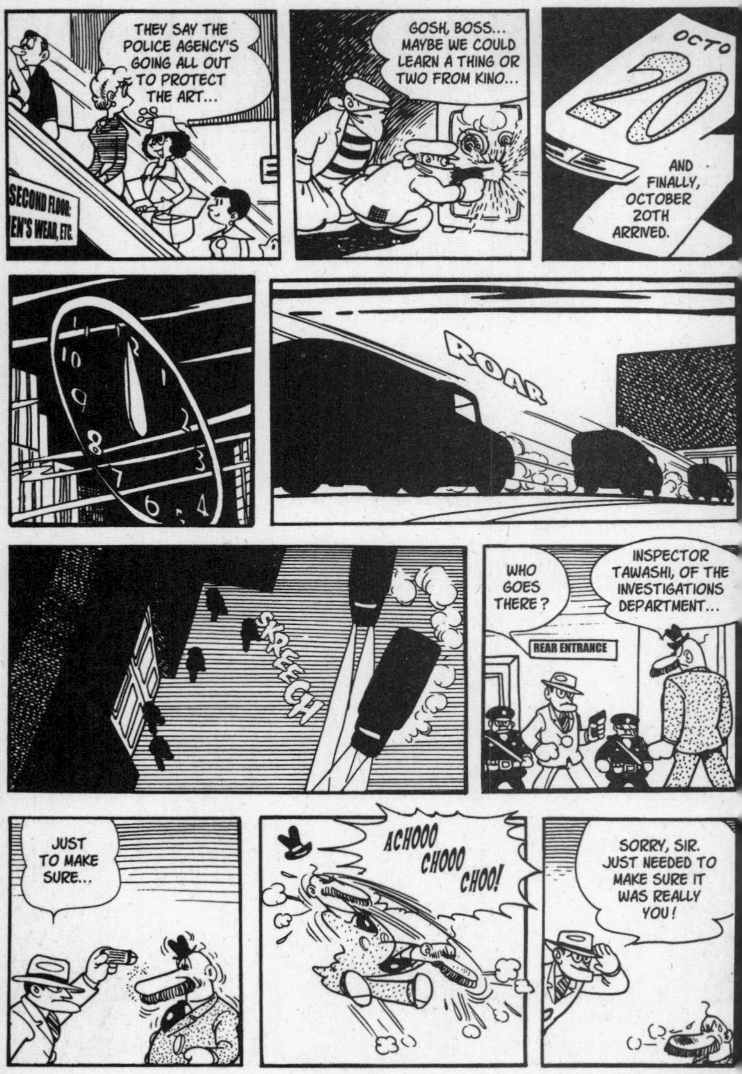
THEY SAY THE POLICE AGENCY'S GOING ALL OUT TO PROTECT THE ART...
SECOND FLOOR: EN'S WEAR, ETC.
GOSH, BOSS... MAYBE WE COULD LEARN A THING OR TWO FROM KINO...
OCTO
20
AND FINALLY, OCTOBER 20TH ARRIVED.
ROAR
SKREECH
WHO GOES THERE?
INSPECTOR TAWASHI, OF THE INVESTIGATIONS DEPARTMENT...
REAR ENTRANCE
JUST TO MAKE SURE...
ACHOOO CHOOO CHOO!
SORRY, SIR. JUST NEEDED TO MAKE SURE IT WAS REALLY YOU!

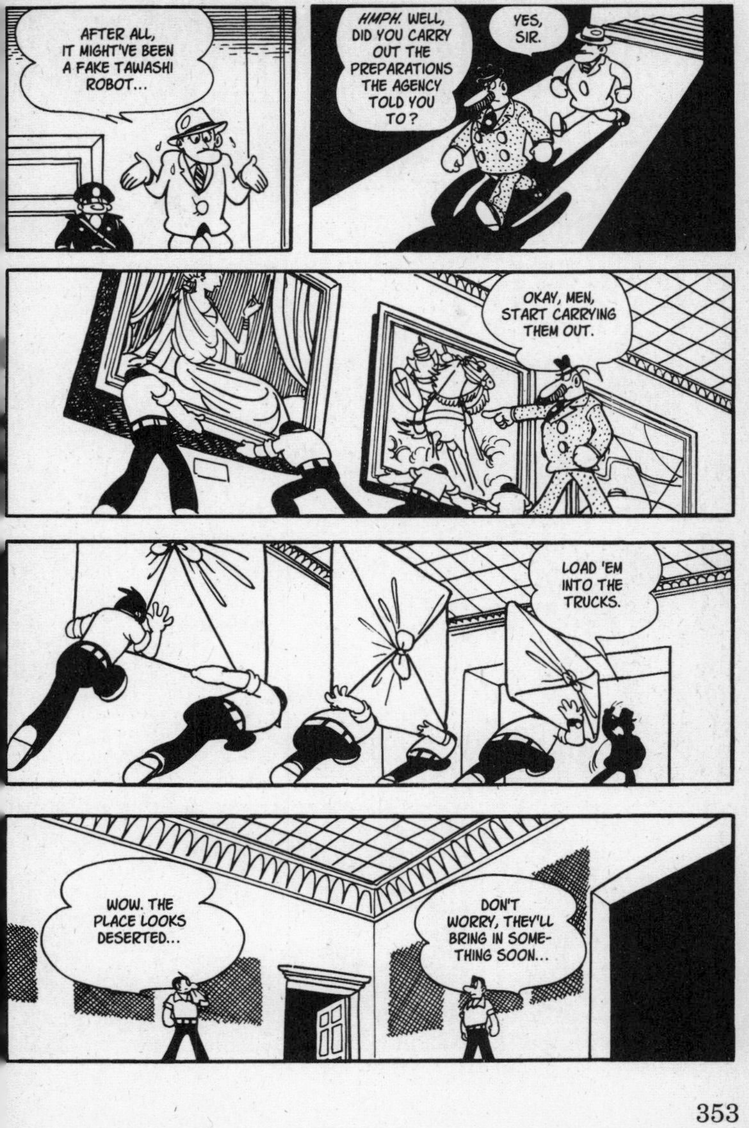
AFTER ALL, IT MIGHT'VE BEEN A FAKE TAWASHI ROBOT...
HMPH. WELL, DID YOU CARRY OUT THE PREPARATIONS THE AGENCY TOLD YOU TO?
YES, SIR.
OKAY, MEN, START CARRYING THEM OUT.
LOAD 'EM INTO THE TRUCKS.
WOW. THE PLACE LOOKS DESERTED...
DON'T WORRY, THEY'LL BRING IN SOME-THING SOON...

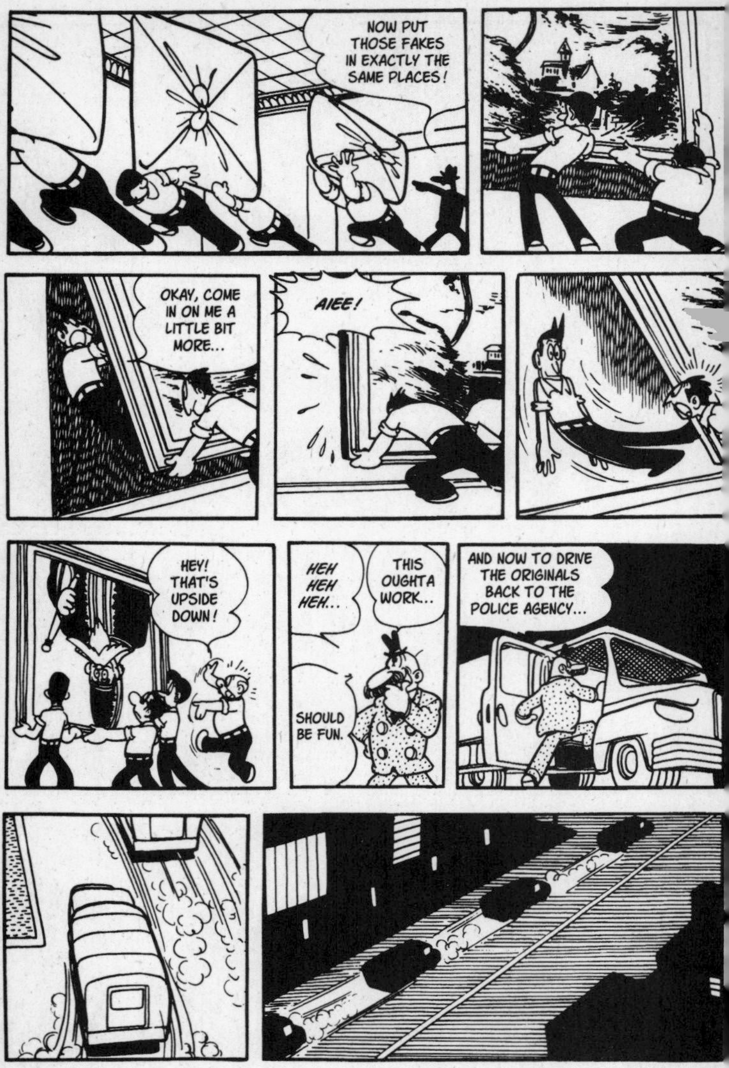
NOW PUT THOSE FAKES IN EXACTLY THE SAME PLACES!
OKAY, COME IN ON ME A LITTLE BIT MORE...
AIEE!
HEY! THAT'S UPSIDE DOWN!
HEH HEH HEH...
THIS OUGHTA WORK...
SHOULD BE FUN.
AND NOW TO DRIVE THE ORIGINALS BACK TO THE POLICE AGENCY...

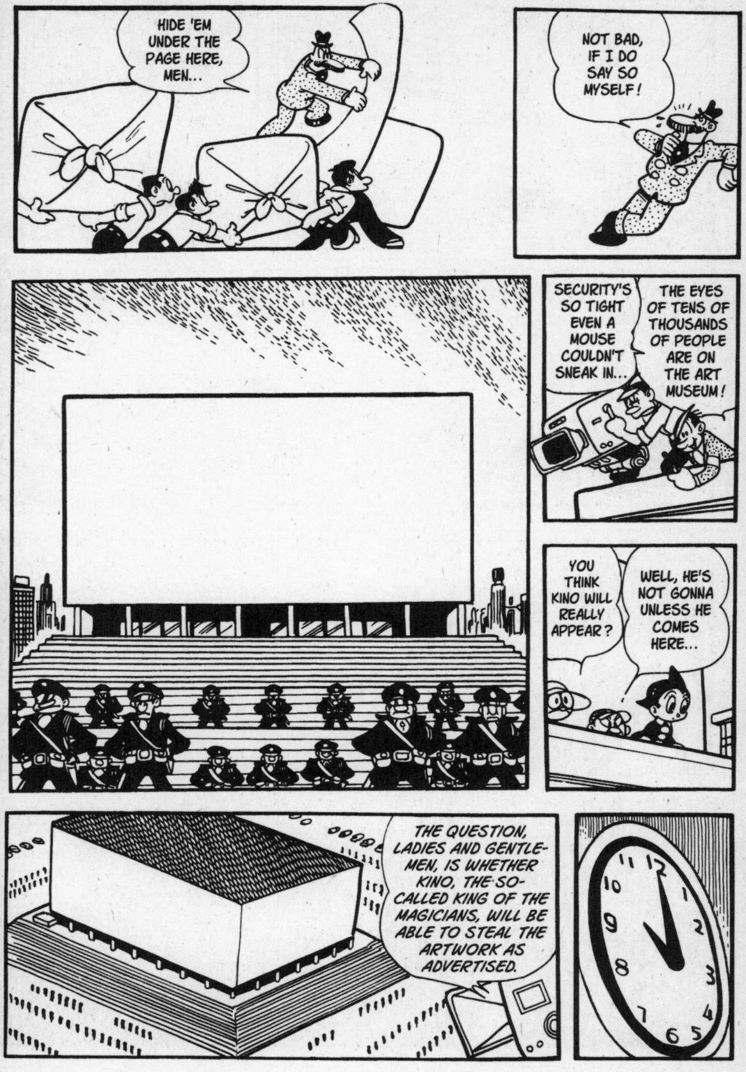
HIDE 'EM UNDER THE PAGE HERE, MEN...
NOT BAD, IF I DO SAY SO MYSELF!
SECURITY'S SO TIGHT EVEN A MOUSE COULDN'T SNEAK IN...
THE EYES OF TENS OF THOUSANDS OF PEOPLE ARE ON THE ART MUSEUM!
YOU THINK KINO WILL REALLY APPEAR?
WELL, HE'S NOT GONNA UNLESS HE COMES HERE...
THE QUESTION, LADIES AND GENTLEMEN, IS WHETHER KINO, THE SO-CALLED KING OF THE MAGICIANS, WILL BE ABLE TO STEAL THE ARTWORK AS ADVERTISED.

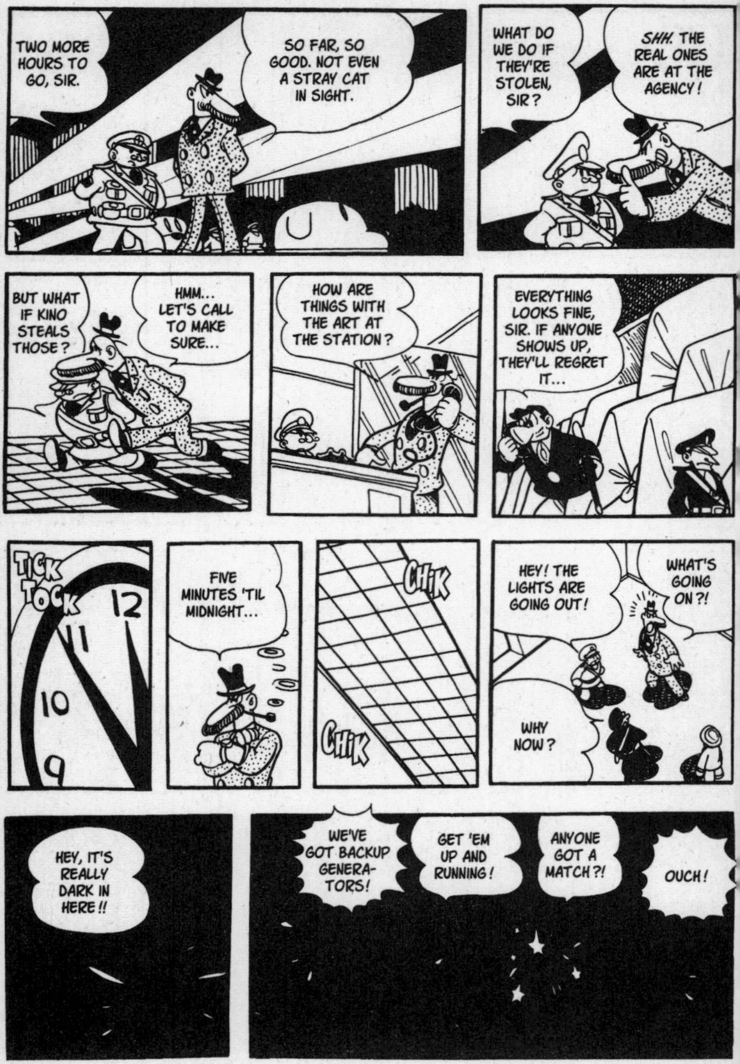
TWO MORE HOURS TO GO, SIR.
SO FAR, SO GOOD. NOT EVEN A STRAY CAT IN SIGHT.
WHAT DO WE DO IF THEY'RE STOLEN, SIR?
SHH. THE REAL ONES ARE AT THE AGENCY!
BUT WHAT IF KINO STEALS THOSE?
HMM... LET'S CALL TO MAKE SURE...
HOW ARE THINGS WITH THE ART AT THE STATION?
EVERYTHING LOOKS FINE, SIR. IF ANYONE SHOWS UP, THEY'LL REGRET IT...
TICK TOCK
12
11
10
9
FIVE MINUTES 'TIL MIDNIGHT...
CHIK
CHIK
HEY! THE LIGHTS ARE GOING OUT!
WHAT'S GOING ON?!
WHY NOW?
HEY, IT'S REALLY DARK IN HERE!!
WE'VE GOT BACKUP GENERA-TORS!
GET 'EM UP AND RUNNING!
ANYONE GOT A MATCH?!
OUCH!

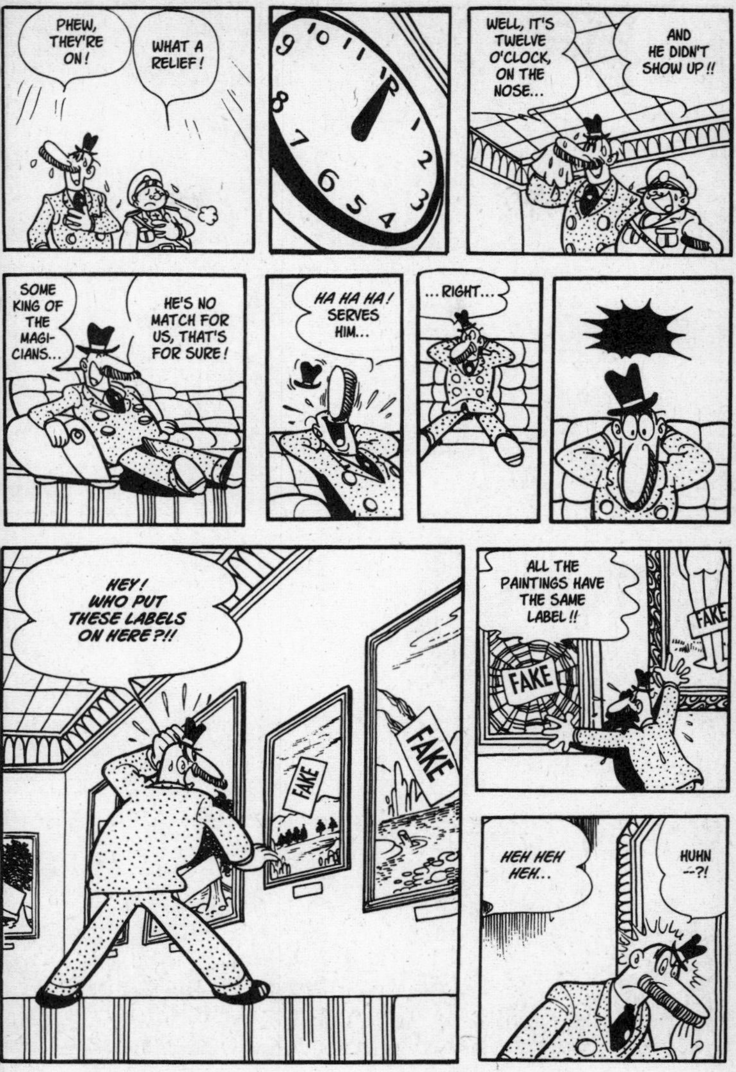
PHEW, THEY'RE ON!
WHAT A RELIEF!
WELL, IT'S TWELVE O'CLOCK, ON THE NOSE...
AND HE DIDN'T SHOW UP!!
SOME KING OF THE MAGI-CIANS...
HE'S NO MATCH FOR US, THAT'S FOR SURE!
HA HA HA! SERVES HIM...
...RIGHT...
HEY! WHO PUT THESE LABELS ON HERE?!!
FAKE
FAKE
ALL THE PAINTINGS HAVE THE SAME LABEL!!
FAKE
FAKE
HEH HEH HEH...
HUHN --?!

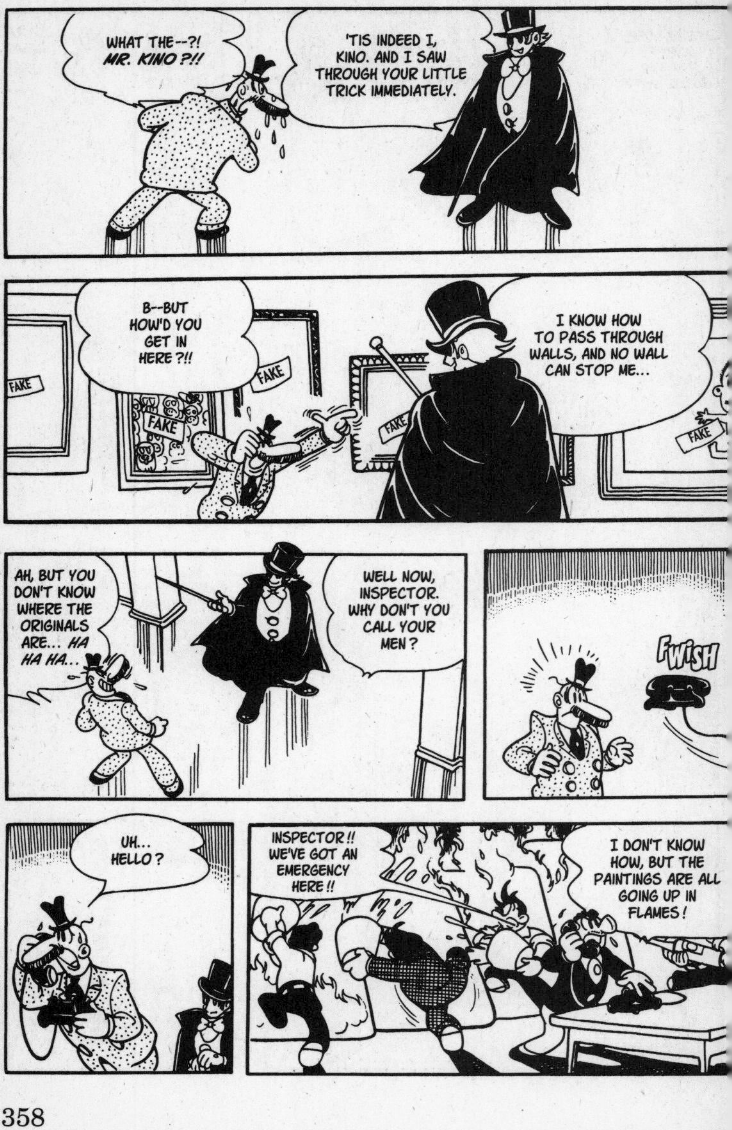

WHAT THE--?! MR. KINO?!!
'TIS INDEED I, KINO. AND I SAW THROUGH YOUR LITTLE TRICK IMMEDIATELY.
B--BUT HOW'D YOU GET IN HERE?!!
FAKE
FAKE
FAKE
FAKE
FAKE
I KNOW HOW TO PASS THROUGH WALLS, AND NO WALL CAN STOP ME...
AH, BUT YOU DON'T KNOW WHERE THE ORIGINALS ARE... HA HA HA...
WELL NOW, INSPECTOR. WHY DON'T YOU CALL YOUR MEN?
FWISH
UH... HELLO?
INSPECTOR!! WE'VE GOT AN EMERGENCY HERE!!
I DON'T KNOW HOW, BUT THE PAINTINGS ARE ALL GOING UP IN FLAMES!

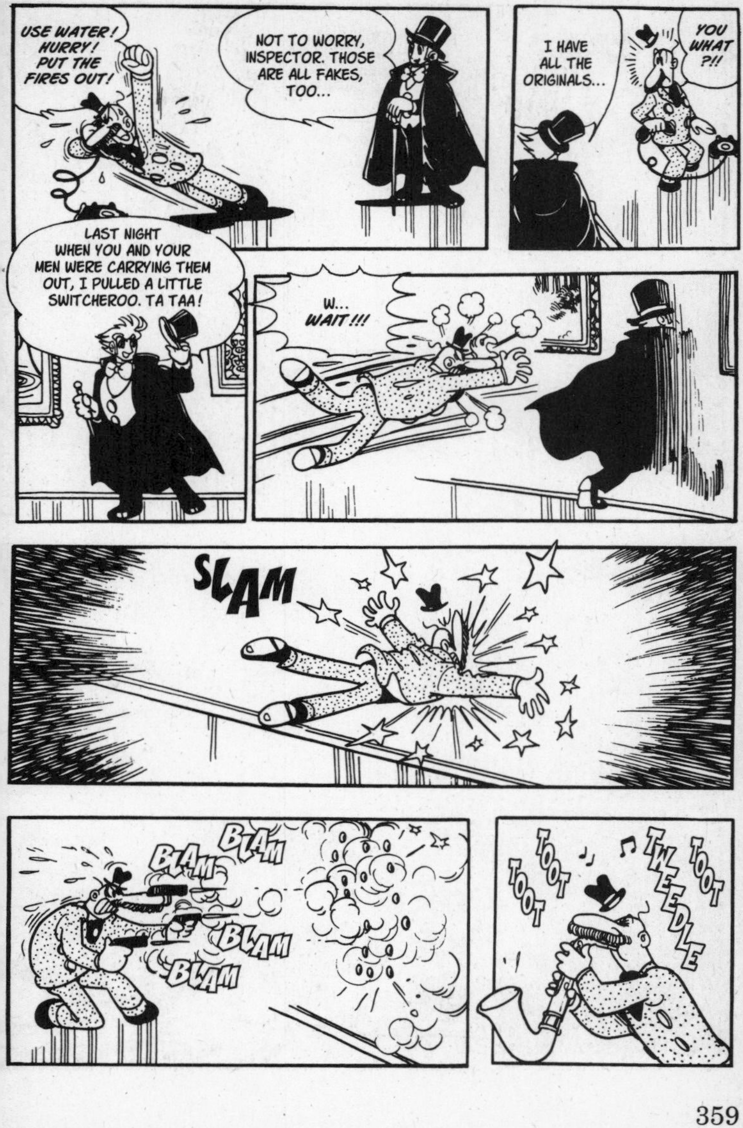
USE WATER! HURRY! PUT THE FIRES OUT!
NOT TO WORRY, INSPECTOR. THOSE ARE ALL FAKES, TOO...
I HAVE ALL THE ORIGINALS...
YOU WHAT ?!!
LAST NIGHT WHEN YOU AND YOUR MEN WERE CARRYING THEM OUT, I PULLED A LITTLE SWITCHEROO. TA TAA!
W... WAIT!!!
SLAM
BLAM
BLAM
BLAM
BLAM
TOOT
TOOT
TWEEDLE
TOOT

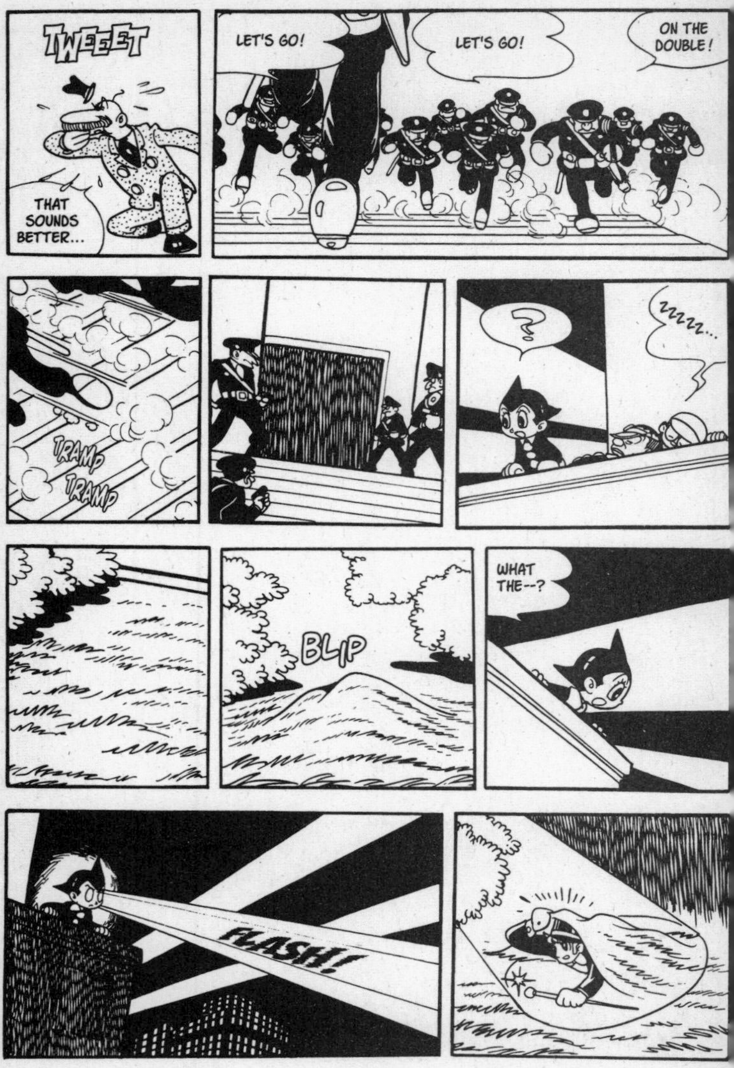
TWEEET
THAT SOUNDS BETTER...
LET'S GO!
LET'S GO!
ON THE DOUBLE!
TRAMP
TRAMP
?
ZZZZ...
BLIP
WHAT THE--?
FLASH!

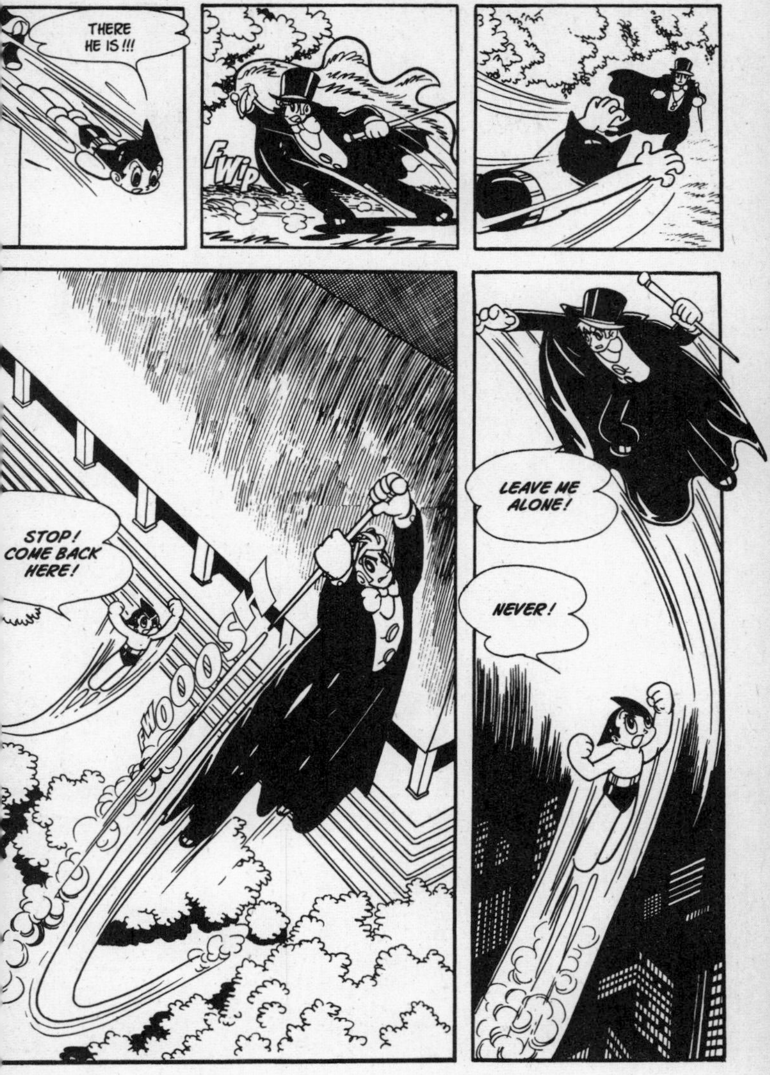
THERE HE IS!!!
FWIP
STOP! COME BACK HERE!
FWOOOSH
LEAVE ME ALONE!
NEVER!

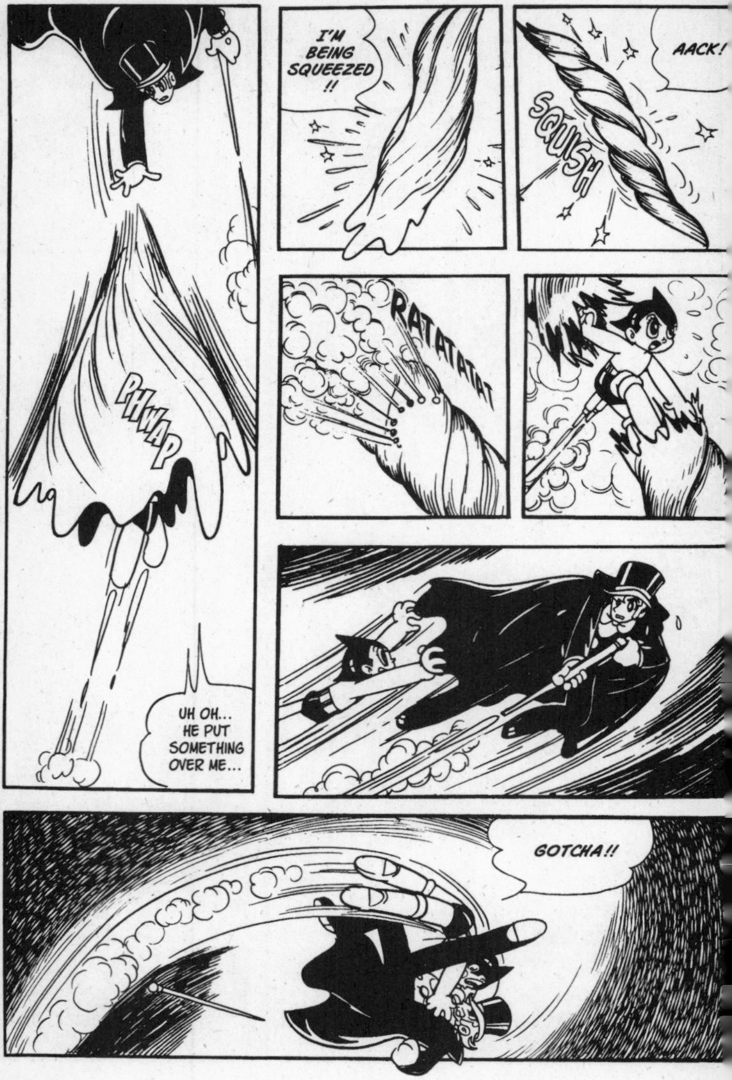
PHWAP
UH OH... HE PUT SOMETHING OVER ME...
I'M BEING SQUEEZED !!
AACK!
SQUISH
RATATATAT
GOTCHA!!

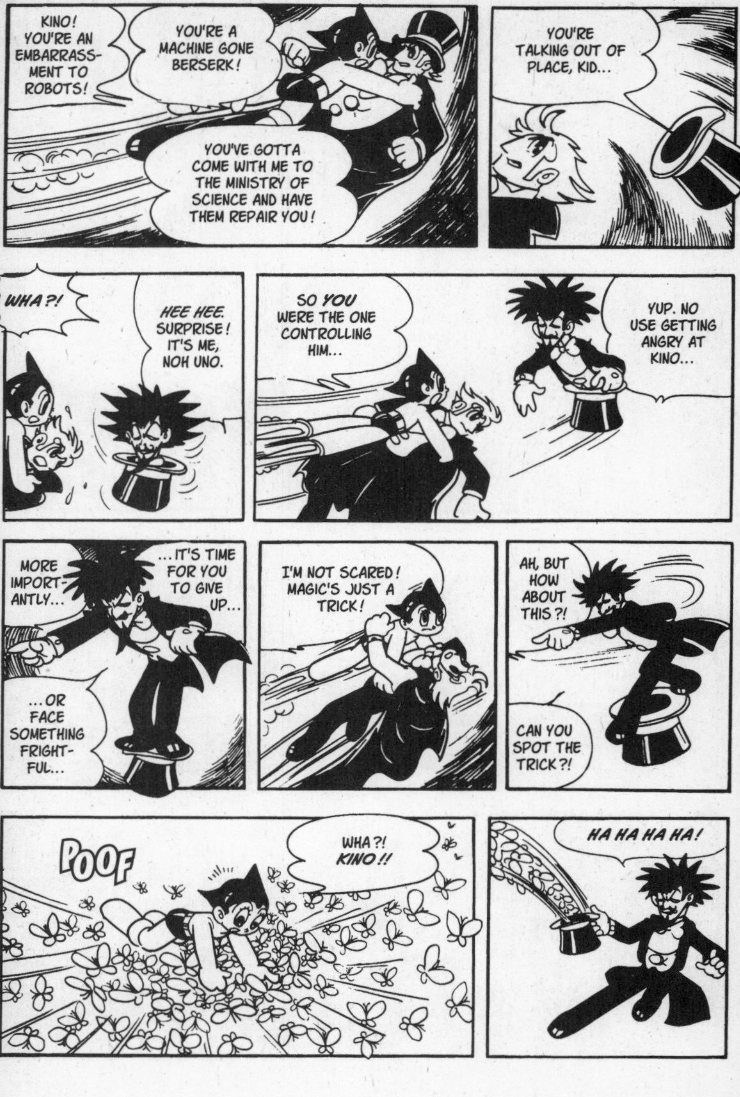
KINO! YOU'RE AN EMBARRASS-MENT TO ROBOTS!
YOU'RE A MACHINE GONE BERSERK!
YOU'VE GOTTA COME WITH ME TO THE MINISTRY OF SCIENCE AND HAVE THEM REPAIR YOU!
YOU'RE TALKING OUT OF PLACE, KID...
WHA?!
HEE HEE. SURPRISE! IT'S ME, NOH UNO.
SO YOU WERE THE ONE CONTROLLING HIM...
YUP. NO USE GETTING ANGRY AT KINO...
MORE IMPORT-ANTLY...
...IT'S TIME FOR YOU TO GIVE UP...
...OR FACE SOMETHING FRIGHT-FUL...
I'M NOT SCARED! MAGIC'S JUST A TRICK!
AH, BUT HOW ABOUT THIS?!
CAN YOU SPOT THE TRICK?!
POOF
WHA?! KINO!!
HA HA HA HA!

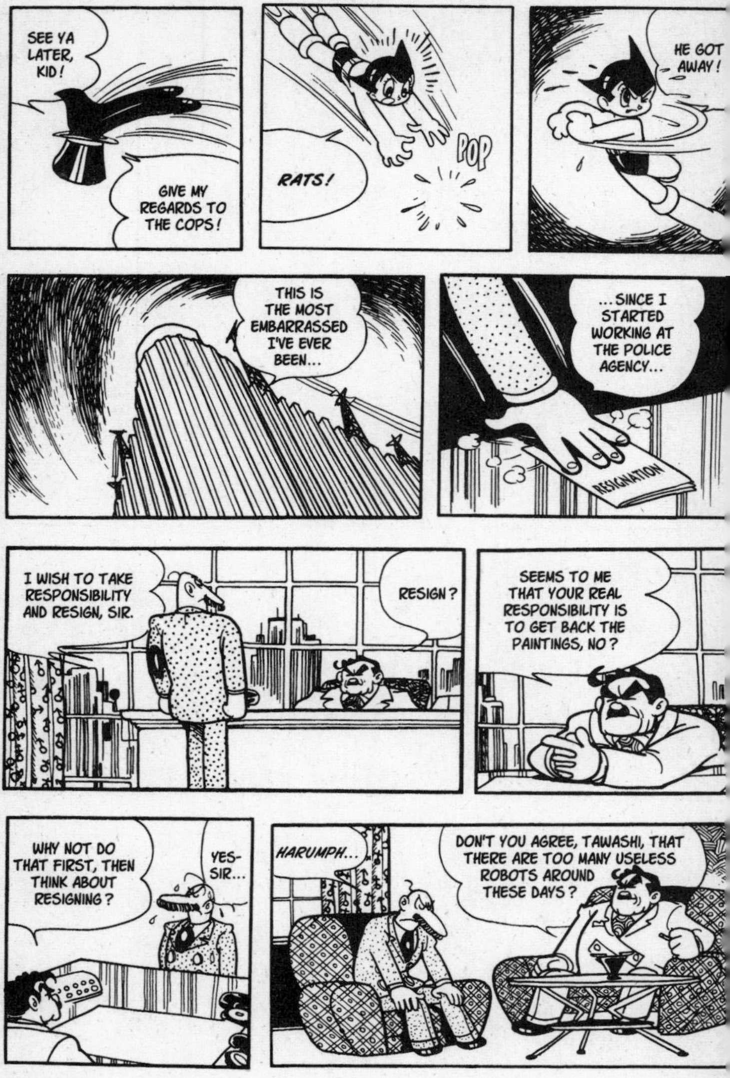
SEE YA LATER, KID!
GIVE MY REGARDS TO THE COPS!
RATS!
POP
HE GOT AWAY!
THIS IS THE MOST EMBARRASSED I'VE EVER BEEN...
...SINCE I STARTED WORKING AT THE POLICE AGENCY...
RESIGNATION
I WISH TO TAKE RESPONSIBILITY AND RESIGN, SIR.
RESIGN?
SEEMS TO ME THAT YOUR REAL RESPONSIBILITY IS TO GET BACK THE PAINTINGS, NO?
WHY NOT DO THAT FIRST, THEN THINK ABOUT RESIGNING?
YES-SIR...
HARUMPH...
DON'T YOU AGREE, TAWASHI, THAT THERE ARE TOO MANY USELESS ROBOTS AROUND THESE DAYS?

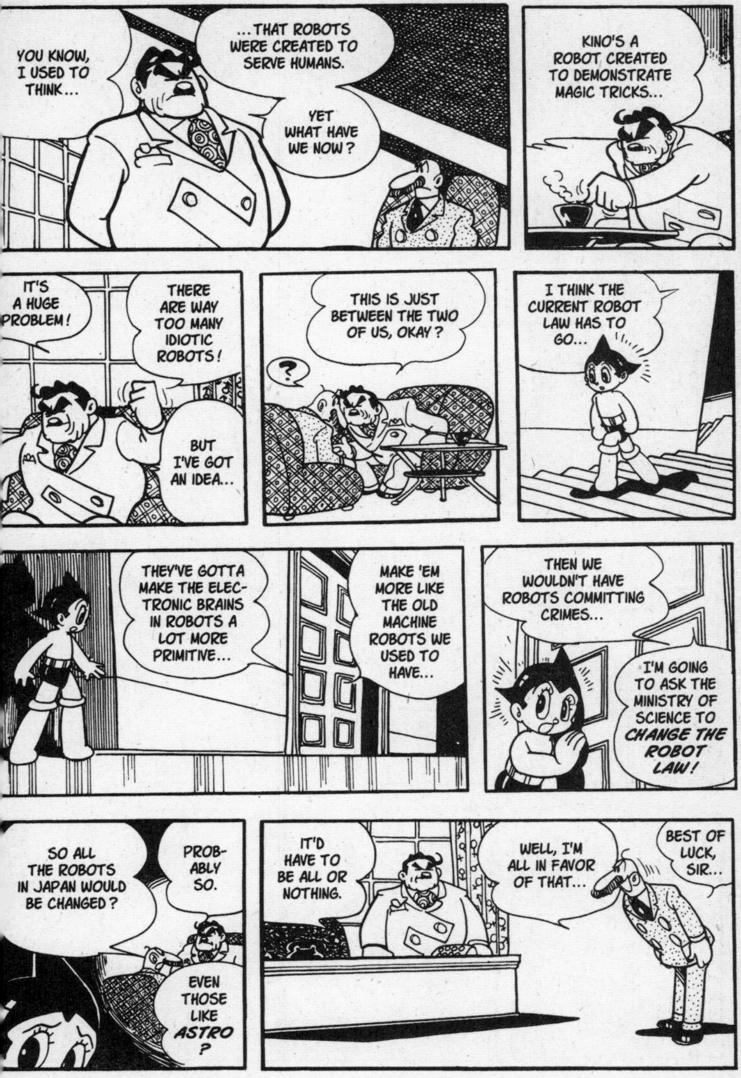
YOU KNOW, I USED TO THINK...
...THAT ROBOTS WERE CREATED TO SERVE HUMANS.
YET WHAT HAVE WE NOW?
KINO'S A ROBOT CREATED TO DEMONSTRATE MAGIC TRICKS...
IT'S A HUGE PROBLEM!
THERE ARE WAY TOO MANY IDIOTIC ROBOTS!
BUT I'VE GOT AN IDEA...
THIS IS JUST BETWEEN THE TWO OF US, OKAY?
?
I THINK THE CURRENT ROBOT LAW HAS TO GO...
THEY'VE GOTTA MAKE THE ELECTRONIC BRAINS IN ROBOTS A LOT MORE PRIMITIVE...
MAKE 'EM MORE LIKE THE OLD MACHINE ROBOTS WE USED TO HAVE...
THEN WE WOULDN'T HAVE ROBOTS COMMITTING CRIMES...
I'M GOING TO ASK THE MINISTRY OF SCIENCE TO *CHANGE THE ROBOT LAW!*
SO ALL THE ROBOTS IN JAPAN WOULD BE CHANGED?
PROBABLY SO.
EVEN THOSE LIKE *ASTRO*?
IT'D HAVE TO BE ALL OR NOTHING.
WELL, I'M ALL IN FAVOR OF THAT...
BEST OF LUCK, SIR...

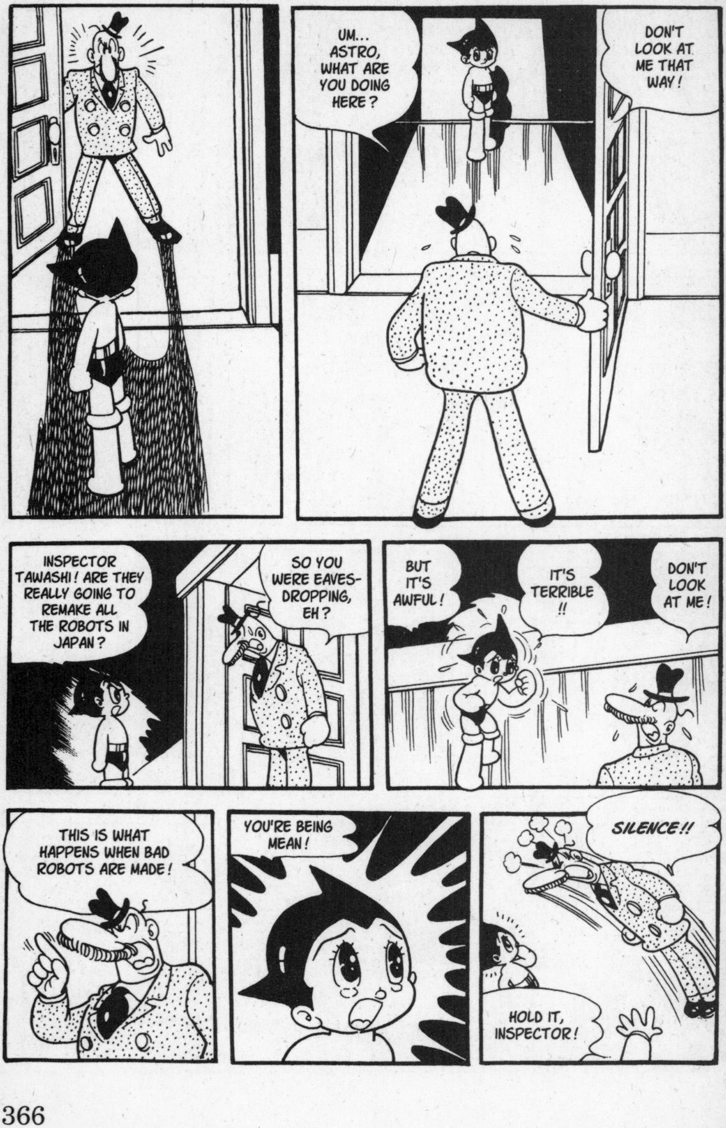
UM... ASTRO, WHAT ARE YOU DOING HERE?
DON'T LOOK AT ME THAT WAY!
INSPECTOR TAWASHI! ARE THEY REALLY GOING TO REMAKE ALL THE ROBOTS IN JAPAN?
SO YOU WERE EAVES-DROPPING, EH?
BUT IT'S AWFUL!
IT'S TERRIBLE!!
DON'T LOOK AT ME!
THIS IS WHAT HAPPENS WHEN BAD ROBOTS ARE MADE!
YOU'RE BEING MEAN!
SILENCE!!
HOLD IT, INSPECTOR!

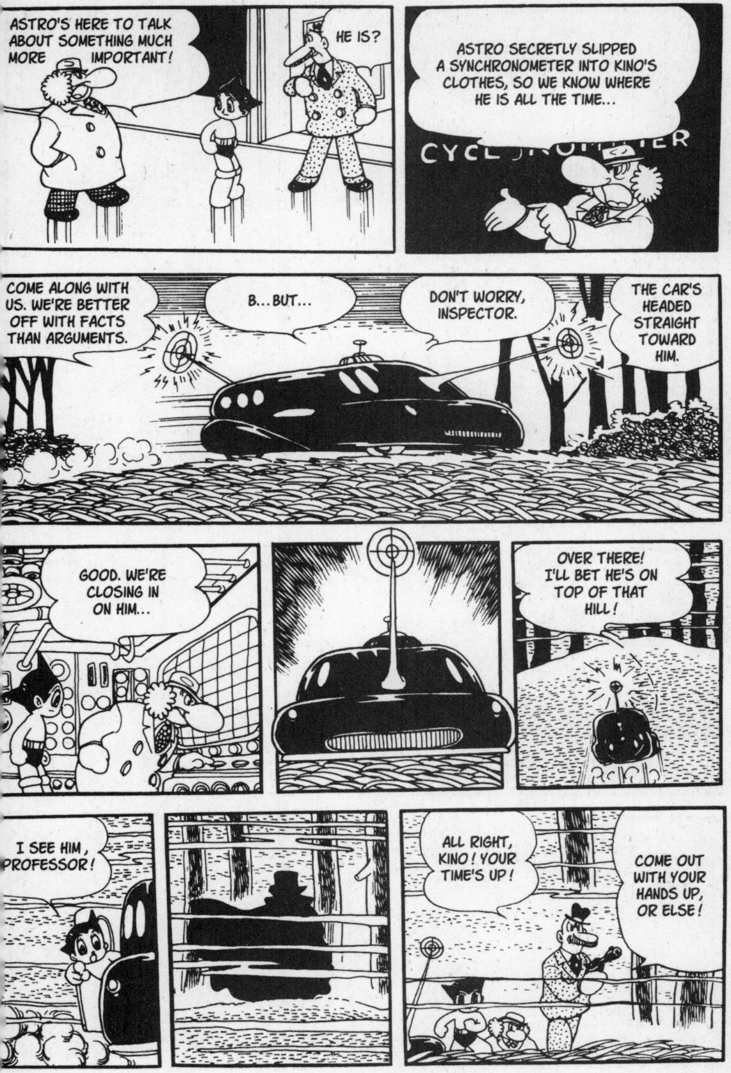

ASTRO'S HERE TO TALK ABOUT SOMETHING MUCH MORE IMPORTANT!
HE IS?
ASTRO SECRETLY SLIPPED A SYNCHRONOMETER INTO KINO'S CLOTHES, SO WE KNOW WHERE HE IS ALL THE TIME...
COME ALONG WITH US. WE'RE BETTER OFF WITH FACTS THAN ARGUMENTS.
B...BUT...
DON'T WORRY, INSPECTOR.
THE CAR'S HEADED STRAIGHT TOWARD HIM.
GOOD. WE'RE CLOSING IN ON HIM...
OVER THERE! I'LL BET HE'S ON TOP OF THAT HILL!
I SEE HIM, PROFESSOR!
ALL RIGHT, KINO! YOUR TIME'S UP!
COME OUT WITH YOUR HANDS UP, OR ELSE!

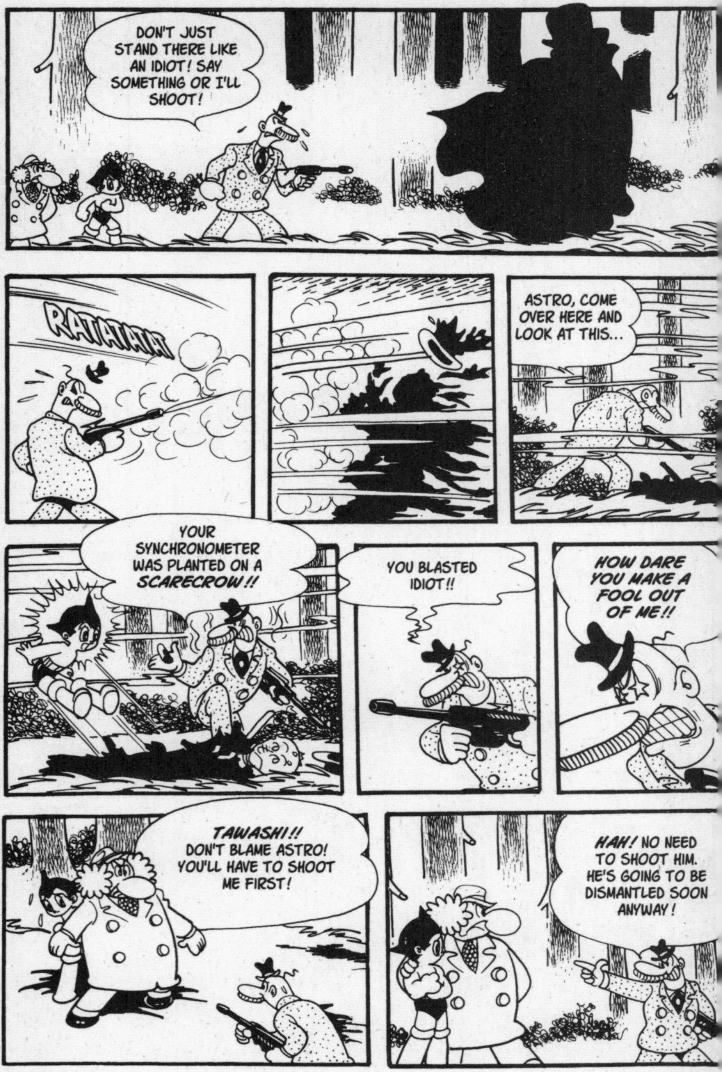
DON'T JUST STAND THERE LIKE AN IDIOT! SAY SOMETHING OR I'LL SHOOT!
RATATATAT
ASTRO, COME OVER HERE AND LOOK AT THIS...
YOUR SYNCHRONOMETER WAS PLANTED ON A SCARECROW!!
YOU BLASTED IDIOT!!
HOW DARE YOU MAKE A FOOL OUT OF ME!!
TAWASHI!! DON'T BLAME ASTRO! YOU'LL HAVE TO SHOOT ME FIRST!
HAH! NO NEED TO SHOOT HIM. HE'S GOING TO BE DISMANTLED SOON ANYWAY!

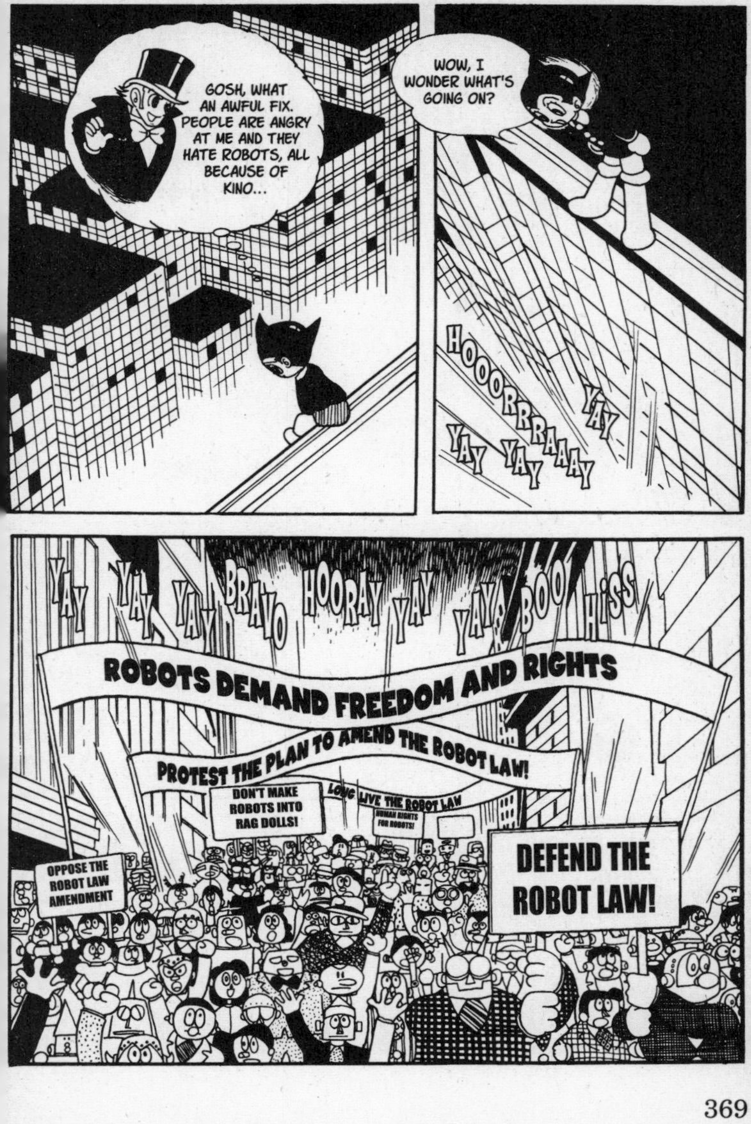
GOSH, WHAT AN AWFUL FIX. PEOPLE ARE ANGRY AT ME AND THEY HATE ROBOTS, ALL BECAUSE OF KINO...
WOW, I WONDER WHAT'S GOING ON?
HOOORRRAAAAY
YAY
YAY YAY
YAY YAY YAY BRAVO HOORAY YAY YAY BOO HISS
ROBOTS DEMAND FREEDOM AND RIGHTS
PROTEST THE PLAN TO AMEND THE ROBOT LAW!
DON'T MAKE ROBOTS INTO RAG DOLLS!
LONG LIVE THE ROBOT LAW
HUMAN RIGHTS FOR ROBOTS!
DEFEND THE ROBOT LAW!
OPPOSE THE ROBOT LAW AMENDMENT

WOW... IT'S A DEMONSTRATION BY ROBOTS!

HEY, EVERYBODY! WAIT! LISTEN TO ME!

WE PROTEST!

IF WE OFFEND THE HUMANS NOW, IT'LL ONLY MAKE THINGS WORSE!

MAYBE SO, KIDDO...

BUT WE CAN'T STOP...

WE JUST DON'T WANT THEM TO CHANGE THE LAW!

FREEDOM FOR ROBOTS!

DEFEN...

NO! STOP!!

THE HAWKS AMONG THE HUMANS'LL SEE THIS...

THEY'LL GET ANGRIER AND REALLY CHANGE THE LAW!

IT'S NO USE... NOBODY'S LISTENING TO ME...

THEY'RE ALREADY STARTING TO FIGHT WITH HUMAN POLICE OVER THERE...

YEAH!

RIGHTS FOR ROBOTS!

THINGS ARE JUST GONNA GET WORSE THIS WAY...

HEY, WHO'S THAT OVER THERE?

370

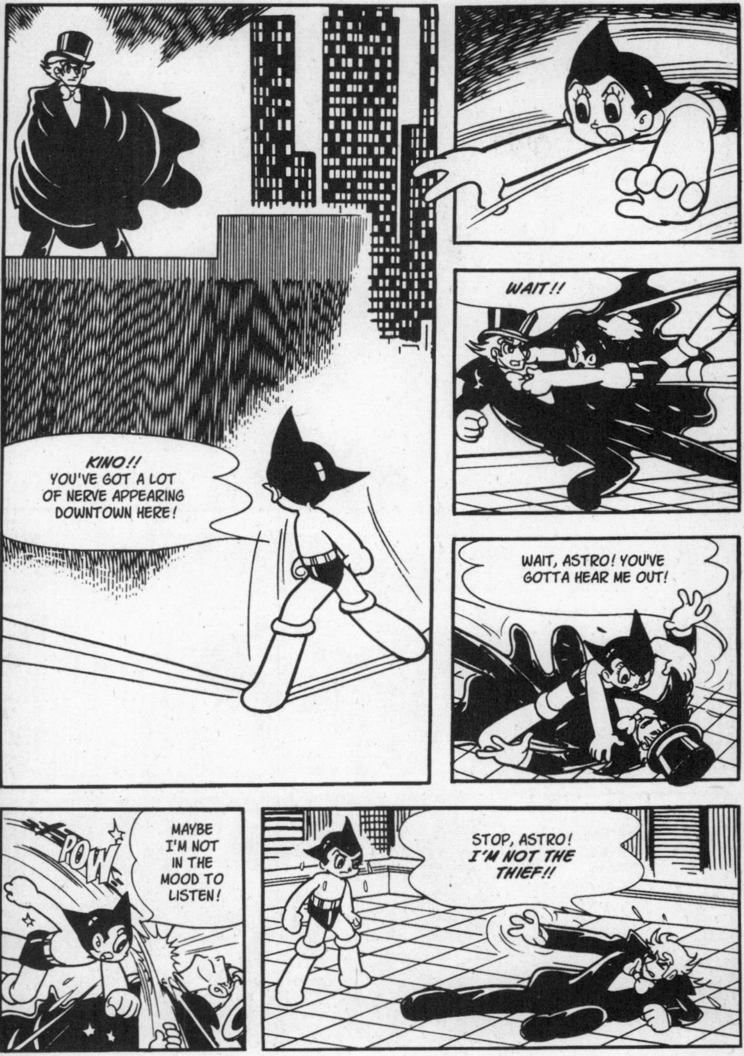
KINO!! YOU'VE GOT A LOT OF NERVE APPEARING DOWNTOWN HERE!
WAIT!!
WAIT, ASTRO! YOU'VE GOTTA HEAR ME OUT!
POW
MAYBE I'M NOT IN THE MOOD TO LISTEN!
STOP, ASTRO! I'M NOT THE THIEF!!

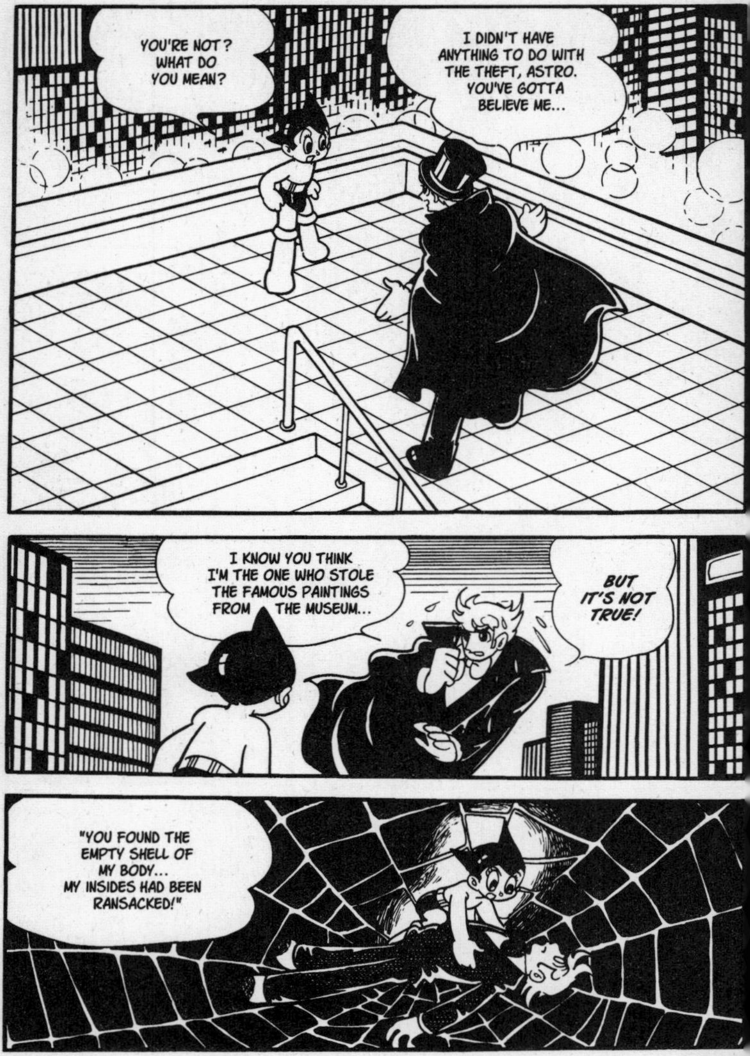
YOU'RE NOT? WHAT DO YOU MEAN?
I DIDN'T HAVE ANYTHING TO DO WITH THE THEFT, ASTRO. YOU'VE GOTTA BELIEVE ME...
I KNOW YOU THINK I'M THE ONE WHO STOLE THE FAMOUS PAINTINGS FROM THE MUSEUM...
BUT IT'S NOT TRUE!
"YOU FOUND THE EMPTY SHELL OF MY BODY... MY INSIDES HAD BEEN RANSACKED!"

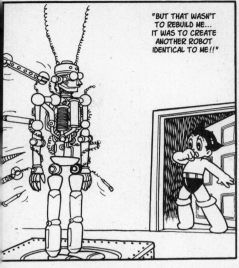

"BUT THAT WASN'T TO REBUILD ME... IT WAS TO CREATE ANOTHER ROBOT IDENTICAL TO ME!!"

A FAKE YOU?

THAT'S RIGHT. UNO CREATED AN IMPOSTOR.

"SO THE KINO, THE THIEF THAT ROBBED THE ART MUSEUM..."

"...THAT WASN'T THE REAL YOU?"

HMM. I'M STARTING TO GET IT. IT WAS AN IMPOSTOR, POSING AS KINO THE MAGICIAN...

AND NOT ONLY WAS HE AN IMPOSTOR, ASTRO... HE WAS CONTROLLED BY *NOH UNO*!!

COME WITH ME, KINO. YOU'VE GOTTA TELL THAT TO EVERYONE!

NO! I CAN'T!

ANY-THING BUT THAT!

373

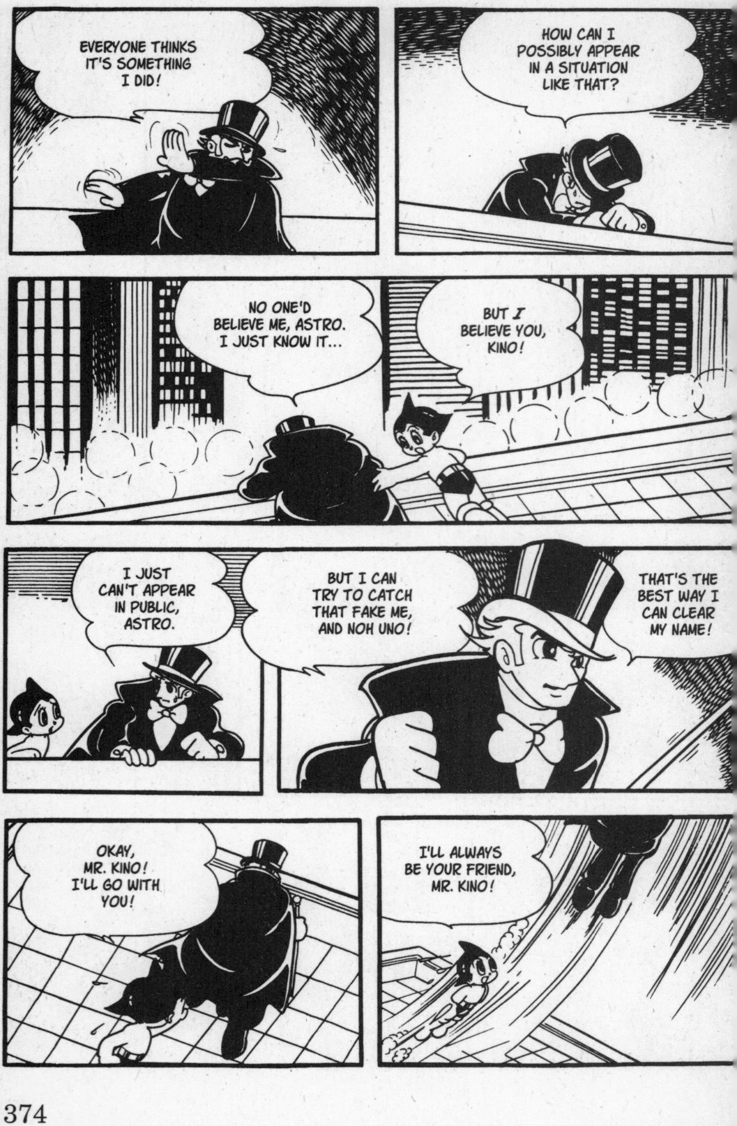
EVERYONE THINKS IT'S SOMETHING I DID!
HOW CAN I POSSIBLY APPEAR IN A SITUATION LIKE THAT?
NO ONE'D BELIEVE ME, ASTRO. I JUST KNOW IT...
BUT *I* BELIEVE YOU, KINO!
I JUST CAN'T APPEAR IN PUBLIC, ASTRO.
BUT I CAN TRY TO CATCH THAT FAKE ME, AND NOH UNO!
THAT'S THE BEST WAY I CAN CLEAR MY NAME!
OKAY, MR. KINO! I'LL GO WITH YOU!
I'LL ALWAYS BE YOUR FRIEND, MR. KINO!

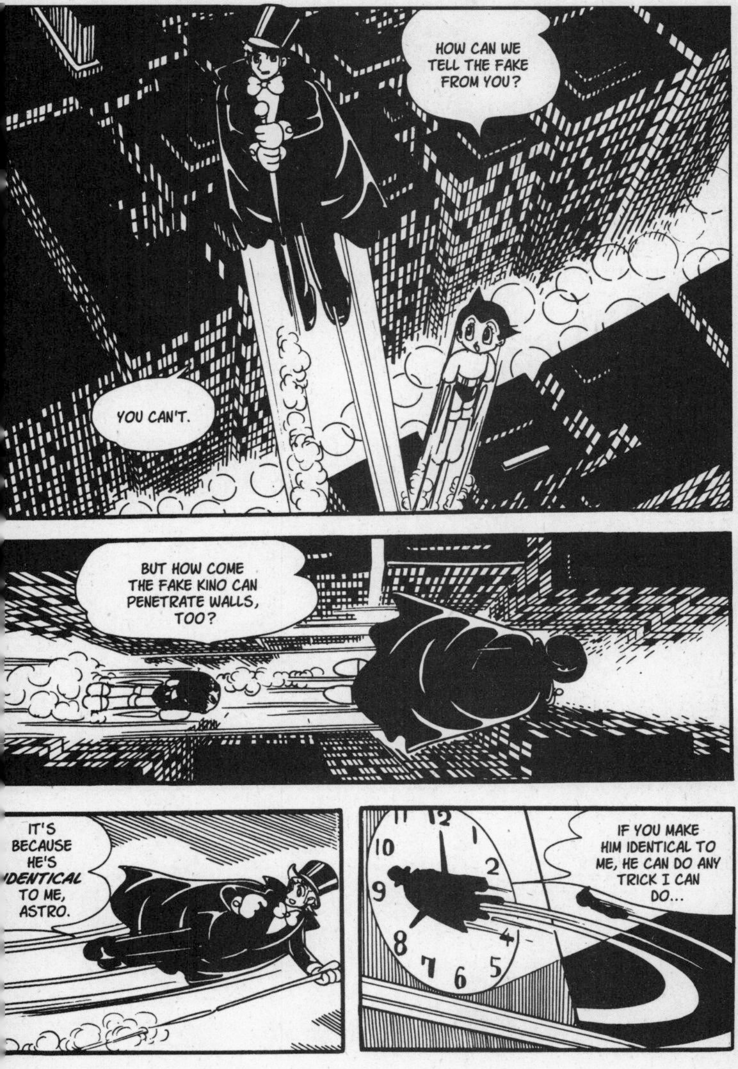
HOW CAN WE TELL THE FAKE FROM YOU?
YOU CAN'T.
BUT HOW COME THE FAKE KINO CAN PENETRATE WALLS, TOO?
IT'S BECAUSE HE'S IDENTICAL TO ME, ASTRO.
IF YOU MAKE HIM IDENTICAL TO ME, HE CAN DO ANY TRICK I CAN DO...

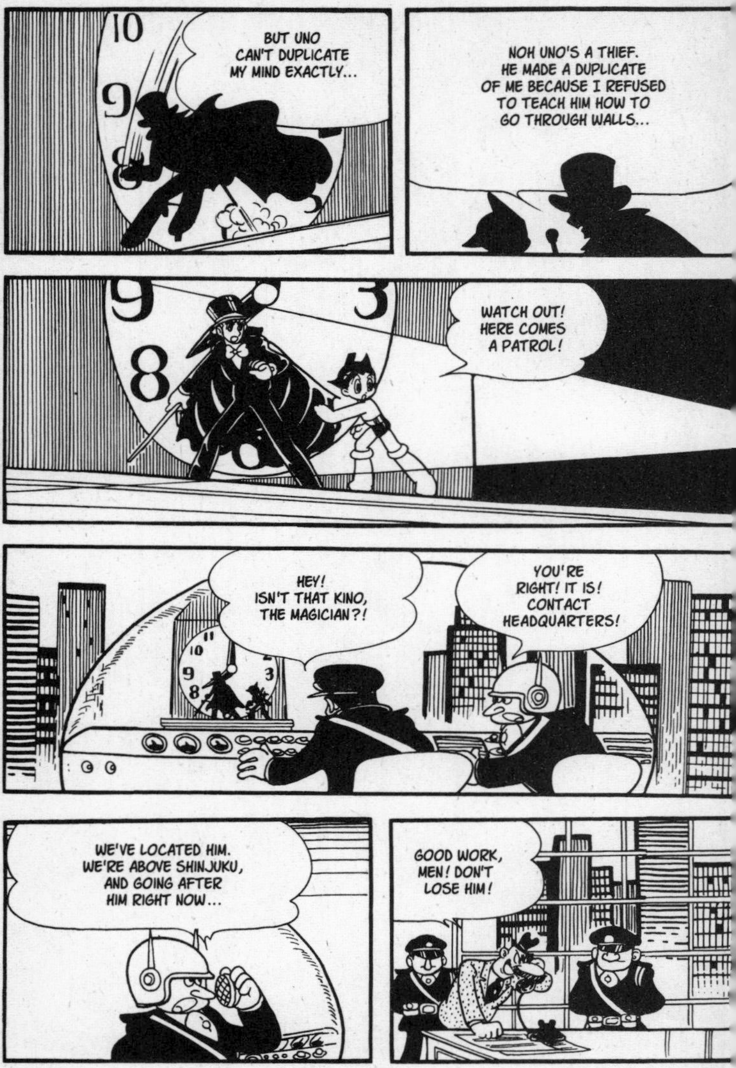
BUT UNO CAN'T DUPLICATE MY MIND EXACTLY...
NOH UNO'S A THIEF. HE MADE A DUPLICATE OF ME BECAUSE I REFUSED TO TEACH HIM HOW TO GO THROUGH WALLS...
WATCH OUT! HERE COMES A PATROL!
HEY! ISN'T THAT KINO, THE MAGICIAN?!
YOU'RE RIGHT! IT IS! CONTACT HEADQUARTERS!
WE'VE LOCATED HIM. WE'RE ABOVE SHINJUKU, AND GOING AFTER HIM RIGHT NOW...
GOOD WORK, MEN! DON'T LOSE HIM!

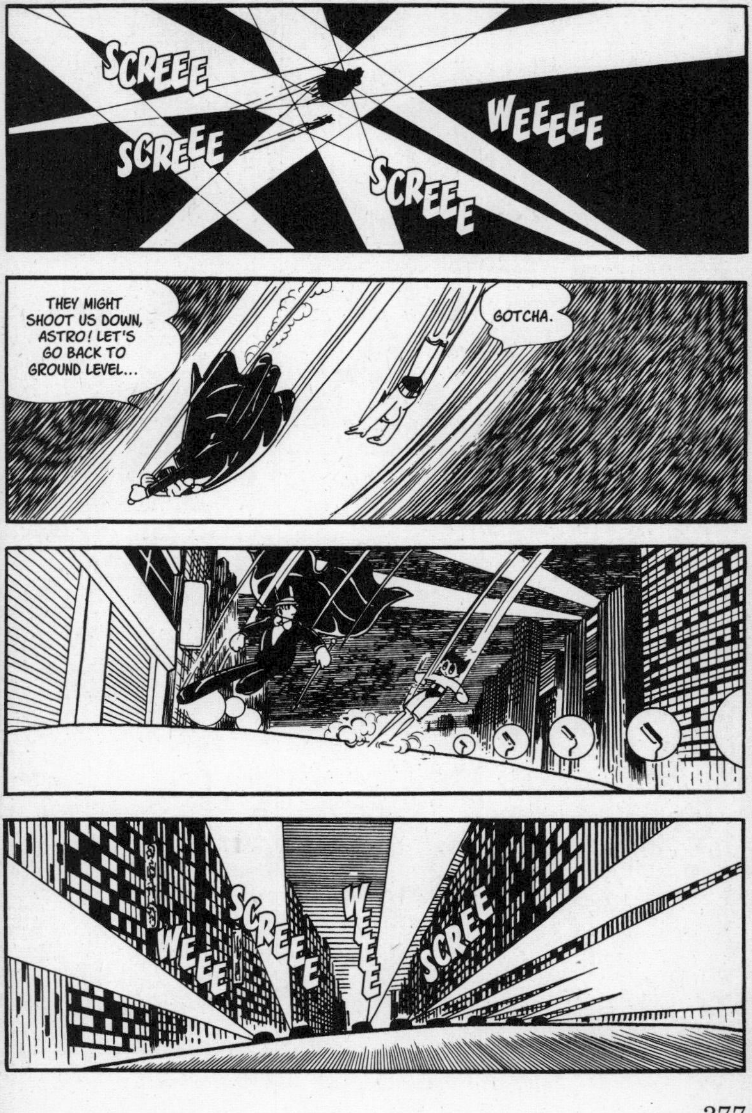
SCREEE
SCREEE
WEEEEE
SCREEE
THEY MIGHT SHOOT US DOWN, ASTRO! LET'S GO BACK TO GROUND LEVEL...
GOTCHA.
WEEE
SCREEEE
WEEE
SCREE

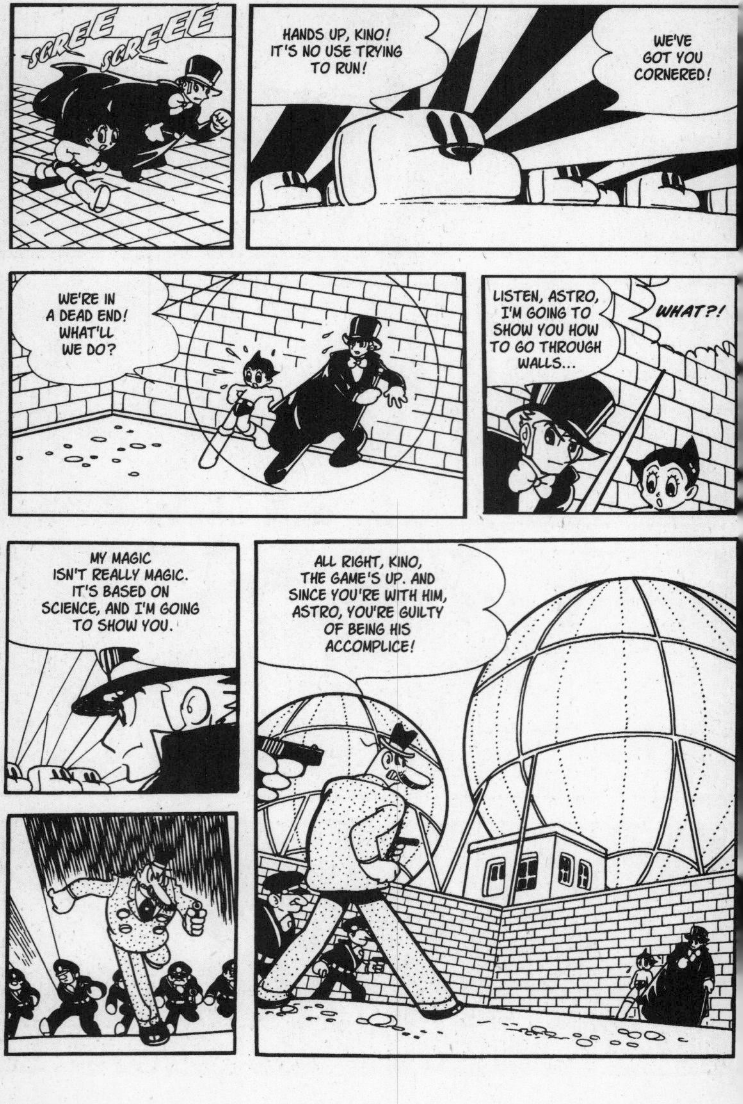
SCREE SCREEE
HANDS UP, KINO! IT'S NO USE TRYING TO RUN!
WE'VE GOT YOU CORNERED!
WE'RE IN A DEAD END! WHAT'LL WE DO?
LISTEN, ASTRO, I'M GOING TO SHOW YOU HOW TO GO THROUGH WALLS...
WHAT?!
MY MAGIC ISN'T REALLY MAGIC. IT'S BASED ON SCIENCE, AND I'M GOING TO SHOW YOU.
ALL RIGHT, KINO, THE GAME'S UP. AND SINCE YOU'RE WITH HIM, ASTRO, YOU'RE GUILTY OF BEING HIS ACCOMPLICE!

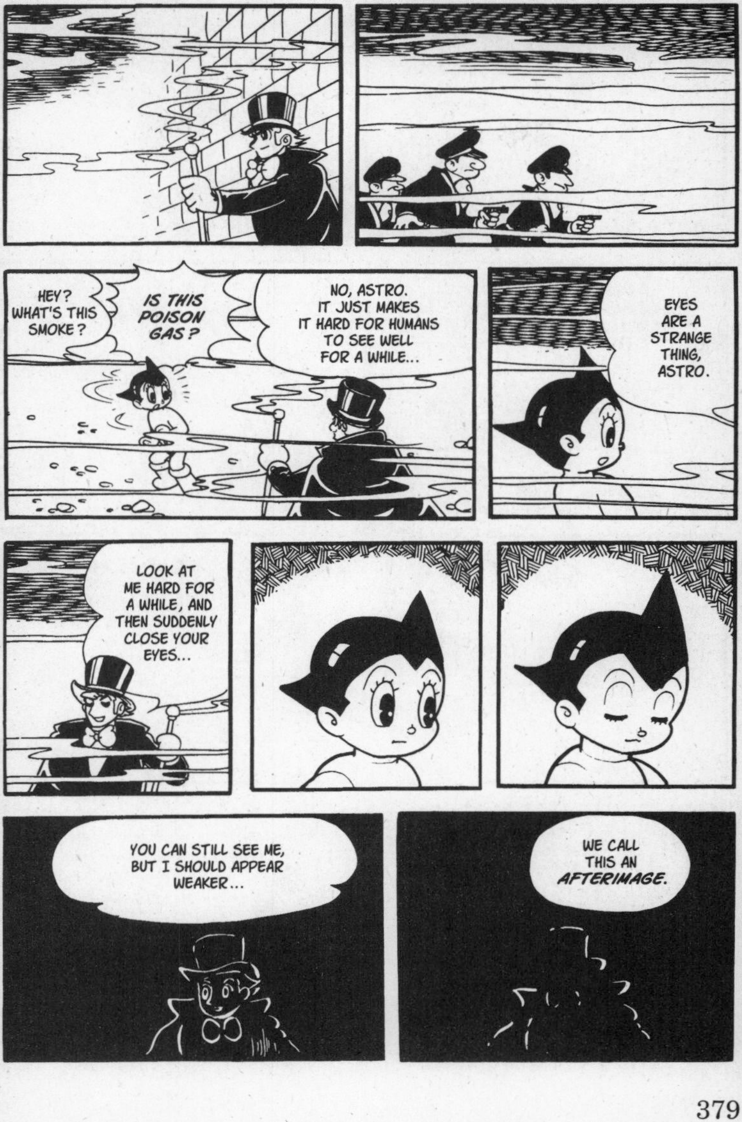
HEY? WHAT'S THIS SMOKE?
IS THIS POISON GAS?
NO, ASTRO. IT JUST MAKES IT HARD FOR HUMANS TO SEE WELL FOR A WHILE...
EYES ARE A STRANGE THING, ASTRO.
LOOK AT ME HARD FOR A WHILE, AND THEN SUDDENLY CLOSE YOUR EYES...
YOU CAN STILL SEE ME, BUT I SHOULD APPEAR WEAKER...
WE CALL THIS AN *AFTERIMAGE*.

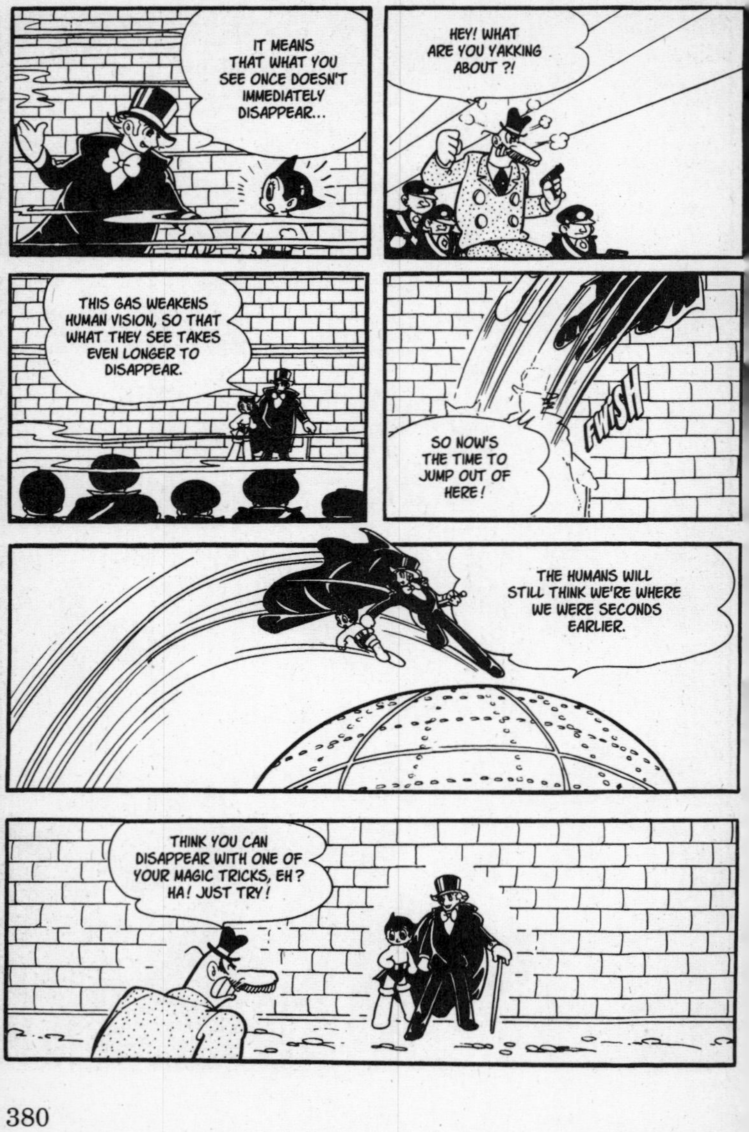
IT MEANS THAT WHAT YOU SEE ONCE DOESN'T IMMEDIATELY DISAPPEAR...
HEY! WHAT ARE YOU YAKKING ABOUT ?!
THIS GAS WEAKENS HUMAN VISION, SO THAT WHAT THEY SEE TAKES EVEN LONGER TO DISAPPEAR.
SO NOW'S THE TIME TO JUMP OUT OF HERE!
FWISH
THE HUMANS WILL STILL THINK WE'RE WHERE WE WERE SECONDS EARLIER.
THINK YOU CAN DISAPPEAR WITH ONE OF YOUR MAGIC TRICKS, EH? HA! JUST TRY!

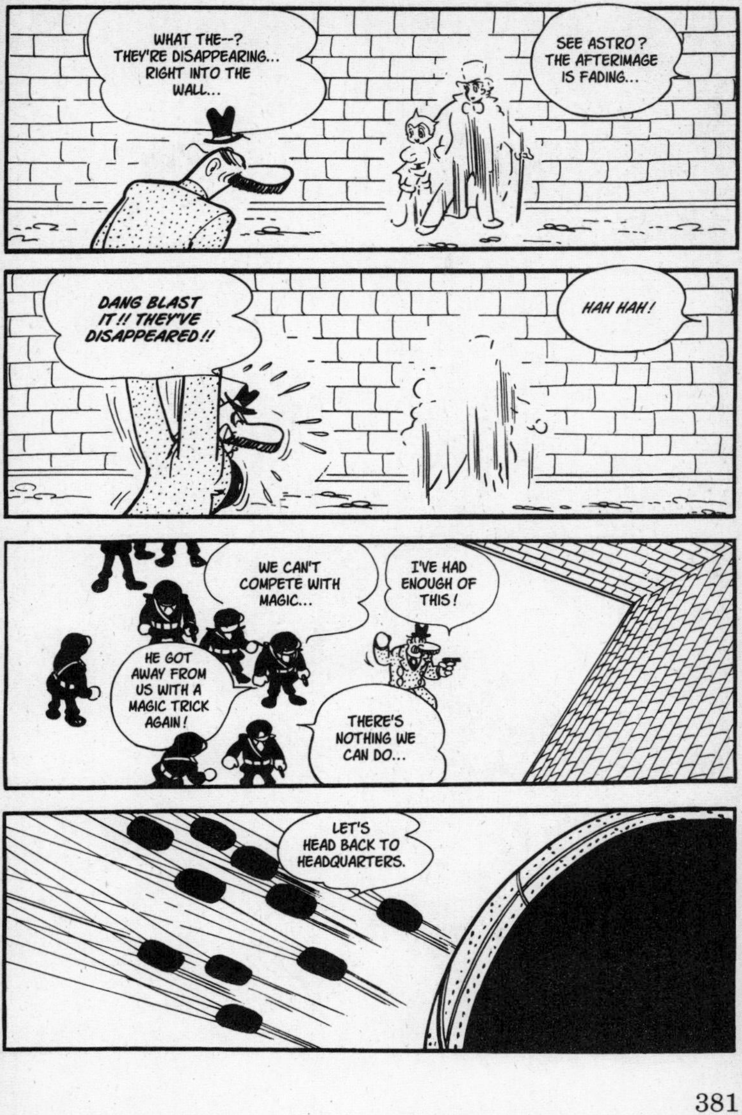
WHAT THE--? THEY'RE DISAPPEARING... RIGHT INTO THE WALL...
SEE ASTRO? THE AFTERIMAGE IS FADING...
DANG BLAST IT!! THEY'VE DISAPPEARED!!
HAH HAH!
WE CAN'T COMPETE WITH MAGIC...
I'VE HAD ENOUGH OF THIS!
HE GOT AWAY FROM US WITH A MAGIC TRICK AGAIN!
THERE'S NOTHING WE CAN DO...
LET'S HEAD BACK TO HEADQUARTERS.

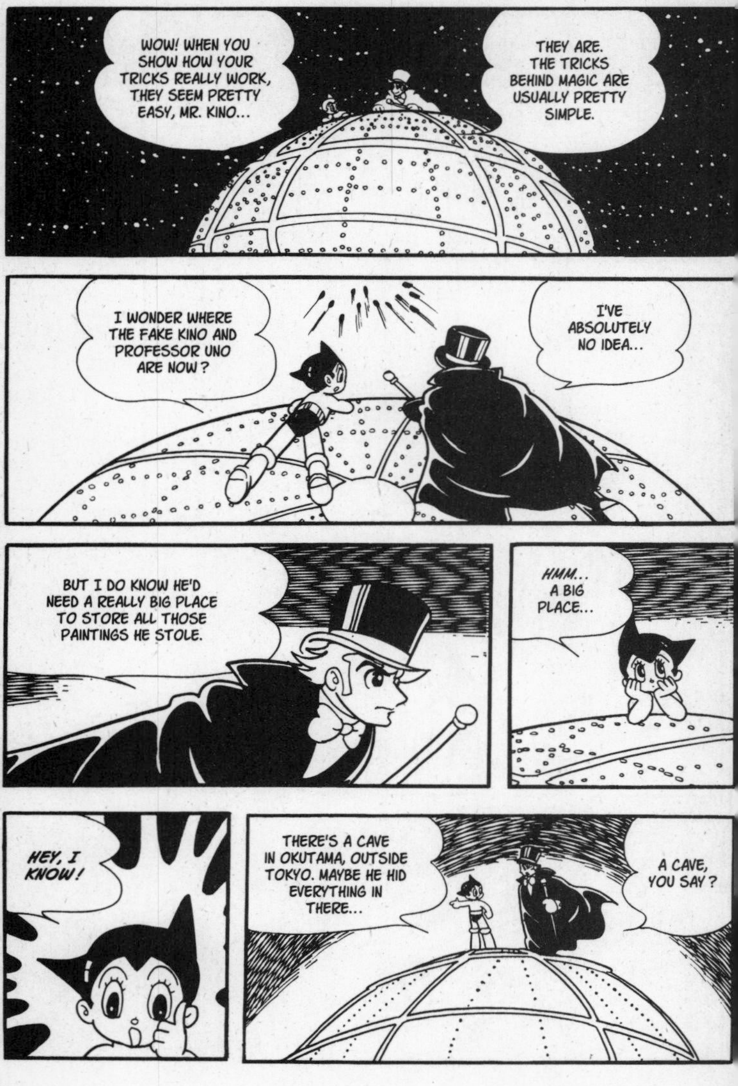

WOW! WHEN YOU SHOW HOW YOUR TRICKS REALLY WORK, THEY SEEM PRETTY EASY, MR. KINO...
THEY ARE. THE TRICKS BEHIND MAGIC ARE USUALLY PRETTY SIMPLE.
I WONDER WHERE THE FAKE KINO AND PROFESSOR UNO ARE NOW?
I'VE ABSOLUTELY NO IDEA...
BUT I DO KNOW HE'D NEED A REALLY BIG PLACE TO STORE ALL THOSE PAINTINGS HE STOLE.
HMM... A BIG PLACE...
HEY, I KNOW!
THERE'S A CAVE IN OKUTAMA, OUTSIDE TOKYO. MAYBE HE HID EVERYTHING IN THERE...
A CAVE, YOU SAY?

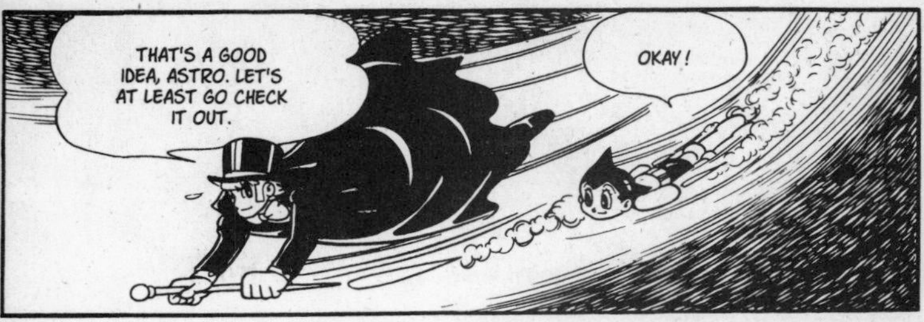
THAT'S A GOOD IDEA, ASTRO. LET'S AT LEAST GO CHECK IT OUT.
OKAY!

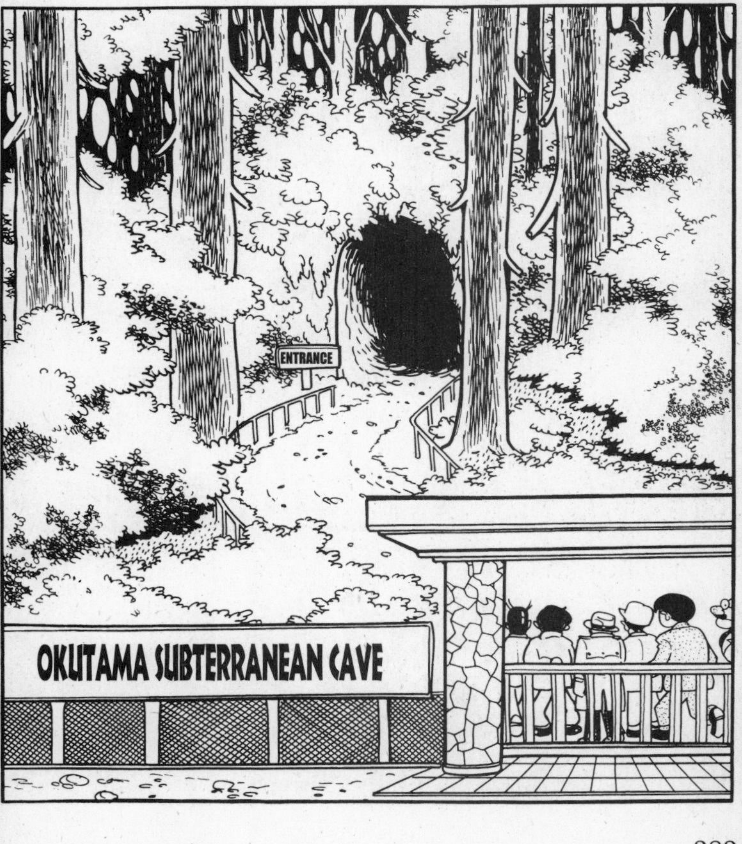
ENTRANCE
OKUTAMA SUBTERRANEAN CAVE

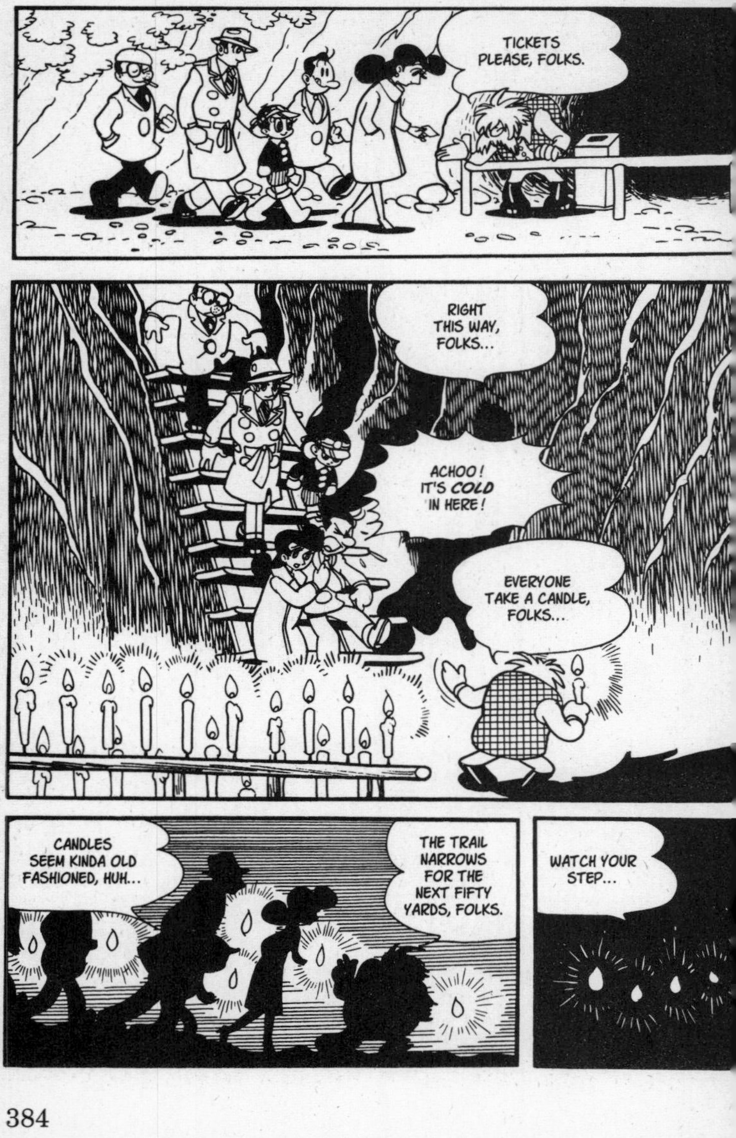
TICKETS PLEASE, FOLKS.
RIGHT THIS WAY, FOLKS...
ACHOO! IT'S *COLD* IN HERE!
EVERYONE TAKE A CANDLE, FOLKS...
CANDLES SEEM KINDA OLD FASHIONED, HUH...
THE TRAIL NARROWS FOR THE NEXT FIFTY YARDS, FOLKS.
WATCH YOUR STEP...

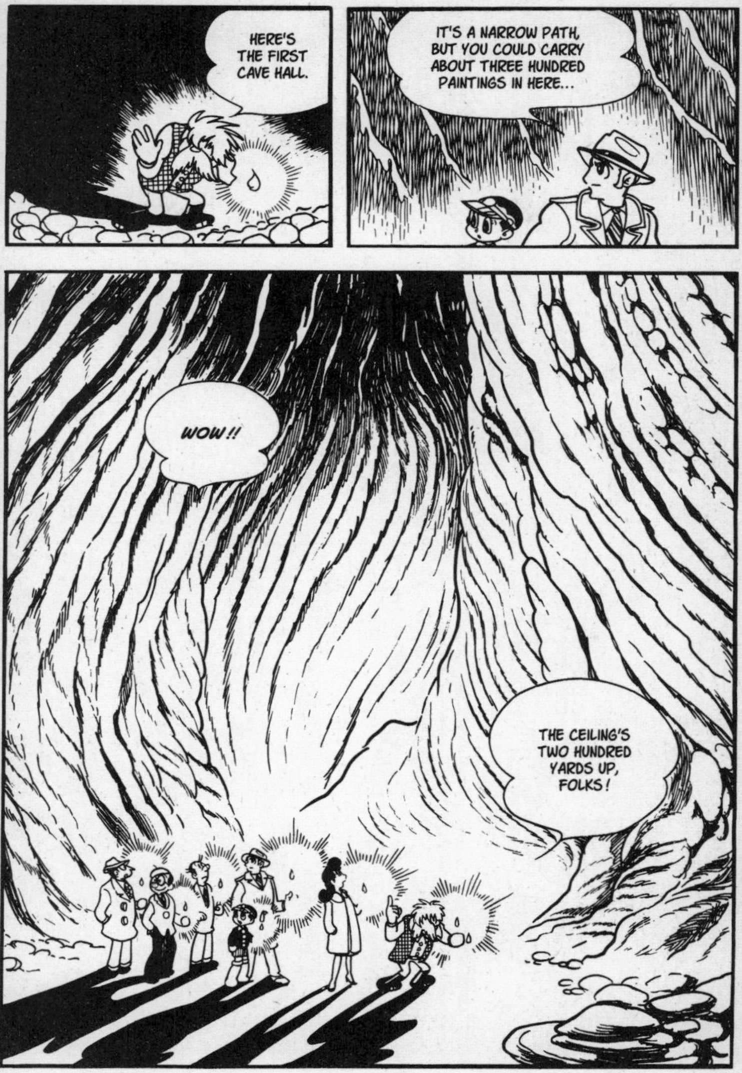
HERE'S THE FIRST CAVE HALL.
IT'S A NARROW PATH, BUT YOU COULD CARRY ABOUT THREE HUNDRED PAINTINGS IN HERE...
WOW!!
THE CEILING'S TWO HUNDRED YARDS UP, FOLKS!

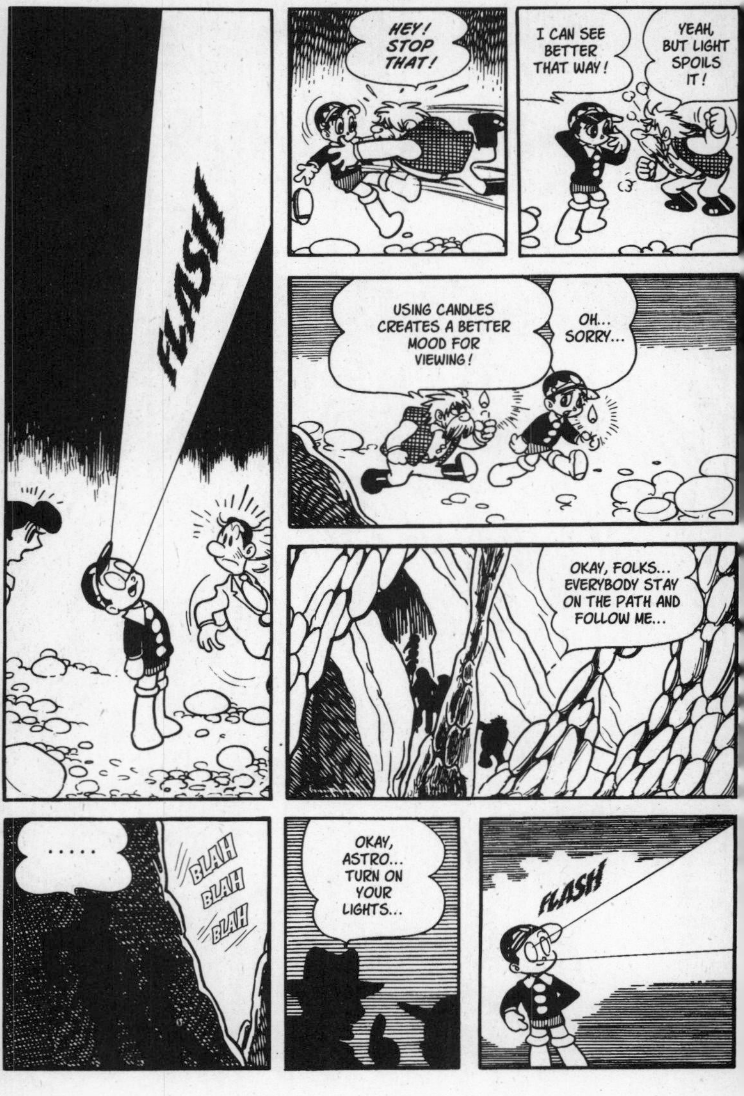
FLASH
HEY! STOP THAT!
I CAN SEE BETTER THAT WAY!
YEAH, BUT LIGHT SPOILS IT!
USING CANDLES CREATES A BETTER MOOD FOR VIEWING!
OH... SORRY...
OKAY, FOLKS... EVERYBODY STAY ON THE PATH AND FOLLOW ME...
.....
BLAH
BLAH
BLAH
OKAY, ASTRO... TURN ON YOUR LIGHTS...
FLASH

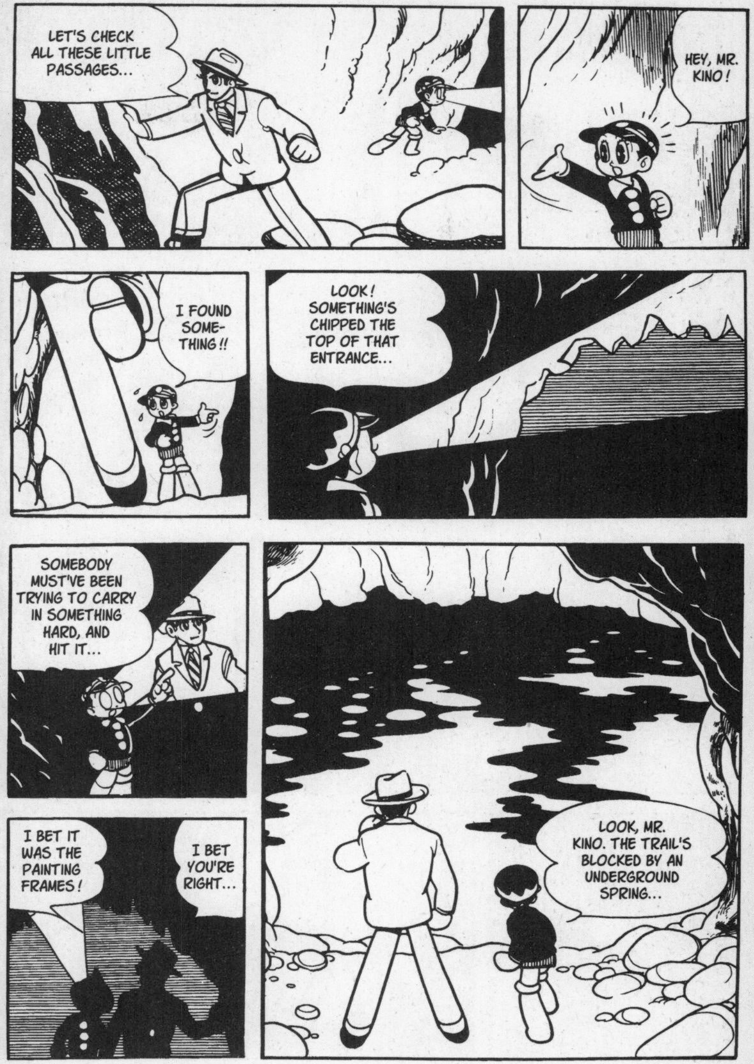
LET'S CHECK ALL THESE LITTLE PASSAGES...
HEY, MR. KINO!
I FOUND SOME-THING!!
LOOK! SOMETHING'S CHIPPED THE TOP OF THAT ENTRANCE...
SOMEBODY MUST'VE BEEN TRYING TO CARRY IN SOMETHING HARD, AND HIT IT...
I BET IT WAS THE PAINTING FRAMES!
I BET YOU'RE RIGHT...
LOOK, MR. KINO. THE TRAIL'S BLOCKED BY AN UNDERGROUND SPRING...

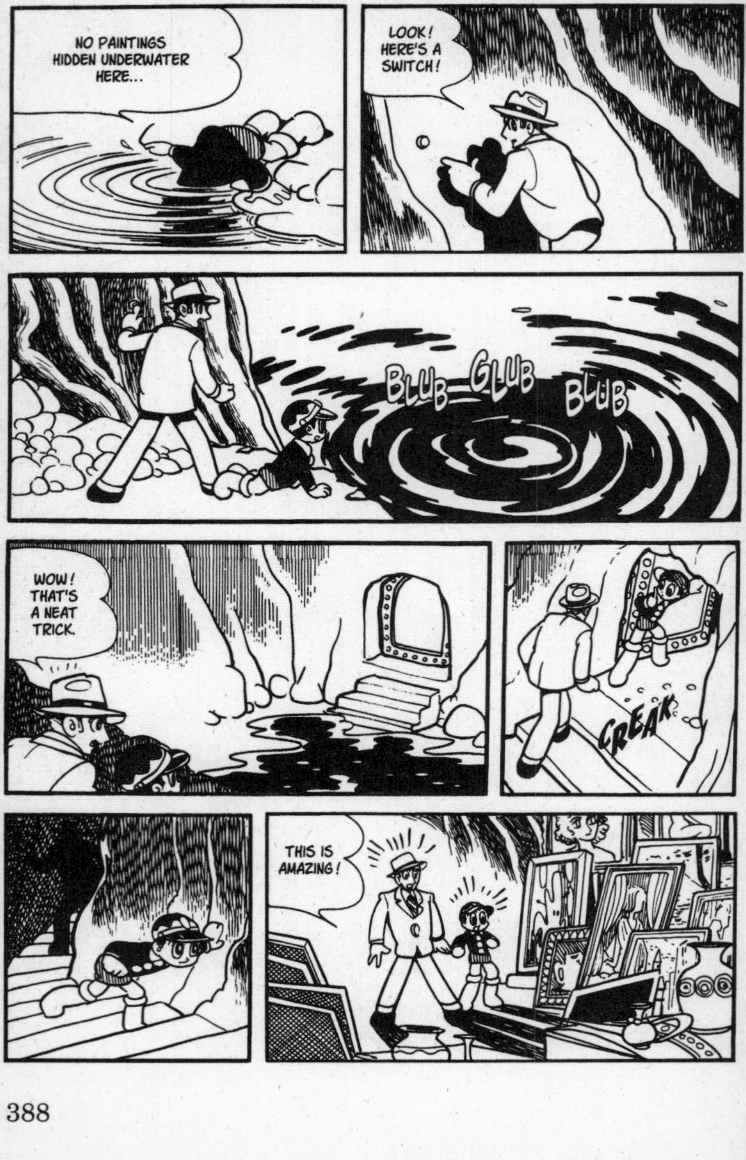
NO PAINTINGS HIDDEN UNDERWATER HERE...
LOOK! HERE'S A SWITCH!
BLUB GLUB BLUB
WOW! THAT'S A NEAT TRICK.
CREAK
THIS IS AMAZING!

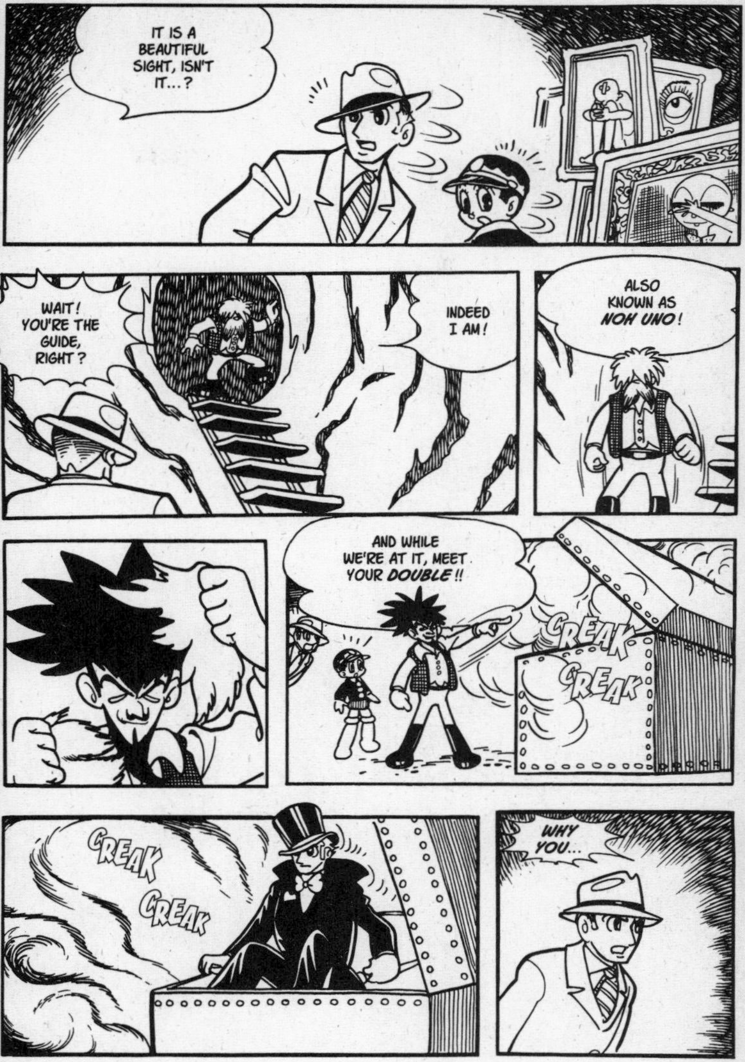
IT IS A BEAUTIFUL SIGHT, ISN'T IT...?
WAIT! YOU'RE THE GUIDE, RIGHT?
INDEED I AM!
ALSO KNOWN AS NOH UNO!
AND WHILE WE'RE AT IT, MEET YOUR DOUBLE!!
CREAK
CREAK
CREAK
CREAK
WHY YOU...

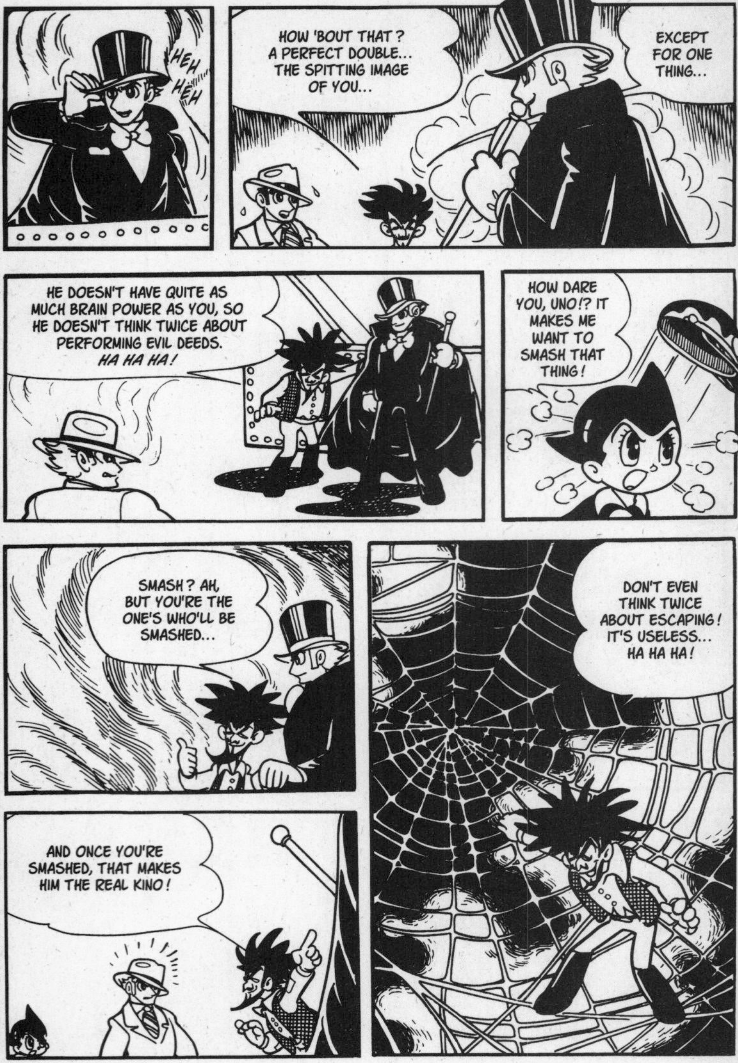
HEH HEH
HOW 'BOUT THAT? A PERFECT DOUBLE... THE SPITTING IMAGE OF YOU...
EXCEPT FOR ONE THING...
HE DOESN'T HAVE QUITE AS MUCH BRAIN POWER AS YOU, SO HE DOESN'T THINK TWICE ABOUT PERFORMING EVIL DEEDS. *HA HA HA!*
HOW DARE YOU, UNO!? IT MAKES ME WANT TO SMASH THAT THING!
SMASH? AH, BUT YOU'RE THE ONE'S WHO'LL BE SMASHED...
AND ONCE YOU'RE SMASHED, THAT MAKES HIM THE REAL KINO!
DON'T EVEN THINK TWICE ABOUT ESCAPING! IT'S USELESS... HA HA HA!

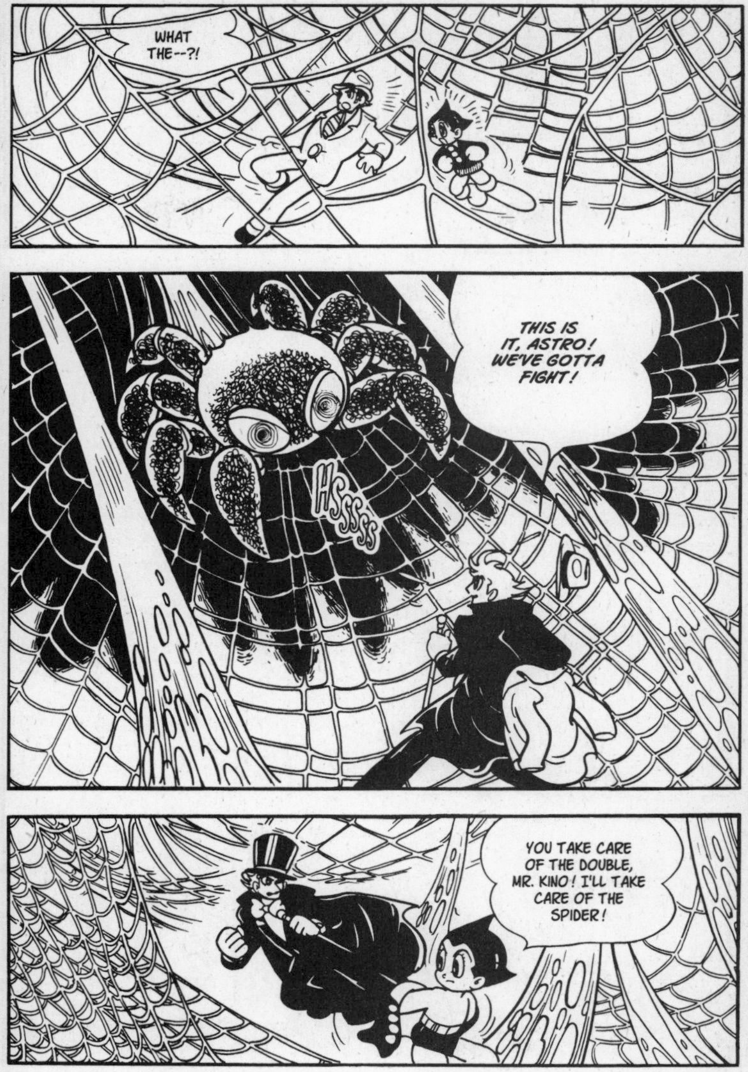
WHAT THE--?!
THIS IS IT, ASTRO! WE'VE GOTTA FIGHT!
HSSSSS
YOU TAKE CARE OF THE DOUBLE, MR. KINO! I'LL TAKE CARE OF THE SPIDER!

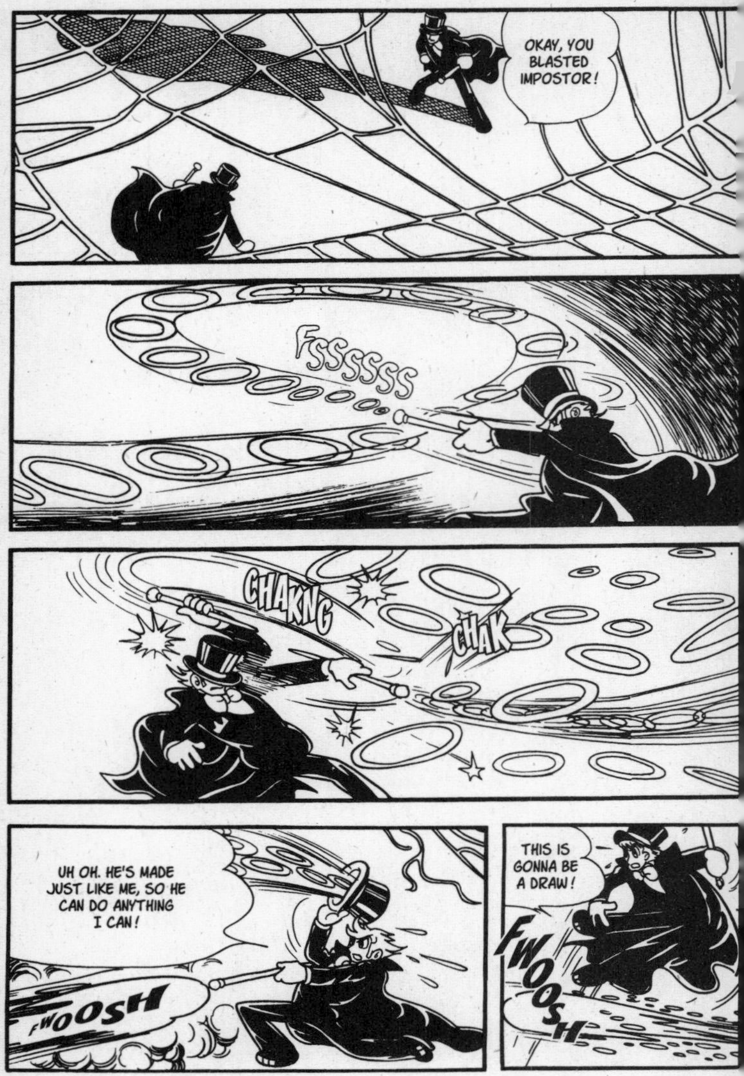
OKAY, YOU BLASTED IMPOSTOR!
FSSSSSS
CHAKNG
CHAK
UH OH. HE'S MADE JUST LIKE ME, SO HE CAN DO ANYTHING I CAN!
FWOOSH
THIS IS GONNA BE A DRAW!
FWOOSH

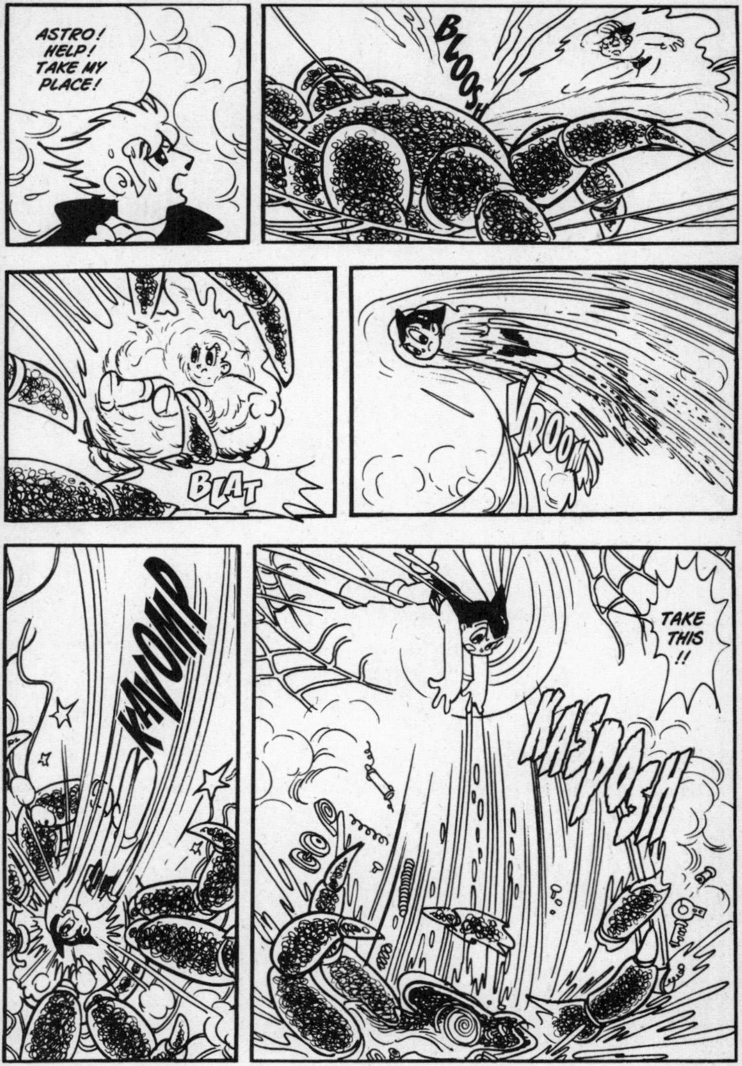
ASTRO! HELP! TAKE MY PLACE!
BLOOSH
BLAT
VROOM
KAVOMP
TAKE THIS !!
KAESPOSH

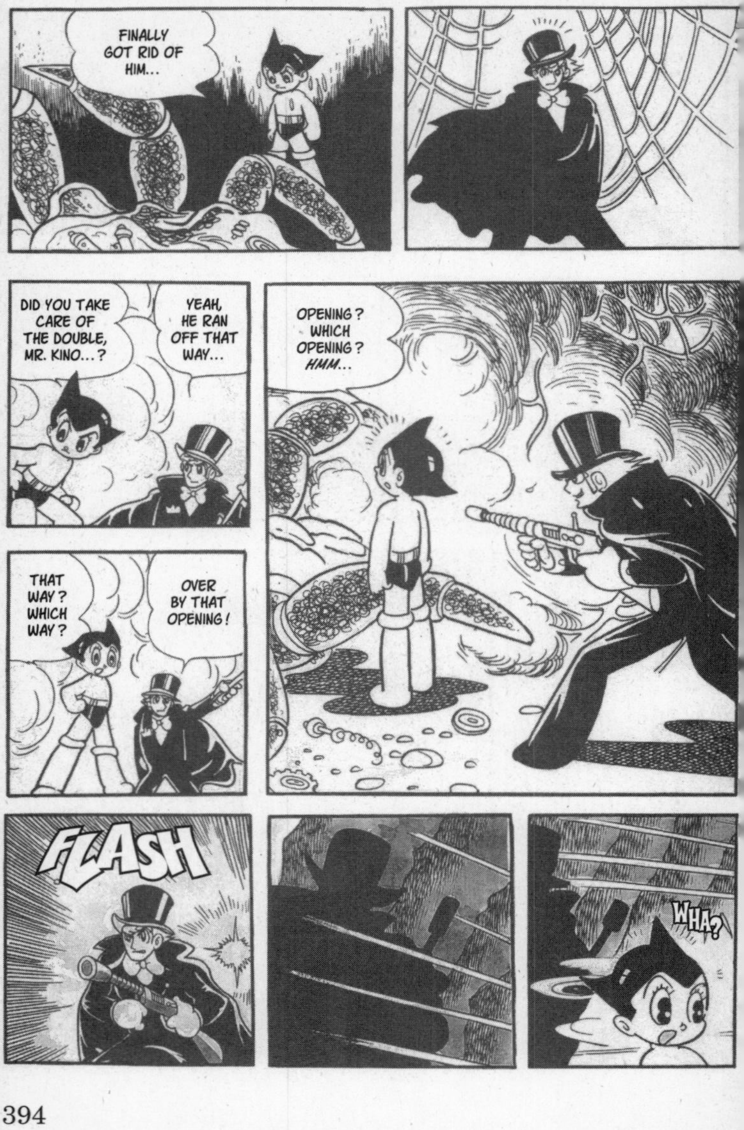
FINALLY GOT RID OF HIM...
DID YOU TAKE CARE OF THE DOUBLE, MR. KINO...?
YEAH, HE RAN OFF THAT WAY...
THAT WAY? WHICH WAY?
OVER BY THAT OPENING!
OPENING? WHICH OPENING? *HMM...*
FLASH
WHA?

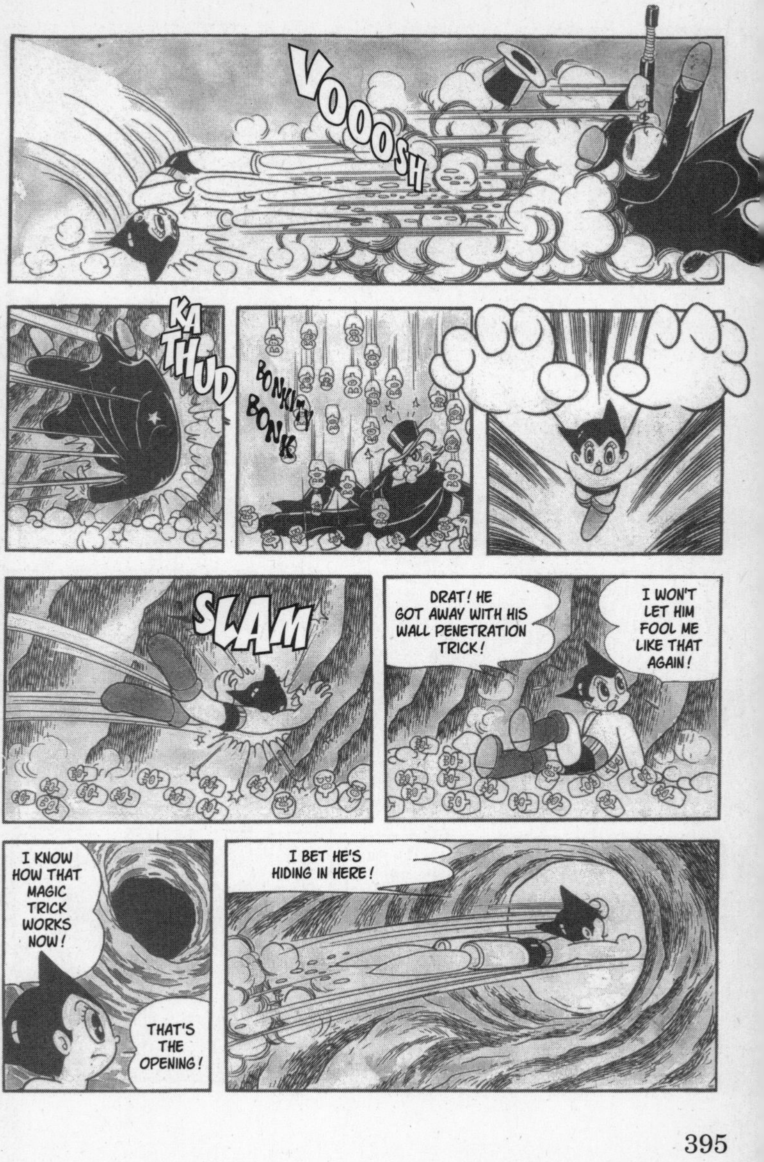

VOOOOSH
KA THUD
BONKITY BONK
SLAM
DRAT! HE GOT AWAY WITH HIS WALL PENETRATION TRICK!
I WON'T LET HIM FOOL ME LIKE THAT AGAIN!
I KNOW HOW THAT MAGIC TRICK WORKS NOW!
THAT'S THE OPENING!
I BET HE'S HIDING IN HERE!

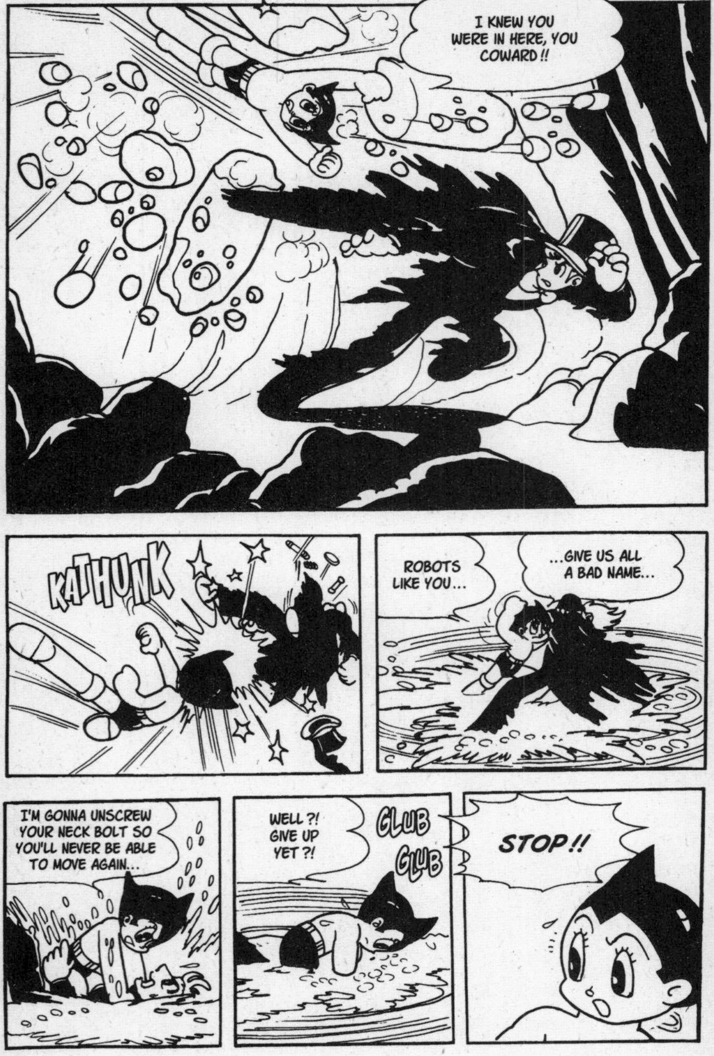
I KNEW YOU WERE IN HERE, YOU COWARD!!
KATHUNK
ROBOTS LIKE YOU...
...GIVE US ALL A BAD NAME...
I'M GONNA UNSCREW YOUR NECK BOLT SO YOU'LL NEVER BE ABLE TO MOVE AGAIN...
WELL?! GIVE UP YET?!
GLUB
GLUB
STOP!!

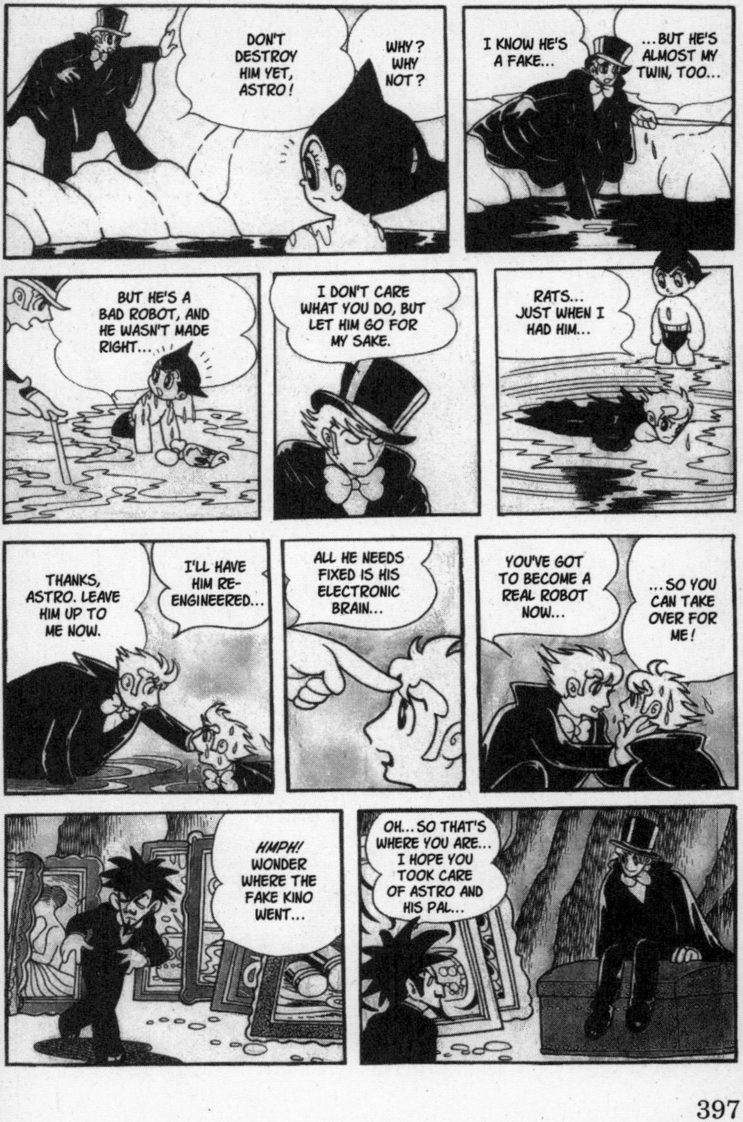
DON'T DESTROY HIM YET, ASTRO!
WHY? WHY NOT?
I KNOW HE'S A FAKE...
...BUT HE'S ALMOST MY TWIN, TOO...
BUT HE'S A BAD ROBOT, AND HE WASN'T MADE RIGHT...
I DON'T CARE WHAT YOU DO, BUT LET HIM GO FOR MY SAKE.
RATS... JUST WHEN I HAD HIM...
THANKS, ASTRO. LEAVE HIM UP TO ME NOW.
I'LL HAVE HIM RE-ENGINEERED...
ALL HE NEEDS FIXED IS HIS ELECTRONIC BRAIN...
YOU'VE GOT TO BECOME A REAL ROBOT NOW...
...SO YOU CAN TAKE OVER FOR ME!
HMPH! WONDER WHERE THE FAKE KINO WENT...
OH...SO THAT'S WHERE YOU ARE... I HOPE YOU TOOK CARE OF ASTRO AND HIS PAL...

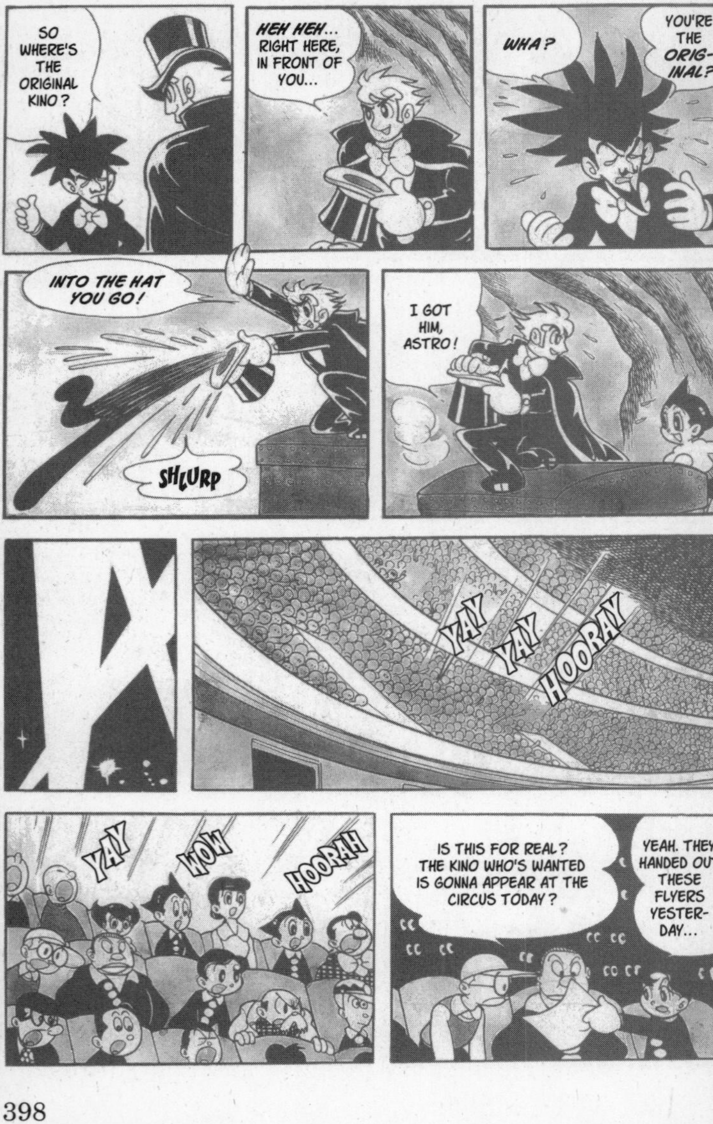
SO WHERE'S THE ORIGINAL KINO?
HEH HEH... RIGHT HERE, IN FRONT OF YOU...
WHA?
YOU'RE THE ORIGINAL?
INTO THE HAT YOU GO!
SHLURP
I GOT HIM, ASTRO!
YAY
YAY
HOORAY
YAY
WOW
HOORAH
IS THIS FOR REAL? THE KINO WHO'S WANTED IS GONNA APPEAR AT THE CIRCUS TODAY?
YEAH. THEY HANDED OUT THESE FLYERS YESTERDAY...

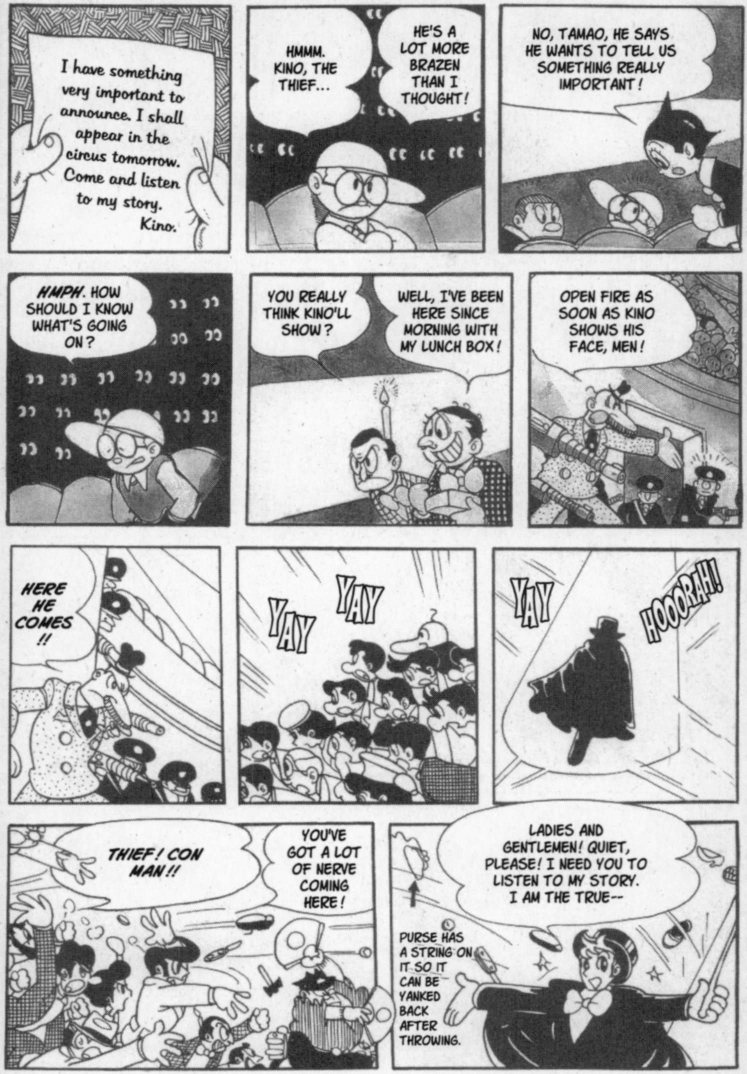

I have something very important to announce. I shall appear in the circus tomorrow. Come and listen to my story. Kino.
HMMM. KINO, THE THIEF...
HE'S A LOT MORE BRAZEN THAN I THOUGHT!
NO, TAMAO, HE SAYS HE WANTS TO TELL US SOMETHING REALLY IMPORTANT!
HMPH. HOW SHOULD I KNOW WHAT'S GOING ON?
YOU REALLY THINK KINO'LL SHOW?
WELL, I'VE BEEN HERE SINCE MORNING WITH MY LUNCH BOX!
OPEN FIRE AS SOON AS KINO SHOWS HIS FACE, MEN!
HERE HE COMES!!
YAY
YAY
YAY
HOOORAH!
THIEF! CON MAN!!
YOU'VE GOT A LOT OF NERVE COMING HERE!
LADIES AND GENTLEMEN! QUIET, PLEASE! I NEED YOU TO LISTEN TO MY STORY. I AM THE TRUE--
PURSE HAS A STRING ON IT SO IT CAN BE YANKED BACK AFTER THROWING.

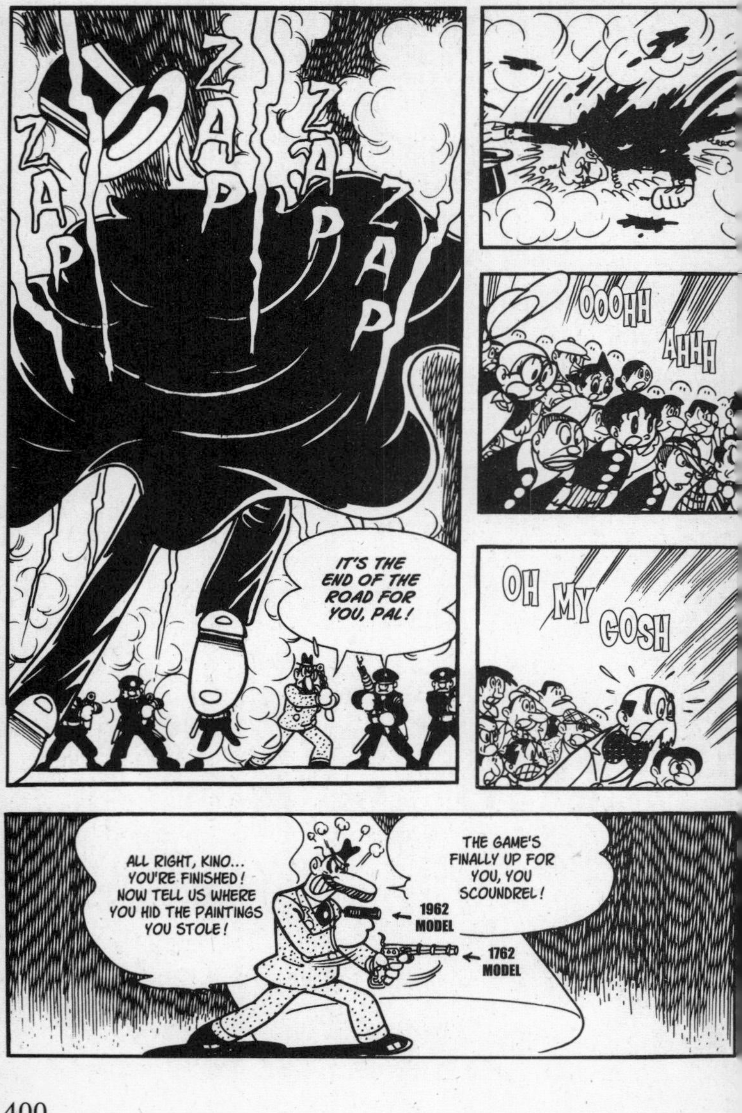
ZAP
ZAP
ZAP
ZAP
IT'S THE END OF THE ROAD FOR YOU, PAL!
OOOHH
AHHH
OH MY GOSH
ALL RIGHT, KINO... YOU'RE FINISHED! NOW TELL US WHERE YOU HID THE PAINTINGS YOU STOLE!
THE GAME'S FINALLY UP FOR YOU, YOU SCOUNDREL!
1962 MODEL
1762 MODEL

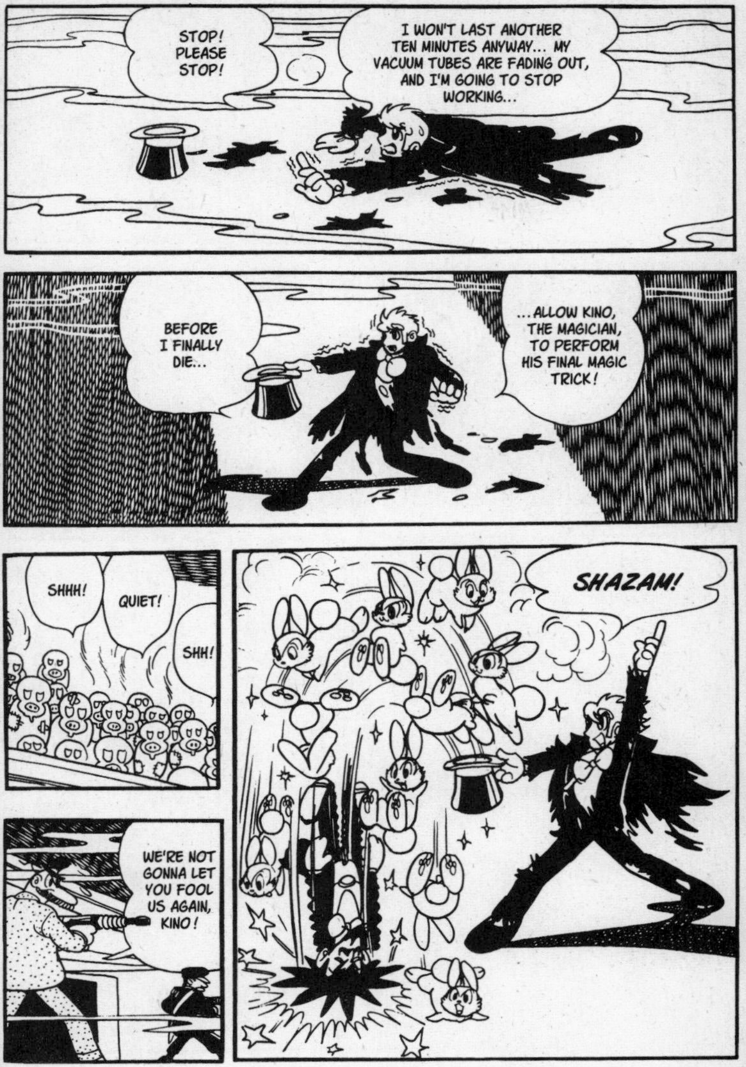
STOP! PLEASE STOP!
I WON'T LAST ANOTHER TEN MINUTES ANYWAY... MY VACUUM TUBES ARE FADING OUT, AND I'M GOING TO STOP WORKING...
BEFORE I FINALLY DIE...
...ALLOW KINO, THE MAGICIAN, TO PERFORM HIS FINAL MAGIC TRICK!
SHHH!
QUIET!
SHH!
WE'RE NOT GONNA LET YOU FOOL US AGAIN, KINO!
SHAZAM!

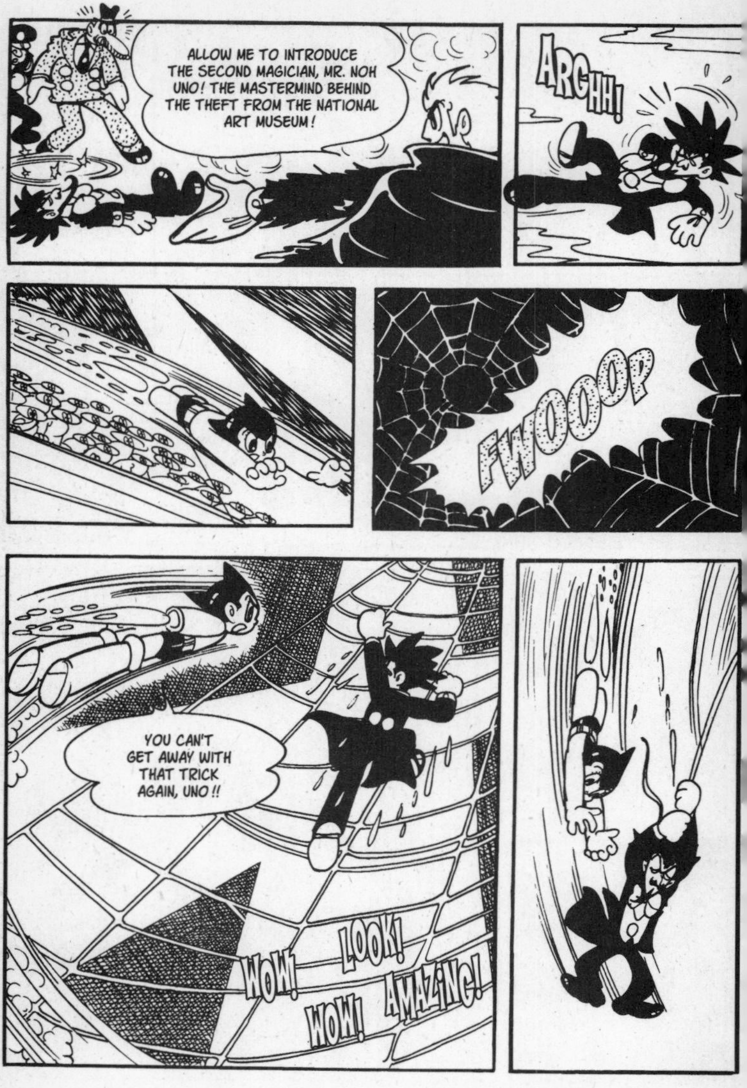
ALLOW ME TO INTRODUCE THE SECOND MAGICIAN, MR. NOH UNO! THE MASTERMIND BEHIND THE THEFT FROM THE NATIONAL ART MUSEUM!
ARGHH!
FWOOOP
YOU CAN'T GET AWAY WITH THAT TRICK AGAIN, UNO!!
WOW!
LOOK!
WOW!
AMAZING!

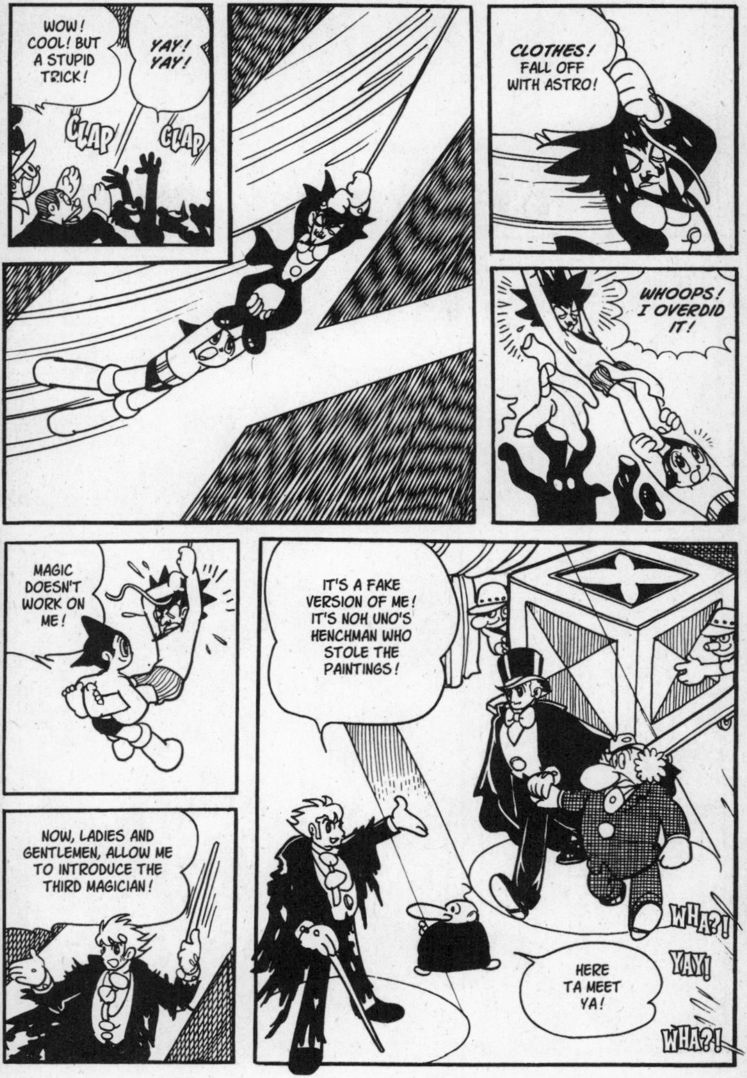
WOW! COOL! BUT A STUPID TRICK!
YAY! YAY!
CLAP
CLAP
CLOTHES! FALL OFF WITH ASTRO!
WHOOPS! I OVERDID IT!
MAGIC DOESN'T WORK ON ME!
IT'S A FAKE VERSION OF ME! IT'S NOH UNO'S HENCHMAN WHO STOLE THE PAINTINGS!
NOW, LADIES AND GENTLEMEN, ALLOW ME TO INTRODUCE THE THIRD MAGICIAN!
WHA?!
YAY!
HERE TA MEET YA!
WHA?!

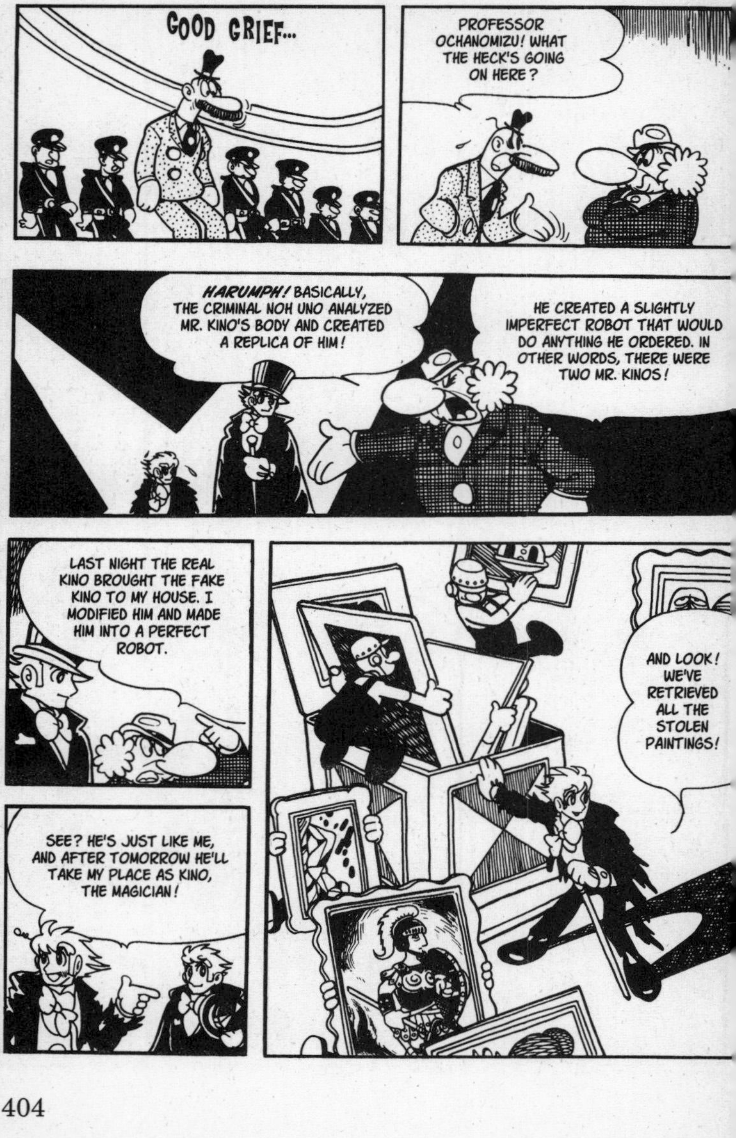
GOOD GRIEF...
PROFESSOR OCHANOMIZU! WHAT THE HECK'S GOING ON HERE?
HARUMPH! BASICALLY, THE CRIMINAL NOH UNO ANALYZED MR. KINO'S BODY AND CREATED A REPLICA OF HIM!
HE CREATED A SLIGHTLY IMPERFECT ROBOT THAT WOULD DO ANYTHING HE ORDERED. IN OTHER WORDS, THERE WERE TWO MR. KINOS!
LAST NIGHT THE REAL KINO BROUGHT THE FAKE KINO TO MY HOUSE. I MODIFIED HIM AND MADE HIM INTO A PERFECT ROBOT.
SEE? HE'S JUST LIKE ME, AND AFTER TOMORROW HE'LL TAKE MY PLACE AS KINO, THE MAGICIAN!
AND LOOK! WE'VE RETRIEVED ALL THE STOLEN PAINTINGS!

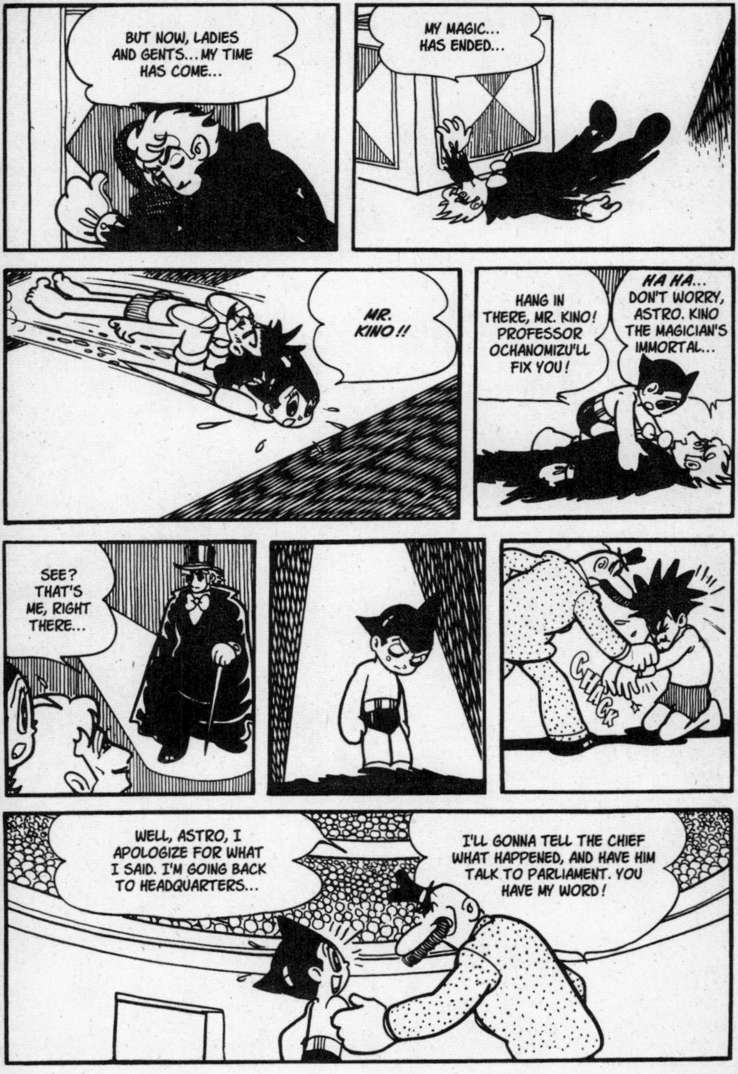
BUT NOW, LADIES AND GENTS... MY TIME HAS COME...
MY MAGIC... HAS ENDED...
MR. KINO!!
HANG IN THERE, MR. KINO! PROFESSOR OCHANOMIZU'LL FIX YOU!
HA HA... DON'T WORRY, ASTRO. KINO THE MAGICIAN'S IMMORTAL...
SEE? THAT'S ME, RIGHT THERE...
CHACK
WELL, ASTRO, I APOLOGIZE FOR WHAT I SAID. I'M GOING BACK TO HEADQUARTERS...
I'LL GONNA TELL THE CHIEF WHAT HAPPENED, AND HAVE HIM TALK TO PARLIAMENT. YOU HAVE MY WORD!

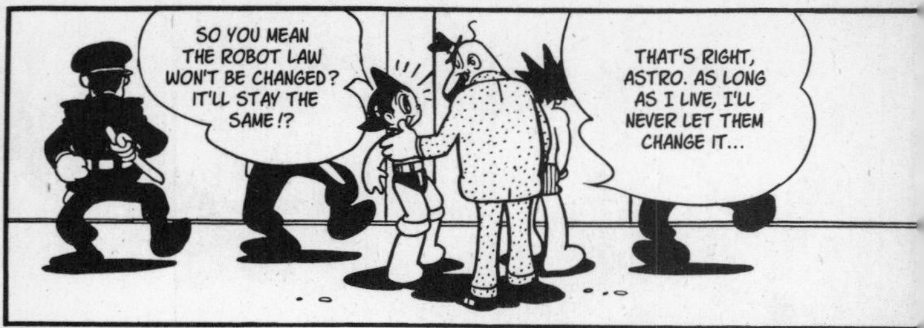
SO YOU MEAN THE ROBOT LAW WON'T BE CHANGED? IT'LL STAY THE SAME!?
THAT'S RIGHT, ASTRO. AS LONG AS I LIVE, I'LL NEVER LET THEM CHANGE IT...
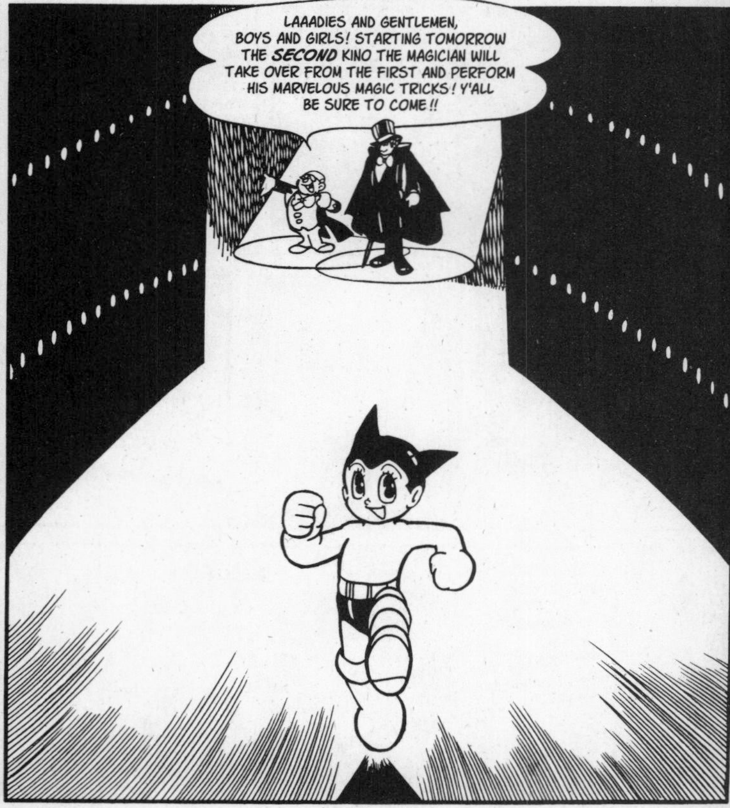
LAAADIES AND GENTLEMEN, BOYS AND GIRLS! STARTING TOMORROW THE *SECOND* KINO THE MAGICIAN WILL TAKE OVER FROM THE FIRST AND PERFORM HIS MARVELOUS MAGIC TRICKS! Y'ALL BE SURE TO COME!!

WHITE PLANET

First published in the special expanded 1963
New Year's edition of *Shonen* magazine.

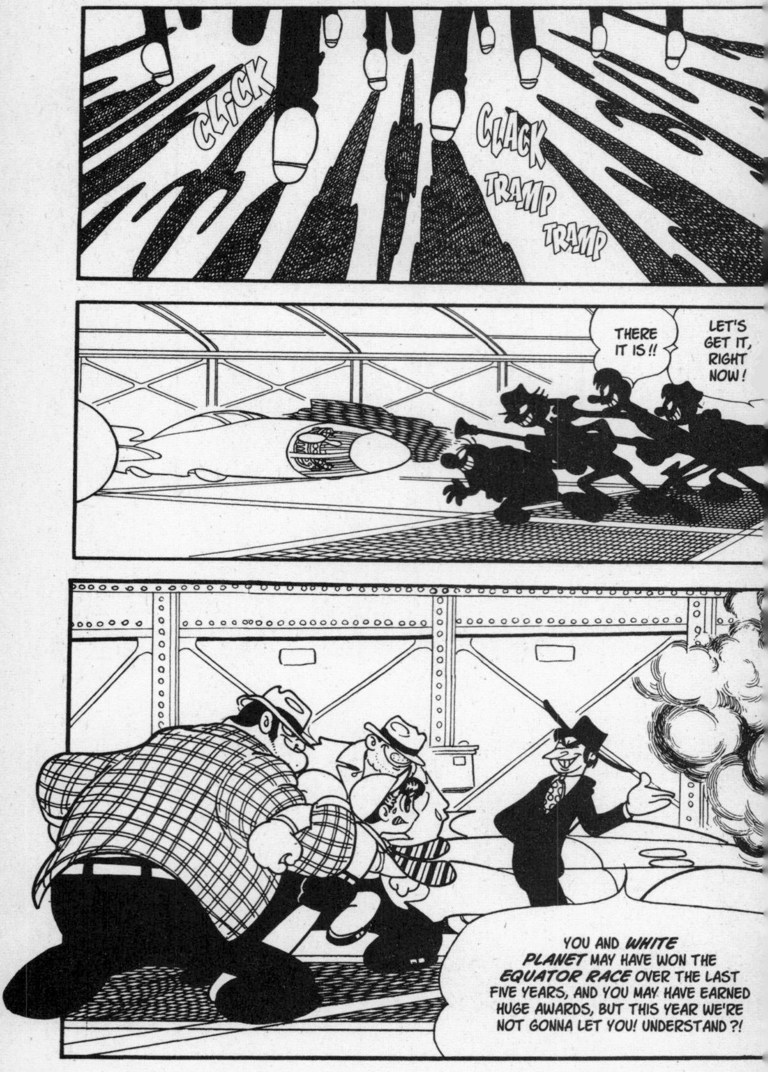
CLICK
CLACK
TRAMP
TRAMP
THERE IT IS!!
LET'S GET IT, RIGHT NOW!
YOU AND WHITE PLANET MAY HAVE WON THE EQUATOR RACE OVER THE LAST FIVE YEARS, AND YOU MAY HAVE EARNED HUGE AWARDS, BUT THIS YEAR WE'RE NOT GONNA LET YOU! UNDERSTAND?!

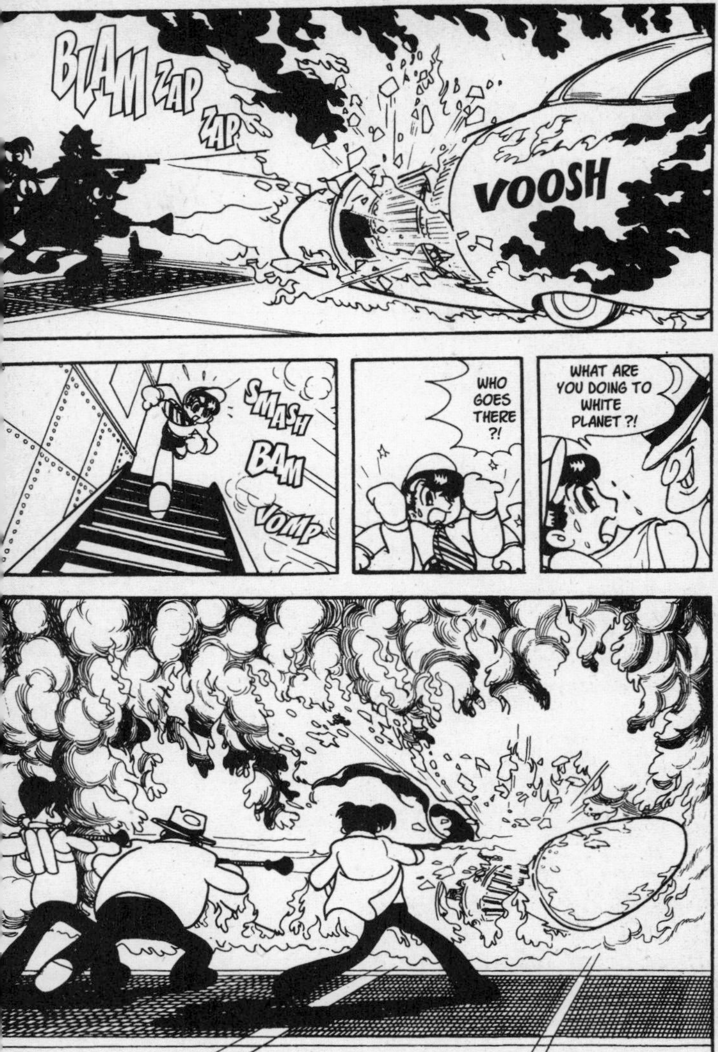
BLAM
ZAP
ZAP
VOOSH
SMASH
BAM
VOMP
WHO GOES THERE ?!
WHAT ARE YOU DOING TO WHITE PLANET ?!

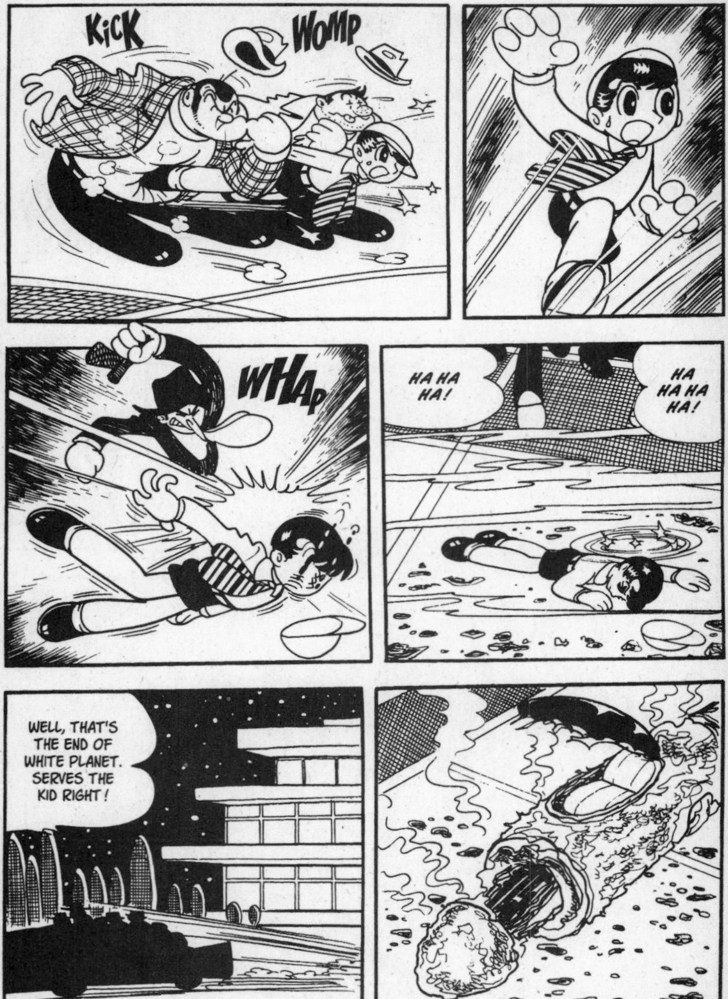
KICK
WOMP
WHAP
HA HA HA!
HA HA HA HA!
WELL, THAT'S THE END OF WHITE PLANET. SERVES THE KID RIGHT!

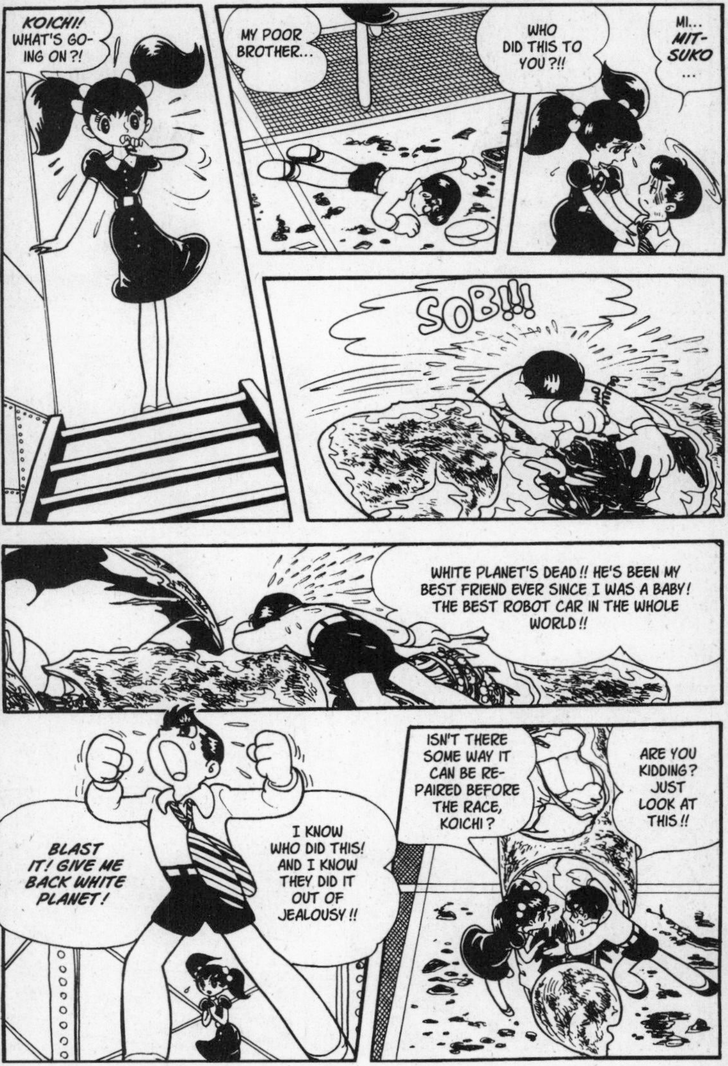
KOICHI! WHAT'S GOING ON?!
MY POOR BROTHER...
WHO DID THIS TO YOU?!!
MI... MITSUKO ...
SOB!!!
WHITE PLANET'S DEAD!! HE'S BEEN MY BEST FRIEND EVER SINCE I WAS A BABY! THE BEST ROBOT CAR IN THE WHOLE WORLD!!
BLAST IT! GIVE ME BACK WHITE PLANET!
I KNOW WHO DID THIS! AND I KNOW THEY DID IT OUT OF JEALOUSY!!
ISN'T THERE SOME WAY IT CAN BE REPAIRED BEFORE THE RACE, KOICHI?
ARE YOU KIDDING? JUST LOOK AT THIS!!

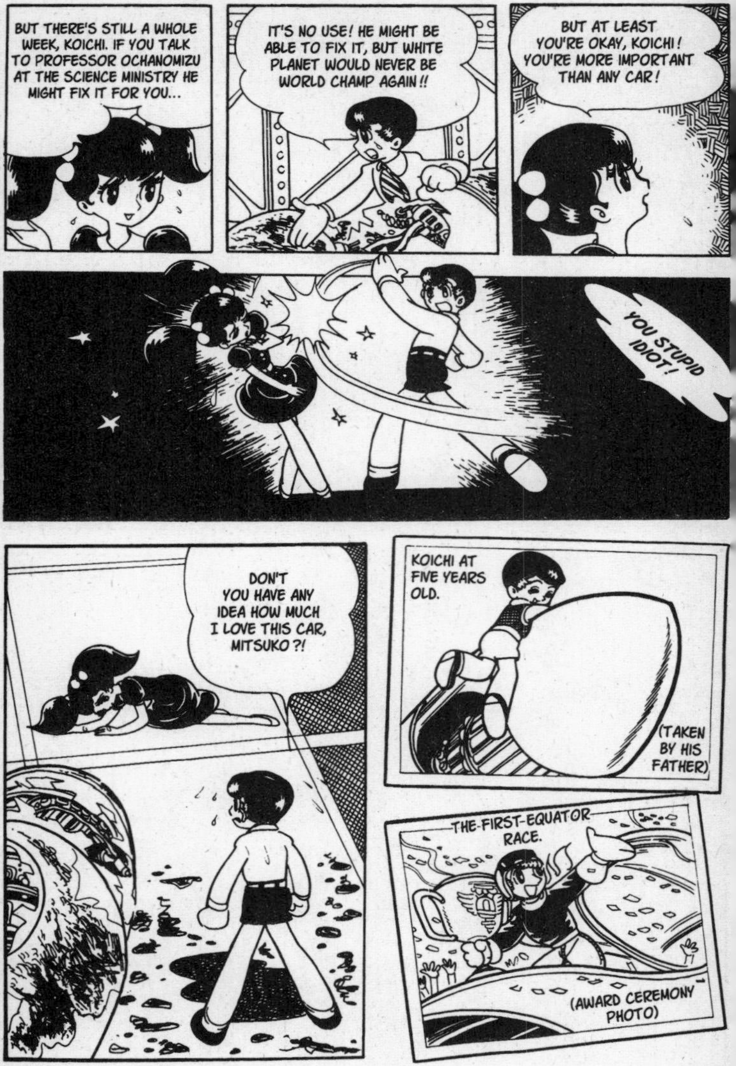
BUT THERE'S STILL A WHOLE WEEK, KOICHI. IF YOU TALK TO PROFESSOR OCHANOMIZU AT THE SCIENCE MINISTRY HE MIGHT FIX IT FOR YOU...
IT'S NO USE! HE MIGHT BE ABLE TO FIX IT, BUT WHITE PLANET WOULD NEVER BE WORLD CHAMP AGAIN!!
BUT AT LEAST YOU'RE OKAY, KOICHI! YOU'RE MORE IMPORTANT THAN ANY CAR!
YOU STUPID IDIOT!
DON'T YOU HAVE ANY IDEA HOW MUCH I LOVE THIS CAR, MITSUKO?!
KOICHI AT FIVE YEARS OLD.
(TAKEN BY HIS FATHER)
THE FIRST EQUATOR RACE.
(AWARD CEREMONY PHOTO)

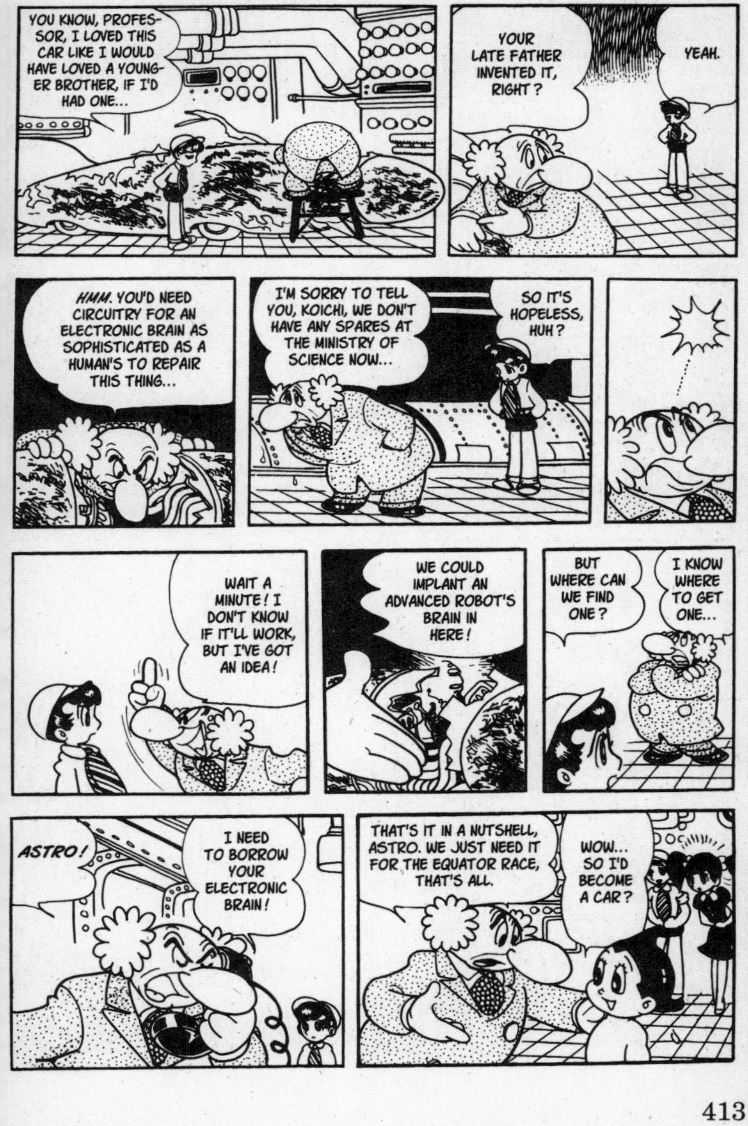
YOU KNOW, PROFESSOR, I LOVED THIS CAR LIKE I WOULD HAVE LOVED A YOUNGER BROTHER, IF I'D HAD ONE...
YOUR LATE FATHER INVENTED IT, RIGHT?
YEAH.
HMM. YOU'D NEED CIRCUITRY FOR AN ELECTRONIC BRAIN AS SOPHISTICATED AS A HUMAN'S TO REPAIR THIS THING...
I'M SORRY TO TELL YOU, KOICHI, WE DON'T HAVE ANY SPARES AT THE MINISTRY OF SCIENCE NOW...
SO IT'S HOPELESS, HUH?
WAIT A MINUTE! I DON'T KNOW IF IT'LL WORK, BUT I'VE GOT AN IDEA!
WE COULD IMPLANT AN ADVANCED ROBOT'S BRAIN IN HERE!
BUT WHERE CAN WE FIND ONE?
I KNOW WHERE TO GET ONE...
ASTRO!
I NEED TO BORROW YOUR ELECTRONIC BRAIN!
THAT'S IT IN A NUTSHELL, ASTRO. WE JUST NEED IT FOR THE EQUATOR RACE, THAT'S ALL.
WOW... SO I'D BECOME A CAR?

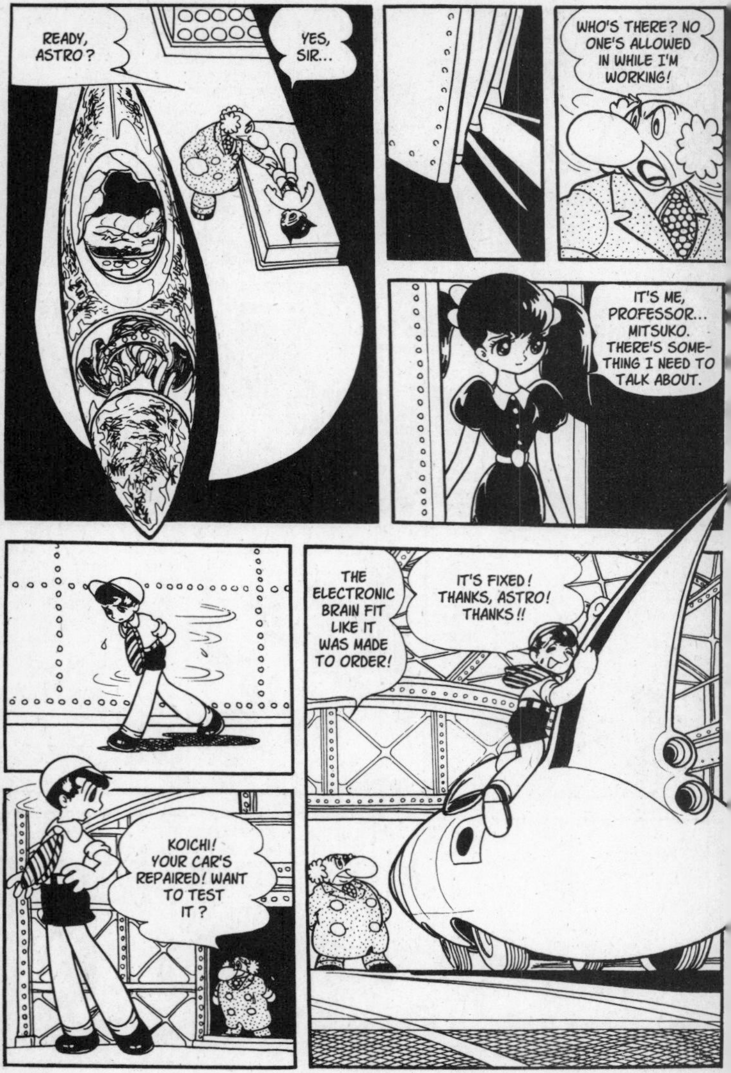

READY, ASTRO?
YES, SIR...
WHO'S THERE? NO ONE'S ALLOWED IN WHILE I'M WORKING!
IT'S ME, PROFESSOR... MITSUKO. THERE'S SOMETHING I NEED TO TALK ABOUT.
THE ELECTRONIC BRAIN FIT LIKE IT WAS MADE TO ORDER!
IT'S FIXED! THANKS, ASTRO! THANKS!!
KOICHI! YOUR CAR'S REPAIRED! WANT TO TEST IT?

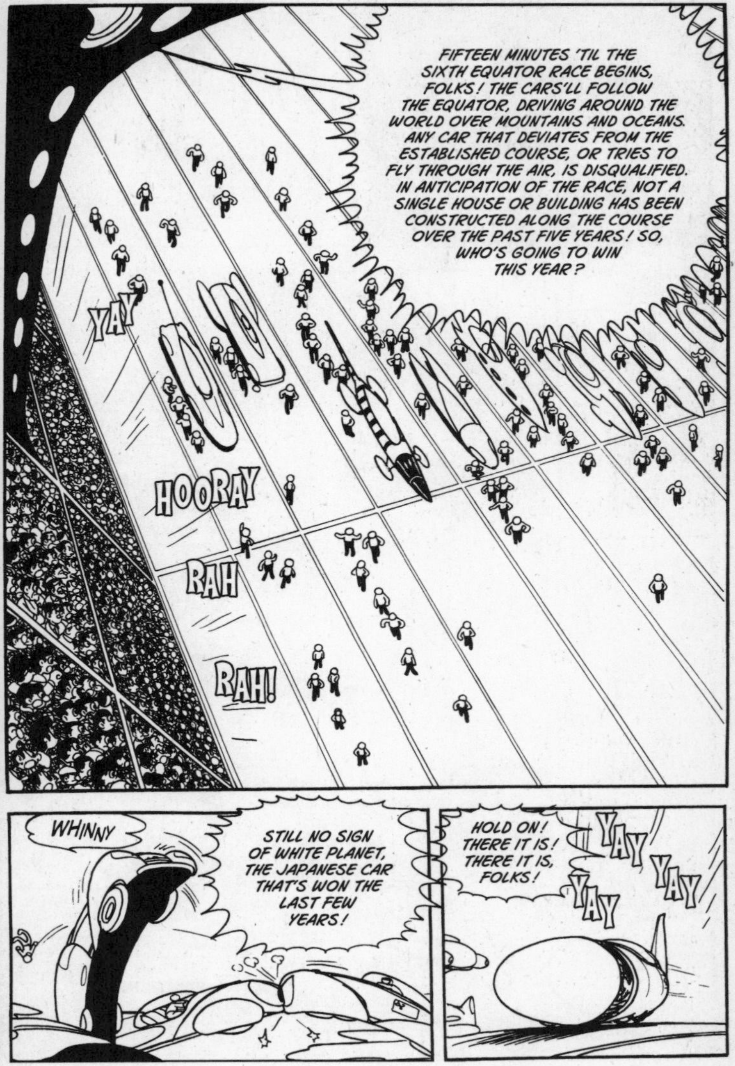
FIFTEEN MINUTES 'TIL THE SIXTH EQUATOR RACE BEGINS, FOLKS! THE CARS'LL FOLLOW THE EQUATOR, DRIVING AROUND THE WORLD OVER MOUNTAINS AND OCEANS. ANY CAR THAT DEVIATES FROM THE ESTABLISHED COURSE, OR TRIES TO FLY THROUGH THE AIR, IS DISQUALIFIED. IN ANTICIPATION OF THE RACE, NOT A SINGLE HOUSE OR BUILDING HAS BEEN CONSTRUCTED ALONG THE COURSE OVER THE PAST FIVE YEARS! SO, WHO'S GOING TO WIN THIS YEAR?
YAY
HOORAY
RAH
RAH!
WHINNY
STILL NO SIGN OF WHITE PLANET, THE JAPANESE CAR THAT'S WON THE LAST FEW YEARS!
HOLD ON! THERE IT IS! THERE IT IS, FOLKS!
YAY
YAY
YAY

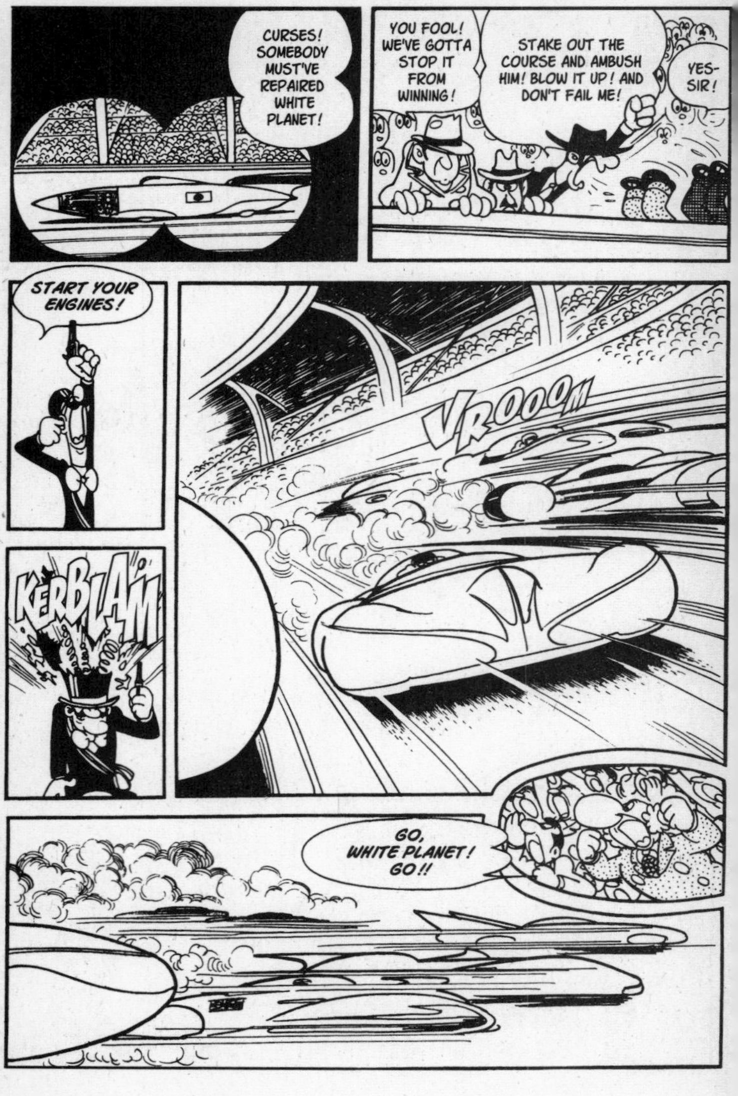
CURSES! SOMEBODY MUST'VE REPAIRED WHITE PLANET!
YOU FOOL! WE'VE GOTTA STOP IT FROM WINNING!
STAKE OUT THE COURSE AND AMBUSH HIM! BLOW IT UP! AND DON'T FAIL ME!
YES-SIR!
START YOUR ENGINES!
KERBLAM
VROOOM
GO, WHITE PLANET! GO!!

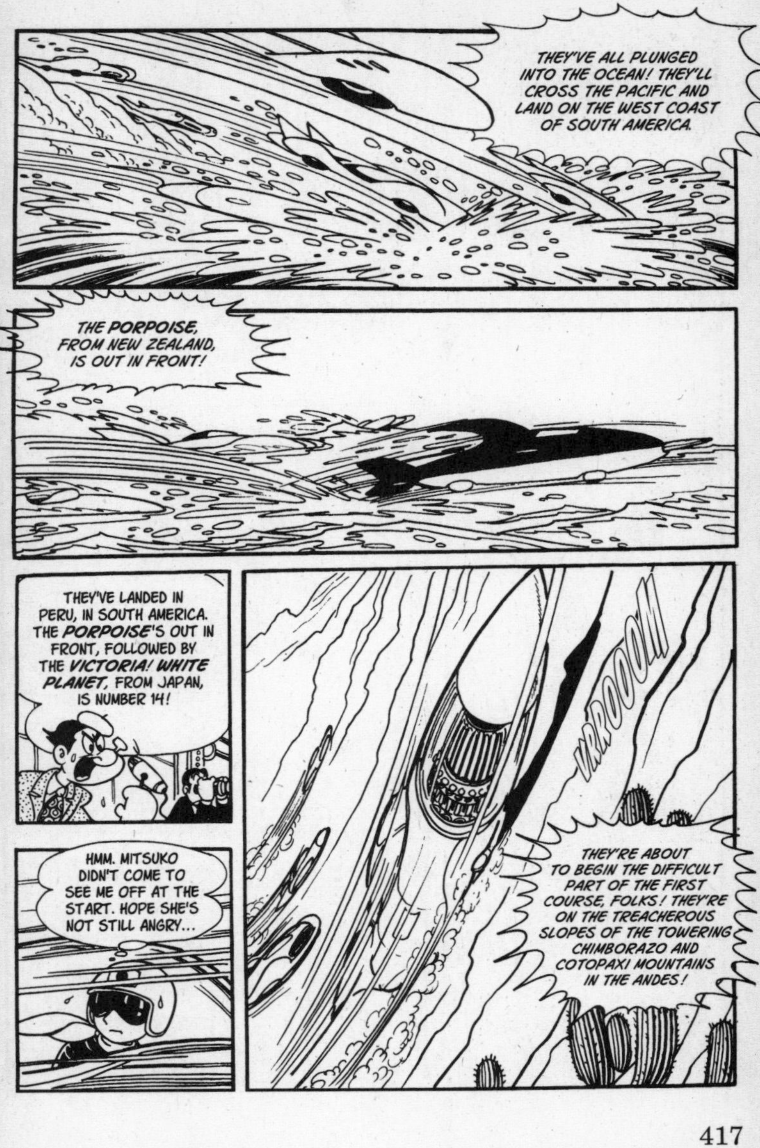
THEY'VE ALL PLUNGED INTO THE OCEAN! THEY'LL CROSS THE PACIFIC AND LAND ON THE WEST COAST OF SOUTH AMERICA.
THE PORPOISE, FROM NEW ZEALAND, IS OUT IN FRONT!
THEY'VE LANDED IN PERU, IN SOUTH AMERICA. THE PORPOISE'S OUT IN FRONT, FOLLOWED BY THE VICTORIA! WHITE PLANET, FROM JAPAN, IS NUMBER 14!
HMM. MITSUKO DIDN'T COME TO SEE ME OFF AT THE START. HOPE SHE'S NOT STILL ANGRY...
VRROOOOM
THEY'RE ABOUT TO BEGIN THE DIFFICULT PART OF THE FIRST COURSE, FOLKS! THEY'RE ON THE TREACHEROUS SLOPES OF THE TOWERING CHIMBORAZO AND COTOPAXI MOUNTAINS IN THE ANDES!

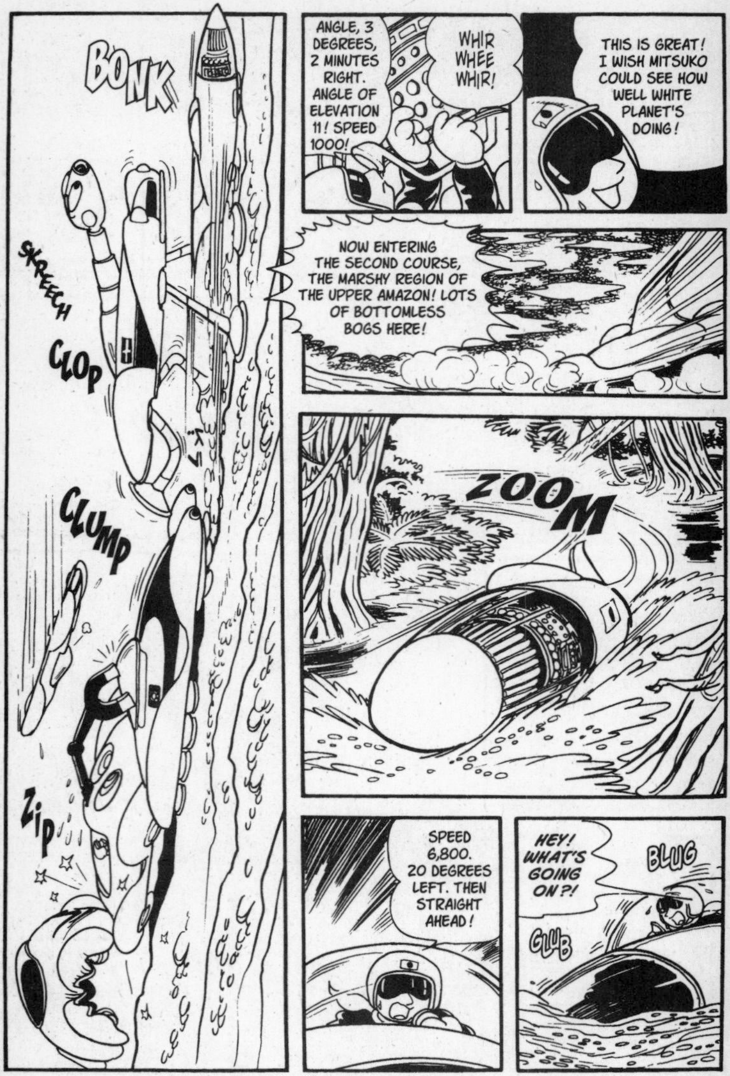
BONK
SKREECH
CLOP
CLUMP
ZIP
ANGLE, 3 DEGREES, 2 MINUTES RIGHT. ANGLE OF ELEVATION 11! SPEED 1000!
WHIR WHEE WHIR!
THIS IS GREAT! I WISH MITSUKO COULD SEE HOW WELL WHITE PLANET'S DOING!
NOW ENTERING THE SECOND COURSE, THE MARSHY REGION OF THE UPPER AMAZON! LOTS OF BOTTOMLESS BOGS HERE!
ZOOM
SPEED 6,800. 20 DEGREES LEFT. THEN STRAIGHT AHEAD!
HEY! WHAT'S GOING ON?!
BLUG
GLUB

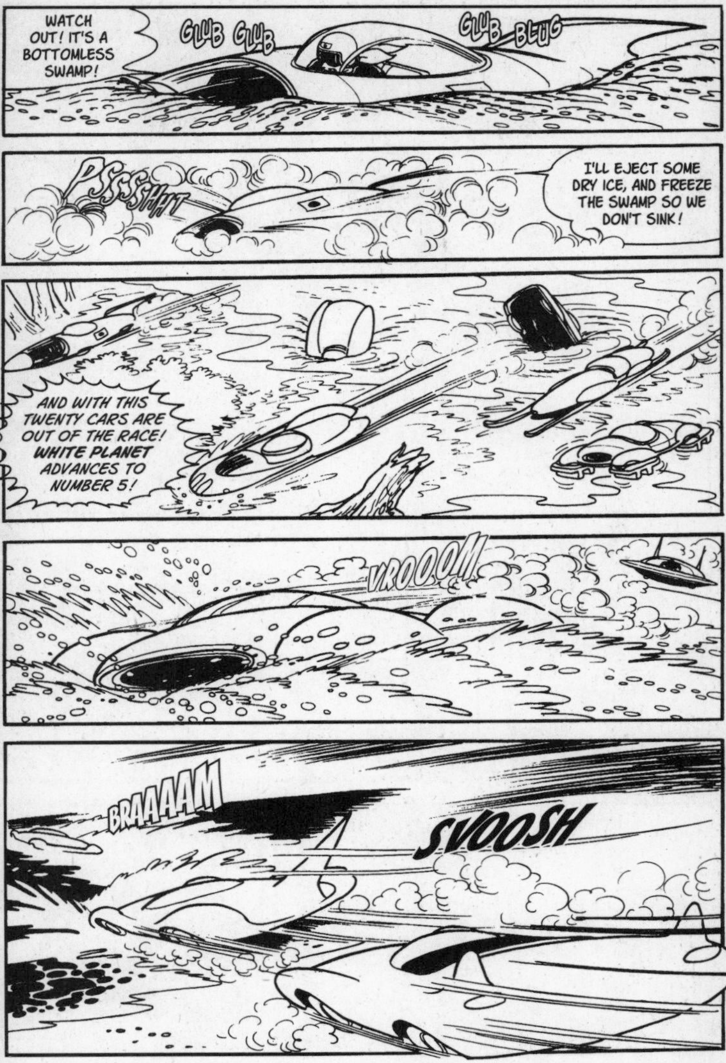
WATCH OUT! IT'S A BOTTOMLESS SWAMP!
GLUB GLUB
GLUB BLUG
PSSSSHHT
I'LL EJECT SOME DRY ICE, AND FREEZE THE SWAMP SO WE DON'T SINK!
AND WITH THIS TWENTY CARS ARE OUT OF THE RACE! WHITE PLANET ADVANCES TO NUMBER 5!
VROOOM
BRAAAAM
SVOOSH

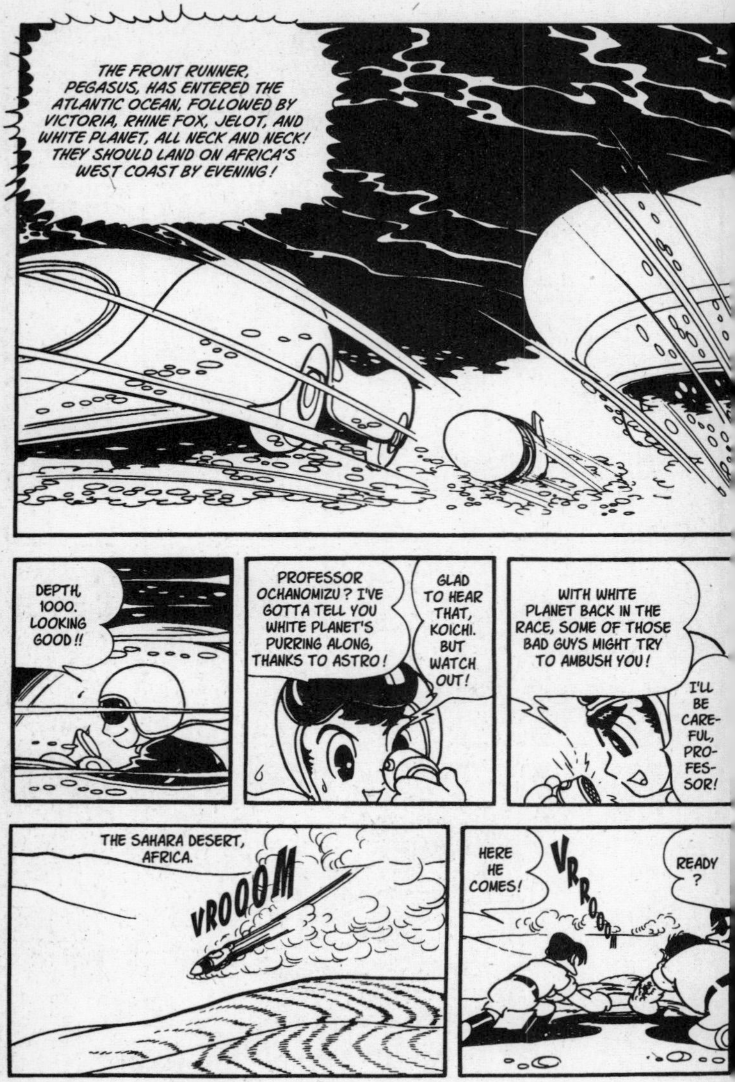
THE FRONT RUNNER, PEGASUS, HAS ENTERED THE ATLANTIC OCEAN, FOLLOWED BY VICTORIA, RHINE FOX, JELOT, AND WHITE PLANET, ALL NECK AND NECK! THEY SHOULD LAND ON AFRICA'S WEST COAST BY EVENING!
DEPTH, 1000. LOOKING GOOD!!
PROFESSOR OCHANOMIZU? I'VE GOTTA TELL YOU WHITE PLANET'S PURRING ALONG, THANKS TO ASTRO!
GLAD TO HEAR THAT, KOICHI. BUT WATCH OUT!
WITH WHITE PLANET BACK IN THE RACE, SOME OF THOSE BAD GUYS MIGHT TRY TO AMBUSH YOU!
I'LL BE CAREFUL, PROFESSOR!
THE SAHARA DESERT, AFRICA.
VROOOOM
HERE HE COMES!
VRROOOOM
READY?

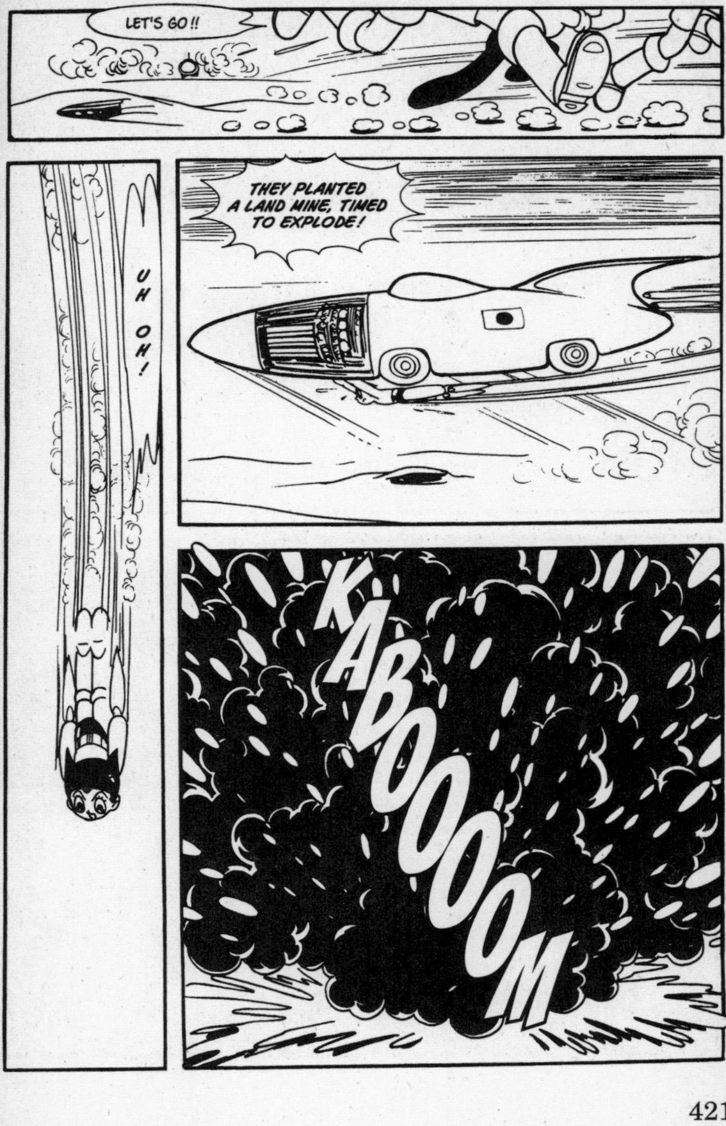
LET'S GO!!
UH OH!
THEY PLANTED A LAND MINE, TIMED TO EXPLODE!
KABOOOOOM

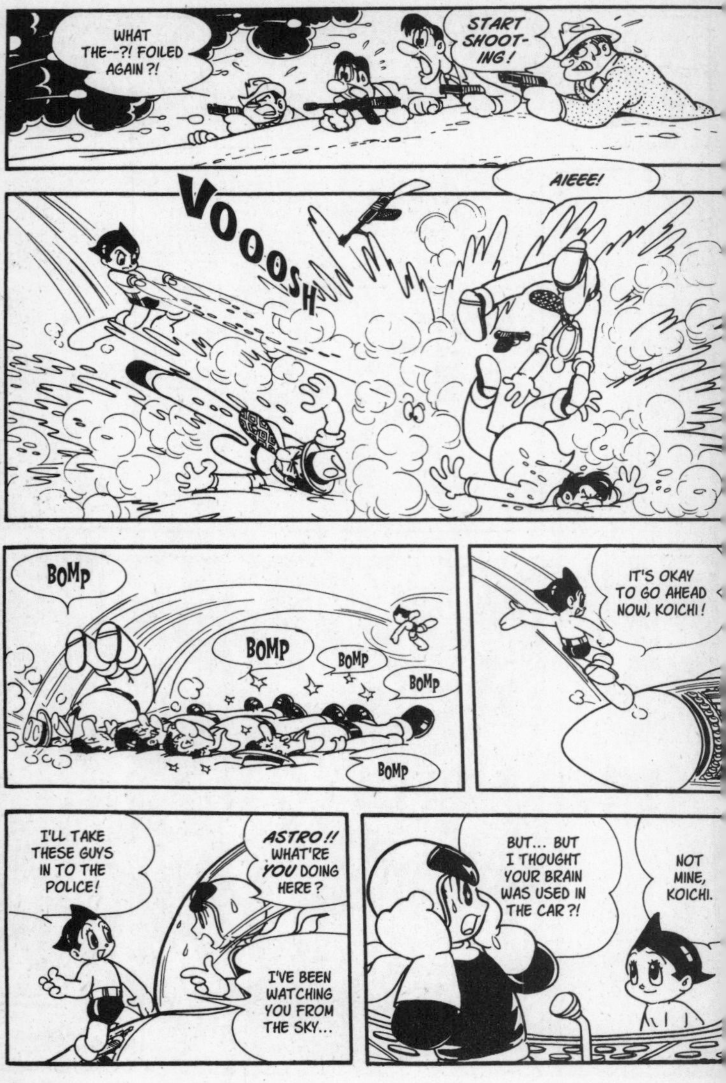
WHAT THE--?! FOILED AGAIN?!
START SHOOT-ING!
VOOOSH
AIEEE!
BOMP
BOMP
BOMP
BOMP
BOMP
IT'S OKAY TO GO AHEAD NOW, KOICHI!
I'LL TAKE THESE GUYS IN TO THE POLICE!
ASTRO!! WHAT'RE YOU DOING HERE?
I'VE BEEN WATCHING YOU FROM THE SKY...
BUT... BUT I THOUGHT YOUR BRAIN WAS USED IN THE CAR?!
NOT MINE, KOICHI.

WHEN YOUR FATHER MADE WHITE PLANET, HE WAS CAREFUL TO MAKE AN EXTRA ELECTRONIC BRAIN.

BUT WHERE WAS IT?

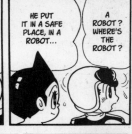

HE PUT IT IN A SAFE PLACE, IN A ROBOT...

A ROBOT? WHERE'S THE ROBOT?

IT'S YOUR SISTER, MIT- SUKO...

MY SISTER?!

RIGHT. I KNOW YOU THINK OF HER AS YOUR SISTER, BUT SHE'S REALLY A ROBOT, KOICHI.

SHE SECRETLY TOLD US, AND SAID SHE WANTED TO BECOME PART OF WHITE PLANET.

SO IT WAS YOU, MITSUKO...

MITSUKO NO LONGER EXISTS NOW, KOICHI. BUT SHE'S BEEN REBORN IN WHITE PLANET!

MITSUKO... I'LL DO MY BEST FOR YOU... AND WITH YOUR HELP, WE'LL WIN!

AND IT'S *WHITE PLANET* FIRST OVER THE FINISH LINE! ONE MORE TIME, THE CHAMPIONSHIP THIS YEAR GOES TO *WHITE PLANET!*

VROOOM

THE END

423

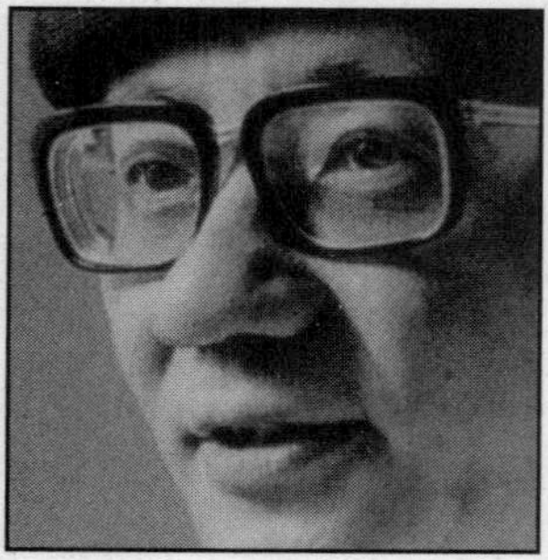

Osamu Tezuka was born in the city of Toyonaka, in Osaka, Japan, on November 3, 1928, and raised in Takarazuka, in Hyogo prefecture. He graduated from the Medical Department of Osaka University and was later awarded a Doctorate of Medicine.

In 1946 Tezuka made his debut as a manga artist with the work *Ma-chan's Diary*, and in 1947 he had his first big hit with *New Treasure Island*. In over forty years as a cartoonist, Tezuka produced in excess of an astounding 150,000 pages of manga, including the creation of *Metropolis, Mighty Atom* (a.k.a. *Astro Boy*), *Jungle Emperor* (a.k.a. *Kimba the White Lion*), *Black Jack, Phoenix, Buddha*, and many more.

Tezuka's fascination with Disney cartoons led him to begin his own animation studio, creating the first serialized Japanese cartoon series, which was later exported to America as *Astro Boy* in 1963. Tezuka Productions went on to create animated versions of *Kimba the White Lion* (*Jungle Emperor*) and *Phoenix*, among others.

He received numerous awards during his life, including the Bungei Shunju Manga Award, the Kodansha Manga Award, the Shogakukan Manga Award, and the Japan Cartoonists' Association Special Award for Excellence. He also served a variety of organizations. He was a director of the Japan Cartoonists' Association, the chairman of the Japan Animation Association, and a member of the Manga Group, Japan Pen Club, and the Japan SF Authors' Club, among others. Tezuka became Japan's "comics ambassador," taking Japan's comics culture to the world. In 1980, he toured and lectured in America, including a speech at the United Nations.

Regarded as a national treasure, Osamu Tezuka died on February 9, 1989 at the age of 60. In April 1994, the Osamu Tezuka Manga Museum opened in the city of Takarazuka, where he was raised. His creations remain hugely popular in Japan and are printed in many languages throughout the world, where he is acclaimed as one of the true giants of comics and animation, his work as vital and influential today as it was half a century ago.

"Comics are an international language," Tezuka said. "They can cross boundaries and generations. Comics are a bridge between all cultures."

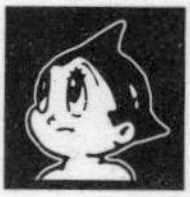